Philosophy and The Human Condition

An Anthology

EDITED BY
BRIAN R. CLACK & TYLER HOWER
University of San Diego

New York   Oxford
OXFORD UNIVERSITY PRESS

Oxford University Press is a department of the University of Oxford.
It furthers the University's objective of excellence in research,
scholarship, and education by publishing worldwide.
Oxford is a registered trademark of Oxford University Press
in the UK and certain other countries.

Published in the United States of America by Oxford University Press
198 Madison Avenue, New York, NY 10016, United States of America.

Library of Congress Cataloging-in-Publication Data

Names: Clack, Brian R., editor.
Title: Philosophy and the human condition : an anthology / edited by
Brian R.
   Clack & Tyler Hower Brian Clack.
Description: 1 [edition]. | New York : Oxford University Press, 2017.
Identifiers: LCCN 2017021621 | ISBN 9780190253585 (pbk.)
Subjects: LCSH: Philosophy.
Classification: LCC B21 .P555 2017 | DDC 100—dc23 LC record available at
https://lccn.loc.gov/2017021621

9 8 7 6 5 4 3 2 1

Printed by LSC Communications, Inc.

For
Sabrina & Fernando

CONTENTS

PART FOUR: Renaissance and Modern Works

PART FIVE: Late Modern Writings

PART SIX: **Twentieth Century and Contemporary Voices**

ACKNOWLEDGMENTS

We are grateful to Robert Miller and Alyssa Palazzo at Oxford University Press for their support and guidance in the composition of this book. We are thankful for the helpful and insightful comments of reviewers of the proposal for this work. Accordingly, we would like to thank Carlos Atalay, Michael Carper, Jeffrey Jordan, Crystal L'Hôte, Ryan M. Lozano, Ryan P. Mott, Herminia Reyes, David Rodick, Gregory Straughn, and Marisola Xhelili. Without the talented eye of our copyeditor Elizabeth Bortka this work would not have been possible. We would also like to express thanks to colleagues at the University of San Diego whose help is deeply appreciated by us: in particular we wish to thank Leeanna Cummings, Lance Nelson, Noelle Norton, Karma Lekshe Tsomo, Lindy Villa, and Lori Watson. We dedicate the book to Fernando Bosco and Sabrina Kaiser, to whom the deepest gratitude is owed.

PREFACE

T he importance of self-knowledge is one constant in the long history and broad scope of philosophy. Philosophers of all stripes and eras have turned their eyes on themselves to ask who and what they are. Hindu and Confucian philosophers have called us to examine our actions and thoughts and very natures. Buddhist thought has questioned whether there is even a self of which we could be aware. The Abrahamic religions and philosophies that have grown out of them began by positioning us in relation to God and the rest of creation and from there asking how we ought to live.

In Western philosophy, Socrates set the tone for all those who have come after, adopting the Delphic inscription "Know thyself" as a guiding principle. Together with his dictum in the *Apology*, "The unexamined life is not a fully human life (or worth living)," this has placed the duty to know better who and what we are at the very center of his and the philosophical enterprise.

Before we can know our selves as individual selves, we have to know what kinds of individuals we are; since we are human beings, we have to know what we are as human beings. We even have to ask if there is something that we all are as humans or if there is something distinct about us that separates us from the rest of the animals. Our task here is to begin to explore what the human condition is.

We have collected in this work some of the many approaches to answering just what human beings are like. We have included selections representing different approaches, methods, and voices. No collection can be exhaustive or fully comprehensive, but we hope that the pieces here can serve as a starting point and inspiration in the readers' own explorations of themselves and the shared human condition.

Philosophizing About the Human Condition

"I have become a problem to myself..."
St. Augustine

The Nature of Philosophy and Philosophical Questions

It is customary in an introductory text such as this to supply the reader with a description of what philosophy is. This is no straightforward task. For one thing, philosophy as a discipline has changed over time as certain elements originally within its purview (biology and cosmology, for example) branched off to become independent disciplines. Moreover, philosophers tend to disagree about the nature of their subject, the definition of philosophy being a hotly debated topic. One might here note that this is one thing that marks off the peculiarity of philosophy as a subject. Practitioners of other subjects—geologists or chemists, for example—do not spend a great deal of their research time trying to work out what their subject *is*, but philosophers actually do that, and such work forms in fact an important part of philosophical inquiry. We are not going to offer here our own definition of philosophy, but will instead briefly survey some ways in which it has been characterized. This should serve to frame a helpful composite picture of the nature both of philosophy and of philosophical questions.

Building upon a familiar characterization of philosophy as *thinking about thinking*, the British philosopher Anthony Quinton offered the following definition, which both preserves that important insight and indicates the major subdivisions of the subject: "Philosophy is rationally critical thinking of a more or less systematic kind about the general nature of the world (metaphysics or theory of existence), the justification of belief

1

(epistemology or theory of knowledge), and the conduct of life (ethics or theory of value)."[1] Each of these three elements has "a non-philosophical counterpart" active in the (mostly unarticulated) worldview of each and every person. That is to say, everyone has some general conception of the world they live in, some doubts—at least from time to time—about the veracity of their beliefs, and some set of values by which they govern their conduct and make judgments on the conduct of others. The activity of the philosopher can be seen to consist, at least in part, in the rational evaluation and criticism of the assumptions involved in those counterparts and in the development of more systematic and well-founded accounts of reality and the world, belief and knowledge, and value and moral conduct. Here philosophy can be seen to possess two dimensions, one critical and the other constructive.

A variant approach lays considerably less emphasis on any constructive dimension, instead characterizing philosophy as a *clarificatory* activity. A succinct expression of this idea can be found in the work of Ludwig Wittgenstein, one of the most significant philosophers of the twentieth century:

> Philosophy aims at the logical clarification of thoughts.
>
> Philosophy is not a body of doctrine but an activity. . . .
>
> Philosophy does not result in "philosophical propositions," but rather in the clarification of propositions.
>
> Without philosophy thoughts are, as it were, cloudy and indistinct: its task is to make them clear and give them sharp boundaries.[2]

This clarificatory conception may sound appealing to all those people who have ever felt frustrated by the occasional opacity and blurriness of human discourse, something often experienced when contested and mysterious topics are being discussed, topics such as freedom, the soul, immortality, happiness, and so on. One of Wittgenstein's interpreters, the philosopher Friedrich Waismann, wrote that this sense of blurriness will typically be felt by anyone brooding over a seemingly intractable philosophical question (the question of time, for example), and that this

---

[1]   Anthony Quinton, "Philosophy," in *The Oxford Companion to Philosophy*, ed. Ted Honderich (Oxford: Oxford University Press, 1995), 666.

[2]   Ludwig Wittgenstein, *Tractatus Logico-Philosophicus* (London: Routledge & Kegan Paul, 1961 [1922]), 4.112.

peculiar "dizziness" can be undone by the clarification of one's thoughts.[3] Here we encounter a dual conception of philosophy as (1) a set of dizzying problems and (2) a technique whereby that dizziness may be cured. While the entirety of that conception may be peculiar to the Wittgensteinian school, philosophy's clarity-throwing, meaning-seeking ideal is probably one of its greatest qualities.

The goal of clarification is likewise stressed in an interesting discussion of the nature of philosophical questions found in the work of the influential twentieth century philosopher Isaiah Berlin. "The goal of philosophy," Berlin writes, "is always the same, to assist men to understand themselves and thus operate in the open, and not wildly, in the dark."[4] Berlin's account is also useful in helping us to see the differences between philosophical questions and the questions addressed in other disciplines (such as history or mathematics or natural science). There is something peculiar about a philosophical question ("Are there other minds in the universe besides my own?" for example), a peculiarity that is absent in those other questions. In those latter cases (Berlin's examples include "Did the battle of Waterloo take place in the seventeenth century?" and "What is the cube root of 729?"), we generally know how to set about answering the question, but in philosophy it is otherwise: there is no generally agreed-upon method of discovering the solution to philosophical questions, and yet these questions seem real enough, often generating the most intensely tormenting intellectual engagement. It is to that lack of methodological agreement—a lack that has been regarded by some as something of a scandal—that we owe the great diversity of responses to philosophical questions: that diversity is the history of philosophy itself.

It is a distinguishing feature of philosophical questions, Berlin writes, that they are *neither empirical nor formal*. What this means is that questions like "What is the supreme good for human beings?" or "Do things continue to exist when they are unobserved?" can be answered neither by appeal to observation and experience (the technique of both science and everyday common sense) nor by the use of formal deductive reasoning (such as is utilized in logic or mathematics). It was mentioned earlier that the scope of philosophical concern has altered over time as certain elements of it developed into independent subjects: for Berlin, that development occurred precisely as the result of the disentanglement

---

[3]   See Friedrich Waismann, *The Principles of Linguistic Philosophy* (London: Macmillan, 1997), 5–9.

[4]   Isaiah Berlin, *The Power of Ideas* (Princeton, NJ: Princeton University Press, 2000), 35.

from philosophy of all those problems found to be either empirically or formally soluble. What was left was "a nucleus of unresolved (and largely unanalysed) questions, whose generality, obscurity and, above all, apparent (or real) insolubility by empirical or formal methods gives them a status of their own which we tend to call philosophical."[5]

This sense of insoluble obscurity informs the attitude of uncertainty typically present in the philosophical stance. Against dogmatism, always questioning and always probing—this stance has been definitive of the philosopher since the subject's inception. Socrates—the founding martyr of Western philosophy—famously declared his ignorance, maintaining that he was wiser than others simply because they mistakenly thought they knew something whereas he was aware of his own ignorance. Two and a half thousand years later, Bertrand Russell noted that the philosophical attitude leads to an all-encompassing puzzlement. "As soon as we begin to philosophize," he wrote, "we find that even the most everyday things lead to problems to which only very incomplete answers can be given."[6]

Russell's comment on how, for the philosopher, everyday things become problematic is interesting, and alerts us to another salient feature of philosophy. It is this: *philosophy takes nothing for granted*. The philosopher looks on things—which, for a great number of people are obvious, accepted, or presupposed—as ambiguous, disputable, and extraordinary. Note here Wittgenstein's words about the human activities—typically taken for granted—of reading a novel and looking at art: "Don't take it as a matter of course, but as a remarkable fact, that pictures and fictitious narratives give us pleasure, occupy our minds."[7] With this evocation of astonishment at the everyday, we are not too far from Aristotle's familiar judgment that philosophy originates in a sense of *wonder*: "For it is owing to their wonder that men both now begin and at first began to philosophize."[8]

To speak in this way of a sense of wonder brings to prominence the fact that philosophy is a manifestation of human beings' engagement with the world, an engagement that provokes astonishment and curiosity. The impulse to philosophize might here be regarded as a part of "the natural

---

[5]   Ibid., 38.

[6]   Bertrand Russell, *The Problems of Philosophy* (Oxford: Oxford University Press, 1912), 157.

[7]   Ludwig Wittgenstein, *Philosophical Investigations* (Oxford: Basil Blackwell, 1953), §524.

[8]   Aristotle, *Metaphysics*, in *The Complete Works of Aristotle*, vol. 2, ed. Jonathan Barnes (Princeton, NJ: Princeton University Press, 1984), 1554 (982b).

history of human beings"[9] (to use a phrase of Wittgenstein's), and seems indeed to be distinctively human: whatever the extent of animal intelligence, the ability to think about the meaning of life, the nature of time, to make one's own existence an object of investigation, seems a uniquely human thing. Recognition of this distinctive quality may even function as a source of consolation and happiness for us, as it did for one such as Blaise Pascal. Though tormented by the apparently wretched nature of the human condition, Pascal nonetheless took comfort in the fact that we are *aware* of that wretchedness in a way that nothing else—no animal, no plant—can be. As a result, our wretchedness had something great about it, "the wretchedness of a great lord." This was felt by him to be the case, even in the face of death:

> Man is only a reed, the weakest in nature, but he is a thinking reed. There is no need for the whole universe to take up arms to crush him: a vapour, a drop of water is enough to kill him. But even if the universe were to crush him, man would still be nobler than his slayer, because he knows that he is dying, and the advantage the universe has over him. The universe knows none of this.[10]

Even more than this rather downbeat assessment, philosophy might provide positive delight; our pleasure in thinking about life's most intractable and ultimate questions itself making life worthwhile and meaningful. "And so they tell us," writes Aristotle, "that Anaxagoras answered a man who was raising problems of this sort and was asking why one should choose rather to be born than not—'for the sake of viewing the heavens and the whole order of the universe.'"[11]

The great Stoic philosopher Epictetus held that philosophy originated, not in a general sense of wonder, but rather in the recognition of the conflict between opinions.[12] We have seen that, with regard to philosophical matters, a conflict of views will be inescapable. Rather, therefore, than sharing Epictetus's hope that the work of philosophy would discover a standard whereby that conflict might be finally resolved, one might need to find a way to tolerate the great diversity of philosophical positions and views. It might be helpful in this context to make appeal to the idea of a *conversation* and to depict philosophy in those terms. As emphasized by the political

---

[9] Wittgenstein, *Philosophical Investigations*, §415.

[10] Blaise Pascal, *Pensées* (Harmondsworth: Penguin, 1966), 95.

[11] Aristotle, *Ethica Eudemia* (Oxford: Clarendon Press, 1915), 1216a.

[12] See *The Discourses of Epictetus*, Book II, Chapter XI (any edition).

philosopher Michael Oakeshott, in a conversation "the participants are not engaged in an enquiry or a debate; there is no 'truth' to be discovered, no proposition to be proved, no conclusion sought"; a conversation is "an un-rehearsed intellectual adventure," exhibiting "a tension between serious-ness and playfulness"; and in it "everything is permitted which can get itself accepted into the flow of speculation."[13] While this conversational model should not be allowed to compromise or overshadow the rigor required of philosophical argumentation, it nonetheless captures something of the character of the lively and open-ended exchange of diverse views within philosophy. The model of a conversation, moreover, conjures up an image of something warm and inviting, and it also suggests a way to approach the discussion of problems having the kind of insoluble form earlier described, as we saw, by Berlin. Finally, the set of problems pertaining to the human condition would appear precisely to have been the focus of a vibrant and centuries-long philosophical conversation. To the nature of these prob-lems we will now turn.

Philosophical Questions about the Human Condition

When we speak here of "the human condition" we are referring to that collection of existential qualities and problems that together comprise the distinctively human state of being, a state of being that is both a puzzle and a predicament. It is natural and fitting that our own con-dition in the world should be the focus of philosophical investigation: "The proper study of mankind," wrote the poet Alexander Pope, "is man." And when Pope described the human being as the "glory, jest, and riddle of the world" he was giving memorable expression to our paradoxical, contradictory and enigmatic condition: a part of nature yet somehow distinct from it; an animal, yes, yet with a capacity for reflection and creativity beyond anything found elsewhere in the animal kingdom; a creature capable of great love and compassion but with a propensity for extraordinary violence; a capacity for joy and yet frequently sunk in de-spair; and with an intuition of our lasting significance, countered by an all-too-painful awareness of our transience. Such are the tensions provid-ing the context for philosophical investigations into the human condition.

We have selected five major areas of controversy that have preoccupied thinkers from ancient times to the present day. These are: the relation of

---

[13] Michael Oakeshott, *The Voice of Poetry in the Conversation of Mankind* (London: Bowes & Bowes, 1959), 10–14.

mind and body; the threat of death and the promise of immortality; the debate about free will and determinism; the question of the essential benevolence or viciousness of human beings; and the nature and possibility of happiness. With all of these questions there is, as Quinton noted, a "nonphilosophical counterpart," each person (whether philosophically inclined or not) having a more or less articulated opinion about whether they possess something that might be called "a soul," whether they will live on after physical death, whether they are free and therefore responsible for their actions, whether they and their fellow humans are gentle or cruel, whether (and how) they can attain happiness. In the writings of the philosophers assembled in this book, varieties of each of these "counterparts" are presented, questioned, criticized and defended. They are exposed, in short, to rational evaluation. To these five perennial themes we have added a sixth: issues concerning race and gender. Throughout the history of philosophy, both women and people of color have been treated with contempt and with neglect, their perspectives on the human condition sidelined and they themselves subjected to sexist and racist invectives. We here illustrate this unpleasant fact by including selections of misogynistic and racist claims uttered by major thinkers, and we also include extracts from the frequently neglected work of women philosophers and philosophers of color.

After an initial set of readings drawn from religious texts, this book is arranged chronologically rather than thematically. This allows the reader to be immersed in the grand historical sweep of the subject, but it does also mean that the six themes are dispersed throughout the book, rather than separately treated. It will be beneficial, therefore, to map out the terrain of each theme, indicating the ideas and thinkers central to each broad topic. We will start with the contentious issue of the relation between mind and body.

Mind and Body

We have something in common with the other animals. It is something we share also with plants and with such mundane objects as tables and chairs and pebbles: we are physical beings and parts of the physical universe. That is simply to say that we are—at least in part—physical matter. Some people might want to balk at the claim that we *are* physical matter, but it seems clear to most that we at least possess a physical part; I have a body, even if I am not that body. Only the rare religious or philosophical idealist has denied this fact; however, such thinkers do so at the cost of denying the existence of any physical matter or the physical universe as physical. If we aren't willing to go that far with them, then we have to see ourselves with at least one foot in the physical. In philosophical discussion, this has usually been formulated as the claim that we are/have bodies, where "body" is meant to refer to any physical object, whether living or not.

If it is obvious that we have a physical component, it has seemed just as obvious to many that we are more than *just* a body. Of course, we are living, and this separates us from the tables and chairs and pebbles, but we also seem to have capacities that raise us above other living things, including the other animals. In particular, we reason; we have a deeper understanding of the world; we exhibit self-consciousness, if not always self-awareness; and, we do things like engage in philosophical speculation.

We have, it seems, not just bodies, but also *minds*. This claim that humans are composed of two parts, a body and a mind, is a form of what is called *dualism*. In particular, it is *mind-body dualism* or *substance dualism*, because it claims that there are two independent types of things or *substances* that make us up. For many of us, including many philosophers, this view matches our most basic conceptions of ourselves. On this view, the mind is something wholly other than the body. Whatever the mind is, it is not a part of the body or a physical thing like the body. It is *not* the brain.

The idea that we have a part that is wholly distinct and separate from the physical world can be very appealing. It helps makes sense of the beliefs in survival after death that many of us hold. Of course, when humans die, their bodies decompose. That is, the body clearly does not and cannot survive death, but if there is a part of a human being that is not physical, it is at least plausible that that part, not being subject to the laws of the physical universe, might survive the body's death. In any case, the death of the body would not necessitate the death of a nonphysical mind. Insofar as we might believe or hope that we survive bodily death, this conception of the mind can be very reassuring. It might also be reassuring to those who worry that we couldn't really exhibit free will if we were merely bodies. Many philosophers argue that the physical world and its constituents obey deterministic physical laws. If we were *merely* physical beings, they reason, we would also be subject to such deterministic laws. This would make our apparently free choices really the result of those laws. That, they believe, means that we could never be truly free. If, however, there is a part of us that is independent of the physical world, we can make more sense of our freedom, since this part of us would not be subject to the physical laws, whatever other laws they may be bound by.

We address both of these questions in more detail elsewhere, but it is worth noting here that none of these questions stands entirely alone.

Mind-body dualism has a long pedigree both in philosophy and in nonphilosophical—particularly religious—thought. We can see an ancestor of this view in the creation narrative in the biblical book of Genesis, in which humans, but no other animals, receive the breath of God, or in the idea from Hinduism that the same self lives through many bodies, only to finally be reunited with the ultimate reality. The idea of a soul or spirit that resides in a body from which it is distinct is, in many ways, the same view as mind-body dualism seen from a different, religious perspective. In philosophy, this view goes back at least as far as Plato's arguments for a real distinction between the mind and body in texts such as *Phaedo* and *Alcibiades*. That reference to *argument* is here worth emphasizing: philosophers do not merely *state* a position but provide *arguments* in support of it. In *Alcibiades*, for example, Plato (through the mouth of Socrates) operates with a distinction between *user* and *thing used*. A shoemaker is distinct from the things he uses in shoemaking (his tools); since he also uses his hands and his eyes and his entire body, whatever he is must be distinct from his body; this leads Plato to a conception of the soul as "the user of the body," and therefore to a conception of the genuine separateness of mind/soul and body.[14]

Substance dualism gets its strongest presentation in the work of the seventeenth century philosopher Rene Descartes. In both the *Meditations* and *The Discourse on Method*, Descartes provides an array of arguments in support of the dualist conception. Minds and bodies, he argues, since they differ in their essential properties—one as thinking and nonextended and the other unthinking and extended—must be regarded as different kinds of thing. Moreover, these two distinct things can be conceived as existing separately and apart from one another: I can, for example, imagine myself without (or losing) my body and yet still remaining myself, this demonstrating that I am in essence a thinking thing in some fashion harnessed to, or "intimately conjoined" with, an unthinking body. By means of this argument from conceivability, Descartes can persuade himself (and perhaps also others) that "it is certain that this I (that is to say, my soul by which I am what I am), is entirely and absolutely distinct from my body, and can exist without it)."[15] A further argument, known as the argument from *poverty*, stresses that a purely physical (or bodily) thing, however complex it might be, could

---

[14]   See the selections from Plato's *Alcibiades* included in this volume.

[15]   Rene Descartes, *Meditations*, in *The Philosophical Works of Descartes*, vol. 1 (Cambridge: Cambridge University Press, 1931), 54.

never be expected to produce thought, creativity, and speech. Matter is, by itself, too paltry a thing (in other words, too *impoverished*) to do that. Animals, he notoriously claims, though having machine-like bodies as complex as those of human beings, neither reason nor talk: they are merely machines (this being the notorious Cartesian doctrine of the *bête-machine*). Humans, though having machine-like bodies, have something invaluable in addition: minds, the possession of which accounts for our intellectual abilities.

Almost as soon as Descartes formulated his arguments in favor of substance dualism, correspondents, especially Princess Elisabeth of Bohemia, began to question how it could be possible for two such vastly different substances to interact. This is a significant problem. Descartes holds the mind and the body to be two wholly distinct substances. Indeed, he defines mind and body by way of completely opposite sets of qualities: thinking/unthinking; immaterial/material; nonextended/extended. But how can two wholly distinct substances *causally interact*? We understand perfectly well how two physical things can interact with each other, one causing the other to move or to change. But how could something entirely *immaterial* cause something material to move, alter, or do anything at all? Though she is often overlooked in histories of philosophy, Elisabeth's important question, now known as the *interaction problem*, has driven much of the discussion of the mind and body to this day. Descartes himself had no satisfactory answer beyond attempting to locate the interaction of the mind and body in the pineal gland of the brain, while leaving the nature of that interaction a mystery.

When I look out the window and think to myself how nice it would be to go outdoors, that thought has a role in causing my escape from my office. When, on my way out, I bang my shin against a door, it leads to my pain and my thought that I oughtn't do that again. Our thoughts cause our bodily actions—or, at any rate, certainly seem to—and what impinges on our bodies leads to thoughts. That fact has seemed obvious to almost everyone; most efforts at explaining how that might be have fared no better than Descartes's abortive attempt. For example, the great German philosopher G. W. Leibniz argues that, in order to explain how there can be minds or mental properties at all, we must posit that the most basic constituents of the universe are not physical atoms, but *monads*, which already have a very basic sort of consciousness. To solve the problem of how those monads that make up a body interact with those that compose a mind, Leibniz argued that between all the monads in the universe there was a *pre-established harmony*. In other words, the monads and the minds and bodies they make up run in parallel, much like two clocks wound, in this case by God, and set at the same time: they continue to reflect one another's readings, but not because they interact in any way. As interesting as this *parallelism* might be, it explains away the apparent interaction of mind and body by claiming that it really is *merely* apparent. Moreover, it does this at the cost of claiming that there is consciousness in everything, whether minds or physical objects like chairs. *Panpsychism*, the claim that there is consciousness in everything, does have some prominent defenders today, but because of the way it attempts to solve the so-called *hard problem*—this is the question how consciousness could ever arise in any physical object like a body or a brain—most find it implausible.

Another account of the interaction of mind and body is *epiphenomenalism*, the claim that activities in the body cause states in the mind—my stubbing my toe leads to my feeling of pain—but that those pains and thoughts and beliefs are causally inert, causing neither further mental states nor any states of the body. Some sort of epiphenomenalism pops up even outside of dualism, but as a type of dualism it suffers from two problems: It still doesn't tell us how the physical body is able to interact with the nonphysical mind, since it's as much a problem in one direction as it is in two; and, we are left without any sense of *mental causation*. It certainly seems that our thoughts have effects, both in the world and on other thoughts, but epiphenomenalism says this is illusory. It might turn out that our intuitions are wrong, but that will take a lot of argument and convincing.

Dualism presents other problems. Since I know about my own mind through *introspection*—I know my mind immediately and by looking inside—it would appear that I can never be certain that anyone else has a mind. This is the *problem of other minds*. Moreover, if dualism is true there can never be a complete scientific account of nature, since the mind would still need to be explained. It posits a great divide between us and the rest of the natural world. It calls into question our relationship to the rest of the animals: Do they all have minds? Do they altogether lack minds, as Descartes believed? Do they have minds that are similar or different to ours? What, if anything, can be said positively about the nature of the nonphysical mind beyond that it is a *res cogitans*, a thinking thing? What began as an intuitively appealing view leaves us in mystery.

The root of difficulties of substance dualism is the division of the world into two substances opposite in their essential qualities.[16] If there are two different kinds of substance, then we have to find a way for them to interact and coexist in the one world we know. If the problems do indeed result from the positing of two substances, many philosophers have thought the answer might be found in some sort of *monism*, a view on which there is only one sort of substance. Monism comes in two varieties: *physicalism* (or *materialism*) and *idealism*.[17] Idealism is the view that all that really exists are minds and thoughts, in other words that the mental is all of reality. While it has had many proponents in the history of philosophy, idealism is still very much a minority view. In their holding that *Brahman* is the true reality and all distinctions are mere illusions, some of the *Upanishads* might be seen as putting forth a version of idealism. George Berkeley and others have represented it in the history of philosophy.

However, physicalism has been far better represented in that history. Physicalism is the view that all that exists are physical objects, or whatever is part of the final or complete physical theory.[18] This view has antecedents as far back as the atomism of Democritus and Lucretius. Aristotle's *hylomorphism*, on which the human is composed of *form* (the soul, including the rational soul) and *matter* (the body), can also be seen as a kind of physicalism, inasmuch as Aristotle denies that form can exist without matter, implying that the soul is the organization of the body and not something independent of the matter it organizes. Elisabeth, in her correspondence with Descartes, hints that it would best solve her worries. It is represented throughout the history of philosophy by figures as diverse as Thomas Hobbes, Julian Offray de La Mettrie, Karl Marx, Friedrich Nietzsche, Sigmund Freud, Gilbert Ryle, and most contemporary philosophers of mind.

While physicalism has become close to the orthodox view in contemporary philosophy, it has its own set of concerns. Perhaps the most important issue for any physicalist account is what to say about mental states: What are they? What is my belief that it's sunny today? What is

---

[16] There is another version of dualism: *property dualism*. On this view, there is only one kind of substance, which exhibits two different sorts of properties which cannot be reduced to one another: physical properties and mental properties. Most, if not all, of the mysteries that arise for substance dualism cause problems for property dualism, as well.

[17] Spinoza's view that there is only one substance, God, of which the mind and body are aspects, is another type of monism that is not easily categorized.

[18] To see how this reliance on a physics we don't yet (and may never) have raises problems, see especially Debra Montero, "The Body Problem," *Noûs* 33, no. 2 (1999), 183–200.

my desire to go to the beach? It's one thing to say, with Ryle, that talk of the mind and talk of the body are just two ways of talking about the same thing, exhausted in his case by descriptions of bodily behavior and dispositions; but that doesn't tell us quite how to map one language onto the other. Some physicalists, the *identity theorists*, argue that mental states are just brain states and can be mapped onto them one-to-one. Others believe that having a particular mental state is just having some brain state that carries out a certain function. Much as you might have different machines all of which carry out the function of adding—for instance, an abacus, a mechanical calculator, a digital calculator, a computer—you might have different brain and other physical states all of which could be said to be mental states. This view is called *functionalism*. Still others, *eliminativists*, argue that our talking in terms of thoughts and beliefs and desires and pains is an artifact of an outdated language, one which will be replaced as our understanding of the brain increases.[19]

Even if we settle on the most compelling physicalism available, other questions remain. One of the most important is the so-called *hard problem* mentioned above, namely how it is that any physical substance could come to have subjective states or consciousness. For many, this question and the subjectivity of mental states—your pains are your pains and the way they feel (their *qualia*) are essential to them—contrasted to the necessary objectivity of the sciences that describe the physical world—they deal in what is observable to all—call into question both the plausibility and possibility of any physicalist account of thought. Another important concern is one shared with dualism, namely what to say about the causal power of thought. If my thought is really just some physical state of mine, then it can cause movement in my body in virtue of its physical (e.g., electrochemical) properties. If that is the way a thought causes actions, then the fact that it is a thought, that it is mental, that it seems or feels a certain way to me, just doesn't matter. Once again the mental properties of the thought are superfluous. We are back at epiphenomenalism.

The fact that we—and who knows how many other creatures—have both physical and mental properties or bodies and minds is at once obvious and mysterious. As with many philosophical questions and especially those about our natures, it continues to fascinate and puzzle, awaiting a final explanation, if one can be provided.

---

[19]   On eliminative materialism, see the selection from Paul Churchland included in this volume.

Death and Immortality

In relation to death, John Hick writes, "Man is unique among the animal species, and indeed doubly unique. For alone among the animals he knows that he is going to die; and further, he not only knows it but—in an important sense—does not believe it."[20] Hick's words illustrate the two complementary issues to be explored within this book's second theme: the proper attitude to be adopted toward our mortality and the nature and possibility of survival after bodily death.

Death appears to be something to be feared, not merely on account of the possible pain involved in the process, but more profoundly in the mystery of what might follow (Hamlet's "undiscovered country") or in the terror of complete annihilation and loss of being. The work of philosophers has on occasion served to give clear articulation to, and rational justifications for, those fears and anxieties. The French existentialist Jean-Paul Sartre, for example, saw in any individual's death, in the final analysis unpredictable and unexpected, confirmation of life's superfluous insignificance; while Pascal's fertile imagination conjured up truly disquieting images of what it must mean to die: "The last act is bloody, however fine the rest of the play. They throw earth over your head and it is finished for ever."[21] The neuroscientist David Eagleman's description of the "three deaths" adds another terror, that of being forgotten:

> There are three deaths. The first is when the body ceases to function. The second is when the body is consigned to the grave. The third is that moment, sometime in the future, when your name is spoken for the last time.[22]

It is no wonder that people should try to shield their minds from such painful realities. According to Pascal, this is typically achieved by means of the construction of "diversions" of one kind or other (he mentions gaming and hunting, noise and bustle, while we might add to his list our contemporary diversions: sports, social media, reality TV, and so on). Anything, he thinks, will suffice, so long as it stops us from thinking too much. It is not that Pascal endorsed the pursuit of diversions. On the contrary, he thought it vital to face up to, rather than ignore, what was inevitable: "We run heedlessly into the abyss after putting

---

[20]   John Hick, *Death and Eternal Life* (London: Collins, 1976), 55.

[21]   Pascal, *Pensées*, 82.

[22]   David Eagleman, *Sum* (New York: Random House, 2009), 23.

something in front of us to stop us seeing it."[23] There are echoes of this in the philosophy of Martin Heidegger. He saw the death-evasive strategies utilized by people—including the belief in an afterlife—as exercises in inauthenticity, futile denials of the human being's unavoidable destiny as "being-towards-death."[24]

While these distinctly troubled perspectives are striking, perhaps the more familiar stance of philosophers has been to stress a calm acceptance of death, this being achieved by denying either the perceived terrors of nothingness or the finality of death.[25] An attitude of acceptance is, indeed, so thoroughly associated with philosophy that a person behaving in a resigned or dignified manner, particularly in the face of adversity, is commonly described as "being philosophical." Such an attitude might also be dubbed "stoical," and this with good reason, as a brief account of the essentials of the Stoic tradition will show. As presented by Epictetus, Stoicism operates upon the basis of a belief in the rational harmony of the universe and a division between those things that are in our power and those that are not in our power. While it is reasonable to attempt to alter for the better those things that lie within our power, it is futile to fret about, or rage against, those things that are outside of our control. Since death falls squarely within the latter category, the attitude a person takes toward it should be one of resigned acceptance, an attitude strengthened by that aforementioned belief that in a rationally ordered cosmos all must ultimately be for the best: whatever will be, will be. While a great many people have found consolation and strength from the Stoic perspective on death, others have not been persuaded: Hume found it irritating, La Rochefoucauld insincere.[26]

It was to help people overcome their fear of death, and by so doing attain a state of mental tranquility (or *ataraxia*), that another classical philosopher, Epicurus, offered an influential argument aiming to show that one cannot rationally fear death:

> Grow accustomed to the belief that death is nothing to us, since every good and evil lie in sensation. However, death is the deprivation of

---

[23] Pascal, *Pensées*, 82.

[24] See the selections from Heidegger later in this volume.

[25] A great many of these strategies are utilized by Plutarch in his beautiful "Letter of Condolence to Apollonius," selections from which are included in this book.

[26] See the selections from Hume and La Rochefoucauld later in this volume. The Stoic approach to death is represented in this book by the inclusion of extracts from the work of both Epictetus and Seneca.

sensation. . . . Death, therefore—the most dreadful of evils—is nothing to us, since while we exist, death is not present, and whenever death is present, we do not exist. It is nothing either to the living or the dead, since it does not exist for the living, and the dead no longer are.[27]

For this argument to be persuasive, one needs to distinguish clearly (as Stephen Rosenbaum has)[28] between three senses of "death": (i) the process of dying; (ii) the moment at which a person dies, passing from the state of life to the state of death; and (iii) the state of being dead. A person might rationally fear (i), because of the potential pain and distress involved in the process of dying; (ii) might (arguably) be thought of as an event in a person's life, though its momentary duration should rob that of its terrors; but it seems entirely irrational to fear (iii) since the dead person will no longer be able to experience any sensation. To put this in another way, there is no such sensation as "the sensation of being dead," and it is therefore not to be feared.

The Epicurean argument has generated an industry of commentary. It has its detractors and its defenders. Some have felt that, even on Epicurus's own terms, the sensationless state of death is rightly to be feared. Bad things can happen to a person, for example, even if that person is unaware of the occurrence of those things—a partner's never-discovered infidelity could be one such example—and the state of death might be one such "unexperienced evil." Other criticisms focus on death as an important kind of *loss*: since the loss of something treasured (a home, a wedding ring) is bad for a person, the loss of his or her *life* (the most treasured thing of all) must be regarded as hugely regrettable and something reasonably to be feared.[29] Writers of an Epicurean persuasion will remain unswayed by such criticisms. Lucretius, for example, mocks those critics, who proceed as though the dead person is longing for his lost existence or regretting her name being spoken no more. But there is no realm of nonbeing within which the dead person mournfully recalls the lost enjoyments of his or her life, and nothing therefore to fear. The Epicurean controversy is a lively and ongoing one.

---

27 Epicurus, "Letter to Menoeceus," in *The Essential Epicurus*, ed. Eugene O'Connor (Amherst, NY: Prometheus Books, 1993), 63.

28 See Stephen E. Rosenbaum, "How to Be Dead and Not Care: A Defense of Epicurus," in *The Metaphysics of Death*, ed. John Martin Fischer (Stanford, CA: Stanford University Press, 1993), 119–34.

29 See Thomas Nagel, "Death," in *Mortal Questions* (Cambridge: Cambridge University Press, 1979), 1–10.

To return to the Stoics for a moment, at one point in his argument Epictetus appeals to the example of Socrates: "Death is nothing dreadful, or else Socrates [in other words, the wisest of men] would have thought it so."[30] Though Socrates certainly did not fear death, his reasons differed markedly from the stoical acceptance of an inevitability. For Socrates, death could be welcomed as a new beginning, and not as something final at all. What would commence at death was indeed something preferable to this flesh-and-blood life. For the great Dr. Johnson, it is only this, the promise "of another and better state," and not the empty philosophical assurances of the Stoics and Epicureans, that can justify calmness in the face of death.[31]

Socrates and Johnson have in this manner guided us into our next topic: the nature and possibility of *immortality*. The philosophical tasks in this regard are: to consider the different models entertained by human beings of life after death, and to establish whether each model is either coherent or incoherent (whether, in other words, the model *makes sense*); to consider whether there are good grounds for believing that a life after death, in the form of one or other of the proposed models, happens (whether, in other words, we have any *evidence*, either conceptual or empirical, for its occurrence); and to consider the *desirability* of such a prospect. Only when such a thorough evaluation has been undertaken might one be in position to accept Johnson's contention that our fear and sadness in the face of death can be banished by the promise of immortality.

The first model of life after death—and the one held by Socrates—is the model of *immortality of the disembodied soul*. Clearly predicated upon a dualist conception of the human person (and its plausibility therefore determined by the truth or falsity of substance dualism), this model conceives of death simply as a "release and separation"[32] of the mind (or soul) from the body. As a material and composite structure, the body is subject to death and dissolution; not so the mind/soul which, as immaterial and simple, cannot suffer destruction. As well as having to dispense with notable criticisms of dualism, proponents of this model need also to rebuff concerns about both the intelligibility and the desirability of disembodied existence. Is it really possible to imagine oneself existing without a body, without any senses? And even if one can do this, a large question mark must surely hang over the desirability of such an existence.

---

[30] Epictetus, "The Manual of Epictetus," in *The Discourses and Manual* (Oxford: Clarendon Press, 1916), 215.

[31] See Samuel Johnson, *Consolation in the Face of Death*, in this volume.

[32] The phrasing is Plato's. See *Phaedo*, the relevant extract from which is included below.

It would seem to consist of a life of pure thought, lacking any kind of physical stimulation and sensuous content. For Plato, of course, this was precisely the great appeal of a disembodied existence: the prospect of concentrated thought, uninterrupted by the needs, desires and follies of the body. Less cerebral types may not share Plato's enthusiasm for such a form of existence. Even professional philosophers have their doubts. Sir Peter Strawson, for example, argues that a disembodied life would be entirely solitary, characterized by immersion in personal memories or in a remote and impotent interest in the affairs of others. Strawson—along with a great many others, presumably—finds this an unattractive prospect, and probably as much to be feared as annihilation itself.[33]

The most valiant and imaginative defense of disembodied existence, as both an intelligible and a desirable proposition, belongs to H. H. Price. A substantial extract from his notable paper, "Two Conceptions of the Next World," is included in this anthology. Price appeals to the experience of *dreaming* in order to throw light on the possible nature of an afterlife. The senses are not operative during dreaming, and yet this does not stop dreams from being exceedingly vibrant and lively; hence a disembodied existence—a dream, perhaps, from which we never awake—might consist of a great deal more than abstract thought and the mere poring over of memories. Price confronts the allegedly (and unappealingly) solitary nature of disembodied existence by raising the possibility of post-mortem telepathic communication between like-minded individuals and the possession in the afterlife of an "image body" allowing recognition and social interaction to occur. Skeptics are likely to scoff at Price's speculations. Is not all this talk of telepathic communication in the afterlife rather extravagant and baseless? Can dreams occur in the absence of a brain? These are not insignificant questions. Readers will need to judge for themselves whether Price has been successful in the task of presenting an intelligible account of disembodied existence.

Those responding to requests for *evidence* that the soul survives the death of the body have a number of strategies open to them. Firstly, a robust defense of substance dualism might produce an assurance that the mind/soul is of an indestructible nature and that survival of death is accordingly a natural implication of the human person's ontological constitution. A belief in the persistence of personality after death might

---

[33]   See the selection from Strawson's *Individuals* (New York: Doubleday Anchor, 1963), included below.

also be supported by the findings of investigators into the paranormal: reported ghostly encounters might throw doubt on the sufficiency of a materialistic worldview, thereby diminishing the perceived unlikelihood of a life beyond the grave, while the phenomenon of so-called "near-death experiences" would appear to support the contention that a person's consciousness, separated from the body at the point of death, survives and persists. This latter phenomenon has been a cause of much controversy, some writers detecting in the typically uniform structure of such experiences a mark of their genuine insight into the afterlife, while more skeptical commentators (Patricia Churchland, for example) see in these experiences little more than the frenetic activity of brains under extreme stress.

A second model of life after death is that of *resurrection of the body.* Its depiction of the afterlife as an embodied state circumvents some of the intelligibility and desirability problems attending the concept of disembodied existence: the physical delights of an earthly life will, presumably, still be available to us in the post-mortem world. According to this model, which deserves to be called the orthodox Christian position, the individual person is recreated by God in a physical form, either at some point in the distant future or in some other "resurrection world." While this model might indeed rate highly on the desirability stakes, it is vulnerable to two significant criticisms. Firstly, it lacks real evidential support: the faithful might appeal to its biblical support (see the vision of Ezekiel, included in this volume, and the story of the resurrection of Jesus), but this is unlikely to sway inquirers of a less committed nature. And secondly, it appears to become badly entangled in certain problems concerning *personal identity.* A word about this is in order.

The issue of personal identity broadly concerns what it is that constitutes the continued identity of a person over time. Clearly a person undergoes substantial changes during the course of his or her life. These changes refer not just to tastes, beliefs, and opinions but also to physical appearance and structure. What is it that can justify, amid all those considerable alterations, the assertion of continued identity across time, so that one might say that an elderly person is *the same person as—* or *has a continued identity with—*the baby born eighty years previously (or even the zygote formed soon after his or her conception)? Some philosophers—notably John Locke—located the criterion for identity in *memory*: I am the same person now, at fifty years old, as I was at twenty, because I can *recall* certain events happening to me those thirty years ago. There are a great many objections to this appeal to memory.[34] For one thing, very few of us can remember anything at all of our earliest experiences (and not a single person has memories of life as a zygote). On the memory criterion, the conclusion would appear to follow that I am not the same person as the baby born fifty years ago, and that seems unpalatable. An alternative, and perhaps more promising, approach stresses *spatio-temporal continuity* (or *bodily continuity*) as the proper criterion for personal identity. Being *the same person* consists in having a single, uninterrupted "body history."[35] There is, as it were, a continuous unbroken line, along which all the moments of my bodily life have occurred, which links my life now all the way back to my conception, and which secures my identity as "the same person."

An acceptance of spatio-temporal continuity as the criterion for identity poses enormous problems for the resurrection model of life after death. For it is precisely a person's "body history" that is interrupted in the case of resurrection: a person dies, and is subsequently "recreated" at some different time or in some different space, and that hiatus between death and re-creation is what raises a question about continued identity. It would appear that rather than an individual surviving death in a recreated, physical form, we simply seem to have the creation of a perfect replica of that person, and that would seem to be of little interest or consolation to anyone troubled by the prospect of annihilation. To put this another way, the identity of the resurrected person with the pre-resurrected person would appear to be that of *qualitative identity* only (two things having the same qualities) and not *numerical identity* (two things being one and the same). And qualitative identity doesn't secure personal survival. The imaginative thought experiments of John Hick, included in this book, are intended to resolve these identity issues. Readers will have to judge for themselves whether or not Hick succeeds.

The third and final model of life after death is that of *reincarnation*. According to this model, the soul of a person departs the body at death and is subsequently reborn in a new (and possibly very different) form. The Bhagavad Gita, one of the great texts of the Hindu tradition, explains this by an analogy with a person changing his or her clothes: "As a man, casting off old clothes, puts on others and new ones, so the embodied self

---

[34]   See, for example, the objections raised by the Scottish philosopher Thomas Reid, included in this anthology.

[35]   See Jack S. Crumley II, *Introducing Philosophy: Knowledge and Reality* (Peterborough: Broadview, 2016), 244–48.

casting off old bodies, goes to others and new ones." It is the quality of a person's actions (one's *karma*) in this life that determines the nature and quality of their next one. This was an idea imaginatively explored by the neo-Platonist philosopher Plotinus: those who murdered will return to be murdered; those who misused their wealth will be poor; torpid and lethargic individuals will be reborn as trees; and so on.

Major philosophical problems attend the concept of reincarnation. It shares with the model of disembodied existence a reliance on substance dualism, since only on such a basis might a soul leave one body and take up home in another. Hence reincarnation (sometimes called *transmigration of the soul*) must likewise find answers to the criticisms leveled at dualism. It also finds itself entangled in the most difficult problems regarding personal identity, problems shared with the resurrection model but in a more extreme form. For what now secures the identity between individual a_1, who lived as a wealthy but irresponsible American woman, and the person she is reincarnated as, individual a_2, an impoverished yet compassionate Englishman? The character traits are different, no relevant physical features are common, and a_2 has no recollection of ever having been a_1. In these circumstances it seems most unreasonable to claim that there is any form of identity—let alone numerical identity—between a_1 and a_2. And accordingly there seems here to be little hope offered to one worried at the prospect of death. As Leibniz concluded at the end of his discussion of an individual suddenly being born anew as the King of China but with no recollection of his own previous life: "This particular individual has no reason to desire this." It is indeed hard to see why anyone should care as to whether they are to be reincarnated or not.

We need to touch on one last thing. There are a number of more general criticisms of the belief in immortality that should be registered. For certain writers, the whole idea is simply implausible. Baron d'Holbach, for example, held it to be "an illusion of the brain," generated by the desire for self-preservation but fundamentally incoherent: "To say, that the soul shall feel, shall think, shall enjoy, shall suffer, after the death of the body, is to pretend, that a clock, shivered into a thousand pieces, will continue to strike the hour, and have the faculty of marking the progress of time."[36] Lucretius, comparably, found the belief to be both incoherent and undignified, urging his readers to "put away all that is unbecoming to your years

---

[36]   Baron d'Holbach, *The System of Nature* (New York: Burt Franklin, 1868 [1770]), 119.

and compose your mind to make way for others. . . . To none is life given in freehold; to all on lease."[37] The apparent attractiveness of immortality has even come under attack from certain quarters. The twentieth-century philosopher Bernard Williams held immortality to be a quite dreadful prospect, ultimately productive only of tedium, memorably noting that, after enough time, "I would eventually have had altogether too much of myself."[38] Finally, the feeling that may lie at the root of the desire for a life after death—the feeling that the shortness of life robs it of all significance if there is no life to come—was challenged powerfully by Sigmund Freud, the founder of psychoanalysis. Against the view that the ephemerality of a thing compromised its meaningfulness, Freud asserted the opposite, and did this by means of a simple formula: "Transience value is scarcity value in time." As a flower's evanescence does not diminish its beauty, increasing it instead, so the bittersweet transience of our time here enhances the significance of life. Hence, as a way of securing life's meaning, the belief in immortality might actually be unnecessary, and even counterproductive.

Freedom and Determinism

Few things are more obvious than that we sometimes make decisions to act one way rather than another. Many people think this fact about us is one of the things distinguishing us from the other animals; while they act on instinct, we make choices, informed not just by desire and impulse but also by reason. Whether it's choosing what to wear in the morning, whether to have a muffin with my coffee, or whether and whom to marry, it certainly seems to me that *I* am making a choice in each of these cases. I might be constrained by limited options—I only have so many shirts or suitors from which to choose—but the final impetus in picking among my options is fully a choice that originates with me. For instance, there may be only a blue shirt and a gray one from which to pick, but at the final moment which one is picked is not determined by anything other than my totally free choice. If I chose the blue one, I could have chosen the gray one; things might have turned out differently in a world that was otherwise exactly the same.

This idea that I alone am ultimately responsible for what I choose is *libertarianism*. Such libertarianism is important to many of our basic

---

[37] Lucretius, *On the Nature of the Universe* (Harmondsworth: Penguin, 1951), 125.

[38] Bernard Williams, *Problems of the Self* (Cambridge: Cambridge University Press, 1973), 100. Comparable to Williams's claim is that made by Grace Jantzen in her article "Do We Need Immortality?" Both pieces are included in this anthology.

assumptions about ourselves and many of our practices. When we praise or blame others for their actions, we are holding *them* responsible for what they have done. It would make no sense to evaluate them in the same way if they had had no choice or if they couldn't have done differently than they did. It doesn't make any sense, for instance, to blame people for their height or their age, but it does to blame them for their treatment of their children or maybe even what they're wearing. The difference in the two cases is just that people don't, in the normal case, choose their height or their age, but we do take them to choose the way they treat others or what they wear.

It should be obvious, for these same reasons, that we couldn't make sense of morality if we didn't hold ourselves and others to be free in their choices. If you are told that you *ought* to be more charitable, this implies that you have some say in how charitable you are. If it is outside of your control, it makes no more sense to say that you ought to be charitable than it would to say that you ought to fly under your own power. Since you *can't* do either of those, you *ought* not either.

The idea that I am responsible for what I do is also a central part of my self-concept. I see myself as the author and creator of my actions. To remove that idea would leave me little more than a cog in a machine, a machine being operated by someone or something else. That is not what I think I am.

While it is obvious that I make decisions and some of them, at least, are free, it is much less obvious how this could be so. After all, each one of us is a physical being—or has a physical body—and whatever actions we undertake are physical actions, occurrences in the physical universe. Occurrences in the physical universe, however, are subject to physical laws. They have physical causes and those physical causes are sufficient for their effects. If my choice is a cause, then, it has to be a physical occurrence—say, an event in my brain. If it is also a physical occurrence, then it has a physical cause. This also has a physical cause. It's not hard to see that this chain of causes will begin outside of me and before my existence. That's just to say that my choice and action are determined by causes outside my control and outside of myself. The theory that our choices and actions are determined in this way is *determinism*. Of course, our actions don't seem determined to us, but this is just because we're unable to see the big picture. As Hobbes describes his view, we only see through introspection the last step in the chain, that of deliberation, and so we see ourselves making a choice, but this does nothing to remove the importance of all the previous links in the chain; we merely see the last step in the process and erroneously take it to be the whole process. Laplace goes as far as to argue that if we knew all the physical facts about the world and the people in it and all the physical laws, we could correctly predict all future events including those involving action; humans and our actions are no different from any of the other occurrences in the world. On this view, and in the words of d'Holbach, "Man's life is a line that nature commands him to describe upon the surface of the earth, without his ever being able to swerve from it, even for an instant."[39]

It's worth noticing that some people, going as far back as Lucretius, at least, have attempted to make room for our freedom, our *free will*, by claiming that not all physical laws are deterministic. Lucretius thought his atoms might sometimes *swerve* in a non-deterministic way; comparably, people today sometimes point to the indeterminacy of physics introduced by quantum mechanics. But we don't have to have the correct interpretation of quantum mechanics to see that this won't solve our quandary. Whether the physical causes are deterministic or not, their beginning lies far outside of me. Indeterminacy, at best, introduces the idea that my actions might have random and unpredictable causes, but that's not the same as my being the cause of them.

There is another strain of argument in favor of determinism (prominent, for example, in the work of Arthur Schopenhauer) that relies not on the physical antecedents of an act but the psychological ones.[40] When we act, we act for reasons, but those themselves are facts about us that are not chosen. I might choose the blue shirt rather than the gray one because I prefer blue to gray, but this preference is not something I chose. This psychological fact about me is itself the result of other facts and other occurrences. It might, as Schopenhauer thought, be the result of innate facts about my character. It might be the result of the way I was raised, or the environment in which I grew up, or the society around me, or any number of other things. Whichever it is, my psychological states are the result of other facts over which I had no choice. We've reached determinism by another road. Of course, psychological facts about us, as well as tastes and preferences, may change over time, but they do so because of other psychological facts about which the same causal story can be told.

---

[39]   d'Holbach, *System of Nature*, 88.

[40]   This approach is given its strongest contemporary form in Galen Strawson's "Basic Argument." See "The Impossibility of Moral Responsibility," *Philosophical Studies* 75 (1994): 5–24.

Not least because of the ways in which giving up on our free will means abandoning—or reevaluating—our practices of evaluation and rethinking our conceptions of ourselves, many philosophers have rejected determinism. They instead opt for the libertarianism mentioned above. They hold to the view that human beings are free in at least some of their actions. This needn't be a denial that physical or psychological facts influence the decisions that we make. I might be influenced in my choice of rhubarb rather than peach pie by the availability of rhubarb in my hometown and pleasant memories I have, but the libertarian claims those facts and that past is not sufficient to push the choice in one direction rather than another. At the last moment, I have the ability to choose either of two (or more) options; the decision is ultimately and utterly mine.

From Plato onward, libertarianism has been the dominant view in philosophy. For some philosophers, including existentialists like Sartre, it is our absolute freedom that is definitive of our human nature; in our free choices we create our own essence. Because of its dominance and its intuitive appeal, libertarianism has often been assumed rather than strongly argued for. Quite often, the argument for libertarianism amounts to little more than the statement that it is obvious that we make free and undetermined choices and that we can see ourselves doing so. Something like this is the argument of Aristotle and Aquinas. The problem with such arguments is, of course, that introspection is not a good guide to the truth. Maybe Hobbes is correct that when we look inside, we do see the moment of choice, but are unable to see all the antecedent causes.

The deeper problem for the libertarian is explaining the nature of our free choices. For any decision I might make, it makes sense to ask why I made that choice. Either I will have a reason or I will not have a reason. If I do have a reason, then we can ask the question again and we are off and running toward determinism. If I don't have a reason or if the reasons come to an end at some point, then it looks as if I have not really made a choice, but have done something more akin to flipping a coin. Whatever we want to say about the choices that matter most to us, it isn't that they are like coin flips. We think that our choices are more than arbitrary.

Moreover, free will seems to require that we can interfere with the chain of physical causes in which our physical brains and physical actions are ensconced. If the choice is itself a physical event in our brain, then it will have a physical cause. If the choice is a nonphysical event, perhaps in a nonphysical mind, then we are thrown back onto all the problems of substance dualism, as previously enumerated. In short, we will be left with an unexplained mystery that we should accept *because we all know that we make choices.* This is unsatisfactory, even for those of us who are tempted to believe that we are free.

Some philosophers have attempted to reconcile determinism and libertarianism in a view called *compatibilism* or *soft determinism.* This view has antecedents as far back as early Buddhist scripture. It's David Hume's view, it's related to—if not identical to—Immanuel Kant's view, and it has many proponents in contemporary debates. In short, the compatibilist believes that human actions are determined by antecedent causes—the determinist is correct—but we nonetheless make real choices—the libertarian is correct, as well. Not all compatibilists argue in the same way. However, one common way of explaining the view is to distinguish between coerced or unfree acts and those we normally take to be free.[41] If I am abducted, strapped to a chair, head restrained, my eyes held open, and placed before a screen playing silent films on endless loop, I have no choice in the matter and it would be right to say that my viewing wasn't free, or wasn't really an action. If, on the other hand, I go to a theater playing a silent film, this is a free action, even though—the compatibilist would say—my choice to do so was the result of a chain of causes and effects that ultimately stretches outside my being, even though the roots of my desire have causes over which I am not ultimately responsible. Freedom, then, is a matter of doing what we want. The fact that what we want is itself beyond our control—is determined by other factors—doesn't negate this sort of freedom. In short, the compatibilist can be seen as looking at our freedom and our determinism from two different perspectives: the ultimate and the personal, or the external and the internal. Ultimately— or looking at ourselves as just another thing in the physical world—we can't help seeing ourselves as determined, but as a person—seen from the inside—we can't help seeing ourselves as free.

Whether compatibilism really gives us the kind of freedom we think we have or want to have is an open question. There might still seem to be something unjust in blaming or praising others for what they do and desire to do when they could not have desired (or chosen) to do anything other than what they did.

We are left with the puzzle with which we began. Most of us have a sense that we are fully responsible for at least some of our actions. For many of us, the idea that we might be fully determined is horrific, robbing us of something essential to our humanity, our *agency.* Even if we can be convinced to

---

[41]   This is the strategy of W. T. Stace, Harry Frankfurt, and others.

deny this in the midst of reading or hearing a compelling argument, in the moment of choice, as the libertarians have claimed, we *know*—or think very strongly—that we are free. Squaring this deeply held intuition with what we know about the rest of the world is no easy task and one that has not yet been achieved in anything like a fully satisfactory manner.

Human Nature: Good or Bad?

After the expulsion from the Garden of Eden, we are told, humanity went into a steep moral decline. A witness to the escalating violence, God "saw that the wickedness of humankind was great in the earth, and that every inclination of the thoughts of their hearts was only evil continually." "I am sorry that I have made them," laments the Creator.[42]

Undoubtedly, the nastiness of human beings presents itself to us, not only as an indictment, but also as an intellectual problem.[43] Is it a fundamental part of human nature, ever present and ineradicable, or is it merely a consequence of the corruption of that nature which, originally and at root, is benevolent and kind? The terms of this controversy are most explicitly to be seen in the clash between the theories of Thomas Hobbes and Jean-Jacques Rousseau, so this will be a good place for us to start.

Both theories involve dramatic depictions of what is known as "the state of nature," namely the real or hypothetical conditions human beings would have lived in prior to or without society and political association. Hobbes, the seventeenth-century philosopher and author of the hugely influential political treatise *Leviathan*, provides a harrowing account of that state of nature, depicted as a "warre of every man against every man."[44] This war arises from, and is driven by, two unalterable characteristics of human nature: a colossal egoism untouched by concern for others; and the fear of death. These characteristics are to the fore in Hobbes's enumeration of the "three principal causes of quarrell. First, Competition; Secondly, Diffidence; Thirdly, Glory."[45] Human beings, in

---

[42] Genesis 6:5–7 (New Revised Standard Version).

[43] The word "nastiness" here is intended to be broad enough to cover the entire range of unpleasant and distressing human actions, from the extreme evils of murder, genocide, and torture down to more everyday petty cruelties such as malicious gossip, *schadenfreude*, lying, and cheating.

[44] Thomas Hobbes, *Leviathan* (London: Penguin, 1985 [1651]), 188.

[45] Ibid., 185.

other words, enter situations of conflict when they find themselves desiring possession of the same thing and which they both cannot have; when the fearful anticipation of being themselves attacked provokes a preemptive strike; and when they wish to advance their standing or position. Given this inauspicious combination of factors, it is clear how human beings will behave in a state devoid of authority to keep them all in check. Guided only by the desires for self-preservation and self-advancement, each person will exist in a state of conflict with everybody else, the resulting unchecked violence making "the life of man, solitary, poore, nasty, brutish, and short."[46]

The central element of this account, of course, is Hobbes's emphasis on the extraordinarily self-centered nature of human beings. This egoism is for him unbounded and exclusive. Even the most conspicuous acts of apparent benevolence are reinterpreted by Hobbes so as to reveal an egoistic motive: *charity*, for example, is an expression of power; while *pity* is a fearful imagination of the pitied person's fate befalling oneself. It is a bleak picture. No compassion to counteract the competition, no mutual trust to mitigate the mutual fear. Hobbes is aware that his readers might find this dreadful picture implausible, might reject his thorough indictment of our kind. Hobbes cedes no ground. If you really think of your fellow human beings in a kindlier light, he rhetorically asks, then why do you lock your doors at night? This, it must be said, is not entirely persuasive: we lock our doors, not because we think that *all* people are out to get us and wish to rob us of all we have, but simply because there may be *a few* people around with such nefarious intentions. Hobbes's words on this matter nonetheless reveal his anxieties about human beings: entirely governed by self-interest, not one of us is to be trusted.

It is, perhaps ironically, self-interest that leads the way out of the terrible state of nature. Each person recognizing the precariousness of their existence in a state of nature, they agree to surrender a part of their freedom and place it, for the purposes of protection, into the hands of some authority, or monarch, able to make laws and to enforce them. This, of course, is the famous "social contract." Underlying Hobbes's version of this theory is the idea that without some powerful wielder of sanctions and punishments, nothing can stop the worst of human violence. This suspicion is no Hobbesian idiosyncrasy. It has been felt by many a thinker that, if unwatched, or if the possibility of detection and punishment is

---

[46] Ibid., 186.

absent, humans will behave terribly. The haunting story of the "Ring of Gyges," told by the character of Glaucon in Plato's *Republic*, has precisely this as its point. The ability to become invisible would provide opportunities for outrageous misconduct which no person could—or, Glaucon contends, should—resist. The conclusion is an unsettling one: all people would prefer to behave immorally if only they could get away with it; goodness is, as it were, something grudgingly adopted. This is a significant challenge, both to morality and to a friendly conception of human beings and their desires. The need to address its possible implications is so great that Plato's *Republic* might even be regarded as one monumental and circuitous attempt to answer Glaucon's challenge.

Rousseau's opposition to the dismal Hobbesian view takes the form of a critique both of the idea of an original "state of war" and of the theory of exclusive egoism. Underlying Rousseau's criticisms is the suspicion that Hobbes has been unable to distinguish *original human nature* from *human nature as it currently exists*. A lack of imagination precludes Hobbes from thinking that human beings could be, or might ever have been, anything other than how he encountered them in his own time, the markedly violent England of the seventeenth century. In truth, contends Rousseau, the state of nature could not have been a "state of war," since wars arise only over disputes about *property*, and property would have been altogether lacking in the original condition of humankind. Rousseau presents that condition in fairly idyllic terms. It would have consisted, he thinks, of individuals wandering the world, with neither permanent relationships nor attachments. His vision is of one of these original men "satisfying his hunger at the first oak, and slaking his thirst at the first brook: finding his bed at the foot of the tree which afforded him a repast; and, with that, all his wants supplied."[47] These peaceful beginnings were disrupted with the birth of private property, when the first greedy individuals, digging ditches and erecting fences, took sole possession of desirable pieces of land. From this act sprung inequality, resentment and conflict. The wars that have marred history are not a consequence of an unchangeably selfish and violent human nature, but rather of a sad perversion of an originally generous and pacific one.

As with Hobbes, at the root of Rousseau's depiction of the state of nature lies a particular account of human psychology. Rousseau does

---

[47] Jean-Jacques Rousseau, *A Discourse on the Origin of Inequality* in *The Social Contract and Discourses* (London: J. M. Dent, 1913), 52.

not deny that there is a large element of self-interest at work in human actions. He calls this *amour de soi* ("self-love" or "self-regard"). It is not, however, the sort of rapacious egoism described by Hobbes, but simply refers to the need, shared with animals, to take care of pressing biological needs. At any rate, this self-love is balanced by the presence of a second characteristic—*pitié* (or compassion)—having as its focus of concern not our own well-being but the well-being of others. This, Rousseau believes, is a very strong impulse in human beings and is seen everyday, from the active assistance given to the needy to the tears provoked even by fictitious accounts of human suffering: "Nature, in giving men tears, bears witness that she gave the human race the softest hearts."[48] Rousseau certainly holds, and probably with good reason, that his account is better suited than the Hobbesian one of exclusive egoism to explain the persistence of our species. Without the presence of some degree of compassion, it is indeed hard to imagine that the species could have survived the carnival of mutual destruction that would have engulfed it.

Raising the issue of survival in this way inevitably brings us to Charles Darwin. The picture of a great "struggle for existence" put forward in *The Origin of Species*, may make it appear—as it did to some nineteenth century proponents of unbridled laissez-faire capitalism—that natural selection is a result precisely of a Hobbesian-style war of all against all, the fittest surviving and the weakest going to the wall. Darwin's picture, however, is more nuanced than that. The struggle, he writes, is of a threefold form, "either one individual with another of the same species, or with the individuals of distinct species, or with the physical conditions of life."[49] Humanity's struggle with those physical conditions bespeaks a *co-operative* triumph—of working together, rather than in competition—and indeed, in his later *Descent of Man*, Darwin devotes much energy to an exploration of the human concern for others, seeing it as serving some vital evolutionary function. Whatever its explanation, this concern for others seems to form a natural part of human psychology.

The human capacity for both violence and compassion is certainly puzzling, and the best accounts of human nature will be those that stress a tension in the human heart, with competing tendencies vying for supremacy. It is an old refrain, this story of the internal battle between

---

[48] These words, by the Roman poet Juvenal, are quoted approvingly by Rousseau in the *Discourse on Inequality*.

[49] Charles Darwin, *On the Origin of Species* (London: John Murray, 1859), 63.

one's own dark impulses and (what Lincoln famously called) "the better angels of our nature." St. Paul dwells on this inner turmoil ("I do not do the good I want, but the evil I do not want is what I do"),[50] while David Hume stresses the chimerical nature of the human being in memorable words: "There is some benevolence, however small, infused into our bosom; some spark of friendship for human kind; some particle of the dove kneaded into our frame, along with the elements of the wolf and serpent."[51]

Of these mixed accounts, Arthur Schopenhauer's is among the best and is certainly the most harrowing. Schopenhauer isolates three distinct incentives of human action. The first (and principal) incentive is *egoism*, from which most human actions spring, and by which all people will the preservation of their existence, seek pleasures and avoid pains. Egoism is not the exclusive motivation, however, since two other incentives exist alongside it. Like Rousseau before him, Schopenhauer notes the presence of *compassion* in the human heart. This second incentive, however small its presence, forms the basis of the moral life: it is our duty, Schopenhauer thinks, to cultivate and deepen that compassionate element within us. Neither egoism nor compassion can account for the very worst of human conduct, which Schopenhauer traces back to a third (and terrible) incentive: *malice*. Malice actively seeks another person's woe, without bringing any benefit to the agent himor herself, and is accordingly distinct from a merely egoistic action. It is this feature that underscores Schopenhauer's bitter and despairing denunciation of human beings: "Man is at bottom a savage, horrible beast. . . . No animal ever torments another for the mere purpose of tormenting, but man does it, and it is this that constitutes that diabolical feature in his character which is so much worse than the merely animal."[52]

This vision of a frightening human nature provided by the likes of Schopenhauer and Hobbes has a political corollary, as do the more upbeat perspectives of Rousseau and his ilk. These competing corollaries would appear to revolve around differing views on the desirability of *chains*. Schopenhauer writes of the dangers of human nature revealing itself in all its anger, "waiting only for an opportunity of venting itself, and then, like a demon unchained, of storming and raging."[53] This coheres with a

---

[50]   Romans 7:19 (New Revised Standard Version).

[51]   David Hume, *An Enquiry Concerning the Principles of Morals* (Oxford: Clarendon Press, 1902 [1751]), 271.

[52]   Arthur Schopenhauer, *On Human Nature* (London: Swan Sonnenschein & Co., 1897), 18, 21.

[53]   Ibid., 20.

traditional conservative view of government, in which laws are vener-
ated as "the Chains that tie up our unruly Passions, which else, like Wild
Beasts let loose, would reduce the World into its first State of Barbarism
and Hostility."[54] Such an idea is echoed by the greatest of conservative
thinkers, Edmund Burke, who, noting the unruly and potentially evil
nature of human passions, accordingly writes, "the restraints on men,
as well as their liberties, are to be reckoned among their rights."[55] On the
other, radical end of the political spectrum, the chains placed on human
beings are seen, contrariwise, to thwart potential, blight lives and stunt
possibilities. They are, accordingly, to be removed. This theme runs from
the opening words of Rousseau's *Social Contract*—"Man is born free; and
everywhere he is in chains"[56]—through to the closing call to arms of *The
Communist Manifesto*: "The proletarians have nothing to lose but their
chains. They have a world to win."[57]

The view of Marx on these matters is in reality an interesting
variant on this old debate about the inherent goodness or badness of
human nature. Instead of siding one way or the other, Marx stresses
the malleability of human nature, which is continuously being changed
throughout history and is determined by the conditions of the particular society into which individual humans are born. The self-centered and
aggressive nature of human beings as we experience them is not, on this
view, to be taken for an essential or unalterable characteristic, but rather
as a microcosmic reflection of a society built upon and valorizing such
qualities. In short, if people are rapacious and nasty, it is because society
has made them that way. That contention has far-reaching consequences.
If the conditions of society were to be changed, one would see a corresponding alteration in the character of human beings. Human nature
would then have been changed. Such a "blank slate" view—which in
some fashion might be traced back to the work of John Locke—supports
the ideas of those who hope for unconstrained human improvement,
those radical thinkers who see in political activity not merely the sadly

---

[54] Sir George Savile, Marquis of Halifax, *The Character of a Trimmer* (London: Richard Baldwin, 1688), 1.

[55] Edmund Burke, *Reflections on the Revolution in France* (Oxford: Oxford University Press, 1999 [1790]), 60.

[56] Jean-Jacques Rousseau, *The Social Contract and Discourses* (London: J. M. Dent, 1913), 5.

[57] Karl Marx & Friedrich Engels, *The Communist Manifesto* (London: Penguin, 1967 [1848]), 120–21.

necessary work of restraining a wild beast but the opportunity of realizing humanity's full potential. In the work of a philosopher such as the Marquis de Condorcet that unlimited human potential includes unlimited happiness, the fifth theme of this book.

The Nature and Possibility of Happiness

We will start with perhaps the bleakest assessment of the possibility of happiness, that contained within Sigmund Freud's deeply pessimistic *Civilization and Its Discontents*. This can be read, in part, as a contribution to the Hobbes/Rousseau debate, as discussed earlier, since Freud is addressing why people believe (as Rousseau did) that the demands and restrictions of civilization contribute to human unhappiness. In his distinctive account, Freud combines the most despairing parts of the rival analyses. From the Hobbesian tradition, he takes the idea of a fundamentally egoistic and ineradicably aggressive human nature; while, somewhat in the spirit of Rousseau, he holds that the thwarting of our instinctual impulses by civilization has resulted in distressing and neurotic disorders. The problem is insoluble. The frighteningly aggressive nature of human beings needs to be restrained (and for that one reason alone we should be grateful for civilization), but those restraints contribute to our unhappy state. Caught between violence and frustration, unhappiness appears to be the fate of human beings.

Other factors undermine the possibility of happiness. Freud isolates three perennial sources of suffering. The first of these is by now familiar to us: our relations with *other people* are not infrequently a source of pain, human nastiness (whatever its origin) posing a considerable threat to any person's prospects for a happy life. A second source of suffering is found in the *external world*, with natural phenomena large and small (from earthquakes and hurricanes all the way down to bacteria and viruses) able to bring us low and even destroy our lives entirely and at a stroke. It is, of course, possible that an individual person may be fortunate enough not to experience suffering either at the hands of other people or as a result of impersonal nature. But none of us can hope to escape the third source of suffering: *our own bodies*, essentially transient structures doomed to decay and dissolution. In contrast to the ease with which unhappiness tracks us down, happiness is hard to find. Consisting of "strong feelings of pleasure," it is "only possible as an episodic phenomenon" and is even only felt as pleasure when contrasted with pain. Freud's conclusion is emphatic and barbed: "One feels inclined to say that the intention that man should be 'happy' is not included in the plan of 'Creation.'"[58]

Freud's account is not at all uncontroversial. John Stuart Mill, for example, is one who would demur from such a bleak prognosis. Certainly, Mill is not himself entirely sanguine about the ease with which happiness can be attained, his extraordinary essay on "Nature" graphically detailing the power of hostile natural forces to destroy and mutilate human lives. In *Utilitarianism*, on the other hand, he presents to us depictions of both "the happy life" and "the satisfied life," neither of which would seem to be unattainable, at least for a great many people. Rejecting the impossible notion of "a continuity of highly pleasurable excitement" (the kind of experience that Freud seems to think happiness would have to consist in), Mill instead describes the happy life as "an existence made up of few and transitory pains, many and various pleasures, with a decided predominance of the active over the passive, and having as the foundation of the whole, not to expect more from life than it is capable of bestowing." And people, Mill thinks, have been satisfied with even less than this. The satisfied life is one characterized by either tranquility or excitement: "With much tranquility, many find that they can be content with very little pleasure: with much excitement, many can reconcile themselves to a considerable quantity of pain."[59] While there may not be anything especially ecstatic about Mill's account of the happy life, it does provide a degree more hope than the Freudian conception of a life so difficult that we can only look for ways to minimize and palliate the amount of pain that will inevitably come our way.

Among those who accept the possibility of human happiness, there are strong divergences of view as to whether this is to be found in either sensuous or intellectual fulfillment. As representatives of the first view we may note the Roman poet Martial, the eighteenth century French philosopher Julien Offray de la Mettrie, and the British philosopher and founder of utilitarianism Jeremy Bentham. In his poem "On the Happy Life," Martial does not entirely ignore matters of the intellect—mentioning the value of a "calm mind," especially with regard to mortality—but his list is of a markedly physical nature, including sexual satisfaction, food and wine, good health, and inherited wealth (having to work for a living is, as God told Adam, truly a curse). La Mettrie, true to the vigorous physicalism of

---

[58] Sigmund Freud, *Civilization and Its Discontents* (New York: W. W. Norton & Co., 1961[1930]), 24.

[59] John Stuart Mill, *Utilitarianism* (London: Longman, Green, Reader, and Dyer, 1871), 18–19.

his philosophy as a whole, turns his back on the joys and consolations of the intellect: "We shall be all body and ignore our souls." It is the organs of the body that deliver happiness to us, the pleasant stimulation of these organs making life enjoyable. The evidence La Mettrie marshals for this account is drawn from the lives of ignorant people (frequently happier than melancholic philosophical types), from those of animals (more tranquil than us), and from the delightful—and decidedly nonintellectual—sensations produced by the use of narcotics such as opium: "And what would be the fate of someone whose organisation was all his life as it is when under the influence of that divine remedy! How happy he would be!"[60] Comparable thoughts are voiced by Bentham. All of human life being governed by the "sovereign masters" of pleasure and pain, anything that maximizes the amount of pleasure in a person's life is to be pursued. In that direction lies happiness. And very frequently the greatest pleasures are of a nonintellectual kind, more intense, less ponderous. The silly game of pushpin, he notoriously remarked, may be preferable to poetry.

It is fair to say that, at least amongst philosophers, the sensuous account of happiness has been greeted with a degree of scorn. Seneca (himself the focus of La Mettrie's sensualist attack) voiced this scorn in the strongest manner: "Why do you mention pleasure to me? I seek the good of a man, not of his belly, which has greater room in cattle and wild beasts."[61] This is a sentiment that tends to be shared by proponents of more refined and cerebral views of happiness. Mill, for example, although reluctant to surrender the equation of happiness with pleasure, nonetheless made a vital distinction between "lower pleasures" (the pleasures of the body) and "higher pleasures" (cultivated pleasures of the mind and spirit, such as the enjoyment of art and literature). Though the former pleasures may be more intense, the higher varieties demand our allegiance since they are peculiar to our unique human condition. What a waste of one's human potential if the pleasures one seeks (food, sex, sleep, and so on) are those that are also sought by animals. This is the case, he holds, even if the animalistic pursuits of the ignorant produce a greater yield of pleasure: "It is better to be a human being dissatisfied than a pig satisfied; better to be Socrates dissatisfied than a fool satisfied."[62]

---

[60] Julien Offray de la Mettrie, "Anti-Seneca or the Sovereign Good," in *Machine Man and Other Writings* (Cambridge: Cambridge University Press, 1996), 119, 123–24.

[61] Seneca, "On the Happy Life," in *Dialogues and Essays* (Oxford: Oxford University Press), 93.

[62] Mill, *Utilitarianism*, 14.

The difference of view between Bentham and Mill on the parity of pleasures is a fundamental one. Readers will need to judge for themselves where their own sympathies and inclinations lie.

Robert Nozick's thought-experiment of "the experience machine" throws some further light on these issues.[63] Nozick asks us to imagine that a machine has been constructed that can deliver to us a series of entirely pleasurable virtual experiences, tailored to meet each individual's desires. Once inside the machine, the individual will not know that the experiences are only virtual, and will take them instead for reality. One is now faced with a choice: a real human life, filled with the usual mixture of sadness and delight, trials and triumphs; or a purely virtual life, though one in which all experiences—though unreal—are pleasurable and there are neither pains nor disappointments. It is telling, Nozick believes, that most people would decline to enter the experience machine. This may indicate that what people desire—a happy life—is more than merely a collection of pleasurable experiences.

What, then, do the opponents of the pleasure conception depict the happy life to be? One possibility is found in the work of Seneca, already here mentioned. Recognizing the troubles attending human life, this Stoic view locates happiness in the ability to transcend those difficulties, being indifferent to fortune and to riches, accepting calmly the inevitability of death, and generally recognizing our place in an ordered universe. (It is this kind of view, of course, that La Mettrie wants to ridicule, seeing something entirely joyless in that conception of happiness, and describing Seneca as "a sort of leper well armed against the pleasures of life. I believe that the first member of that sect [the Stoics] must have been a hypochondriac.") A crucial element in Seneca's account is the sense that happiness must be something *secure*: if happiness depends upon external things—excellent food, opulent dwellings, social status, and so on—then it is a very fragile thing; if, contrariwise, it is rooted in a person's mental state or outlook, then it cannot easily be taken away, even in the most extreme of circumstances. The classic case here is that of the Roman philosopher Boethius, languishing in prison and awaiting execution, and yet able to find deep consolation in philosophical contemplation. This would appear to be a great strength of the nonsensuous account: Martial-type happiness seems a thing easily lost, while the intellectual kind appears, at least potentially, to be something bulletproof and unassailable.

---

[63]   Robert Nozick, *Anarchy, State, and Utopia* (Oxford: Basil Blackwell, 1974), 42–45.

These ideas are examined with forensic intensity in Aristotle's *Nicomachean Ethics*, perhaps the most vital text for discussions about the nature of happiness. Aristotle argues that the highest of all goods for human beings is *eudaimonia* (a Greek word meaning "happiness" or "flourishing"). All agree, he says, that happiness is what people seek, though there is disagreement over precisely what this means. That disagreement is shown, indeed, in the varying ways people structure their individual lives, and Aristotle surveys and documents these differences. Most people, he writes, appear to identify happiness with pleasure, but this is a woeful conception more suitable for animal lives, a criticism we have already noted. Improvements upon the bovine conception are located in those lives that seem to equate happiness either with honor or with wealth. Aristotle supplies trenchant criticisms of these. With regard to honor, the criticism stresses the insecurity of honor-based happiness: honor depends upon those who bestow it and thus can easily be lost. Happiness, by contrast, must be secure and "something of one's own." Such a criticism can also be leveled against a wealth-based conception of happiness—if one's wealth were to be lost then so would one's happiness— and Aristotle adds a separate point too, namely that wealth cannot be the final goal of human activity and is useful merely as a means to an end, not as the end itself. Advancing his own view, Aristotle holds that the highest and most perfect conception of happiness must be one that is self-sufficient, noble and characteristically human. This he locates in *theoretical contemplation*, an activity the characteristics of which promise the greatest happiness: it is, he says, *self-sufficient*, as we can engage in contemplation without the aid of anyone or anything else; it is *an end in itself*, and enjoyable in and of itself; it employs the highest and noblest of human capacities, namely the exercise of *reason*; and it is *a god-like activity*, since the blessedness of God's life consists in thought and we are, accordingly, most like divine beings when we think.

A notable—and religious—variant on this Aristotelian account is provided by St. Thomas Aquinas. Having reiterated Aristotle's criticisms of pleasure-, honor- and wealth-based views of happiness, Aquinas endorses the contention that the happy life is one of contemplation. Not just any kind of contemplation will do, however. Contemplation of things of this world is of a less elevated and less joyful nature than the contemplation of the highest and the best. From this it follows that happiness lies in the contemplation of the most perfect thing of all, namely God. Since our knowledge of God is, in this life, imperfect, we must wait until the next life to attain that perfect contemplation; this—coupled with a number of other happiness-compromising aspects of earthly life, such as our ever-present anxiety about death—means, Aquinas holds, that humankind's ultimate happiness must lie in the afterlife, as a reward in heaven.

It is worth saying some brief words here about a question which would appear to go hand in hand with discussions about the possibility of happiness: the question of whether or not human life is meaningful. It is important in this context to distinguish clearly between two senses of "meaning" as this word pertains to questions of existence. Firstly, an individual person might reflect on the details of his or her own life and conclude that it either does or does not hold meaning and significance (for him- or herself). Such a judgment will (typically) be the result of reflecting on whether work is rewarding or repetitively empty, whether personal relations and family life are fulfilling, whether one's hopes and dreams for life have been realized or thwarted, and so on. We might call this *individual meaning* or *Meaning (A)*. This can be contrasted with *cosmic meaning* or *Meaning (B)*, which concerns—not the details of individual human lives, which in some cases may be meaningful and in other cases may not be—but with existence in its entirety. For *Meaning (B)*, the question is not whether I find my life rewarding or significant, but whether the phenomenon of human life as a whole, embedded in the vastness of the universe, can be said to have a meaning.

Paradigmatically, it is *religion* that offers putative answers to the question of *Meaning (B)*. Among their other functions, the great religions of the world will typically provide narratives about the origins of human-kind and our place in the world. Within the teachings of the major mono-theistic faiths, for example, human beings are presented as having been intentionally created by a divine being. This suggests that human life has a purpose and a meaning, and that we are part of a plan envisioned and set in motion by God. Those standing outside of a religious tradition may be less sanguine on the question of life's meaning. Freud, for example, concluded that "the idea of life having a purpose stands and falls with the religious system": consistent with that claim, Freud's atheism led him to deny that life had any meaning at all. For the most pessimistic thinkers—Schopenhauer, for instance—this perceived lack of purpose is combined with a recognition of the widespread pain of the human condi-tion to produce a truly nightmarish conclusion: the suffering that we are subject to is entirely without purpose or significance, our suffering entirely in vain. The Italian poet Giacomo Leopardi, voicing this concern, writes of the world being "dirt," our strivings being "to no purpose" and of our insignificant little lives being drowned in "the immeasurable emptiness of all things."[64] The bleakness of this conclusion, if accepted, might lead to dreadful thoughts: Sophocles (among others) wondered whether it might have been better never to have been born; while the French philosopher Albert Camus saw this as occasioning the one truly serious philosophical problem, namely why do humans, sensing the absurd meaninglessness of life, not simply commit suicide? When one thinks about the human condition, there is probably no more wrenching issue than these questions concerning meaning and happiness, and of the six themes in this book, this is probably the one in which the reader's individual temperament will most determine his or her judgment and conclusions.

Issues of Race and Gender

When discussing the human condition, philosophers have typically spoken in rather general terms, as though the human person could be abstracted from the particularities of any distinct social or historical situation. Karl Marx evidently had this tendency in his sights when he wrote that "man is no abstract being squatting outside the world."[65] On this view, there may not be any such thing as *the* human condition; at the very least, what philosophers have commonly presented as the (universal) human condition may in reality reflect merely the condition of a specific group of people, predominantly male and predominantly white. Writing about this matter, the African-American philosopher Charles Mills suggests that "sometimes it is only through the emergence of alternative views and voices that one begins to appreciate how much of what had seemed genuinely universalistic was really particular."[66] Among those "alternative voices" are the voices of women and people of color, two groups that have not, it is fair to say, been treated well in the history of philosophy: their specific perspectives have been neglected, their mental and moral capacities ridiculed and condemned. In this anthology we bring these issues to prominence by (a) providing a snapshot of the sometimes misogynistic and racist views of philosophers, and (b) including selections of great significance from those voices that have been overlooked and often silenced by the tradition.

---

[64]   See Leopardi's poem "To Himself," this volume.

[65]   Karl Marx, *A Contribution to the Critique of Hegel's "Philosophy of Right"* (Cambridge: Cambridge University Press, 1970 [1843]), 131.

[66]   Charles W. Mills, *Blackness Visible* (Ithaca, NY: Cornell University Press, 1998), xi.

Regarding derogatory attitudes toward women, it might be felt that the very first selection in this anthology sets the tone perfectly. In the second chapter of the book of Genesis, we are told that God created Adam; realizing that it was not good for the man to be alone, God looked around for an appropriate companion and, finding nothing suitable among the animals, created a woman, Eve. God's decision would produce puzzlement in one of the greatest of Christian philosophers, St. Augustine. Augustine struggled to understand why, if Adam really needed a companion in work and for conversation, God did not simply create another male, the physical strength of a man, not to mention his intellectual ability, far exceeding that of a woman and making him considerably more useful. Augustine's solution to this quandary stressed the fundamentally *biological* value of the female: "I cannot work out what help a wife could have been made to provide the man with, if you take away the purpose of childbearing."[67] The secondary nature of the woman is apparent in the creation story: she is God's afterthought. And not only that, but she is a *disastrous* afterthought, ushering in the fall of humanity. Her frail intellect unable to withstand the persuasion of the serpent, Eve tempts her husband to eat the forbidden fruit from the tree of the knowledge of good and evil. God's ensuing punishment condemns Adam and Eve—and all subsequent generations—to the pains of the human condition: work, toil, and death. The divine punishment meted out to women has its distinctive elements: pain in childbirth and submission to the husband's rule. The lesson of the Genesis narrative regarding woman's responsibility for human misery was not lost on the author of the Bible's deuterocanonical book of Sirach: "From a woman sin had a beginning, and because of her we all die."[68]

Though Jesus's own words are free of misogynistic bile, the denigration of women continues in the New Testament. Witness St. Paul:

> I permit no woman to teach or to have authority over a man; she is to keep silent. For Adam was formed first, then Eve; and Adam was not deceived, but the woman was deceived and became a transgressor. Yet she will be saved through childbearing, provided they continue in faith and love and holiness, with modesty.[69]

---

[67] St. Augustine, *The Literal Meaning of Genesis* (Hyde Park, NY: New City Press, 2002), 380.

[68] Sirach 25:24 (New Revised Standard Version).

[69] 1 Timothy 2:12–15 (New Revised Standard Version).

Familiar themes converge here. Woman as afterthought. Woman as temptress and transgressor. The need for submission. Childbearing as the meaning of a woman's life. And underlying Paul's prohibition on women teachers may be the twofold judgment: suspicion that nothing is to be learned from the inferior female intellect, and fear that a woman's influence—as it was in Eden—is generally a dangerous and disruptive one.

It would be unfair to single out the Bible as the prime sexist villain. Thinkers and philosophers of all ages and cultures would appear to have given expression to comparable opinions. Woman is frequently seen to be of a secondary character, deficient in comparison with the male, while in that perennial division between mind and body, the male was identified predominantly with the intellect, the female with the physical. Aristotle (and in this he was followed by St. Thomas Aquinas) describes her as a "misbegotten" or "mutilated" male, suited by nature to be ruled over by a man. These slurs and discriminatory prescriptions roll on throughout the long history of philosophy.[70] Here are some fairly representative samples. According to Rousseau, men should be "strong and active," women "weak and passive." Kant declares that "laborious learning or painful pondering" destroy the light-hearted charms of the fair sex. Schopenhauer's bitterly misogynistic words castigate both the mental and the moral capacities of women, depicted as "childish, frivolous and shortsighted; . . . big children all their life long," suited only to be the nurses of young children and submissive yet "patient and cheering" wives. "Everything in woman is a riddle," writes Nietzsche, "and everything in woman hath one solution—it is called pregnancy"; when going among women he urges men not to forget "thy whip." Freud provides a psychoanalytic variation on the Aristotelian theme of mutilation when he theorizes that all women suffer from the effects of "penis envy," the unconscious sense of being a castrated male. The young Wittgenstein confides to a friend that he opposes women's suffrage on the grounds that "all the women he knows are such idiots."[71] Even the substantially more progressive Plato, while opening up all professions to women in his ideal republic, cannot resist commenting that in all activities men, of course, will be better and more able.

Criticisms of such perspectives have typically taken the form of refutations of the *gender essentialism* on which these sexist views are based.

---

[70] For a substantial treatment of (and selections from) this history, see Beverley Clack (ed.), *Misogyny in the Western Philosophical Tradition* (London: Macmillan, 1999).

[71] Brian McGuinness, *Wittgenstein: A Life* (London: Duckworth, 1988), 121.

If it is the case that men have distinguished themselves more than women in the fields of art, literature, science and philosophy, this is not necessarily attributable to a set of innate and essential differences suiting men for intellectual enterprises and women for nonintellectual ones (motherhood, homemaking, and so on). It may be a particular form of social organization—and therefore something contingent and arbitrary—that has yielded differences in performance and achievement. Rousseau was earlier put in the list of the denigrators of women, but in a lesser-known piece of writing (a fragment titled "On Women") he pursues this alternative line: had women not been "deprived of their freedom by the tyranny of men," who is to say that they would not have matched or exceeded the achievements of men? "I repeat it, all proportions maintained, women would have been able to give greater examples of greatness of soul and love of virtue and in greater number than men have ever done if our injustice had not despoiled, along with their freedom, all the occasions to manifest them to the eyes of the world."[72]

Similar ideas are found, though worked out in far greater detail, in the work of both Mary Wollstonecraft and John Stuart Mill. Writing in the 1790s, Wollstonecraft said that women had been "rendered weak and wretched by a variety of concurring causes," principally a deficient education.[73] The word "rendered" here is the vital one: if women have been intellectually weak, this is not an innate feature of their female nature. Social causes are to blame. Mill's great essay *The Subjection of Women*, which he said was co-written with his wife Harriet Taylor Mill, continues and deepens this anti-essentialist critique: "I deny that any one knows or can know, the nature of the two sexes, as long as they have only been seen in their present relation to one another."[74] What are perceived by some to be natural inequalities between the sexes are in fact the result of purely conventional inequalities in education and permitted social status; only the removal of those baseless discrepancies of treatment will allow us to see the real capacities of each of the sexes. Mill's thought thus combines philosophical critique with an egalitarian call to action.

---

[72]   Jean-Jacques Rousseau, "On Women," in *Rousseau on Women, Love, and Family*, ed. C. Kelly & E. Grace (Hanover, NH: Dartmouth College Press, 2009), 63–64.

[73]   Mary Wollstonecraft, *A Vindication of the Rights of Woman* (Oxford: Oxford University Press, 1999 [1792]), 71.

[74]   John Stuart Mill, *The Subjection of Women* (London: Longmans, Green, Reader & Dyer, 1869), 38.

Another way to combat the misogyny of the philosophers is, not to explain why women may have fallen short of men intellectually, but to show how women have produced work of philosophical brilliance, work that has been unjustly sidelined and kept in the shadows by those keen to preserve the maleness of the discipline. We have already had cause to mention Mary Wollstonecraft, and the greatness of her work would be one such exhibit in this case. It is in this spirit that this anthology showcases the work of a good number of women philosophers. The chosen selections sometimes relate to the question of gender (see the extracts from the work of both Simone de Beauvoir and Genevieve Lloyd, for example); others address a different philosophical issue (as in the selections drawn from the work of Princess Elisabeth of Bohemia, for instance, or from that of Hannah Arendt). These pieces are significant on their own terms, namely as contributions to ongoing philosophical debates, but they are also important in bringing neglected female perspectives to light. In so doing, a different philosophical standpoint is perhaps revealed. As Charles Mills has said about philosophical work on gender: "New conceptual and theoretical philosophical horizons have been opened up, revealing realities that in a sense were always there but that were either not seen or not deemed worth mapping."[75]

In this light it is worth saying a brief word about the case of Émilie du Châtelet, whose *Discourse on Happiness* is included in this book. A thinker of brilliance, translator of Isaac Newton, with research interests extending from science and mathematics to the study of the Bible, du Châtelet would surely have ranked amongst the top flight of eighteenth century philosophers had she only been a man. Her work, however, was treated with dreadful condescension by Kant—"A woman who . . . carries on fundamental controversies about mechanics, like the Marquise de Châtelet, might as well even have a beard; for perhaps that would express more obviously the mien of profundity for which she strives"[76]—and it received largely a muted reception. Rather than being recognized as an important philosopher in her own right, du Châtelet has been most commonly defined in relation to another philosopher—Voltaire—and in that relation defined indeed by a particular, and very physical, role: that of lover. Sadly, this is not atypical. A woman's fate in philosophy has commonly been to be harnessed in the popular imagination to a male figure,

---

[75] Mills, *Blackness Visible*, xi–xii.

[76] Immanuel Kant, *Observations on the Feeling of the Beautiful and Sublime* (Berkeley, CA: University of California Press, 1960), 78.

in whose shadow she languishes, and with whom she has a (real or perceived) amatory relationship. In this manner, the female's secondary and largely physical nature has been reinforced, even in the case of the most intellectual of women. Du Châtelet did not suffer this fate alone. The cases of Hannah Arendt (in relation to Martin Heidegger) and Simone de Beauvoir (forever linked to Jean-Paul Sartre) bear the same imprint.

Du Châtelet's work is fully worthy of investigation.[77] Her distinctive perspective is on clear display in the *Discourse on Happiness*, which deserves a place alongside the best and most famous treatments of that subject. Shunning a monochrome and one-dimensional account of what constitutes happiness, du Châtelet offers a colorful and multifaceted alternative. To be happy one must have a mind free from prejudice, a life devoid of immorality, and a cultivation of the love of study (this last being particularly true for a woman, for whom "only study remains to console her for all the exclusions and all the dependencies to which she finds herself condemned by her place in society"); alongside these intellectual determinants of happiness, du Châtelet lists some more sensuous delights: the pleasures of love, for example, as well as some of her personal sources of excitement, such as gambling and the collecting of snuffboxes. The whole account suggests a full and well-rounded life, and is vastly different from the entirely dispassionate and coldly intellectual perspectives of (at least many) male philosophers. Du Châtelet analyzes and critiques like the best of philosophers, but she also surprises us by peppering her account with revelations of her own idiosyncratic pleasures and with heartbreaking words about her own romantic experiences. Her exemplary openness to the variability of human life is revealed in the *Discourse*'s closing words, in which we are urged to "choose for ourselves our path in life, and let us try to strew that path with flowers."[78]

Attention to the work of women philosophers certainly helps to open those "new horizons" that Charles Mills speaks of, throwing light on the traditional "maleness" of orthodox philosophy. Mills himself notes some "welcome signs that parallel possibilities may be opening up around the question of race,"[79] developments that might comparably reveal the "whiteness" of philosophy.

---

[77] See Émilie du Châtelet, *Selected Philosophical and Scientific Writings* (Chicago: University of Chicago Press, 2009), and Judith P. Zinsser, *Emilie du Châtelet: Daring Genius of the Enlightenment* (London: Penguin, 2007).

[78] Émilie du Châtelet, *Discourse on Happiness*, in *Selected Philosophical and Scientific Writings*, 357, 365.

[79] Mills, *Blackness Visible*, xii.

Though less prevalent than the misogynistic attitudes earlier surveyed, explicitly racist utterances are sadly to be found in the writings of the philosophers. Kant is one such example. "The Negroes of Africa," he wrote, "have by nature no feeling that rises above the trifling"; they appear incapable of producing "anything great in art or science or any other praiseworthy quality"; and of a particular man "a clear proof that what he said was stupid" was simply that "this fellow was quite black from head to foot." Kant bewails the loquacious character of blacks, "so talkative that they must be driven apart from each other with thrashings."[80]

That last quoted remark is especially chilling since it evokes images of the appalling treatment endured by people of color at the hands of white slave masters. Philosophers have certainly had a hand in the defense of the idea of slavery, Aristotle, for example, declaring "that some men are by nature free, and others slaves, and that for these latter slavery is both expedient and right."[81] The fruit of such an attitude appears centuries later in Thomas Carlyle's horrific "Occasional Discourse on the Negro Question." It makes for uncomfortable reading. Carlyle laments the demise of slavery, in part because that demise threatens the flow of spices into Europe, but mainly because it subverts the natural order of things, in which some are masters and some slaves. Black people are described in animalistic terms, "their beautiful muzzles up to the ears in pumpkins"; the black man "a handsome glossy thing . . . a merry-hearted, grinning, dancing, singing, affectionate kind of creature," yet prone to laziness and devoid of the white man's characteristic industriousness. Reluctant independently to exert himself, the black man "with the beneficent whip, since other methods avail not, will be compelled to work."

Carlyle's words provoked an impressive and humane response from the redoubtable John Stuart Mill. Mill attacks all of Carlyle's positions, denying the latter's stress on the soul-improving value of work ("There is nothing laudable in work for work's sake," Mill writes) before exploding Carlyle's central claim, namely that "one kind of human beings are born servants to another kind." This "damnable" idea results from the groundless belief that there exist innate differences of quality and capacity between groups of people. His argument here is the same as that previously noted in *The Subjection of Women*: differences are due to a broad range of social and environmental factors, and not to anything innate; Carlyle's disregard of "the analytical examination of human nature" makes him see natural inequalities

---

[80] Kant, *Observations*, 110–13.

[81] Aristotle, *The Politics* (Oxford: Oxford University Press, 1905), 34 (Book I, Part 5).

where there are only conventional (and unfair) ones. There are no natural slaves, therefore, and the institution of slavery is "a true work of the devil": "I have yet to learn that anything more detestable than this has been done by human beings towards human beings in any part of the earth."[82]

The racism of the likes of Kant and Carlyle notwithstanding, there is truth in Charles Mills's judgment that the attitude of philosophers toward black people has largely been one of exclusion and silence, of a complete lack of interest. The black experience finds no home in the philosophical account of the human person, an account operating too often with abstractions, and with insufficient attention to concrete situations (including situations of oppression). Mills's treatment of Descartes's skeptical questioning is here apposite. Descartes's worries—about what he can know, about whether there are other people, about whether he might not himself even exist—cannot be features of a universal predicament, cannot (for example) be part of the experience of those oppressed because of their color. For how can the oppressed really doubt the existence of their oppressors? Under this aspect, traditional philosophical problems might appear as pseudo-problems rather than real problems, the frivolous playthings of a privileged and ruling group, "just white guys jerking off."[83]

Other selections in this anthology drawn from the work of African-American writers can be used as a corrective to the abstract perspective of the philosopher. The former slave Frederick Douglass writes of the humanity of a person "possessing a soul, eternal and indestructible; capable of endless happiness, or immeasurable woe" being "smitten and blasted" by the dreadful institution of slavery. W. E. B. Du Bois reflects on "how it feels to be a problem" and in so doing develops the concept of "double consciousness," denoting the internal conflict felt by members of a subordinated group when they struggle to reconcile the two cultures (in this case, African and American) composing their identity. And in the work of Patricia Hill Collins, an epistemology is developed that respects and reflects the experience of black women. These perspectives—and those of the women writers considered earlier—serve to undermine the plausibility of that old philosophical ideal of a detached and objective "view from nowhere." All views seem to be embedded in some concrete situation, and the best measure we can perhaps get of "the human condition" is

---

[82]　Selections from Carlyle/Mill debate on "The Negro Question" are included in this anthology.

[83]　Mills, *Blackness Visible*, 4. See also the entire selection from Mills, this volume.

to take as many of these divergently situated views into account and to provide a richly composite and varied picture. In the words of the great African-American author Alice Walker, "What is always needed in the appreciation of art, or life, is the larger perspective . . . , to encompass in one's glance at the varied world the common thread, the unifying theme through immense diversity."[84] It would be hard to find better words to summarize our desire in assembling this entire collection of varied readings: the desire to attain a larger perspective on our human condition and to find common threads unifying us all amid our diversity.

Using this Book: Advice to Instructors, Students, and the General Reader

We have produced this anthology with the intention and the hope that it might be enjoyed both inside and outside of classrooms. Instructors designing an introductory level philosophy class will find here an extensive range of materials from which to draw. The book might be used as the basis either for a class taking the form of a historical survey of philosophy or for those that are more thematically arranged. In the latter cases, an instructor might, for example, construct a class around two of the book's organizing themes (coupling *mind and body* with *death and immortality*, perhaps, or exploring how the *aggressiveness* of human beings might hinder the search for *happiness*, and so on). An instructor might then choose to supplement the materials assembled in *Philosophy and the Human Condition* with another text, diving more deeply into one of the classic works selected from here (Descartes's *Meditations*, say, or the primary sources in the Hobbes/Rousseau debate: *Leviathan* and the *Discourse on the Origin of Inequality*) or else picking a contemporary text and examining how a present-day philosopher is addressing one or more of the themes explored in this collection.

The last mentioned course of action might in fact be particularly fruitful. Since our own policy has been to present substantial extracts from acknowledged classics, this has inevitably resulted in a scantier representation of contemporary work. This is in no way to be taken as a judgment on the quality of the work of more recent philosophers, but is

---

[84] Alice Walker, *In Search of our Mothers' Gardens* (New York: Harcourt Brace Jovanovich, 1983), 5. Walker's words are quoted approvingly by Patricia Hill Collins in the selection from her work included in this anthology.

simply in this context an indicator of two things: firstly, of the uncertainty involved in judging the significance of recent work at such close quarters (one can never be sure what will be of abiding importance, what will be judged a classic rather than a fad); and secondly, of the historical character of our subject (while Whitehead's famous characterization of philosophy as "a series of footnotes to Plato" may be an exaggeration, its central point—namely, that philosophical investigations take place within a historical tradition of thought and activity—is certainly true). Combining the use of this anthology with a text by a contemporary author would serve both to place that later work in the context of a centuries-long conversation and to alert students to the fact that philosophy is not merely a historical curiosity but a living and vibrant enterprise.

Readers of this book, we hope, will come away with a sense of the beauty and richness of philosophy and of the varying ways in which human beings, across centuries and cultures, have sought to understand themselves and their condition. As for those readers, you might be a student, perhaps coming to philosophy for the first time and opening this book with excitement, with trepidation, or simply out of duty, or you might be an interested general reader, for whom the question *"What kind of thing am I?"* has suddenly, or once again, taken hold. Whatever your situation, and whatever your motive, here you will find fellow human beings addressing life's most pressing questions: Am I free? Can I be happy? And if so, in what does happiness consist? Are we all basically good or is there an ineradicable core of aggression and nastiness in all of us? Is there a spiritual component to my being, able to survive my physical death and live on, perhaps for eternity? Or am I simply a purely material bag of guts, ultimately transient and destined for annihilation? These questions seem inescapable. They call to be addressed, at least by serious and thoughtful people. And who would not wish to be counted amongst that number?

We earlier described the philosophical investigation into the human condition as an ongoing conversation between voices of great variety. This book is an invitation to take part in that conversation.

PART ONE

Religious Scriptures

1

═══ ☙ ═══

The Hebrew Bible

....

The books composing the Hebrew Bible were written over a period of around a thousand years, between 1200 and 100 BCE. It is a holy book both of the Jewish faith and of Christianity, referred to by the latter religion as the "Old Testament," and is of great importance for the philosophical and religious investigation of the human condition, as the following extracts demonstrate.

The first selection is drawn from the book of Genesis, and describes God's creation of the world and of human beings, the origin of sin and evil, and the spiraling violence that led God to regret creating humans in the first place. In these passages we also see a depiction of the differences between the sexes. The Genesis account indicates a great tension in the nature of the human being. Specially created by God in his image, humans occupy a privileged place in the world, and yet we have a mortal lifespan: made from dust, we return to dust. This tension is explored in the selections from the Psalms and from the book of Ecclesiastes, one of the most haunting philosophical meditations on the problems and seemingly meaningless nature of human life. The final selection is drawn from the book of the prophet Ezekiel and can be seen to suggest one possible model for a life after death: the resurrection of the human body.

....

From the Holy Bible (King James Version): Genesis 1–4:15; 6:1–7; Psalms 8; 51; 103:6–19; Ecclesiastes 1–4:3; 9, 11–12; Ezekiel 37:1–14.

Genesis

Chapter 1

In the beginning God created the heaven and the earth. And the earth was without form, and void; and darkness was upon the face of the deep. And the Spirit of God moved upon the face of the waters. And God said, Let there be light: and there was light. And God saw the light, that it was good: and God divided the light from the darkness. And God called the light Day, and the darkness he called Night. And the evening and the morning were the first day. And God said, Let there be a firmament in the midst of the waters, and let it divide the waters from the waters. And God made the firmament, and divided the waters which were under the firmament from the waters which were above the firmament: and it was so. And God called the firmament Heaven. And the evening and the morning were the second day. And God said, Let the waters under the heaven be gathered together unto one place, and let the dry land appear: and it was so. And God called the dry land Earth; and the gathering together of the waters called he Seas: and God saw that it was good. And God said, Let the earth bring forth grass, the herb yielding seed, and the fruit tree yielding fruit after his kind, whose seed is in itself, upon the earth: and it was so. And the earth brought forth grass, and herb yielding seed after his kind, and the tree yielding fruit, whose seed was in itself, after his kind: and God saw that it was good. And the evening and the morning were the third day. And God said, Let there be lights in the firmament of the heaven to divide the day from the night; and let them be for signs, and for seasons, and for days, and years. And let them be for lights in the firmament of the heaven to give light upon the earth: and it was so. And God made two great lights; the greater light to rule the day, and the lesser light to rule the night: he made the stars also. And God set them in the firmament of the heaven to give light upon the earth. And to rule over the day and over the night, and to divide the light from the darkness: and God saw that it was good. And the evening and the morning were the fourth day. And God said, Let the waters bring forth abundantly the moving creature that hath life, and fowl that may fly above the earth in the open firmament of heaven. And God created great whales, and every living creature that moveth, which the waters brought forth abundantly, after their kind, and every winged fowl after his kind: and God saw that it was good. And God blessed them, saying, Be fruitful, and multiply, and fill the waters in the seas, and let fowl multiply in the earth. And the evening and the morning were the fifth day. And God said, Let the earth bring forth the living creature after his kind, cattle, and creeping thing, and beast of the earth after his kind: and it was so. And God made the beast of the earth after his kind, and cattle after their kind, and every thing that creepeth upon the earth after his kind: and God saw that it was good. And God said, Let us make man in our image, after our likeness: and let them have dominion over the fish of the sea, and over the fowl of the air, and over the cattle, and over all the earth, and over every creeping thing that creepeth upon the earth. So God created man in his own image, in the image of God created he him; male and female created he them. And God blessed them, and God said unto them, Be fruitful, and multiply, and replenish the earth, and subdue it: and have dominion over the fish of the sea, and over the fowl of the air, and over every living thing that moveth upon the earth. And God said, Behold, I have given you every herb bearing seed, which is upon the face of all the earth, and every tree, in the which is the fruit of a tree yielding seed; to you it shall be for meat. And to every beast of the earth, and to every fowl of the air, and to every thing that creepeth upon the earth, wherein there is life, I have given every green herb for meat: and it was so. And God saw every thing that he had made, and, behold, it was very good. And the evening and the morning were the sixth day.

Chapter 2

Thus the heavens and the earth were finished, and all the host of them. And on the seventh day God ended his work which he had made; and he rested on the seventh day from all his work which he had made. And God blessed the seventh day, and sanctified it: because that in it he had rested from all his work which God created and made. These are the generations of the heavens and of the earth when they were created, in the day that the LORD God made the earth and the heavens. And every plant of the field before it was in the earth, and every herb of the field before it grew: for the LORD God had not caused it to rain upon the earth, and there was not a man to till the ground. But there went up a mist from the earth, and watered the whole face of the ground. And the LORD God formed man of the dust of the ground, and breathed into his nostrils the breath of life; and man became a living soul. And the LORD God planted a garden eastward in Eden; and there he put the man whom he had formed. And out of the ground made the LORD God to grow every tree that is pleasant to the sight, and good for food; the tree of life also in the midst of the garden, and the tree of knowledge of good and evil. And a river went out of Eden to water the garden; and from thence it was parted, and became into four heads. The name of the first is Pison: that is it which compasseth the whole land of Havilah, where there is gold; And the gold of that land is good: there is bdellium and the onyx stone. And the name of the second river is Gihon: the same is it that compasseth the whole land of Ethiopia. And the name of the third river is Hiddekel: that is it which goeth toward the east of Assyria. And the fourth river is Euphrates. And the LORD God took the man, and put him into the garden of Eden to dress it and to keep it. And the LORD God commanded the man, saying, Of every tree of the garden thou mayest freely eat: But of the tree of the knowledge of good and evil, thou shalt not eat of it: for in the day that thou eatest thereof thou shalt surely die. And the LORD God said, It is not good that the man should be alone; I will make him an help meet for him. And out of the ground the LORD God formed every beast of the field, and every fowl of the air; and brought them unto Adam to see what he would call them: and whatsoever Adam called every living creature, that was the name thereof. And Adam gave names to all cattle, and to the fowl of the air, and to every beast of the field; but for Adam there was not found an help meet for him. And the LORD God caused a deep sleep to fall upon Adam, and he slept: and he took one of his ribs, and closed up the flesh instead thereof; And the rib, which the LORD God had taken from man, made he a woman, and brought her unto the man. And Adam said, This is now bone of my bones, and flesh of my flesh: she shall be called Woman, because she was taken out of Man. Therefore shall a man leave his father and his mother, and shall cleave unto his wife: and they shall be one flesh. And they were both naked, the man and his wife, and were not ashamed.

Chapter 3

Now the serpent was more subtil than any beast of the field which the LORD God had made. And he said unto the woman, Yea, hath God said, Ye shall not eat of every tree of the garden? And the woman said unto the serpent, We may eat of the fruit of the trees of the garden: But of the fruit of the tree which is in the midst of the garden, God hath said, Ye shall not eat of it, neither shall ye touch it, lest ye die. And the serpent said unto the woman, Ye shall not surely die: For God doth know that in the day ye eat thereof, then your eyes shall be opened, and ye shall be as gods, knowing good and evil. And when the woman saw that the tree was good for food, and that it was pleasant to the eyes, and a tree to be desired to make one wise, she took of the fruit thereof, and did eat, and gave also unto her husband with her; and he did eat. And the eyes of them both were opened, and they knew that they were naked; and they sewed fig leaves together, and made themselves aprons. And they heard the voice of the LORD God walking in the garden in the cool of the day: and Adam and his wife hid themselves from the presence of the LORD God amongst the trees of the garden. And the LORD God called unto Adam, and said unto him, Where art thou? And he said, I heard thy voice in the garden, and I was afraid, because I was naked; and I hid myself. And he said, Who told thee that thou wast naked? Hast thou eaten of the tree, whereof I commanded thee that thou shouldest not eat? And the man said, The woman whom thou gavest to be with me, she gave me of the tree, and I did eat. And the LORD God said unto the woman, What is this that thou hast done? And the woman said, The serpent beguiled me, and I did eat. And the LORD God said unto the serpent, Because thou hast done this, thou art cursed above all cattle, and above every beast of the field; upon thy belly shalt thou go, and dust shalt thou eat all the days of thy life: And I will put enmity between thee and the woman, and between thy seed and her seed; it shall bruise thy head, and thou shalt bruise his heel. Unto the woman he said, I will greatly multiply thy sorrow and thy conception; in sorrow thou shalt bring forth children; and thy desire shall be to thy husband, and he shall rule over thee. And unto Adam he said, Because thou hast hearkened unto the voice of thy wife, and hast eaten of the tree, of which I commanded thee, saying, Thou shalt not eat of it: cursed is the ground for thy sake; in sorrow shalt thou eat of it all the days of thy life; Thorns also and thistles shall it bring forth to thee; and thou shalt eat the herb of the field; In the sweat of thy face shalt thou eat bread, till thou return unto the ground; for out of it wast thou taken: for dust thou art, and unto dust shalt thou return. And Adam called his wife's name Eve; because she was the mother of all living. Unto Adam also and to his wife did the LORD God make coats of skins, and clothed them. And the LORD God said, Behold, the man is become as one of us, to know good and evil: and now, lest he put forth his hand, and take also of the tree of life, and eat, and live for ever: Therefore the LORD God sent him forth from the garden of Eden, to till the ground from whence he was taken. So he drove out the man; and he placed at the east of the garden of Eden Cherubims, and a flaming sword which turned every way, to keep the way of the tree of life.

Chapter 4:1–15

And Adam knew Eve his wife; and she conceived, and bare Cain, and said, I have gotten a man from the LORD. And she again bare his brother Abel. And Abel was a keeper of sheep, but Cain was a tiller of the ground. And in process of time it came to pass, that Cain brought of the fruit of the ground an offering unto the LORD. And Abel, he also brought of the firstlings of his flock and of the fat thereof. And the LORD had respect unto Abel and to his offering: But unto Cain and to his offering he had not respect. And Cain was very wroth, and his countenance fell. And the LORD said unto Cain, Why art thou wroth? and why is thy countenance fallen? If thou doest well, shalt thou not be accepted? and if thou doest not well, sin lieth at the door. And unto thee shall be his desire, and thou shalt rule over him. And Cain talked with Abel his brother: and it came to pass, when they were in the field, that Cain rose up against Abel his brother, and slew him. And the LORD said unto Cain, Where is Abel thy brother? And he said, I know not: Am I my brother's keeper? And he said, What hast thou done? the voice of thy brother's blood crieth unto me from the ground. And now art thou cursed from the earth, which hath opened her mouth to receive thy brother's blood from thy hand; When thou tillest the ground, it shall not henceforth yield unto thee her strength; a fugitive and a vagabond shalt thou be in the earth. And Cain said unto the LORD, My punishment is greater than I can bear. Behold, thou hast driven me out this day from the face of the earth; and from thy face shall I be hid; and I shall be a fugitive and a vagabond in the earth; and it shall come to pass, that every one that findeth me shall slay me. And the LORD said unto him, Therefore whosoever slayeth Cain, vengeance shall be taken on him sevenfold. And the LORD set a mark upon Cain, lest any finding him should kill him.

Chapter 6:1–7

And it came to pass, when men began to multiply on the face of the earth, and daughters were born unto them, That the sons of God saw the daughters of men that they were fair; and they took them wives of all which they chose. And the LORD said, My spirit shall not always strive with man, for that he also is flesh: yet his days shall be an hundred and twenty years. There were giants in the earth in those days; and also after that, when the sons of God came in unto the daughters of men, and they bare children to them, the same became mighty men which were of old, men of renown. And GOD saw that the wickedness of man was great in the earth, and that every imagination of the thoughts of his heart was only evil continually. And it repented the LORD that he had made man on the earth, and it grieved him at his heart. And the LORD said, I will destroy man whom I have created from the face of the earth; both man, and beast, and the creeping thing, and the fowls of the air; for it repenteth me that I have made them.

Psalm 8

O LORD our Lord, how excellent is thy name in all the earth! who hast set thy glory above the heavens. Out of the mouth of babes and sucklings hast thou ordained strength because of thine enemies, that thou mightest still the enemy and the avenger. When I consider thy heavens, the work of thy fingers, the moon and the stars, which thou hast ordained; What is man, that thou art mindful of him? and the son of man, that thou visitest him? For thou hast made him a little lower than the angels, and hast crowned him with glory and honour. Thou madest him to have dominion over the works of thy hands; thou hast put all things under his feet: All sheep and oxen, yea, and the beasts of the field; The fowl of the air, and the fish of the sea, and whatsoever passeth through the paths of the seas. O LORD our Lord, how excellent is thy name in all the earth!

Psalm 51

Have mercy upon me, O God, according to thy lovingkindness: according unto the multitude of thy tender mercies blot out my transgressions. Wash me thoroughly from mine iniquity, and cleanse me from my sin. For I acknowledge my transgressions: and my sin is ever before me. Against thee, thee only, have I sinned, and done this evil in thy sight: that thou mightest be justified when thou speakest, and be clear when thou judgest. Behold, I was shapen in iniquity; and in sin did my mother conceive me. Behold, thou desirest truth in the inward parts: and in the hidden part thou shalt make me to know wisdom. Purge me with hyssop, and I shall be clean: wash me, and I shall be whiter than snow. Make me to hear joy and gladness; that the bones which thou hast broken may rejoice. Hide thy face from my sins, and blot out all mine iniquities. Create in me a clean heart, O God; and renew a right spirit within me. Cast me not away from thy presence; and take not thy holy spirit from me.

Restore unto me the joy of thy salvation; and uphold me with thy free spirit. Then will I teach transgressors thy ways; and sinners shall be converted unto thee. Deliver me from bloodguiltiness, O God, thou God of my salvation: and my tongue shall sing aloud of thy righteousness. O Lord, open thou my lips; and my mouth shall shew forth thy praise. For thou desirest not sacrifice; else would I give it: thou delightest not in burnt offering. The sacrifices of God are a broken spirit: a broken and a contrite heart, O God, thou wilt not despise. Do good in thy good pleasure unto Zion: build thou the walls of Jerusalem. Then shalt thou be pleased with the sacrifices of righteousness, with burnt offering and whole burnt offering: then shall they offer bullocks upon thine altar.

Psalm 103:6–19

The LORD executeth righteousness and judgment for all that are oppressed. He made known his ways unto Moses, his acts unto the children of Israel. The LORD is merciful and gracious, slow to anger, and plenteous in mercy. He will not always chide: neither will he keep his anger for ever. He hath not dealt with us after our sins; nor rewarded us according to our iniquities. For as the heaven is high above the earth, so great is his mercy toward them that fear him. As far as the east is from the west, so far hath he removed our transgressions from us. Like as a father pitieth his children, so the LORD pitieth them that fear him. For he knoweth our frame; he remembereth that we are dust. As for man, his days are as grass: as a flower of the field, so he flourisheth. For the wind passeth over it, and it is gone; and the place thereof shall know it no more. But the mercy of the LORD is from everlasting to everlasting upon them that fear him, and his righteousness unto children's children; To such as keep his covenant, and to those that remember his commandments to do them. The LORD hath prepared his throne in the heavens; and his kingdom ruleth over all.

Ecclesiastes

Chapter 1

The words of the Preacher, the son of David, king in Jerusalem. Vanity of vanities, saith the Preacher, vanity of vanities; all is vanity. What profit hath a man of all his labour which he taketh under the sun? One generation passeth away, and another generation cometh: but the earth abideth for ever. The sun also ariseth, and the sun goeth down, and hasteth to his place where he arose. The wind goeth toward the south, and turneth about unto the north; it whirleth about continually, and the wind returneth again according to his circuits. All the rivers run into the sea; yet the sea is not full; unto the place from whence the rivers come, thither they return again. All things are full of labour; man cannot utter it: the eye is not satisfied with seeing, nor the ear filled with hearing. The thing that hath been, it is that which shall be; and that which is done is that which shall be done: and there is no new thing under the sun. Is there any thing whereof it may be said, See, this is new? it hath been already of old time, which was before us. There is no remembrance of former things; neither shall there be any remembrance of things that are to come with those that shall come after. I the Preacher was king over Israel in Jerusalem. And I gave my heart to seek and search out by wisdom concerning all things that are done under heaven: this sore travail hath God given to the sons of man to be exercised therewith. I have seen all the works that are done under the sun; and, behold, all is vanity and vexation of spirit. That which is crooked cannot be made straight: and that which is wanting cannot be numbered. I communed with mine own heart, saying, Lo, I am come to great estate, and have gotten more wisdom than all they that have been before me in Jerusalem: yea, my heart had great experience of wisdom and knowledge. And I gave my heart to know wisdom, and to know madness and folly: I perceived that this also is vexation of spirit. For in much wisdom is much grief: and he that increaseth knowledge increaseth sorrow.

Chapter 2

I said in mine heart, Go to now, I will prove thee with mirth, therefore enjoy pleasure: and, behold, this also is vanity. I said of laughter, It is mad: and of mirth, What doeth it? I sought in mine heart to give myself unto wine, yet acquainting mine heart with wisdom; and to lay hold on folly, till I might see what was that good for the sons of men, which they should do under the heaven all the days of their life. I made me great works; I builded me houses; I planted me vineyards: I made me gardens and orchards, and I planted trees in them of all kind of fruits: I made me pools of water, to water therewith the wood that bringeth forth trees: I got me servants and maidens, and had servants born in my house; also I had great possessions of great and small cattle above all that were in Jerusalem before me:

I gathered me also silver and gold, and the peculiar treasure of kings and of the provinces: I gat me men singers and women singers, and the delights of the sons of men, as musical instruments, and that of all sorts. So I was great, and increased more than all that were before me in Jerusalem: also my wisdom remained with me. And whatsoever mine eyes desired I kept not from them, I withheld not my heart from any joy; for my heart rejoiced in all my labour: and this was my portion of all my labour. Then I looked on all the works that my hands had wrought, and on the labour that I had laboured to do: and, behold, all was vanity and vexation of spirit, and there was no profit under the sun. And I turned myself to behold wisdom, and madness, and folly: for what can the man do that cometh after the king? even that which hath been already done. Then I saw that wisdom excelleth folly, as far as light excelleth darkness. The wise man's eyes are in his head; but the fool walketh in darkness: and I myself perceived also that one event happeneth to them all. Then said I in my heart, As it happeneth to the fool, so it happeneth even to me; and why was I then more wise? Then I said in my heart, that this also is vanity. For there is no remembrance of the wise more than of the fool for ever; seeing that which now is in the days to come shall all be forgotten. And how dieth the wise man? as the fool. Therefore I hated life; because the work that is wrought under the sun is grievous unto me: for all is vanity and vexation of spirit. Yea, I hated all my labour which I had taken under the sun: because I should leave it unto the man that shall be after me. And who knoweth whether he shall be a wise man or a fool? yet shall he have rule over all my labour wherein I have laboured, and wherein I have shewed myself wise under the sun. This is also vanity. Therefore I went about to cause my heart to despair of all the labour which I took under the sun. For there is a man whose labour is in wisdom, and in knowledge, and in equity; yet to a man that hath not laboured therein shall he leave it for his portion. This also is vanity and a great evil. For what hath man of all his labour, and of the vexation of his heart, wherein he hath laboured under the sun? For all his days are sorrows, and his travail grief; yea, his heart taketh not rest in the night. This is also vanity. There is nothing better for a man, than that he should eat and drink, and that he should make his soul enjoy good in his labour. This also I saw, that it was from the hand of God. For who can eat, or who else can hasten hereunto, more than I? For God giveth to a man that is good in his sight wisdom, and knowledge, and joy: but to the sinner he giveth travail, to gather and to heap up, that he may give to him that is good before God. This also is vanity and vexation of spirit.

Chapter 3

To every thing there is a season, and a time to every purpose under the heaven: A time to be born, and a time to die; a time to plant, and a time to pluck up that which is planted; A time to kill, and a time to heal; a time to break down, and a time to build up; A time to weep, and a time to laugh; a time to mourn, and a time to dance; A time to cast away stones, and a time to gather stones together; a time to embrace, and a time to refrain from embracing; A time to get, and a time to lose; a time to keep, and a time to cast away; A time to rend, and a time to sew; a time to keep silence, and a time to speak; A time to love, and a time to hate; a time of war, and a time of peace. What profit hath he that worketh in that wherein he laboureth? I have seen the travail, which God hath given to the sons of men to be exercised in it. He hath made every thing beautiful in his time: also he hath set the world in their heart, so that no man can find out the work that God maketh from the beginning to the end. I know that there is no good in them, but for a man to rejoice, and to do good in his life. And also that every man should eat and drink, and enjoy the good of all his labour, it is the gift of God. I know that, whatsoever God doeth, it shall be for ever: nothing can be put to it, nor any thing taken from it: and God doeth it, that men should fear before him. That which hath been is now; and that which is to be hath already been; and God requireth that which is past. And moreover I saw under the sun the place of judgment, that wickedness was there; and the place of righteousness, that iniquity was there. I said in mine heart, God shall judge the righteous and the wicked: for there is a time there for every purpose and for every work. I said in mine heart concerning the estate of the sons of men, that God might manifest them, and that they might see that they themselves are beasts. For that which befalleth the sons of men befalleth beasts; even one thing befalleth them: as the one dieth, so dieth the other; yea, they have all one breath; so that a man hath no preeminence above a beast: for all is vanity. All go unto one place; all are of the dust, and all turn to dust again. Who knoweth the spirit of man that goeth upward, and the spirit of the beast that goeth downward to the earth? Wherefore I perceive that there is nothing better, than that a man should rejoice in his own works; for that is his portion: for who shall bring him to see what shall be after him?

Chapter 4:1–3

So I returned, and considered all the oppressions that are done under the sun: and behold the tears of such as were oppressed, and they had no comforter; and on the side of their oppressors there was power; but they had no comforter. Wherefore I praised the dead which are already dead more than the living which are yet alive. Yea, better is he than both they, which hath not yet been, who hath not seen the evil work that is done under the sun.

Chapter 9

For all this I considered in my heart even to declare all this, that the righteous, and the wise, and their works, are in the hand of God: no man knoweth either love or hatred by all that is before them. All things come alike to all: there is one event to the righteous, and to the wicked; to the good and to the clean, and to the unclean; to him that sacrificeth, and to him that sacrificeth not: as is the good, so is the sinner; and he that sweareth, as he that feareth an oath. This is an evil among all things that are done under the sun, that there is one event unto all: yea, also the heart of the sons of men is full of evil, and madness is in their heart while they live, and after that they go to the dead. For to him that is joined to all the living there is hope: for a living dog is better than a dead lion. For the living know that they shall die: but the dead know not any thing, neither have they any more a reward; for the memory of them is forgotten. Also their love, and their hatred, and their envy, is now perished; neither have they any more a portion for ever in any thing that is done under the sun. Go thy way, eat thy bread with joy, and drink thy wine with a merry heart; for God now accepteth thy works. Let thy garments be always white; and let thy head lack no ointment. Live joyfully with the wife whom thou lovest all the days of the life of thy vanity, which he hath given thee under the sun, all the days of thy vanity: for that is thy portion in this life, and in thy labour which thou takest under the sun. Whatsoever thy hand findeth to do, do it with thy might; for there is no work, nor device, nor knowledge, nor wisdom, in the grave, whither thou goest. I returned, and saw under the sun, that the race is not to the swift, nor the battle to the strong, neither yet bread to the wise, nor yet riches to men of understanding, nor yet favour to men of skill; but time and chance happeneth to them all. For man also knoweth not his time: as the fishes that are taken in an evil net, and as the birds that are caught in the snare; so are the sons of men snared in an evil time, when it falleth suddenly upon them. This wisdom have I seen also under the sun, and it seemed great unto me: There was a little city, and few men within it; and there came a great king against it, and besieged it, and built great bulwarks against it: Now there was found in it a poor wise man, and he by his wisdom delivered the city; yet no man remembered that same poor man. Then said I, Wisdom is better than strength: nevertheless the poor man's wisdom is despised, and his words are not heard. The words of wise men are heard in quiet more than the cry of him that ruleth among fools. Wisdom is better than weapons of war: but one sinner destroyeth much good.

Chapter 11

Cast thy bread upon the waters: for thou shalt find it after many days. Give a portion to seven, and also to eight; for thou knowest not what evil shall be upon the earth. If the clouds be full of rain, they empty themselves upon the earth: and if the tree fall toward the south, or toward the north, in the place where the tree falleth, there it shall be. He that observeth the wind shall not sow; and he that regardeth the clouds shall not reap. As thou knowest not what is the way of the spirit, nor how the bones do grow in the womb of her that is with child: even so thou knowest not the works of God who maketh all. In the morning sow thy seed, and in the evening withhold not thine hand: for thou knowest not whether shall prosper, either this or that, or whether they both shall be alike good. Truly the light is sweet, and a pleasant thing it is for the eyes to behold the sun: But if a man live many years, and rejoice in them all; yet let him remember the days of darkness; for they shall many. All that cometh is vanity. Rejoice, O young man, in thy youth; and let thy heart cheer thee in the days of thy youth, and walk in the ways of thine heart, and in the sight of thine eyes: but know thou, that for all these things God will bring thee into judgment. Therefore remove sorrow from thy heart, and put away evil from thy flesh: for childhood and youth are vanity.

Chapter 12

Remember now thy Creator in the days of thy youth, while the evil days come not, nor the years draw nigh, when thou shalt say, I have no pleasure in them; While the sun, or the light, or the moon, or the stars, be not darkened, nor the clouds return after the rain: In the day when the keepers of the house shall tremble, and the strong men shall bow themselves, and the grinders cease because they are few, and those that look out of the windows be darkened, And the doors shall be shut in the streets, when the sound of the grinding is low, and he shall rise up at the voice of the bird, and all the daughters of musick shall be brought low; Also when they shall be afraid of that which is high, and fears shall be in the way, and the almond tree shall flourish, and the grasshopper shall be a burden, and desire shall fail: because man goeth to his long home, and the mourners go about the streets: Or ever the silver cord be loosed, or the golden bowl be broken, or the pitcher be broken at the fountain, or the wheel broken at the cistern. Then shall the dust return to the earth as it was: and the spirit shall return unto God who gave it. Vanity of vanities, saith the preacher; all is vanity. And moreover, because the preacher was wise, he still taught the people knowledge; yea, he gave good heed, and sought out, and set in order many proverbs. The preacher sought to find out acceptable words: and that which was written was upright, even words of truth. The words of the wise are as goads, and as nails fastened by the masters of assemblies, which are given from one shepherd. And further, by these, my son, be admonished: of making many books there is no end; and much study is a weariness of the flesh. Let us hear the conclusion of the whole matter: Fear God, and keep his commandments: for this is the whole duty of man. For God shall bring every work into judgment, with every secret thing, whether it be good, or whether it be evil.

Ezekiel

Chapter 37:1–14

The hand of the LORD was upon me, and carried me out in the spirit of the LORD, and set me down in the midst of the valley which was full of bones, And caused me to pass by them round about: and, behold, there were very many in the open valley; and, lo, they were very dry. And he said unto me, Son of man, can these bones live? And I answered, O Lord GOD, thou knowest. Again he said unto me, Prophesy upon these bones, and say unto them, O ye dry bones, hear the word of the LORD. Thus saith the Lord GOD unto these bones; Behold, I will cause breath to enter into you, and ye shall live: And I will lay sinews upon you, and will bring up flesh upon you, and cover you with skin, and put breath in you, and ye shall live; and ye shall know that I am the LORD. So I prophesied as I was commanded: and as I prophesied, there was a noise, and behold a shaking, and the bones came together, bone to his bone. And when I beheld, lo, the sinews and the flesh came up upon them, and the skin covered them above: but there was no breath in them. Then said he unto me, Prophesy unto the wind, prophesy, son of man, and say to the wind, Thus saith the Lord GOD; Come from the four winds, O breath, and breathe upon these slain, that they may live. So I prophesied as he commanded me, and the breath came into them, and they lived, and stood up upon their feet, an exceeding great army. Then he said unto me, Son of man, these bones are the whole house of Israel: behold, they say, Our bones are dried, and our hope is lost: we are cut off for our parts. Therefore prophesy and say unto them, Thus saith the Lord GOD; Behold, O my people, I will open your graves, and cause you to come up out of your graves, and bring you into the land of Israel. And ye shall know that I am the LORD, when I have opened your graves, O my people, and brought you up out of your graves, And shall put my spirit in you, and ye shall live, and I shall place you in your own land: then shall ye know that I the LORD have spoken it, and performed it, saith the LORD.

======= ॐ =======

The Upanishads

. . . .

The *Upanishads* (from the Sanskrit "sitting down near," indicating the attitude of listening to a teacher) are comprised of verse and prose teachings on the nature of brahman (ultimate reality), atman (the soul or self), the beginning and nature of the sensible universe, and the relation between brahman and atman. As Hindu scriptures they also contain a recipe (or recipes) for their readers to come to ultimate salvation, conceived as moksha (release or liberation) from the cycle of samsara (death and rebirth) and realization of and entry into the true relation of brahman and atman.

Composed over many centuries—beginning in the eighth century BCE—and comprising at least 108 works, the Upanishads do not present one unified picture. There are competing views about each of the questions addressed. There is not just one picture of brahman—is this something like a personal god or can we say anything positive about it?—or atman—is this a separately existing soul or is this separation illusory leading to a view similar to the Buddhist anatman?—or, because of this, what moksha is—after release do we enjoy a beatific vision or do we cease to exist? What we instead find are different thinkers approaching these questions each in their own way.

The texts selected here are from the earliest works. In the selection from the Brihadaranyaka Upanishad, the sage Yajñavalkya explains the nature of atman or the soul to King Janaka. In the Chandogya Upanishad, an analogy is drawn between the ubiquity of salt in salt water and the indwelling of brahman in all of reality, including atman. The selection from the Kaushitaki Upanishad

From Müller, Max (ed.) *The Sacred Books of the East*, vol I (Chandogya, Kaushitaki) and XV (Brihadaranyaka, Katha) Clarendon 1879, 1884.

emphasizes the relationship between prâna (the universal life force) and self-consciousness as well as the importance of knowing the origins of phenomena rather than the phenomena themselves and, by extension, the importance of answering ultimate questions. The Katha Upanishad is structured as the teaching of Yama (Death) to Nachiketa, a child whose father curses him by "sending him to death," (think of telling someone to "go to hell") when Nachiketa questions the values of his father's sacrifices. Yama instructs his charge on the nature of atman, its eternality, and its identification with brahman before returning him to the world of the living.

Brihadaranyaka Upanishad

In the beginning this was Self alone, in the shape of a person. He looking round saw nothing but his Self. He first said, "This is I," therefore he became I by name. Therefore even now, if a man is asked, he first says, "This is I," and then pronounces the other name which he may have. And because before all this, he (the Self) burnt down all evils, therefore he was a person. Verily he who knows this, burns down every one who tries to be before him.

He feared, and therefore any one who is lonely fears. He thought, "As there is nothing but myself, why should I fear?" Thence his fear passed away. For what should he have feared? Verily fear arises from a second only.

But he felt no delight. Therefore a man who is lonely feels no delight. He wished for a second. He was so large as man and wife together. He then made this his Self to fall in two (pat), and thence arose husband and wife. Therefore Yâgñavalkya said: "We two are thus (each of us) like half a shell." Therefore the void which was there, is filled by the wife. He embraced her, and men were born.

She thought, "How can he embrace me, after having produced me from himself? I shall hide myself."

She then became a cow, the other became a bull and embraced her, and hence cows were born. The one became a mare, the other a stallion; the one a male ass, the other a female ass. He embraced her, and hence one-hoofed animals were born. The one became a she-goat, the other a he-goat; the one became a ewe, the other a ram. He embraced her, and hence goats and sheep were born. And thus he created everything that exists in pairs, down to the ants.

He knew, "I indeed am this creation, for I created all this." Hence he became the creation, and he who knows this lives in this his creation.

Next he thus produced fire by rubbing. From the mouth, as from the fire-hole, and from the hands he created fire. Therefore both the mouth and the hands are inside without hair, for the fire-hole is inside without hair.

And when they say, "Sacrifice to this or sacrifice to that god," each god is but his manifestation, for he is all gods.

Now, whatever there is moist, that he created from seed; this is Soma. So far verily is this universe either food or eater. Soma indeed is food, Agni eater. This is the highest creation of Brahman, when he created the gods from his better part, and when he, who was (then) mortal, created the immortals. Therefore it was the highest creation. And he who knows this, lives in this his highest creation.

Now all this was then undeveloped. It became developed by form and name, so that one could say, "He, called so and so, is such a one." Therefore at present also all this is developed by name and form, so that one can say, "He, called so and so, is such a one."

He (Brahman or the Self) entered thither, to the very tips of the finger-nails, as a razor might be fitted in a razor-case, or as fire in a fire-place.

He cannot be seen, for, in part only, when breathing, he is breath by name; when speaking, speech by name; when seeing, eye by name; when hearing, ear by name; when thinking, mind by name. All these are but the names of his acts. And he who worships him as the one or the other, does not know him, for he is apart from this by the one or the other. Let men worship him as Self, for in the Self all these are one. This Self is the footstep of everything, for through it one knows everything. And as one can find again by footsteps what was lost, thus he who knows this finds glory and praise.

. . .

Ganaka Vaideha, descending from his throne, said: "I bow to you, O Yâgñavalkya, teach me."

Yâgñavalkya said: "Your Majesty, as a man who wishes to make a long journey, would furnish himself with a chariot or a ship, thus is your mind well furnished by these Upanishads. You are honourable, and wealthy, you have learnt the Vedas and been told the Upanishads. Whither then will you go when departing hence?"

Ganaka Vaideha said: "Sir, I do not know whither I shall go."
Yâgñavalkya said: "Then I shall tell you this, whither you will go."
Ganaka Vaideha said: "Tell it, Sir."

. . .

"And he [Âtman, or Self] can only be described by No, no! He is incomprehensible, for he cannot be comprehended; he is undecaying, for he cannot decay; he is not attached, for he does not attach himself; he is unbound, he does not suffer, he does not perish. O Ganaka, you have indeed reached fearlessness,"—thus said Yâgñavalkya.

Then Ganaka said: "May that fearlessness come to you also who teachest us fearlessness. I bow to you. Here are the Videhas, and here am I (thy slave)."

Chandogya Upanishad

"Place this salt in water, and then wait on me in the morning."

The son did as he was commanded.

The father said to him: "Bring me the salt, which you placed in the water last night."

The son having looked for it, found it not, for, of course, it was melted.

The father said: "Taste it from the surface of the water. How is it?"

The son replied: "It is salt."

"Taste it from the middle. How is it?"

The son replied: "It is salt."

"Taste it from the bottom. How is it?"

The son replied "It is salt."

The father said: "Throw it away and then wait on me."

He did so; but salt exists for ever.

Then the father said: "Here also, in this body, forsooth, you do not perceive the True, my son; but there indeed it is."

"That which is the subtle essence, in it all that exists has its self. It is the True. It is the Self, and thou, O Svetaketu, art it."

"Please, Sir, inform me still more," said the son.

"Be it so, my child," the father replied.

Kaushitaki Upanishad

Man lives deprived of speech, for we see dumb people. Man lives deprived of sight, for we see blind people. Man lives deprived of hearing, for we see deaf people. Man lives deprived of mind, for we see infants. Man lives deprived of his arms, deprived of his legs, for we see it thus. But prâna [breath, or life force] alone is the conscious self, and having laid hold of this body, it makes it rise up. Therefore it is said, Let man worship it alone as uktha. What is prâna, that is pragñâ (self-consciousness); what is pragñâ, that is prâna, for together they live in this body, and together they go out of it. Of that, this is the evidence, this is the understanding. When a man, being thus asleep, sees no dream whatever, he becomes one with that prâna alone. Then speech goes to him with all names, the eye with all forms, the ear with all sounds, the mind with all thoughts. And when he awakes, then, as from a burning fire sparks proceed in all directions, thus from that self the prânâs (speech, etc.) proceed, each towards its place; from the prânas the gods, from the gods the worlds.

Of this, this is the proof, this is the understanding. When a man is thus sick, going to die, falling into weakness and faintness, they say: "His thought has departed, he hears not, he sees not, he speaks not, he thinks not." Then he becomes one with that prâna alone. Then speech goes to him with all names, the eye with all forms, the ear with all sounds, the mind with all thoughts. And when he departs from this body, he departs together with all these. Let no man try to find out what speech is, let him know the speaker. Let no man try to find out what odour is, let him know him who smells. Let no man try to find out what form is, let him know the seer. Let no man try to find out what sound is, let him know the hearer. Let no man try to find out the tastes of food, let him know the knower of tastes. Let no man try to find out what action is, let him know the agent. Let no man try to find out what pleasure and pain are, let him know the knower of pleasure and pain. Let no man try to find out what happiness, joy, and offspring are, let him know the knower of happiness, joy, and offspring. Let no man try to find out what movement is, let him know the mover. Let no man try to find out what mind is, let him know the thinker. These ten objects (what is spoken, smelled, seen, etc.) have reference to pragñâ, the ten subjects (speech, the senses, mind) have reference to objects. If there were no objects, there would be no subjects; and if there were no subjects, there would be no objects. For on either side alone nothing could be achieved. But that (the self of pragñâ, and prâna) is not many, (but one). For as in a car the circumference of a wheel is placed on the spokes, and the spokes on the nave, thus are these objects placed on the subjects, and the subjects on the prâna. And that prâna indeed is the self of pragñâ, blessed, imperishable, immortal. He does not increase by a good action, nor decrease by a bad action. For he (the self of prâna and pragñâ) makes him, whom he wishes to lead up from these worlds, do a good deed; and the same makes him, whom he wishes to lead down from these worlds, do a bad deed. And he is the guardian of the world, he is the king of the world, he is the lord of the universe,—and he is my (Indra's) self, thus let it be known, yea, thus let it be known!

Katha Upanishad

Vâgasravasa, desirous (of heavenly rewards), surrendered (at a sacrifice) all that he possessed. He had a son of the name of Nakiketas.

When the presents were being given (to the priests), faith entered into the heart of Nakiketas, who was still a boy, and he thought:

"Unblessed, surely, are the worlds to which a man goes by giving cows which have drunk water, eaten hay, given their milk, and are barren."

He (knowing that his father had promised to give up all that he possessed, and therefore his son also) said to his father: "Dear father, to whom wilt thou give me?" He said it a second and a third time. Then the father replied (angrily):

"I shall give thee unto Death."

(The father, having once said so, though in haste, had to be true to his word and to sacrifice his son.)

The son said: "I go as the first, at the head of many (who have still to die); I go in the midst of many (who are now dying). What will be the work of Yama (the ruler of the departed) which to-day he has to do unto me?"

. . .

"The wise who, by means of meditation on his Self, recognises the Ancient, who is difficult to be seen, who has entered into the dark, who is hidden in the cave, who dwells in the abyss, as God, he indeed leaves joy and sorrow far behind."

"A mortal who has heard this and embraced it, who has separated from it all qualities, and has thus reached the subtle Being, rejoices, because he has obtained what is a cause for rejoicing. The house (of Brahman) is open, I believe, O Nakiketas."

Nakiketas said: "That which thou seest as neither this nor that, as neither effect nor cause, as neither past nor future, tell me that."

Yama said: "That word (or place) which all the Vedas record, which all penances proclaim, which men desire when they live as religious students, that word I tell thee briefly, it is Om."

"That (imperishable) syllable means Brahman, that syllable means the highest (Brahman); he who knows that syllable, whatever he desires, is his."

"This is the best support, this is the highest support; he who knows that support is magnified in the world of Brahmâ."

"The knowing (Self) is not born, it dies not; it sprang from nothing, nothing sprang from it. The Ancient is unborn, eternal, everlasting; he is not killed, though the body is killed."

"If the killer thinks that he kills, if the killed thinks that he is killed, they do not understand; for this one does not kill, nor is that one killed."

"The Self, smaller than small, greater than great, is hidden in the heart of that creature. A man who is free from desires and free from grief, sees the majesty of the Self by the grace of the Creator."

"Though sitting still, he walks far; though lying down, he goes everywhere. Who, save myself, is able to know that God who rejoices and rejoices not?"

"The wise who knows the Self as bodiless within the bodies, as unchanging among changing things, as great and omnipresent, does never grieve."

"That Self cannot be gained by the Veda, nor by understanding, nor by much learning. He whom the Self chooses, by him the Self can be gained. The Self chooses him (his body) as his own."

"But he who has not first turned away from his wickedness, who is not tranquil, and subdued, or whose mind is not at rest, he can never obtain the Self (even) by knowledge!"

"Who then knows where He is, He to whom the Brahmans and Kshatriyas are (as it were) but food, and death itself a condiment?"

. . .

"Know the Self to be sitting in the chariot, the body to be the chariot, the intellect the charioteer, and the mind the reins."

"The senses they call the horses, the objects of the senses their roads. When he (the Highest Self) is in union with the body, the senses, and the mind, then wise people call him the Enjoyer."

"He who has no understanding and whose mind (the reins) is never firmly held, his senses (horses) are unmanageable, like vicious horses of a charioteer."

"But he who has understanding and whose mind is always firmly held, his senses are under control, like good horses of a charioteer."

"He who has no understanding, who is unmindful and always impure, never reaches that place, but enters into the round of births."

"But he who has understanding, who is mindful and always pure, reaches indeed that place, from whence he is not born again."

"But he who has understanding for his charioteer, and who holds the reins of the mind, he reaches the end of his journey, and that is the highest place of Vishnu."

"Beyond the senses there are the objects, beyond the objects there is the mind, beyond the mind there is the intellect, the Great Self is beyond the intellect."

"Beyond the Great there is the Undeveloped, beyond the Undeveloped there is the Person. Beyond the Person there is nothing—this is the goal, the highest road."

"That Self is hidden in all beings and does not shine forth, but it is seen by subtle seers through their sharp and subtle intellect."

. . .

"What is here (visible in the world), the same is there (invisible in Brahman); and what is there, the same is here. He who sees any difference here (between Brahman and the world), goes from death to death."

"Even by the mind this (Brahman) is to be obtained, and then there is no difference whatsoever. He goes from death to death who sees any difference here."

"The person, of the size of a thumb, stands in the middle of the Self, as lord of the past and the future, and henceforward fears no more. This is that."

"That person, of the size of a thumb, is like a light without smoke, lord of the past and the future, he is the same to-day and to-morrow. This is that."

"As rain-water that has fallen on a mountain-ridge runs down the rocks on all sides, thus does he, who sees a difference between qualities, run after them on all sides."

"As pure water poured into pure water remains the same, thus, O Gautama, is the Self of a thinker who knows."

. . .

"He (the Self) cannot be reached by speech, by mind, or by the eye. How can it be apprehended except by him who says: "He is?""

"By the words "He is," is he to be apprehended, and by (admitting) the reality of both (the invisible Brahman and the visible world, as coming from Brahman). When he has been apprehended by the words "He is," then his reality reveals itself."

"When all desires that dwell in his heart cease, then the mortal becomes immortal, and obtains Brahman."

"When all the ties of the heart are severed here on earth, then the mortal becomes immortal—here ends the teaching."

. . .

"There are a hundred and one arteries of the heart, one of them penetrates the crown of the head. Moving upwards by it, a man (at his death) reaches the Immortal; the other arteries serve for departing in different directions."

"The Person not larger than a thumb, the inner Self, is always settled in the heart of men. Let a man draw that Self forth from his body with steadiness, as one draws the pith from a reed. Let him know that Self as the Bright, as the Immortal; yes, as the Bright, as the Immortal."

Having received this knowledge taught by Death and the whole rule of Yoga, Nâkiketa became free from passion and death, and obtained Brahman. Thus it will be with another also who knows thus what relates to the Self.

May He protect us both! May He enjoy us both! May we acquire Strength together! May our knowledge become bright! May we never quarrel! Om! Peace! peace! peace! Harih, Om!

3

Confucian Sources

Confucius (Kong Fuzi, that is, "Grand Master Kong") lived from 551–479 BCE, mostly in the Chinese state of Lu, in today's Shandong Province. He gained a reputation for wisdom and rectitude as a government minister. After a setback in his career, he went into a self-imposed exile, traveling from one state to another, spreading his views. Near the end of his life, he returned to Lu and spent the rest of his years teaching some seventy disciples.

As with Socrates, our evidence for his teaching comes from his disciples. The *Analects* are a collection of his teachings and practices collected by his followers in the centuries following his death. The system that begins with the teachings in the Analects formed the basis for much Chinese education and government well into the twentieth century. Confucian principles, including an emphasis on fulfilling one's role, respect for elders and rulers, and the importance of propriety, maintain their importance throughout many countries, where his teachings spread.

In the selection here from Book X of the *Analects*, Confucius (the Master) demonstrates the value of human life above property. In that from Book XII, he explains the importance of propriety, the virtues of a good person ("the superior man," cf., the Aristotelian virtuous person or the Stoic sage). He also emphasizes the importance of love and knowledge of one's fellows. In the selection from Book XV, he fills out his picture of the superior man as one focused on individual virtue, and for whom being remembered after death is important.

From Legge, James (trans.) *Analects of Confucius*, Oxford University Press, 1893 and Mencius, Oxford University Press, 1895.

Mencius (Mengzi or "Master Meng") lived in the fourth century BCE. He was born in the state of Zhou, also in today's Shandong Province. After training in the Confucian school, he became an itinerant sage. For a time, he was an ultimately unsuccessful official in the Qi state.

In the selection here from the Book of Mencius, the sage explains to the king that only righteousness and benevolence are important in human life and in government.

....

Confucian Analects

Book X

The stable being burned down, when he was at court, on his return he said, "Has any man been hurt?" He did not ask about the horses.

Book XII

Yen Yuan asked about perfect virtue. The Master said, "To subdue one's self and return to propriety, is perfect virtue. If a man can for one day subdue himself and return to propriety, all under heaven will ascribe perfect virtue to him. Is the practice of perfect virtue from a man himself, or is it from others?"

Yen Yuan said, "I beg to ask the steps of that process." The Master replied, "Look not at what is contrary to propriety; listen not to what is contrary to propriety; speak not what is contrary to propriety; make no movement which is contrary to propriety." Yen Yuan then said, "Though I am deficient in intelligence and vigor, I will make it my business to practice this lesson."

Chung-kung asked about perfect virtue. The Master said, "It is, when you go abroad, to behave to every one as if you were receiving a great guest; to employ the people as if you were assisting at a great sacrifice; not to do to others as you would not wish done to yourself; to have no murmuring against you in the country, and none in the family." Chung-kung said, "Though I am deficient in intelligence and vigor, I will make it my business to practice this lesson."

Sze-ma Niu asked about perfect virtue.

The Master said, "The man of perfect virtue is cautious and slow in his speech."

"Cautious and slow in his speech!" said Niu, "is this what is meant by perfect virtue?" The Master said, "When a man feels the difficulty of doing, can he be other than cautious and slow in speaking?"

Sze-ma Niu asked about the superior man. The Master said, "The superior man has neither anxiety nor fear."

"Being without anxiety or fear!" said Nui, "does this constitute what we call the superior man?"

The Master said, "When internal examination discovers nothing wrong, what is there to be anxious about, what is there to fear?"

Sze-ma Niu, full of anxiety, said, "Other men all have their brothers, I only have not."

Tsze-hsia said to him, "There is the following saying which I have heard—'Death and life have their determined appointment; riches and honors depend upon Heaven.'"

"Let the superior man never fail reverentially to order his own conduct, and let him be respectful to others and observant of propriety:— then all within the four seas will be his brothers. What has the superior man to do with being distressed because he has no brothers?"

Tsze-chang asked what constituted intelligence. The Master said, "He with whom neither slander that gradually soaks into the mind, nor statements that startle like a wound in the flesh, are successful may be called intelligent indeed. Yea, he with whom neither soaking slander, nor startling statements, are successful, may be called farseeing."

. . .

The Master said, "The superior man seeks to perfect the admirable qualities of men, and does not seek to perfect their bad qualities. The mean man does the opposite of this."

. . .

Fan Ch'ih rambling with the Master under the trees about the rain altars, said, "I venture to ask how to exalt virtue, to correct cherished evil, and to discover delusions."

The Master said, "Truly a good question!

"If doing what is to be done be made the first business, and success a secondary consideration:—is not this the way to exalt virtue? To assail one's own wickedness and not assail that of others;—is not this the way to correct cherished evil? For a morning's anger to disregard one's own life, and involve that of his parents;—is not this a case of delusion?"

Fan Ch'ih asked about benevolence. The Master said, "It is to love all men." He asked about knowledge. The Master said, "It is to know all men."

Fan Ch'ih did not immediately understand these answers.

The Master said, "Employ the upright and put aside all the crooked; in this way the crooked can be made to be upright."

Fan Ch'ih retired, and, seeing Tsze-hsia, he said to him, "A little while ago, I had an interview with our Master, and asked him about knowledge. He said, 'Employ the upright, and put aside all the crooked;—in this way, the crooked will be made to be upright.' What did he mean?"

Tsze-hsia said, "Truly rich is his saying!"

. . .

Tsze-kung asked about friendship. The Master said, "Faithfully admonish your friend, and skillfully lead him on. If you find him impracticable, stop. Do not disgrace yourself."

The philosopher Tsang said, "The superior man on grounds of culture meets with his friends, and by friendship helps his virtue."

Book XV

The Master said, "The superior man in everything considers righteousness to be essential. He performs it according to the rules of propriety. He brings it forth in humility. He completes it with sincerity. This is indeed a superior man."

The Master said, "The superior man is distressed by his want of ability. He is not distressed by men's not knowing him."

The Master said, "The superior man dislikes the thought of his name not being mentioned after his death."

The Master said, "What the superior man seeks, is in himself. What the mean man seeks, is in others."

The Master said, "The superior man is dignified, but does not wrangle. He is sociable, but not a partisan."

The Master said, "The superior man does not promote a man simply on account of his words, nor does he put aside good words because of the man."

Tsze-kung asked, saying, "Is there one word which may serve as a rule of practice for all one's life?" The Master said, "Is not RECIPROCITY such a word? What you do not want done to yourself, do not do to others."

The Master said, "In my dealings with men, whose evil do I blame, whose goodness do I praise, beyond what is proper? If I do sometimes exceed in praise, there must be ground for it in my examination of the individual."

The Book of Mencius

Chapter I

Mencius went to see king Hûi of Liang.

The king said, "Venerable sir, since you have not counted it far to come here, a distance of a thousand lî, may I presume that you are provided with counsels to profit my kingdom?"

Mencius replied, "Why must your Majesty use that word 'profit?' What I am provided with are counsels to benevolence and righteousness, and these are my only topics."

"If your Majesty say, 'What is to be done to profit my kingdom?' the great officers will say, 'What is to be done to profit our families?' and the inferior officers and the common people will say, 'What is to be done to profit our persons?' Superiors and inferiors will try to snatch this profit the one from the other, and the kingdom will be endangered. In the kingdom of ten thousand chariots, the murderer of his sovereign shall be the chief of a family of a thousand chariots. In the kingdom of a thousand chariots, the murderer of his prince shall be the chief of a family of a hundred chariots. To have a thousand in ten thousand, and a hundred in a thousand, cannot be said not to be a large allotment, but if righteousness be put last, and profit be put first, they will not be satisfied without snatching all."

"There never has been a benevolent man who neglected his parents. There never has been a righteous man who made his sovereign an after consideration."

"Let your Majesty also say, 'Benevolence and righteousness, and let these be your only themes.'"

"Why must you use that word—'profit?'"

. . .

"If the seasons of husbandry be not interfered with, the grain will be more than can be eaten. If close nets are not allowed to enter the pools and ponds, the fishes and turtles will be more than can be consumed. If the axes and bills enter the hills and forests only at the proper time, the wood will be more than can be used. When the grain and fish and turtles are more than can be eaten, and there is more wood than can be used, this enables the people to nourish their living and mourn for their dead, without any feeling against any. This condition, in which the people nourish their living and bury their dead without any feeling against any, is the first step of royal government."

"Let mulberry trees be planted about the homesteads with their five mâu, and persons of fifty years may be clothed with silk. In keeping fowls, pigs, dogs, and swine, let not their times of breeding be neglected, and persons of seventy years may eat flesh. Let there not be taken away the time that is proper for the cultivation of the farm with its hundred mâ, and the family of several mouths that is supported by it shall not suffer from hunger. Let careful attention be paid to education in schools, inculcating in it especially the filial and fraternal duties, and grey-haired men will not be seen upon the roads, carrying burdens on their backs or on their heads. It never has been that the ruler of a State, where such results were seen,—persons of seventy wearing silk and eating flesh, and the black-haired people suffering neither from thunder nor cold,—did not attain to the royal dignity."

"Your dogs and swine eat the food of men, and you do not make any restrictive arrangements. There are people dying from famine on the roads, and you do not issue the stores of your granaries for them. When people die, you say, 'It is not owing to me; it is owing to the year.' In what does this differ from stabbing a man and killing him, and then saying—'It was not I; it was the weapon?' Let your Majesty cease to lay the blame on the year, and instantly from all the nation the people will come to you."

4

Buddhist Scriptures

The Buddhist account of the human condition is characterized by the claims that all things are impermanent, that life is full of suffering, and that there is no such thing as the self or ego. It is the nature of these contentions that are explored in the selections from the Buddhist scriptures that follow, while all three of these claims are pithily condensed in the final reading included here ("The Three Characteristics").

The founder of Buddhism, Siddhartha Gautama, was born in the sixth century BCE in what is now Nepal. Born into a life of royal luxury and secluded from the world by his father, the young Siddhartha eventually saw four signs of the world's suffering (old age, disease, death, and poverty) and, disturbed by what he had seen, renounced his privilege and set out on a quest to understand the meaning of suffering and how to overcome it. His conclusions, by means of which he awoke and became the Buddha (a title meaning "one who has woken up"), are presented in the Four Noble Truths, the heart of Buddhist teaching and the subject of the first reading below. The Four Noble Truths are akin to a medical diagnosis of the human condition, isolating a problem (suffering, or dukkha), the cause of that problem (craving, or tanha), the remedy for that problem (cessation of craving, or nirvana), and a prescription for the attainment of the remedy (the Noble Eightfold Path, or marga). The Buddha devoted the remainder of his life to the teaching of this Dhamma ("way" or "Truth"), dying around the age of eighty years old. His final words are held to have been: "All things are impermanent. Strive on with awareness."

This emphasis on impermanence (anitya) can be seen in the readings taken from the *Samyutta Nikāya* and the *Majjhima Nikāya* respectively. In these we find the Buddha describing the nature of the human person in terms of "five aggregates" (or skandhas): the materialbodyorform(rūpakkhandha);feelingorsensation(vedanākhandha); perception (saññākhandha); volitional or mental formations (samkhārakkhandha); and consciousness (viññānakkhandha). The human person is a temporary amalgamation of these; since none of the five is permanent, the human person lacks permanence also, and hence the Buddhist doctrine of "No-Self" (anattā). The Buddha contends that it is attachment (or clinging) to the aggregates that leads to suffering; accordingly, the attainment of an attitude of nonattachment will remove this burden from humans. The suffering-inducing nature of attachment to the passions and sensations of mind and body is vividly depicted in the Buddha's "Fire Sermon," and is to be noted that nonattachment is to be extended not merely to sensations that are ultimately unpleasant but to all things, and even to the most valuable thing of all: the Dhamma. This is the subject matter of the "Simile of the Raft."

The next set of selections is drawn from The Questions of King Milinda (or *Milindapañha*), a text composed probably during the first century CE. It reports the conversations between Nâgasena, a Buddhist sage, and King Milinda, a Greco-Bactrian king who ruled in the east Punjab for a lengthy period during the second and first centuries BCE. The readings included here focus on questions of personal identity, the body, and rebirth. One thing of especial significance here to be noted is that Nâgasena's explicit denial of the existence of the soul leads to a conception of rebirth markedly different from the non-Buddhist notion of reincarnation as transmigration of the soul (as found, for example, in the Bhagavad Gita). Part of the significance of the Milindapañha as a text—particularly in the context of this anthology—is that it shows the basic ideas of an Eastern philosophy being explained to a king whose outlook is, as Edward Conze put it, "half-European."

Dhamma-Kakka-Ppavattana-Sutta

Reverence to the Blessed One, the Holy One, the Fully-Enlightened One;

Thus have I heard. The Blessed One was once staying at Benares, at the hermitage called Migadftya. And there the Blessed One addressed the company of the five Bhikkhus [monks], and said: . . .

"Now this, O Bhikkhus, is the noble truth concerning suffering.

"Birth is attended with pain, decay is painful, disease is painful, death is painful. Union with the unpleasant is painful, painful is separation from the pleasant; and any craving that is unsatisfied, that too is painful. In brief, the five aggregates which spring from attachment (the conditions of individuality and their cause) are painful.

"This then, O Bhikkhus, is the noble truth concerning suffering.

"Now this, O Bhikkhus, is the noble truth concerning the origin of suffering.

"Verily, it is that thirst (or craving), causing the renewal of existence, accompanied by sensual delight, seeking satisfaction now here, now there—that is to say, the craving for the gratification of the passions, or the craving for (a future) life, or the craving for success (in this present life).

"This then, O Bhikkhus, is the noble truth concerning the origin of suffering.

"Now this, O Bhikkhus, is the noble truth concerning the destruction of suffering.

"Verily, it is the destruction, in which no passion remains, of this very thirst; the laying aside of, the getting rid of, the being free from, the harbouring no longer of this thirst.

"This then, O Bhikkhus, is the noble truth concerning the destruction of suffering.

"Now this, O Bhikkhus, is the noble truth concerning the way which leads to the destruction of sorrow. Verily! it is this noble eightfold path; that is to say:

> Right views;
> Right aspirations;
> Right speech;

From the Buddha's teaching of the Four Noble Truths, from the *Dhamma-kakka-ppavattana-Sutta* ("The Foundation of the Kingdom of Righteousness") (Sections 1–9, 23, 24 in Buddhist Sutras (translated by T. W. Rhys Davids) (Oxford: Oxford University Press, 1881) pp.146–150, 153).

Right conduct;
Right livelihood;
Right effort;
Right mindfulness;
and Right contemplation.

"This then, O Bhikkhus, is the noble truth concerning the destruction of sorrow.

"That this was the noble truth concerning sorrow, was not, O Bhikkhus, among the doctrines handed down, but there arose within me the eye (to perceive it), there arose the knowledge (of its nature), there arose the understanding (of its cause), there arose the wisdom (to guide, in the path of tranquility), there arose the light (to dispel darkness from it)."

. . .

"And now this knowledge and this insight has arisen within me. Immovable is the emancipation of my heart. This is my last existence. There will now be no rebirth for me!"

Samyutta Nikāya

The Burden

At Sāvatthi . . . There the Blessed One said this: "Bhikkhus, I will teach you the burden, the carrier of the burden, the taking up of the burden, and the laying down of the burden. Listen to that." . . . "And what, Bhikkhus, is the burden? It should be said: the five aggregates subject to clinging. What five? The form aggregate subject to clinging, the feeling aggregate subject to clinging, the perception aggregate subject to clinging, the volitional formations aggregate subject to clinging, the consciousness aggregate subject to clinging. This is called the carrier of the burden:

"And what, Bhikkhus, is the carrier of the burden? It should be said: the person, this venerable one of such a name and clan is called the carrier of the burden.

"And what, Bhikkhus, is the taking up of the burden? It is this craving that leads to renewed existence accompanied by delight and lust, seeking delight here and there; that is, craving for sensual pleasures, craving for existence; craving for extermination. This is called the taking up of the burden.

From the Buddha on the Five Aggregates (or khandhas] and Impermanence, from the Samyutta Nikāya: (22) "The Burden" (pp.871–872) and the Majjhima Nikāya: Sutta 22, sections 25–29 (pp.232–233).

"And what, Bhikkhus, is the laying down of the burden? It is the remainderless fading away and cessation of that same craving, the giving up and relinquishing of it, freedom from it, non-reliance on it. This is called the laying down of the burden."

This is what the Blessed One said. Having said this, the Fortunate One, the Teacher, further said this:

> "The five aggregates are truly burdens,
> The burden-carrier is the person.
> Taking up the burden is suffering in the world.
> Laying the burden down is blissful.
> Having laid the heavy burden down,
> Without taking up another burden,
> Having drawn out craving with its root,
> One is free from hunger fully quenched."

Majjhima Nikāya

"Bhikkhus, there being a self, would there be what belongs to my self?"—"Yes, venerable sir." "Or, there being what belongs to a self, would there be my self?"—"Yes, venerable sir."—"Bhikkhus, since a self and what belongs to a self are not apprehended as true and established, then this standpoint for views, namely, 'This is self, this the world; after death I shall be permanent, everlasting, eternal, not subject to change; I shall endure as long as eternity'—would it not be an utterly and completely foolish teaching?"

"What else could it be, venerable sir? It would be an utterly and completely foolish teaching."

"Bhikkhus, what do you think? Is material form permanent or impermanent?—"Impermanent, venerable sir."—"Is what is impermanent suffering or happiness?"—"Suffering, venerable sir."—"Is what is impermanent, suffering, and subject to change, fit to be regarded thus: 'This is mine, this I am, this is my self?'"—"No, venerable sir."

"Bhikkhus, what do you think? Is feeling . . . Is perception . . . Are formations . . . Is consciousness permanent or impermanent?"—"Impermanent, venerable sir."—"Is what is impermanent suffering or happiness?"—"Suffering, venerable sir."—"Is what is impermanent, suffering, and subject to change, fit to be regarded thus: 'This is mine, this I am, this is my self?'"—"No, venerable sir."

Mahā-Yagga

The Fire Sermon

Then the Blessed One, having dwelt in Uravelā as long as he wished, proceeded on his wanderings in the direction of Gayā Head, accompanied by a great congregation of priests, a thousand in number, who had all of them aforetime been monks with matted hair. And there in Gayā, on Gayā Head, the Blessed One dwelt, together with the thousand priests.

And there the Blessed One addressed the priests:—

"All things, O priests, are on fire. And what, O priests, are all these things which are on fire?

"The eye, O priests, is on fire; forms are on fire; eye-consciousness is on fire; impressions received by the eye are on fire; and whatever sensation, pleasant, unpleasant, or indifferent, originates in dependence on impressions received by the eye, that also is on fire.

"And with what are these on fire?

"With the fire of passion, say I, with the fire of hatred, with the fire of infatuation; with birth, old age, death, sorrow, lamentation, misery, grief, and despair are they on fire.

"The ear is on fire; sounds are on fire; ... the nose is on fire; odors are on fire; ... the tongue is on fire; tastes are on fire; ... the body is on fire; things tangible are on fire; ... the mind is on fire; ideas are on fire; ... mind-consciousness is on fire; impressions received by the mind are on fire; and whatever sensation, pleasant, unpleasant, or indifferent, originates in dependence on impressions received by the mind, that also is on fire.

"And with what are these on fire?

"With the fire of passion, say I, with the fire of hatred, with the fire of infatuation; with birth, old age, death, sorrow, lamentation, misery, grief, and despair are they on fire.

"Perceiving this, O priests, the learned and noble disciple conceives an aversion for the eye, conceives an aversion for forms, conceives an aversion for eye-consciousness, conceives an aversion for the impressions received by the eye and whatever sensation, pleasant, unpleasant,

---

From the Buddha on aversion to passion: "The Fire Sermon" (in *Buddhism in Translations* (translated by Henry Clarke Warren) (Cambridge, MA: Harvard University Press, 1896), pp.351–352).

or indifferent, originates in dependence on impressions received by the eye, for that also he conceives an aversion. Conceives an aversion for the ear, conceives an aversion for sounds, . . . conceives an aversion for the nose, conceives an aversion for odors, . . . conceives an aversion for the tongue, conceives an aversion for tastes, . . . conceives an aversion for the body, conceives an aversion for things tangible, . . . conceives an aversion for the mind, conceives an aversion for ideas, conceives an aversion for mind-consciousness, conceives an aversion for the impressions received by the mind; and whatever sensation, pleasant, unpleasant, or indifferent, originates in dependence on impressions received by the mind, for this also he conceives an aversion. And in conceiving this aversion, he becomes divested of passion, and by the absence of passion he becomes free, and when he is free he becomes aware that he is free; and he knows that rebirth is exhausted, that he has lived the holy life, that he has done what it behooved him to do, and that he is no more for this world."

Now while this exposition was being delivered, the minds of the thousand priests became free from attachment and delivered from the depravities.

Alagaddupama-Sutta

The Simile of the Raft

"Bhikkhus, I shall show you how the Dhamma is similar to a raft, being for the purpose of crossing over; not for the purpose of grasping. Listen and attend closely to what I shall say."—"Yes, venerable sir," the Bhikkhus replied.

The Blessed One said this:

"Bhikkhus, suppose a man in the course of a journey saw a great expanse of water, whose near shore was dangerous and fearful and whose further shore was safe and free from fear, but there was no ferryboat or bridge going to the far shore. Then he thought: 'There is this great expanse of water, whose near shore is dangerous and fearful and whose further shore is safe and free from fear, but there is no ferryboat or bridge going to the far shore. Suppose I collect grass, twigs, branches, and leaves and

---

From the Buddha on non-attachment: "The Simile of the Raft" (from the Majjhima Nikāya: Sutta 22, section 13–14 (pp. 228–229).

bind them together into a raft, and supported by the raft and making an effort with my hands and feet got safely across to the far shore.' And then the man collected grass, twigs, branches, and leaves and bound them together into a raft, and supported by the raft and making an effort with his hands and feet, he got safely across to the far shore. Then, when he had got across and had arrived at the far shore, he might think thus: 'This raft has been very helpful to me; since supported by it and making an effort with my hands and feet I got safely across to the far shore. Suppose I were to hoist it on my head or load it on my shoulder, and then go wherever I want.' Now, Bhikkhus, what do you think? By doing so would that man be doing what should be done with that raft?"

"No, venerable sir."

"By doing what would that man be doing what should be done with that raft? Here, Bhikkhus, when that man got across and had arrived at the far shore he might think thus: 'This raft has been very helpful to me since supported by it and making an effort with my hands and feet I got safely across to the far shore. Suppose I were to haul it onto dry land or set it adrift in the water, and then go wherever I want.' Now, Bhikkhus, it is by so doing that that man would be doing what should be done with that raft. So I have shown you how the Dhamma is similar to a raft, being for the purpose of crossing over, not for the purpose of grasping.

"Bhikkhus, when you know the Dhamma to be similar to a raft; you should abandon even good states, how much more so bad states."

The Questions of King Milinda

Book II, Chapter 1

The Chariot

Now Milinda the king went up to where the venerable Nâgasena was, and addressed him with the greetings and compliments of friendship and courtesy, and took his seat, respectfully apart. And Nâgasena reciprocated his courtesy, so that the heart of the king was propitiated.

And Milinda began by asking, "How is your Reverence known, and what, Sir, is your name?"

Selections from *The Questions of King Milinda* (translated by T. W. Rhys Davids) (Oxford: Oxford University Press, 1890 (Volume One) and 1894 (Volume Two)).

"I am known as Nâgasena, O king, and it is by that name that my brethren in the faith address me. But although parents, O king, give such a name as Nâgasena, or Sûrasena, or Vîrasena, or Sîhasena, yet this, Sire,—Nâgasena and so on—is only a generally understood term, a designation in common use. For there is no permanent individuality (no soul) involved in the matter."

Then Milinda called upon the Yonakas [Greek-speakers] and the brethren to witness: "This Nâgasena says there is no permanent individuality implied in his name. Is it now even possible to approve him in that?" And turning to Nâgasena, he said: "If, most reverend Nâgasena, there be no permanent individuality involved in the matter, who is it, pray, who gives to you members of the Order your robes and food and lodging and necessaries for the sick? Who is it who enjoys such things when given? Who is it who lives a life of righteousness? Who is it who devotes himself to meditation? Who is it who attains to the goal of the Excellent Way, to the Nirvâna of Arahatship? And who is it who destroys living creatures? who is it who takes what is not his own? who is it who lives an evil life of worldly lusts, who speaks lies, who drinks strong drink, who commits any one of the five sins which work out their bitter fruit even in this life? If that be so there is neither merit nor demerit; there is neither doer nor causer of good or evil deeds there is neither fruit nor result of good or evil Karma.—If, most reverend Nâgasena, we are to think that were a man to kill you there would be no murder then it follows that there are no real masters or teachers in your Order, and that your ordinations are void.—You tell me that your brethren in the Order are in the habit of addressing you as Nâgasena. Now what is that Nâgasena? Do you mean to say that the hair is Nâgasena?"

"I don't say that, great king."

"Or the hairs on the body, perhaps?"

"Certainly not."

"Or is it the nails, the teeth, the skin, the flesh, the nerves, the bones, the marrow, the kidneys, the heart, the liver, the abdomen, the spleen, the lungs, the larger intestines, the lower intestines, the stomach, the faeces, the bile, the phlegm, the pus, the blood, the sweat, the fat, the tears, the serum, the saliva, the mucus, the oil that lubricates the joints, the urine, or the brain, or any or all of these, that is Nâgasena?" And to each of these he answered no.

"Is it the outward form then that is Nâgasena, or the sensations, or the ideas, or the confections (the constituent elements of character), or the consciousness, that is Nâgasena?"

And to each of these also he answered no.

"Then is it all these Skandhas combined that are Nâgasena?"

"No! great king."

"But is there anything outside the five Skandhas that is Nâgasena?"

And still he answered no.

"Then thus, ask as I may, I can discover no Nâgasena. Nâgasena is a mere empty sound. Who then is the Nâgasena that we see before us? It is a falsehood that your reverence has spoken, an untruth!"

And the venerable Nâgasena said to Milinda the king: "You, Sire, have been brought up in great luxury, as beseems your noble birth. If you were to walk this dry weather on the hot and sandy ground, trampling under foot the gritty, gravelly grains of the hard sand, your feet would hurt you. And as your body would be in pain, your mind would be disturbed, and you would experience a sense of bodily suffering. How then did you come, on foot, or in a chariot?"

"I did not come, Sir, on foot. I came in a carriage."

"Then if you came, Sire, in a carriage, explain to me what that is. Is it the pole that is the chariot?

"I did not say that."

"Is it the axle that is the chariot?"

"Certainly not."

"Is it the wheels, or the framework, or the ropes, or the yoke, or the spokes of the wheels, or the goad, that are the chariot?"

And to all these he still answered no.

"Then is it all these parts of it that are the chariot?"

"No, Sir."

"But is there anything outside them that is the chariot?"

And still he answered no.

"Then thus, ask as I may, I can discover no chariot. Chariot is a mere empty sound. What then is the chariot you say you came in? It is a falsehood that your Majesty has spoken, an untruth! There is no such thing as a chariot! You are king over all India, a mighty monarch. Of whom then are you afraid that you speak untruth? And he called upon the Yonakas and the brethren to witness, saying: "Milinda the king here has said that he came by carriage. But when asked in that case to explain what the carriage was, he is unable to establish what he averred. Is it, forsooth, possible to approve him in that?"

When he had thus spoken the five hundred Yonakas shouted their applause, and said to the king:

"Now let your Majesty get out of that if you can?"

And Milinda the king replied to Nâgasena, and said: "I have spoken no untruth, reverend Sir. It is on account of its having all these things—the pole, and the axle, the wheels, and the framework, the ropes, the yoke, the spokes, and the goad—that it comes under the generally understood term, the designation in common use, of 'chariot.'"

"Very good! Your Majesty has rightly grasped the meaning of 'chariot.' And just even so it is on account of all those things you questioned me about—the thirty-two kinds of organic matter in a human body, and the five constituent elements of being—that I come under the generally understood term, the designation in common use, of 'Nâgasena.'

"For it was said, Sire, by our Sister Vagirâ, in the presence of the Blessed One:

'Just as it is by the condition precedent of the co-existence of its various parts that the word "chariot" is used, just so is it that when the Skandhas are there we talk of a "being."'"

"Most wonderful, Nâgasena, and most strange. Well has the puzzle put to you, most difficult though it was, been solved. Were the Buddha himself here he would approve your answer. Well done, well done, Nâgasena!"

Chapter 2

The king said "He who is born, Nâgasena, does he remain the same or become another?

"Neither the same nor another."

"Give me an illustration."

"Now what do you think, O king? You were once a baby, a tender thing, and small in size, lying flat on your back. Was that the same as you who are now grown up?"

"No. That child was one, I am another."

"If you are not that child, it will follow that you have had neither mother nor father, no! nor teacher. You cannot have been taught either learning, or behaviour, or wisdom. What, great king! is the mother of the embryo in the first stage different from the mother of the embryo in the second stage, or the third, or the fourth? Is the mother of the baby a different person from the mother of the grown-up man? Is the person who goes to school one, and the same when he has finished his schooling another? Is it one who commits a crime, another who is punished by having his hands or feet cut off?

"Certainly not. But what would you, Sir, say to that?"

The Elder replied: "I should say that I am the same person, now I am grown up, as I was when I was a tender tiny baby, flat on my back. For all these states are included in one by means of this body.

"Give me an illustration."

"Suppose a man, O king, were to light a lamp, would it burn the night through?"

"Yes, it might do so."

"Now, is it the same flame that burns in the first watch of the night, Sir, and in the second?"

"No."

"Or the same that burns in the second watch and in the third?"

"No."

"Then is there one lamp in the first watch, and another in the second, and another in the third?"

"No. The light comes from the same lamp all the night through."

"Just so, O king, is the continuity of a person or thing maintained. One comes into being, another passes away; and the rebirth is, as it were, simultaneous. Thus neither as the same nor as another does a man go on to the last phase of his self-consciousness."

"Give me a further illustration."

"It is like milk, which when once taken from the cow, turns, after a lapse of time, first to curds, and then from curds to butter, and then from butter to ghee. Now would it be right to say that the milk was the same thing as the curds, or the butter, or the ghee?"

"Certainly not; but they are produced out of it." "Just so, O king, is the continuity of a person or thing maintained. One comes into being, another passes away; and the rebirth is, as it were, simultaneous. Thus neither as the same nor as another does a man go on to the last phase of his self-consciousness."

"Well put, Nâgasena!"

The king said: "What is it, Nâgasena, that is reborn?"

"Name-and-form is reborn."

"What, is it this same name-and-form that is reborn?"

"No, but by this name-and-form deeds are done, good or evil, and by these deeds (this Karma) another name-and-form is reborn."

"If that be so, Sir, would not the new being be released from its evil Karma?"

The Elder replied: "Yes, if it were not reborn. But just because it is reborn, O king, it is therefore not released from its evil Karma?"

"Give me an illustration."

"Suppose, O king, some man were to steal a mango from another man, and the owner of the mango were to seize him and bring him before the king, and charge him with the crime. And the thief were to say: 'Your Majesty! I have not taken away this man's mangoes. Those that he put in the ground are different from the ones I took, I do not deserve to be punished.' How then? would he be guilty?"

"Certainly, Sir. He would deserve to be punished."

"But on what ground?"

"Because, in spite of whatever he may say, he would be guilty in respect of the last mango which resulted from the first one (the owner set in the ground)."

"Just so, great king, deeds good or evil are done by this name-and-form and another is reborn. But that other is not thereby released from its deeds (its Karma)."

"Give me a further illustration."

"It is like rice or sugar so stolen, of which the same might be said as of the mango. Or it is like the fire which a man, in the cold season, might kindle, and when he had warmed himself, leave still burning, and go away. Then if that fire were to set another man's field on fire, and the owner of the field were to seize him, and bring him before the king, and charge him with the injury, and he were to say: "Your Majesty! It was not I who set this man's field on fire. The fire I left burning was a different one from that which burnt his field. I am not guilty." Now would the man, O king, be guilty?"

"Certainly, Sir."

"But why?"

"Because, in spite of whatever he might say, he would be guilty in respect of the subsequent fire that resulted from the previous one."

"Just so, great king, deeds good or evil are done by this name-and-form and another is reborn. But that other is not thereby released from its deeds (its Karma)."

"Give me a further illustration."

"Suppose, O king, a man were to take a lamp and go up into the top story of his house, and there eat his meal. And the lamp blazing up were to set the thatch on fire, and from that the house should catch fire, and that house having caught fire the whole village should be burnt. And they should seize him and ask: "What, you fellow, did you set our village on fire for?" And he should reply: "I've not set your village on fire! The flame of the lamp, by the light of which I was eating, was one thing; the fire which burnt your village was another thing!" Now if they, thus disputing, should go to law before you, O king, in whose favour would you decide the case?"

"In the villagers' favour."

"But why?"

"Because, Sir, in spite of whatever the man might say, the one fire was produced from the other."

"Just so, great king, it is one name-and-form which has its end in death, and another name-and-form which is reborn. But the second is the result of the first, and is therefore not set free from its evil deeds.

"Give me a further illustration."

"Suppose, O king, a man were to choose a young girl in marriage, and give a price for her and go away. And she in due course should grow up to full age, and then, another man were to pay a price for her and marry her. And when the first one had come back he should say: "Why, you fellow, have you carried off my wife?" And the other were to reply: "It's not your wife I have carried off! The little girl, the mere child, whom you chose in marriage and paid a price for is one; the girl grown up to full age whom I chose in marriage and paid a price for, is another." Now if they, thus disputing, were to go to law about it before you, O king, in whose favour would you decide the case?"

"In favour of the first."

"But why?"

"Because, in spite of whatever the second might say, the grown-up girl would have been derived from the other girl."

"Just so, great king, it is one name-and-form which has its end in death, and another name-and-form which is reborn. But the second is the result of the first, and is therefore not set free from its evil deeds."

"Give me a further illustration."

"Suppose a man, O king, were to buy of a herdsman a vessel of milk, and go away leaving it in his charge, saying: "I will come for it tomorrow;" and the next day it were to become curds. And when the man should come and ask for it, then suppose the other were to offer him the curds, and he should say: "It was not curds I bought of you; give me my vessel of milk." And the other were to reply: "Without any fault of mine your milk has turned to curds." Now if they, thus disputing, were to go to law about it before you, O king, in whose favour would you decide the case?"

"In favour of the herdsman."

"But why?"

"Because, in spite of whatever the other might say, the curds were derived from the milk."

"Just so, great king, it is one name-and-form that finds its end in death, and another that is reborn. But that other is the result of the first, and is therefore not thereby released from its evil deeds (its bad Karma)."

"Very good, Nâgasena!"

Book III, Chapter 4

The king said: "Is cessation Nirvâna?"

"Yes, your Majesty."

"How is that, Nâgasena?"

"All foolish individuals, O king, take pleasure in the senses and in the objects of sense, find delight in them, continue to cleave to them. Hence are they carried down by that flood (of human passions), they are not set free from birth, old age, and death, from grief, lamentation, pain, sorrow, and despair,—they are not set free, I say, from suffering. But the wise, O king, the disciple of the noble ones, neither takes pleasure in those things, nor finds delight in them, nor continues cleaving to them. And inasmuch as he does not, in him craving ceases, and by the cessation of craving grasping ceases, and by the cessation of grasping becoming ceases, and when becoming has ceased birth ceases, and with its cessation birth, old age, and death, grief, lamentation, pain, sorrow, and despair cease to exist. Thus is the cessation brought about the end of all that aggregation of pain. Thus is it that cessation is Nirvâna."

"Very good, Nâgasena!"

The king said: "Venerable Nâgasena, do all men receive Nirvâna?"

"Not all, O king. But he who walks righteously, who admits those conditions which ought to be admitted, perceives clearly those conditions which ought to be clearly perceived, abandons those conditions which ought to be abandoned, practises himself in those conditions which ought to be practised, realises those conditions which ought to be realised—he receives Nirvâna."

"Very good, Nâgasena!"

Chapter 5

The king said: "Where there is no transmigration, Nâgasena, can there be rebirth?"

"Yes, there can."

"But how can that be? Give me an illustration."

"Suppose a man, O king, were to light a lamp from another lamp, can it be said that the one transmigrates from, or to, the other?"

"Certainly not."

"Just so, great king, is rebirth without transmigration."

"Give me a further illustration."

"Do you recollect, great king, having learnt, when you were a boy, some verse or other from your teacher?"

"Yes, I recollect that."

"Well then, did that verse transmigrate from your teacher?"

"Certainly not."

"Just so, great king, is rebirth without transmigration."

"Very good Nâgasena!"

The king said: "Is there such a thing, Nâgasena, as the soul?"

"In the highest sense, O king, there is no such thing."

"Very good, Nâgasena!"

The king said: "Is there any being, Nâgasena, who transmigrates from this body to another?"

"No, there is not."

"But if so, would it not get free from its evil deeds."

"Yes, if it were not reborn; but if it were, no."

"Give me an illustration."

"Suppose, O king, a man were to steal another man's mangoes, would the thief deserve punishment?"

"Yes."

"But he would not have stolen the mangoes the other set in the ground. Why would he deserve punishment?"

"Because those he stole were the result of those that were planted."

"Just so, great king, this name-and-form commits deeds, either pure or impure, and by that Karma another name-and-form is reborn. And therefore is it not set free from its evil deeds?"

"Very good, Nâgasena!"

The king said: "When deeds are committed, Nâgasena, by one name-and-form, what becomes of those deeds?"

"The deeds would follow it, O king, like a shadow that never leaves it."

"Can any one point out those deeds, saying: 'Here are those deeds, or there'?"

"No."

"Give me an illustration."

"Now what do you think, O king? Can any one point out the fruits which a tree has not yet produced, saying: 'Here they are, or there'?"

"Certainly not, Sir."

"Just so, great king, so long as the continuity of life is not cut off, it is impossible to point out the deeds that are done."

"Very good, Nâgasena!"

Chapter 6

The king said: "Is the body, Nâgasena, dear to you recluses?"

"No, they love not the body."

"Then why do you nourish it and lavish attention upon it?"

"In all the times and places, O king, that you have gone down to battle, did you never get wounded by an arrow?"

"Yes, that has happened to me."

"In such cases, O king, is not the wound anointed with salve, and smeared with oil, and bound up in a bandage?"

"Yes, such things are done to it."

"What then? Is the wound dear to you that you treat it so tenderly, and lavish such attention upon it?"

"No, it is not dear to me in spite of all that, which is only done that the flesh may grow again."

"Just so, great king, with the recluses and the body. Without cleaving to it do they bear about the body for the sake of righteousness of life. The body, O king, has been declared by the Blessed One to be like a wound. And therefore merely as a sore, and without cleaving to it, do the recluses bear about the body. For it has been said by the Blessed One: 'Covered with clammy skin, an impure thing and foul, nine-apertured, it oozes, like a sore!'"

"Well answered, Nâgasena!"

The Three Characteristics

Whether Buddhas arise, O priests, or whether Buddhas do not arise, it remains a fact and the fixed and necessary constitution of being, that all its constituents are transitory. This fact a Buddha discovers and masters, and when he has discovered and mastered it, he announces, teaches, publishes, proclaims, discloses, minutely explains, and makes it clear, that all the constituents of being are transitory.

Whether Buddhas arise, O priests, or whether Buddhas do not arise, it remains a fact and the fixed and necessary constitution of being, that all its constituents are misery. This fact a Buddha discovers and masters, and when he has discovered and mastered it, he announces, teaches, publishes, proclaims, discloses, minutely explains, and makes it clear, that all the constituents of being are misery.

Whether Buddhas arise, O priests, or whether Buddhas do not arise, it remains a fact and the fixed and necessary constitution of being, that all its elements are lacking in an Ego. This fact a Buddha discovers and masters, and when he has discovered and mastered it, he announces, teaches, publishes, proclaims, discloses, minutely explains, and makes it clear, that all the elements of being are lacking in an Ego.

From "The Three Characteristics" (from the Anguttara-Nikāya) (in Buddhism in Translations (translated by Henry Clarke Warren) (Cambridge, MA: Harvard University Press, 1896).

====== 🐦 ======

The Bhagavad Gita

The *Bhagavad Gita* (from the Sanskrit for "Song of the Lord"), is part of the much longer Hindu epic *Mahabharata*. The Mahabarhata was composed sometime between the fifth and second century BCE. By tradition, the author of the entire work is the legendary sage Vyasa.

The Gita is an epic poem within the poem in which the sage Sanjaya narrates the battlefield conversation between a warrior and his charioteer. It is set during a war for the throne of the kingdom of Kuru, between two branches of one family, the Pandavas (the younger branch) and the Kauravas (the elder branch). On the eve of battle, Arjuna, a Pandava, starts to question whether he should kill his own relatives in this war. His charioteer, Krishna, an avatar of the god Vishnu (and thus the Lord of the title), enters into a dialogue with him convincing him that it is his dharma (duty or righteous act) as a member of a warrior caste and as an individual warrior to fight. Krishna further argues that Arjuna should not consider the consequences of his action, but only focus on doing the right thing. In some ways, this argument can be seen as of a piece with the later deontological theories of philosophers like Immanuel Kant.

Here we have selected representative passages from several chapters. As with the Upanishads, it is not possible to cover all the themes in this important work. From the first chapter, we have selected the passage in which Arjuna explains his reluctance to enter into the war, the second chapter in which Lord Krishna ("The Deity") discusses both his own nature and the nature of all humans, claiming that all

From Müller, Max (ed.) Telang, KÂSHINÂTH TRIMBAK (trans.) THE BHAGAVADGÎTÂ WITH THE SANATSUGÂTÎYA AND THE ANUGÎTÂ, Volume 8, The Sacred Books of the East, 1882).

are immortal. Throughout life, death, and the acquisition of new bodies, the same being persists. For this reason, he argues, Arjuna should not concern himself with the deaths he might bring about, nor his own death, as these are merely sensible and seemingly illusory facts, the real facts being about the immortal self and the immortal God. As the same person remains throughout many changes of clothes, he says, the same self remains through many changes of body. There is one indestructible and immortal self. For these reasons, Arjuna should concern himself only with doing his duty and not its outcomes in the sensible world. We have also included selections from the fifth chapter, in which Krishna extols both asceticism and devotion to duty as roads to happiness, but situates duty as a higher asceticism. In the selection from the sixth chapter, Krishna explains the process of rebirth as it leads to ultimate happiness, even in those who fail in achieving perfection in this life. Finally, in the selection from the eleventh chapter, Krishna reiterates the way in which doing one's duty is making oneself an instrument of God and, thus, the right path. Here Krishna comes close to enunciating a form of determinism or fatalism.

....

Chapter I

Arjuna said:

Seeing these kinsmen, O Krishna! standing (here) desirous to engage in battle, my limbs droop down; my mouth is quite dried up; a tremor comes on my body; and my hairs stand on end; the Gândîva (bow) slips from my hand; my skin burns intensely. I am unable, too, to stand up; my mind whirls round, as it were; O Kesava! I see adverse omens; and I do not perceive any good after killing kinsmen in the battle. I do not wish for victory, O Krishna! nor sovereignty, nor pleasures: what is sovereignty to us, O Govinda! what enjoyments, and even life? Even those, for whose sake we desire sovereignty, enjoyments, and pleasures, are standing here for battle, abandoning life and wealth-preceptors, fathers, sons as well as grandfathers, maternal uncles, fathers-in-law, grandsons, brothers-in-law, as also (other) relatives. These I do not wish to kill, though they kill (me), O destroyer of Madhu! even for the sake of sovereignty over the three worlds, how much less then for this earth? What joy shall be ours, O Ganârdana! after killing Dhritarâshtra's sons?

Chapter II

You have grieved for those who deserve no grief, and you talk words of wisdom. Learned men grieve not for the living nor the dead. Never did I not exist, nor you, nor these rulers of men; nor will any one of us ever hereafter cease to be. As, in this body, infancy and youth and old age (come) to the embodied (self), so does the acquisition of another body; a sensible man is not deceived about that. The contacts of the senses, O son of Kuntî! which produce cold and heat, pleasure and pain, are not permanent, they are ever coming and going. Bear them, O descendant of Bharata! For, O chief of men! that sensible man whom they (pain and pleasure being alike to him) afflict not, he merits immortality. There is no existence for that which is unreal; there is no non-existence for that which is real. And the conclusion about both is perceived by those who perceive the truth. Know that to be indestructible which pervades all this; the destruction of that inexhaustible (principle) none can bring about. These bodies appertaining to the embodied (self) which is eternal, indestructible, and indefinable, are said to be perishable; therefore do engage in battle, O descendant of Bharata! He who thinks it to be the killer and he who thinks it to be killed, both know nothing. It kills not, is not killed. It is not born, nor does it ever die, nor, having existed, does it exist no more. Unborn, everlasting, unchangeable, and primeval, it is not killed when the body is killed. O son of Prithâ! how can that man who knows it thus to be indestructible, everlasting, unborn, and inexhaustible, how and whom can he kill, whom can he cause to be killed? As a man, casting off old clothes, puts on others and new ones, so the embodied (self) casting off old bodies, goes to others and new ones. Weapons do not divide it; fire does not burn it, waters do not moisten it; the wind does not dry it up. It is not divisible; it is not combustible; it is not to be moistened; it is not to be dried up. It is everlasting, all-pervading, stable, firm, and eternal. It is said to be unperceived, to be unthinkable, to be unchangeable. Therefore knowing it to be such, you ought not to grieve, But even if you think that it is constantly born, and constantly dies, still, O you of mighty arms! you ought not to grieve thus. For to one that is born, death is certain; and to one that dies, birth is certain. Therefore about (this) unavoidable thing, you ought not to grieve. The source of things, O descendant of Bharata!

is unperceived; their middle state is perceived; and their end again is unperceived. What lamentation regarding them? One looks upon it as a wonder; another similarly speaks of it as a wonder; another too hears of it as a wonder; and even after having heard of it, no one does really know it. This embodied (self), O descendant of Bharata! within every one's body is ever indestructible. Therefore you ought not to grieve for any being. Having regard to your own duty also, you ought not to falter, for there is nothing better for a Kshatriya [the ruling and military class] than a righteous battle. Happy those Kshatriyas, O son of Pritha! who can find such a battle—come of itself—an open door to heaven! But if you will not fight this righteous battle, then you will have abandoned your own duty and your fame, and you will incur sin. All beings, too, will tell of your everlasting infamy; and to one who has been honoured, infamy is greater than death. (Warriors who are) masters of great cars will think that you abstained from the battle through fear, and having been highly thought of by them, you will fall down to littleness. Your enemies, too, decrying your power, will speak much about you that should not be spoken. And what, indeed, more lamentable than that? Killed, you will obtain heaven; victorious, you will enjoy the earth. Therefore arise, O son of Kunti! resolved to battle. Looking alike on pleasure and pain, on gain and loss, on victory and defeat, then prepare for battle, and thus you will not incur sin. The knowledge here declared to you is that relating to the Sânkhya. Now hear that relating to the Yoga. Possessed of this knowledge, O son of Pritha! you will cast off the bonds of action.

. . .

Your business is with action alone; not by any means with fruit. Let not the fruit of action be your motive. Let not your attachment be on inaction. Having recourse to devotion, O Dhanañgaya! perform actions, casting off attachment, and being equable in success or ill-success; (such) equability is called devotion. Action, O Dhanañgaya! is far inferior to the devotion of the mind. In that devotion seek shelter. Wretched are those whose motive is the fruit (of action). He who has obtained devotion in this world casts off both merit and sin. Therefore apply yourself to devotion; devotion in actions is wisdom. The wise who have obtained devotion cast off the fruit of action; and released from the shackles of (repeated) births, repair to that seat where there is no unhappiness.

. . .

The man who ponders over objects of sense forms an attachment to them; from attachment is produced desire; and from desire anger is produced; from anger results want of discrimination; from want of discrimination, confusion of the memory; from confusion of the memory, loss of reason; and in consequence of loss of reason he is utterly ruined. But the self-restrained man who moves among objects with senses under the control of his own self, and free from affection and aversion, obtains tranquillity. When there is tranquillity, all his miseries are destroyed, for the mind of him whose heart is tranquil soon becomes steady.

Chapter V

The Deity said:

Renunciation and pursuit of action are both instruments of happiness. But of the two, pursuit of action is superior to renunciation of action. He should be understood to be always an ascetic, who has no aversion and no desire. For, O you of mighty arms! he who is free from the pairs of opposites is easily released from (all) bonds. Children—not wise men—talk of sânkhya and yoga as distinct. One who pursues either well obtains the fruit of both. The seat which the sânkhyas obtain is reached by the yogas also. He sees (truly), who sees the sânkhya and yoga as one. Renunciation, O you of mighty arms! is difficult to reach without devotion; the sage possessed of devotion attains Brahman without delay. He who is possessed of devotion, whose self is pure, who has restrained his self, and who has controlled his senses, and who identifies his self with every being, is not tainted though he performs (actions).

. . .

He who knows Brahman, whose mind is steady, who is not deluded, and who rests in Brahman, does not exult on finding anything agreeable, nor does he grieve on finding anything disagreeable. One whose self is not attached to external objects, obtains the happiness that is in (one's) self; and by means of concentration of mind, joining one's self (with the Brahman), one obtains indestructible happiness. For the enjoyments born of contact (between senses and their objects) are, indeed, sources of misery; they have a beginning as well as an end. O son of Kunti! a wise man feels no pleasure in them. He who even in this world, before his release from the body, is able to bear the agitations produced from desire and wrath, is a devoted man, he is a happy man. The devotee whose happiness is within, whose recreation is within, and whose light (of knowledge) also is within, becoming (one with) the Brahman, obtain the Brahmic bliss.

Chapter VI

The Deity said:

O son of Prithâ! neither in this world nor the next, is ruin for him; for, O dear friend! none who performs good comes to an evil end. He who is fallen from devotion attains the worlds of those who perform meritorious acts, dwells for many a year, and is afterwards born into a family of holy and illustrious men. Or he is even born into a family of talented devotees; for such a birth as that in this world is more difficult to obtain. There he comes into contact with the knowledge which belonged to him in his former body, and then again, O descendant of Kuru! he works for perfection. For even though reluctant, he is led away by the self-same former practice, and although he only wishes to learn devotion, he rises above the (fruits of action laid down in the) divine word. But the devotee working with great efforts, and cleared of his sins, attains perfection after many births, and then reaches the supreme goal. The devotee is esteemed higher than the performers of penances, higher even than the men of knowledge, and the devotee is higher than the men of action; therefore, O Arjuna! become a devotee. And even among all devotees, he who, being full of faith, worships me, with his inmost self intent on me, is esteemed by me to be the most devoted.

Chapter XI

The Deity said:

I am death, the destroyer of the worlds, fully developed, and I am now active about the overthrow of the worlds. Even without you, the warriors standing in the adverse hosts, shall all cease to be. Therefore, be up, obtain glory, and vanquishing foes, enjoy a prosperous kingdom. All these have been already killed by me. Be only the instrument, O Savyasâkin! Drona, and Bhîshma, and Gayadratha, and Karna, and likewise other valiant warriors also, whom I have killed, do you kill. Be not alarmed. Do fight. And in the battle you will conquer your foes.

6

=== ❧ ===

The New Testament

....

The New Testament, a collection of twenty-seven books written in the first and second centuries, is the second part of the Christian biblical canon, the first being the Hebrew Bible (or "Old Testament"). The focus of the New Testament is on the life and significance of Jesus of Nazareth, believed by Christians to be the Son of God: it contains four narratives of Jesus's life and teachings (the "Gospels"), an account of the apostles' activities in the early church, twenty-one letters (or "Epistles") by various authors (including St. Paul) concerning church doctrine and instruction, and a book of prophecy (the Book of Revelation) dealing with end times.

The opening selections are drawn from the Gospels: the first is the three chapters of the Gospel of St. Matthew known as the "Sermon on the Mount," and are a condensed account of Jesus's teaching, in which the rules and principles of moral conduct are outlined and in which Jesus also outlines how to live without avoidable anxieties. The remainder of the selections come from the Epistles. In St. Paul's Epistle to the Romans we see him powerfully expressing the inner conflict that human beings feel between our inclinations and our felt duties, and there are also words of hope in the face of "the sufferings of this present time," a hope that is rooted in Paul's fervent belief in the love of God for humanity. Hope is also uppermost in the subsequent selection, drawn from the First Epistle to the Corinthians, in which Paul discusses the possibility and character of the resurrection of the dead. The final selection, from the First Epistle to Timothy,

---

From the Holy Bible (Revised Standard Version): Matthew 5–7; Romans 7:14–25, 8:18–39; 1 Corinthians 15:12–57; 1 Timothy 2.)

(traditionally though perhaps not accurately attributed to Paul) is included to illustrate the submissive character apparently demanded of women in the early church.

....

Matthew

Chapter 5

Seeing the crowds, he went up on the mountain, and when he sat down his disciples came to him. And he opened his mouth and taught them, saying: "Blessed are the poor in spirit, for theirs is the kingdom of heaven. Blessed are those who mourn, for they shall be comforted. Blessed are the meek, for they shall inherit the earth. Blessed are those who hunger and thirst for righteousness, for they shall be satisfied. Blessed are the merciful, for they shall obtain mercy. Blessed are the pure in heart, for they shall see God. Blessed are the peacemakers, for they shall be called sons of God. Blessed are those who are persecuted for righteousness' sake, for theirs is the kingdom of heaven. Blessed are you when men revile you and persecute you and utter all kinds of evil against you falsely on my account."

"Rejoice and be glad, for your reward is great in heaven, for so men persecuted the prophets who were before you."

"You are the salt of the earth; but if salt has lost its taste, how shall its saltness be restored? It is no longer good for anything except to be thrown out and trodden under foot by men."

"You are the light of the world. A city set on a hill cannot be hid. Nor do men light a lamp and put it under a bushel, but on a stand, and it gives light to all in the house. Let your light so shine before men, that they may see your good works and give glory to your Father who is in heaven."

"Think not that I have come to abolish the law and the prophets; I have come not to abolish them but to fulfil them. For truly, I say to you, till heaven and earth pass away, not an iota, not a dot, will pass from the law until all is accomplished. Whoever then relaxes one of the least of these commandments and teaches men so, shall be called least in the kingdom of heaven; but he who does them and teaches them shall be called great in the kingdom of heaven."

"For I tell you, unless your righteousness exceeds that of the scribes and Pharisees, you will never enter the kingdom of heaven. You have heard that it was said to the men of old, 'You shall not kill; and whoever kills shall be liable to judgment.' But I say to you that every one who is angry with his brother shall be liable to judgment; whoever insults his brother shall be liable to the council, and whoever says, 'You fool!' shall be liable to the hell of fire."

"So if you are offering your gift at the altar, and there remember that your brother has something against you, leave your gift there before the altar and go; first be reconciled to your brother, and then come and offer your gift."

"Make friends quickly with your accuser, while you are going with him to court, lest your accuser hand you over to the judge, and the judge to the guard, and you be put in prison; truly, I say to you, you will never get out till you have paid the last penny."

"You have heard that it was said, 'You shall not commit adultery.' But I say to you that every one who looks at a woman lustfully has already committed adultery with her in his heart."

"If your right eye causes you to sin, pluck it out and throw it away; it is better that you lose one of your members than that your whole body be thrown into hell. And if your right hand causes you to sin, cut it off and throw it away; it is better that you lose one of your members than that your whole body go into hell."

"It was also said, 'Whoever divorces his wife, let him give her a certificate of divorce.' But I say to you that every one who divorces his wife, except on the ground of unchastity, makes her an adulteress; and whoever marries a divorced woman commits adultery."

"Again you have heard that it was said to the men of old, 'You shall not swear falsely, but shall perform to the Lord what you have sworn.' But I say to you, Do not swear at all, either by heaven, for it is the throne of God, or by the earth, for it is his footstool, or by Jerusalem, for it is the city of the great King. And do not swear by your head, for you cannot make one hair white or black. Let what you say be simply 'Yes' or 'No'; anything more than this comes from evil."

"You have heard that it was said, 'An eye for an eye and a tooth for a tooth.' But I say to you, Do not resist one who is evil. But if any one strikes you on the right cheek, turn to him the other also; and if any one would sue you and take your coat, let him have your cloak as well; and if any one forces you to go one mile, go with him two miles. Give to him who begs from you, and do not refuse him who would borrow from you."

"You have heard that it was said, 'You shall love your neighbor and hate your enemy.' But I say to you, Love your enemies and pray for those who persecute you, so that you may be sons of your Father who is in heaven; for he makes his sun rise on the evil and on the good, and sends rain on the just and on the unjust. For if you love those who love you, what reward have you? Do not even the tax collectors do the same? And if you salute only your brethren, what more are you doing than others? Do not even the Gentiles do the same?"

"You, therefore, must be perfect, as your heavenly Father is perfect."

Chapter 6

"Beware of practicing your piety before men in order to be seen by them; for then you will have no reward from your Father who is in heaven."

"Thus, when you give alms, sound no trumpet before you, as the hypocrites do in the synagogues and in the streets, that they may be praised by men. Truly, I say to you, they have received their reward. But when you give alms, do not let your left hand know what your right hand is doing, so that your alms may be in secret; and your Father who sees in secret will reward you."

"And when you pray, you must not be like the hypocrites; for they love to stand and pray in the synagogues and at the street corners, that they may be seen by men. Truly, I say to you, they have received their reward. But when you pray, go into your room and shut the door and pray to your Father who is in secret; and your Father who sees in secret will reward you."

"And in praying do not heap up empty phrases as the Gentiles do; for they think that they will be heard for their many words. Do not be like them, for your Father knows what you need before you ask him. Pray then like this:

> Our Father who art in heaven,
> Hallowed be thy name.
> Thy kingdom come.
> Thy will be done,
> On earth as it is in heaven.
> Give us this day our daily bread;
> And forgive us our debts,
> As we also have forgiven our debtors;

And lead us not into temptation,
But deliver us from evil."

"For if you forgive men their trespasses, your heavenly Father also will forgive you; but if you do not forgive men their trespasses, neither will your Father forgive your trespasses."

"And when you fast, do not look dismal, like the hypocrites, for they disfigure their faces that their fasting may be seen by men. Truly, I say to you, they have received their reward. But when you fast, anoint your head and wash your face, that your fasting may not be seen by men but by your Father who is in secret; and your Father who sees in secret will reward you."

"Do not lay up for yourselves treasures on earth, where moth and rust consume and where thieves break in and steal, but lay up for yourselves treasures in heaven, where neither moth nor rust consumes and where thieves do not break in and steal. For where your treasure is, there will your heart be also."

"The eye is the lamp of the body. So, if your eye is sound, your whole body will be full of light; but if your eye is not sound, your whole body will be full of darkness. If then the light in you is darkness, how great is the darkness!"

"No one can serve two masters; for either he will hate the one and love the other, or he will be devoted to the one and despise the other. You cannot serve God and mammon."

"Therefore I tell you, do not be anxious about your life, what you shall eat or what you shall drink, nor about your body, what you shall put on. Is not life more than food, and the body more than clothing? Look at the birds of the air: they neither sow nor reap nor gather into barns, and yet your heavenly Father feeds them. Are you not of more value than they? And which of you by being anxious can add one cubit to his span of life? And why are you anxious about clothing? Consider the lilies of the field, how they grow; they neither toil nor spin; yet I tell you, even Solomon in all his glory was not arrayed like one of these. But if God so clothes the grass of the field, which today is alive and tomorrow is thrown into the oven, will he not much more clothe you, O men of little faith? Therefore do not be anxious, saying, 'What shall we eat?' or 'What shall we drink?' or 'What shall we wear?' For the Gentiles seek all these things; and your heavenly Father knows that you need them all. But seek first his kingdom and his righteousness, and all these things shall be yours as well."

"Therefore do not be anxious about tomorrow, for tomorrow will be anxious for itself. Let the day's own trouble be sufficient for the day."

Chapter 7

"Judge not, that you be not judged. For with the judgment you pronounce you will be judged, and the measure you give will be the measure you get. Why do you see the speck that is in your brother's eye, but do not notice the log that is in your own eye? Or how can you say to your brother, 'Let me take the speck out of your eye,' when there is the log in your own eye? You hypocrite, first take the log out of your own eye, and then you will see clearly to take the speck out of your brother's eye."

"Do not give dogs what is holy; and do not throw your pearls before swine, lest they trample them under foot and turn to attack you."

"Ask, and it will be given you; seek, and you will find; knock, and it will be opened to you. For every one who asks receives, and he who seeks finds, and to him who knocks it will be opened. Or what man of you, if his son asks him for bread, will give him a stone? Or if he asks for a fish, will give him a serpent? If you then, who are evil, know how to give good gifts to your children, how much more will your Father who is in heaven give good things to those who ask him! So whatever you wish that men would do to you, do so to them; for this is the law and the prophets."

"Enter by the narrow gate; for the gate is wide and the way is easy, that leads to destruction, and those who enter by it are many. For the gate is narrow and the way is hard, that leads to life, and those who find it are few."

"Beware of false prophets, who come to you in sheep's clothing but inwardly are ravenous wolves. You will know them by their fruits. Are grapes gathered from thorns, or figs from thistles? So, every sound tree bears good fruit, but the bad tree bears evil fruit. A sound tree cannot bear evil fruit, nor can a bad tree bear good fruit. Every tree that does not bear good fruit is cut down and thrown into the fire. Thus you will know them by their fruits."

"Not every one who says to me, 'Lord, Lord,' shall enter the kingdom of heaven, but he who does the will of my Father who is in heaven. On that day many will say to me, 'Lord, Lord, did we not prophesy in your name, and cast out demons in your name, and do many mighty works in your name?' And then will I declare to them, 'I never knew you; depart from me, you evildoers.'"

"Every one then who hears these words of mine and does them will be like a wise man who built his house upon the rock; and the rain fell, and the floods came, and the winds blew and beat upon that house, but it did not fall, because it had been founded on the rock. And every one who hears these words of mine and does not do them will be like a foolish man who built his house upon the sand; and the rain fell, and the floods came, and the winds blew and beat against that house, and it fell; and great was the fall of it."

And when Jesus finished these sayings, the crowds were astonished at his teaching, for he taught them as one who had authority, and not as their scribes.

Romans

Chapter 7

. . . For we know that the law is spiritual; but I am of the flesh, sold into slavery under sin. I do not understand my own actions. For I do not do what I want, but I do the very thing I hate. Now if I do what I do not want, I agree that the law is good. But in fact it is no longer I that do it, but sin that dwells within me. For I know that nothing good dwells within me, that is, in my flesh. I can will what is right, but I cannot do it. For I do not do the good I want, but the evil I do not want is what I do. Now, if I do what I do not want, it is no longer I that do it, but sin that dwells within me.

So I find it to be a law that when I want to do what is good, evil lies close at hand. For I delight in the law of God in my inmost self, but I see in my members another law at war with the law of my mind, making me captive to the law of sin that dwells in my members. Wretched man that I am! Who will rescue me from this body of death? Thanks be to God through Jesus Christ our Lord!

So then, with my mind I am a slave to the law of God, but with my flesh I am a slave to the law of sin.

Chapter 8

. . . I consider that the sufferings of this present time are not worth comparing with the glory about to be revealed to us. For the creation waits with eager longing for the revealing of the children of God; for the creation was subjected to futility, not of its own will but by the will of the one who subjected it, in hope that the creation itself will be set free from its bondage to decay and will obtain the freedom of the glory of the children of God. We know that the whole creation has been groaning in labor pains until now; and not only the creation, but we ourselves, who have the first fruits of the Spirit, grown inwardly while we wait for adoption, the redemption of our bodies. For in hope we were saved. Now hope that is seen is not hope. For who hopes for what is seen? But if we hope for what we do not see, we wait for it with patience.

. . .

What then are we to say about these things? If God is for us, who is against us? He who did not withhold his own Son, but gave him up for all of us, will he not with him also give us everything else? Who will bring any charge against God's elect? It is God who justifies. Who is to condemn? It is Christ Jesus, who died, yes, who was raised, who is at the right hand of God, who indeed intercedes for us. Who will separate us from the love of Christ? Will hardship, or distress, or persecution, or famine, or nakedness, or peril, or sword? As it is written,

"For your sake we are being killed all day long;
we are accounted as sheep to be slaughtered."

No, in all these things we are more than conquerors through him who loved us. For I am convinced that neither death, nor life, nor angels, nor rulers, nor things present, nor things to come, nor powers, nor height, nor depth, nor anything else in all creation, will be able to separate us form the love of God in Christ Jesus our Lord.

1 Corinthians

Chapter 15

Now if Christ is preached as raised from the dead, how can some of you say that there is no resurrection of the dead? But if there is no resurrection of the dead, then Christ has not been raised; if Christ has not been raised, then our preaching is in vain and your faith is in vain. We are even found to be misrepresenting God, because we testified of God that he raised Christ, whom he did not raise if it is true that the dead are not raised. For if the dead are not raised, then Christ has not been raised. If Christ has not been raised, your faith is futile and you are still in your sins. Then those also who have fallen asleep in Christ have perished. If for this life only we have hoped in Christ, we are of all men most to be pitied.

But in fact Christ has been raised from the dead, the first fruits of those who have fallen asleep. For as by a man came death, by a man has come also the resurrection of the dead. For as in Adam all die, so also in Christ shall all be made alive. But each in his own order: Christ the first fruits, then at his coming those who belong to Christ. Then comes the end, when he delivers the kingdom to God the Father after destroying every rule and every authority and power. For he must reign until he has put all his enemies under his feet. The last enemy to be destroyed is death.

"For God has put all things in subjection under his feet." But when it says, "All things are put in subjection under him," it is plain that he is excepted who put all things under him. When all things are subjected to him, then the Son himself will also be subjected to him who put all things under him, that God may be everything to every one.

Otherwise, what do people mean by being baptized on behalf of the dead? If the dead are not raised at all, why are people baptized on their behalf?

Why am I in peril every hour? I protest, brethren, by my pride in you which I have in Christ Jesus our Lord, I die every day! What do I gain if, humanly speaking, I fought with beasts at Ephesus? If the dead are not raised, "Let us eat and drink, for tomorrow we die."

Do not be deceived: "Bad company ruins good morals." Come to your right mind, and sin no more. For some have no knowledge of God. I say this to your shame.

But some one will ask, "How are the dead raised? With what kind of body do they come?"

You foolish man! What you sow does not come to life unless it dies. And what you sow is not the body which is to be, but a bare kernel, perhaps of wheat or of some other grain. But God gives it a body as he has chosen, and to each kind of seed its own body. For not all flesh is alike, but there is one kind for men, another for animals, another for birds, and another for fish. There are celestial bodies and there are terrestrial bodies; but the glory of the celestial is one, and the glory of the terrestrial is another. There is one glory of the sun, and another glory of the moon, and another glory of the stars; for star differs from star in glory. So is it with the resurrection of the dead. What is sown is perishable, what is raised is imperishable. It is sown in dishonor, it is raised in glory. It is sown in weakness, it is raised in power. It is sown a physical body, it is raised a spiritual body. If there is a physical body, there is also a spiritual body.

Thus it is written, "The first man Adam became a living being"; the last Adam became a life-giving spirit. But it is not the spiritual which is first but the physical, and then the spiritual. The first man was from the earth, a man of dust; the second man is from heaven. As was the man of dust, so are those who are of the dust; and as is the man of heaven, so are those who are of heaven. Just as we have borne the image of the man of dust, we shall also bear the image of the man of heaven.

I tell you this, brethren flesh and blood cannot inherit the kingdom of God, nor does the perishable inherit the imperishable. Lo! I tell you a mystery. We shall not all sleep, but we shall all be changed, in a moment, in the twinkling of an eye, at the last trumpet. For the trumpet will sound, and the dead will be raised imperishable, and we shall be changed. For this perishable nature must put on the imperishable, and this mortal nature must put on immortality. When the perishable puts on the imperishable, and the mortal puts on immortality, then shall come to pass the saying that is written "Death is swallowed up in victory."

"O death, where is thy victory? O death, where is thy sting?" The sting of death is sin, and the power of sin is the law. But thanks be to God, who gives us the victory through our Lord Jesus Christ.

1 Timothy

Chapter 2

First of all, then, I urge that supplications, prayers, intercessions, and thanksgivings be made for all men, for kings and all who are in high positions, that we may lead a quiet and peaceable life, godly and respectful in every way. This is good, and it is acceptable in the sight of God our Savior, who desires all men to be saved and to come to the knowledge of the truth. For there is one God, and there is one mediator between God and men, the man Christ Jesus, who gave himself as a ransom for all, the testimony to which was borne at the proper time.

For this I was appointed a preacher and apostle (I am telling the truth, I am not lying), a teacher of the Gentiles in faith and truth. I desire then that in every place the men should pray, lifting holy hands without anger or quarreling; also that women should adorn themselves modestly and sensibly in seemly apparel, not with braided hair or gold or pearls or costly attire but by good deeds, as befits women who profess religion. Let a woman learn in silence with all submissiveness. I permit no woman to teach or to have authority over men; she is to keep silent. For Adam was formed first, then Eve; and Adam was not deceived, but the woman was deceived and became a transgressor. Yet woman will be saved through bearing children, if she continues in faith and love and holiness, with modesty.

= 𝔰 =

The Qur'an

The *Qur'an* (Arabic for "the recitation") is supposed to have been revealed to the possibly illiterate Prophet Muhammad by *Allah* (God) through the angel *Jibril* (Gabriel) in the cities of Medina and Mecca in what is now Saudi Arabia in the early seventh century. It forms the basis of Islam, supplemented by the *hadith*, or sayings and acts of Muhammad. Much of the narrative of the Qur'an retells the story of the Hebrew Scriptures and the Christian New Testament from the creation of humanity, through the covenant with *Ibrahim* (Abraham), continuing with the ministry of *Isa* (Jesus).

Here we have included selections from several *suras* (chapters) discussing the origins of humans, the promised afterlife for the faithful, the method of pleasing Allah, as well as those human faults that can make this difficult. We have also included sections dealing with the role and place of women and the universality—comprehending all races and ethnicities and defined only by belief—of the message and community. Finally, we have concluded with a few of the shorter suras in their entirety, to provide a better feel for the style of the text.

Qur'an, Max Müller (ed.), E.H. Palmer (trans.) *Sacred Books of the East*, volume 6, Oxford University Press, 1880.

Sura 2: "The Heifer"

And when thy Lord said unto the angels, "I am about to place a vicegerent in the earth," they said, "Wilt Thou place therein one who will do evil therein and shed blood? we celebrate Thy praise and hallow Thee." Said (the Lord), "I know what ye know not." And He taught Adam the names, all of them; then He propounded them to the angels and said, "Declare to me the names of these, if ye are truthful." They said, "Glory be to Thee! no knowledge is ours but what Thou thyself hast taught us, verily, Thou art the knowing, the wise." Said the Lord, "O Adam declare to them their names"; and when he had declared to them their names He said, "Did I not say to you, I know the secrets of the heavens and of the earth, and I know what ye show and what ye were hiding?" And when we said to the angels, "Adore Adam," they adored him save only Iblîs [the Devil], who refused and was too proud and became one of the misbelievers. And we said, "O Adam dwell, thou and thy wife, in Paradise, and eat therefrom amply as you wish; but do not draw near this tree or ye will be of the transgressors." And Satan made them backslide therefrom and drove them out from what they were in, and we said, "Go down, one of you the enemy of the other, and in the earth there is an abode and a provision for a time." And Adam caught certain words from his Lord, and He turned towards him, for He is the compassionate one easily turned. We said, "Go down therefrom altogether and haply there may come from me a guidance, and whoso follows my guidance, no fear is theirs, nor shall they grieve.

. . .

But those who misbelieve, and call our signs lies, they are the fellows of the Fire, they shall dwell therein for aye."

Sura 3: "Imran's Family"

Verily, those are the true stories, and there is no god but God, and, verily, God He is the mighty, the wise; but if they turn back, God knows the evildoers.

Say, "O ye people of the Book, come to a word laid down plainly between us and you, that we will not serve other than God, nor associate aught with him, nor take each other for lords rather than God." But if they turn back then say, "Bear witness that we are resigned."

O people of the Book, why do ye dispute about Abraham, when the law and the gospel were not revealed until after him? What! do ye not understand? Here ye are, disputing about what ye have some knowledge of; why then do ye dispute about what ye have no knowledge of? God knows and ye know not.

Abraham was not a Jew, nor yet a Christian, but he was a "Hanîf [believer, righteous one] resigned, and not of the idolaters. Verily, the people most worthy of Abraham are those who follow him and his prophets, and those who believe;—God is the patron of the believers.

Sura 4: "The Women"

In the name of the merciful and compassionate God.

O ye folk! fear your Lord, who created you from one soul, and created therefrom its mate, and diffused from them twain many men and women. And fear God, in whose name ye beg of one another, and the wombs; verily, God over you doth watch.

And give unto the orphans their property, and give them not the vile in exchange for the good, and devour not their property to your own property; verily, that were a great sin. But if ye fear that ye cannot do justice between orphans, then marry what seems good to you of women, by twos, or threes, or fours; and if ye fear that ye cannot be equitable, then only one, or what your right hands possess. That keeps you nearer to not being partial.

And give women their dowries freely; and if they are good enough to remit any of it of themselves, then devour it with good digestion and appetite.

. . .

God instructs you concerning your children; for a male the like of the portion of two females, and if there be women above two, then let them have two-thirds of what (the deceased) leaves; and if there be but one, then let her have a half; and as to the parents, to each of them a sixth of what he leaves, if he has a son; but if he have no son, and his parents inherit, then let his mother have a third, and if he have brethren, let his mother have a sixth after payment of the bequest he bequeaths and of his debt.

. . .

But whosoever of you cannot go the length of marrying marriageable women who believe, then take of what your right hands possess, of your maidens who believe;—though God knows best about your faith. Ye come one from the other; then marry them with the permission of their people, and give them their hire in reason, they being chaste and not fornicating, and not receivers of paramours.

But when they are married, if they commit fornication, then inflict upon them half the penalty for married women; that is for whomsoever of you fears wrong; but that ye should have patience is better for you, and God is forgiving and merciful.

. . .

Men stand superior to women in that God hath preferred some of them over others, and in that they expend of their wealth: and the virtuous women, devoted, careful (in their husbands') absence, as God has cared for them. But those whose perverseness ye fear, admonish them and remove them into bed-chambers and beat them; but if they submit to you, then do not seek a way against them; verily, God is high and great.

Sura 23: "The Believers"

In the name of the merciful and compassionate God.

Prosperous are the believers who in their prayers are humble, and who from vain talk turn aside, and who in almsgiving are active. And who guard their private parts—except for their wives or what their right hands possess for then, verily, they are not to be blamed;—but whoso craves aught beyond that, they are the transgressors—and who observe their trusts and covenants, and who guard well their prayers: these are the heirs who shall inherit Paradise; they shall dwell therein for aye!

We have created man from an extract of clay; then we made him a clot in a sure depository; then we created the clot congealed blood, and we created the congealed blood a morsel; then we created the morsel bone, and we clothed the bone with flesh; then we produced it another creation; and blessed be God, the best of creators!

Then shall ye after that surely die; then shall ye on the day of resurrection be raised.

Sura 24: "The Light"

In the name of the merciful and compassionate God.

A chapter which we have sent down and determined, and have sent down therein manifest signs; haply ye may be mindful.

The whore and the whoremonger. Scourge each of them with a hundred stripes, and do not let pity for them take hold of you in God's religion, if ye believe in God and the last day; and let a party of the believers witness their torment. And the whoremonger shall marry none but a whore or an idolatress; and the whore shall none marry but an adulterer or an idolater; God has prohibited this to the believers; but those who cast (imputations) on chaste women and then do not bring four witnesses, scourge them with eighty stripes, and do not receive any testimony of theirs ever, for these are the workers of abomination. Except such as repent after that and act aright, for, verily, God is forgiving and compassionate.

And those who cast (imputation) on their wives and have no witnesses except themselves, then the testimony of one of them shall be to testify four times that, by God, he is of those who speak the truth; and the fifth testimony shall be that the curse of God shall be on him if he be of those who lie. And it shall avert the punishment from her if she bears testimony four times that, by God, he is of those who lie; and the fifth that the wrath of God shall be on her if he be of those who speak the truth. . . .

Sura 70: "The Ascents"

Verily, man is by nature rash! when evil touches him, very impatient; when good touches him, niggardly; all save those who pray, who remain at their prayers, and in whose wealth is a reasonable due (set aside) for him who asks and him who is kept from asking, and those who believe in a day of judgment, and those who shrink in terror from the torment of their Lord;—verily, the torment of their Lord is not safe;—and those who guard their private parts, except for their wives or the (slave girls) whom their right hands possess, for they are not to be blamed; but whoso craves beyond this, they are the transgressors; and those who observe their trusts and their compacts, and those who are upright in their testimonies, and those who keep their prayers, these shall dwell in gardens honoured. . . .

Sura 74: "The Covered"

In the name of the merciful and compassionate God.

O thou who art covered! rise up and warn! And thy Lord magnify!

And thy garments purify!

And abomination shun!

And grant not favours to gain increase!

And for thy Lord await!

And when the trump is blown,—for that day is a difficult day! for the misbelievers aught but easy!

Leave me alone with him I have created, and for whom I have made extensive wealth, and sons that he may look upon, and for whom I have smoothed things down. Then he desires that I should increase! nay, verily, he is hostile to our signs! I will drive him up a hill! Then he reflected and planned! May he be killed,—how he planned! Again, may he be killed,— how he planned! Then he looked; then he frowned and scowled; then he retreated and was big with pride and said, "This is only magic exhibited! this is only mortal speech!"—I will broil him in hell-fire! and what shall make thee know what hell-fire is? It will not leave and will not let alone. It scorches the flesh; over it are nineteen (angels).

We have made only angels guardians of the fire, and we have only made their number a trial to those who misbelieve; that those who have been given the Book may be certain, and that those who believe may be increased in faith; and that those who have been given the Book and the believers may not doubt; and that those in whose hearts is sickness, and the misbelievers may say, "What does God mean by this as a parable?"

Thus God leads astray whom He pleases, and guides him He pleases: and none knows the hosts of thy Lord save Himself; and it is only a reminder to mortals!

Nay, by the moon!

And the night when it retires!

And the morning when it brightly dawns!

Verily, it is one of the greatest misfortunes; a warning to mortals; for him amongst you who wishes to press forward or to tarry!

Every soul is pledged for what it earns; except the fellows of the right: in gardens shall they ask each other about the sinners!—"What drove you into hell-fire?"

They shall say, "We weren't of those who prayed; we didn't feed the poor; but we did plunge into discussion with those who plunged, and we called the judgment day a lie until the certainty did come to us!"

But there shall not profit them the intercession of the intercessors.

What ailed them that they turned away from the memorial as though they were timid asses fleeing from a lion?

Nay, every man of them wished that he might have given him books spread open!

Nay, but they did not fear the hereafter!

Nay, it is a memorial! and let him who will remember it; but none will remember it except God please. He is most worthy of fear; and he is most worthy to forgive!

Sura 113: "The Daybreak"

In the name of the merciful and compassionate God.

Say, "I seek refuge in the Lord of the daybreak, from the evil of what He has created; and from the evil of the night when it cometh on; and from the evil of the blowers upon knots; and from the evil of the envious when he envies."

Sura 114: "Men"

In the name of the merciful and compassionate God.

Say, "I seek refuge in the Lord of men, the King of men, the God of men, from the evil of the whisperer, who slinks off, who whispers into the hearts of men!—from ginns and men!"

PART TWO

Classical Sources

8

Plato

While Alfred North Whitehead's claim that Western philosophy is simply "a series of footnotes to Plato" may have been an exaggeration, the significance of this greatest of classical philosophers is immense and abiding. Plato (c. 427–347 BCE) was a friend and follower of Socrates (469–399 BCE), the brilliant and argumentative Athenian "gadfly." Appalled by Socrates's execution, Plato immortalized his teacher in a series of dialogues focused upon an enormous number of issues (including the nature of knowledge, love, poetry, morality, and politics), and in so doing developed his own far-reaching philosophical system. Plato founded in Athens the Academy, an educational institution dedicated to philosophy, and which would become the prototype of the university. The following readings address a great number of issues relating to the human condition. For the sake of clarity they will be introduced individually.

[1] The account of the human person held by Plato is known as "substance dualism": human beings consist of two parts (or substances), the mental (soul or mind) and the physical (body). Plato does not merely assert this, but provides arguments in favor of this position. In this extract, we see Socrates, in dialogue with Alcibiades, arguing for dualism on the basis of a distinction between *user* and *thing used*.

Alcibiades I

SOCRATES: And can we ever know what art makes a man better, if we do not know what we are ourselves?

ALCIBIADES: Impossible.

And is self-knowledge such an easy thing, and was he to be lightly esteemed who inscribed the text on the temple at Delphi? Or is self-knowledge a difficult thing, which few are able to attain?

At times I fancy, Socrates, that anybody can know himself; at other times the task appears to be very difficult.

But whether easy or difficult, Alcibiades, still there is no other way; knowing what we are, we shall know how to take care of ourselves, and if we are ignorant we shall not know.

That is true.

Well, then, let us see in what way the self-existent can be discovered by us; that will give us a chance of discovering our own existence, which otherwise we can never know.

You say truly.

Come, now, I beseech you, tell me with whom you are conversing? with whom but with me?

Yes.

As I am, with you?

Yes.

That is to say, I, Socrates, am talking?

Yes.

And Alcibiades is my hearer?

Yes.

And I in talking use words?

Certainly.

And talking and using words have, I suppose, the same meaning?

To be sure.

And the user is not the same as the thing which he uses?

What do you mean?

I will explain; the shoemaker, for example, uses a square tool, and a circular tool, and other tools for cutting?

Yes.

Alcibiades I, from *The Dialogues of Plato* (translated by B. Jowett) (Two Volumes) (New York: Random House, 1937; copyright Macmillan, 1892), vol.2, pp. 763–766.

But the tool is not the same as the cutter and user of the tool?

Of course not.

And in the same way the instrument of the harper is to be distinguished from the harper himself?

It is.

Now the question which I asked was whether you conceive the user to be always different from that which he uses?

I do.

Then what shall we say of the shoemaker? Does he cut with his tools only or with his hands?

With his hands as well.

He uses his hands too?

Yes.

And does he use his eyes in cutting leather?

He does.

And we admit that the user is not the same with the things which he uses?

Yes.

Then the shoemaker and the harper are to be distinguished from the hands and feet which they use?

Clearly.

And does not a man use the whole body?

Certainly.

And that which uses is different from that which is used?

True.

Then a man is not the same as his own body?

That is the inference.

What is he, then?

I cannot say.

Nay, you can say that he is the user of the body.

Yes.

And the user of the body is the soul?

Yes, the soul.

And the soul rules?

Yes.

Let me make an assertion which will, I think, be universally admitted.

What is it?

That man is one of three things.

What are they?

Soul, body, or both together forming a whole.

Certainly.

But did we not say that the actual ruling principle of the body is man?

Yes, we did.

And does the body rule over itself?

Certainly not.

It is subject, as we were saying?

Yes.

Then that is not the principle which we are seeking?

It would seem not.

But may we say that the union of the two rules over the body, and consequently that this is man?

Very likely.

The most unlikely of all things; for if one of the members is subject, the two united cannot possibly rule.

True.

But since neither the body, nor the union of the two, is man, either man has no real existence, or the soul is man?

Just so.

Is anything more required to prove that the soul is man?

. . . .

[2] Just as Plato provides an argument in support of substance dualism, so he offers an argument for the immortality of the soul, based upon the purported inability of the immaterial to be destroyed by any evil.

. . . .

Republic

Book X

"Are you not aware," I said, "That the soul of man is immortal and imperishable?"

He looked at me in astonishment, and said: "No, by heaven: And are you really prepared to maintain this?"

Proof of the immortality of the soul: The Republic (Jowett translation), from *The Dialogues of Plato*, vol. 1, pp. 866–869.

"Yes," I said, "I ought to be, and you too—there is no difficulty in proving it."

"I see a great difficulty; but I should like to hear you state this argument of which you make so light."

"Listen then."

"I am attending."

"There is a thing which you call good and another which you call evil?"

"Yes," he replied.

"Would you agree with me in thinking that the corrupting and destroying element is the evil, and the saving and improving element the good?"

"Yes."

"And you admit that every thing has a good and also an evil; as ophthalmia is the evil of the eyes and disease of the whole body; as mildew is of corn, and rot of timber, or rust of copper and iron: in everything, or in almost everything, there is an inherent evil and disease?"

"Yes," he said.

"And anything which is infected by any of these evils is made evil, and at last wholly dissolves and dies?"

"True."

"The vice and evil which is inherent in each is the destruction of each; and if this does not destroy them there is nothing else that will; for good certainly will not destroy them nor again, that which is neither good nor evil."

"Certainly not."

"If, then, we find any nature which having this inherent corruption cannot be dissolved or destroyed, we may be certain that of such a nature there is no destruction?"

"That may be assumed."

"Well," I said, "and is there no evil which corrupts the soul?"

"Yes," he said, "there are all the evils which we were just now passing in review: unrighteousness, intemperance, cowardice, ignorance."

"But does any of these dissolve or destroy her?—and here do not let us fall into the error of supposing that the unjust and foolish man, when he is detected, perishes through his own injustice, which is an evil of the soul. Take the analogy of the body: The evil of the body is a disease which wastes and reduces and annihilates the body; and all the things of which we were just now speaking come to annihilation through their own corruption attaching to them and inhering in them and so destroying them. Is not this true?"

"Yes."

"Consider the soul in like manner. Does the injustice or other evil which exists in the soul waste and consume her? Do they by attaching to the soul and inhering in her at last bring her to death, and so separate her from the body?"

"Certainly not."

"And yet," I said, "it is unreasonable to suppose that anything can perish from without through affection of external evil which could not be destroyed from within by a corruption of its own?"

"It is," he replied.

"Consider," I said, "Glaucon, that even the badness of food, whether staleness, decomposition, or any other bad quality, when confined to the actual food, is not supposed to destroy the body; although, if the badness of food communicates corruption to the body, then we should say that the body has been destroyed by a corruption of itself, which is disease, brought on by this; but that the body, being one thing, can be destroyed by the badness of food, which is another, and which does not engender any natural infection—this we shall absolutely deny?"

"Very true."

"And, on the same principle, unless some bodily evil can produce an evil of the soul, we must not suppose that the soul, which is one thing, can be dissolved by any merely external evil which belongs to another?"

"Yes," he said, "there is reason in that."

"Either then, let us refute this conclusion, or, while it remains unrefuted, let us never say that fever, or any other disease, or the knife put to the throat, or even the cutting up of the whole body into the minutest pieces, can destroy the soul, until she herself is proved to become more unholy or unrighteous in consequence of these things being done to the body; but that the soul, or anything else if not destroyed by an internal evil, can be destroyed by an external one, is not to be affirmed by any man."

"And surely," he replied, "no one will ever prove that the souls of men become more unjust in consequence of death."

"But if some one who would rather not admit the immortality of the soul boldly denies this, and says that the dying do really become more evil and unrighteous, then, if the speaker is right, I suppose that injustice, like disease, must be assumed to be fatal to the unjust, and that those who take this disorder die by the natural inherent power of destruction which evil has, and which kills them sooner or later, but in quite another way from that in which, at present, the wicked receive death at the hands of others as the penalty of their deeds?"

"Nay," he said, "in that case injustice, if fatal to the unjust, will not be so very terrible to him, for he will be delivered from evil. But I rather suspect the opposite to be the truth, and that injustice which, if it have the power, will murder others, keeps the murderer alive—aye, and well awake too; so far removed is her dwelling-place from being a house of death."

"True," I said; "If the inherent natural vice or evil of the soul is unable to kill or destroy her, hardly will that which is appointed to be the destruction of some other body, destroy a soul or anything else except that of which it was appointed to be the destruction."

"Yes, that can hardly be."

"But the soul which cannot be destroyed by an evil, whether inherent or external, must exist for ever, and if existing for ever, must be immortal?"

"Certainly."

....

[3] In the next passage, from *Phaedo*, we find Socrates expressing to his friend Simmias, in the final hours before his execution, his calmness in the face of death. This calm disposition is due to Socrates's confidence in both the immortality of the soul and the benefits that flow from finally being released from the limitations of the body.

....

Phaedo

"We believe, do we not, that death is the separation of the soul from the body, and that the state of being dead is the state in which the body is separated from the soul and exists alone by itself and the soul is separated from the body and exists alone by itself? Is death anything other than this?"

"No, it is this," said he.

"Now, my friend, see if you agree with me; for, if you do, I think we shall get more light on our subject. Do you think a philosopher would

---

From Phaedo (translated by H.N.Fowler) (Cambridge, MA: Harvard University Press, 1914), pp. 223–237.

be likely to care much about the so-called pleasures, such as eating and drinking?"

"By no means, Socrates," said Simmias.

"How about the pleasures of love?"

"Certainly not."

"Well, do you think such a man would think much of the other cares of the body—I mean such as the possession of fine clothes and shoes and the other personal adornments? Do you think he would care about them or despise them, except so far as it is necessary to have them?"

"I think the true philosopher would despise them," he replied.

"Altogether, then, you think that such a man would not devote himself to the body, but would, so far as he was able, turn away from the body and concern himself with the soul?"

"Yes."

"To begin with, then, it is clear that in such matters the philosopher, more than other men, separates the soul from communion with the body?"

"It is."

"Now certainly most people think that a man who takes no pleasure and has no part in such things doesn't deserve to live, and that one who cares nothing for the pleasures of the body is about as good as dead."

"That is very true."

"Now, how about the acquirement of pure knowledge? Is the body a hindrance or not, if it is made to share in the search for wisdom? What I mean is this: Have the sight and hearing of men any truth in them, or is it true, as the poets are always telling us, that we neither hear nor see any thing accurately? And yet if these two physical senses are not accurate or exact, the rest are not likely to be, for they are inferior to these. Do you not think so?"

"Certainly I do," he replied.

"Then," said he, "when does the soul attain to truth? For when it tries to consider anything in company with the body, it is evidently deceived by it."

"True."

"In thought, then, if at all, something of the realities becomes clear to it?"

"Yes."

"But it thinks best when none of these things troubles it, neither hearing nor sight, nor pain nor any pleasure, but it is, so far as possible, alone by itself, and takes leave of the body, and avoiding, so far as it can, all association or contact with the body, reaches out toward the reality."

"That is true."

"In this matter also, then, the soul of the philosopher greatly despises the body and avoids it and strives to be alone by itself?"

"Evidently."

"Now how about such things as this, Simmias? Do we think there is such a thing as absolute justice, or not?"

"We certainly think there is."

"And absolute beauty and goodness."

"Of course."

"Well, did you ever see anything of that kind with your eyes?"

"Certainly not," said he.

"Or did you ever reach them with any of the bodily senses? I am speaking of all such things, as size, health, strength, and in short the essence or underlying quality of everything. Is their true nature contemplated by means of the body? Is it not rather the case that he who prepares himself most carefully to understand the true essence of each thing that he examines would come nearest to the knowledge of it?"

"Certainly."

"Would not that man do this most perfectly who approaches each thing, so far as possible, with the reason alone, not introducing sight into his reasoning nor dragging in any of the other senses along with his thinking, but who employs pure, absolute reason in his attempt to search out the pure, absolute essence of things, and who removes himself, so far as possible, from eyes and ears, and, in a word, from his whole body, because he feels that its companionship disturbs the soul and hinders it from attaining truth and wisdom? Is not this the man, Simmias, if anyone, to attain to the knowledge of reality?"

"That is true as true can be, Socrates," said Simmias.

"Then," said he, "all this must cause good lovers of wisdom to think and say one to the other something like this: 'There seems to be a short cut which leads us and our argument to the conclusion in our search that so long as we have the body, and the soul is contaminated by such an evil, we shall never attain completely what we desire, that is, the truth. For the body keeps us constantly busy by reason of its need of sustenance; and moreover, if diseases come upon it they hinder our pursuit of the truth. And the body fills us with passions and desires and fears, and all sorts of fancies and foolishness, so that, as they say, it really and truly makes it impossible for us to think at all. The body and its desires are the only cause of wars and factions and battles; for all wars arise for the sake of gaining money, and we are compelled to gain money for the sake of the body. We are slaves to its service. And so, because of all these things, we have no leisure for philosophy. But the worst of all is that if we do get a bit of leisure and turn to philosophy, the body is constantly breaking in upon our studies and disturbing us with noise and confusion, so that it prevents our beholding the truth, and in fact we perceive that, if we are ever to know anything absolutely, we must be free from the body and must behold the actual realities with the eye of the soul alone. And then, as our argument shows, when we are dead we are likely to possess the wisdom which we desire and claim to be enamored of, but not while we live. For, if pure knowledge is impossible while the body is with us, one of two things must follow, either it cannot be acquired at all or only when we are dead; for then the soul will be by itself apart from the body, but not before. And while we live, we shall, I think, be nearest to knowledge when we avoid, so far as possible, intercourse and communion with the body, except what is absolutely necessary, and are not filled with its nature, but keep ourselves pure from it until God himself sets us free. And in this way, freeing ourselves from the foolishness of the body and being pure, we shall, I think, be with the pure and shall know of ourselves all that is pure,—and that is, perhaps, the truth. For it cannot be that the impure attain the pure.' Such words as these, I think, Simmias, all who are rightly lovers of knowledge must say to each other and such must be their thoughts. Do you not agree?"

"Most assuredly, Socrates."

"Then," said Socrates, "if this is true, my friend, I have great hopes that when I reach the place to which I am going, I shall there, if anywhere, attain fully to that which has been my chief object in my past life, so that the journey which is now imposed upon me is begun with good hope; and the like hope exists for every man who thinks that his mind has been purified and made ready."

"Certainly," said Simmias.

"And does not the purification consist in this which has been mentioned long ago in our discourse, in separating, so far as possible, the soul from the body and teaching the soul the habit of collecting and bringing itself together from all parts of the body, and living, so far as it can, both now and hereafter, alone by itself, freed from the body as from fetters?"

"Certainly," said he.

"Well, then, this is what we call death, is it not, a release and separation from the body?"

"Exactly so," said he.

"But, as we hold, the true philosophers and they alone are always most eager to release the soul, and just this—the release and separation of the soul from the body—is their study, is it not?"

"Obviously."

"Then, as I said in the beginning, it would be absurd if a man who had been all his life fitting himself to live as nearly in a state of death as he could, should then be disturbed when death came to him. Would it not be absurd?"

"Of course."

"In fact, then, Simmias," said he, "the true philosophers practice dying, and death is less terrible to them than to any other men. Consider it in this way. They are in every way hostile to the body and they desire to have the soul apart by itself alone. Would it not be very foolish if they should be frightened and troubled when this very thing happens, and if they should not be glad to go to the place where there is hope of attaining what they longed for all through life—and they longed for wisdom—and of escaping from the companionship of that which they hated? When human loves or wives or sons have died, many men have willingly gone to the other world led by the hope of seeing there those whom they longed for, and of being with them; and shall he who is really in love with wisdom and has a firm belief that he can find it nowhere else than in the other world grieve when he dies and not be glad to go there? We cannot think that, my friend, if he is really a philosopher; for he will confidently believe that he will find pure wisdom nowhere else than in the other world. And if this is so, would it not be very foolish for such a man to fear death?"

....

[4] In the Myth of Er, Plato provides a memorable account of the rewards and punishments of the hereafter. The speaker is Socrates.

....

Republic

Book X

"Well," I said, "I will tell you a tale; not one of the tales which Odysseus tells to the hero Alcinous, yet this too is a tale of a hero, Er the son of Armenius, a Pamphylian by birth. He was slain in battle, and ten days afterwards, when the bodies of the dead were taken up already in a state of corruption, his body was found unaffected by decay, and carried away home to be buried. And on the twelfth day, as he was lying on the funeral pile, he returned to life and told them what he had seen in the other world. He said that when his soul left the body he went on a journey with a great company, and that they came to a mysterious place at which there were two openings in the earth; they were near together, and over against them were two other openings in the heaven above. In the intermediate space there were judges seated, who commanded the just, after they had given judgment on them and had bound their sentences in front of them, to ascend by the heavenly way on the right hand; and in like manner the unjust were bidden by them to descend by the lower way on the left hand; these also bore the symbols of their deeds, but fastened on their backs. He drew near, and they told him that he was to be the messenger who would carry the report of the other world to men, and they bade him hear and see all that was to be heard and seen in that place. Then he beheld and saw on one side the souls departing at either opening of heaven and earth when sentence had been given on them; and at the two other openings other souls, some ascending out of the earth dusty and worn with travel, some descending out of heaven clean and bright. And arriving ever and anon they seemed to have come from a long journey, and they went forth with gladness into the meadow, where they encamped as at a festival; and those who knew one another embraced and conversed, the souls which came from earth curiously enquiring about the things above, and the souls which came from heaven about the things beneath. And they told one another of what had happened by the way, those from below weeping and sorrowing at the remembrance of the things which they had endured and seen in their journey beneath the earth (now the journey lasted a thousand years), while those from above were describing heavenly delights and visions of inconceivable beauty. The story, Glaucon, would take too long to tell; but the sum was this:—He said that for every wrong which they had done to any one they suffered tenfold; or once in a hundred years—such being reckoned to be the length of man's life, and the penalty being thus paid ten times in a thousand years. If, for example, there were any who had been the cause of many deaths, or had betrayed or enslaved cities or armies, or been guilty of any other evil behaviour, for each and all of their offences they received punishment ten times over, and the rewards of beneficence and justice and holiness were in the same proportion. I need hardly repeat what he said concerning young children dying almost as soon as they were born. Of piety and impiety to gods and parents, and of murderers, there were retributions other and greater far which he described. He mentioned that he was present when one of the spirits asked another, 'Where is Ardiaeus the Great?' (Now this Ardiaeus lived a thousand years before the time of Er: he had been the tyrant of some city of Pamphylia, and had murdered his aged father and his elder brother, and was said to have committed many other abominable crimes.) The answer of the other spirit was: 'He comes not hither and will never come. And this,' said he, 'was one of the dreadful sights which we ourselves witnessed. We were at the mouth of the cavern, and, having completed all our experiences, were about to reascend, when of a sudden Ardiaeus appeared and several others, most of whom were tyrants; and there were also besides the tyrants private individuals who had been great criminals: they were just, as they fancied, about to return into the upper world, but the mouth, instead of admitting them, gave a roar, whenever any of these incurable sinners or some one who had not been sufficiently punished tried to ascend; and then wild men of fiery aspect, who were standing by and heard the sound, seized and carried them off; and Ardiaeus and others they bound head and foot and hand, and threw them down and flayed them with scourges, and dragged them along the road at the side, carding them on thorns like wool, and declaring to the passers-by what were their crimes, and that they were being taken away to be cast into hell.' And of all the many terrors which they had endured, he said that there was none like the terror which each of them felt at that moment, lest they should hear the voice; and when there was silence, one by one they ascended with exceeding joy. 'These,' said Er, 'were the penalties and retributions, and there were blessings as great.'"

··

[5] The following selection, from Plato's *Meno*, concerns the evil actions of human beings, and are claimed to be the product of ignorance rather than willful wickedness: all wrongdoing, Socrates famously contends, is involuntary.

··

Meno

"[T]ell me what virtue is in the universal; and do not make a singular into a plural, as the facetious say of those who break a thing, but deliver virtue to me whole and sound, and not broken into a number of pieces: I have given you the pattern."

"Well then, Socrates, virtue, as I take it, is when he, who desires the honourable, is able to provide it for himself; so the poet says, and I say too—'Virtue is the desire of things honourable and the power of attaining them.'"

"And does he who desires the honourable also desire the good?"

"Certainly."

"Then are there some who desire the evil and others who desire the good? Do not all men, my dear sir, desire good?"

"I think not."

"There are some who desire evil?"

"Yes."

"Do you mean that they think the evils which they desire, to be good; or do they know that they are evil and yet desire them?"

"Both, I think."

"And do you really imagine, Meno, that a man knows evils to be evils and desires them notwithstanding?"

"Certainly I do."

"And desire is of possession?"

"Yes, of possession."

"And does he think that the evils will do good to him who possesses them, or does he know that they will do him harm?"

"There are some who think that the evils will do them good, and others who know that they will do them harm."

"And, in your opinion, do those who think that they will do them good know that they are evils?"

"Certainly not."

"Is it not obvious that those who are ignorant of their nature do not desire them; but they desire what they suppose to be goods although they are really evils; and if they are mistaken and suppose the evils to be goods they really desire goods?"

"Yes, in that case."

"Well, and do those who, as you say, desire evils, and think that evils are hurtful to the possessor of them, know that they will be hurt by them?"

"They must know it."

"And must they not suppose that those who are hurt are miserable in proportion to the hurt which is inflicted upon them?"

"How can it be otherwise?"

"But are not the miserable ill-fated?"

"Yes, indeed."

"And does any one desire to be miserable and ill-fated?"

"I should say not, Socrates."

"But if there is no one who desires to be miserable, there is no one, Meno, who desires evil; for what is misery but the desire and possession of evil?"

"That appears to be the truth, Socrates, and I admit that nobody desires evil."

....

[6] The substantial set of selections that come next are drawn from *The Republic*. An investigation into the nature of justice, *The Republic* begins with a number of skeptical challenges to the reality of morality, which Socrates aims to meet and counter. Amongst these challenges is the haunting story of the "Ring of Gyges," told by the character Glaucon in order to suggest that any person would behave immorally if they could get away with so doing (as they could if they were to have the power of becoming invisible at will). Socrates's response to this challenge is to explore the ideal of justice in an ideal republic before transferring the results of that investigation to the case of justice in the individual person. This republic is divided into three classes of people (a ruling class, a military class, and a laboring class), and Socrates's dissection of the human personality (or soul) reveals therein three corresponding qualities (reason, spirit, appetite). It is the establishing of a balance between these three qualities of the soul that provides the stability and happiness of a life, as well

as providing the answer to Glaucon's challenge: acting immorally disturbs the proper balance of the soul and thus, as a kind of mental disorder, can never be good for a person.

....

Republic

Book II

Glaucon: They say that to do injustice is, by nature, good; to suffer injustice, evil; but that the evil is greater than the good. And so when men have both done and suffered injustice and have had experience of both, not being able to avoid the one and obtain the other, they think that they had better agree among themselves to have neither; hence there arise laws and mutual covenants; and that which is ordained by law is termed by them lawful and just. This they affirm to be the origin and nature of justice;—it is a mean or compromise, between the best of all, which is to do injustice and not be punished, and the worst of all, which is to suffer injustice without the power of retaliation; and justice, being at a middle point between the two, is tolerated not as a good, but as the lesser evil, and honoured by reason of the inability of men to do injustice. For no man who is worthy to be called a man would ever submit to such an agreement if he were able to resist; he would be mad if he did. Such is the received account, Socrates, of the nature and origin of justice.

Now that those who practise justice do so involuntarily and because they have not the power to be unjust will best appear if we imagine something of this kind: having given both to the just and the unjust power to do what they will, let us watch and see whither desire will lead them; then we shall discover in the very act the just and unjust man to be proceeding along the same road, following their interest, which all natures deem to be their good, and are only diverted into the path of justice by the force of law. The liberty which we are supposing may be most completely given to them in the form of such a power as is said to have been possessed by Gyges the ancestor of Croesus the Lydian. According to the tradition, Gyges was a shepherd

---

On the nature of the soul and the desire to do evil: The Republic (Jowett translation), from *The Dialogues of Plato*, vol. 1, pp. 622–624, 694, 702–705, 707–709.

in the service of the king of Lydia; there was a great storm, and an earthquake made an opening in the earth at the place where he was feeding his flock. Amazed at the sight, he descended into the opening, where, among other marvels, he beheld a hollow brazen horse, having doors, at which he stooping and looking in saw a dead body of stature, as appeared to him, more than human, and having nothing on but a gold ring; this he took from the finger of the dead and reascended. Now the shepherds met together, according to custom, that they might send their monthly report about the flocks to the king; into their assembly he came having the ring on his finger, and as he was sitting among them he chanced to turn the collet of the ring inside his hand, when instantly he became invisible to the rest of the company and they began to speak of him as if he were no longer present. He was astonished at this, and again touching the ring he turned the collet outwards and reappeared; he made several trials of the ring, and always with the same result—when he turned the collet inwards he became invisible, when outwards he reappeared. Whereupon he contrived to be chosen one of the messengers who were sent to the court; where as soon as he arrived he seduced the queen, and with her help conspired against the king and slew him, and took the kingdom. Suppose now that there were two such magic rings, and the just put on one of them and the unjust the other; no man can be imagined to be of such an iron nature that he would stand fast in justice. No man would keep his hands off what was not his own when he could safely take what he liked out of the market, or go into houses and lie with any one at his pleasure, or kill or release from prison whom he would, and in all respects be like a God among men. Then the actions of the just would be as the actions of the unjust; they would both come at last to the same point. And this we may truly affirm to be a great proof that a man is just, not willingly or because he thinks that justice is any good to him individually, but of necessity, for wherever any one thinks that he can safely be unjust, there he is unjust. For all men believe in their hearts that injustice is far more profitable to the individual than justice, and he who argues as I have been supposing, will say that they are right. If you could imagine any one obtaining this power of becoming invisible, and never doing any wrong or touching what was another's, he would be thought by the lookers-on to be a most wretched idiot, although they would praise him to one another's faces, and keep up appearances with one another from a fear that they too might suffer injustice. Enough of this.

Book IV

"Temperance," I replied, "is the ordering or controlling of certain pleasures and desires; this is curiously enough implied in the saying of 'a man being his own master' and other traces of the same notion may be found in language."

"No doubt," he said.

"There is something ridiculous in the expression 'master of himself'; for the master is also the servant and the servant the master; and in all these modes of speaking the same person is denoted."

"Certainly."

"The meaning is, I believe, that in the human soul there is a better and also a worse principle; and when the better has the worse under control, then a man is said to be master of himself; and this is a term of praise: but when, owing to evil education or association, the better principle, which is also the smaller, is overwhelmed by the greater mass of the worse—in this case he is blamed and is called the slave of self and unprincipled."

. . .

"Would you not say that thirst is one of these essentially relative terms, having clearly a relation—"

"Yes, thirst is relative to drink."

"And a certain kind of thirst is relative to a certain kind of drink; but thirst taken alone is neither of much nor little, nor of good nor bad, nor of any particular kind of drink, but of drink only?"

"Certainly."

Then the soul of the thirsty one, in so far as he is thirsty, desires only drink; for this he yearns and tries to obtain it?"

"That is plain."

"And if you suppose something which pulls a thirsty soul away from drink, that must be different from the thirsty principle which draws him like a beast to drink; for, as we were saying, the same thing cannot at the same time with the same part of itself act in contrary ways about the same."

"Impossible."

"No more than you can say that the hands of the archer push and pull the bow at the same time, but what you say is that one hand pushes and the other pulls."

"Exactly so," he replied.

"And might a man be thirsty, and yet unwilling to drink?"

"Yes," he said, "it constantly happens."

"And in such a case what is one to say? Would you not say that there was something in the soul bidding a man to drink, and something else forbidding him, which is other and stronger than the principle which bids him?"

"I should say so."

"And the forbidding principle is derived from reason, and that which bids and attracts proceeds from passion and disease?"

"Clearly."

"Then we may fairly assume that they are two, and that they differ from one another; the one with which man reasons, we may call the rational principle of the soul, the other, with which he loves and hungers and thirsts and feels the flutterings of any other desire, may be termed the irrational or appetitive, the ally of sundry pleasures and satisfactions?"

"Yes," he said, "we may fairly assume them to be different."

"Then let us finally determine that there are two principles existing in the soul. And what of passion, or spirit? Is it a third, or akin to one of the preceding?"

"I should be inclined to say—akin to desire."

"Well," I said, "there is a story which I remember to have heard, and in which I put faith. The story is, that Leontius, the son of Aglaion, coming up one day from the Piraeus, under the north wall on the outside, observed some dead bodies lying on the ground at the place of execution. He felt a desire to see them, and also a dread and abhorrence of them; for a time he struggled and covered his eyes, but at length the desire got the better of him; and forcing them open, he ran up to the dead bodies, saying, Look, ye wretches, take your fill of the fair sight."

"I have heard the story myself," he said.

"The moral of the tale is, that anger at times goes to war with desire, as though they were two distinct things."

"Yes; that is the meaning," he said.

"And are there not many other cases in which we observe that when a man's desires violently prevail over his reason, he reviles himself, and is angry at the violence within him, and that in this struggle, which is like the struggle of factions in a State, his spirit is on the side of his reason;—but for the passionate or spirited element to take part with the desires when reason decides that she should not be opposed, is a sort of thing which I believe that you never observed occurring in yourself, nor, as I should imagine, in any one else?"

"Certainly not."

"Suppose that a man thinks he has done a wrong to another, the nobler he is the less able is he to feel indignant at any suffering, such as hunger, or cold, or any other pain which the injured person may inflict upon him—these he deems to be just, and, as I say, his anger refuses to be excited by them."

"True," he said.

"But when he thinks that he is the sufferer of the wrong, then he boils and chafes, and is on the side of what he believes to be justice; and because he suffers hunger or cold or other pain he is only the more determined to persevere and conquer. His noble spirit will not be quelled until he either slays or is slain; or until he hears the voice of the shepherd, that is, reason, bidding his dog bark no more."

"The illustration is perfect," he replied; "and in our State, as we were saying, the auxiliaries were to be dogs, and to hear the voice of the rulers, who are their shepherds."

"I perceive," I said, "that you quite understand me; there is, however, a further point which I wish you to consider."

"What point?"

"You remember that passion or spirit appeared at first sight to be a kind of desire, but now we should say quite the contrary; for in the conflict of the soul spirit is arrayed on the side of the rational principle."

"Most assuredly."

"But a further question arises: Is passion different from reason also, or only a kind of reason; in which latter case, instead of three principles in the soul, there will only be two, the rational and the concupiscent; or rather, as the State was composed of three classes, traders, auxiliaries, counsellors, so may there not be in the individual soul a third element which is passion or spirit, and when not corrupted by bad education is the natural auxiliary of reason."

"Yes," he said, "there must be a third."

"Yes," I replied, "if passion, which has already been shown to be different from desire, turn out also to be different from reason."

"But that is easily proved:—We may observe even in young children that they are full of spirit almost as soon as they are born, whereas some of them never seem to attain to the use of reason, and most of them late enough."

"Excellent," I said, "and you may see passion equally in brute animals, which is a further proof of the truth of what you are saying.

And we may once more appeal to the words of Homer, which have been already quoted by us, 'He smote his breast, and thus rebuked his soul,' for in this verse Homer has clearly supposed the power which reasons about the better and worse to be different from the unreasoning anger which is rebuked by it."

. . .

"But in reality justice was such as we were describing, being concerned however, not with the outward man, but with the inward, which is the true self and concernment of man: for the just man does not permit the several elements within him to interfere with one another, or any of them to do the work of others,—he sets in order his own inner life, and is his own master and his own law, and at peace with himself; and when he has bound together the three principles within him, which may be compared to the higher, lower, and middle notes of the scale, and the intermediate intervals—when he has bound all these together, and is no longer many, but has become one entirely temperate and perfectly adjusted nature, then he proceeds to act, if he has to act, whether in a matter of property, or in the treatment of the body, or in some affair of politics or private business; always thinking and calling that which preserves and co-operates with this harmonious condition, just and good action, and the knowledge which presides over it, wisdom, and that which at any time impairs this condition, he will call unjust action, and the opinion which presides over it ignorance."

"You have said the exact truth, Socrates."

"Very good; and if we were to affirm that we had discovered the just man and the just State, and the nature of justice in each of them, we should not be telling a falsehood?"

"Most certainly not."

"May we say so, then?"

"Let us say so."

"And now," I said, "injustice has to be considered."

"Clearly."

"Must not injustice be a strife which arises among the three principles—a meddlesomeness, and interference, and rising up of a part of the soul against the whole, an assertion of unlawful authority, which is made by a rebellious subject against a true prince, of whom he is the natural vassal,—what is all this confusion and delusion but injustice, and intemperance and cowardice and ignorance, and every form of vice?"

"Exactly so."

"And if the nature of justice and injustice be known, then the meaning of acting unjustly and being unjust, or, again, of acting justly, will also be perfectly clear?"

"What do you mean?" he said.

"Why," I said, "they are like disease and health; being in the soul just what disease and health are in the body."

"How so?" he said.

"Why," I said, "that which is healthy causes health, and that which is unhealthy causes disease."

"Yes."

"And just actions cause justice, and unjust actions cause injustice?"

"That is certain."

"And the creation of health is the institution of a natural order and government of one by another in the parts of the body; and the creation of disease is the production of a state of things at variance with this natural order?"

"True."

"And is not the creation of justice the institution of a natural order and government of one by another in the parts of the soul, and the creation of injustice the production of a state of things at variance with the natural order?"

"Exactly so," he said.

"Then virtue is the health and beauty and well-being of the soul, and vice the disease and weakness and deformity of the same?"

"True."

"And do not good practices lead to virtue, and evil practices to vice?"

"Assuredly."

"Still our old question of the comparative advantage of justice and injustice has not been answered: Which is the more profitable, to be just and act justly and practise virtue, whether seen or unseen of gods and men, or to be unjust and act unjustly, if only unpunished and unreformed?"

"In my judgment, Socrates, the question has now become ridiculous. We know that, when the bodily constitution is gone, life is no longer endurable, though pampered with all kinds of meats and drinks, and having all wealth and all power; and shall we be told that when the very essence of the vital principle is undermined and corrupted, life is still worth having to a man, if only he be allowed to do whatever he likes with the single exception that he is not to acquire justice and virtue, or to escape from injustice and vice; assuming them both to be such as we have described?"

....

[7] The following passage from the *Republic* displays an attitude towards women that is simultaneously ahead of its time and yet nonetheless derogatory: in the ideal republic women should be freed from a merely domestic life and permitted the same occupations as men; they will inevitably, however, be less good than men at those occupations.

....

Book V

"What I mean may be put into the form of a question," I said: "Are dogs divided into hes and shes, or do they both share equally in hunting and in keeping watch and in the other duties of dogs? or do we entrust to the males the entire and exclusive care of the flocks, while we leave the females at home, under the idea that the bearing and suckling their puppies is labour enough for them?"

"No," he said, "they share alike; the only difference between them is that the males are stronger and the females weaker."

"But can you use different animals for the same purpose, unless they are bred and fed in the same way?"

"You cannot."

"Then, if women are to have the same duties as men, they must have the same nurture and education?"

"Yes."

"The education which was assigned to the men was music and gymnastic."

"Yes."

"Then women must be taught music and gymnastic and also the art of war, which they must practise like the men?"

"That is the inference, I suppose."

"I should rather expect," I said, "that several of our proposals, if they are carried out, being unusual, may appear ridiculous."

"No doubt of it."

"Yes, and the most ridiculous thing of all will be the sight of women naked in the palaestra, exercising with the men, especially when they are no longer young; they certainly will not be a vision of beauty, any more than the enthusiastic old men who in spite of wrinkles and ugliness continue to frequent the gymnasia."

"Yes, indeed," he said: "According to present notions the proposal would be thought ridiculous."

"But then," I said, "as we have determined to speak our minds, we must not fear the jests of the wits which will be directed against this sort of innovation; how they will talk of women's attainments both in music and gymnastic, and above all about their wearing armour and riding upon horseback!"

"Very true," he replied.

"Yet having begun we must go forward to the rough places of the law; at the same time begging of these gentlemen for once in their life to be serious. Not long ago, as we shall remind them, the Hellenes were of the opinion, which is still generally received among the barbarians, that the sight of a naked man was ridiculous and improper; and when first the Cretans and then the Lacedaemonians introduced the custom, the wits of that day might equally have ridiculed the innovation."

"No doubt."

"But when experience showed that to let all things be uncovered was far better than to cover them up, and the ludicrous effect to the outward eye vanished before the better principle which reason asserted, then the man was perceived to be a fool who directs the shafts of his ridicule at any other sight but that of folly and vice, or seriously inclines to weigh the beautiful by any other standard but that of the good."

"Very true," he replied.

"First, then, whether the question is to be put in jest or in earnest, let us come to an understanding about the nature of woman: Is she capable of sharing either wholly or partially in the actions of men, or not at all? And is the art of war one of those arts in which she can or can not share? That will be the best way of commencing the enquiry, and will probably lead to the fairest conclusion."

"That will be much the best way."

"Shall we take the other side first and begin by arguing against ourselves? In this manner the adversary's position will not be undefended."

"Why not?" he said.

"Then let us put a speech into the mouths of our opponents. They will say: 'Socrates and Glaucon, no adversary need convict you, for you yourselves, at the first foundation of the State, admitted the principle that everybody was to do the one work suited to his own nature.' And certainly, if I am not mistaken, such an admission was made by us. 'And do not the natures of men and women differ very much indeed?' And we shall reply: Of course they do. Then we shall be asked, 'Whether the tasks assigned to men and to women should not be different, and such as are agreeable to their different natures?' Certainly they should. 'But if so, have you not fallen into a serious inconsistency in saying that men and women, whose natures are so entirely different, ought to perform the same actions?'—What defence will you make for us, my good Sir, against any one who offers these objections?"

"That is not an easy question to answer when asked suddenly; and I shall and I do beg of you to draw out the case on our side."

"These are the objections, Glaucon, and there are many others of a like kind, which I foresaw long ago; they made me afraid and reluctant to take in hand any law about the possession and nurture of women and children."

"By Zeus," he said, "the problem to be solved is anything but easy."

"Why yes," I said, "but the fact is that when a man is out of his depth, whether he has fallen into a little swimming bath or into mid-ocean, he has to swim all the same."

"Very true."

"And must not we swim and try to reach the shore: we will hope that Arion's dolphin or some other miraculous help may save us?"

"I suppose so," he said.

"Well then, let us see if any way of escape can be found. We acknowledged—did we not? that different natures ought to have different pursuits, and that men's and women's natures are different. And now what are we saying?—that different natures ought to have the same pursuits,—this is the inconsistency which is charged upon us."

"Precisely."

"Verily, Glaucon," I said, "glorious is the power of the art of contradiction!"

"Why do you say so?"

"Because I think that many a man falls into the practice against his will. When he thinks that he is reasoning he is really disputing, just because he cannot define and divide, and so know that of which he is speaking; and he will pursue a merely verbal opposition in the spirit of contention and not of fair discussion."

"Yes," he replied, "such is very often the case; but what has that to do with us and our argument?"

"A great deal; for there is certainly a danger of our getting unintentionally into a verbal opposition."

"In what way?"

"Why, we valiantly and pugnaciously insist upon the verbal truth, that different natures ought to have different pursuits, but we never considered at all what was the meaning of sameness or difference of nature, or why we distinguished them when we assigned different pursuits to different natures and the same to the same natures."

"Why, no," he said, "that was never considered by us."

I said: "Suppose that by way of illustration we were to ask the question whether there is not an opposition in nature between bald men and hairy men; and if this is admitted by us, then, if bald men are cobblers, we should forbid the hairy men to be cobblers, and conversely?"

"That would be a jest," he said.

"Yes," I said, "a jest; and why? because we never meant when we constructed the State, that the opposition of natures should extend to every difference, but only to those differences which affected the pursuit in which the individual is engaged; we should have argued, for example, that a physician and one who is in mind a physician may be said to have the same nature."

"True."

"Whereas the physician and the carpenter have different natures?"

"Certainly."

"And if," I said, "the male and female sex appear to differ in their fitness for any art or pursuit, we should say that such pursuit or art ought to be assigned to one or the other of them; but if the difference consists only in women bearing and men begetting children, this does not amount to a proof that a woman differs from a man in respect of the sort of education she should receive; and we shall therefore continue to maintain that our guardians and their wives ought to have the same pursuits."

"Very true," he said.

"Next, we shall ask our opponent how, in reference to any of the pursuits or arts of civic life, the nature of a woman differs from that of a man?"

"That will be quite fair."

"And perhaps he, like yourself, will reply that to give a sufficient answer on the instant is not easy; but after a little reflection there is no difficulty."

"Yes, perhaps."

"Suppose then that we invite him to accompany us in the argument, and then we may hope to show him that there is nothing peculiar in the constitution of women which would affect them in the administration of the State."

"By all means."

"Let us say to him: Come now, and we will ask you a question:—when you spoke of a nature gifted or not gifted in any respect, did you mean to say that one man will acquire a thing easily, another with difficulty; a little learning will lead the one to discover a great deal; whereas the other, after much study and application, no sooner learns than he forgets; or again, did you mean, that the one has a body which is a good servant to his mind, while the body of the other is a hindrance to him?—would not these be the sort of differences which distinguish the man gifted by nature from the one who is ungifted?"

"No one will deny that."

"And can you mention any pursuit of mankind in which the male sex has not all these gifts and qualities in a higher degree than the female? Need I waste time in speaking of the art of weaving, and the management of pancakes and preserves, in which womankind does really appear to be great, and in which for her to be beaten by a man is of all things the most absurd?"

"You are quite right," he replied, "in maintaining the general inferiority of the female sex: although many women are in many things superior to many men, yet on the whole what you say is true."

"And if so, my friend," I said, "there is no special faculty of administration in a state which a woman has because she is a woman, or which a man has by virtue of his sex, but the gifts of nature are alike diffused in both; all the pursuits of men are the pursuits of women also, but in all of them a woman is inferior to a man."

"Very true."

"Then are we to impose all our enactments on men and none of them on women?"

"That will never do."

"One woman has a gift of healing, another not; one is a musician, and another has no music in her nature?"

"Very true."

"And one woman has a turn for gymnastic and military exercises, and another is unwarlike and hates gymnastics?"

"Certainly."

"And one woman is a philosopher, and another is an enemy of philosophy; one has spirit, and another is without spirit?"

"That is also true."

"Then one woman will have the temper of a guardian, and another not. Was not the selection of the male guardians determined by differences of this sort?"

"Yes."

"Men and women alike possess the qualities which make a guardian; they differ only in their comparative strength or weakness."

"Obviously."

"And those women who have such qualities are to be selected as the companions and colleagues of men who have similar qualities and whom they resemble in capacity and in character?"

"Very true."

"And ought not the same natures to have the same pursuits?"

"They ought."

"Then, as we were saying before, there is nothing unnatural in assigning music and gymnastic to the wives of the guardians—to that point we come round again."

"Certainly not."

"The law which we then enacted was agreeable to nature, and therefore not an impossibility or mere aspiration; and the contrary practice, which prevails at present, is in reality a violation of nature."

....

[8] The final selection here is probably the most famous passage in Plato's writings: the celebrated "Simile of the Cave," at once a vision of the merely shadow-like status of this material world and a moving portrayal of the philosopher's vocation.

....

Book VII

"And now," I said, "let me show in a figure how far our nature is enlightened or unenlightened:—Behold! human beings living in a underground den, which has a mouth open towards the light and reaching all along the den; here they have been from their childhood, and have their legs and necks chained so that they cannot move, and can only see before them,

---

The Allegory of the Cave: The Republic (Jowett translation), from *The Dialogues of Plato*, vol. 1, pp. 773–777.

being prevented by the chains from turning round their heads. Above and behind them a fire is blazing at a distance, and between the fire and the prisoners there is a raised way; and you will see, if you look, a low wall built along the way, like the screen which marionette players have in front of them, over which they show the puppets."

"I see."

"And do you see," I said, "men passing along the wall carrying all sorts of vessels, and statues and figures of animals made of wood and stone and various materials, which appear over the wall? Some of them are talking, others silent."

"You have shown me a strange image, and they are strange prisoners."

"Like ourselves," I replied; "And they see only their own shadows, or the shadows of one another, which the fire throws on the opposite wall of the cave?"

"True," he said; "How could they see anything but the shadows if they were never allowed to move their heads?"

"And of the objects which are being carried in like manner they would only see the shadows?"

"Yes," he said.

"And if they were able to converse with one another, would they not suppose that they were naming what was actually before them?"

"Very true."

"And suppose further that the prison had an echo which came from the other side, would they not be sure to fancy when one of the passers-by spoke that the voice which they heard came from the passing shadow?"

"No question," he replied.

"To them," I said, "the truth would be literally nothing but the shadows of the images."

"That is certain."

"And now look again, and see what will naturally follow if the prisoners are released and disabused of their error. At first, when any of them is liberated and compelled suddenly to stand up and turn his neck round and walk and look towards the light, he will suffer sharp pains; the glare will distress him, and he will be unable to see the realities of which in his former state he had seen the shadows; and then conceive some one saying to him, that what he saw before was an illusion, but that now, when he is approaching nearer to being and his eye is turned towards more real existence, he has a clearer vision,—what will be his reply? And you may further imagine that his instructor is pointing to the objects as they pass and requiring him to name them,—will he not be perplexed? Will he not fancy that the shadows which he formerly saw are truer than the objects which are now shown to him?"

"Far truer."

"And if he is compelled to look straight at the light, will he not have a pain in his eyes which will make him turn away to take and take in the objects of vision which he can see, and which he will conceive to be in reality clearer than the things which are now being shown to him?"

"True," he said.

"And suppose once more, that he is reluctantly dragged up a steep and rugged ascent, and held fast until he's forced into the presence of the sun himself, is he not likely to be pained and irritated? When he approaches the light his eyes will be dazzled, and he will not be able to see anything at all of what are now called realities."

"Not all in a moment," he said.

"He will require to grow accustomed to the sight of the upper world. And first he will see the shadows best, next the reflections of men and other objects in the water, and then the objects themselves; then he will gaze upon the light of the moon and the stars and the spangled heaven; and he will see the sky and the stars by night better than the sun or the light of the sun by day?"

"Certainly."

"Last of all he will be able to see the sun, and not mere reflections of him in the water, but he will see him in his own proper place, and not in another; and he will contemplate him as he is."

"Certainly."

"He will then proceed to argue that this is he who gives the season and the years, and is the guardian of all that is in the visible world, and in a certain way the cause of all things which he and his fellows have been accustomed to behold?"

"Clearly," he said, "he would first see the sun and then reason about him."

"And when he remembered his old habitation, and the wisdom of the den and his fellow-prisoners, do you not suppose that he would felicitate himself on the change, and pity them?"

"Certainly, he would."

"And if they were in the habit of conferring honours among themselves on those who were quickest to observe the passing shadows and to remark which of them went before, and which followed after, and which were together; and who were therefore best able to draw conclusions as to the future, do you think that he would care for such honours and glories, or envy the possessors of them? Would he not say with Homer,

> Better to be the poor servant of a poor master, and to endure anything, rather than think as they do and live after their manner?

"Yes," he said, "I think that he would rather suffer anything than entertain these false notions and live in this miserable manner."

"Imagine once more," I said, "such an one coming suddenly out of the sun to be replaced in his old situation; would he not be certain to have his eyes full of darkness?"

"To be sure," he said.

"And if there were a contest, and he had to compete in measuring the shadows with the prisoners who had never moved out of the den, while his sight was still weak, and before his eyes had become steady (and the time which would be needed to acquire this new habit of sight might be very considerable) would he not be ridiculous? Men would say of him that up he went and down he came without his eyes; and that it was better not even to think of ascending; and if any one tried to loose another and lead him up to the light, let them only catch the offender, and they would put him to death."

"No question," he said.

"This entire allegory," I said, "you may now append, dear Glaucon, to the previous argument; the prison-house is the world of sight, the light of the fire is the sun, and you will not misapprehend me if you interpret the journey upwards to be the ascent of the soul into the intellectual world according to my poor belief, which, at your desire, I have expressed whether rightly or wrongly God knows. But, whether true or false, my opinion is that in the world of knowledge the idea of good appears last of all, and is seen only with an effort; and, when seen, is also inferred to be the universal author of all things beautiful and right, parent of light and of the lord of light in this visible world, and the immediate source of reason and truth in the intellectual; and that this is the power upon which he who would act rationally, either in public or private life must have his eye fixed."

"I agree," he said, "as far as I am able to understand you."

"Moreover," I said, "you must not wonder that those who attain to this beatific vision are unwilling to descend to human affairs; for their souls are ever hastening into the upper world where they desire to dwell; which desire of theirs is very natural, if our allegory may be trusted."

"Yes, very natural."

"And is there anything surprising in one who passes from divine contemplations to the evil state of man, misbehaving himself in a ridiculous manner; if, while his eyes are blinking and before he has become accustomed to the surrounding darkness, he is compelled to fight in courts of law, or in other places, about the images or the shadows of images of justice, and is endeavouring to meet the conceptions of those who have never yet seen absolute justice?"

"Anything but surprising," he replied.

9

Aristotle

Aristotle (384–322 BCE), sometimes called "the Stagirite" from the place of his birth, was the most famous of Plato's students and later teachers at the Academy. After Plato's death, Aristotle set out on his own series of scientific and philosophical pursuits, writing on a wide range of topics including economics, rhetoric, theater, logic, biology, anatomy, physics, metaphysics, ethics, and politics. While Plato's work can be characterized—as Aristotle himself does—as dealing with the abstract and the ideal, Aristotle begins his work from a reflection on experience, so that he stands in a tradition with later empiricist thinkers like Hume and Locke, even if his results are often radically different. He later became the tutor to the boy who would become Alexander the Great. With the wealth and status he gained, he returned to Athens and opened the Lyceum, a school to rival the Platonic Academy. He had a great influence on later thinkers, particularly during the high middle ages when Thomas Aquinas would refer to him simply as "the Philosopher."

In these selections from the *Nicomachean Ethics*, we see him set out in some detail a view of happiness as a kind of flourishing peculiar to humans, fulfilling of the end or *telos* of humanity, in connection with those excellences that he identifies as virtues. Interestingly, among the virtues he gives an account of the virtue of friendship. He also identifies a way in which the human, through contemplation, attains to something almost divine.

In the selection from the *Politics*, we see the way in which Aristotle attempts to justify the position of women in his society by drawing just the kind of distinction between men and women that Plato denied in his *Republic*. He also sets out a theory of "natural slavery," and elaborates the way that both women and slaves should be governed.

In the selections from *On the Soul*, Aristotle gives an account of the hylomorphic relationship between the soul and body that differs considerably from that of his teacher and prefigures the functionalist accounts of the mind-body relationship of the twentieth and twenty-first centuries. Importantly, he suggests that the soul is inseparable from the body.

Finally, in the selection from the *Eudemian Ethics*, Aristotle addresses the question posed to the philosopher Anaxagoras whether it is better never to have been born.

Nicomachean Ethics

Book I

Let us resume our inquiry and state, in view of the fact that all knowledge and every pursuit aims at some good, what it is that we say political science aims at and what is the highest of all goods achievable by action. Verbally there is very general agreement; for both the general run of men and people of superior refinement say that it is happiness, and identify living well and doing well with being happy; but with regard to what happiness is they differ, and the many do not give the same account as the wise. For the former think it is some plain and obvious thing, like pleasure, wealth, or honour; they differ, however, from one another and often even the same man identifies it with different things, with health when he is ill, with wealth when he is poor; but, conscious of their ignorance, they admire those who proclaim some great ideal that is above their comprehension. Now some thought that apart from these many goods there is another which is self-subsistent and causes the goodness of all these as well. To examine all the opinions that have been held were perhaps somewhat fruitless; enough to examine those that are most prevalent or that seem to be arguable.

From Ross, WD (trans), *Nicomachean Ethics*, Oxford: Clarendon Press, 1908.

. . . [W]e must begin with things known to us. Hence any one who is to listen intelligently to lectures about what is noble and just, and generally, about the subjects of political science must have been brought up in good habits. For the fact is the starting-point, and if this is sufficiently plain to him, he will not at the start need the reason as well; and the man who has been well brought up has or can easily get starting-points. And as for him who neither has nor can get them, let him hear the words of Hesiod:

> Far best is he who knows all things himself;
> Good, he that hearkens when men counsel right;
> But he who neither knows, nor lays to heart
> Another's wisdom, is a useless wight.

. . .

Let us, however, resume our discussion from the point at which we digressed. To judge from the lives that men lead, most men, and men of the most vulgar type, seem (not without some ground) to identify the good, or happiness, with pleasure; which is the reason why they love the life of enjoyment. For there are, we may say, three prominent types of life—that just mentioned, the political, and thirdly the contemplative life. Now the mass of mankind are evidently quite slavish in their tastes, preferring a life suitable to beasts, but they get some ground for their view from the fact that many of those in high places share the tastes of Sardanapallus. A consideration of the prominent types of life shows that people of superior refinement and of active disposition identify happiness with honour; for this is, roughly speaking, the end of the political life. But it seems too superficial to be what we are looking for, since it is thought to depend on those who bestow honour rather than on him who receives it, but the good we divine to be something proper to a man and not easily taken from him. Further, men seem to pursue honour in order that they may be assured of their goodness; at least it is by men of practical wisdom that they seek to be honoured, and among those who know them, and on the ground of their virtue; clearly, then, according to them, at any rate, virtue is better. And perhaps one might even suppose this to be, rather than honour, the end of the political life. But even this appears somewhat incomplete; for possession of virtue seems actually compatible with being asleep, or with lifelong inactivity, and, further, with the greatest sufferings and misfortunes; but a man who was living so no one would call happy, unless he were maintaining a thesis at all costs. But enough of this;

for the subject has been sufficiently treated even in the current discussions. Third comes the contemplative life, which we shall consider later.

The life of money-making is one undertaken under compulsion, and wealth is evidently not the good we are seeking; for it is merely useful and for the sake of something else. And so one might rather take the aforenamed objects to be ends; for they are loved for themselves. But it is evident that not even these are ends; yet many arguments have been thrown away in support of them. Let us leave this subject, then.

We had perhaps better consider the universal good and discuss thoroughly what is meant by it, although such an inquiry is made an uphill one by the fact that the Forms have been introduced by friends of our own. Yet it would perhaps be thought to be better, indeed to be our duty, for the sake of maintaining the truth even to destroy what touches us closely, especially as we are philosophers or lovers of wisdom; for, while both are dear, piety requires us to honour truth above our friends.

. . .

. . . [G]oods must be spoken of in two ways, and some must be good in themselves, the others by reason of these. Let us separate, then, things good in themselves from things useful, and consider whether the former are called good by reference to a single Idea. What sort of goods would one call good in themselves? Is it those that are pursued even when isolated from others, such as intelligence, sight, and certain pleasures and honours? Certainly, if we pursue these also for the sake of something else, yet one would place them among things good in themselves. Or is nothing other than the Idea of good good in itself? In that case the Form will be empty. But if the things we have named are also things good in themselves, the account of the good will have to appear as something identical in them all, as that of whiteness is identical in snow and in white lead. But of honour, wisdom, and pleasure, just in respect of their goodness, the accounts are distinct and diverse. The good, therefore, is not some common element answering to one Idea.

. . .

Let us again return to the good we are seeking, and ask what it can be. It seems different in different actions and arts; it is different in medicine, in strategy, and in the other arts likewise. What then is the good of each? Surely that for whose sake everything else is done. In medicine this is health, in strategy victory, in architecture a house, in any other sphere something else, and in every action and pursuit the end; for it is for the sake of this that all men do whatever else they do. Therefore, if there is an end for all that we do, this will be the good achievable by action, and if there are more than one, these will be the goods achievable by action.

So the argument has by a different course reached the same point; but we must try to state this even more clearly. Since there are evidently more than one end, and we choose some of these (e.g., wealth, flutes, and in general instruments) for the sake of something else, clearly not all ends are final ends; but the chief good is evidently something final. Therefore, if there is only one final end, this will be what we are seeking, and if there are more than one, the most final of these will be what we are seeking. Now we call that which is in itself worthy of pursuit more final than that which is worthy of pursuit for the sake of something else, and that which is never desirable for the sake of something else more final than the things that are desirable both in themselves and for the sake of that other thing, and therefore we call final without qualification that which is always desirable in itself and never for the sake of something else.

Now such a thing happiness, above all else, is held to be; for this we choose always for self and never for the sake of something else, but honour, pleasure, reason, and every virtue we choose indeed for themselves (for if nothing resulted from them we should still choose each of them), but we choose them also for the sake of happiness, judging that by means of them we shall be happy. Happiness, on the other hand, no one chooses for the sake of these, nor, in general, for anything other than itself.

From the point of view of self-sufficiency the same result seems to follow; for the final good is thought to be self-sufficient. Now by self-sufficient we do not mean that which is sufficient for a man by himself, for one who lives a solitary life, but also for parents, children, wife, and in general for his friends and fellow citizens, since man is born for citizenship. But some limit must be set to this; for if we extend our requirement to ancestors and descendants and friends' friends we are in for an infinite series. Let us examine this question, however, on another occasion; the self-sufficient we now define as that which when isolated makes life desirable and lacking in nothing; and such we think happiness to be; and further we think it most desirable of all things, without being counted as one good thing among others—if it were so counted it would clearly be made more desirable by the addition of even the least of goods; for that which is added becomes an excess of goods, and of goods the greater is always more desirable. Happiness, then, is something final and self-sufficient, and is the end of action.

Presumably, however, to say that happiness is the chief good seems a platitude, and a clearer account of what it is still desired. This might perhaps be given, if we could first ascertain the function of man. For just as for a flute-player, a sculptor, or an artist, and, in general, for all things that have a function or activity, the good and the "well" is thought to reside in the function, so would it seem to be for man, if he has a function. Have the carpenter, then, and the tanner certain functions or activities, and has man none? Is he born without a function? Or as eye, hand, foot, and in general each of the parts evidently has a function, may one lay it down that man similarly has a function apart from all these? What then can this be? Life seems to be common even to plants, but we are seeking what is peculiar to man. Let us exclude, therefore, the life of nutrition and growth. Next there would be a life of perception, but it also seems to be common even to the horse, the ox, and every animal. There remains, then, an active life of the element that has a rational principle; of this, one part has such a principle in the sense of being obedient to one, the other in the sense of possessing one and exercising thought. And, as 'life of the rational element' also has two meanings, we must state that life in the sense of activity is what we mean; for this seems to be the more proper sense of the term. Now if the function of man is an activity of soul which follows or implies a rational principle, and if we say "so-and-so" and "a good so-and-so" have a function which is the same in kind, e.g., a lyre, and a good lyre-player, and so without qualification in all cases, eminence in respect of goodness being added to the name of the function (for the function of a lyre-player is to play the lyre, and that of a good lyre-player is to do so well): if this is the case, and we state the function of man to be a certain kind of life, and this to be an activity or actions of the soul implying a rational principle, and the function of a good man to be the good and noble performance of these, and if any action is well performed when it is performed in accordance with the appropriate excellence: if this is the case, human good turns out to be activity of soul in accordance with virtue, and if there are more than one virtue, in accordance with the best and most complete.

But we must add "in a complete life." For one swallow does not make a summer, nor does one day; and so too one day, or a short time, does not make a man blessed and happy.

. . .

Book II

Next we must consider what virtue is. Since things that are found in the soul are of three kinds—passions, faculties, states of character, virtue must be one of these. By passions I mean appetite, anger, fear, confidence, envy, joy, friendly feeling, hatred, longing, emulation, pity, and in general the feelings that are accompanied by pleasure or pain; by faculties the things in virtue of which we are said to be capable of feeling these, e.g., of becoming angry or being pained or feeling pity; by states of character the things in virtue of which we stand well or badly with reference to the passions, e.g., with reference to anger we stand badly if we feel it violently or too weakly, and well if we feel it moderately; and similarly with reference to the other passions.

Now neither the virtues nor the vices are passions, because we are not called good or bad on the ground of our passions, but are so called on the ground of our virtues and our vices, and because we are neither praised nor blamed for our passions (for the man who feels fear or anger is not praised, nor is the man who simply feels anger blamed, but the man who feels it in a certain way), but for our virtues and our vices we are praised or blamed.

Again, we feel anger and fear without choice, but the virtues are modes of choice or involve choice. Further, in respect of the passions we are said to be moved, but in respect of the virtues and the vices we are said not to be moved but to be disposed in a particular way.

For these reasons also they are not faculties; for we are neither called good nor bad, nor praised nor blamed, for the simple capacity of feeling the passions; again, we have the faculties by nature, but we are not made good or bad by nature; we have spoken of this before. If, then, the virtues are neither passions nor faculties, all that remains is that they should be states of character.

Book VIII

After what we have said, a discussion of friendship would naturally follow, since it is a virtue or implies virtue, and is besides most necessary with a view to living. For without friends no one would choose to live, though he had all other goods; even rich men and those in possession of office and of dominating power are thought to need friends most of all; for what is the use of such prosperity without the opportunity of beneficence, which is exercised chiefly and in its most laudable form towards friends? Or how can prosperity be guarded and preserved without friends? The greater it is, the more exposed is it to risk. And in poverty and in other misfortunes men think friends are the only refuge. It helps the young, too, to keep from error; it aids older people by ministering to their needs and supplementing the activities that are failing from weakness; those in the prime of life it stimulates to noble actions—"two going together"—for with friends men are more able both to think and to act. Again, parent seems by nature to feel it for offspring and offspring for parent, not only among men but among birds and among most animals; it is felt mutually by members of the same race, and especially by men, whence we praise lovers of their fellowmen. We may even in our travels [see] how near and dear every man is to every other. Friendship seems too to hold states together, and lawgivers to care more for it than for justice; for unanimity seems to be something like friendship, and this they aim at most of all, and expel faction as their worst enemy; and when men are friends they have no need of justice, while when they are just they need friendship as well, and the truest form of justice is thought to be a friendly quality.

But it is not only necessary but also noble; for we praise those who love their friends, and it is thought to be a fine thing to have many friends; and again we think it is the same people that are good men and are friends.

. . .

The kinds of friendship may perhaps be cleared up if we first come to know the object of love. For not everything seems to be loved but only the lovable, and this is good, pleasant, or useful; but it would seem to be that by which some good or pleasure is produced that is useful, so that it is the good and the useful that are lovable as ends. Do men love, then, the good, or what is good for them? These sometimes clash. So too with regard to the pleasant. Now it is thought that each loves what is good for himself, and that the good is without qualification lovable, and what is good for each man is lovable for him; but each man loves not what is good for him but what seems good. This however will make no difference; we shall just have to say that this is "that which seems lovable." Now there are three grounds on which people love; of the love of lifeless objects we do not use the word "friendship"; for it is not mutual love, nor is there a wishing of good to the other (for it would surely be ridiculous to wish wine well; if one wishes anything for it, it is that it may keep, so that one may have it oneself); but to a friend we say we ought to wish what is good for his sake. But to those who thus wish good we ascribe only goodwill, if the wish is not reciprocated; goodwill when it is reciprocal being friendship. Or must we add "when it is recognized"? For many people have goodwill to those whom they have not seen but judge to be good or useful; and one of these might return this feeling. These people seem to bear goodwill to each other; but how could one call them friends when they do not know their mutual feelings? To be friends, then, they must be mutually recognized as bearing goodwill and wishing well to each other for one of the aforesaid reasons.

. . .

Now these reasons differ from each other in kind; so, therefore, do the corresponding forms of love and friendship. There are therefore three kinds of friendship, equal in number to the things that are lovable; for with respect to each there is a mutual and recognized love, and those who love each other wish well to each other in that respect in which they love one another. Now those who love each other for their utility do not love each other for themselves but in virtue of some good which they get from each other. So too with those who love for the sake of pleasure; it is not for their character that men love ready-witted people, but because they find them pleasant. Therefore those who love for the sake of utility love for the sake of what is good for themselves, and those who love for the sake of pleasure do so for the sake of what is pleasant to themselves, and not in so far as the other is the person loved but in so far as he is useful or pleasant. And thus these friendships are only incidental; for it is not as being the man he is that the loved person is loved, but as providing some good or pleasure. Such friendships, then, are easily dissolved, if the parties do not remain like themselves; for if the one party is no longer pleasant or useful the other ceases to love him.

Now the useful is not permanent but is always changing. Thus when the motive of the friendship is done away, the friendship is dissolved, inasmuch as it existed only for the ends in question. This kind of friendship seems to exist chiefly between old people (for at that age people pursue not the pleasant but the useful) and, of those who are in their prime or young, between those who pursue utility. And such people do not live much with each other either; for sometimes they do not even find each other pleasant; therefore they do not need such companionship unless they are useful to each other; for they are pleasant to each other only in so far as they rouse in each other hopes of something good to come. Among such friendships people also class the friendship of a host and guest. On the other hand the friendship of young people seems to aim at pleasure; for they live under the guidance of emotion, and pursue above all what is pleasant to themselves and what is immediately before them; but with increasing age their pleasures become different. This is why they quickly become friends and quickly cease to be so; their friendship changes with the object that is found pleasant, and such pleasure alters quickly. Young people are amorous too; for the greater part of the friendship of love depends on emotion and aims at pleasure; this is why they fall in love and quickly fall out of love, changing often within a single day. But these people do wish to spend their days and lives together; for it is thus that they attain the purpose of their friendship.

Perfect friendship is the friendship of men who are good, and alike in virtue; for these wish well alike to each other qua good, and they are good themselves. Now those who wish well to their friends for their sake are most truly friends; for they do this by reason of own nature and not incidentally; therefore their friendship lasts as long as they are good— and goodness is an enduring thing. And each is good without qualification and to his friend, for the good are both good without qualification and useful to each other. So too they are pleasant; for the good are pleasant both without qualification and to each other, since to each his own activities and others like them are pleasurable, and the actions of the good are the same or like. And such a friendship is as might be expected permanent, since there meet in it all the qualities that friends should have. For all friendship is for the sake of good or of pleasure—good or pleasure either in the abstract or such as will be enjoyed by him who has the friendly feeling—and is based on a certain resemblance; and to a friendship of good men all the qualities we have named belong in virtue of the nature of the friends themselves; for in the case of this kind of friendship the other qualities also are alike in both friends, and that which is good without qualification is also without qualification pleasant, and these are the most lovable qualities. Love and friendship therefore are found most and in their best form between such men.

But it is natural that such friendships should be infrequent; for such men are rare. Further, such friendship requires time and familiarity; as the proverb says, men cannot know each other till they have "eaten salt together"; nor can they admit each other to friendship or be friends till each has been found lovable and been trusted by each. Those who quickly show the marks of friendship to each other wish to be friends, but are not friends unless they both are lovable and know the fact; for a wish for friendship may arise quickly, but friendship does not.

Book X

If happiness is activity in accordance with virtue, it is reasonable that it should be in accordance with the highest virtue; and this will be that of the best thing in us. Whether it be reason or something else that is this element which is thought to be our natural ruler and guide and to take thought of things noble and divine, whether it be itself also divine or only the most divine element in us, the activity of this in accordance with its proper virtue will be perfect happiness. That this activity is contemplative we have already said.

Now this would seem to be in agreement both with what we said before and with the truth. For, firstly, this activity is the best (since not only is reason the best thing in us, but the objects of reason are the best of knowable objects); and secondly, it is the most continuous, since we can contemplate truth more continuously than we can do anything. And we think happiness has pleasure mingled with it, but the activity of philosophic wisdom is admittedly the pleasantest of virtuous activities; at all events the pursuit of it is thought to offer pleasures marvellous for their purity and their enduringness, and it is to be expected that those who know will pass their time more pleasantly than those who inquire. And the self-sufficiency that is spoken of must belong most to the contemplative activity. For while a philosopher, as well as a just man or one possessing any other virtue, needs the necessaries of life, when they are sufficiently equipped with things of that sort the just man needs people towards whom and with whom he shall act justly, and the temperate man, the brave man, and each of the others is in the same case, but the philosopher, even when by himself, can contemplate truth, and the better the wiser he is; he can perhaps do so better if he has fellow-workers, but still he is the most self-sufficient. And this activity alone would seem to be loved for its own sake; for nothing arises from it apart from the contemplating, while from practical activities we gain more or less apart from the action. And happiness is thought to depend on leisure; for we are busy that we may have leisure, and make war that we may live in peace. Now the activity of the practical virtues is exhibited in political or military affairs, but the actions concerned with these seem to be unleisurely. Warlike actions are completely so (for no one chooses to be at war, or provokes war, for the sake of being at war; any one would seem absolutely murderous if he were to make enemies of his friends in order to bring about battle and slaughter); but the action of the statesman is also unleisurely, and—apart from the political action itself—aims at despotic power and honours, or at all events happiness, for him and his fellow citizens—a happiness different from political action, and evidently sought as being different. So if among virtuous actions political and military actions are distinguished by nobility and greatness, and these are unleisurely and aim at an end and are not desirable for their own sake, but the activity of reason, which is contemplative, seems both to be superior in serious worth and to aim at no end beyond itself, and to have its pleasure proper to itself (and this augments the activity), and the self-sufficiency, leisureliness, unweariedness (so far as this is possible for man), and all the other attributes ascribed to the supremely happy man are evidently those connected with this activity, it follows that this will be the complete happiness of man, if it be allowed a complete term of life (for none of the attributes of happiness is incomplete).

But such a life would be too high for man; for it is not in so far as he is man that he will live so, but in so far as something divine is present in him; and by so much as this is superior to our composite nature is its activity superior to that which is the exercise of the other kind of virtue. If reason is divine, then, in comparison with man, the life according to it is divine in comparison with human life. But we must not follow those who advise us, being men, to think of human things, and, being mortal, of mortal things, but must, so far as we can, make ourselves immortal, and strain every nerve to live in accordance with the best thing in us; for even if it be small in bulk, much more does it in power and worth surpass everything. This would seem, too, to be each man himself, since it is the authoritative and better part of him. It would be strange, then, if he were to choose not the life of his self but that of something else. And what we said before will apply now; that which is proper to each thing is by nature best and most pleasant for each thing; for man, therefore, the life according to reason is best and pleasantest, since reason more than anything else is man. This life therefore is also the happiest.

. . .

But in a secondary degree the life in accordance with the other kind of virtue is happy; for the activities in accordance with this befit our human estate. Just and brave acts, and other virtuous acts, we do in relation to each other, observing our respective duties with regard to contracts and services and all manner of actions and with regard to passions; and all of these seem to be typically human. Some of them seem even to arise from the body, and virtue of character to be in many ways bound up with the passions. Practical wisdom, too, is linked to virtue of character, and this to practical wisdom, since the principles of practical wisdom are in accordance with the moral virtues and rightness in morals is in accordance with practical wisdom. Being connected with the passions also, the moral virtues must belong to our composite nature; and the virtues of our composite nature are human; so, therefore, are the life and the happiness which correspond to these. The excellence of the reason is a thing apart; we must be content to say this much about it, for to describe it precisely is a task greater than our purpose requires. It would seem, however, also to need external equipment but little, or less than moral virtue does. Grant that both need the necessaries, and do so equally, even if the statesman's work is the more concerned with the body and things of that sort; for there will be little difference there; but in what they need for the exercise of their activities there will be much difference. The liberal man will need money for the doing of his liberal deeds, and the just man too will need it for the returning of services (for wishes are hard to discern, and even people who are not just pretend to wish to act justly); and the brave man will need power if he is to accomplish any of the acts that correspond to his virtue, and the temperate man will need opportunity; for how else is either he or any of the others to be recognized? It is debated, too, whether the will or the deed is more essential to virtue, which is assumed to involve both; it is surely clear that its perfection involves both; but for deeds many things are needed, and more, the greater and nobler the deeds are. But the man who is contemplating the truth needs no such thing, at least with a view to the exercise of his activity; indeed they are, one may say, even hindrances, at all events to his contemplation; but in so far as he is a man and lives with a number of people, he chooses to do virtuous acts; he will therefore need such aids to living a human life.

But that perfect happiness is a contemplative activity will appear from the following consideration as well. We assume the gods to be above all other beings blessed and happy; but what sort of actions must we assign to them? Acts of justice? Will not the gods seem absurd if they make contracts and return deposits, and so on? Acts of a brave man, then, confronting dangers and running risks because it is noble to do so? Or liberal acts? To whom will they give? It will be strange if they are really to have money or anything of the kind. And what would their temperate acts be? Is not such praise tasteless, since they have no bad appetites? If we were to run through them all, the circumstances of action would be found trivial and unworthy of gods. Still, every one supposes that they live and therefore that they are active; we cannot suppose them to sleep like Endymion. Now if you take away from a living being action, and still more production, what is left but contemplation? Therefore the activity of God, which surpasses all others in blessedness, must be contemplative; and of human activities, therefore, that which is most akin to this must be most of the nature of happiness.

This is indicated, too, by the fact that the other animals have no share in happiness, being completely deprived of such activity. For while the whole life of the gods is blessed, and that of men too in so far as some likeness of such activity belongs to them, none of the other animals is happy, since they in no way share in contemplation. Happiness extends, then, just so far as contemplation does, and those to whom contemplation more fully belongs are more truly happy, not as a mere concomitant but in virtue of the contemplation; for this is in itself precious. Happiness, therefore, must be some form of contemplation.

But, being a man, one will also need external prosperity; for our nature is not self-sufficient for the purpose of contemplation, but our body also must be healthy and must have food and other attention. Still, we must not think that the man who is to be happy will need many things or great things, merely because he cannot be supremely happy without external goods; for self-sufficiency and action do not involve excess, and we can do noble acts without ruling earth and sea; for even with moderate advantages one can act virtuously (this is manifest enough; for private persons are thought to do worthy acts no less than despots— indeed even more); and it is enough that we should have so much as that; for the life of the man who is active in accordance with virtue will be happy. Solon, too, was perhaps sketching well the happy man when he described him as moderately furnished with externals but as having done (as Solon thought) the noblest acts, and lived temperately; for one can with but moderate possessions do what one ought. Anaxagoras also seems to have supposed the happy man not to be rich nor a despot, when he said that he would not be surprised if the happy man were to seem to most people a strange person; for they judge by externals, since these are all they perceive. The opinions of the wise seem, then, to harmonize with our arguments. But while even such things carry some conviction, the truth in practical matters is discerned from the facts of life; for these are the decisive factor. We must therefore survey what we have already said, bringing it to the test of the facts of life, and if it harmonizes with the facts we must accept it, but if it clashes with them we must suppose it to be mere theory. Now he who exercises his reason and cultivates it seems to be both in the best state of mind and most dear to the gods. For if the gods have any care for human affairs, as they are thought to have, it would be reasonable both that they should delight in that which was best and most akin to them (i.e. reason) and that they should reward those who love and honour this most, as caring for the things that are dear to them and acting both rightly and nobly. And that all these attributes belong most of all to the philosopher is manifest. He, therefore, is the dearest to the gods. And he who is that will presumably be also the happiest; so that in this way too the philosopher will more than any other be happy.

Politics

Book I

But is there any one thus intended by nature to be a slave, and for whom such a condition is expedient and right, or rather is not all slavery a violation of nature?

There is no difficulty in answering this question, on grounds both of reason and of fact. For that some should rule and others be ruled is a thing not only necessary, but expedient; from the hour of their birth, some are marked out for subjection, others for rule.

And there are many kinds both of rulers and subjects (and that rule is the better which is exercised over better subjects—for example, to rule over men is better than to rule over wild beasts; for the work is better which is executed by better workmen, and where one man rules and another is ruled, they may be said to have a work); for in all things which form a composite whole and which are made up of parts, whether continuous or discrete, a distinction between the ruling and the subject element comes to light. Such a duality exists in living creatures, but not in them only; it originates in the constitution of the universe; even in things which have no life there is a ruling principle, as in a musical mode.

From Jowett, Benjamin (trans), *Politics*.

But we are wandering from the subject. We will therefore restrict ourselves to the living creature, which, in the first place, consists of soul and body: and of these two, the one is by nature the ruler, and the other the subject. But then we must look for the intentions of nature in things which retain their nature, and not in things which are corrupted. And therefore we must study the man who is in the most perfect state both of body and soul, for in him we shall see the true relation of the two; although in bad or corrupted natures the body will often appear to rule over the soul, because they are in an evil and unnatural condition. At all events we may firstly observe in living creatures both a despotical and a constitutional rule; for the soul rules the body with a despotical rule, whereas the intellect rules the appetites with a constitutional and royal rule. And it is clear that the rule of the soul over the body, and of the mind and the rational element over the passionate, is natural and expedient; whereas the equality of the two or the rule of the inferior is always hurtful. The same holds good of animals in relation to men; for tame animals have a better nature than wild, and all tame animals are better off when they are ruled by man; for then they are preserved. Again, the male is by nature superior, and the female inferior; and the one rules, and the other is ruled; this principle, of necessity, extends to all mankind.

Where then there is such a difference as that between soul and body, or between men and animals (as in the case of those whose business is to use their body, and who can do nothing better), the lower sort are by nature slaves, and it is better for them as for all inferiors that they should be under the rule of a master. For he who can be, and therefore is, another's and he who participates in rational principle enough to apprehend, but not to have, such a principle, is a slave by nature. Whereas the lower animals cannot even apprehend a principle; they obey their instincts. And indeed the use made of slaves and of tame animals is not very different; for both with their bodies minister to the needs of life. Nature would like to distinguish between the bodies of freemen and slaves, making the one strong for servile labor, the other upright, and although useless for such services, useful for political life in the arts both of war and peace. But the opposite often happens—that some have the souls and others have the bodies of freemen. And doubtless if men differed from one another in the mere forms of their bodies as much as the statues of the Gods do from men, all would acknowledge that the inferior class should be slaves of the superior. And if this is true of the body, how much more just that a similar distinction should exist in the soul? but the beauty of the body is seen, whereas the beauty of the soul is not seen. It is clear, then, that some men are by nature free, and others slaves, and that for these latter slavery is both expedient and right.

. . .

Of household management we have seen that there are three parts— one is the rule of a master over slaves, which has been discussed already, another of a father, and the third of a husband. A husband and father, we saw, rules over wife and children, both free, but the rule differs, the rule over his children being a royal, over his wife a constitutional rule. For although there may be exceptions to the order of nature, the male is by nature fitter for command than the female, just as the elder and full-grown is superior to the younger and more immature. But in most constitutional states the citizens rule and are ruled by turns, for the idea of a constitutional state implies that the natures of the citizens are equal, and do not differ at all. Nevertheless, when one rules and the other is ruled we endeavor to create a difference of outward forms and names and titles of respect, which may be illustrated by the saying of Amasis about his foot-pan. The relation of the male to the female is of this kind, but there the inequality is permanent. The rule of a father over his children is royal, for he rules by virtue both of love and of the respect due to age, exercising a kind of royal power. And therefore Homer has appropriately called Zeus "father of Gods and men," because he is the king of them all. For a king is the natural superior of his subjects, but he should be of the same kin or kind with them, and such is the relation of elder and younger, of father and son.

. . .

Thus it is clear that household management attends more to men than to the acquisition of inanimate things, and to human excellence more than to the excellence of property which we call wealth, and to the virtue of freemen more than to the virtue of slaves. A question may indeed be raised, whether there is any excellence at all in a slave beyond and higher than merely instrumental and ministerial qualities—whether he can have the virtues of temperance, courage, justice, and the like; or whether slaves possess only bodily and ministerial qualities. And, whichever way we answer the question, a difficulty arises; for, if they have virtue, in what will they differ from freemen? On the other hand, since they are men and share in rational principle, it seems absurd to say that they have no virtue. A similar question may be raised about women and children, whether they too have virtues: ought a woman to be temperate and brave and just, and is a child to be called temperate, and intemperate, or not? So in general we may ask about the natural ruler, and the natural subject, whether they have the same or different virtues. For if a noble nature is equally required in both, why should one of them always rule, and the other always be ruled? Nor can we say that this is a question of degree, for the difference between ruler and subject is a difference of kind, which the difference of more and less never is. Yet how strange is the supposition that the one ought, and that the other ought not, to have virtue! For if the ruler is intemperate and unjust, how can he rule well? If the subject, how can he obey well? If he be licentious and cowardly, he will certainly not do his duty. It is evident, therefore, that both of them must have a share of virtue, but varying as natural subjects also vary among themselves. Here the very constitution of the soul has shown us the way; in it one part naturally rules, and the other is subject, and the virtue of the ruler we in maintain to be different from that of the subject; the one being the virtue of the rational, and the other of the irrational part. Now, it is obvious that the same principle applies generally, and therefore almost all things rule and are ruled according to nature. But the kind of rule differs; the freeman rules over the slave after another manner from that in which the male rules over the female, or the man over the child; although the parts of the soul are present in and of them, they are present in different degrees. For the slave has no deliberative faculty at all; the woman has, but it is without authority, and the child has, but it is immature. So it must necessarily be supposed to be with the moral virtues also; all should partake of them, but only in such manner and degree as is required by each for the fulfillment of his duty. Hence the ruler ought to have moral virtue in perfection, for his function, taken absolutely, demands a master artificer, and rational principle is such an artificer; the subjects, on the other hand, require only that measure of virtue which is proper to each of them. Clearly, then, moral virtue belongs to all of them; but the temperance of a man and of a woman, or the courage and justice of a man and of a woman, are not, as Socrates maintained, the same; the courage of a man is shown in commanding, of a woman in obeying. And this holds of all other virtues, as will be more clearly seen if we look at them in detail, for those who say generally that virtue consists in a good disposition of the soul, or in doing rightly, or the like, only deceive themselves. Far better than such definitions is their mode of speaking, who, like Gorgias, enumerate the virtues. All classes must be deemed to have their special attributes; as the poet says of women, "Silence is a woman's glory," but this is not equally the glory of man. The child is imperfect, and therefore obviously his virtue is not relative to himself alone, but to the perfect man and to his teacher, and in like manner the virtue of the slave is relative to a master. Now we determined that a slave is useful for the wants of life, and therefore he will obviously require only so much virtue as will prevent him from failing in his duty through cowardice or lack of self-control. Some one will ask whether, if what we are saying is true, virtue will not be required also in the artisans, for they often fail in their work through the lack of self control? But is there not a great difference in the two cases? For the slave shares in his master's life; the artisan is less closely connected with him, and only attains excellence in proportion as he becomes a slave. The meaner sort of mechanic has a special and separate slavery; and whereas the slave exists by nature, not so the shoemaker or other artisan. It is manifest, then, that the master ought to be the source of such excellence in the slave, and not a mere possessor of the art of mastership which trains the slave in his duties. Wherefore they are mistaken who forbid us to converse with slaves and say that we should employ command only, for slaves stand even more in need of admonition than children.

So much for this subject; the relations of husband and wife, parent and child, their several virtues, what in their intercourse with one another is good, and what is evil, and how we may pursue the good and good and escape the evil, will have to be discussed when we speak of the different forms of government. For, inasmuch as every family is a part of a state, and these relationships are the parts of a family, and the virtue of the part must have regard to the virtue of the whole, women and children must be trained by education with an eye to the constitution, if the virtues of either of them are supposed to make any difference in the virtues of the state. And they must make a difference: for the children grow up to be citizens, and half the free persons in a state are women.

On the Soul

Book II

That is why the soul is the first grade of actuality of a natural body having life potentially in it. The body so described is a body which is organized. The parts of plants in spite of their extreme simplicity are

From Smith, JA (trans), *On the Soul*, 1931.

"organs"; e.g., the leaf serves to shelter the pericarp, the pericarp to shelter the fruit, while the roots of plants are analogous to the mouth of animals, both serving for the absorption of food. If, then, we have to give a general formula applicable to all kinds of soul, we must describe it as the first grade of actuality of a natural organized body. That is why we can wholly dismiss as unnecessary the question whether the soul and the body are one: it is as meaningless as to ask whether the wax and the shape given to it by the stamp are one, or generally the matter of a thing and that of which it is the matter. Unity has many senses (as many as "is" has), but the most proper and fundamental sense of both is the relation of an actuality to that of which it is the actuality. We have now given an answer to the question, What is soul?—an answer which applies to it in its full extent. It is substance in the sense which corresponds to the definitive formula of a thing's essence. That means that it is "the essential whatness" of a body of the character just assigned. Suppose that what is literally an "organ," like an axe, were a natural body, its "essential whatness," would have been its essence, and so its soul; if this disappeared from it, it would have ceased to be an axe, except in name. As it is, it is just an axe; it wants the character which is required to make its whatness or formulable essence a soul; for that, it would have had to be a natural body of a particular kind, viz. one having in itself the power of setting itself in movement and arresting itself. Next, apply this doctrine in the case of the "parts" of the living body. Suppose that the eye were an animal—sight would have been its soul, for sight is the substance or essence of the eye which corresponds to the formula, the eye being merely the matter of seeing; when seeing is removed the eye is no longer an eye, except in name—it is no more a real eye than the eye of a statue or of a painted figure. We must now extend our consideration from the "parts" to the whole living body; for what the departmental sense is to the bodily part which is its organ, that the whole faculty of sense is to the whole sensitive body as such.

. . .

[A]s the pupil plus the power of sight constitutes the eye, so the soul plus the body constitutes the animal.

From this it indubitably follows that the soul is inseparable from its body, or at any rate that certain parts of it are (if it has parts) for the actuality of some of them is nothing but the actualities of their bodily parts. Yet some may be separable because they are not the actualities of any body at all. Further, we have no light on the problem whether the soul may not be the actuality of its body in the sense in which the sailor is the actuality of the ship.   •

. . .

It follows that first of all we must treat of nutrition and reproduction, for the nutritive soul is found along with all the others and is the most primitive and widely distributed power of soul, being indeed that one in virtue of which all are said to have life. The acts in which it manifests itself are reproduction and the use of food—reproduction, I say, because for any living thing that has reached its normal development and which is unmutilated, and whose mode of generation is not spontaneous, the most natural act is the production of another like itself, an animal producing an animal, a plant a plant, in order that, as far as its nature allows, it may partake in the eternal and divine. That is the goal towards which all things strive, that for the sake of which they do whatsoever their nature renders possible. The phrase "for the sake of which" is ambiguous; it may mean either (a) the end to achieve which, or (b) the being in whose interest, the act is done. Since then no living thing is able to partake in what is eternal and divine by uninterrupted continuance (for nothing perishable can for ever remain one and the same), it tries to achieve that end in the only way possible to it, and success is possible in varying degrees; so it remains not indeed as the self-same individual but continues its existence in something like itself—not numerically but specifically one.

The soul is the cause or source of the living body. The terms cause and source have many senses. But the soul is the cause of its body alike in all three senses which we explicitly recognize. It is (a) the source or origin of movement, it is (b) the end, it is (c) the essence of the whole living body.

That it is the last, is clear; for in everything the essence is identical with the ground of its being, and here, in the case of living things, their being is to live, and of their being and their living the soul in them is the cause or source. Further, the actuality of whatever is potential is identical with its formulable essence.

. . .

It is manifest that the soul is also the final cause of its body. For Nature, like mind, always does whatever it does for the sake of something, which something is its end. To that something corresponds in the case of animals the soul and in this it follows the order of nature; all natural bodies are organs of the soul. This is true of those that enter into the constitution of plants as well as of those which enter into that of animals. This shows that that the sake of which they are is soul. We must here recall the two senses of "that for the sake of which," viz. (a) the end to achieve which, and (b) the being in whose interest, anything is or is done.

We must maintain, further, that the soul is also the cause of the living body as the original source of local movement. The power of loco-motion is not found, however, in all living things. But change of quality and change of quantity are also due to the soul. Sensation is held to be a qualitative alteration, and nothing except what has soul in it is capable of sensation. The same holds of the quantitative changes which constitute growth and decay; nothing grows or decays naturally except what feeds itself, and nothing feeds itself except what has a share of soul in it.

Eudemian Ethics

Book I

About many other things it is difficult to judge well, but most difficult about that on which judgement seems to all easiest and the knowledge of it in the power of any man—viz. what of all that is found in living is desir-able, and what, if attained, would satisfy our desire. For there are many consequences of life that make men fling away life, as disease, excessive pain, storms, so that it is clear that, if one were given the power of choice, not to be born at all would, as far at least as these reasons go, have been desirable. Further, the life we lead as children is not desirable, for no one in his senses would consent to return again to this. Further, many inci-dents involving neither pleasure nor pain or involving pleasure but not of a noble kind are such that, as far as they are concerned, non-existence is preferable to life. And generally, if one were to bring together all that all men do and experience but not willingly because not for its own sake, and were to add to this an existence of infinite duration, one would none the more on account of these experiences choose existence rather than non-existence. But further, neither for the pleasure of eating alone or that of sex, if all the other pleasures were removed that knowing or seeing or any other sense provides men with, would a single man value existence, unless he were utterly servile, for it is clear that to the man making this choice there would be no difference between being born a brute and a

From Solomon, J (trans), *Eudemian Ethics*, OUP, 1915.

man; at any rate the ox in Egypt, which they reverence as Apis, in most of such matters has more power than many monarchs. We may say the same of the pleasure of sleeping. For what is the difference between sleeping an unbroken sleep from one's first day to one's last, say for a thousand or any number of years, and living the life of a plant? Plants at any rate seem to possess this sort of existence, and similarly children; for children, too, continue having their nature from their first coming into being in their mother's womb, but sleep the entire time. It is clear then from these considerations that men, though they look, fail to see what is well-being, what is the good in life.

And so they tell us that Anaxagoras answered a man who was raising problems of this sort and asking why one should choose rather to be born than not—"for the sake of viewing the heavens and the whole order of the universe." He, then, thought the choice of life for the sake of some sort of knowledge to be precious; but those who felicitate Sardanapallus or Smindyrides the Sybarite or any other of those who live the voluptuary's life, these seem all to place happiness in the feeling of pleasure. But others would rather choose virtuous deeds than either any sort of wisdom or sensual pleasures; at any rate some choose these not only for the sake of reputation, but even when they are not going to win credit by them; but most "political" men are not truly so called; they are not in truth "political" for the "political" man is one who chooses noble acts for their own sake, while most take up the "political" life for the sake of money and greed.

From what has been said, then, it is clear that all connect happiness with one or other of three lives, the "political," the philosophic, and the voluptuary's. Now among these the nature and quality and sources of the pleasure of the body and sensual enjoyment are clear, so that we have not to inquire what such pleasures are, but whether they tend to happiness or not and how they tend, and whether—supposing it right to attach to the noble life certain pleasures—it is right to attach these, or whether some other sort of participation in these is a necessity, but the pleasures through which men rightly think the happy man to live pleasantly and not merely painlessly are different.

10

Epicurus

The system of thought of the Greek philosopher Epicurus (341–270 BCE) consists of a component dealing with physics and a component dealing with the good life. Epicurus's system of physics is materialistic in nature: the universe consists of the random motion of physical atoms in an infinity of empty space ("the void"); human beings (and their minds) are likewise to be understood materialistically, from which it follows that the human condition is one of final mortality. Famously, this ushers in the characteristic Epicurean contention that one should not fear death: since there will be no sensations to experience after death (since nothing will *happen* once one no longer exists), there is nothing whatsoever to fear in death. The Epicurean system of ethics was very simple: all that is needed for a good and happy life is a life lived among friends, a body free from pain, and a mind free from anxiety; in short, seek happiness and avoid pain. Many moralists regarded the Epicurean emphasis on pleasure as base and contemptible, though—as can be seen in the extracts to follow—Epicurus was not recommending anything like an orgiastic life of sensuous luxury. Indeed, in the "Vatican Sayings" he wrote: "Sexual pleasure has never done anybody any good. One must be content if it has not done actual harm." The idea that the good life is to be characterized in terms of pleasure would be resoundingly embraced centuries later by Jeremy Bentham and John Stuart Mill as the very foundation of their utilitarian philosophy.

The first selection below is extracted from the "Letter to Herodotus" and outlines Epicurus's views concerning the infinity of the universe, the motion of atoms, and the purely material nature of the soul. The "Letter to Menoeceus" (reproduced in its entirety) and some selections from the "Principal Doctrines" follow. Their focus is on how to secure happiness and avoid pain, and this goal is in fact emblematic of Epicurus's goals as a philosopher: "Vain is the word of a philosopher, by which no mortal suffering is healed. Just as medicine confers no benefit if it does not drive away bodily disease, so is philosophy useless if it does not drive away the suffering of the mind" (Epicurus, Fragment 54, in *The Essential Epicurus*, 97).

Letter to Herodotus

The Universe and Its Constituent Elements

Bodies and Void

[T]he universe consists of bodies and void: that bodies exist, perception itself in all men bears witness; it is through the senses that we must by necessity form a judgment about the imperceptible by means of reason, just as I argued above. But if that which we call void and place and impalpable substance did not exist, bodies would have no place to be nor anything through which to move, as they are clearly seen to be moving. Beyond this, nothing can even be thought of, either by the understanding or on analogy with things comprehensible, as are graspable as entire substances and not spoken of as attributes or accidents of them. And of the bodies some are compounds and others are those from which the compounds have been formed: these latter are indivisible and unchangeable if everything is not about to be reduced to nonexistence; but some strong element remains in the breakup of the compounds, one that is solid by nature and incapable of being dissolved. As a result, the first beginnings must be indivisible bodily substances.

The Infinity of the Universe

Furthermore, the universe is without limit. For that which is limited has an outermost edge; the outermost edge will be seen against something else.

From *The Essential Epicurus* (translated and edited by Eugene O'Connor) (Buffalo, NY: Prometheus Books, 1993 (pp. 21–23, 32–34, 61–68, 69–76).

As a result, the universe, having no outermost edge, has no limit; having no limit it would be boundless and unlimited. Also, the universe is boundless both in the number of the bodies and the magnitude of the void. If the void were limitless and the bodies limited, the bodies would not remain anywhere, but be borne and scattered into the limitless void, having nothing to support them and check them by colliding with them. But if the void were limited, there would not be enough room in it for a limitless number of bodies. . . .

Atoms' Motion

The atoms move continuously forever, some . . . standing at a long distance from one another, others in turn maintaining their rapid vibration, whenever they happen to be checked by their interlacing with others or covered by the interlaced atoms. It is both the nature of the void separating each atom by itself that effects this, since it is unable to furnish any resistance, and the hardness belonging to the atoms that makes them rebound after colliding, to the extent that their interlacing grants them a return to their former position following collision. Of their motions there is no beginning; the atoms and the void are the cause.

The Soul

Its Composition

Next you must, referring to the perceptions and the feelings—for in these there will lie the most reliable certainty—consider that the soul is a body of fine particles dispersed throughout the entire organism and most resembling a wind that contains a certain mixture of heat, in some ways resembling this (the wind) and in others this (the heat). And there is a part of the soul that is very different even from these in subtlety of composition and is therefore more interactive, or more in sympathy, with the rest of the organism. All this is made evident by the powers of the mind, its feelings, its mobility, and those faculties of which we are deprived when we die.

The Soul and Sensation

Furthermore, you must understand that the soul is the chief cause of sensation. But it would not have acquired this faculty, if it were not somehow enclosed by the rest of the body.

The rest of the body, having provided to the soul this cause of sensation, has itself acquired from the soul a share in this capacity, although not all the sensations that the soul has acquired. For this reason, the body has no sensation once the soul departs. For the body did not acquire this power on its own, but made it possible for the companion being that came into existence at the same time. . . .

It is not possible to imagine the soul existing and having sensation without the body, and experiencing these movements when there no longer exists that which encloses and surrounds the soul, in which it now exists and has these movements.

The Material Nature of the Soul

We must, in addition, note that the word "incorporeal" is most commonly applied to what may be thought of as existing by itself. It is impossible to imagine the incorporeal as an independent existence except as the void. The void can neither act nor be acted upon, but only furnishes to bodies motion through it. For this reason, those who claim that the soul is incorporeal are talking rubbish, for the soul would not be able to act or be acted upon if that were so. But as the case stands, both these occurrences are clearly distinguished in connection with the soul. Therefore, anyone who refers all these considerations concerning the soul to his feelings and sensations, remembering what was said at the beginning, will observe that they are comprehended by these general principles in a manner sufficient to enable him to work out the details for himself with certainty, starting from these general formulae.

Letter to Menoeceus

Introduction

Let no one put off studying philosophy when he is young, nor when old grow weary of its study. For no one is too young or too far past his prime to achieve the health of his soul. The man who alleges that he is not yet ready for philosophy or that the time for it has passed him by, is like the man who says that he is either too young or too old for happiness. Therefore, we should study philosophy both in youth and in old age, so that we, though growing old, may be young in blessings through the pleasant memory of what has been; and when young we may be old as well, because we harbor no fear over what lies ahead. We must, therefore, pursue the things that make for happiness, seeing that when happiness is present, we have everything; but when it is absent, we do everything to possess it.

First Principles

The Gods

The things which I used constantly to recommend to you, these things do and pursue, realizing that they are the fundamental principles of the good life. First of all, regard the god as an immortal and blessed being, as the concept of deity is commonly presented, but do not apply to him anything foreign to his immortality or out of keeping with his blessedness; believe instead, concerning him, everything that can safeguard his blessedness along with his immortality. For the gods exist; of them we have distinct knowledge. But they are not such as the majority think them to be. For they do not maintain a consistent view of what they think the gods are. The impious man is not he who confutes the gods of the majority, but he who applies to the gods the majority's opinions. For the assertions of the many concerning the gods are conceptions grounded not in experience but in false assumptions, according to which the greatest misfortunes are brought upon the evil by the gods and the greatest benefits upon the good. Men being always at home with their own virtues, they embrace those like themselves and regard everything unlike themselves as alien.

Death

Grow accustomed to the belief that death is nothing to us, since every good and evil lie in sensation. However, death is the deprivation of sensation. Therefore, correct understanding that death is nothing to us makes a mortal life enjoyable, not by adding an endless span of time but by taking away the longing for immortality. For there is nothing dreadful in life for the man who has truly comprehended that there is nothing terrible in not living. Therefore, foolish is the man who says that he fears death, not because it will cause pain when it arrives but because anticipation of it is painful. What is no trouble when it arrives is an idle worry in anticipation. Death, therefore—the most dreadful of evils—is nothing to us, since while we exist, death is not present, and whenever death is present, we do not exist. It is nothing either to the living or the dead, since it does not exist for the living, and the dead no longer are.

The majority, however, sometimes flee from death as the greatest of evils, and other times choose it for themselves as a respite from the evils in life. The wise man neither rejects life nor fears not living. Life is not objectionable to him, nor is not living regarded as an evil. Just as he assuredly chooses not the greatest quantity of food but the most tasty, so does he enjoy the fruits not of the lengthiest period of time but of the most pleasant.

He who advises the youth to live well but the old man to die well is foolish, not only because of the desirability of life but also because the training for living well and dying well is the same. Much worse is he who says that it is good not to be born and "once born to pass through the gates of death as quickly as possible." If a man says this with conviction, how can he avoid departing from life? For this road is open to him, if he has firmly resolved to do it. If, however, he has spoken in jest, he is considered foolish among men who cannot welcome his words.

We must keep in mind that the future is neither completely ours nor not ours, so that we should not fully expect it to come, nor lose hope, as if it were not coming at all.

The Moral Theory

The Various Desires

We must consider that of the desires some are natural and others idle: of the natural desires, some are necessary while others are natural only. Of the necessary desires, there are those that are necessary for happiness, those that are necessary for the body's freedom from disturbance, and those that are necessary for life itself. A firm understanding of these things enables us to refer every choice and avoidance to the health of the body or the calm of the soul, since this is the goal of a happy life. Everything we do is for the sake of this, namely, to avoid pain and fear. Once this is achieved, all the soul's trouble is dispelled, as the living being does not have to go in search of something missing or to seek something else, by which the good of the soul and of the body will be fulfilled. For we have need of pleasure at that time when we feel pain owing to the absence of pleasure. When we do not feel pain, it is because we no longer have need of pleasure. Therefore, we declare that pleasure is the beginning and the goal of a happy life. For we recognize pleasure as the first good and as inborn; it is from this that we begin every choice and every avoidance. It is to pleasure that we have recourse, using the feeling as our standard for judging every good.

Pleasure and Pain

Since pleasure is the first good and natural to us, it is for this reason also that we do not choose every pleasure; instead, there are times when we pass over many pleasures, whenever greater difficulty follows from them. Also, we regard many pains as better than pleasures, since a greater pleasure will attend us after we have endured pain for a long time. Every pleasure, therefore, because of its natural relationship to us, is good, but not every pleasure is to be chosen. Likewise, every pain is an evil, but not every pain is of a nature always to be avoided. Yet it is proper to judge all these things by a comparison and a consideration of both their advantages and disadvantages. For on certain occasions we treat the good as bad and, conversely, the bad as good.

Self-Sufficiency

We regard self-sufficiency as a great good, not that we may always have the enjoyment of but a few things, but that if we do not have many, we may have but few enjoyments in the genuine conviction that they take the sweetest pleasure in luxury who have least need of it, and that everything easy to procure is natural while everything difficult to obtain is superfluous. Plain dishes offer the same pleasure as a luxurious table, when the pain that comes from want is taken away. Bread and water offer the greatest pleasure when someone in need partakes of them. Becoming accustomed, therefore, to simple and not luxurious fare is productive of health and makes humankind resolved to perform the necessary business of life. When we approach luxuries after long intervals, it makes us better disposed toward them and renders us fearless of fortune.

Genuine Pleasure

When we say that pleasure is the goal, we are not talking about the pleasure of profligates or that which lies in sensuality, as some ignorant persons think, or else those who do not agree with us or have followed our argument badly; rather, it is freedom from bodily pain and mental anguish. For it is not continuous drinking and revels, nor the enjoyment of women and young boys, nor of fish and other viands that a luxurious table holds, which make for a pleasant life, but sober reasoning, which examines the motives for every choice and avoidance, and which drives away those opinions resulting in the greatest disturbance to the soul.

Prudence

The beginning and the greatest good of all these is prudence. For this reason prudence is more valuable even than philosophy: from it derive all the other virtues. Prudence teaches us how impossible it is to live pleasantly without living wisely, virtuously, and justly, just as we cannot live wisely, virtuously, and justly without living pleasantly. For the virtues arise naturally with the pleasant life; indeed, the pleasant life cannot be separated from them. Who, do you think, is better than the man who keeps a reverent opinion about the gods, and is altogether fearless of death and has reasoned out the end of nature; who understands that the limit of good things is easy to attain and easy to procure, while the limit of evils is but brief in duration and small in pain; who laughs at fate, which is painted by some as the mistress over all things? . . . Some things happen by necessity, others as the result of chance; other things are subject to our control. Because necessity is not accountable to anyone, he sees that chance is unstable, but what lies in our control is subject to no master; it naturally follows, then, that blame or praise attend our decisions.

Indeed, it would be better to accept the myths about the gods than to be a slave to the "destiny" of the physical philosophers. The myths present the hope of appeasing the gods through worship, while the other is full of unappeasable necessity. Understanding that chance is neither a god, as the majority think (for nothing is done by a god in an irregular fashion), nor an unstable cause of all things, the wise man does not think that either good or evil is furnished by chance to humankind for the purpose of living a happy life, but that the opportunities for great good or evil are bestowed by it. He thinks that it is preferable to remain prudent and suffer ill fortune than to enjoy good luck while acting foolishly. It is better in human actions that the sound decision fail than that the rash decision turn out well due to luck.

Conclusion

Take thought, then, for these and kindred matters day and night, on your own or in the company of someone like yourself. You shall be disturbed neither waking nor sleeping, and you shall live as a god among men. For the man who dwells among immortal blessings is not like a mortal being.

Principal Doctrines (Selections)

1. The blessed and immortal is itself free from trouble nor does it cause trouble for anyone else; therefore, it is not constrained either by anger or by favor. For such sentiments exist only in the weak.

2. Death is nothing to us. For what has been dispersed has no sensation. And what has no sensation is nothing to us.

3. The limit of the extent of pleasure is the removal of all pain. Wherever pleasure is present, for however long a time, there can be no pain or grief, or both at once.

4. Pain does not dwell continuously in the flesh. Extreme pain is present but a very brief time, and that which barely exceeds bodily pleasure continues no more than a few days. . . .

5. It is impossible to live pleasantly without living prudently, well, and justly, nor is it possible to live prudently, well, and justly without living pleasantly. . . .

6. Whatever you can provide yourself with to secure protection from men is a natural good.

8. No pleasure is evil in itself; but the means of obtaining some pleasures bring in their wake troubles many times greater than the pleasures.

12. It is impossible for anyone to dispel his fear over the most important matters, if he does not know what is the nature of the universe but instead suspects something that happens in myth. Therefore, it is impossible to obtain unmitigated pleasure without natural science.

13. There is no benefit in securing protection from men if things above and beneath the earth and indeed all the limitless universe are made matters for suspicion.

14. The most perfect means of securing safety from men, which arises, to some extent, from a certain power to expel, is the assurance that comes from quietude and withdrawal from the world.

15. Natural wealth is limited and easily obtained; the riches of idle fancies go on forever.

16. In few instances does chance intrude upon the wise man, but reason has administered his greatest and most important affairs, and will continue to do so throughout his whole life.

17. The just man is most free of perturbation, while the unjust man is full of the greatest disturbance.

20. The flesh considers the limits of pleasure to be boundless, and only infinite time makes it possible. But the mind, having gained a reasonable understanding of the end and limit of the flesh, and having expelled fears about eternity, furnishes the complete life, and we no longer have any need for time without end. But the mind does not flee from pleasure nor, when circumstances bring about the departure from life, does it take its leave as though falling short somehow of the best life.

27. Of all the things that wisdom provides for living one's entire life in happiness, the greatest by far is the possession of friendship.

28. The same knowledge that makes one confident that nothing dreadful is eternal or long-lasting, also recognizes in the face of these limited evils the security afforded by friendship.

11

Lucretius

Lucretius (c. 100–55 BCE) was a Roman citizen and an enthusiastic exponent of Epicureanism. Very little is known of his life, and the most famous story about him—namely that he was driven mad by a love-philtre and wrote *On the Nature of the Universe* during lucid intervals—appears to be entirely untrue. In the selections below, we first see Lucretius setting out the atomistic physics of Epicureanism and describing the random movements of atoms by means of a memorable analogy with dust particles in a shaft of sunlight. Next, Lucretius supports the materialistic Epicurean view of the mind by means of a number of arguments, for example that the mind develops and declines along with the body, that it is affected by wine and medicinal drugs, and so on. Finally, he provides a discussion and defense of the Epicurean denial that there is anything to fear in death.

On the Nature of the Universe

Book I

You will find that anything that can be named is either a property or an accident of these two. A *property* is something that cannot be detached or separated from a thing without destroying it, as weight is a property of

Approximately two thousand six hundred and ninety-four (2,694) words from ON THE NATURE OF THE UNIVERSE by Lucretius, translated and introduced by R.E. Latham (Penguin Classics, 1951). Copyright © R.E. Latham, 1951.

rocks, heat of fire, fluidity of water, tangibility of all bodies, intangibility of vacuum. On the other hand, servitude and liberty, poverty and riches, war and peace, and all other things whose advent or departure leaves the essence of a thing intact, all these it is our practice to call by their appropriate name, *accidents*.

. . .

Certainly the atoms did not post themselves purposefully in due order by an act of intelligence, nor did they stipulate what movements each should perform. As they have been rushing everlastingly throughout all space in their myriads, undergoing a myriad changes under the disturbing impact of collisions, they have experienced every variety of movement and conjunction till they have fallen into the particular pattern by which this world of ours is constituted.

Book II

This process, as I might point out, is illustrated by an image of it that is continually taking place before our very eyes. Observe what happens when sunbeams are admitted into a building and shed light on its shadowy places. You will see a multitude of tiny particles mingling in a multitude of ways in the empty space within the light of the beam, as though contending in everlasting conflict, rushing into battle rank upon rank with never a moment's pause in a rapid sequence of unions and disunions. From this you may picture what it is for the atoms to be perpetually tossed about in the illimitable void. To some extent a small thing may afford an illustration and an imperfect image of great things. Besides, there is a further reason why you should give your mind to these particles that are seen dancing in a sunbeam: their dancing is an actual indication of underlying movements of matter that are hidden from our sight. There you will see many particles under the impact of invisible blows changing their course and driven back upon their tracks, this way and that, in all directions. You must understand that they all derive this restlessness from the atoms. It originates with the atoms, which move of themselves. Then those small compound bodies that are least removed from the impetus of the atoms are set in motion by the impact of their invisible blows and in turn cannon against slightly larger bodies. So the movement mounts up from the atoms and gradually emerges to the level of our senses, so that those bodies are in motion that we see in sunbeams, moved by blows that remain invisible.

Book III

The same reasoning proves that *mind and spirit are both composed of matter*. We see them propelling the limbs, rousing the body from sleep, changing the expression of the face and guiding and steering the whole man—activities that all clearly involve touch, as touch in turn involves matter. How then can we deny their material nature? You see the mind sharing in the body's experiences and sympathizing with it. When the nerve-racking impact of a spear gashes bones and sinews, even if it does not penetrate to the seat of life, there ensues faintness and a tempting inclination earthwards and on the ground a turmoil in the mind and an intermittent faltering impulse to stand up again. The substance of the mind must therefore be material, since it is affected by the impact of material weapons.

. . .

My next point is this: you must understand that the *minds of living things and the light fabric of their spirits are neither birth-less nor death-less*. To this end I have long been mustering and inventing verses with a labour that is also a joy. Now I will try to set them out in a style worthy of your career.

Please note that both objects are to be embraced under one name. When, for instance, I proceed to demonstrate that "spirit" is mortal, you must understand that this applies equally to "mind," since the two are so conjoined as to constitute a single substance.

. . .

Again, we are conscious that mind and body are born together, grow up together and together decay. With the weak and delicate frame of wavering childhood goes a like infirmity of judgement. The robust vigour of ripening years is accompanied by a steadier resolve and a maturer strength of mind. Later, when the body is palsied by the potent forces of age and the limbs begin to droop with blunted vigour, the understanding limps, the tongue falters and the mind totters: everything weakens and gives way at the same time. It is thus natural that the vital spirit should evaporate like smoke, soaring into the gusty air, since we have seen that it shares in the body's birth and growth and wearies with the weariness of age.

Furthermore, as the body suffers the horrors of disease and the pangs of pain, so we see the mind stabbed with anguish, grief, and fear. What more natural than that it should likewise have a share in death? Often enough in the body's illness the mind wanders. It raves and babbles distractedly. At times it drifts on a tide of drowsiness, with drooping eyelids and nodding head, into a deep and endless sleep, from which it cannot hear the voices or recognize the faces of those who stand around with streaming eyes and tear-stained cheeks, striving to recall it to life. Since the mind is thus invaded by the contagion of disease, you must acknowledge that it is destructible. For pain and sickness are the artificers of death, as we have been taught by the fate of many men before us.

. . .

You must admit, therefore, that when the body has perished there is an end also of the spirit diffused through it. It is surely crazy to couple a mortal object with an eternal and suppose that they can work in harmony and mutually interact. What can be imagined more incongruous, what more repugnant and discordant, than that a mortal object and one that is immortal and everlasting should unite to form a compound and jointly weather the storms that rage about them?

. . .

From all this it follows that *death is nothing to us* and no concern of ours, since our tenure of the mind is mortal. In days of old, we felt no disquiet when the hosts of Carthage poured in to battle on every side— when the whole earth, dizzied by the convulsive shock of war, reeled sickeningly under the high ethereal vault, and between realm and realm the empire of mankind by land and sea trembled in the balance. So, when we shall be no more—when the union of body and spirit that engenders us has been disrupted—to us, who shall then be nothing, nothing by any hazard will happen any more at all. Nothing will have power to stir our senses, not though earth be fused with sea and sea with sky.

If any feeling remains in mind or spirit after it has been torn from our body, that is nothing to us, who are brought into being by the wedlock of body and spirit, conjoined and coalesced. Or even if the matter that composes us should be reassembled by time after our death and brought back into its present state—if the light of life were given to us anew—even that contingency would still be no concern of ours once the chain of our identity had been snapped. We who are now are not concerned with ourselves in any previous existence: the sufferings of those selves do not touch us. When you look at the immeasurable extent of time gone by and the multiform movements of matter, you will readily credit that these same atoms that compose us now must many a time before have entered into the selfsame combinations as now. But our mind cannot recall this to remembrance. For between then and now is interposed a breach in life, and all the atomic motions have been wandering far astray from sentience.

If the future holds travail and anguish in store, the self must be in existence, when that time comes, in order to experience it. But from this fate we are redeemed by death, which denies existence to the self that might have suffered these tribulations. Rest assured, therefore, that we have nothing to fear in death. One who no longer is cannot suffer, or differ in any way from one who has never been born, when once this mortal life has been usurped by death the immortal.

When you find a man treating it as a grievance that after death he will either moulder in the grave or fall a prey to flames or to the jaws of predatory beasts, be sure that his utterance does not ring true. Subconsciously his heart is stabbed by a secret dread, however loudly the man himself may disavow the belief that after death he will still experience sensation. I am convinced that he does not grant the admission he professes, nor the grounds of it; he does not oust and pluck himself root and branch out of life, but all unwittingly makes something of himself linger on. When a living man confronts the thought that after death his body will be mauled by birds and beasts of prey, he is filled with self-pity. He does not banish himself from the scene nor distinguish sharply enough between himself and that abandoned carcass. He visualizes that object as himself and infects it with his own feelings as an onlooker. That is why he is aggrieved at having been created mortal. He does not see that in real death there will be no other self alive to mourn his own decease—no other self standing by to flinch at the agony he suffers lying there being mangled, or indeed being cremated. For if it is really a bad thing after death to be mauled and crunched by ravening jaws, I cannot see why it should not be disagreeable to roast in the scorching flames of a funeral pyre, or to lie embalmed in honey, stifled and stiff with cold, on the surface of a chilly slab, or to be squashed under a crushing weight of earth.

"Now it is all over. Now the happy home and the best of wives will welcome you no more, nor winsome children rush to snatch the first kiss at your coming and touch your heart with speechless joy. No chance now to further your fortune or safeguard your family. Unhappy man," they cry, "unhappily cheated by one treacherous day out of all the uncounted blessings of life!" But they do not go on to say: "And now no repining for these lost joys will oppress you any more." If they perceived this clearly with their minds and acted according to the words, they would free their breasts from a great load of grief and dread.

"Ah yes! *You* are at peace now in the sleep of death, and so you will stay to the end of time. Pain and sorrow will never touch you again. But to *us*, who stood weeping inconsolably while you were consumed to ashes on the dreadful pyre—to us no day will come that will lift the undying sorrow from our hearts." Ask the speaker, then, what is so heart-rending about this. If something returns to sleep and peace what reason is that for pining in inconsolable grief?

Here, again, is the way men often talk from the bottom of their hearts when they recline at a banquet, goblet in hand and brows decked with garlands: "How all too short are these good times that come to us poor creatures! Soon they will be past and gone, and there will be no recalling them." You would think the crowning calamity in store for them after death was to be parched and shrivelled by a tormenting thirst or oppressed by some other vain desire. But even in sleep, when mind and body alike are at rest, no one misses himself or sighs for life. If such sleep were prolonged to eternity, no longing for ourselves would trouble us. And yet the vital atoms in our limbs cannot be far removed from their sensory motions at a time when a mere jolt out of sleep enables a man to pull himself together. Death, therefore, must be regarded, so far as we are concerned, as having much less existence than sleep, if anything can have less existence than what we perceive to be nothing. For death is followed by a far greater dispersal of the seething mass of matter: once that icy breach in life has intervened, there is no more waking.

Suppose that Nature herself were suddenly to find a voice and round upon one of us in these terms: "What is your grievance, mortal, that you give yourself up to this whining and repining? Why do you weep and wail over death? If the life you have lived till now has been a pleasant thing—if all its blessings have not leaked away like water poured into a cracked pot and run to waste unrelished—why then, you silly creature, do you not retire as a guest who has had his fill of life and take your care-free rest with a quiet mind? Or, if all your gains have been poured profitless away and life has grown distasteful, why do you seek to swell the total? The new can but turn out as badly as the old and perish as unprofitably. Why not rather make an end of life and labour? Do you expect me to invent some new contrivance for your pleasure? I tell you, there is none. All things are always the same. If your body is not yet withered with age, nor your limbs decrepit and flagging, even so there is nothing new to look forward to—not though you should outlive all living creatures, or even though you should never die at all." What are we to answer, except that Nature's rebuttal is justified and the plea she puts forward is a true one?

But suppose it is some man of riper years who complains—some dismal greybeard who frets unconscionably at his approaching end. Would she not have every right to protest more vehemently and repulse him in stern tones: "Away with your tears, old reprobate! Have done with your grumbling! You are withering now after tasting all the joys of life. But, because you are always pining for what is not and unappreciative of the things at hand, your life has slipped away unfulfilled and unprized. Death has stolen upon you unawares, before you are ready to retire from life's banquet filled and satisfied. Come now, put away all that is unbecoming to your years and compose your mind to make way for others. You have no choice." I cannot question but she would have right on her side; her censure and rebuke would be well merited. The old is always thrust aside to make way for the new, and one thing must be built out of the wreck of another. There is no murky pit of Hell awaiting anyone. There is need of matter, so that later generations may arise; when they have lived out their span, they will all follow you. Bygone generations have taken your road, and those to come will take it no less. So one thing will never cease to spring from another. To none is life given in freehold; to all on lease. Look back at the eternity that passed before we were born and mark how utterly it counts to us as nothing. This is a mirror that Nature holds up to us, in which we may see the time that shall be after we are dead. Is there anything terrifying in the sight—anything depressing—anything that is not more restful than the soundest sleep?

12

🐎

Seneca

....

Lucius Annaeus Seneca (c. 1 BCE–65 CE) was a philosopher, dramatist, and exponent of Stoicism. This philosophical tradition, so named because it was taught by its founder Zeno of Citium (c. 334–c. 262 BCE) from the Stoa Poikile (or "Painted Porch") in Athens, stressed the rational order of the universe and the need for fortitude in the face of life's inevitable difficulties. The following reading is a very brief extract from his essay on the happy life, identified here—against the views of the multitude—with virtue rather than pleasure, and with a life free from both fear and desire.

....

On the Happy Life

When we discuss the happy life, there is no reason for you to give me the well-known reply familiar from vote-counting: "This side seems to be in the majority." For that is why it is the worse side. Human concerns are not so happily arranged that the majority prefers the better things: evidence of the worst choice is the crowd. So let us enquire what is the best, not what is the most customary, thing to do, and what establishes our claim to unending happiness, not what the rabble, that worst of truth's exponents, has set its stamp of approval on. But by rabble I mean grand

DIALOGUES AND ESSAYS translated by Davie (2007) 1,460w from pp. 3, 7, 9, 15, 20, 86–88, 90–91, 93, 98, 101–102. By permission of Oxford University Press UK.

people just as much as ordinary folk; for I have no regard for the colour of clothing that adorns the body. In judging a man I do not trust my eyes, I have a better and more reliable light by which to distinguish truth from falsehood: let the soul's goodness be discovered by the soul. . . .

Let us seek something that is good not merely in outward appearance, something that is solid, balanced, and more beautiful in that part which is more hidden; let this be what we try to unearth. And it is not situated far away: it will be found, you need only know where to stretch out your hand; as it is, we pass by things that are near us, as though we are in darkness, and stumble over the very objects of our desire.

But not wishing to haul you through circuitous details, I will pass over without comment the opinions of other thinkers. . . . In the meantime, as is agreed among all Stoics, Nature is the guide I choose; wisdom lies in not wandering from her path and in moulding oneself in accordance with her law and example.

Accordingly, the happy life is the one that is in harmony with its own nature, and the only way it can be achieved is if, first, the mind is sound and constantly in possession of its sanity, and secondly, if it is brave and vigorous, and, in addition, attentive to the body and to all that affects it, but not in an anxious way, and, finally, if it concerns itself with all the things that enhance life, without showing undue respect for any one of them, taking advantage of Fortune's gifts, but not becoming their slave.

You understand, even if I were not to make this further point, that, once the things that either exasperate or scare us are banished, there follows a state of peace, of freedom, that knows no end; for once pleasures and pains have been scorned, then, in place of those things that are trivial and fragile and, because of their noxious effects, harmful, we experience a great joy that is steadfast and constant, then peace and harmony of mind and the greatness that goes with benevolence; for every impulse to cruelty is born from weakness. . . .

Even those who have stated that the highest good is located in the belly see in how dishonourable a place they have placed it. Accordingly, they say that pleasure cannot be separated from virtue, and they claim that no one can live honourably unless he also lives pleasantly, or pleasantly unless he also lives honourably. I fail to see how things so different from each other belong to the same potter's wheel. . . . Why do you seek to join two things that are not alike, indeed opposites? Virtue is something lofty, elevated, regal, unconquerable, and untiring: pleasure is something lowly and slavish, weak and destructible, whose haunt and living-quarters are brothels and taverns. Virtue you will find in a temple, in the forum, in the senate house, standing in front of the city walls, dusty and stained, with hands that are calloused: pleasure you will find more often lurking out of sight and searching for darkness around the baths and sweating-rooms and places that fear the aedile, soft and drained of strength, soaked with wine and perfume, with features that are pale or painted and tricked out with cosmetics like a corpse. The highest good is untouched by death, it knows no ending, it tolerates neither excess nor regret; for the upright mind never turns from its course, or succumbs to self-loathing or alters anything, being perfect. But pleasure is extinguished at the very moment it gives delight; it occupies only a small place, and therefore speedily fills it, and, becoming weary, loses its energy after the first assault. . . .

Why do you mention pleasure to me? I seek the good of a man, not of his belly, which has greater room in cattle and wild beasts. . . .

How can a man like this obey God and accept with cheerful heart whatever happens, not complaining about fate but interpreting in a genial spirit his own misfortunes, if he is disconcerted by the tiny pinpricks of pain and pleasure? But he is not even a good protector or champion of his homeland, or a defender of his friends, if he inclines towards pleasures. Accordingly, let the highest good ascend to a place from which no power can drag it down, where there can be no access for pain or hope or fear, or for anything which can diminish the authority of the highest good; but only Virtue is able to make the ascent to that place. It is her steps we must follow if that ascent is to be mastered; she will stand bravely and endure whatever happens, not only with patience but also with good cheer, knowing that every difficulty that time brings proceeds from a law of Nature, and, like a good soldier, she will bear her wounds, count her scars, and, as she dies, pierced by weapons, she will love the one in whose service she falls, her commander; she will keep in mind that old precept: follow God. But whoever complains and weeps and groans, is compelled by force to carry out commands, and, though unwilling, is hurried on regardless to perform his bidden tasks. But what lunacy to prefer to be dragged than to follow! This is tantamount, believe me, to the folly and ignorance of one's lot demonstrated when you grieve because you lack something or have suffered a rather harsh experience, or, equally, when you feel surprise or resentment at those things that happen to good people as much as to bad, I mean illness and death and infirmities, and all the other ills that strike at human life from unexpected quarters. Whatever we have to suffer as a result of the way the universe is framed, let it be endured with great fortitude; this is the solemn obligation to which we have sworn, that we will submit to our mortal lot and not be confounded by those things it is not in our power to avoid. We have been born under a monarchy: obedience to God is our liberty. . . .

The man who has set before him such ideals as these: "For my part, I shall look upon death with the same expression as when I hear of it. For my part, I shall undergo all hardships, however great they may be, supporting my body by means of my mind. For my part, I will hold riches in contempt, no less when they are mine to enjoy than when they are not, feeling no more dejected if they lie elsewhere, and no more emboldened if they shine around me. For my part, I will be indifferent to Fortune, whether she flows towards me or ebbs away. For my part, I shall view all lands as my own, and my own as belonging to others. For my part, I shall live as if I knew that I was born to benefit others, thanking Nature on this account: for in what way could my business prosper better? She has made a gift of me, the individual, to all men, and of all men to me, the individual. Whatever I possess, I shall not guard it in a miserly fashion, or squander it like a spendthrift. . . . I shall know that my homeland is the world, and that its rulers are the gods, and that they are the ones who stand above and around me, examining my acts and words with a severe eye. And whenever my breath of life is demanded back by Nature or re-leased by my own reason, I shall take my leave, having shown to all that I have loved a good conscience and noble aspirations, and that by no action of mine has any man's freedom been impaired, least of all my own—the man who shall resolve, shall wish, and shall attempt to do these things will be travelling the road that leads to the gods, yes, and such a man, even if he does not complete his journey,

Yet fails in no weak enterprise." (Ovid, *Metamorphoses* 2.328)

=== 🐌 ===

13

Martial

Marcus Valerius Martialis (c. 38–102), known more commonly as Martial, was born in Spain but moved to Rome when he was in his mid-twenties, spending most of the remainder of his life there. His 1,561 poems bring the life of Rome and its citizens wittily to life. In the selection included here, Martial presents to us what he sees as the elements of a happy life. In contrast to other writers who—as we frequently see in this anthology—stress that happiness is to be attained from a certain independence from worldly things, Martial's account is profoundly earthy: happiness is seen here to reside in the enjoyment of a number of material comforts and physical pleasures, alongside the attainment of a calm state of mind and an absence of anxiety with regard to one's own mortality.

X: 47

Of what does the happy life consist,
My dear friend, Julius? Here's a list:
Inherited wealth, no need to earn,
Fires that continually burn,
And fields that give a fair return,
No lawsuits, formal togas worn

From Martial, *Epigrams* (selected and translated by James Michie), (New York: Modern Library, 2002) (Epigram 47, p. 125).

Seldom, a calm mind, the freeborn
Gentleman's health and good physique.
Tact with the readiness to speak
Openly, friends of your own mind.
Guests of an easy-going kind,
Plain food, a table simply set,
Nights sober but wine-freed from fret,
A wife who's true to you and yet
No prude in bed, and sleep so sound
It makes the dawn come quickly round.
Be pleased with what you are, keep hope
Within that self-appointed scope;
Neither uneasily apprehend,
Nor morbidly desire the end.

===== 🐚 =====

14

Plutarch

....

Plutarch (c. 46–120) was a biographer and Platonist philosopher, best known for his *Parallel Lives* and also for his *Moralia*, a collection of ethical and philosophical essays, from which the following selection is taken. In these extracts from the lengthy "Letter of Condolence to Apollonius," Plutarch offers thoughts of consolation to his friend Apollonius following the untimely death of the latter's son. Concerned to show how "reason is the best remedy for the cure of grief," Plutarch draws on a great range of philosophical and literary insights and dwells on the deeply pessimistic thought that it would be better never to have been born. In Plutarch's hands, these thoughts are not merely an academic and intellectual exercise, but are intended for the sake of consolation and to demonstrate how a philosophical understanding of the nature of the human condition can produce tranquility, even in the face of the very saddest events.

....

Letter of Condolence to Apollonius

Reason is the best remedy for the cure of grief, reason, and the preparedness through reason for all the changes of life. For one ought to realize, not merely that he himself is mortal by nature, but also that he is allotted

---

From Plutarch, "A Letter of Condolence to Apollonius", from Plutarch's Moralia (in Sixteen Volumes), Vol. II (Cambridge, MA: Harvard University Press, 1928), pp. 119, 137, 139, 141, 149, 151, 157, 159, 177, 179, 181.

to a life that is mortal and to conditions which readily reverse themselves. For men's bodies are indeed mortal, lasting but a day, and mortal is all that they experience and suffer, and, in a word, everything in life; and all this

[m]ay not be escaped nor avoided by mortals [Homer's *Illiad*]

at all, but

The depths of unseen Tartarus hold you fast by hard-forged necessities,

as Pindar says. Whence Demetrius of Phalerum was quite right when, in reference to a saying of Euripides:

Wealth is inconstant, lasting but a day,

and also:

Small things may cause an overthrow; one day
Puts down the mighty and exalts the low,

he said that it was almost all admirably put, but it would have been better if he had said not "one day," but "one second of time."

Socrates said that death resembles either a very deep sleep or a long and distant journey, or, thirdly, a sort of destruction and extinction of both the body and the soul, but that by no one of these possibilities is it an evil. Each of these conceptions he pursued further, and the first one first. For if death is a sleep, and there is nothing evil in the state of those who sleep, it is evident that there is likewise nothing evil in the state of those who are dead. Nay, what need is there even to state that the deepest sleep is indeed the sweetest? For the fact is of itself patent to all men, and Homer bears witness by saying regarding it:

Slumber the deepest and sweetest, and nearest to death in its semblance.

In another place also he says:

Here she chanced to encounter the brother of Death, which is Slumber, and

> Slumber and Death, the twin brothers,

thereby indicating their similarity in appearance, for twins show most similarity. And again somewhere he says that death is a "brazen sleep" in allusion to our insensibility in it.

If death indeed resembles a journey, even so it is not an evil. On the contrary, it may even be a good. For to pass one's time unenslaved by the flesh and its emotions, by which the mind is distracted and tainted with human folly, would be a blessed piece of good fortune.

If, however, death is really a complete destruction and dissolution of both body and soul (for this was the third of Socrates's conjectures), even so it is not an evil. For, according to him, there ensues a sort of insensibility and a liberation from all pain and anxiety. For just as no good can attach to us in such a state, so also can no evil; for just as the good, from its nature, can exist only in the case of that which is and has substantiality, so it is also with the evil. But in the case of that which is not, but has been removed from the sphere of being, neither of them can have any real existence. Now those who have died return to the same state in which they were before birth; therefore, as nothing was either good or evil for us before birth, even so will it be with us after death. And just as all events before our lifetime were nothing to us, even so will all events subsequent to our lifetime be nothing to us. For in reality

> No suffering affects the dead,

since

> Not to be born I count the same as death [Euripides, *Trojan Women*].

For the condition after the end of life is the same as that before birth. But do you imagine that there is a difference between not being born at all, and being born and then passing away? Surely not, unless you assume also that there is a difference in a house or a garment of ours after its destruction, as compared with the time when it had not yet been fashioned. But if there is no difference in these cases, it is evident that there is no difference in the case of death, either, as compared with the condition before birth. Arcesilaus puts the matter neatly: "This that we call an evil, death, is the only one of the supposed evils which, when present, has never caused anybody any pain, but causes pain when it is not present but merely expected."

In general everyone ought to hold the conviction, if he seriously reviews the facts both by himself and in the company of another, that not the longest life is the best, but the most efficient. For it is not the man who has played the lyre the most, or made the most speeches, or piloted the most ships, who is commended, but he who has done these things excellently. Excellence is not to be ascribed to length of time, but to worth and timely fitness. For these have come to be regarded as tokens of good fortune and of divine favour. It is for this reason, at any rate, that the poets have traditionally represented those of the heroes who were preeminent and sprung from the gods as quitting this life before old age, like him

> Who to the heart of great Zeus and Apollo was held to be dearest,
> Loved with exceeding great love; but of eld he reached not the
> threshold [Homer, *Odyssey*].

For we everywhere observe that it is a happy use of opportunity, rather than a happy old age, that wins the highest place. For of trees and plants the best are those that in a brief time produce the most crops of fruit, and the best of animals are those from which in no long time we have the greatest service toward our livelihood. The terms "long" and "short" obviously appear to lose their difference if we fix our gaze on eternity. For a thousand or ten thousand years, according to Simonides, are but a vague second of time, or rather the smallest fraction of a second. Take the case of those creatures which they relate exist on the shores of the Black Sea, and have an existence of only one day, being born in the morning, reaching the prime of life at mid-day, and toward evening growing old and ending their existence; would there not be in those creatures this same feeling which prevails with us, if each of them had within him a human soul and power to reason, and would not the same relative conditions obviously obtain there, so that those who departed this life before mid-day would cause lamentation and tears, while those who lived through the day would be accounted altogether happy? The measure of life is its excellence, not its length in years.

. . .

We must regard as vain and foolish such exclamations as these: "But he ought not to have been snatched away while young!" For who may say what ought to be? Many other things, of which one may say "they ought not to have been done," have been done, and are done, and will be done over and over again. For we have come into this world, not to make laws for its governance, but to obey the commandments of the gods who preside over the universe, and the decrees of Fate or Providence.

. . .

Not merely now, but long ago, as Crantor says, the lot of man has been bewailed by many wise men, who have felt that life is a punishment and that for man to be born at all is the greatest calamity. Aristotle says that Silenus when he was captured declared this to Midas. It is better to quote the very words of the philosopher. He says, in the work which is entitled *Eudemus,* or *Of the Soul,* the following: "'Wherefore, O best and blessedest of all, in addition to believing that those who have ended this life are blessed and happy, we also think that to say anything false or slanderous against them is impious, from our feeling that it is directed against those who have already become our betters and superiors. And this is such an old and ancient belief with us that no one knows at all either the beginning of the time or the name of the person who first promulgated it, but it continues to be a fixed belief for all time. And in addition to this you observe how the saying, which is on the lips of all men, has been passed from mouth to mouth for many years.' 'What is this?' said he. And the other, again taking up the discourse, said: 'That not to be born is the best of all, and that to be dead is better than to live. And the proof that this is so has been given to many men by the deity. So, for example, they say that Silenus, after the hunt in which Midas of yore had captured him, when Midas questioned and inquired of him what is the best thing for mankind and what is the most preferable of all things, was at first unwilling to tell, but maintained a stubborn silence. But when at last, by employing every device, Midas induced him to say something to him, Silenus, forced to speak, said: "Ephemeral offspring of a travailing genius and of harsh fortune, why do you force me to speak what it were better for you men not to know? For a life spent in ignorance of one's own woes is most free from grief. But for men it is utterly impossible that they should obtain the best thing of all, or even have any share in its nature (for the best thing for all men and women is not to be born); however, the next best thing to this, and the first of those to which man can attain, but nevertheless only the second best, is, after being born, to die as quickly

as possible." It is evident, therefore, that he made this declaration with the conviction that the existence after death is better than that in life.'"
One might cite thousands and thousands of examples under this same head, but there is no need to be prolix.

. . .

We ought not, therefore, to lament those who die young on the ground that they have been deprived of those things which in a long life are accounted good; for this is uncertain, as we have often said—whether the things of which they have been deprived are good or evil; for the evils are much the more numerous. And whereas we acquire the good things only with difficulty and at the expense of many anxieties, the evils we acquire very easily. For they say that the latter are compact and conjoined, and are brought together by many influences, while the good things are disjoined, and hardly manage to unite towards the very end of life. We therefore resemble men who have forgotten, not merely, as Euripides says, that

Mortals are not the owners of their wealth,

but also that they do not own a single one of human possessions. Wherefore we must say in regard to all things that

We keep and care for that which is the gods',
And when they will they take it back again.

15

Epictetus

Epictetus (55–135) was a major exponent of Stoicism. Born in Phrygia (in what is now southwestern Turkey), Epictetus came to Rome as a slave; later freed, he opened his own school in Greece. A story—possibly apocryphal—about Epictetus's life as a slave seems emblematic of his philosophical outlook and its recommendations regarding the proper response to suffering. On an occasion when his master, Epaphroditus, was torturing him by violently twisting his leg, Epictetus calmly warned that to continue twisting in that manner would result in his leg being broken; when his leg did indeed break, Epictetus simply said, "There, did I not tell you it would break?" In the selections from *The Manual* (or *Enchiridion*) below, this attitude of acceptance of things that lie beyond one's control—the very heart of Stoicism—is clearly outlined and described.

The Manual (or Enchiridion)

1. Of all existing things some are in our power, and others are not in our power. In our power are thought, impulse, will to get and will to avoid, and, in a word, everything which is our own doing. Things not in our power include the body, property,

Selections from "The Manual of Epictetus", in Epictetus, The Discourses and Manual (translated by P. E. Matheson) (Oxford: Clarendon Press, 1916).

reputation, office, and, in a word, everything which is not our own doing. Things in our power are by nature free, unhindered, untrammelled; things not in our power are weak, servile, subject to hindrance, dependent on others. Remember then that if you imagine that what is naturally slavish is free, and what is naturally another's is your own, you will be hampered, you will mourn, you will be put to confusion, you will blame gods and men; but if you think that only your own belongs to you, and that what is another's is indeed another's, no one will ever put compulsion or hindrance on you, you will blame none, you will accuse none, you will do nothing against your will, no one will harm you, you will have no enemy, for no harm can touch you. . . . Make it your study then to confront every harsh impression with the words, "You are but an impression, and not at all what you seem to be." Then test it by those rules that you possess; and first by this—the chief test of all—"Is it concerned with what is in our power or with what is not in our power?" And if it is concerned with what is not in our power, be ready with the answer that it is nothing to you.

3. When anything, from the meanest thing upwards, is attractive or serviceable or an object of affection, remember always to say to yourself, "What is its nature?" If you are fond of a jug, say you are fond of a jug; then you will not be disturbed if it be broken. If you kiss your child or your wife, say to yourself that you are kissing a human being, for then if death strikes it you will not be disturbed.

5. What disturbs men's minds is not events but their judgements on events: For instance, death is nothing dreadful, or else Socrates would have thought it so. No, the only dreadful thing about it is men's judgement that it is dreadful. And so when we are hindered, or disturbed, or distressed, let us never lay the blame on others, but on ourselves, that is, on our own judgements. To accuse others for one's own misfortunes is a sign of want of education; to accuse oneself shows that one's education has begun; to accuse neither oneself nor others shows that one's education is complete.

8. Ask not that events should happen as you will, but let your will be that events should happen as they do, and you shall have peace.

11. Never say of anything, "I lost it," but say, "I gave it back." Has your child died? It was given back. Has your wife died? She was given back. Has your estate been taken from you? Was not this

also given back? But you say, "He who took it from me is wicked." What does it matter to you through whom the Giver asked it back? As long as He gives it you, take care of it, but not as your own; treat it as passers-by treat an inn.

14. It is silly to want your children and your wife and your friends to live for ever, for that means that you want what is not in your control to be in your control, and what is not your own to be yours. . . . Let him then who wishes to be free not wish for anything or avoid anything that depends on others; or else he is bound to be a slave.

17. Remember that you are an actor in a play, and the Playwright chooses the manner of it: if he wants it short, it is short; if long, it is long. If he wants you to act a poor man you must act the part with all your powers; and so if your part be a cripple or a magistrate or a plain man. For your business is to act the character that is given you and act it well; the choice of the cast is Another's.

20. Remember that foul words or blows in themselves are no outrage, but your judgement that they are so. So when any one makes you angry, know that it is your own thought that has angered you. Wherefore make it your first endeavour not to let your impressions carry you away. For if once you gain time and delay, you will find it easier to control yourself.

26. It is in our power to discover the will of Nature from those matters on which we have no difference of opinion. For instance, when another man's slave has broken the wine-cup we are very ready to say at once, "Such things must happen." Know then that when your own cup is broken, you ought to behave in the same way as when your neighbour's was broken. Apply the same principle to higher matters. Is another's child or wife dead? Not one of us but would say, "Such is the lot of man"; but when one's own dies, straightway one cries, "Alas! miserable am I." But we ought to remember what our feelings are when we hear it of another.

31. For piety towards the gods know that the most important thing is this: to have right opinions about them—that they exist, and that they govern the universe well and justly—and to have set yourself to obey them, and to give way to all that happens, following events with a free will, in the belief that they are fulfilled by the highest mind. For thus you will never blame the gods, nor accuse them of neglecting you. But this you cannot achieve, unless you apply your

conception of good and evil to those things only which are in our power, and not to those which are out of our power.

33. In your conversation avoid frequent and disproportionate mention of your own doings or adventures; for other people do not take the same pleasure in hearing what has happened to you as you take in recounting your adventures.

34. When you imagine some pleasure, beware that it does not carry you away, like other imaginations. Wait a while, and give yourself pause. Next remember two things: how long you will enjoy the pleasure, and also how long you will afterwards repent and revile yourself. And set on the other side the joy and self-satisfaction you will feel if you refrain. And if the moment seems come to realize it, take heed that you be not overcome by the winning sweetness and attraction of it; set in the other scale the thought how much better is the consciousness of having vanquished it.

41. It is a sign of a dull mind to dwell upon the cares of the body, to prolong exercise, eating, drinking, and other bodily functions. These things are to be done by the way; all your attention must be given to the mind.

48. The ignorant man's position and character is this: he never looks to himself for benefit or harm, but to the world outside him. The philosopher's position and character is that he always looks to himself for benefit and harm.

===== 𝕤 =====

Plotinus

....

The Enneads of Plotinus (204–270) is both the principal exposition of Neoplatonism (a philosophy developed from the teachings of Plato and known for describing the derivation of reality from a single principle, called "the One") and a classic of Western mysticism. In the first set of readings, we find Plotinus discussing reincarnation, and the laws that determine what a person's subsequent life will be, while the second selection concerns free will, the "spring" of which, according to Plotinus, is "the activity of Intellectual-Principle, the highest in our being."

....

The Enneads

III.2.13. And we must not despise the familiar observation that there is something more to be considered than the present. There are the periods of the past and, again, those in the future; and these have everything to do with fixing worth of place.

Thus a man, once a ruler, will be made a slave because he abused his power and because the fall is to his future good. Those that have misused money will be made poor—and to the good poverty is no hindrance. Those that have unjustly killed, are killed in turn, unjustly as regards the

From Plotinus, The Enneads (translated by Stephen MacKenna) (London: Faber & Faber, 1956).

murderer but justly as regards the victim, and those that are to suffer are thrown into the path of those that administer the merited treatment.

It is not an accident that makes a man a slave; no one is a prisoner by chance; every bodily outrage has its due cause. The man once did what he now suffers. A man that murders his mother will become a woman and be murdered by a son; a man that wrongs a woman will become a woman, to be wronged.

Hence arises that awesome word Adrasteia (the Inevadable Retribution); for in very truth this ordinance is an Adrasteia, Justice itself and a wonderful wisdom.

We cannot but recognize from what we observe in this universe that some such principle of order prevails throughout the entire of existence—the minutest of things a tributary to the vast total; the marvellous art shown not merely in the mightiest works and sublimest members of the All, but even amid such littleness as one would think Providence must disdain: the varied workmanship of wonder in any and every animal form; the world of vegetation, too; the grace of fruits and even of leaves, the lavishness, the delicacy, the diversity of exquisite bloom: and all this not issuing once, and then to die out, but made ever and ever anew as the Transcendent Beings move variously over this earth.

In all the changing, there is no change by chance: there is no taking of new forms but to desirable ends and in ways worthy of Divine Powers. All that is Divine executes the Act of its quality; its quality is the expression of its essential Being: and this essential Being in the Divine is the Being whose activities produce as one thing the desirable and the just—for if the good and the just are not produced there, where, then, have they their being?

III.4.2. It is of this Soul especially that we read "All Soul has care for the Soulless"—though the several souls thus care in their own degree and way. The passage continues—"Soul passes through the entire heavens in forms varying with the variety of place"—the sensitive form, the reasoning form, even the vegetative form—and this means that in each "place" the phase of the Soul there dominant carries out its own ends while the rest, not present there, is idle.

Now, in humanity the lower is not supreme; it is an accompaniment; but neither does the better rule unfailingly; the lower element also has a footing, and Man, therefore, lives in part under sensation, for he has the organs of sensation, and in large part even by the merely vegetative principle, for the body grows and propagates: all the graded phases are in a collaboration, but the entire form, man, takes rank by the dominant, and when the life-principle leaves the body it is what it is, what it most intensely lived.

This is why we must break away towards the High: we dare not keep ourselves set towards the sensuous principle, following the images of sense, or towards the merely vegetative, intent upon the gratifications of eating and procreation; our life must be pointed towards the Intellective, towards the Intellectual-Principle, towards God.

Those that have maintained the human level are men once more. Those that have lived wholly to sense become animals—corresponding in species to the particular temper of the life—ferocious animals where the sensuality has been accompanied by a certain measure of spirit, gluttonous and lascivious animals; where all has been appetite and satiation of appetite. Those who in their pleasures have not even lived by sensation, but have gone their way in a torpid grossness become mere growing things, for only or mainly the vegetative principle was active in them, and such men have been busy be-treeing themselves. Those, we read, that, otherwise untainted, have loved song become vocal animals; kings ruling unreasonably but with no other vice are eagles; futile and flighty visionaries ever soaring skyward, become high-flying birds; observance of civic and secular virtue makes man again, or where the merit is less marked, one of the animals of communal tendency, a bee or the like.

VI.8.1. Can there be question as to whether the gods have voluntary action? Or are we to take it that while we may well inquire in the case of men with their combination of powerlessness and hesitating power, the gods must be declared omnipotent, not merely some things but all lying at their nod? Or is power entire, freedom of action in all things, to be reserved to one alone, of the rest some being powerful, others powerless, others again a blend of power and impotence?

All this must come to the test: we must dare it even of the Firsts and of the All-Transcendent and if we find omnipotence possible work out how far freedom extends. The very notion of power must be scrutinized lest in this ascription we be really setting up an antithesis of power (potency) and Act, and identifying power with Act not yet achieved.

But for the moment we may pass over these questions to deal with the traditional problem of freedom of action in ourselves. To begin with, what must be intended when we assert that something is in our power; what is the conception here?

To establish this will help to show whether we are to ascribe freedom to the gods and still more to God, or to refuse it, or again, while asserting it, to question still, in regard both to the higher and lower, the mode of its presence.

What then do we mean when we speak of freedom in ourselves and why do we question it?

My own reading is that, moving as we do amid adverse fortunes, compulsions, violent assaults of passion crushing the soul, feeling ourselves mastered by these experiences, playing slave to them, going where they lead, we have been brought by all this to doubt whether we are anything at all and dispose of ourselves in any particular.

This would indicate that we think of our free act as one which we execute of our own choice, in no servitude to chance or necessity or overmastering passion, nothing thwarting our will; the voluntary is conceived as an event amenable to will and occurring or not as our will dictates. Everything will be voluntary that is produced under no compulsion and with knowledge; our free act is what we are masters to perform.

Differing conceptually, the two conditions will often coincide but sometimes will clash. Thus a man would be master to kill but the act will not be voluntary if in the victim he had failed to recognize his own father. Perhaps, however, that ignorance is not compatible with real freedom: for the knowledge necessary to a voluntary act cannot be limited to certain particulars but must cover the entire field. Why, for example, should killing be involuntary in the failure to recognize a father and not so in the failure to recognize the wickedness of murder? If because the killer ought to have learned, still ignorance of the duty of learning and the cause of that ignorance remain alike involuntary.

2. A cardinal question is where are we to place the freedom of action ascribed to us.

It must be founded in impulse or in some appetite, as when we act or omit in lust or rage or upon some calculation of advantage accompanied by desire.

But if rage or desire implied freedom we must allow freedom to animals, infants, maniacs, the distraught, the victims of malpractice producing incontrollable delusions. And if freedom turns on calculation with desire, does this include faulty calculation? Sound calculation, no doubt, and sound desire; but then comes the question whether the appetite stirs the calculation or the calculation the appetite.

Where the appetites are dictated by the very nature they are either the desires of the conjoint of soul and body and then soul lies under physical compulsions; or they spring in the soul as an independent, and then much that we take to be voluntary is in reality outside of our free act. Further, does the soul advance any reasoning which is free from emotion, and can a compelling imagination, an appetite drawing us where it will, be supposed to leave us masters in the ensuing act? How can we be masters when we are compelled? Need, inexorably craving satisfaction, is not free in face of that to which it is forced: and how at all can a thing have efficiency of its own when it rises from an extern, has an extern for very principle, thence taking its being as it stands?

It lives by that extern, lives as it has been moulded: if this be freedom, there is freedom in even the soulless; fire acts in accordance with its characteristic being.

We may be reminded that the Living Form and the Soul know what they do, But if this is knowledge by perception it does not help towards the freedom of the act; perception gives awareness, not mastery: if true knowing is meant, either this is the knowing of something happening—once more awareness—with the motive-force still to seek, or the reasoning and knowledge have acted to quell the appetite; then we have to ask to what this repression is to be referred and where it has taken place. If it is that the mental process sets up an opposing desire we must assure ourselves how; if it merely stills the appetite with no further efficiency and this is our freedom, then freedom does not depend upon act but is a thing of the mind—and in truth all that has to do with act, the very most reasonable, is still of mixed value and cannot carry freedom.

3. All this calls for examination; the inquiry must bring us close to the solution as regards the gods.

We have traced self-disposal to will, will to reasoning and, next step, to right reasoning; perhaps to right reasoning we must add knowledge, for however sound opinion and act may be they do not yield true freedom when the adoption of the right course is the result of hazard or of some presentment from the fancy with no knowledge of the foundations of that rightness.

Taking it that the presentment of fancy is not a matter of our will and choice, how can we think those acting at its dictation to be free agents? Fancy strictly, in our use, takes its rise from conditions of the body; lack of food and drink sets up presentments and so does the meeting of these needs; similarly with seminal abundance and other humours of the body. We refuse to range under the principle of freedom those whose conduct is directed by such fancy: the baser sort, therefore, mainly so guided, cannot be credited with self-disposal or voluntary act. Self-disposal, to us, belongs to those who, through the activities of the Intellectual-Principle, live above the states of the body. The spring of freedom is the activity of Intellectual-Principle, the highest in our being; the proposals emanating thence are freedom; such desires as are formed in the exercise of the Intellectual act cannot be classed as involuntary; the gods, therefore, that live in this state, living by Intellectual-Principle and by desire conformed to it, possess freedom.

PART THREE

Medieval Texts

17

Augustine

....

Born to a pagan father and Christian mother (St. Monica) in North Africa in the Roman Empire, Augustine (354–430) spent part of his youth as a follower of the dualistic religion of the Manichaeans. When he broke with them, he explored Platonism, resisting his mother's Christianity and its demands of chastity, famously praying, "God, make me chaste, but not yet!" He fathered a son, Adeodatus, with a long-term companion. His career teaching rhetoric took him to Milan—then the capital of the Roman Empire—where he met St. Ambrose and, having heard a child's voice calling out "Tolle et lege," ("Take up and read"), he picked up the nearest book, a New Testament, and was converted.

Augustine turned his classical learning to an exploration and explanation of his new faith, creating a synthesis that endures in Christian thought. In many ways, he became a second St. Paul. His works have been taken as authoritative throughout most of Western Christianity and debates about the meaning of his interpretations of Christianity motivated many of the fights of the Reformation and Counter-Reformation and those between the Jansenists and Pascal and the Jesuits, with every side claiming him.

He became a priest and then the bishop of Hippo, again in North Africa. He died in that city with his people during a siege by the Vandals.

In the selection here from the *Confessions*, a very early example of autobiography, Augustine gives an account of the depravity he finds in all human nature.

In the selections from *On the Free Choice of the Will*, Augustine addresses the role of reason in human life and the freedom of the will and its value in spite of its role in evildoing.

In the selection from *On Genesis*, Augustine muses as to the purpose of the creation of men and women, rather than just men.

Finally, in the short selection from *The City of God*, we see Augustine proving that he can know at least that he exists, a precursor of Descartes' "I think, therefore I am."

....

Confessions

Book I

Hear, O God. Alas, for man's sin! So saith man, and Thou pitiest him; for Thou madest him, but sin in him Thou madest not. Who remindeth me of the sins of my infancy? for in Thy sight none is pure from sin, not even the infant whose life is but a day upon the earth. Who remindeth me? doth not each little infant, in whom I see what of myself I remember not? What then was my sin? was it that I hung upon the breast and cried? for should I now so do for food suitable to my age, justly should I be laughed at and reproved. What I then did was worthy reproof; but since I could not understand reproof, custom and reason forbade me to be reproved. For those habits, when grown, we root out and cast away. Now no man, though he prunes, wittingly casts away what is good. Or was it then good, even for a while, to cry for what, if given, would hurt? bitterly to resent, that persons free, and its own elders, yea, the very authors of its birth, served it not? that many besides, wiser than it, obeyed not the nod of its good pleasure? to do its best to strike and hurt, because commands were not obeyed, which had been obeyed to its hurt? The weakness then of infant limbs, not its will, is its innocence. Myself have seen and known even a baby envious; it could not speak, yet it turned pale and looked bitterly on its foster-brother. Who knows not this? Mothers and nurses tell you that they allay these things by I know not what remedies. Is that too innocence, when the

---

From Pusey, EB (trans), *Confessions* 1838 Book I, 1, Book II, 1, 3–5.

fountain of milk is flowing in rich abundance, not to endure one to share it, though in extremest need, and whose very life as yet depends thereon? We bear gently with all this, not as being no or slight evils, but because they will disappear as years increase; for, though tolerated now, the very same tempers are utterly intolerable when found in riper years.

Book II

I will now call to mind my past foulness, and the carnal corruptions of my soul; not because I love them, but that I may love Thee, O my God. For love of Thy love I do it; reviewing my most wicked ways in the very bitterness of my remembrance, that Thou mayest grow sweet unto me (Thou sweetness never failing, Thou blissful and assured sweetness); and gathering me again out of that my dissipation, wherein I was torn piecemeal, while turned from Thee, the One Good, I lost myself among a multiplicity of things. For I even burnt in my youth heretofore, to be satiated in things below; and I dared to grow wild again, with these various and shadowy loves: my beauty consumed away, and I stank in Thine eyes; pleasing myself, and desirous to please in the eyes of men.

. . .

Behold with what companions I walked the streets of Babylon, and wallowed in the mire thereof, as if in a bed of spices and precious ointments. And that I might cleave the faster to its very centre, the invisible enemy trod me down, and seduced me, for that I was easy to be seduced. Neither did the mother of my flesh (who had now fled out of the centre of Babylon, yet went more slowly in the skirts thereof as she advised me to chastity, so heed what she had heard of me from her husband, as to restrain within the bounds of conjugal affection (if it could not be pared away to the quick) what she felt to be pestilent at present and for the future dangerous. She heeded not this, for she feared lest a wife should prove a clog and hindrance to my hopes. Not those hopes of the world to come, which my mother reposed in Thee; but the hope of learning, which both my parents were too desirous

I should attain; my father, because he had next to no thought of Thee, and of me but vain conceits; my mother, because she accounted that those usual courses of learning would not only be no hindrance, but even some furtherance towards attaining Thee. For thus I conjecture, recalling, as well as I may, the disposition of my parents. The reins, meantime, were slackened to me, beyond all temper of due severity, to spend my time in sport, yea, even unto dissoluteness in whatsoever I affected. And in all was a mist, intercepting from me, O my God, the brightness of Thy truth; and mine iniquity burst out as from very fatness.

...

Theft is punished by Thy law, O Lord, and the law written in the hearts of men, which iniquity itself effaces not. For what thief will abide a thief? not even a rich thief, one stealing through want. Yet I lusted to thieve, and did it, compelled by no hunger, nor poverty, but through a cloyedness of well-doing, and a pamperedness of iniquity. For I stole that, of which I had enough, and much better. Nor cared I to enjoy what I stole, but joyed in the theft and sin itself. A pear tree there was near our vineyard, laden with fruit, tempting neither for colour nor taste. To shake and rob this, some lewd young fellows of us went, late one night (having according to our pestilent custom prolonged our sports in the streets till then), and took huge loads, not for our eating, but to fling to the very hogs, having only tasted them. And this, but to do what we liked only, because it was misliked. Behold my heart, O God, behold my heart, which Thou hadst pity upon in the bottom of the bottomless pit. Now, behold, let my heart tell Thee what it sought there, that I should be gratuitously evil, having no temptation to ill, but the ill itself. It was foul, and I loved it; I loved to perish, I loved mine own fault, not that for which I was faulty, but my fault itself. Foul soul, falling from Thy firmament to utter destruction; not seeking aught through the shame, but the shame itself!

...

For there is an attractiveness in beautiful bodies, in gold and silver, and all things; and in bodily touch, sympathy hath much influence, and each other sense hath his proper object answerably tempered. Wordly honour hath also its grace, and the power of overcoming, and of mastery; whence springs also the thirst of revenge. But yet, to obtain all these, we may not depart from Thee, O Lord, nor decline from Thy law. The life also which here we live hath its own enchantment, through a certain proportion of its own, and a correspondence with all things beautiful here below. Human friendship also is endeared with a sweet tie, by reason of the unity formed of many souls. Upon occasion of all these, and the like, is sin committed, while through an immoderate inclination towards these goods of the lowest order, the better and higher are forsaken,—Thou, our Lord God, Thy truth, and Thy law. For these lower things have their delights, but not like my God, who made all things; for in Him doth the righteous delight, and He is the joy of the upright in heart.

On Free Choice of the Will

Augustine. This is what I mean: whatever it is that sets man above beast—whether it is called mind or spirit (or, more correctly, both, since we find both in the Holy Scriptures)—if it controls and commands whatever else man consists of, then man is ordered in the highest degree. We see that we have many things in common not only with beasts, but even with trees and plants. Trees, though they are on the lowest plane of life, take nourishment, grow, reproduce, and become strong. Furthermore, beasts see, hear, and can perceive corporeal things by touch, taste, and smell more keenly than we. Add to this energy, power, strength of limb, speed, and agility of bodily motion. In all of these faculties we excel some, equal others, and to some are inferior.

Things of this sort we clearly share with beasts. Indeed, to seek the pleasures of the body and to avoid harm constitute the entire activity of a beast's life. There are other things which do not seem to fall to the lot of beasts, but which nevertheless are not the highest attributes of man: jesting and laughing, for example, which anyone who judges human nature correctly judges to be human, though he rates them low. Again, there are the love of praise and glory and the desire for power; while beasts do not have these, nevertheless we are not to be judged better than beasts because of them. For this craving, when not subject to reason, makes men wretched, and no one has ever thought himself superior to another because of his own wretchedness. When reason is master of these emotions, a man may be said to be well ordered. No order in which the better are subject to the worse can be called right, or can even be called order at all. Do you agree?

Evodius. It is obvious.

A. Therefore, when reason, whether mind or spirit, rules the irrational emotions, then there exists in man the very mastery which the law that we know to be eternal prescribes.

E. I understand and follow.

No one can force the soul to be a slave to lust.

E. But let us take up some other arguments. We have already proved that governance by the human mind is human wisdom, and that the mind may not always rule.

From Benjamin, Anna S., and Hackstaff, L.H. (trans.), *On Free Choice of the Will*, Indianapolis: Bobbs Merrill, 1964, p. 18–19, 20–21, 36.

A. Do you think that any lust can overpower that mind to which we know dominion over lusts has been granted by eternal law? I myself do not think so. For the order [of the universe] would not be the most excellent possible if the weaker commanded the stronger. Therefore, it necessarily follows that the mind is more powerful than desire, because it is right and just that it should rule desire.

E. I think so too.

A. We would not hesitate, would we, to prefer every virtue to every vice, so that the stronger and more invincible a virtue is, the better and nobler it is?

E. Of course not.

A. Therefore, no vicious spirit overcomes the spirit armed by virtue.

E. Very true.

A. I think that you will not deny that any spirit what-ever is better and more powerful than any body.

E. No one denies it who sees, as he easily may, that a living substance is to be preferred to a non-living one, and that the thing that gives life is to be preferred to that which receives it.

A. So much the less, then, does the body, whatever it may be, overcome the spirit endowed with virtue.

E. Obviously.

A. What then? Can the just spirit, and the mind that is watchful over its own right and rule, throw down from its citadel another mind which rules with justice and virtue, and subjugate it to lust?

E. By no means; not only because the same excellence is in each, but also because the former mind will fall away from justice and become sinful; it will become weaker in trying to make the other sinful.

A. You understand well. It remains for you to answer this, if you can: do you think there is anything more excellent than a rational and wise mind?

E. Nothing, I think, except God.

A. This is my opinion too. But though we accept this with the strongest faith, understanding it is a very difficult matter. This is not the time to take it up, since our investigation of this question must be careful and systematic.

. . .

A. If man is a goody [a good thing], and cannot act rightly unless he wills to do so, then he must have free will, without which he cannot act rightly. We must not believe that God gave us free will so that we might sin, just because sin is committed through free-will. It is sufficient for our question, why free will should have been given to man, to know that without it man cannot live rightly. That it was given for this reason can be understood from the following: if anyone uses free will for sinning, he incurs divine punishment. This would be unjust if free will had been given, not only that man might live rightly, but also that he might sin. For how could a man justly incur punishment who used free will to do the thing for which it was given?—When God punishes a sinner, does He not seem to say, "Why have you not used free will for the purpose for which I gave it to you, to act rightly"? Then too if man did not have free choice of will, how could there exist the good according to which it is just to condemn evildoers and reward those who act rightly? What was not done by will would be neither evildoing nor right action. Both punishment and reward would be unjust if man did not have free will.

Moreover, there must needs be justice both in punishment and in reward, since justice is one of the goods that are from God. Therefore, God must needs have given free will to man.

On Genesis

Or if it was not for help in producing children that a wife was made for the man, then what other help was she made for? If it was to till the earth together, with him, there was as yet no hard toil to need such assistance; and if there had been the need, a male would have made a better help. The same can be said about companionship, should he grow tired of solitude. How much more agreeably, after all, for conviviality and conversation would two male friends live together on equal terms than man and wife? While if it was expedient that one should be in charge and the other should comply, to avoid a clash of wills disturbing the peace of the household, such an arrangement would have been ensured by one being made first, the other later, especially if the latter were created from the former, as the female was in fact created. Or would anyone say that God was only able to make a female from the man's rib, and not also a male if he so wished? For these reasons I cannot work out what help a wife could have been made to provide the man with, if you take away the purpose of childbearing.

From Hill, Edmund, OP (trans) *On Genesis*, Hyde Park, New York: New City Press, 2002, p. 380.

The City of God

Book XI, Chapter 26

For we both are, and know that we are, and delight in our being, and our knowledge of it. Moreover, in these three things no true-seeming illusion disturbs us; for we do not come into contact with these by some bodily sense, as we perceive the things outside of us,—colors, e.g., by seeing, sounds by hearing, smells by smelling, tastes by tasting, hard and soft objects by touching,—of all which sensible objects it is the images resembling them, but not themselves which we perceive in the mind and hold in the memory, and which excite us to desire the objects. But, without any delusive representation of images or phantasms, I am most certain that I am, and that I know and delight in this. In respect of these truths, I am not at all afraid of the arguments of the Academicians, who say, What if you are deceived? For if I am deceived, I am. For he who is not, cannot be deceived; and if I am deceived, by this same token I am. And since I am if I am deceived, how am I deceived in believing that I am? For it is certain that I am if I am deceived. Since, therefore, I, the person deceived, should be, even if I were deceived, certainly I am not deceived in this knowledge that I am. And, consequently, neither am I deceived in knowing that I know. For, as I know that I am, so I know this also, that I know. And when I love these two things, I add to them a certain third thing, namely, my love, which is of equal moment. For neither am I deceived in this, that I love, since in those things which I love I am not deceived; though even if these were false, it would still be true that I loved false things. For how could I justly be blamed and prohibited from loving false things, if it were false that I loved them? But, since they are true and real, who doubts that when they are loved, the love of them is itself true and real? Further, as there is no one who does not wish to be happy, so there is no one who does not wish to be. For how can he be happy, if he is nothing?

From Dods, Marcus (trans), *The City of God*, 1876.

18

Boethius

Ancius Boethius (c. 480–524) was a Roman philosopher and public political figure during the reign of the Gothic emperor Theodoric. He rose to the level of consul, but was later imprisoned and executed on charges of treason and conspiracy. Whilst awaiting execution, Boethius composed his masterpiece, *The Consolation of Philosophy*, a conversation between the ailing prisoner and his "nurse," Lady Philosophy. The first readings address the capricious nature of fortune and the proper route to happiness. The second set concerns free will, and deals both with its nature and with the threat posed to its possibility by the existence of an omniscient God who, it would appear, must know all the future actions of human beings.

The Consolation of Philosophy

Book II, Chapter 2

"I would like to continue our discussion a while by using Fortune's own arguments, and I would like you to consider whether her demands are just. 'Why do you burden me each day, mortal man,' she asks, 'with your querulous accusations? What harm have I done you? What possessions of yours have I stolen? Choose any judge you like and sue me for possession

---

Boethius, *The Consolation of Philosophy* (translated by Victor E. Watts) (London: Penguin, 1969), pp. 56–57, 90–92, 99–100, 149–150, 150–151, 152–153, 163–164, 165.

of wealth and rank, and if you can show that any part of these belongs by right to any mortal man, I will willingly concede that what you are seeking to regain really did belong to you. When nature brought you forth from your mother's womb I received you naked and devoid of everything and fed you from my own resources. I was inclined to favour you, and I brought you up—and this is what makes you lose patience with me—with a measure of indulgence, surrounding you with all the splendour and affluence at my command. Now I have decided to withdraw my hand. You have been receiving a favour as one who has had the use of another's possessions, and you have no right to complain as if what you have lost was fully your own. You have no cause to begin groaning at me: I have done you no violence. Wealth, honours, and the like are all under my jurisdiction. They are my servants and know their mistress. When I come, they come with me, and when I go, they leave as well. I can say with confidence that if the things whose loss you are bemoaning were really yours, you could never have lost them. Surely I am not the only one to be denied the exercise of my rights? The heavens are allowed to bring forth the bright daylight and lay it to rest in the darkness of night: the year is allowed alternately to deck the face of the earth with fruit and flowers and to disfigure it with cloud and cold. The sea is allowed either to be calm and inviting or to rage with storm-driven breakers. Shall man's insatiable greed bind me to a constancy which is alien to my ways? Inconstancy is my very essence; it is the game I never cease to play as I turn my wheel in its ever changing circle, filled with joy as I bring the top to the bottom and the bottom to the top. Yes, rise up on my wheel if you like, but don't count it an injury when by the same token you begin to fall, as the rules of the game will require. . . . '"

Book III, Chapter 7

"Of bodily pleasure I can think of little to say. Its pursuit is full of anxiety and its fulfilment full of remorse. Frequently, like a kind of reward for wickedness, it causes great illness and unbearable pain for those who make it their source of enjoyment. I do not know what happiness lies in its passions, but that the end of pleasure is sorrow is known to everyone who cares to recall his own excesses. But if bodily pleasure can produce happiness, there is no need to deny that animals are happy, since their whole aim in life is directed towards the fulfilment of bodily needs. The pleasures derived from a wife and children are indeed most honest;

but there is a story all too natural that a certain man found his children tormentors. How painful the condition of every such man is, there is no need to remind you, since you have experienced such conditions yourself, and are still not free from anxiety."

Book III, Chapter 8

"There is no doubt, then, that these roads to happiness are side-tracks and cannot bring us to the destination they promise. The evils with which they are beset are great, as I will briefly show you. If you try to hoard money, you will have to take it by force. If you want to be resplendent in the dignities of high office, you will have to grovel before the man who bestows it: in your desire to outdo others in high honour you will have to cheapen and humiliate yourself by begging. If you want power, you will have to expose yourself to the plots of your subjects and run danger-ous risks. If fame is what you seek, you will find yourself on a hard road, drawn this way and that until you are worn with care. Decide to lead a life of pleasure, and there will be no one who will not reject you with scorn as the slave of that most worthless and brittle master, the human body.

"For think how puny and fragile a thing men strive to possess when they set the good of the body before them as their aim. As if you could sur-pass the elephant in size, the bull in strength, or the tiger in speed! Look up at the vault of heaven: see the strength of its foundation and the speed of its movement, and stop admiring things that are worthless. Yet the heavens are less wonderful for their foundation than for the order that rules them.

"The sleek looks of beauty are fleeting and transitory, more ephem-eral than the blossom in spring. If, as Aristotle said, we had the piercing eyesight of the mythical Lynceus and could see right through things, even the body of an Alcibiades, so fair on the surface, would look thoroughly ugly once we had seen the bowels inside. Your own nature doesn't make you look beautiful. It is due to the weak eyesight of the people who see you. Think how excessive this desire for the good of the body is, when, as you know, all that you admire can be reduced to nothing by three days of burning fever."

Book III, Chapter 10

"As to where it [happiness] is to be found, then, you should think as fol-lows. It is the universal understanding of the human mind that God, the author of all things, is good. Since nothing can be conceived better than God, everyone agrees that that which has no superior is good. Reason shows that God is so good that we are convinced that His goodness is perfect. Otherwise He couldn't be the author of creation. There would have to be something else possessing perfect goodness over and above God, which would seem to be superior to Him and of greater antiquity. For all perfect things are obviously superior to those that are imperfect. Therefore, to avoid an unending argument, it must be admitted that the supreme God is to the highest degree filled with supreme and perfect goodness. But we have agreed that perfect good is true happiness; so that it follows that true happiness is to be found in the supreme God."

Book V, Chapter 2

". . . [I]s there room in this chain of close-knit causes for any freedom of the will? Or does the chain of Fate bind even the impulses of the human mind?"

"There is freedom," she said. "For it would be impossible for any rational nature to exist without it. Whatever by nature has the use of reason has the power of judgement to decide each matter. It can distinguish by itself between what to avoid and what to desire. But man pursues what he judges to be desirable and avoids that which he thinks undesirable. So that those creatures who have an innate power of reason also have the freedom to will or not to will, though I do not claim that this freedom is equal in all. Celestial and divine beings possess clear sighted judgement, uncorrupted will, and the power to effect their desires. Human souls are of necessity more free when they continue in the contemplation of the mind of God and less free when they descend to bodies, and less still when they are imprisoned in earthly flesh and blood. They reach an extremity of enslavement when they give themselves up to wickedness and lose possession of their proper reason. Once they have turned their eyes away from the light of truth above to things on a lower and dimmer level, they are soon darkened by the mists of ignorance. Destructive passions torment them, and by yielding and giving in to them, they only aid the slavery they have brought upon themselves and become in a manner prisoners of their own freedom. Even so, this is visible to the eye of Providence as it looks out at all things from eternity and arranges predestined rewards according to each man's merit."

Book V, Chapter 3

"Look," I said, "there is something even more difficult which I find perplexing and confusing."

"Tell me," she said, "though I can guess what is troubling you."

"Well, the two seem contrary and opposite, God's universal foreknowledge and freedom of the will. If God foresees all things and cannot be mistaken in any way, what Providence has foreseen as a future event must happen. So that if from eternity Providence foreknows not only men's actions but also their thoughts and desires, there will be no freedom of will. No action or desire will be able to exist other than that which God's infallible Providence has foreseen. For if they can be changed and made different from how they were foreseen, there will be no sure foreknowledge of the future, only an uncertain opinion; and this I do not think can be believed of God.

"I do not agree with the argument by which some people believe they can cut this Gordian knot. They say that it is not because Providence has foreseen something as a future event that it must happen, but the other way round, that because something is to happen it cannot be concealed from divine Providence. In this way the necessity is passed to the other side. It is not necessary, they say, that what is foreseen must happen, but it is necessary that what is destined to happen must be foreseen, as though the point at issue was which is the cause; does foreknowledge of the future cause the necessity of events, or necessity cause the foreknowledge? But what I am trying to show is that, whatever the order of the causes, the coming to pass of things foreknown is necessary even if the foreknowledge of future events does not seem to impose the necessity on them. . . .

"If there can be no uncertainty at that most sure fount of all things, the coming to pass of those things which God firmly foreknows as future events is certain. Therefore, human thoughts and actions have no freedom, because the divine mind in foreseeing all things without being led astray by falseness binds human thoughts and actions to a single manner of occurrence.

"Once this has been admitted, the extent of the disruption in human affairs is obvious. In vain is reward offered to the good and punishment to the bad, because they have not been deserved by any free and willed movement of the mind. That which is now judged most equitable, the punishment of the wicked and the reward of the good, will be seen to be the most unjust of all; for men are driven to good or evil not by their own will but by the fixed necessity of what is to be. Neither vice nor virtue will have had any existence; but all merit will have been mixed up and undifferentiated. Nothing more wicked can be conceived than this, for as the whole order of things is derived from Providence and there is no room for human thoughts, it follows that our wickedness, too, is derived from the Author of all good."

Book V, Chapter 6

"Since, [Philosophy replied,] . . . every object of knowledge is known not as a result of its own nature, but of the nature of those who comprehend it, let us now examine, as far as we may, the nature of the divine substance, so that we may also learn what is its mode of knowledge.

"It is the common judgement, then, of all creatures that live by reason that God is eternal. So let us consider the nature of eternity, for this will make clear to us both the nature of God and his manner of knowing. Eternity, then, is the complete, simultaneous and perfect possession of everlasting life; this will be clear from a comparison with creatures that exist in time. Whatever lives in time exists in the present and progresses from the past to the future, and there is nothing set in time which can embrace simultaneously the whole extent of its life: it is in the position of not yet possessing tomorrow when it has already lost yesterday. In this life of today you do not live more fully than in that fleeting and transitory moment. Whatever, therefore, suffers the condition of being in time, even though it never had any beginning, never has any ending and its life extends into the infinity of time, as Aristotle thought was the case of the world, it is still not such that it may properly be considered eternal.

"Its life may be infinitely long, but it does not embrace and comprehend its whole extent simultaneously. It still lacks the future, while already having lost the past. So that that which embraces and possesses simultaneously the whole fullness of everlasting life, which lacks nothing of the future and has lost nothing of the past, that is what may properly be said to be eternal. Of necessity it will always be present to itself, controlling itself, and have present the infinity of fleeting time.

"Those philosophers are wrong, therefore, who when told that Plato believed the world had had no beginning in time and would have no end, maintain that the created world is co-eternal with the Creator. For it is one thing to progress like the world in Plato's theory through everlasting life, and another thing to have embraced the whole of everlasting life in one simultaneous present. This is clearly a property of the mind of God. God ought not to be considered as older than the created world in extent of time, but rather in the property of the immediacy of His nature. . . .

"Since, therefore, all judgement comprehends those things that are subject to it according to its own nature, and since the state of God is ever that of eternal presence, His knowledge, too, transcends all temporal change and abides in the immediacy of His presence. It embraces all the infinite recesses of past and future and views them in the immediacy of its knowing as though they are happening in the present. If you wish to consider, then, the foreknowledge or prevision by which He discovers all things, it will be more correct to think of it not as a kind of foreknowledge of the future, but as the knowledge of a never ending presence. So that it is better called providence or 'looking forth' than prevision or 'seeing beforehand.' For it is far removed from matters below and looks forth at all things as though from a lofty peak above them."

19

Maimonides

Moses ben Maimon (or Maimonides) (c. 1135–1204) was a rabbi, an authoritative commentator on Scripture and the Talmud, a physician, an astronomer, and philosopher. He was born in Islamic Spain and died in Egypt. During his lifetime, his work was known, consulted, and sometimes opposed throughout the Sephardic Jewish and Islamic world, where his philosophical and medical and other works were read in Arabic.

In the selections from *The Guide for the Perplexed*, a manual for those troubled by both theological and philosophical puzzles, he addresses the relationship between the form and matter, the soul and body, that makes up human beings and lays blame for all the failings and ills of humanity firmly with the body and concern for it, and with lust and intemperance. He also counteracts the claims of pessimists who see the world as it is as mostly evil, arguing that they have also mistaken the relative importance of the soul and the body.

In the selection from the *Treatise on the Resurrection*, he continues this dualist theme by arguing that, though religion requires a belief in bodily resurrection, the life of the world to come is one of pure soul.

Guide for the Perplexed

Chapter VIII

Transient bodies are only subject to destruction through their substance and not through their form, nor can the essence of their form be destroyed; in this respect they are permanent. The generic forms, as you know, are all permanent and stable. Form can only be destroyed accidentally, i.e., on account of its connexion with substance, the true nature of which consists in the property of never being without a disposition to receive form. This is the reason why no form remains permanently in a substance; a constant change takes place, one form is taken off and another is put on. How wonderfully wise is the simile of King Solomon, in which he compares matter to a faithless wife; for matter is never found without form, and is therefore always like such a wife who is never without a husband, never single; and yet, though being wedded, constantly seeks another man in the place of her husband; she entices and attracts him in every possible manner till he obtains from her what her husband has obtained. The same is the case with matter. Whatever form it has, it is disposed to receive another form; it never leaves off moving and casting off the form which it has in order to receive another. The same takes place when this second form is received. It is therefore clear that all corruption, destruction, or defect comes from matter. Take, e.g., man; his deformities and unnatural shape of limbs; all weakness, interruption, or disorder of his actions, whether innate or not, originate in the transient substance, not in the form. All other living beings likewise die or become ill through the substance of the body and not through its form. Man's shortcomings and sins are all due to the substance of the body and not to its form; while all his merits are exclusively due to his form. Thus the knowledge of God, the formation of ideas, the mastery of desire and passion, the distinction between that which is to be chosen and that which is to be rejected, all these man owes to his form; but eating, drinking, sexual intercourse, excessive lust, passion, and all vices, have their origin in the substance of his body. Now it was clear that this was the case,—it was impossible, according to the wisdom of God, that substance should exist without form, or any of the forms of the bodies without substance, and it was necessary that the very noble form of man, which is the image and likeness of God;

Friedlander, M (trans), *The Guide for the Perplexed*, New York: EP Dutton & Co, 1928.

as has been shown by us, should be joined to the substance of dust and darkness, the source of all defect and loss. For these reasons the Creator gave to the form of man power, rule, and dominion over the substance;— the form can subdue the substance, refuse the fulfilment of its desires, and reduce them, as far as possible, to a just and proper measure.

. . .

This is exactly the difference in the conduct of different men. Some consider, as we just said, all wants of the body as shame, disgrace, and defect to which they are compelled to attend; this is chiefly the case with the sense of touch, which is a disgrace to us according to Aristotle, and which is the cause of our desire for eating, drinking, and sensuality. Intelligent persons must, as much as possible, reduce these wants, guard against them, feel grieved when satisfying them, abstain from speaking of them, discussing them, and attending to them in company with others. Man must have control over all these desires, reduce them as much as possible, and only retain of them as much as is indispensable. His aim must be the aim of man as man, viz., the formation of ideas, and nothing else. The best and sublimest among them is the idea which man forms of God, angels, and the rest of the creation according to his capacity. Such men are always with God, and of them it is said, "Ye are princes, and all of you are children of the Most High" (Ps. lxxvii. 6). This is man's task and purpose. Others, however, that are separated from God form the multitude of fools, and do just the opposite. They neglect all thought and all reflection on ideas, and consider as their task the cultivation of the sense of touch,—that sense which is the greatest disgrace; they only think and reason about eating and love. Thus it is said of the wicked who are drowned in eating, drinking, and love, "They also have erred through wine, and through strong drink are out of the way," etc. (Isa. xxviii. 7), "for all tables are full of vomit and filthiness, so that there is no place clean" (ver. 8); again, "And women rule over them" (ibid. iii. 2),—the opposite of that which man was told in the beginning of the creation, "And for thy husband shall thy desire be, and he shall rule over thee" (Gen. iii. 16). The intensity of their lust is then described thus, "Every one neighed after his neighbour's wife," etc. (Jer. v. 8); "they are all adulter-ers, an assembly of treacherous men" (ibid. ix. 2). The whole book of the Proverbs of Solomon treats of this subject, and exhorts to abstain from lust and intemperance. These two vices ruin those that hate God and keep far from Him; to them the following passages may be applied, "They are not the Lord's" (ibid. v. 10); "Cast them out of my sight, and let them go forth" (ibid. xv. 1). As regards the portion beginning, "Who can find a virtuous woman?" it is clear what is meant by the figurative expression, "a virtuous woman." When man possesses a good sound body that does not overpower him nor disturb the equilibrium in him, he possesses a divine gift. In short, a good constitution facilitates the rule of the soul over the body, but it is not impossible to conquer a bad constitution by training.

Chapter XII

Men frequently think that the evils in the world are more numerous than the good things; many sayings and songs of the nations dwell on this idea. They say that a good thing is found only exceptionally, whilst evil things are numerous and lasting. Not only common people make this mistake, but even many who believe that they are wise. Al-Razi wrote a well-known book *On Metaphysics* [or *Theology*]. Among other mad and foolish things, it contains also the idea, discovered by him, that there exists more evil than good. For if the happiness of man and his pleasure in the times of prosperity be compared with the mishaps that befall him,—such as grief, acute pain, defects, paralysis of the limbs, fears, anxieties, and troubles,—it would seem as if the existence of man is a punishment and a great evil for him. This author commenced to verify his opinion by counting all the evils one by one; by this means he opposed those who hold the correct view of the benefits bestowed by God and His evident kindness, viz., that God is perfect goodness, and that all that comes from Him is absolutely good. The origin of the error is to be found in the circumstance that this ignorant man, and his party among the common people, judge the whole universe by examining one single person. For an ignorant man believes that the whole universe only exists for him; as if nothing else required any consideration. If, therefore, anything happens to him contrary to his expectation, he at once concludes that the whole universe is evil. If, however, he would take into consideration the whole universe, form an idea of it, and comprehend what a small portion he is of the Universe, he will find the truth. For it is clear that persons who have fallen into this widespread error as regards the multitude of evils in the world, do not find the evils among the angels, the spheres and stars, the elements, and that which is formed of them, viz., minerals and plants, or in the various species of living beings, but only in some individual instances of mankind. They wonder that a person, who became leprous in consequence of bad food, should be afflicted with so great an illness and suffer such a misfortune; or that he who indulges so much in sensuality as to weaken his sight, should be struck with blindness and the like. What we have, in truth, to consider is this:—The whole mankind at present in existence, and a fortiori, every other species of animals, form an infinitesimal portion of the permanent universe.

Treatise on the Resurrection

Book I

... However, the world to come is totally forgotten. Furthermore, we explained there that the resurrection of the dead is one of the cornerstones of the Torah of Moses our Teacher of blessed memory, but it is not the ultimate goal. Rather, the ultimate goal is the world to come and all this (lengthy discussion concerning the world to come) is to clarify the great doubt which is pondered (by the masses), i.e., that there is no reward or punishment (described) in the Torah except in relation to the present world, and that there is no reward or punishment clearly mentioned in relation to the world to come. And we elucidated from the words of the Torah, according to the Rabbis' interpretations thereof, that the Torah's intent in regard to reward is to the ultimate goal which is the life in the world to come, and in regard to punishment is to the ultimate end which is extinction from the world to come. And these very subjects are those which we elucidated and also explained at great length in our Composition in Hilchoth Teshuvah.

But in the chapter Chelek we explained—as anyone who delves therein will observe—that after we spoke at length about the world to come, we asserted that the resurrection of the dead is a cornerstone of the Torah and that there is no portion for him that denies that it is part of the Torah of Moses our Teacher, but it is nevertheless not the ultimate goal. So, too, in our Composition we enumerated those who do not have a share in the world to come, and we listed them (again) by number and said that they are twenty-four for fear lest a copyist omit one of them and someone say that we did not mention him. Among the twenty-four that we enumerated there is one who denies the resurrection of the dead. And when we mentioned the world to come, we also explained there that it is the ultimate goal and we said as follows; "and this recompense is such that there is none higher and a bliss beyond which there is none more blissful."

We have also explained that in the world to come there is no corporeal existence, as the Sages, of blessed memory, said: "[T]here is no eating and no drinking and no sexual intercourse (in the world to come)." It would be false, however, to assume that a person has these organs for no purpose; Heaven forbid, God would not create anything for naught. For if a person would have a mouth and a stomach and a liver and sex organs but not eat and not drink and not procreate, then his existence would be absolutely for naught. A person should not argue with these essentials concerning which there are logical proofs through simple expositions which are worthy of being said before women in the house of a mourner.

Book IV

... Verily, we have already explained that the existence of the entire body is for a single goal and that is to receive nutrition for the maintenance of the body and for the bearing of children in the likeness (of the parents) in order to maintain the human race. And when that goal is removed because there is no longer a need therefor, that is to say in the world to come—and this has already been explained to us by many of our Sages that "there is no eating or drinking or sexual intercourse there"—it is clear that the body will not exist.

For the Lord, blessed be He, would not let anything exist without a purpose and would not create anything except for a reason. God forbid that His perfect actions be compared to the actions of idol worshippers: they have eyes but they see not, they have ears but they hear not. So is God, may He be exalted, in the opinion of those (misbelievers), in that He creates bodies, that is to say, organs which do not at all serve the purpose for which they were created, nor serve any other purpose. Perhaps to those (misbelievers), the people in the world to come do not have organs but nevertheless have physical bodies; or perhaps they are hard balls or columns or cubes. Such suggestions are really ludicrous: Oh that ye would altogether hold your peace, and it would be your wisdom.

20

Thomas Aquinas

Thomas Aquinas (1225–1274), the son of an Italian noble family, entered the order of mendicant Dominican friars against his family's desire for a more prominent career. During his training, he was exposed by Albertus Magnus to the trove of lost and disregarded Aristotelian texts making their way to Western Europe in Latin translations of texts preserved and commented on in the Islamic world. Aquinas's great contribution was to synthesize the philosophy of Aristotle ("the Philosopher") with the theology of the Catholic Church, represented in the Scriptures and Augustine, and itself influenced by Platonism. The depth, breadth, and originality of that synthesis makes his work a high point in the scholasticism against which modern philosophy rebelled, even as it borrowed from it.

In the selections from the *Summa Theologica*, Aquinas addresses the nature of the soul, the relation between the soul and the body, the relation between the soul and the whole person, the incorruptibility of the soul even at death, and what happens to the soul when it is separated from the body. He also considers "synderesis," an innate orientation toward the good. Finally, in these selections, he addresses in what sense we can say humans have free will, even if we are not the originators of ourselves or our characters. These texts also give the reader a flavor for the exhaustive way in which he treats all questions.

In the selection from the *Summa Contra Gentiles,* Aquinas considers what human happiness is and why it must ultimately be found beyond this life.

....

Summa Theologica

Ia.75.1—Whether the Soul Is a Body

. . . I answer that, To seek the nature of the soul, we must premise that the soul is defined as the first principle of life of those things which live: for we call living things "animate," [i.e., having a soul], and those things which have no life, "inanimate." Now life is shown principally by two actions, knowledge and movement. The philosophers of old, not being able to rise above their imagination, supposed that the principle of these actions was something corporeal: for they asserted that only bodies were real things; and that what is not corporeal is nothing: hence they maintained that the soul is something corporeal. This opinion can be proved to be false in many ways; but we shall make use of only one proof, based on universal and certain principles, which shows clearly that the soul is not a body.

It is manifest that not every principle of vital action is a soul, for then the eye would be a soul, as it is a principle of vision; and the same might be applied to the other instruments of the soul: but it is the "first" principle of life, which we call the soul. Now, though a body may be a principle of life, or to be a living thing, as the heart is a principle of life in an animal, yet nothing corporeal can be the first principle of life. For it is clear that to be a principle of life, or to be a living thing, does not belong to a body as such; since, if that were the case, every body would be a living thing, or a principle of life. Therefore a body is competent to be a living thing or even a principle of life, as "such" a body. Now that it is actually such a body, it owes to some principle which is called its act. Therefore the soul, which is the first principle of life, is not a body, but the act of a body; thus heat, which is the principle of calefaction, is not a body, but an act of a body.

From Summa Theologica, translated by the Fathers of the English Dominican Province, Cincinnati: Benziger Brothers, 1917.

Ia.75.2—Whether the Human Soul Is Something Subsistent

. . . I answer that, It must necessarily be allowed that the principle of intellectual operation which we call the soul, is a principle both incorporeal and subsistent. For it is clear that by means of the intellect man can have knowledge of all corporeal things. Now whatever knows certain things cannot have any of them in its own nature; because that which is in it naturally would impede the knowledge of anything else. Thus we observe that a sick man's tongue being vitiated by a feverish and bitter humor, is insensible to anything sweet, and everything seems bitter to it. Therefore, if the intellectual principle contained the nature of a body it would be unable to know all bodies. Now every body has its own determinate nature. Therefore it is impossible for the intellectual principle to be a body. It is likewise impossible for it to understand by means of a bodily organ; since the determinate nature of that organ would impede knowledge of all bodies; as when a certain determinate color is not only in the pupil of the eye, but also in a glass vase, the liquid in the vase seems to be of that same color.

Therefore the intellectual principle which we call the mind or the intellect has an operation "per se" apart from the body. Now only that which subsists can have an operation "per se." For nothing can operate but what is actual: for which reason we do not say that heat imparts heat, but that what is hot gives heat. We must conclude, therefore, that the human soul, which is called the intellect or the mind, is something incorporeal and subsistent.

. . .

Reply to Objection 3: The body is necessary for the action of the intellect, not as its origin of action, but on the part of the object; for the phantasm is to the intellect what color is to the sight. Neither does such a dependence on the body prove the intellect to be non-subsistent; otherwise it would follow that an animal is non-subsistent, since it requires external objects of the senses in order to perform its act of perception.

Ia.75.4—Whether the Soul Is Man

. . . On the contrary, Augustine (De Civ. Dei xix, 3) commends Varro as holding that "man is not a mere soul, nor a mere body; but both soul and body."

I answer that, The assertion "the soul is man," can be taken in two senses. First, that man is a soul; though this particular man, Socrates, for instance, is not a soul, but composed of soul and body. I say this, forasmuch as some held that the form alone belongs to the species; while matter is part of the individual, and not the species. This cannot be true; for to the nature of the species belongs what the definition signifies; and in natural things the definition does not signify the form only, but the form and the matter. Hence in natural things the matter is part of the species; not, indeed, signate matter, which is the principle of individuality; but the common matter. For as it belongs to the notion of this particular man to be composed of this soul, of this flesh, and of these bones; so it belongs to the notion of man to be composed of soul, flesh, and bones; for whatever belongs in common to the substance of all the individuals contained under a given species, must belong to the substance of the species.

It may also be understood in this sense, that this soul is this man; and this could be held if it were supposed that the operation of the sensitive soul were proper to it, apart from the body; because in that case all the operations which are attributed to man would belong to the soul only; and whatever performs the operations proper to a thing, is that thing; wherefore that which performs the operations of a man is man. But it has been shown that sensation is not the operation of the soul only. Since, then, sensation is an operation of man, but not proper to him, it is clear that man is not a soul only, but something composed of soul and body. Plato, through supposing that sensation was proper to the soul, could maintain man to be a soul making use of the body.

Ia.75.5—Whether the Soul Is Composed of Matter and Form

. . . On the contrary, Augustine (Gen. ad lit. vii, 7,8,9) proves that the soul was made neither of corporeal matter, nor of spiritual matter.

I answer that, the soul has no matter. We may consider this question in two ways. First, from the notion of a soul in general; for it belongs to the notion of a soul to be the form of a body. Now, either it is a form by virtue of itself, in its entirety, or by virtue of some part of itself. If by virtue of itself in its entirety, then it is impossible that any part of it should be matter, if by matter we understand something purely potential: for a form, as such, is an act; and that which is purely potentiality cannot be part of an act, since potentiality is repugnant to actuality as being opposite thereto. If, however, it be a form by virtue of a part of itself, then we call that part the soul: and that matter, which it actualizes first, we call the "primary animate."

Secondly, we may proceed from the specific notion of the human soul inasmuch as it is intellectual. For it is clear that whatever is received into something is received according to the condition of the recipient. Now a thing is known in as far as its form is in the knower. But the intellectual soul knows a thing in its nature absolutely: for instance, it knows a stone absolutely as a stone; and therefore the form of a stone absolutely, as to its proper formal idea, is in the intellectual soul. Therefore the intellectual soul itself is an absolute form, and not something composed of matter and form. For if the intellectual soul were composed of matter and form, the forms of things would be received into it as individuals, and so it would only know the individual: just as it happens with the sensitive powers which receive forms in a corporeal organ; since matter is the principle by which forms are individualized. It follows, therefore, that the intellectual soul, and every intellectual substance which has knowledge of forms absolutely, is exempt from composition of matter and form.

Ia.75.6 Whether the Human Soul Is Incorruptible

Objection 1: It would seem that the human soul is corruptible. For those things that have a like beginning and process seemingly have a like end. But the beginning, by generation, of men is like that of animals, for they are made from the earth. And the process of life is alike in both; because "all things breathe alike, and man hath nothing more than the beast," as it is written (Eccles. 3:19). Therefore, as the same text concludes, "the death of man and beast is one, and the condition of both is equal." But the souls of brute animals are corruptible. Therefore, also, the human soul is corruptible. . . .

Objection 3: Further, nothing is without its own proper operation. But the operation proper to the soul, which is to understand through a phantasm, cannot be without the body. For the soul understands nothing without a phantasm; and there is no phantasm without the body as the Philosopher says (De Anima i, 1). Therefore the soul cannot survive the dissolution of the body.

On the contrary, Dionysius says (Div. Nom. iv) that human souls owe to Divine goodness that they are "intellectual," and that they have "an incorruptible substantial life."

I answer that, We must assert that the intellectual principle which we call the human soul is incorruptible. For a thing may be corrupted in two ways—"per se," and accidentally. Now it is impossible for any substance to be generated or corrupted accidentally, that is, by the generation or corruption of something else. For generation and corruption belong to a thing, just as existence belongs to it, which is acquired by generation and lost by corruption. Therefore, whatever has existence "per se" cannot be generated or corrupted except "per se"; while things which do not subsist, such as accidents and material forms, acquire existence or lost it through the generation or corruption of composite things. [T]he souls of brutes are not self-subsistent, whereas the human soul is; so that the souls of brutes are corrupted, when their bodies are corrupted; while the human soul could not be corrupted unless it were corrupted "per se." This, indeed, is impossible, not only as regards the human soul, but also as regards anything subsistent that is a form alone. For it is clear that what belongs to a thing by virtue of itself is inseparable from it; but existence belongs to a form, which is an act, by virtue of itself. Wherefore matter acquires actual existence as it acquires the form; while it is corrupted so far as the form is separated from it. But it is impossible for a form to be separated from itself; and therefore it is impossible for a subsistent form to cease to exist. . . .

Reply to Objection 1: Solomon reasons thus in the person of the foolish, as expressed in the words of Wisdom 2. Therefore the saying that man and animals have a like beginning in generation is true of the body; for all animals alike are made of earth. But it is not true of the soul. For the souls of brutes are produced by some power of the body; whereas the human soul is produced by God. To signify this it is written as to other animals: "Let the earth bring forth the living soul" (Gn. 1:24): while of man it is written (Gn. 2:7) that "He breathed into his face the breath of life." And so in the last chapter of Ecclesiastes (12:7) it is concluded: "(Before) the dust return into its earth from whence it was; and the spirit return to God Who gave it." Again the process of life is alike as to the body, concerning which it is written (Eccles. 3:19): "All things breathe alike," and (Wis. 2:2), "The breath in our nostrils is smoke." But the process is not alike of the soul; for man is intelligent, whereas animals are not. Hence it is false to say: "Man has nothing more than beasts." Thus death comes to both alike as to the body, by not as to the soul. . . .

Reply to Objection 3: To understand through a phantasm is the proper operation of the soul by virtue of its union with the body. After separation from the body it will have another mode of understanding, similar to other substances separated from bodies.

Ia.76.8 Whether the Soul Is in Each Part of the Body

. . . I answer that, As we have said, if the soul were united to the body merely as its motor, we might say that it is not in each part of the body, but only in one part through which it would move the others. But since the soul is united to the body as its form, it must necessarily be in the whole body, and in each part thereof. For it is not an accidental form, but the substantial form of the body. Now the substantial form perfects not only the whole, but each part of the whole. For since a whole consists of parts, a form of the whole which does not give existence to each of the parts of the body, is a form consisting in composition and order, such as the form of a house; and such a form is accidental. But the soul is a substantial form; and therefore it must be the form and the act, not only of the whole, but also of each part. Therefore, on the withdrawal of the soul, as we do not speak of an animal or a man unless equivocally, as we speak of a painted animal or a stone animal; so is it with the hand, the eye, the flesh and bones, as the Philosopher says (De Anima ii, 1). A proof of which is, that on the withdrawal of the soul, no part of the body retains its proper action; although that which retains its species, retains the action of the species. But act is in that which it actuates: wherefore the soul must be in the whole body, and in each part thereof. . . .

Ia.79.12—Whether Synderesis Is a Special Power of the Soul Distinct from the Others?

. . . I answer that, "Synderesis" is not a power but a habit; though some held that it is a power higher than reason; while others said that it is reason itself, not as reason, but as a nature. In order to make this clear we must observe that man's act of reasoning, since it is a kind of movement, proceeds from the understanding of certain things—namely, those which are naturally known without any investigation on the part of reason, as from an immovable principle—and ends also at the understanding, inasmuch as by means of those principles naturally known, we judge of those things which we have discovered by reasoning. Now it is clear that, as the speculative reason argues about speculative things, so that practical reason argues about practical things. Therefore we must have, bestowed on us by nature, not only speculative principles, but also practical principles. Now the first speculative principles bestowed on us by nature do not belong to a special power, but to a special habit, which is called "the understanding of principles," as the Philosopher explains (Ethic. vi, 6). Wherefore the first practical principles, bestowed on us by nature, do not belong to a special power, but to a special natural habit, which we call "synderesis." Whence "synderesis" is said to incite to good, and to murmur at evil, inasmuch as through first principles we proceed to discover, and judge of what we have discovered. It is therefore clear that "synderesis" is not a power, but a natural habit. . . .

Ia.83.1—Whether Man Has Free-Will

Objection 1: It would seem that man has not free-will. For whoever has free-will does what he wills. But man does not what he wills; for it is written (Rom. 7:19): "For the good which I will I do not, but the evil which I will not, that I do." Therefore man has not free-will. . . .

Objection 3: Further, what is "free is cause of itself," as the Philosopher says (Metaph. i, 2). Therefore what is moved by another is not free. But God moves the will, for it is written (Prov. 21:1): "The heart of the king is in the hand of the Lord; whithersoever He will He shall turn it" and (Phil. 2:13): "It is God Who worketh in you both to will and to accomplish." Therefore man has not free-will. . . .

Objection 5: Further, the Philosopher says (Ethic. iii, 5): "According as each one is, such does the end seem to him." But it is not in our power to be of one quality or another; for this comes to us from nature. Therefore it is natural to us to follow some particular end, and therefore we are not free in so doing.

On the contrary, It is written (Ecclus. 15:14): "God made man from the beginning, and left him in the hand of his own counsel"; and the gloss adds: "That is of his free-will."

I answer that, Man has free-will: otherwise counsels, exhortations, commands, prohibitions, rewards, and punishments would be in vain. In order to make this evident, we must observe that some things act without judgment; as a stone moves downwards; and in like manner all things which lack knowledge. And some act from judgment, but not a free judgment; as brute animals. For the sheep, seeing the wolf, judges it a thing to be shunned, from a natural and not a free judgment, because it judges, not from reason, but from natural instinct. And the same thing is to be said of any judgment of brute animals. But man acts from judgment, because by his apprehensive power he judges that something should be avoided or sought. But because this judgment, in the case of some particular act, is not from a natural instinct, but from some act of comparison in the reason, therefore he acts from free judgment and retains the power of being inclined to various things. For reason in contingent matters may follow opposite courses, as we see in dialectic syllogisms and rhetorical arguments. Now particular operations are contingent, and therefore in such matters the judgment of reason may follow opposite courses, and is not determinate to one. And forasmuch as man is rational is it necessary that man have a free-will.

Reply to Objection 1: [T]he sensitive appetite, though it obeys the reason, yet in a given case can resist by desiring what the reason forbids. This is therefore the good which man does not when he wishes—namely, "not to desire against reason," as Augustine says. . . .

Reply to Objection 3: Free-will is the cause of its own movement, because by his free-will man moves himself to act. But it does not of necessity belong to liberty that what is free should be the first cause of itself, as neither for one thing to be cause of another need it be the first cause. God, therefore, is the first cause, Who moves causes both natural and voluntary. And just as by moving natural causes He does not prevent their acts being natural, so by moving voluntary causes He does not deprive their actions of being voluntary: but rather is He the cause of this very thing in them; for He operates in each thing according to its own nature. . . .

Reply to Objection 5: Quality in man is of two kinds: natural and adventitious. Now the natural quality may be in the intellectual part, or in the body and its powers. From the very fact, therefore, that man is such by virtue of a natural quality which is in the intellectual part, he naturally desires his last end, which is happiness. Which desire, indeed, is a natural desire, and is not subject to free-will. But on the part of the body and its powers man may be such by virtue of a natural quality, inasmuch as he is of such a temperament or disposition due to any impression whatever produced by corporeal causes, which cannot affect the intellectual part, since it is not the act of a corporeal organ. And such as a man is by virtue of a corporeal quality, such also does his end seem to him, because from such a disposition a man is inclined to choose or reject something. But these inclinations are subject to the judgment of reason, which the lower appetite obeys. Wherefore this is in no way prejudicial to free-will.

The adventitious qualities are habits and passions, by virtue of which a man is inclined to one thing rather than to another. And yet even these inclinations are subject to the judgment of reason. Such qualities, too, are subject to reason, as it is in our power either to acquire them, whether by causing them or disposing ourselves to them, or to reject them. And so there is nothing in this that is repugnant to free-will.

Summa Contra Gentiles

Book III, Part I

Chapter 25

That to Understand God Is the End of Every Intellectual Substance

Since all creatures, even those devoid of understanding, are ordered to God as an ultimate end, all achieve this end to the extent that they participate somewhat in His likeness. Intellectual creatures attain it in a more special way, that is, through their proper operation of understanding Him. Hence, this must be the end of the intellectual creature, namely to understand God. . . .

Now, the ultimate end of man, and of every intellectual substance, is called felicity or happiness, because this is what every intellectual substance desires as an ultimate end, for its own sake alone. Therefore, the ultimate happiness and felicity of every intellectual substance is to know God. . . .

Chapter 27

That Human Felicity Does Not Consist in Pleasures of the Flesh

Now, it is clear . . . that it is impossible for human felicity to consist in bodily pleasures, the chief of which are those of food and sex.

In fact, we have shown that in the order of nature pleasure depends on operation, and not the converse.

So, if operations are not the ultimate end, the pleasures that result from them are not the ultimate end, either. . . . So, felicity is not to be located in these pleasures. . . .

Besides, felicity is a certain kind of good, appropriate to man. Indeed, brute animals cannot be deemed happy, unless we stretch the meaning of the term. But these pleasures that we are talking about are common to men and brutes. So, felicity should not be attributed to them. . . .

Again, something which is not good unless it be moderated is not good of itself; rather, it receives goodness from the source of moderation. Now, the enjoyment of the aforementioned pleasures is not good for man unless it be moderated; otherwise, these pleasures will interfere with each other. So, these pleasures are not of themselves the good for man. . . .

Furthermore, the ultimate end of everything is God. . . . So, we should consider the ultimate end of man to be that whereby he most closely approaches God. But, through the aforesaid pleasures, man is kept away from God, for this approach is effected through contemplation, and the aforementioned pleasures are the chief impediment to contemplation, since they plunge man very deep into sensible things, consequently distracting him from intelligible objects. Therefore, human felicity must not be located in bodily pleasures.

Through this conclusion we are refuting the errors of the Epicureans, who placed man's felicity in these enjoyments. . . .

Chapter 34

That Man's Ultimate Felicity Does Not Lie in Acts of the Moral Virtues

It is clear, too, that the ultimate felicity of man does not consist in moral actions.

In fact, human felicity is incapable of being ordered to a further end, if it is ultimate. But all moral operations can be ordered to something else. This is evident from the most important instances of these actions. The operations of fortitude, which are concerned with warlike activities, are ordered to victory and to peace. Indeed, it would be foolish to make war merely for its own sake. Likewise, the operations of justice are ordered for the preservation of peace among men, by means of each man having his own possessions undisturbed. And the same is evident for all the other virtues. Therefore, man's ultimate felicity does not lie in moral operations. . . .

Moreover, . . . the ultimate end of all things is to become like unto God. So, that whereby man is made most like unto God will be his felicity. Now, this is not a function of moral acts, since such acts cannot be attributed to God, except metaphorically. Indeed, it does not befit God to have passions, or the like, with which moral acts are concerned. Therefore, man's ultimate felicity, that is, his ultimate end, does not consist in moral actions. . . .

Chapter 37

That the Ultimate Felicity of Man Consists in the Contemplation of God

So, if the ultimate felicity of man does not consist in external things which are called the goods of fortune, nor in the goods of the body, nor in the goods of the soul according to its sensitive part, nor as regards the intellective part according to the activity of the moral virtues, nor according to the intellectual virtues that are concerned with action, that is, art and prudence—we are left with the conclusion that the ultimate felicity of man lies in the contemplation of truth.

Indeed, this is the only operation of man which is proper to him, and in it he shares nothing in common with the other animals.

So, too, this is ordered to nothing else as an end, for the contemplation of truth is sought for its own sake.

Also, through this operation man is united by way of likeness with beings superior to him, since this alone of human operations is found also in God and in separate substances.

Indeed, in this operation he gets in touch with these higher beings by knowing them in some way.

Also, for this operation man is rather sufficient unto himself, in the sense that for it he needs little help from external things.

In fact, all other human operations seem to be ordered to this one, as to an end. For, there is needed for the perfection of contemplation a soundness of body, to which all the products of art that are necessary for life are directed. Also required are freedom from the disturbances of the passions—this is achieved through the moral virtues and prudence—and freedom from external disorders, to which the whole program of government in civil life is directed. And so, if they are rightly considered, all human functions may be seen to subserve the contemplation of truth.

However, it is not possible for man's ultimate felicity to consist in the contemplation which depends on the understanding of principles, for that is very imperfect, being most universal, including the potential cognition of things. Also, it is the beginning, not the end, of human enquiry, coming to us from nature and not because of our search for truth. Nor, indeed, does it lie in the area of the sciences which deal with lower things, because felicity should lie in the working of the intellect in relation to the noblest objects of understanding. So, the conclusion remains that man's ultimate felicity consists in the contemplation of wisdom, based on the considering of divine matters.

From this, that is also clear . . . that man's ultimate felicity consists only in the contemplation of God. . . .

Chapter 48

That Man's Ultimate Felicity Does Not Come in This Life

If . . . it is not possible in this life to reach a higher knowledge of God so as to know Him through His essence. . . ; and if it is necessary to identify ultimate felicity with some sort of knowledge of God, as we proved above; then it is not possible for man's ultimate felicity to come in this life.

Again, the ultimate end of man brings to a termination man's natural appetite, in the sense that, once the end is acquired, nothing else will be sought. For, if he is still moved onward to something else, he does not yet have the end in which he may rest. Now, this termination cannot occur in this life. For, the more a person understands, the more is the desire to understand increased in him, and this is natural to man, unless, per-chance, there be someone who understands all things. But in this life this does not happen to anyone who is a mere man. . . . Therefore, it is not possible for man's ultimate felicity to be in this life.

Besides, everything that is moved toward an end naturally desires to be stationed at, and at rest in, that end; consequently, a body does not move away from the place to which it is moved naturally, unless by virtue of a violent movement which runs counter to its appetite. Now, felicity is the ultimate end which man naturally desires. So, there is a natural desire of man to be established in felicity. Therefore, unless along with felicity such an unmoving stability be attained, he is not yet happy, for his natural desire is not yet at rest. And so, when a person attains felicity he likewise attains stability and rest, and that is why this is the notion of all men concerning felicity, that it requires stability as part of its essential character. For this reason, the Philosopher [Aristotle] says, in *Ethics* I, that "we do not regard the happy man as a sort of chameleon." Now, in this life there is no certain stability, for to any man, no matter how happy he is reputed to be, illnesses and misfortunes may possibly come, and by them he may be hindered in that operation, whatever it may be, with which felicity is identified. Therefore, it is not possible for man's ultimate felicity to be in this life. . . .

Furthermore, all men admit that felicity is a perfect good; otherwise it could not satisfy desire. Now, a perfect good is one which lacks any admixture of evil, just as a perfect white thing is unmixed with black. Of course, it is not possible for man in the present state of life to be entirely free from evils, not only from corporeal ones, such as hunger, thirst, heat and cold, and other things of this kind, but also from evils of the soul. . . . Therefore, no person is happy in this life.

Again, man naturally shrinks from death, and is sorrowful at its prospect, not only at the instant when he feels its threat and tries to avoid it, but even when he thinks back on it. But freedom from death is something man cannot achieve in this life. Therefore, it is not possible for man in this life to be entirely happy. . . .

Furthermore, the more a thing is desired and loved, the more does its loss bring sorrow and sadness. Now, felicity is what is most desired and loved. Therefore, its loss holds the greatest prospect of sorrow. But, if ultimate felicity were possible in this life, it is certain that it would be lost, at least by death. And it is not certain whether it would last until death, since for any man in this life there is the possibility of sickness, by which he may be completely impeded from the work of virtue: such things as mental illness and the like, by which the use of reason is halted. So, such felicity always will have sorrow naturally associated with it. Therefore, it will not be perfect felicity. . . .

And so, man's ultimate felicity will lie in the knowledge of God that the human mind has after this life, according to the way in which separate substances know Him. For which reason our Lord promises us "a reward in heaven" and says that the saints "shall be as the angels . . . who always see God in heaven," as it is said (Matt. 5:12; 22:30; 18:10).

PART IV

Renaissance and Modern Works

=== 🐝 ===

21

Michel de Montaigne

....

Renaissance philosopher Michel de Montaigne (1533–1592) remains one of the most influential essayists of all time. His essays range over an enormous variety of subjects and include anecdotes and personal judgments. The following selection is a meditation on Ovid's remark that no person can be regarded as having had a happy life until they have died, the manner of their death determining our judgment on their overall character.

....

That We Should Not Be Deemed Happy Till After Our Death

[A] *Scilicet ultima semper*
Expectanda dies homini est, dicique beatus
Ante obitum nemo, supremaque funera debet.

—Ovid

[You must always await a man's last day: before his death and last funeral rites, no one should be called happy.]

There is a story about this which children know; it concerns King Croesus: having been taken by Cyrus and condemned to death, he cried

---

out as he awaited execution, "O Solon, Solon!" This was reported to Cyrus who inquired of him what it meant. Croesus explained to him that Solon had once given him a warning which he was now proving true to his own cost: that men, no matter how Fortune may smile on them, can never be called happy until you have seen them pass through the last day of their life, on account of the uncertainty and mutability of human affairs which lightly shift from state to state, each one different from the other. That is why Agesilaus replied to someone who called the King of Persia happy because he had come so young to so great an estate, "Yes: but Priam was not wretched when he was that age." Descendants of Alexander the Great, themselves kings of Macedonia, became cabinet-makers and scriveners in Rome; tyrants of Sicily became schoolteachers in Corinth. A conqueror of half the world, a general of numerous armies, became a wretched suppliant to the beggarly officials of the King of Egypt: that was the cost of five or six more months of life to Pompey the Great. And during our fathers' lifetime Ludovico Sforza, the tenth Duke of Milan, who for so long had been the driving force in Italy, was seen to die prisoner at Loches—but (and that was the worst of it) only after living there ten years. The fairest Queen, widow of the greatest King in Christendom, has she not just died by the hand of the executioner? There are hundreds of other such examples. For just as storms and tempests seem to rage against the haughty arrogant height of our buildings, so it could seem that there are spirits above us, envious of any greatness here below.

> *Usque adeo res humanas vis abdita quædam*
> *Obterit, et pulchros fasces sævasque secures*
> *Proculcare, ac ludibrio sibi habere videtur.*
>
> —Lucretius

[Some hidden force apparently topples the affairs of men, seeming to trample down the resplendent fasces and the lictor's unyielding axe, holding them in derision.]

Fortune sometimes seems precisely to lie in ambush for the last day of a man's life in order to display her power to topple in a moment what she had built up over the length of years, and to make us follow Laberius and exclaim: "*Nimirum hac die una plus inxi, mihi quam vivendum fuit*" [I have lived this day one day longer than I ought to have lived.]

The good counsel of Solon could be taken that way. But he was a philosopher: for such, the favours and ill graces of Fortune do not rank as happiness or unhappiness and for them great honours and powers are non-essential properties, counted virtually as things indifferent. So it seems likely to me that he was looking beyond that, intending to tell us that happiness in life (depending as it does on the tranquillity and contentment of a spirit well-born and on the resolution and assurance of an ordered soul) may never be attributed to any man until we have seen him act out the last scene in his play, which is indubitably the hardest. In all the rest he can wear an actor's mask: those fine philosophical arguments may be only a pose, or whatever else befalls us may not assay us to the quick, allowing us to keep our countenance serene. But in that last scene played between death and ourself there is no more feigning; we must speak straightforward French; we must show whatever is good and clean in the bottom of the pot:

> *Nam veræ voces tum demum pectore ab imo*
> *Ejiciuntur, et eripitur persona, manet res*
>
> —Lucretius

[Only then are true words uttered from deep in our breast. The mask is ripped off; reality remains.]

That is why all the other actions in our life must be tried on the touchstone of this final deed. It is the Master-day, the day which judges all the others; it is (says one of the Ancients) the day which must judge all my years now past. The assay of the fruits of my studies is postponed unto death. Then we shall see if my arguments come from my lips or my heart.

I note that several men by their death have given a good or bad reputation to their entire life. Scipio, Pompey's father-in-law, redeemed by good death the poor opinion people had had of him until then. And when asked which of three men he judged most worthy of honour, Chabrias, Iphicrates or himself, Epaminondas replied, "Before deciding that you must see us die." (Indeed Epaminondas would be robbed of a great deal if anyone were to weigh his worth without the honour and greatness of his end.)

In my own times three of the most execrable and ill-famed men I have known, men plunged into every kind of abomination, died deaths which were well-ordered and in all respects perfectly reconciled: such was God's good pleasure.

Some deaths are fine and fortunate. I knew a man whose thread of life was progressing towards brilliant preferment when it was snapped; his end was so splendid that in my opinion, his great-souled search after honor held nothing so sublime as that snapping asunder: the goal he aimed for he reached before he had even set out; that was more grand and more glorious than anything he had wished or hoped for. As he fell, he surpassed the power and reputation towards which his course aspired.

When judging another's life I always look to see how its end was borne: and one of my main concerns for my own is that it be borne well, that is, in a quiet and muted manner.

William Shakespeare

Many regard William Shakespeare (1564–1616) as the greatest writer in the English language, and his plays contain a wealth of philosophical and psychological insight into the human condition. As a sample of his thoughts, three selections are here included: Jaques's speech from *As You Like It* on the progression of human life from infancy to the "second childishness" of old age; Hamlet's melancholic assessment of humanity's place in the world; and Macbeth's nihilistic judgment of the pointlessness of life. In the first and last selections, Shakespeare's vision of a human life as being akin to the role of an actor upon a stage is clearly seen: for Jaques, a person plays many parts, according to their stage in life; for Macbeth, the play is ephemeral and meaningless, "a tale told by an idiot, . . . signifying nothing."

As You Like It

Act II, scene vii

> All the world's a stage,
> And all the men and women merely players:
> They have their exits and their entrances;
> And one man in his time plays many parts,

From Shakespeare, William, *As You Like It*, Act II, scene vii.

His acts being seven ages. At first the infant,
Mewling and puking in the nurse's arms.
And then the whining schoolboy, with his satchel
And shining morning face, creeping like snail
Unwillingly to school. And then the lover,
Sighing like furnace, with a woeful ballad
Made to his mistress' eyebrow. Then the soldier,
Full of strange oaths, and bearded like the pard,
Jealous in honour, sudden and quick in quarrel,
Seeking the bubble's reputation
Even in the cannon's mouth. And then the justice,
In fair round belly with good capon lined,
With eyes severe and beard of formal cut,
Full of wise saws and modern instances;
And so he plays his part. The sixth age shifts
Into the lean and slipper'd pantaloons,
With spectacles on nose and pouch on side;
For his shrunk shank; and his big manly voice,
Turning again toward childish treble, pipes
And whistles in his sound. Last scene of all,
That ends this strange eventful history,
Is second childishness and mere oblivion,
Sans teeth, sans eyes, sans taste, sans every thing.

Hamlet

Act II, scene ii

I have of late—but wherefore I know not—lost all my mirth, forgone all custom of exercises; and, indeed, it goes so heavily with my disposition that this goodly frame, the earth, seems to me a sterile promontory; this most excellent canopy, the air, look you, this brave o'erhanging firmament, this majestical roof fretted with golden fire,—why it appears no other thing to me than a foul and pestilent congregation of vapours. What a piece of work is man! how noble in reason! how infinite in faculty! in form and moving how express and admirable! in action how like an angel! in apprehension how like a god! the beauty of the world! the paragon of animals! And yet, to me, what is this quintessence of dust?

From Shakespeare, William, *Hamlet*, Act II, scene ii.

Macbeth

Act V, scene v

> To-morrow, and to-morrow, and to-morrow,
> Creeps in this petty pace from day to day,
> To the last syllable of recorded time;
> And all our yesterdays have lighted fools
> The way to dusty death. Out, out, brief candle!
> Life's but a walking shadow; a poor player,
> That struts and frets his hour upon the stage,
> And then is heard no more: it is a tale
> Told by an idiot, full of sound and fury,
> Signifying nothing.

From Shakespeare, William, *Macbeth*, Act V, scene v.

===== ♄ =====

23

Thomas Hobbes

One of the greatest of all political philosophers, Thomas Hobbes (1588–1679) was born in Malmesbury, England. The bleakness of his account of the natural human condition—with its emphasis upon the fear of violence and the need for security—has been seen by some (notably Rousseau) to be a product of the turbulent period of civil war through which Hobbes lived. The selections below concern three separable matters: his physicalist account of the person and his attack on the concept of the soul as an "incorporeal substance"; his attendant thoughts on volition and free will; and his famous account of the pre-societal "Naturall Condition," in which the life of human beings would have been "solitary, poore, nasty, brutish, and short."

Leviathan

Concerning the Thoughts of man, I will consider them first *Singly*, and afterwards in *Trayne*, or dependance upon one another. *Singly*, they are every one a *Representation* or *Apparence*, of some quality, or other Accident of a body without us; which is commonly called an *Object*. Which Object worketh on the Eyes, Eares, and other parts of mans body; and by diversity of working, produceth diversity of Apparences.

Approximately three thousand two hundred and ninety-seven (3,297) words from LEVIATHAN by Thomas Hobbes, edited by C.B. MacPherson (Penguin, 1968). Introduction and notes copyright © C.B. MacPherson, 1968.

The Originall of them all, is that which we call SENSE; (For there is no conception in a mans mind, which hath not at first, totally, or by parts, been begotten upon the organs of Sense.) The rest are derived from that originall. . . .

. . .

When a man reckons without the use of words, which may be done in particular things, (as when upon the sight of any one thing, wee conjecture what was likely to have preceded, or is likely to follow upon it;) if that which he thought likely to follow, followes not; or that which he thought likely to have preceded it, hath not preceded it, this is called ERROR; to which even the most prudent men are subject. But when we Reason in Words of generall signification, and fall upon a generall inference which is false; though it be commonly called *Error*, it is indeed an ABSURDITY, or senseless Speech. For Error is but a deception, in presuming that somewhat is past, or to come; of which, though it were not past, or not to come; yet there was no impossibility discoverable. But when we make a generall assertion, unless it be a true one, the possibility of it is unconceivable. And words whereby we conceive nothing but the sound, are those we call *Absurd, Insignificant*, and *Non-sense*. And therefore if a man should talk to me of a *round Quadrangle*; or *accidents of Bread in Cheese*; or *Immaterial Substances*; or of *A free Subject; A free-Will*; or any *Free*, but free from being hindred by opposition, I should not say he were in an Errour; but that his words were without meaning; that is to say, Absurd.

. . .

The Word *Body*, in the most generall acceptation, signifieth that which filleth, or occupyeth some certain room, or imagined place; and dependeth not on the imagination, but is a reall part of that we call the *Universe*. For the *Universe,* being the Aggregate of all Bodies, there is no reall part thereof that is not also *Body*; nor any thing properly a *Body*, that is not also part of (that Aggregate of all *Bodies*) the *Universe*. The same also, because Bodies are subject to change, that is to say, to variety of apparence to the sense of living creatures, is called *Substance*, that is to say, *Subject*, to various accidents, as sometimes to be Moved, sometimes to stand Still; and to seem to our senses sometimes Hot, sometimes Cold, sometimes of one Colour, Smel, Tast, or Sound, sometimes of another. And this diversity of Seeming, (produced by the diversity of the operation of bodies, on the organs of our sense) we attribute to alterations of the Bodies that operate, & call them *Accidents* of those Bodies. And according to this acceptation of the word, *Substance* and *Body*, signifie the same thing; and therefore *Substance incorporeall* are words, which when they are joined together, destroy one another, as if a man should say, an *Incorporeall Body*.

***

There be in Animals, two sorts of *Motions* peculiar to them: One called *Vitall*; begun in generation, and continued without interruption through their whole life; such as are the *course* of the *Bloud*, the *Pulse*, the *Breathing*, the *Concoction*, *Nutrition*, *Excretion*, &c; to which Motions there needs no help of Imagination: The other is *Animal motion*, otherwise called *Voluntary motion*; as to *go*, to *speak*, to *move* any of our limbes, in such manner as is first fancied in our minds. That Sense, is Motion in the organs and interiour parts of mans body, caused by the action of the things we See, Heare, &c.; . . . And because *going*, *speaking*, and the like Voluntary motions, depend alwayes upon a precedent thought of *whither*, *which way*, and *what*; it is evident, that the Imagination is the first internall beginning of all Voluntary Motion. And although unstudied men, doe not conceive any motion at all to be there, where the thing moved is invisible; or the space it is moved in, is (for the shortnesse of it) insensible; yet that doth not hinder, but that such Motions are. For let a space be never so little, that which is moved over a greater space, whereof that little one is part, must first be moved over that. These small beginnings of Motion, within the body of Man, before they appear in walking, speaking, striking, and other visible actions, are commonly called ENDEAVOUR.

This Endeavour, when it is toward something which causes it, is called APPETITE, or DESIRE; the later, being the generall name; and the other, oftentimes restrayned to signifie the Desire of Food, namely *Hunger* and *Thirst*. And when the Endeavour is fromward something, it is generally called AVERSION. These words *Appetite*, and *Aversion* we have from the *Latines*; and they both of them signifie the motions, one of approaching, the other of retiring. . . .

That which men Desire, they are also sayd to LOVE; and to HATE those things, for which they have Aversion. So that Desire, and Love, are the same thing; save that by Desire, we alwayes signifie the Absence of the Object; by Love, most commonly the Presence of the same. So also by Aversion, we signifie the Absence; and by Hate, the Presence of the Object.

Of Appetites, and Aversions, some are born with men; as Appetite of food, Appetite of excretion, and exoneration, (which may also and more properly be called Aversions, from somewhat they feele in their Bodies;)

and some other Appetites, not many. The rest, which are Appetites of particular things, proceed from Experience, and triall of their effects upon themselves, or other men. For of things wee know not at all, or believe not to be, we can have no further Desire, than to tast and try. But Aversion wee have for things, not onely which we know have hurt us; but also that we do not know whether they will hurt us, or not.

Those things which we neither Desire, nor Hate, we are said to *Contemne*: CONTEMPT being nothing else but an immobility, or contumacy of the Heart, in resisting the action of certain things; and proceeding from that the Heart is already moved otherwise, by either more potent objects; or from want of experience of them.

And because the constitution of a mans Body, is in continuall mutation; it is impossible that all the same things should alwayes cause in him the same Appetites, and Aversions: much lesse can all men consent, in the Desire of almost any one and the same Object.

But whatsoever is the object of any mans Appetite or Desire; that is it, which he for his part calleth *Good*: And the object of his Hate, and Aversion, *Evill*; And of his Contempt, *Vile*, and *Inconsiderable*. For these words of Good, Evill, and Contemptible, are ever used with relation to the person that useth them: There being nothing simply and absolutely so; nor any common Rule of Good and Evill, to be taken from the nature of the objects themselves; but from the Person of the man (where there is no Common-wealth;) or, (in a Common-wealth,) from the Person that representeth it; or from an Arbitrator or Judge, whom men disagreeing shall by consent set up, and make his sentence the Rule thereof.

. . .

When in the mind of man, Appetites, and Aversions, Hopes, and Feares, concerning one and the same thing, arise alternately; and divers good and evill consequences of the doing, or omitting the thing propounded, come successively into our thoughts; so that sometimes we have an Appetite to it, sometimes an Aversion from it; sometimes Hope to be able to do it; sometimes Despaire, or Feare to attempt it; the whole sum of Desires, Aversions, Hopes, and Feares, continued till the thing be either done, or thought impossible, is that we call DELIBERATION.

Therefore of things past, there is no *Deliberation*; because manifestly impossible to be changed: nor of things known to be impossible, or thought so; because men know, or think such Deliberation vain. But of things impossible, which we think possible, we may Deliberate; not knowing it is in vain. And it is called *Deliberation*; because it is a putting an end to the *Liberty* we had of doing, or omitting, according to our own Appetite, or Aversion.

This alternate Succession of Appetites, Aversions, Hopes and Fears, is no lesse in other living Creatures than in Man: and therefore Beasts also Deliberate.

Every *Deliberation* is then sayd to *End* when that whereof they Deliberate, is either done, or thought impossible; because till then wee retain the liberty of doing, or omitting, according to our Appetite, or Aversion.

In *Deliberation*, the last Appetite, or Aversion, immediately adhæring to the action, or to the omission thereof, is that wee call the WILL; the Act, (not the faculty,) of *Willing*. And Beasts that have Deliberation must necessarily also have *Will*. The Definition of the *Will*, given commonly by the Schooles, that it is a *Rationall Appetite*, is not good. For if it were, then could there be no Voluntary Act against Reason. For a *Voluntary Act* is that, which proceedeth from the *will*, and no other. But if in stead of a Rationall Appetite, we shall say an Appetite resulting from a precedent Deliberation, then the Definition is the same that I have given here. *Will*, therefore, *is the last Appetite In Deliberating*. And though we say in common Discourse, a man had a Will once to do a thing, that neverthelesse he forbore to do; yet that is properly but an Inclination, which makes no Action Voluntary; because the action depends not of it, but of the last Inclination, or Appetite. For if the intervenient Appetites make any action Voluntary, then by the same reason all intervenient Aversions should make the same action Involuntary; and so one and the same action should be both Voluntary & Involuntary.

By this it is manifest, that not onely actions that have their beginning from Covetousness, Ambition, Lust, or other Appetites to the thing propounded; but also those that have their beginning from Aversion, or Feare of those consequences that follow the omission, are *voluntary actions*.

. . .

Continuall Successe in obtaining those things which a man from time to time desireth, that is to say, continuall prospering, is that men call FELICITY; I mean the Felicity of this life. For there is no such thing as perpetuall Tranquillity of mind, while we live here; because Life it selfe is but Motion, and can never be without Desire, nor without Feare, no more than without Sense. What kind of Felicity God hath ordained to them that devoutly honour him, a man shall no sooner know, than enjoy;

being joyes, that now are as incomprehensible, as the word of School-men, *Beatificall Vision*, is unintelligible.

***

Nature hath made men so equall, in the faculties of body, and mind; as that though there bee found one man sometimes manifestly stronger in body, or of quicker mind then another; yet when all is reckoned together, the difference between man, and man, is not so considerable, as that one man can thereupon claim to himselfe any benefit, to which another may not pretend, as well as he. For as to the strength of body, the weakest has strength enough to kill the strongest, either by secret machination, or by confederacy with others, that are in the same danger with himselfe.

And as to the faculties of the mind, . . . I find yet a greater equality amongst men, than that of strength. For Prudence, is but Experience; which equall time, equally bestowes on all men, in those things they equally apply themselves unto. That which may perhaps make such equality incredible, is but a vain conceipt of ones owne wisdome, which almost all men think they have in a greater degree, than the Vulgar; that is, than all men but themselves, and a few others, whom by Fame, or for concurring with themselves, they approve. For such is the nature of men, that howsoever they may acknowledge many others to be more witty, or more eloquent, or more learned; Yet they will hardly believe there be many so wise as themselves: For they see their own wit at hand, and other mens at a distance. But this proveth rather that men are in that point equall, than unequall. For there is not ordinarily a greater signe of the equall distribution of any thing, than that every man is contented with his share.

From this equality of ability, ariseth equality of hope in the attaining of our Ends. And therefore if any two men desire the same thing, which neverthelesse they cannot both enjoy, they become enemies; and in the way to their End, (which is principally their owne conservation, and sometimes their delectation only,) endeavour to destroy, or subdue one an other. And from hence it comes to passe, that where an Invader hath no more to feare, than an other mans single power; if one plant, sow, build, or possesse a convenient Seat, others may probably be expected to come prepared with forces united, to dispossesse, and deprive him, not only of the fruit of his labour, but also of his life, or liberty. And the Invader again is in the like danger of another.

And from this diffidence of one another, there is no way for any man to secure himselfe, so reasonable, as Anticipation; that is, by force, or wiles, to master the persons of all men he can, so long, till he see no other power great enough to endanger him: And this is no more than his own conservation requireth, and is generally allowed. Also because there be some, that taking pleasure in contemplating their own power in the acts of conquest, which they pursue farther than their security requires; if others, that otherwise would be glad to be at ease within modest bounds, should not by invasion increase their power, they would not be able, long time, by standing only on their defence, to subsist. And by consequence, such augmentation of dominion over men, being necessary to a mans conservation, it ought to be allowed him.

Againe, men have no pleasure, (but on the contrary a great deale of griefe) in keeping company, where there is no power able to over-awe them all. For every man looketh that his companion should value him, at the same rate he sets upon himselfe: And upon all signes of contempt, or undervaluing, naturally endeavours, as far as he dares (which amongst them that have no common power, to keep them in quiet, is far enough to make them destroy each other,) to extort a greater value from his contemners, by dommage; and from others, by the example.

So that in the nature of man, we find three principall causes of quarrell. First, Competition; Secondly, Diffidence; Thirdly, Glory.

The first, maketh men invade for Gain; the second, for Safety; and the third, for Reputation. The first use Violence, to make themselves Masters of other mens persons, wives, children, and cattell; the second, to defend them; the third, for trifles, as a word, a smile, a different opinion, and any other signe of undervalue, either direct in their Persons, or by reflexion in their Kindred, their Friends, their Nation, their Profession, or their Name.

Hereby it is manifest, that during the time men live without a common Power to keep them all in awe, they are in that condition which is called Warre; and such a warre, as is of every man, against every man. For WARRE, consisteth not in Battell onely, or the act of fighting; but in a tract of time, wherein the Will to contend by Battell is sufficiently known: and therefore the notion of *Time*, is to be considered in the nature of Warre; as it is in the nature of Weather. For as the nature of Foule weather, lyeth not in a showre or two of rain; but in an inclination thereto of many dayes together: So the nature of War, consisteth not in actuall fighting; but in the known disposition thereto, during all the time there is no assurance to the contrary. All other time is PEACE.

Whatsoever therefore is consequent to a time of Warre, where every man is Enemy to every man; the same is consequent to the time, wherein men live without other security, than what their own strength, and their own invention shall furnish them withall. In such condition, there is no place for Industry; because the fruit thereof is uncertain: and consequently no Culture of the Earth; no Navigation, nor use of the commodities that may be imported by Sea; no commodious Building; no Instruments of moving, and removing such things as require much force; no Knowledge of the face of the Earth; no account of Time; no Arts; no Letters; no Society; and which is worst of all, continuall feare, and danger of violent death; And the life of man, solitary, poore, nasty, brutish, and short.

It may seem strange to some man, that has not well weighed these things; that Nature should thus dissociate, and render men apt to invade, and destroy one another: and he may therefore, not trusting to this Inference, made from the Passions, desire perhaps to have the same confirmed by Experience. Let him therefore consider with himselfe, when taking a journey, he armes himselfe, and seeks to go well accompanied; when going to sleep, he locks his dores; when even in his house he locks his chests; and this when he knows there bee Lawes, and publike Officers, armed, to revenge all injuries shall bee done him; what opinion he has of his fellow subjects, when he rides armed; of his fellow Citizens, when he locks his dores; and of his children, and servants, when he locks his chests. Does he not there as much accuse mankind by his actions, as I do by my words? But neither of us accuse mans nature in it. The Desires, and other Passions of man, are in themselves no Sin. No more are the Actions, that proceed from those Passions, till they know a Law that forbids them: which till Lawes be made they cannot know: nor can any Law be made, till they have agreed upon the Person that shall make it.

It may peradventure be thought, there was never such a time, nor condition of warre as this; and I believe it was never generally so, over all the world: but there are many places, where they live so now. For the savage people in many places of *America*, except the government of small Families, the concord whereof dependeth on naturall lust, have no government at all; and live at this day in that brutish manner, as I said before. Howsoever, it may be perceived what manner of life there would be, where there were no common Power to feare; by the manner of life, which men that have formerly lived under a peacefull government, use to degenerate into, in a civill Warre....

The Passions that encline men to Peace, are Feare of Death; Desire of such things as are necessary to commodious living; and a Hope by their Industry to obtain them. And Reason suggesteth convenient Articles of Peace, upon which men may be drawn to agreement.

24

⸭

René Descartes

René Descartes (1596–1650) lived through a time of great intellectual, spiritual, and political change. He himself took part in the wars of religion tearing at the heart of Europe. He contributed to the new physics and astronomy that upset the established truths of antiquity and the Middle Ages and that caused such trouble for Galileo. He invented new methods in mathematics, giving us the Cartesian coordinate system and developments in analytic geometry. Most importantly, he responded to the tumult and uncertainty of his time by attempting a new philosophical method now called "Cartesian skepticism" in which he doubted everything that could be doubted in order to find a firm, indubitable, certain foundation for all true knowledge. He found the one indubitable fact to be that he was thinking and therefore existed, the famous *Cogito ergo sum*, mirroring Augustine's argument that we know our own existence even in being deceived.

From this Descartes argued that he knew himself as a thinking thing, as a mind, and not as a body. He argued for a form of substance dualism, claiming that the mind and the body are each different substances. Because of this strict distinction, he argued that animals were mere bodies and therefore, whatever the appearances to the contrary, animals had no part in thinking, or even sensations such as pain.

Here, we have selected parts of his *Discourse on Method*, in which he sets out the differences between the world as explored in physics and biology and the mind. We have also included the second of his *Meditations*, in which he gives his account of the human as a thinking thing.

Discourse on Method

Part V

... From the description of inanimate bodies and plants, I passed to animals, and particularly to man. But since I had not as yet sufficient knowledge to enable me to treat of these in the same manner as of the rest, that is to say, by deducing effects from their causes, and by showing from what elements and in what manner Nature must produce them, I remained satisfied with the supposition that God formed the body of man wholly like to one of ours, as well in the external shape of the members as in the internal conformation of the organs, of the same matter with that I had described, and at first placed in it no Rational Soul, nor any other principle, in room of the Vegetative or Sensitive Soul, beyond kindling in the heart one of those fires without light, such as I had already described, and which I thought was not different from the heat in hay that has been heaped together before it is dry, or that which causes fermentation in new wines before they are run clear of the fruit. For, when I examined the kind of functions which might, as consequences of this supposition, exist in this body, I found precisely all those which may exist in us independently of all power of thinking, and consequently without being in any measure owing to the soul; in other words, to that part of us which is distinct from the body, and of which it has been said above that the nature distinctively consists in thinking,—functions in which the animals void of Reason may be said wholly to resemble us; but among which I could not discover any of those that, as dependent on thought alone, belong to us as men, while, on the other hand, I did afterwards discover these as soon as I supposed God to have created a Rational Soul, and to have annexed it to this body in a particular manner which I described. ...

I had expounded all these matters with sufficient minuteness in the Treatise which I formerly thought of publishing. And after these, I had shewn what must be the fabric of the nerves and muscles of the human body to give the animal spirits contained in it the power to move the members, as when we see heads shortly after they have been struck off still move and bite the earth, although no longer animated; what changes must take place in the brain to produce waking, sleep, and dreams; how light,

From René Descartes. (John Veitch, trans.) *Discourse on Method*. (Cambridge: The Harvard Classics. 1909–14.)

sounds, odours, tastes, heat, and all the other qualities of external objects impress it with different ideas by means of the senses; how hunger, thirst, and the other internal affections can likewise impress upon it divers ideas; what must be understood by the common sense (*sensus communis*) in which these ideas are received, by the memory which retains them, by the fantasy which can change them in various ways, and out of them compose new ideas, and which, by the same means, distributing the animal spirits through the muscles, can cause the members of such a body to move in as many different ways, and in a manner as suited, whether to the objects that are presented to its senses or to its internal affections, as can take place in our own case apart from the guidance of the will. Nor will this appear at all strange to those who are acquainted with the variety of movements performed by the different automata, or moving machines fabricated by human industry, and that with help of but few pieces compared with the great multitude of bones, muscles, nerves, arteries, veins, and other parts that are found in the body of each animal. Such persons will look upon this body as a machine made by the hands of God, which is incomparably better arranged, and adequate to movements more admirable than is any machine of human invention. And here I specially stayed to show that, were there such machines exactly resembling in organs and outward form an ape or any other irrational animal, we could have no means of knowing that they were in any respect of a different nature from these animals; but if there were machines bearing the image of our bodies, and capable of imitating our actions as far as it is morally possible, there would still remain two most certain tests whereby to know that they were not therefore really men. Of these the first is that they could never use words or other signs arranged in such a manner as is competent to us in order to declare our thoughts to others; for we may easily conceive a machine to be so constructed that it emits vocables, and even that it emits some correspondent to the action upon it of external objects which cause a change in its organs; for example, if touched in a particular place it may demand what we wish to say to it; if in another it may cry out that it is hurt, and such like; but not that it should arrange them variously so as appositely to reply to what is said in its presence, as men of the lowest grade of intellect can do. The second test is, that although such machines might execute many things with equal or perhaps greater perfection than any of us, they would, without doubt, fail in certain others from which it could be discovered that they did not act from knowledge, but solely from the disposition of their organs: for while Reason is an universal instrument that is alike available on every occasion, these organs, on the contrary, need a particular arrangement for each particular action; whence it must be morally impossible that there should exist in any machine a diversity of organs sufficient to enable it to act in all the occurrences of life, in the way in which our reason enables us to act. Again, by means of these two tests we may likewise know the difference between men and brutes. For it is highly deserving of remark, that there are no men so dull and stupid, not even idiots, as to be incapable of joining together different words, and thereby constructing a declaration by which to make their thoughts understood; and that on the other hand, there is no other animal, however perfect or happily circumstanced, which can do the like. Nor does this inability arise from want of organs: for we observe that magpies and parrots can utter words like ourselves, and are yet unable to speak as we do, that is, so as to show that they understand what they say; in place of which men born deaf and dumb, and thus not less, but rather more than the brutes, destitute of the organs which others use in speaking, are in the habit of spontaneously inventing certain signs by which they discover their thoughts to those who, being usually in their company, have leisure to learn their language. And this proves not only that the brutes have less Reason than man, but that they have none at all: for we see that very little is required to enable a person to speak; and since a certain inequality of capacity is observable among animals of the same species, as well as among men, and since some are more capable of being instructed than others, it is incredible that the most perfect ape or parrot of its species, should not in this be equal to the most stupid infant of its kind, or at least to one that was crack-brained, unless the soul of brutes were of a nature wholly different from ours. And we ought not to confound speech with the natural movements which indicate the passions, and can be imitated by machines as well as manifested by animals; nor must it be thought with certain of the ancients, that the brutes speak, although we do not understand their language. For if such were the case, since they are endowed with many organs analogous to ours, they could as easily communicate their thoughts to us as to their fellows. It is also very worthy of remark, that, though there are many animals which manifest more industry than we in certain of their actions, the same animals are yet observed to show none at all in many others: so that the circumstance that they do better than we does not prove that they are endowed with mind, for it would thence follow that they possessed greater Reason than any of us, and could surpass us in all things; on the contrary, it rather proves that they are destitute of Reason, and that it is Nature which acts in them according to the disposition of their organs: thus it is seen, that a clock composed only of wheels and weights can number the hours and measure time more exactly than we with all our skill.

I had after this described the Reasonable Soul, and shewn that it could by no means be educed from the power of matter, as the other things of which I had spoken but that it must be expressly created; and that it is not sufficient that it be lodged in the human body exactly like a pilot in a ship, unless perhaps to move its members, but that it is necessary for it to be joined and united more closely to the body, in order to have sensations and appetites similar to ours, and thus constitute a real man. I here entered, in conclusion, upon the subject of the soul at considerable length, because it is of the greatest moment: for after the error of those who deny the existence of God, an error which I think I have already sufficiently refuted, there is none that is more powerful in leading feeble minds astray from the straight path of virtue than the supposition that the soul of the brutes is of the same nature with our own; and consequently that after this life we have nothing to hope for or fear, more than flies and ants; in place of which, when we know how far they differ we much better comprehend the reasons which establish that the soul is of a nature wholly independent of the body, and that consequently it is not liable to die with the latter; and, finally, because no other causes are observed capable of destroying it, we are naturally led thence to judge that it is immortal.

Meditations on First Philosophy

Meditation II

"Of the Nature of the Human Mind; and That It Is More Easily Known Than the Body"

The Meditation of yesterday has filled my mind with so many doubts, that it is no longer in my power to forget them. Nor do I see, meanwhile, any principle on which they can be resolved; and, just as if I had fallen all of a sudden into very deep water, I am so greatly disconcerted as to be unable either to plant my feet firmly on the bottom or sustain myself by swimming on the surface. I will, nevertheless, make an effort, and try anew the

---

From *Meditations*, (John Veitch, trans.) 1901.

same path on which I had entered yesterday, that is, proceed by casting aside all that admits of the slightest doubt, not less than if I had discovered it to be absolutely false; and I will continue always in this track until I shall find something that is certain, or at least, if I can do nothing more, until I shall know with certainty that there is nothing certain. Archimedes, that he might transport the entire globe from the place it occupied to another, demanded only a point that was firm and immovable; so, also, I shall be entitled to entertain the highest expectations, if I am fortunate enough to discover only one thing that is certain and indubitable.

I suppose, accordingly, that all the things which I see are false (fictitious); I believe that none of those objects which my fallacious memory represents ever existed; I suppose that I possess no senses; I believe that body, figure, extension, motion, and place are merely fictions of my mind. What is there, then, that can be esteemed true? Perhaps this only, that there is absolutely nothing certain.

But how do I know that there is not something different altogether from the objects I have now enumerated, of which it is impossible to entertain the slightest doubt? Is there not a God, or some being, by whatever name I may designate him, who causes these thoughts to arise in my mind? But why suppose such a being, for it may be I myself am capable of producing them? Am I, then, at least not something? But I before denied that I possessed senses or a body; I hesitate, however, for what follows from that? Am I so dependent on the body and the senses that without these I cannot exist? But I had the persuasion that there was absolutely nothing in the world, that there was no sky and no earth, neither minds nor bodies; was I not, therefore, at the same time, persuaded that I did not exist? Far from it; I assuredly existed, since I was persuaded. But there is I know not what being, who is possessed at once of the highest power and the deepest cunning, who is constantly employing all his ingenuity in deceiving me. Doubtless, then, I exist, since I am deceived; and, let him deceive me as he may, he can never bring it about that I am nothing, so long as I shall be conscious that I am something. So that it must, in fine, be maintained, all things being maturely and carefully considered, that this proposition I am, I exist, is necessarily true each time it is expressed by me, or conceived in my mind.

But I do not yet know with sufficient clearness what I am, though assured that I am; and hence, in the next place, I must take care, lest perchance I inconsiderately substitute some other object in room of what is properly myself, and thus wander from truth, even in that knowledge which I hold to be of all others the most certain and evident. For this reason, I will now consider anew what I formerly believed myself to be, before I entered on the present train of thought; and of my previous opinion I will retrench all that can in the least be invalidated by the grounds of doubt I have adduced, in order that there may at length remain nothing but what is certain and indubitable.

What then did I formerly think I was? Undoubtedly I judged that I was a man. But what is a man? Shall I say a rational animal? Assuredly not; for it would be necessary forthwith to inquire into what is meant by animal, and what by rational, and thus, from a single question, I should insensibly glide into others, and these more difficult than the first; nor do I now possess enough of leisure to warrant me in wasting my time amid subtleties of this sort. I prefer here to attend to the thoughts that sprung up of themselves in my mind, and were inspired by my own nature alone, when I applied myself to the consideration of what I was. In the first place, then, I thought that I possessed a countenance, hands, arms, and all the fabric of members that appears in a corpse, and which I called by the name of body. It further occurred to me that I was nourished, that I walked, perceived, and thought, and all those actions I referred to the soul; but what the soul itself was I either did not stay to consider, or, if I did, I imagined that it was something extremely rare and subtile, like wind, or flame, or ether, spread through my grosser parts. As regarded the body, I did not even doubt of its nature, but thought I distinctly knew it, and if I had wished to describe it according to the notions I then entertained, I should have explained myself in this manner: By body I understand all that can be terminated by a certain figure; that can be comprised in a certain place, and so fill a certain space as therefrom to exclude every other body; that can be perceived either by touch, sight, hearing, taste, or smell; that can be moved in different ways, not indeed of itself, but by something foreign to it by which it is touched and from which it receives the impression; for the power of self-motion, as likewise that of perceiving and thinking, I held as by no means pertaining to the nature of body; on the contrary, I was somewhat astonished to find such faculties existing in some bodies.

But as to myself, what can I now say that I am, since I suppose there exists an extremely powerful, and, if I may so speak, malignant being, whose whole endeavors are directed toward deceiving me? Can I affirm that I possess any one of all those attributes of which I have lately spoken as belonging to the nature of body? After attentively considering them in my own mind, I find none of them that can properly be said to belong to myself. To recount them were idle and tedious. Let us pass, then, to the attributes of the soul. The first mentioned were the powers of nutrition and walking; but, if it be true that I have no body, it is true likewise that I am capable neither of walking nor of being nourished. Perception is another attribute of the soul; but perception too is impossible without the body; besides, I have frequently, during sleep, believed that I perceived objects which I afterward observed I did not in reality perceive. Thinking is another attribute of the soul; and here I discover what properly belongs to myself. This alone is inseparable from me. I am—I exist: this is certain; but how often? As often as I think; for perhaps it would even happen, if I should wholly cease to think, that I should at the same time altogether cease to be. I now admit nothing that is not necessarily true. I am therefore, precisely speaking, only a thinking thing, that is, a mind, understanding, or reason, terms whose signification was before unknown to me. I am, however, a real thing, and really existent; but what thing? The answer was, a thinking thing.

The question now arises, am I aught besides? I will stimulate my imagination with a view to discover whether I am not still something more than a thinking being. Now it is plain I am not the assemblage of members called the human body; I am not a thin and penetrating air diffused through all these members, or wind, or flame, or vapor, or breath, or any of all the things I can imagine; for I supposed that all these were not, and, without changing the supposition, I find that I still feel assured of my existence. But it is true, perhaps, that those very things which I suppose to be non-existent, because they are unknown to me, are not in truth different from myself whom I know. This is a point I cannot determine, and do not now enter into any dispute regarding it. I can only judge of things that are known to me: I am conscious that I exist, and I who know that I exist inquire into what I am. It is, however, perfectly certain that the knowledge of my existence, thus precisely taken, is not dependent on things, the existence of which is as yet unknown to me: and consequently it is not dependent on any of the things I can feign in imagination. Moreover, the phrase itself, I frame an image, reminds me of my error; for I should in truth frame one if I were to imagine myself to be anything, since to imagine is nothing more than to contemplate the figure or image of a corporeal thing; but I already know that I exist, and that it is possible at the same time that all those images, and in general all that relates to the nature of body, are merely dreams or chimeras. From this I discover that it is not more reasonable to say, I will excite my imagination that I may know more distinctly what I am, than to express myself as follows: I am now awake, and perceive something real; but because my perception is not sufficiently clear, I will of express purpose go to sleep that my dreams may represent to me the object of my perception with more truth and clearness. And, therefore, I know that nothing of all that I can embrace in imagination belongs to the knowledge which I have of myself, and that there is need to recall with the utmost care the mind from this mode of thinking, that it may be able to know its own nature with perfect distinctness.

But what, then, am I? A thinking thing, it has been said. But what is a thinking thing? It is a thing that doubts, understands, conceives, affirms, denies, wills, refuses; that imagines also, and perceives.

Assuredly it is not little, if all these properties belong to my nature. But why should they not belong to it? Am I not that very being who now doubts of almost everything; who, for all that, understands and conceives certain things; who affirms one alone as true, and denies the others; who desires to know more of them, and does not wish to be deceived; who imagines many things, sometimes even despite his will; and is likewise percipient of many, as if through the medium of the senses. Is there nothing of all this as true as that I am, even although I should be always dreaming, and although he who gave me being employed all his ingenuity to deceive me? Is there also any one of these attributes that can be properly distinguished from my thought, or that can be said to be separate from myself? For it is of itself so evident that it is I who doubt, I who understand, and I who desire, that it is here unnecessary to add anything by way of rendering it more clear. And I am as certainly the same being who imagines; for although it may be (as I before supposed) that nothing I imagine is true, still the power of imagination does not cease really to exist in me and to form part of my thought. In fine, I am the same being who perceives, that is, who apprehends certain objects as by the organs of sense, since, in truth, I see light, hear a noise, and feel heat. But it will be said that these presentations are false, and that I am dreaming. Let it be so. At all events it is certain that I seem to see light, hear a noise, and feel heat; this cannot be false, and this is what in me is properly called perceiving, which is nothing else than thinking.

From this I begin to know what I am with somewhat greater clearness and distinctness than heretofore. But, nevertheless, it still seems to me, and I cannot help believing, that corporeal things, whose images are formed by thought, which fall under the senses, and are examined by the same, are known with much greater distinctness than that I know not what part of myself which is not imaginable; although, in truth, it may seem strange to say that I know and comprehend with greater distinctness things whose existence appears to me doubtful, that are unknown, and do not belong to me, than others of whose reality I am persuaded, that are known to me, and appertain to my proper nature; in a word, than myself. But I see clearly what is the state of the case. My mind is apt to wander, and will not yet submit to be restrained within the limits of truth. Let us therefore leave the mind to itself once more, and, according to it every kind of liberty, permit it to consider the objects that appear to it from without, in order that, having afterward withdrawn it from these gently and opportunely and fixed it on the consideration of its being and the properties it finds in itself, it may then be the more easily controlled.

Let us now accordingly consider the objects that are commonly thought to be the most easily, and likewise the most distinctly known, viz., the bodies we touch and see; not, indeed, bodies in general, for these general notions are usually somewhat more confused, but one body in particular. Take, for example, this piece of wax; it is quite fresh, having been but recently taken from the beehive; it has not yet lost the sweetness of the honey it contained; it still retains somewhat of the odor of the flowers from which it was gathered; its color, figure, size, are apparent (to the sight); it is hard, cold, easily handled; and sounds when struck upon with the finger. In fine, all that contributes to make a body as distinctly known as possible, is found in the one before us. But, while I am speaking, let it be placed near the fire—what remained of the taste exhales, the smell evaporates, the color changes, its figure is destroyed, its size increases, it becomes liquid, it grows hot, it can hardly be handled, and, although struck upon, it emits no sound. Does the same wax still remain after this change? It must be admitted that it does remain; no one doubts it, or judges otherwise. What, then, was it I knew with so much distinctness in the piece of wax? Assuredly, it could be nothing of all that I observed by means of the senses, since all the things that fell under taste, smell, sight, touch, and hearing are changed, and yet the same wax remains.

It was perhaps what I now think, viz., that this wax was neither the sweetness of honey, the pleasant odor of flowers, the whiteness, the figure, nor the sound, but only a body that a little before appeared to me conspicuous under these forms, and which is now perceived under others. But, to speak precisely, what is it that I imagine when I think of it in this way? Let it be attentively considered, and, retrenching all that does not belong to the wax, let us see what remains. There certainly remains nothing, except something extended, flexible, and movable. But what is meant by flexible and movable? Is it not that I imagine that the piece of wax, being round, is capable of becoming square, or of passing from a square into a triangular figure? Assuredly such is not the case, because I conceive that it admits of an infinity of similar changes; and I am, moreover, unable to compass this infinity by imagination, and consequently this conception which I have of the wax is not the product of the faculty of imagination. But what now is this extension? Is it not also unknown? for it becomes greater when the wax is melted, greater when it is boiled, and greater still when the heat increases; and I should not conceive clearly and according to truth, the wax as it is, if I did not suppose that the piece we are considering admitted even of a wider variety of extension than I ever imagined. I must, therefore, admit that I cannot even comprehend by imagination what the piece of wax is, and that it is the mind alone which perceives it. I speak of one piece in particular; for as to wax in general, this is still more evident. But what is the piece of wax that can be perceived only by the understanding or mind? It is certainly the same which I see, touch, imagine; and, in fine, it is the same which, from the beginning, I believed it to be. But (and this it is of moment to observe) the perception of it is neither an act of sight, of touch, nor of imagination, and never was either of these, though it might formerly seem so, but is simply an intuition of the mind, which may be imperfect and confused, as it formerly was, or very clear and distinct, as it is at present, according as the attention is more or less directed to the elements which it contains, and of which it is composed.

But, meanwhile, I feel greatly astonished when I observe the weakness of my mind, and its proneness to error. For although, without at all giving expression to what I think, I consider all this in my own mind, words yet occasionally impede my progress, and I am almost led into error by the terms of ordinary language. We say, for example, that we see the same wax when it is before us, and not that we judge it to be the same from its retaining the same color and figure: whence I should forthwith be disposed to conclude that the wax is known by the act of sight, and not by the intuition of the mind alone, were it not for the analogous instance of human beings passing on in the street below, as observed from a window. In this case I do not fail to say that I see the men themselves, just as I say that I see the wax; and yet what do I see from the window beyond hats and cloaks that might cover artificial machines, whose motions might be determined by springs? But I judge that there are human beings from these appearances, and thus I comprehend, by the faculty of judgment alone which is in the mind, what I believed I saw with my eyes.

The man who makes it his aim to rise to knowledge superior to the common, ought to be ashamed to seek occasions of doubting from the vulgar forms of speech: instead, therefore, of doing this, I shall proceed with the matter in hand, and inquire whether I had a clearer and more perfect perception of the piece of wax when I first saw it, and when I thought I knew it by means of the external sense itself, or, at all events, by the common sense, as it is called, that is, by the imaginative faculty; or whether I rather apprehend it more clearly at present, after having examined with greater care, both what it is, and in what way it can be known. It would certainly be ridiculous to entertain any doubt on this point. For what, in that first perception, was there distinct? What did I perceive which any animal might not have perceived? But when I distinguish the wax from its exterior forms, and when, as if I had stripped it of its vestments, I consider it quite naked, it is certain, although some error may still be found in my judgment, that I cannot, nevertheless, thus apprehend it without possessing a human mind.

But finally, what shall I say of the mind itself, that is, of myself? for as yet I do not admit that I am anything but mind. What, then! I who seem to possess so distinct an apprehension of the piece of wax, do I not know myself, both with greater truth and certitude, and also much more distinctly and clearly? For if I judge that the wax exists because I see it, it assuredly follows, much more evidently, that I myself am or exist, for the same reason: for it is possible that what I see may not in truth be wax, and that I do not even possess eyes with which to see anything; but it cannot be that when I see, or, which comes to the same thing, when I think I see, I myself who think am nothing. So likewise, if I judge that the wax exists because I touch it, it will still also follow that I am; and if I determine that my imagination, or any other cause, whatever it be, persuades me of the existence of the wax, I will still draw the same conclusion. And what is here remarked of the piece of wax, is applicable to all the other things that are external to me. And further, if the notion or perception of wax appeared to me more precise and distinct, after that not only sight and touch, but many other causes besides, rendered it manifest to my apprehension, with how much greater distinctness must I now know myself, since all the reasons that contribute to the knowledge of the nature of wax, or of any body whatever, manifest still better the nature of my mind? And there are besides so many other things in the mind itself that contribute to the illustration of its nature, that those dependent on the body, to which I have here referred, scarcely merit to be taken into account.

But, in conclusion, I find I have insensibly reverted to the point I desired; for, since it is now manifest to me that bodies themselves are not properly perceived by the senses nor by the faculty of imagination, but by the intellect alone; and since they are not perceived because they are seen and touched, but only because they are understood or rightly comprehended by thought, I readily discover that there is nothing more easily or clearly apprehended than my own mind. But because it is difficult to rid one's self so promptly of an opinion to which one has been long accustomed, it will be desirable to tarry for some time at this stage, that, by long continued meditation, I may more deeply impress upon my memory this new knowledge.

Princess Elisabeth
of Bohemia and René Descartes

Having published his new philosophy, Descartes engaged in a corre-spondence with philosophers throughout Europe, responding to their objections and clarifying his positions. Princess Elisabeth of Bohemia, or of the Palatinate (1618–1680) was the daughter of a once-royal family who ended her life as the abbess of a Protestant convent, but lived it as a participant in the intellectual life of her time. She engaged in a lengthy correspondence with Descartes over nine years, in which she raised the interaction problem. She asked Descartes how it is possible that a fully nonmaterial object, the mind, can affect or interact with a fully material one, the body. Many philosophers continue to find this the thorniest and most damning problem with substance dualism.

Here we have included her initial presentation of her objection, Descartes's attempt to answer it through clarifying what he sees as a problem in talking about the soul or mind alone, the body alone, and their interaction, and Elisabeth's reply, in which she puts forward the plausibility of a materialist account of the soul or mind as more easily explaining mental causation.

Elisabeth

... Given that the soul of a human being is only a thinking substance, how can it affect the bodily spirits, in order to bring about voluntary actions?

... [B]ecause it seems that how a thing moves depends solely on (i) how much it is pushed, (ii) the manner in which it is pushed, or (iii) the surface-texture and shape of the thing that pushes it. The first two of those require contact between the two things, and the third requires that the causally active thing be extended. Your notion of the soul entirely excludes extension, and it appears to me that an immaterial thing can't possibly touch anything else. So I ask you for a definition of the soul that homes in on its nature more thoroughly than does the one you give in your Meditations, i.e., I want one that characterizes what it is as distinct from what it does (namely to think). It looks as though human souls can exist without thinking—e.g. in an unborn child or in someone who has a great fainting spell—but even if that is not so, and the soul's intrinsic nature and its thinking are as inseparable as God's attributes are, we can still get a more perfect idea of both of them by considering them separately. I am freely exposing to you the weaknesses of my soul's speculations; but I know that you are the best physician for my soul, and I hope that you will observe the Hippocratic oath and supply me with remedies without making them public.

Descartes

... No doubt you have noticed this, and have kindly wanted to help me with this by leaving me the traces of your thoughts on paper. I have now read them several times and become accustomed to thinking about them, with the result that I am indeed less dazzled, but am correspondingly more admiring when I see that these thoughts seem ingenious at a first reading and appear increasingly judicious and solid the more I examine them.

In view of my published writings, the question that can most rightly be asked is the very one that you put to me. All the knowledge we can have of the human soul depends on two facts about it: (1) the fact that it thinks, and (2) the fact that being united to the body it can act and be acted on along with it.

I have said almost nothing about (2), focussing entirely on making (1) better understood. That is because my principal aim was to show that the soul is distinct from the body, and (1) was helpful in showing this whereas (2) could have been harmful. But I can't hide anything from eyesight as sharp as yours! So I'll try here to explain how I conceive of the soul's union with the body and how it has the power to move the body....

...I think we have until now (i) confused the notion of the soul's power to act on the body with the body's power to act on other bodies, and have (ii) applied them (not to the soul, for we haven't yet known the soul, but) to various qualities of bodies—weight, heat, and so on—which we have imagined to be real, i.e., to have an existence distinct from that of the body that has them, and thus to be substances though we have called them "qualities."

Trying to understand weight, heat, and the rest, we have applied to them sometimes notions that we have for knowing body and sometimes ones that we have for knowing the soul, depending on whether we were attributing to them something material or something immaterial. Take for example what happens when we suppose that weight is a "real quality" about which we know nothing except that it has the power to move the body that has it toward the centre of the earth. We don't think that this happens through a real contact of one surface against another—as though the weight was a hand pushing the rock downwards! But we have no difficulty in conceiving how it moves the body, nor how the weight and the rock are connected, because we find from our own inner experience that we already have a notion that provides just such a connection. But I believe we are misusing this notion when we apply it to weight—which, as I hope to show in my Physics, is not a thing distinct from the body that has it. For I believe that this notion was given to us for conceiving how the soul moves the body.

If I make this explanation any longer I'll be doing an injustice to your incomparable mind, whereas if I let myself think that what I have written so far will be entirely satisfactory to you I'll be guilty of egotism. I'll try to steer between these by saying just this: if I can write or say something that could please you, I will always take it as a great honour to take up a pen or to go to The Hague for that purpose.... But I can't find here anything that brings into play the Hippocratic oath that you put to me, because everything in the letter deserves to be seen and admired by everyone. Your letter is infinitely precious to me, and I'll treat it in the way misers do their treasures: the more they value them the more they hide them, grudging the sight of them to rest of the world and placing their supreme happiness in looking at them....

Elisabeth

Your goodness shows not only in your (of course) pointing out and correcting the faults in my reasoning but also in your using false praise...so as to make the faults less distressing to me. The false praise wasn't necessary: the life I live here...has made me so familiar with my faults that the thought of them doesn't make me feel anything beyond the desire to remedy them.

So I am not ashamed to admit that I have found in myself all the causes of the error you mention in your letter, and that I can't yet banish them entirely. That's because the life that I am constrained to lead doesn't let me free up enough time to acquire a habit of meditation in accordance with your rules. The interests of my house (which I must not neglect) and conversations and social obligations (which I can't avoid), inflict so much annoyance and boredom on this weak mind that it is useless for anything else for a long time afterward. I hope that this will excuse my stupid inability to grasp. I don't see how the idea that you used to have about weight can guide us to the idea we need in order to judge how the (non-extended and immaterial) soul can move the body....

The old idea about weight may be a fiction produced by ignorance of what really moves rocks toward the centre of the earth (it can't claim the special guaranteed truthfulness that the idea of God has!)....[T]he argument might go like this:

No material cause presents itself to the senses, so this power must be due to the contrary of what is material, i.e., to an immaterial cause.

But I've never been able to conceive of "what is immaterial" in any way except as the bare negative "what is not material," and that can't enter into causal relations with matter!

I have to say that I would find it easier to concede matter and extension to the soul than to concede that an immaterial thing could move and be moved by a body. On the one side, if the soul moves the body through information, the spirits would have to think, and you say that nothing of a bodily kind thinks. On the other side, you show in your Meditations that the body could move the soul, and yet it is hard to understand that a soul (as you have described souls), having become able and accustomed to reasoning well, can lose all that because of some vaporous condition of the body; and that a soul that can exist without the body, and that has nothing in common with the body, is so governed by it.

But now that you have undertaken to instruct me, I entertain these views only as friends whom I don't expect to keep as friends, assuring myself that you will explain the nature of an immaterial substance and the manner in which it acts and is acted on in the body, making as good a job of this as of all the other things that you have undertaken to teach.

================ ॐ ================

François, Duc de La Rochefoucauld

The *Maxims* of La Rochefoucauld (1613–1680) express a bitter and pessimistic view of human life, clearly seen in the motto of that work ("Our virtues are usually only vices in disguise"). La Rochefoucauld aimed to show that egoistic concerns lay at the heart of all human action, and his emphasis on the unknown motives of our own behavior anticipates Freud. The following selections show La Rochefoucauld's cynical stress on self-love, while the lengthiest extract serves as a useful contrast with the familiar (and, to La Rochefoucauld, false) philosophical stance of indifference towards death.

Maxims

19

We all have strength enough to endure the troubles of others.

26

Neither the sun nor death can be looked at steadily.

Approximately one thousand four hundred and eighty-nine words (1489 words) from MAXIMS by La Rochefoucauld (Penguin Books, 1959). This translation and editorial material copyright © 1959 Leonard Tancock. The moral right of the translator has been asserted.

68

It is difficult to define love; what can be said is that in the soul it is a passion to dominate another, in the mind it is mutual understanding, whilst in the body it is simply a delicately veiled desire to possess the beloved after many rites and mysteries.

69

If pure love exists, free from the dross of our other passions, it lies hidden in the depths of our hearts and unknown even to ourselves.

72

If love be judged by most of its visible effects it looks more like hatred than friendship.

76

True love is like ghostly apparitions: everybody talks about them but few have ever seen one.

78

In most men love of justice is only fear of suffering injustice.

81

We cannot love anything except in terms of ourselves, and when we put our friends above ourselves we are only concerned with our own taste and pleasure. Yet it is only through such preference that friendship can be true and perfect.

85

Though we often persuade ourselves that we like people more influential than ourselves, our friendship is really based on self-interest alone. We do not give them our affection for the good we want to do them but for the good we want to get out of them.

87

Social life would not last long if men were not taken in by each other.

93

Old people are fond of giving good advice; it consoles them for no longer being capable of setting a bad example.

114

We cannot get over being deceived by our enemies and betrayed by our friends, yet we are often content to be so treated by ourselves.

115

It is as easy to deceive ourselves without noticing it as it is hard to deceive others without their noticing.

116

Nothing is less sincere than the way people ask and give advice. The asker appears to have deferential respect for his friend's sentiments, although his sole object is to get his own approved and transfer responsibility for his conduct; whereas the giver repays with tireless and disinterested energy the confidence that has been placed in him, although most often the advice he gives is calculated to further his own interests or reputation alone.

119

We are so used to disguising ourselves from others that we end by disguising ourselves from ourselves.

136

Some people would never have fallen in love if they had never heard of love.

137

When vanity is not prompting us we have little to say.

138

We would rather run ourselves down than not talk about ourselves at all.

146

We seldom praise except to get praise back.

178

What makes us like new acquaintances is not so much weariness of the old ones or the pleasure of making a change, as displeasure at not being sufficiently admired by those who know us too well, and the hope of being more admired by those who do not yet know us well enough.

263

What is called generosity is most often just the vanity of giving, which we like more than what we give.

264

Pity is often feeling our own sufferings in those of others, a shrewd precaution against misfortunes that may befall us. We give help to others so that they have to do the same for us on similar occasions, and these kindnesses we do them are, to put it plainly, gifts we bestow on ourselves in advance.

312

The reason why lovers never tire of each other's company is that the conversation is always about themselves.

342

The accent of one's birthplace persists in the mind and heart as much as in speech.

423

Not many know how to be old.

435

Chance and caprice rule the world.

487

We are lazier in mind than in body.

488

Our state of mind is placid or restless not so much because of the really important happenings in our lives as because of convenient or annoying concatenations of trivial daily events.

504

Having discussed the falsity of so many sham virtues, it is fitting that I should say something about the falsity of indifference to death: I mean that indifference to death that pagans pride themselves on drawing from their own strength, and not from the hope of a better life hereafter. Facing death steadfastly and being indifferent to it are not the same thing: the first is not unusual, but I do not think the second is ever genuine. Yet men have written in the most convincing manner to prove that death is no evil, and this opinion has been confirmed on a thousand celebrated occasions by the weakest of men as well as by heroes. Even so I doubt whether any sensible person has ever believed it, and the trouble men take to convince others as well as themselves that they do shows clearly that it is no easy undertaking. We may find various things in life distasteful, but we are never right to make light of death. Even those who deliberately take their own life do not count it so cheap, for they are startled when death comes by some other way than that of their own planning, and resist it as strongly as everybody else. The variations to be seen in the courage of myriads of valiant men come from the different ways their imagination presents death to them, more vividly at one time than another. Thus it comes about that after scorning what they do not know they end by fearing what they know. Unless one is prepared to consider death the direst of all evils, it should never be contemplated with all its attendant circumstances. The wisest and also the bravest are those who find the least shameful pretexts for not contemplating it, but every man capable of seeing death as it really is thinks it a fearful thing.

The inevitability of death underlay all the constancy of the philosophers, who believed in travelling with a good grace along a road there was no avoiding. Not being able to prolong their own lives for ever, they stopped at nothing in order to earn eternal life for their reputation and save from the wreck whatever can be saved. So as to keep in good countenance, let us be content not to admit to ourselves all we think about it, and let us put more trust in our own character than in those feeble arguments that make out that we can draw near to death with indifference. The glory of dying with steadfast courage, the hope of being missed, the desire to leave a fair name, the assurance of being set free from the torments of life and of no longer being dependent upon the whims of fortune are remedies not lightly to be thrust aside, but neither should they be thought infallible. They offer the kind of comfort often given in war by a simple hedge to those obliged to advance towards the enemy's fire: from a distance you imagine it must provide cover, but when you come near you find it gives little help. It is illusory to suppose that death will look the same near at hand as we thought it did at a distance, and that our emotions, which are the very stuff of weakness, will be strong enough not to be daunted by the toughest of all ordeals. And we misunderstand the effects of self-love if we believe it can help us to make light of the very thing that spells its own destruction; the mind, in which we think we can find so many resources, is too feeble at such a juncture to persuade us as we would wish. On the contrary, it is the mind that most often betrays us, for instead of filling us with contempt for death it succeeds in revealing to us its hideous and terrible side, and all it can do for us is to advise us to avert our gaze and look at other things. Cato and Brutus chose glorious things to contemplate, but not so long ago a lackey was quite happy to dance on the scaffold where he was about to be broken on the wheel. And so, although motives differ, they produce the same effects, and it is therefore true that whatever difference there may be between great men and common, thousands of times men of both kinds have been seen to meet death with the same demeanour. But there has always been this distinction: in the indifference to death shown by great men their gaze is turned aside by love of glory, whilst common men are prevented from realizing the full extent of their plight by mere lack of understanding, and that leaves them free to think of something else.

=== ﷼ ===

Blaise Pascal

....

During his short life, the French thinker Blaise Pascal (1623–1662) made significant contributions to mathematics, philosophy, and religious controversies. He published no books, but he left behind a series of fragmentary notes known as the *Pensées*. In the following selections, we see Pascal, in a number of remarkable images, exploring the wretchedness of the human condition, a wretchedness that is in part rectifiable by the acceptance of religious faith. The unhappiness of a life without God is contrasted with the extraordinary happiness of the Christian. The frailty of the human intellect means that humans can never rationally arrive at any certain conclusions concerning the being and nature of God, and so religious faith is to be arrived at by means of an act of will, the famous "Wager."

....

Pensées

We never keep to the present. We recall the past; we anticipate the future as if we found it too slow in coming and were trying to hurry it up, or we recall the past as if to stay its too rapid flight. We are so unwise that we wander about in times that do not belong to us, and do not think of the only one that does; so vain that we dream of times

Approximately two thousand two hundred and ninety-eight words (2298 words) from PENSEES by Blaise Pascal (Penguin Books, 1922). This translation and editorial material copyright © 1966 A.j. Krailsheimer. The moral right of the translator has been asserted.

that are not and blindly flee the only one that is. The fact is that the present usually hurts. We thrust it out of sight because it distresses us, and if we find it enjoyable, we are sorry to see it slip away. We try to give it the support of the future, and think how we are going to arrange things over which we have no control for a time we can never be sure of reaching.

Let us each examine his thoughts; he will find them wholly concerned with the past or the future. We almost never think of the present, and if we do think of it, it is only to see what light it throws on our plans for the future. The present is never our end. The past and the present are our means, the future alone our end. Thus we never actually live, but hope to live, and since we are always planning how to be happy, it is inevitable that we should never be so.
[47]

When I consider the brief span of my life absorbed into the eternity which comes before and after—*as the remembrance of a guest that tarrieth but a day*—the small space I occupy and which I see swallowed up in the infinite immensity of spaces of which I know nothing and which know nothing of me, I take fright, and am amazed to see myself here rather than there: there is no reason for me to be here rather than there, now rather than then. Who put me here? By whose command and act were this time and place allotted to me?
[68]

If our condition were truly happy we should not need to divert ourselves from thinking about it.
[70]

Ecclesiastes shows that man without God is totally ignorant and inescapably unhappy, for anyone is unhappy who wills but cannot do.
[75]

Man's greatness comes from knowing he is wretched: a tree does not know it is wretched.

Thus it is wretched to know that one is wretched, but there is greatness in knowing one is wretched.
[114]

All these examples of wretchedness prove his greatness. It is the wretchedness of a great lord, the wretchedness of a dispossessed king.
[116]

Man's greatness. Man's greatness is so obvious that it can even be deduced from his wretchedness, for what is nature in animals we call wretchedness in man, thus recognizing that, if his nature is today like that of the animals, he must have fallen from some better state which was once his own.
[117]

Diversion. If man were happy, the less he were diverted the happier he would be, like the saints and God.
[132]

Diversion. Being unable to cure death, wretchedness and ignorance, men have decided, in order to be happy, not to think about such things.
[133]

Diversion. Sometimes, when I set to thinking about the various activities of men, the dangers and troubles which they face at Court, or in war, giving rise to so many quarrels and passions, daring and often wicked enterprises and so on, I have often said that the sole cause of man's unhappiness is that he does not know how to stay quietly in his room. A man wealthy enough for life's needs would never leave home to go to sea or besiege some fortress if he knew how to stay at home and enjoy it. Men would never spend so much on a commission in the army if they could bear living in town all their lives, and they only seek after the company and diversion of gambling because they do not enjoy staying at home.

But after closer thought, looking for the particular reasons for all our unhappiness now that I knew its general cause, I found that one very cogent reason in the natural unhappiness of our feeble mortal condition, so wretched that nothing can console us when we really think about it.

Imagine any situation you like, add up all the blessings with which you could be endowed, to be king is still the finest thing in the world; yet if you imagine one with all the advantages of his rank, but no means of diversion, left to ponder and reflect on what he is, this limp felicity will not keep him going; he is bound to start thinking of all the threats facing him, of possible revolts, finally of inescapable death and disease, with the result that if he is deprived of so-called diversion he is unhappy, indeed more unhappy than the humblest of his subjects who can enjoy sport and diversion.

The only good thing for men therefore is to be diverted from thinking of what they are, either by some occupation which takes their mind off it, or by some novel and agreeable passion which keeps them busy, like gambling, hunting, some absorbing show, in short by what is called diversion.

This is why gaming and feminine society, war and high office are so popular. It is not that they really bring happiness, nor that anyone imagines that true bliss comes from possessing the money to be won at gaming or the hare that is hunted: no one would take it as a gift. What people want is not the easy peaceful life that allows us to think of our unhappy condition, nor the dangers of war, nor the burdens of office, but the agitation that takes our mind off it and diverts us. That is why we prefer the hunt to the capture.

That is why men are so fond of hustle and bustle; that is why prison is such a fearful punishment; that is why the pleasures of solitude are so incomprehensible. That, in fact, is the main joy of being a king, because people are continually trying to divert him and procure him every kind of pleasure. A king is surrounded by people whose only thought is to divert him and stop him thinking about himself, because, king though he is, he becomes unhappy as soon as he thinks about himself . . .

[Men] have a secret instinct driving them to seek external diversion and occupation, and this is the result of their constant sense of wretchedness. They have another secret instinct, left over from the greatness of our original nature, telling them that the only true happiness lies in rest and not in excitement. These two contrary instincts give rise to a confused plan buried out of sight in the depths of their soul, which leads them to seek rest by way of activity and always to imagine that the satisfaction they miss will come to them once they have overcome certain obvious difficulties and can open the door to welcome rest.

All our life passes in this way: we seek rest by struggling against certain obstacles, and once they are overcome, rest proves intolerable because of the boredom it produces. We must get away from it and crave excitement.

We think either of present or of threatened miseries, and even if we felt quite safe on every side, boredom on its own account would not fail to emerge from the depths of our hearts, where it is naturally rooted, and poison our whole mind.

[136]

It is absurd of us to rely on the company of our fellows, as wretched and helpless as we are; they will not help us; we shall die alone.

We must act then as if we were alone. If that were so, would we build superb houses, etc.? We should unhesitatingly look for the truth. And, if we refuse, it shows that we have a higher regard for men's esteem than for pursuing the truth.
[151]

The last act is bloody, however fine the rest of the play. They throw earth over your head and it is finished for ever.
[165]

We run heedlessly into the abyss after putting something in front of us to stop us seeing it.
[166]

Man is only a reed, the weakest in nature, but he is a thinking reed. There is no need for the whole universe to take up arms to crush him: a vapour, a drop of water is enough to kill him. But even if the universe were to crush him, man would still be nobler than his slayer, because he knows that he is dying, and the advantage the universe has over him. The universe knows none of this.

Thus all our dignity consists in thought. It is on thought that we must depend for our recovery, not on space and time, which we could never fill. Let us then strive to think well; that is the basic principle of morality.
[200]

The eternal silence of these infinite spaces fills me with dread.
[201]

Christianity is strange; It bids man to recognize that he is vile, and even abominable, and bids him to want to be like God. Without such a counterweight his exaltation would make him horribly vain or his abasement horribly abject.
[351]

The Incarnation shows man the greatest of his wretchedness through the greatness of the remedy required.
[352]

There is no doctrine better suited to man than that which teaches him his dual capacity for receiving and losing grace, on account of the dual danger to which he is always exposed of despair or pride.
[354]

No one is so happy as a true Christian, or so reasonable, virtuous, and lovable.
[357]

How little pride the Christian feels in believing himself united to God! How little he grovels when he likens himself to the earthworm! A fine way to meet life and death, good and evil!
[358]

Let us now speak according to our natural lights.

If there is a God, he is infinitely beyond our comprehension, since, being indivisible and without limits, he bears no relation to us. We are therefore incapable of knowing either what he is or whether he is. That being so, who would dare to attempt an answer to the question? Certainly not we, who bear no relation to him.

Who then will condemn Christians for being unable to give rational grounds for their belief, professing as they do a religion for which they cannot give rational grounds? They declare that it is a folly, *stultitiam*, in expounding it to the world, and then you complain that they do not prove it. If they did prove it they would not be keeping their word. It is by being without proof that they show they are not without sense. "Yes, but although that excuses those who offer their religion as such, and absolves them from the criticism of producing it without rational grounds, it does not absolve those who accept it." Let us then examine this point, and let us say: "Either God is or he is not." But to which view shall we be inclined? Reason cannot decide this question. Infinite chaos separates us. At the far end of this infinite distance a coin is being spun which will come down heads or tails. How will you wager? Reason cannot make you choose either, reason cannot prove either wrong.

Do not condemn as wrong those who have made a choice, for you know nothing about it. "No, but I will condemn them not for having made this particular choice, but any choice, for, although the one who calls heads and the other one are equally at fault, the fact is that they are both at fault: the right thing is not to wager at all."

Yes, but you must wager. There is no choice, you are already committed. Which will you choose then? Let us see: since a choice must be made, let us see which offers you the least interest. You have two things to lose: the true and the good; and two things to stake: your reason and your will, your knowledge and your happiness; and your nature has two things to avoid: error and wretchedness. Since you must necessarily choose, your reason is no more affronted by choosing one rather than the other. That is one point cleared up. But your happiness? Let us weigh up the gain and the loss involved in calling heads that God exists. Let us assess the two cases: if you win you win everything, if you lose you lose nothing. Do not hesitate then; wager that he does exist . . .

"Now what harm will come to you from choosing this course? You will be faithful, honest, humble, grateful, full of good works, a sincere, true friend. . . . It is true you will not enjoy noxious pleasures, glory and good living, but will you not have others?

"I tell you that you will gain even in this life, and that at every step along this road you will see that your gain is so certain and your risk so negligible that in the end you will realize that you have wagered on something certain and infinite for which you have paid nothing."
[418]

Imagine a number of men in chains, all under sentence of death, some of whom are each day butchered in the sight of the others; those remaining see their own condition in that of their fellows, and looking at each other with grief and despair await their turn. This is an image of the human condition.
[434]

28

John Locke

A towering figure in the history of British philosophy, John Locke (1632–1704) was one of the principal architects of *empiricism*, the theory that all knowledge derives ultimately from sense experience. This theory, and its implications, is spelled out in Locke's monumental *Essay Concerning Human Understanding*, from which the selections below are drawn. The first set of selections describes what Locke sees as the original blankness of the human mind (the famous *tabula rasa*) and how it comes to be furnished with contents via experience. The second set is concerned with the question of what constitutes the identity (including the *personal* identity) of a thing: Locke's thoughts on this matter, in which personal identity is located in continued consciousness or memory, are of great significance for discussions about immortality.

An Essay Concerning Human Understanding

Book II, Chapter I: *Of Ideas in General, and Their Original*

§ 1. Every Man being conscious to himself, That he thinks, and that which his Mind is employ'd about whilst thinking, being the *Ideas*, that are there, 'tis past doubt, that Men have in their minds several *Ideas*, such as

From John Locke, "An Essay Concerning Human Understanding" (Oxford: Clarendon Press, 1975 [1690]: Book II, Chapter I, §§1–6, 21–22 (ed.), 23, 25; Book II, Chapter XXVII, §§3–7 (ed.), 9, 16, 19.

are those expressed by the words, *Whiteness, Hardness, Sweetness, Thinking, Motion, Man, Elephant, Army, Drunkenness,* and others: It is in the first place then to be enquired, How he comes by them? . . .

§2. Let us then suppose the Mind to be, as we say, white Paper, void of all Characters, without any *Ideas*; How comes it to be furnished? Whence comes it by that vast store, which the busy and boundless Fancy of Man has painted on it, with an almost endless variety? Whence has it all the materials of Reason and Knowledge? To this I answer, in one word, From *Experience*: In that, all our Knowledge is founded; and from that it ultimately derives it self. Our Observation employ'd either about *external, sensible Objects; or about the internal Operations of our Minds, perceived and reflected on by our selves, is that which supplies our Understandings with all the materials of thinking.* These two are the Fountain of Knowledge, from whence all the *Ideas* we have, or can naturally have, do spring.

§3. First, *Our Senses*, conversant about particular sensible Objects, do *convey into the Mind*, several distinct *Perceptions* of things, according to those various ways, wherein those Objects do affect them: And thus we come by those *Ideas*, we have of *Yellow, White, Heat, Cold, Soft, Hard, Bitter, Sweet,* and all those which we call sensible qualities, which when I say the senses convey into the mind, I mean, they from external Objects convey into the mind what produces there those *Perceptions*. This great Source, of most of the *Ideas* we have, depending wholly upon our Senses, and derived by them to the Understanding, I call *SENSATION*.

§4. Secondly, The other Fountain, from which Experience furnisheth the Understanding with *Ideas*, is the *Perception of the Operations of our own Minds* within us, as it is employ'd about the *Ideas* it has got; which Operations, when the Soul comes to reflect on, and consider, do furnish the Understanding with another set of *Ideas*, which could not be had from things without: and such are, *Perception, Thinking, Doubting, Believing, Reasoning, Knowing, Willing,* and all the different actings of our own Minds; which we being conscious of, and observing in our selves, do from these receive into our Understandings, as distinct *Ideas*, as we do from Bodies affecting our Senses. This Source of *Ideas*, every Man has wholly in himself: And though it be not Sense, as having nothing to do with external Objects; yet it is very like it, and might properly enough be call'd internal Sense. But as I call the other *Sensation*, so I call this *REFLECTION*, the Ideas it affords being such only, as the Mind gets by reflecting on its own Operations within it self. By *REFLECTION* then, in the following part of this Discourse, I would be understood to mean, that notice which the Mind takes of its own Operations, and the manner of them, by reason whereof, there come to be *Ideas* of these Operations in the Understanding. These two, I say, *viz.* External, Material things, as the Objects of *SENSATION*; and the Operations of our own Minds within, as the Objects of *REFLECTION*, are, to me the only Originals, from whence all our *Ideas* take their beginnings. The term *Operations* here, I use in a large sense, as comprehending not barely Actions of the Mind about its *Ideas,* but some sort of Passions arising sometimes from them, such as is the satisfaction or uneasiness arising from any thought.

§ 5. The Understanding seems to me, not to have the least glimmering of any *Ideas,* which it doth not receive from one of these two. *External Objects furnish the Mind with the* Ideas *of sensible qualities*, which are all those different perceptions they produce in us: And the *Mind furnishes the Understanding with* Ideas *of its own Operations.*

These, when we have taken a full survey of them, and their several Modes, Combinations, and Relations, we shall find to contain all our whole stock of *Ideas*; and that we have nothing in our Minds, which did not come in, one of these two ways. Let any one examine his own Thoughts, and thoroughly search into his Understanding, and then let him tell me, Whether all the original *Ideas* he has there, are any other than of the Objects of his *Senses*; or of the Operations of his Mind, considered as Objects of his *Reflection*: and how great a mass of Knowledge soever he imagines to be lodged there, he will, upon taking a strict view, see, that he has *not any* Idea *in his Mind, but what one of these two have imprinted*; though, perhaps, with infinite variety compounded and enlarged by the Understanding, as we shall see hereafter.

§ 6. He that attentively considers the state of a *Child,* at his first coming into the World, will have little reason to think him stored with plenty of *Ideas,* that are to be the matter of his future Knowledge. 'Tis by degrees he comes to be furnished with them: And though the *Ideas* of obvious and familiar qualities, imprint themselves, before the Memory begins to keep a Register of Time and Order, yet 'tis often so late, before some unusual qualities come in the way, that there are few Men that cannot recollect the beginning of their acquaintance with them: And if it were worth while, no doubt a Child might be so ordered, as to have but a very few, even of the ordinary *Ideas,* till he were grown up to a Man. But all that are born into the World being surrounded with Bodies, that perpetually and diversly affect them, variety of *Ideas,* whether care be taken about it or no, are imprinted on the Minds of Children. *Light,* and *Colours,* are busie at hand every where, when the Eye is but open; *Sounds* and some *tangible Qualities* fail not to solicite their proper Senses, and force an entrance to the Mind; but yet, I think, it will be granted easily, That if a Child were kept in a place, where he never saw any other but Black and White, till he were a Man, he would have no more *Ideas* of Scarlet or Green, than he that from his Childhood never tasted an Oyster, or a Pine-Apple, has of those particular Relishes.

. . .

§ 21. He that will suffer himself, to be informed by Observation and Experience, and not make his own Hypothesis the Rule of Nature, will find few Signs of a Soul accustomed to much thinking in a new born Child, and much fewer of any Reasoning at all . . . And he that will consider, that Infants, newly come into the World, spend the greatest part of their time in Sleep, and are seldom awake, but when either Hunger calls for the Teat, or some Pain, (the most importunate of all Sensations) or some other violent Impression on the Body, forces the mind to perceive, and attend to it. He, I say, who considers this, will, perhaps, find Reason to imagine, That a *Foetus in the Mother's Womb, differs not much from the State of a Vegetable*; but passes the greatest part of its time without Perception or Thought, doing very little, but sleep in a Place, where it needs not seek for Food, and is surrounded with Liquor, always equally soft, and near of the same Temper; where the Eyes have no Light, and the Ears, so shut up, are not very susceptible of Sounds; and where there is little or no variety, or change of Objects, to move the Senses.

§ 22. Follow a *Child* from its Birth, and observe the alterations that time makes, and you shall find, as the Mind by the Senses comes more and more to be furnished with *Ideas,* it comes to be more and more awake; thinks more, the more it has matter to think on. After some time, it begins to know the Objects, which being most familiar with it, have made lasting Impressions. Thus it comes, by degrees, to know the Persons it daily converses with, and distinguish them from Strangers; which are Instances and Effects of its coming to retain and distinguish the *Ideas* the Senses convey to it. . . .

§ 23. If it shall be demanded then, *When a man begins to have any Idea?* I think, the true Answer is, When he first has any *Sensation*. . . .

§ 25. In this Part, the *Understanding is* meerly *passive*; and whether or no, it will have these Beginnings, and as it were materials of Knowledge, is not in its own Power. For the Objects of our Senses, do, many of them, obtrude their particular *Ideas* upon our minds, whether we will or no: And the Operations of our minds, will not let us be without, at least some obscure Notions of them. No Man can be wholly ignorant of what he does, when he thinks. These *simple Ideas,* when offered to the mind, *the Understanding* can no more refuse to have, nor alter, when they are imprinted, nor blot them out, and make new ones in it self, than a mirror can refuse, alter, or obliterate the Images or *Ideas,* which, the Objects set before it, do therein produce. As the Bodies that surround us, do diversly affect our Organs, the mind is forced to receive the Impressions; and cannot avoid the Perception of those *Ideas* that are annexed to them.

Book II Chapter XXVII: *Of Identity and Diversity*

§1. ANOTHER occasion, the mind often takes of comparing, is the very Being of things, when considering any thing as existing at any determin'd time and place, we compare it with it self existing at another time, and thereon form the *Ideas* of *Identity* and *Diversity.* . . .

§3. . . . In the state of living Creatures, their Identity depends not on a Mass of the same Particles; but on something else. For in them the variation of great parcels of Matter alters not the Identity: An Oak, growing from a Plant to a great Tree, and then lopp'd, is still the same Oak: And a Colt grown up to a Horse, sometimes fat, sometimes lean, is all the while the same Horse: though, in both these Cases, there may be a manifest change of the parts: So that truly they are not either of them the same Masses of Matter, though they be truly one of them the same Oak, and the other the same Horse. The reason whereof is, that in these two cases of a Mass of Matter, and a living Body, *Identity* is not applied to the same thing.

§4. We must therefore consider wherein an Oak differs from a Mass of Matter, and that seems to me to be in this; that the one is only the Cohesion of Particles of Matter any how united, the other such a disposition of them as constitutes the Parts of an Oak; and such an Organization of those Parts, as is fit to receive, and distribute nourishment, so as to continue, and frame the Wood, Bark, and Leaves, *etc.* of an Oak, in which consists the vegetable Life. That being then one Plant, which has such an Organization of Parts in one coherent Body, partaking of one Common Life, continues to be the same Plant, as long as it partakes of the same Life, though that life be communicated to new Particles of Matter vitally united to the living Plant, in a like continued Organization, conformable to that sort of Plants. For this Organization being at any one instant in any one Collection of *Matter,* is in that particular concrete distinguished from all other, and is that individual Life, which existing constantly from that moment both forwards and backwards in the same continuity of insensibly succeeding Parts united to the living Body of the Plant, it has that Identity, which makes the same Plant, and all the parts of it, parts of the same Plant, during all the time that they exist united in that continued Organization, which is fit to convey that Common Life to all the Parts so united.

§5. The Case is not so much different in *Brutes*, but that any one may hence see what makes an Animal, and continues it the same. . . .

§6. This also shews wherein the Identity of the same *Man* consist; *viz.* in nothing but a participation of the same continued Life, by constantly fleeting Particles of Matter, in succession vitally united to the same organized Body. He that shall place the *Identity* of Man in any thing else, but like that of other Animals in one fitly organized Body taken in any one instant, and from thence continued under one Organization of Life in several successively fleeting Particles of Matter, united to it, will find it hard, to make an *Embryo*, one of Years, mad, and sober, the same Man, by any Supposition, that will not make it possible for *Seth, Ismael, Socrates, Pilate, St. Austin,* and *Cesar Borgia* to be the same Man. For if the *Identity* of Soul alone makes the same Man, and there be nothing in the Nature of Matter, why the same individual Spirit may not be united to different Bodies, it will be possible, that those Men, living in distant Ages, and of different Tempers, may have been the same Man: Which way of speaking must be from a very strange use of the word *Man*, applied to an *Idea*, out of which Body and Shape is excluded: And that way of speaking would agree yet worse with the Notions of those Philosophers, who allow of Transmigration, and are of Opinion that the Souls of Men may, for their Miscarriages, be detruded into the Bodies of Beasts, as fit Habitations with Organs suited to the satisfaction of their Brutal Inclinations. But yet I think no body, could he be sure that the Soul of *Heliogabalus* were in one of his Hogs, would yet say that Hog were a *Man* or *Heliogabalus*.

§7. 'Tis not therefore Unity of Substance that comprehends all sorts of *Identity,* or will determine it in every Case: But to conceive and judge of it aright, we must consider what *Idea* the Word it is applied to stands for: It being one thing to be the same *Substance*, another the same *Man*, and a third the same *Person*, if *Person, Man,* and *Substance,* are three Names standing for three different *Ideas*; for such as is the *Idea* belonging to that Name, such must be the *Identity*: Which if it had been a little more carefully attended to, would possibly have prevented a great deal of that Confusion, which often occurs about this Matter, with no small seeming Difficulties; especially concerning *Personal Identity*, which therefore we shall in the next place a little consider.

. . .

§9. This being premised to find wherein *personal Identity* consists, we must consider what *Person* stands for; which, I think, is a thinking intelligent Being, that has reason and reflection, and can consider it self as it self, the same thinking thing in different times and places; which it does only by that consciousness, which is inseparable from thinking, and as it seems to me essential to it: It being impossible for any one to perceive, without perceiving, that he does perceive. When we see, hear, smell, taste, feel, meditate, or will any thing, we know that we do so. Thus it is always as to our present Sensations and Perceptions: And by this every one is to himself, that which he calls *self*: It not being considered in this case, whether the same *self* be continued in the same, or divers Substances. For since consciousness always accompanies thinking, and 'tis that, that makes every one to be, what he calls *self*; and thereby distinguishes himself from all other thinking things, in this alone consists *personal Identity, i.e.,* the sameness of a rational Being: And as far as this consciousness can be extended backwards to any past Action or Thought, so far reaches the Identity of that *Person*; it is the same *self* now it was then; and 'tis by the same *self* with this present one that now reflects on it, that that Action was done.

. . .

§16. But though the same immaterial Substance or Soul does not alone, where-ever it be, and in whatsoever State, make the same Man; yet 'tis plain consciousness, as far as ever it can be extended, should it be to Ages past, unites Existences, and Actions, very remote in time, into the same Person, as well as it does the Existence and Actions of the immediately preceding moment: So that whatever has the consciousness of present and past Actions, is the same Person to whom they both belong. Had I the same consciousness, that I saw the Ark and *Noah*'s Flood, as that I saw an overflowing of the *Thames* last Winter, or as that I write now, I could no more doubt that I, that write this now, that saw the *Thames* overflowed last Winter, and that view'd the Flood at the general Deluge, was the same *self*, place that *self* in what Substance you please, than that I that write this am the same *my self* now whilst I write (whether I consist of all the same Substance, material or immaterial, or no) that I was Yesterday. For as to this point of being the same *self*, it matters not whether this present *self* be made up of the same or other Substances, I being as much concern'd, and as justly accountable for any Action that was done a thousand Years since, appropriated to me now by this self-consciousness, as I am, for what I did the last moment.

. . .

§19. This may shew us wherein *personal Identity* consists, not in the Identity of Substance, but, as I have said, in the Identity of *consciousness*.

29

Benedict de Spinoza

Baruch (later Benedict de) Spinoza (1632–1677) was a Dutch philosopher raised in the Portuguese Jewish community in Amsterdam.
His highly controversial ideas (including the pantheistic equation of
God with Nature) earned his masterpiece, *The Ethics*, a place on the
Catholic Church's Index of Forbidden Books. The following selection
concerns the mind-body problem: in a position known as "double-
aspect theory," Spinoza argues that, rather than being two distinct
substances, mind and body are two aspects of the same substance.

Ethics

Note.—This is made more clear by what was said in the note to II. vii.,
namely, that mind and body are one and the same thing, conceived first
under the attribute of thought, secondly, under the attribute of extension. Thus it follows that the order or concatenation of things is identical,
whether nature be conceived under the one attribute or the other; consequently the order of states of activity and passivity in our body is simultaneous in nature with the order of states of activity and passivity in the
mind. . . .

Nevertheless, though such is the case, and though there be no further room for doubt, I can scarcely believe, until the fact is proved by
experience, that men can be induced to consider the question calmly and

From Spinoza, Benedictus de, *The Ethics*, Part III, Prop. II (Wordsworth 2001), pp. 131–134.

fairly, so firmly are they convinced that it is merely at the bidding of the mind, that the body is set in motion or at rest, or performs variety of actions depending solely on the mind's will or the exercise of thought. However, no one has hitherto laid down the limits to the powers of the body, that is, no one has as yet been taught by experience what the body can accomplish solely by the laws of nature, in so far as she is regarded as extension. No one hitherto has gained such an accurate knowledge of the bodily mechanism, that he can explain all its functions; nor need I call attention to the fact that many actions are observed in the lower animals, which far transcend human sagacity, and that somnambulists do many things in their sleep, which they would not venture to do when awake: these instances are enough to show, that the body can by the sole laws of its nature do many things which the mind wonders at.

Again, no one knows how or by what means the mind moves the body, nor how many various degrees of motion it can impart to the body, nor how quickly it can move it. Thus, when men say that this or that physical action has its origin in the mind, which latter has dominion over the body, they are using words without meaning, or are confessing in specious phraseology that they are ignorant of the cause of the said action, and do not wonder at it.

But, they will say, whether we know or do not know the means whereby the mind acts on the body, we have, at any rate, experience of the fact that unless the human mind is in a fit state to think, the body remains inert. Moreover, we have experience, that the mind alone can determine whether we speak or are silent, and a variety of similar states which, accordingly, we say depend on the mind's decree. But, as to the first point, I ask such objectors, whether experience does not also teach, that if the body be inactive the mind is simultaneously unfitted for thinking?

For when the body is at rest in sleep, the mind simultaneously is in a state of torpor also, and has no power of thinking, such as it possesses when the body is awake. Again, I think everyone's experience will confirm the statement, that the mind is not at all times equally fit for thinking on a given subject, but according as the body is more or less fitted for being stimulated by the image of this or that object, so also is the mind more or less fitted for contemplating the said object.

But, it will be urged, it is impossible that solely from the laws of nature considered as extended substance, we should be able to deduce the causes of buildings, pictures, and things of that kind, which are produced only by human art; nor would the human body, unless it were determined and led by the mind, be capable of building a single temple. However, I have just pointed out that the objectors cannot fix the limits of the body's power, or say what can be concluded from a consideration of its sole nature, whereas they have experience of many things being accomplished solely by the laws of nature, which they would never have believed possible except under the direction of mind: such are the actions performed by somnambulists while asleep, and wondered at by their performers when awake. I would further call attention to the mechanism of the human body, which far surpasses in complexity all that has been put together by human art, not to repeat what I have already shown, namely, that from nature, under whatever attribute she be considered, infinite results follow. As for the second objection, I submit that the world would be much happier, if men were as fully able to keep silence as they are to speak. Experience abundantly shows that men can govern anything more easily than their tongues, and restrain anything more easily than their appetites; whence it comes about that many believe, that we are only free in respect to objects which we moderately desire, because our desire for such can easily be controlled by the thought of something else frequently remembered, but that we are by no means free in respect to what we seek with violent emotion, for our desire cannot then be allayed with the remembrance of anything else. However, unless such persons had proved by experience that we do many things which we afterwards repent of, and again that we often, when assailed by contrary emotions, see the better and follow the worse, there would be nothing to prevent their believing that we are free in all things. Thus an infant believes that of its own free will it desires milk, an angry child believes that it freely desires vengeance, a timid child believes that it freely desires to run away; further, a drunken man believes that he utters from the free decision of his mind words which, when he is sober, he would willingly have withheld: thus too, a delirious man, a garrulous woman, a child, and others of like complexion, believe that they speak from the free decision of their mind, when they are in reality unable to restrain their impulse to talk. Experience teaches us no less clearly than reason, that men believe themselves to be free, simply because they are conscious of their actions, and unconscious of the causes whereby those actions are determined; and, further, it is plain that the dictates of the mind are but another name for the appetites, and therefore vary according to the varying state of the body. Everyone shapes his actions according to his emotion, those who are assailed by conflicting emotions know not what they wish; those who are not attacked by any emotion are readily swayed this way or that. All these considerations clearly show that a mental decision and a bodily appetite, or determined state, are simultaneous, or rather are one and the same thing, which we call decision, when it is regarded under and explained through the attribute of thought, and a conditioned state, when it is regarded under the attribute of extension, and deduced from the laws of motion and rest.

====== 🐌 ======

30

Gottfried Wilhelm Leibniz

....

The brief extracts included here from the works of the great German philosopher Gottfried Wilhelm Leibniz (1646–1716) are of relevance to a number of the thematic strands of this anthology. In the first, Leibniz's example of an individual suddenly becoming the King of China poses a vital problem for the concept of reincarnation and why one should care about the character and circumstances of one's next life. The second reading describes the theory of *pre-established harmony*, Leibniz's solution to the thorny problem of how mind and body interact. Thirdly, the final two readings concern Leibniz's famous claim that this is "the best of all possible worlds," a cosmic optimism that was to be mercilessly lampooned by Voltaire.

....

Discourse on Metaphysics

Assuming that the bodies which constitute an essential unity, such as man, are substances and that they have substantial forms; assuming, too, that the beasts have souls, one has to admit that these souls and these substantial forms cannot entirely perish, any more than the atoms or ultimate particles of matter that are believed in by other philosophers. For no substance perishes, though it can become quite different. Further, they express the

From the Discourse on Metaphysics, Letter to Basnage, Monadology, all drawn from: Gottfried Wilhelm Leibniz, *Philosophical Writings* (translated by Mary Morris & G. H. R. Parkinson) (London : J. M. Dent, 1973)

entire universe, though in a less perfect way than minds do. But the chief difference is that they know neither what they are nor what they do; consequently, being unable to reflect, they cannot discover necessary and universal truths. It is also for lack of reflexion on themselves that they have no moral quality; the result is that as they pass through a thousand transformations—much as we see a caterpillar change into a butterfly—it is morally or practically the same as if they were said to perish, and we can even say the same in terms of natural science, as when we say that bodies perish by their corruption. But the intelligent soul, knowing what it is and being able to say this "I" which says so much, does not merely remain and subsist metaphysically (which it does more fully than the others), but also remains morally the same and constitutes the same personality. For it is the memory or knowledge of this "I" which makes it capable of reward and punishment. Therefore the immortality which is demanded in morals and in religion does not consist solely in that perpetual subsistence, which belongs to all substances, for without the memory of what one has been it would be in no way desirable. Let us suppose that some individual were suddenly to become King of China, but on condition of forgetting what he has been, as if he had just been born anew. Is not this practically the same, or the same as far as the effects which can be apperceived, as if he were to be annihilated and a King of China were to be created in his place at the same moment? And this particular individual has no reason to desire this.

Letter to H. Basnage de Beauval

I see clearly from your reflexions that I need to throw some light on that idea of mine which a friend caused to be inserted in the *Journal des Savants*. You say, sir, that you do not see how I could prove what I propounded concerning the communication or harmony of two substances as different as the soul and the body. It is true that I thought I had supplied the means of doing so. And I hope that what follows will satisfy you.

Imagine two clocks or watches which are in perfect agreement. Now this agreement may come about *in three ways. The first* consists of a natural influence. This is what M. Huygens tried with a result that surprised him. He suspended two pendulums from the same piece of wood; the continual strokes of the pendulums communicated similar vibrations to the particles of the wood; but since these different vibrations could not well persist independently and without interfering with one another, unless the pendulums were in agreement, it happened by some sort of miracle that even when their strokes had been purposely disturbed, they soon went back to swinging together, rather like two strings which are in unison. *The second method* of achieving the constant agreement of two clocks, albeit imperfect ones, would be to have them continually supervised by a skilful craftsman who should be constantly setting them right. *The third method* is to construct the two clocks so skilfully and accurately at the outset that one could be certain of their subsequent agreement.

Now substitute the soul and the body for these two watches. Their agreement or sympathy will also arise in one of these ways. *The way of influence* is that of ordinary philosophy; but as it is impossible to conceive of either material particles, or immaterial species or qualities, as capable of passing from one of these substances to the other, we are obliged to abandon this view. *The way of assistance* is that of the system of occasional causes. But I hold that this is bringing in the *deus ex machina* for a natural and ordinary thing, where reason requires him to intervene only in the way he concurs with all other things in nature. Thus there remains only my hypothesis, that is to say *the way of pre-established harmony*— pre-established, that is, by a Divine anticipatory artifice, which so formed each of these substances from the beginning, that in merely following its own laws, which it received with its being, it is yet in accord with the other, just as if they mutually influenced one another, or as if, over and above his general concourse, God were for ever putting in his hand to set them right. After this I do not think there is anything for me to prove, unless I am desired to prove that God possesses the cleverness necessary for making use of this anticipatory artifice, of which we see samples even among men, in proportion as they are clever people. And supposing that he can, it is clear that this is the finest way and the worthiest of him.

Monadology

52. ... For when God compares two simple substances he finds in each reasons which oblige him to adapt the other to it, and consequently what is active in certain aspects is *passive* from another point of view: *active* in so far as what is distinctly known in it explains what occurs in another, and passive in so far as the reason for what occurs in it is found in what is distinctly known in another.

53. Now as there is an infinite number of possible universes in the ideas of God, and as only one can exist, there must be a sufficient reason for God's choice, determining him to one rather than to another.

54. And this reason can only be found in the *fitness*, or in the degrees of perfection, which these worlds contain, each possible world

having the right to claim existence in proportion to the perfection which it involves.

55. And it is this which causes the existence of the best, which God knows through his wisdom, chooses through his goodness, and produces through his power.

Theodicy

Some persons of discernment have wished me to make this addition. I have the more readily deferred to their opinion, because of the opportunity thereby gained for meeting certain difficulties, and for making observations on certain matters which were not treated in sufficient detail in the work itself.

Objection I

Whoever does not choose the best course is lacking either in power, or knowledge, or goodness.

God did not choose the best course in creating this world. Therefore God was lacking in power, or knowledge, or goodness.

Answer

I deny the minor, that is to say, the second premiss of this syllogism, and the opponent proves it by this

Prosyllogism

Whoever makes things in which there is evil, and which could have been made without any evil, or need not have been made at all, does not choose the best course. God made a world wherein there is evil; a world, I say, which could have been made without any evil or which need not have been made at all.

Therefore God did not choose the best course.

Answer

I admit the minor of this prosyllogism: for one must confess that there is evil in this world which God has made, and that it would have been possible to make a world without evil or even not to create any world, since its creation depended upon the free will of God. But I deny the major, that is, the first of the two premises of the prosyllogism the major and the minor of this conditional syllogism, and I might content myself with asking for its proof. In order, however, to give a clearer exposition of the matter, I would justify this denial by pointing out that the best course is not always that one which tends towards avoiding evil, since it is possible that the evil may be accompanied by a greater good. For example, the general of an army will prefer a great victory with a slight wound to a state of affairs without wound and without victory. I have proved this in further detail in this work by pointing out, through instances taken from mathematics and elsewhere, that an imperfection in the part may be required for a greater perfection in the whole. I have followed therein the opinion of St. Augustine, who said a hundred times that God permitted evil in order to derive from it a good, that is to say, a greater good; and Thomas Aquinas says (in libr. 2, *Sent. Dist.* 32, qu. 1, art. 1) that the permission of evil tends toward the good of the universe. I have shown that among older writers the fall of Adam was termed *felix culpa,* a fortunate sin, because it had been expiated with immense benefit by the incarnation of the Son of God: for he gave to the universe something more noble than anything there would otherwise have been amongst created beings. For the better understanding of the matter I added, following the example of many good authors, that it was consistent with order and the general good for God to grant to certain of his creatures the opportunity to exercise their freedom, even when he foresaw that they would turn to evil: for God could easily correct the evil, and it was not fitting that in order to prevent sin he should always act in an extraordinary way. It will therefore sufficiently refute the objection to show that a world with evil may be better than a world without evil. But I have gone still further in the work, and have even shown that this universe must be indeed better than every other possible universe.

Objection II

If there is more evil than good in intelligent creatures, there is more evil than good in all God's work.

Now there is more evil than good in intelligent creatures. Therefore, there is more evil than good in all God's work.

Answer

I deny the major and the minor of this conditional syllogism. As for the major, I do not admit it because this supposed inference from the part to the whole, from intelligent creatures to all creatures, assumes tacitly and without proof that creatures devoid of reason cannot be compared or taken into account with those that have reason. But why might not the surplus of good in the non-intelligent creatures that fill the world compensate for and even exceed incomparably the surplus of evil in rational creatures? It is true that the value of the latter is greater; but by way of compensation the others are incomparably greater in number; and it may be that the proportion of number and quantity surpasses that of value and quality.

The minor also I cannot admit, namely, that there is more evil than good in intelligent creatures. One need not even agree that there is more evil than good in the human kind. For it is possible and even a very reasonable thing, that the glory and the perfection of the blessed may be incomparably greater than the misery and imperfection of the damned, and that here the excellence of the total good in the smaller number may exceed the total evil which is in the greater number. The blessed draw near to divinity through a divine Mediator, so far as can belong to these created beings, and make such progress in good as is impossible for the damned to make in evil, even though they should approach as nearly as may be the nature of demons. God is infinite, and the Devil is finite; good can and does go on *ad infinitum*, whereas evil has its bounds. It may be therefore, and it is probable, that there happens in the comparison between the blessed and the damned the opposite of what I said could happen in the comparison between the happy and the unhappy, namely that in the latter the proportion of degrees surpasses that of numbers, while in the comparison between intelligent and non-intelligent the proportion of numbers is greater than that of values. One is justified in assuming that a thing may be so as long as one does not prove that it is impossible, and indeed what is here put forward goes beyond assumption.

But secondly, even should one admit that there is more evil than good in the human kind, one still has every reason for not admitting that there is more evil than good in all intelligent creatures. For there is an inconceivable number of Spirits, and perhaps of other rational creatures besides: and an opponent cannot prove that in the whole City of God, composed as much of Spirits as of rational animals without number and of endless different kinds, the evil exceeds the good. Although one need not, in order to answer an objection, prove that a thing is, when its mere possibility suffices, I have nevertheless shown in this present work that it is a result of the supreme perfection of the Sovereign of the Universe that the kingdom of God should be the most perfect of all states or governments possible, and in consequence what little evil there is should be required to provide the full measure of the vast good existing there.

Alexander Pope

The "Essay on Man," written by the English poet Alexander Pope (1688–1744), constitutes a self-proclaimed attempt to "vindicate the ways of God to man." In the selections included here, we first see Pope declaring his optimistic view of things ("Whatever is, is right"), while the second extract contains the great declaration that humanity's business is to inquire, not into God, but into humanity itself.

Essay on Man

Epistle I

VIII.

> See, through this air, this ocean, and this earth,
> All matter quick, and bursting into birth.
> Above, how high, progressive life may go!
> Around, how wide! how deep extend below!
> Vast chain of being! which from God began,
> Natures ethereal, human, angel, man,

From Alexander Pope, "Essay on Man," in *Essay on Man and Other Poems* (New York: Dover, 1994), pp. 51–53, 53–54.

Beast, bird, fish, insect, what no eye can see,
No glass can reach; from infinite to thee,
From thee to nothing.—On superior powers
Were we to press, inferior might on ours;
Or in the full creation leave a void,
Where, one step broken, the great scale's destroy'd:
From Nature's chain whatever link you strike,
Tenth, or ten thousandth, breaks the chain alike,
And, if each system in gradation roll
Alike essential to the amazing whole,
The least confusion but in one, not all
That system only, but the whole must fall.
Let earth, unbalanced, from her orbit fly,
Planets and suns run lawless through the sky;
Let ruling angels from their spheres be hurl'd,
Being on being wreck'd, and world on world;
Heaven's whole foundations to their centre nod,
And Nature tremble to the throne of God.
All this dread order break—for whom? for thee?
Vile worm!—oh madness! pride! impiety!

IX.

What if the foot, ordain'd the dust to tread,
Or hand, to toil, aspired to be the head?
What if the head, the eye, or ear repined
To serve mere engines to the ruling mind?
Just as absurd for any part to claim
To be another, in this general frame;
Just as absurd, to mourn the tasks or pains
The great Directing Mind of all ordains.
All are but parts of one stupendous whole,
Whose body Nature is, and God the soul;
That, changed through all, and yet in all the same;
Great in the earth, as in the ethereal frame;
Warms in the sun, refreshes in the breeze,
Glows in the stars, and blossoms in the trees;

Lives through all life, extends through all extent;
Spreads undivided, operates unspent!
Breathes in our soul, informs our mortal part,
As full, as perfect, in a hair as heart;
As full, as perfect in vile man that mourns,
As the rapt seraph that adores and burns:
To him no high, no low, no great, no small;
He fills, he bounds, connects, and equals all.

X.

Cease then, nor order imperfection name:
Our proper bliss depends on what we blame.
Know thy own point: this kind, this due degree
Of blindness, weakness, Heaven bestows on thee.
Submit, in this, or any other sphere,
Secure to be as blest as thou canst bear:
Safe in the hand of one Disposing Power,
Or in the natal, or the mortal hour.
All Nature is but art, unknown to thee;
All chance, direction, which thou canst not see;
All discord, harmony not understood;
All partial evil, universal good:
And, spite of pride, in erring reason's spite,
One truth is clear, Whatever is, is right.

Epistle II

. . .

Know then thyself, presume not God to scan,
The proper study of mankind is man.
Placed on this isthmus of a middle state,
A being darkly wise, and rudely great:
With too much knowledge for the sceptic side,
With too much weakness for the stoic's pride,
He hangs between; in doubt to act, or rest;
In doubt to deem himself a god, or beast;

In doubt his mind or body to prefer;
Born but to die, and reasoning but to err;
Alike in ignorance, his reason such,
Whether he thinks too little, or too much:
Chaos of Thought and Passion, all confused;
Still by himself abused or disabused;
Created half to rise, and half to fall;
Great lord of all things, yet a prey to all;
Sole judge of truth, in endless error hurl'd:
The glory, jest, and riddle of the world!

32

Voltaire

In this passage from *Candide,* Voltaire (the *nom de plume* of François-Marie Arouet) (1694–1778), the great French *philosophe* and some-time lover of du Châtelet, lampoons the optimistic claim of Leibniz that this world is "the best of all possible worlds," by having Doctor Pangloss—his stand-in for Leibniz—rehearse a litany of ills that have befallen the friends of Candide and end by once again engaging in a theodicy, or answer to the question how a good God could allow there to be evil in the world.

Candide

Candide, yet more moved with compassion than with horror, gave to this shocking beggar the two florins which he had received from the honest Anabaptist James. The spectre looked at him very earnestly, dropped a few tears, and fell upon his neck. Candide recoiled in disgust.

"Alas!" said one wretch to the other, "Do you no longer know your dear Pangloss?"

"What do I hear? You, my dear master! you in this terrible plight! What misfortune has happened to you? Why are you no longer in the most magnificent of castles? What has become of Miss Cunegonde, the pearl of girls, and nature's masterpiece?"

Voltaire, *Candide* (Philip Littell, trans.) (New York: Boni and Liveright, 1918).

"I am so weak that I cannot stand," said Pangloss.

Upon which Candide carried him to the Anabaptist's stable, and gave him a crust of bread. As soon as Pangloss had refreshed himself a little:

"Well," said Candide, "Cunegonde?"

"She is dead," replied the other.

Candide fainted at this word; his friend recalled his senses with a little bad vinegar which he found by chance in the stable. Candide re-opened his eyes.

"Cunegonde is dead! Ah, best of worlds, where art thou? But of what illness did she die? Was it not for grief, upon seeing her father kick me out of his magnificent castle?"

"No," said Pangloss, "she was ripped open by the Bulgarian soldiers, after having been violated by many; they broke the Baron's head for attempting to defend her; my lady, her mother, was cut in pieces; my poor pupil was served just in the same manner as his sister; and as for the castle, they have not left one stone upon another, not a barn, nor a sheep, nor a duck, nor a tree; but we have had our revenge, for the Abares have done the very same thing to a neighbouring barony, which belonged to a Bulgarian lord."

At this discourse Candide fainted again; but coming to himself, and having said all that it became him to say, inquired into the cause and effect, as well as into the *sufficient reason* that had reduced Pangloss to so miserable a plight.

"Alas!" said the other, "it was love; love, the comfort of the human species, the preserver of the universe, the soul of all sensible beings, love, tender love."

"Alas!" said Candide, "I know this love, that sovereign of hearts, that soul of our souls; yet it never cost me more than a kiss and twenty kicks on the backside. How could this beautiful cause produce in you an effect so abominable?"

Pangloss made answer in these terms: "Oh, my dear Candide, you remember Paquette, that pretty wench who waited on our noble Baroness; in her arms I tasted the delights of paradise, which produced in me those hell torments with which you see me devoured; she was infected with them, she is perhaps dead of them. This present Paquette received of a learned Grey Friar, who had traced it to its source; he had had it of an old countess, who had received it from a cavalry captain, who owed it to a marchioness, who took it from a page, who had received it from a Jesuit, who when a novice had it in a direct line from one of the companions of Christopher Columbus. For my part I shall give it to nobody, I am dying."

"Oh, Pangloss!" cried Candide, "what a strange genealogy! Is not the Devil the original stock of it?"

"Not at all," replied this great man, "it was a thing unavoidable, a necessary ingredient in the best of worlds; for if Columbus had not in an island of America caught this disease, which contaminates the source of life, frequently even hinders generation, and which is evidently opposed to the great end of nature, we should have neither chocolate nor cochineal. We are also to observe that upon our continent, this distemper is like religious controversy, confined to a particular spot. The Turks, the Indians, the Persians, the Chinese, the Siamese, the Japanese, know nothing of it; but there is a sufficient reason for believing that they will know it in their turn in a few centuries. In the meantime, it has made marvellous progress among us, especially in those great armies composed of honest well-disciplined hirelings, who decide the destiny of states; for we may safely affirm that when an army of thirty thousand men fights another of an equal number, there are about twenty thousand of them poxed on each side."

"Well, this is wonderful!" said Candide, "But you must get cured."

"Alas! how can I?" said Pangloss, "I have not a farthing, my friend, and all over the globe there is no letting of blood or taking a glister, without paying, or somebody paying for you."

These last words determined Candide; he went and flung himself at the feet of the charitable Anabaptist James, and gave him so touching a picture of the state to which his friend was reduced, that the good man did not scruple to take Dr. Pangloss into his house, and had him cured at his expense. In the cure Pangloss lost only an eye and an ear. He wrote well, and knew arithmetic perfectly. The Anabaptist James made him his bookkeeper. At the end of two months, being obliged to go to Lisbon about some mercantile affairs, he took the two philosophers with him in his ship. Pangloss explained to him how everything was so constituted that it could not be better. James was not of this opinion.

"It is more likely," said he, "mankind have a little corrupted nature, for they were not born wolves, and they have become wolves; God has given them neither cannon of four-and-twenty pounders, nor bayonets; and yet they have made cannon and bayonets to destroy one another. Into this account I might throw not only bankrupts, but Justice which seizes on the effects of bankrupts to cheat the creditors."

"All this was indispensable," replied the one-eyed doctor, "for private misfortunes make the general good, so that the more private misfortunes there are the greater is the general good."

While he reasoned, the sky darkened, the winds blew from the four quarters, and the ship was assailed by a most terrible tempest within sight of the port of Lisbon.

33

Émilie du Châtelet

Though most commonly remembered now as Voltaire's mistress, Émile du Châtelet (1706–1749) was herself a very fine philosopher and writer on scientific matters. She died tragically young, of a pulmonary embolism, a week after giving birth to a daughter, Stanislas-Adélaïde. Du Châtelet's "Discourse on Happiness" is a neglected *tour de force*, in which, seamlessly moving between philosophical detachment and raw personal confession, she documents the ingredients requisite for a happy life: health, passions, a taste for study, and the pleasures of love.

Discourse on Happiness

It is commonly believed that it is difficult to be happy, and there is much reason for such a belief; but it would be much easier for men to be happy if reflecting on and planning conduct preceded action. One is carried along by circumstances and indulges in hopes that never yield half of what one expects. Finally, one clearly perceives the means to be happy only when age and self-imposed fetters put obstacles in one's way. . . .

In order to be happy, one must have freed oneself of prejudices, one must be virtuous, healthy, have tastes and passions, and be susceptible to illusions; for we owe most of our pleasures to illusions, and unhappy is

Selected philosophical and scientific writings by Du Châtelet, Gabrielle Emilie Le Tonnelier de Breteuil; Zinsser, Judith P. Reproduced with permission of The University of Chicago Press in the format Republish in a book via Copyright Clearance Center.

the one who has lost them. Far then, from seeking to make them disappear by the torch of reason, let us try to thicken the varnish that illusion lays on the majority of objects. It is even more necessary to them than are care and finery to our body.

One must begin by saying to oneself, and by convincing oneself, that we have nothing to do in the world but to obtain for ourselves some agreeable sensations and feelings. The moralists who say to men, curb your passions and master your desires if you want to be happy, do not know the route to happiness. One is only happy because of satisfied tastes and passions. . . .

But, some will object, do not the passions cause more unhappiness than happiness? I do not have the instrument necessary to weigh in general the good and the bad that they have done to men; but one must remark that the unhappy are known because they have need of others, that they love to tell their misfortunes, that they seek in the telling some remedy and physical relief. Happy men and women seek nothing and do not notify others of their happiness; the unhappy are interesting, the happy are unknown.

This is why when two lovers are reconciled, when their jealousy is gone, when the obstacles that separated them have been surmounted, they are no longer proper drama. . . . The same motives move our soul at the theater and in the events of life. So one knows more of love by the unhappiness it causes than by the often obscure happiness it produces in men's lives. But let us suppose for a moment that the passions cause more unhappiness than happiness, I say they are still to be more desired, because they are a necessary condition for the enjoyment of great pleasures. Now, the only point of living is to experience agreeable sensations and feelings; and the stronger the agreeable feelings are, the happier one is. So it is desirable to be susceptible to the passions. . . .

But in order to have passions, to be able to satisfy them, one must certainly be healthy; this is the first good. Now, this good is not as independent of us as one may think. As we are all born healthy (in general that is) and our bodies made to last a certain time, there is no doubt that if we did not destroy our health by overeating, by late nights, in short, by excesses, we would all live approximately to what one calls full adulthood. I exclude from this the violent deaths that one cannot predict, and with which consequently it is useless to concern oneself. . . .

Another source of happiness is to be free from prejudices; and the decision rests with us to rid ourselves of them. We all have a sufficient share of intelligence to examine things that others want to oblige us to believe; to know, for example, if two and two make four, or five,—besides, in this century, there are a great many ways to gain instruction. I know that there are other prejudices than those of religion, and I believe that it is good to shake them off, though no prejudices influence our happiness and our unhappiness so much as those of religion. Prejudice is an opinion that one has accepted without examination, because it would be indefensible otherwise. Error can never be a good, and it is surely a great evil in the things on which the conduct of life depends. . . .

I say that one cannot be happy and immoral, and the demonstration of this axiom lies in the depths of the hearts of all men. I put it to them, even to the most villainous, that there is not one of them to whom the reproaches of his conscience—that is to say, of his innermost feeling, the scorn that he feels he deserves and that he experiences, as soon as he is aware of it—there is not one to whom these are not a kind of torture. By villains I do not mean thieves, assassins, poisoners; they do not belong in the category of those for whom I write. Villains are the false and perfidious, the slanderers, the informers, the ungrateful. In a word, all those who have vices the laws do not curb, but against which custom and society have brought formal judgments. These formal judgments are all the more terrible, as they are always carried out.

I maintain then that there is no one on earth who can feel that he is despised and not feel despair. This public disdain, this turning away of people of good will, is a torture more cruel than all those that the public executioner could inflict, because it lasts much longer, and because hope never accompanies it.

So one must never be immoral if one does not want to be unhappy. But it is not enough for us not to be unhappy; life would not be worth the effort of living if the absence of suffering was our only goal; nothingness would be better; for assuredly, that is the state of least suffering. One must, then, try to be happy. One must be at ease with oneself for the same reason that one must be comfortable in one's own home. We would hope in vain for enjoyment of this satisfaction if we were not virtuous:

> Mortals' eyes are easily dazzled;
> But one cannot deceive the vigilant eye of the gods,

as one of our best poets has said[1]; but it is the ever vigilant eye of one's own conscience that one can never deceive.

---

[1] Voltaire, Sémiramis

One is an exacting judge of oneself, and the more one can bear witness to oneself that one has fulfilled one's duties, done all the good that one could do, that in short, one is virtuous, the more one tastes this interior satisfaction that one can call the health of the soul. I doubt that there is a more delicious feeling than what one experiences after doing a virtuous action, an action that merits the esteem of honorable men. To the inner satisfaction caused by virtuous actions can be added the pleasure of enjoying universal esteem, but even though rogues cannot refuse their esteem to integrity, only the esteem of honorable men is truly worthwhile. Finally, I say that to be happy one must be susceptible to illusion, and this scarcely needs to be proved. . . . Why do I laugh more than anyone else at the puppets, if not because I allow myself to be more susceptible than anyone else to illusion, and that after a quarter of an hour I believe that it is Polichinelle, the puppet, who speaks? Would we have a moment of pleasure at the theater if we did not lend ourselves to the illusion that makes us see famous individuals that we know have been dead for a long time, speaking in Alexandrine verse? Truly, what pleasure would one have at any other spectacle where all is illusion if one was not able to abandon oneself to it? Surely there would be much to lose, and those at the opera who only have the pleasure of the music and the dances have a very meager pleasure, one well below that which this enchanting spectacle viewed as a whole provides. I have cited spectacles, because illusion is easier to perceive there. It is, however, involved in all the pleasures of our life, and provides the polish, the gloss of life. . . .

These are the great machines of happiness, so to speak; but there are yet other, lesser skills that can contribute to our happiness.

The first is to be resolute about what one wants to be and about what one wants to do. This is lacking in almost all men; it is, however, the prerequisite without which there is no happiness at all. Without it, one swims forever in a sea of uncertainties, one destroys in the morning what one made in the evening, life is spent doing stupid things, putting them right, repenting of them.

This feeling of repentance is one of the most useless and most disagreeable that our soul can experience. One of the great secrets is to know how to guard against it. As no two things in life are alike, it is almost always useless to see one's errors, or at least to pause a long time to consider them and to reproach oneself with them. In so doing we cover ourselves with confusion in our own eyes for no gain. One must start from where one is, use all one's sagacity to make amends and to find the means to make amends, but there is no point in looking back, and one must always brush from one's mind the memory of one's errors. The ability to benefit from an initial examination, dismiss sad ideas and substitute agreeable ideas, is one of the mainsprings of happiness, and we have this in our power, at least up to a point. I know that a violent passion that makes us unhappy proves that it does not depend entirely on us to banish from our mind the ideas that distress us; but we are not always in such violent situations, all illnesses are not malign fevers, and the trifling misfortunes, those sensations that are disagreeable, though weak, should be avoided. Death, for example, is an idea that always distresses us whether we foresee our own, or think of that of the people we love. So we must avoid with care all that can remind us of this idea. I very much disagree with Montaigne, who congratulated himself on having so accustomed himself to death that he was sure he would see it approach without being afraid. It may be seen by the complacency with which he reports this victory that it was a costly effort for him. And in this the wise Montaigne had miscalculated, because surely it is a folly to poison with this sad and humiliating idea part of the little time we have to live, all this in order to endure more patiently a moment that bodily sufferings always make very bitter, in spite of our philosophy. Moreover, who knows if the weakening of our mind, caused by illness or old age, will allow us to reap the benefit of our reflections; perhaps our efforts will have been all in vain, as so often happens in this life? When the idea of death recurs, let us always have this line of Gresset in mind: "Suffering is a century, and death a moment."

Let us turn the mind away from all disagreeable ideas; they are the source of all metaphysical anxieties, and it is above all those anxieties that it is almost always in our power to avoid.

Wisdom must always have counters in her hand to play with; *wise* and *happy* mean the same, at least in my dictionary. One must have passions to be happy; but they must be made to serve our happiness, and there are some that must absolutely be prevented from entering our soul. I am not speaking here of the passions that are vices, like hatred, vengeance, rage, but ambition, for example, is a passion that I believe one must defend one's soul against, if one wants to be happy. This is not because it does not give enjoyment, for I believe that this passion can provide that; it is not because ambition can never be satisfied—that is surely a great good. Rather, it is because ambition, of all the passions, makes our happiness dependent on others. Now the less our happiness depends on others the easier it is for us to be happy. Let us not be afraid to reduce our dependence on others too much, *our* happiness will always depend on others quite enough. If we value independence, the love of study is, of all the passions, the one that contributes most to our happiness. This love of study holds within it a passion from which a superior soul is never entirely exempt, that of glory. For half the world, glory can only be obtained in this manner, and it is precisely this half whose education made glory inaccessible and made a taste for it impossible.

Undeniably, the love of study is much less necessary to the happiness of men than it is to that of women. Men have infinite resources for their happiness that women lack. They have many means to attain glory, and it is quite certain that the ambition to make their talents useful to their country and to serve their fellow citizens, perhaps by their competency in the art of war, or by their talents for government, or negotiation, is superior to that which one can gain for oneself by study. But women are excluded, by definition, from every kind of glory, and when, by chance, one is born with a rather superior soul, only study remains to console her for all the exclusions and all the dependencies to which she finds herself condemned by her place in society.

The love of glory that is the source of so many pleasures of the soul and of so many efforts of all sorts that contribute to the happiness, the instruction, and the perfection of society, is entirely founded on illusion. Nothing is so easy as to make the phantom after which all superior souls run disappear; but there would be much to lose for them and for others! I know there is some substance in the love of glory that one can enjoy in one's lifetime; but there are scarcely any heroes, of whatever kind, who would want to close themselves off entirely from the plaudits of posterity, from which one expects more justice than from one's contemporaries. One does not always acknowledge the enjoyment of the ill-defined desire to be spoken of after one has passed out of existence; but it always stays deep in our heart. Philosophy would have us feel the vanity of it; but the feeling prevails, and this pleasure is not an illusion; for it proves to us the very real benefit of enjoying our future reputation. If our only source of good feeling were in the present, our pleasures would be even more limited than they are. We are made happy in the present moment not only by our actual delights but also by our hopes, our reminiscences. The present is enriched by the past and the future. Would we work for our children, for the greatness of our lineage, if we did not enjoy the future? Whatever we do, self-esteem is always the more or less hidden driving force of our actions; it is the wind that fills the sails, without which the boat would not move at all. . . .

One of the great secrets of happiness is to moderate one's desires and to love the things already in one's possession. Nature, whose goal is always our happiness (and by nature, I understand all that is instinctive and without reasoning), nature, I say, only gives us the desires appropriate to our rank and circumstances. We only naturally desire things by degrees and within our purview. . . . So one must allow oneself to desire only the things that can be obtained without too much care and effort, and this is a place where we can do much for our own happiness. To love what one possesses, to know how to enjoy it, to savor the advantages of one's situation in life, not to look too much at those who seem happier than we, to apply oneself to perfect one's own happiness and to make the most of it, this is what is rightly termed happiness. And I believe I define it well in saying that the happiest man is he who least desires to change his rank and circumstances. To enjoy this happiness, one must cure or prevent a sickness of another sort that is entirely opposed to it, but is only too common: restlessness. This state of mind is incompatible with any enjoyment, and, consequently, any kind of happiness. Good philosophy, that is to say, the firm belief that all we have to do in this world is to be happy, is a sure remedy against this sickness of which lively minds—those who are capable of reasoning on first causes and consequences—are almost always exempt.

There is a passion, very unreasonable in the eyes of philosophers and of reason, the motive of which, however disguised it may be, is even humiliating, and should be enough to cure one of it and which, nevertheless can make one happy: it is the passion of gambling. It is a good passion to have, if it can be moderated and kept for the time in our life when this resource will be necessary to us, and this time is old age. There is no doubt that the love of gambling has its source in the love of money; there is no individual for whom playing for high stakes is not an interesting activity (and I call high stakes gambling that can make a difference to our fortune).

Our soul wants to be moved by the passions of hope or fear; it is made happy only by things that cause it to feel alive. Now gambling places us perpetually in the grip of these two passions, and consequently holds our soul in an emotion that is one of the great principles of happiness to be found in us. The pleasure that gambling has given me has often served to console me for not being rich. I believe I have a good enough mind to be happy with what would seem to others a mediocre fortune; and in that case—if I were rich—gambling would become dull for me. At least I was afraid that it would, and this fear of boredom convinced me that I owe the pleasure of gambling to my limited fortune, and that consoled me for not being rich.

There is no doubt that physical needs are the source of the pleasures of the senses, and I am convinced that there is more pleasure in a mediocre fortune than in great abundance. A new snuffbox, a new piece of furniture or of china, is a true delight to me; but if I owned thirty snuffboxes, I would be less appreciative of the thirty-first. Our tastes are easily blunted by satiation, and one must give thanks to God for giving us the necessary privations to preserve them. This is what causes a king to be so often bored, and why it is impossible for him to be happy unless Heaven has given him a soul magnanimous enough to be susceptible to the pleasures of his position, that is to say the pleasure of making a great number of men happy. Then this position becomes the first above all for the happiness it brings, as it is by its power.

I have said that the more our happiness depends on us, the more assured it is; yet the passion that can give us the greatest pleasures and make us happiest, places our happiness entirely in the hands of others. You have already gathered that I am speaking of love.

This passion is perhaps the only one that can make us wish to live, and bring us to thank the author of nature, whoever he is, for giving us life. My Lord Rochester is right to say that the gods have put this heavenly drop in the chalice of life to give us the courage to bear it:

One must love, it is that which sustains us:
Because without love, it is sad to be man.

If this mutual taste, which is a sixth sense, and the most refined, the most delicate, the most precious of all, brings together two souls equally sensitive to happiness, to pleasure, all is said, one need not do anything more to be happy, everything else is inconsequential except for health. All the faculties of one's soul must be used to enjoy this happiness. One must give up life when one loses that happiness, and acknowledge that to have attained Nestor's age is nothing when balanced with a quarter hour of such bliss. It is appropriate that such a happiness should be rare; if it were common, one would choose to be a man rather than a god, at least such as we can conceive of God. The best thing we can do is to persuade ourselves that this happiness is not impossible. However, I do not know if love has ever brought together two people who are so made for each other that they have never known the satiety of delight, nor the cooling of passion caused by a sense of security, nor the indolence and the tedium that arise from the ease and the continuity of a relationship, and whose power of illusion never wanes (for where is illusion more important than in love?); and, last, whose ardor remains the same whether in the enjoyment or in the deprivation of the other's presence, and equally tolerates both unhappiness and pleasure.

The creation of a heart capable of such a love, a soul so tender, and so steadfast appears to exhaust the power of the deity; only one is born in a century. It seems that to produce two such hearts would be beyond the deity's powers, or if he has produced them, and if they could meet, he would be jealous of their pleasures. But love can make us happy at less cost: a tender and sensitive soul is made happy by the sheer pleasure it finds in loving. I do not mean that unrequited love could make one perfectly happy; but I say that, although our ideas of happiness are not entirely satisfied by the love given us, the pleasure we feel in giving ourselves up to our feelings of tenderness can suffice to make us happy. And if this soul still has the good fortune to be susceptible to illusions, it is not impossible that it should not believe itself more loved perhaps than it is in fact. This soul must love so much that it loves for two, and the warmth of its heart supplies what is, in fact, lacking in its happiness. A feeling character, keen and susceptible to the passions, must pay the price of the inconveniences attached to these qualities, and I do not know if I must say they are good or bad; but I believe that however composed one's character, one would still want to have them. A first passion carries a soul tempered in this way so much beyond itself that it is inaccessible to any reflection and to any moderate ideas; this soul can probably look forward to great sorrows; but the greatest inconvenience attached to such sensibility is that someone who loves to this excess cannot possibly be loved, for there is scarcely a man whose amorous inclination does not diminish with the experience of such a passion. That must appear quite strange to him who does not yet know enough about the human heart; but however little one may have reflected about what experience offers us, one will feel that to hold the heart of one's beloved for a long time, hope and fear must always operate on him. Now, a passion, such as I have just depicted, produces an abandon that makes one incapable of any art. Love bursts out on all sides; you are initially adored, it can only be so; but soon the certainty of being loved, and the tedium of having one's wishes always

anticipated, the misfortune of having nothing to fear, dulls one's inclination. Such is the human heart, and no one should think that I speak out
of resentment. I have been endowed by God, it is true, with one of these
loving and steadfast souls that know neither how to disguise nor how to
moderate its passions, that know neither their diminution nor disgust
with them, and whose tenacity can resist everything, even the certainty
of being no longer loved. But I was happy for ten years because of the love
of the man [Voltaire] who had completely seduced my soul; and these ten
years I spent tête-à-tête with him without a single moment of distaste
or hint of melancholy. When age, illness, as well as perhaps the ease of
pleasure made his inclination less, for a long time I did not perceive it; I
was loving for two, I spent all my time with him, and my heart, free from
suspicion, delighted in the pleasure of loving and in the illusion of believing myself loved. True, I have lost this happy state, and this has cost me
many tears. Terrible shocks are needed to break such chains. The wound
to my heart bled for a long time; I had grounds to complain, and I have
pardoned all. I was fair enough to accept that in the whole world, perhaps
only my heart possessed the steadfastness that annihilates the power of
time; that if age and illness had not entirely extinguished his desire, it
would perhaps still have been for me, and that love would have restored
him to me; lastly, that his heart, incapable of love, felt for me the most
tender affection, and caused him to dedicate his life to me. The certainty
that a return of his inclination and his passion was impossible—I know
well that such a return is not in nature—imperceptibly led my heart to the
peaceful feeling of deep affection; and this sentiment, together with the
passion for study, made me happy enough.

But can such a tender heart be satisfied by a sentiment as peaceful
and as weak as that of close friendship? I do not know if one must hope,
or even wish, to cling forever to this sensibility, once one has reached the
kind of apathy to which it is so difficult to lead such a soul. Only lively and
agreeable feelings make one happy; why then forbid oneself love, the most
lively and most agreeable of all? But what one has experienced, the reflections that one has had to make to lead one's heart to this apathy, the very
pain that caused one to bring it to this state—all this must make one fear
to leave a situation that at least is not unhappy, in order to venture out to
meet with the misfortunes which one's age and the loss of one's beauty
would make pointless. . . .

The great secret for preventing love from making us unhappy is
to try never to appear in the wrong with your lover, never to display

eagerness when his love is cooling, and always to be a degree cooler than he. This will not bring him back, but nothing could bring him back; there is nothing for us to do then but to forget someone who ceases to love us. If he still loves you, nothing can revive his love and make it as fiery as it was at first, except the fear of losing you and of being less loved. I know that for the susceptible and sincere this secret is difficult to put into practice; however, no effort will be too great, all the more so as it is much more necessary for the susceptible and sincere than for others. Nothing degrades as much as the steps one takes to regain a cold or in-constant heart. This demeans us in the eyes of the one we seek to keep, and in those of other men who might take an interest in us. But, and this is even worse, it makes us unhappy and uselessly torments us. So we must follow this maxim with unwavering courage and never surrender to our own heart on this point. . . . Lastly, it is for reason to make our happiness. In childhood, our senses alone attend to this task; in youth, the heart and the mind become involved, with the proviso that the heart makes all the decisions; but in middle age reason must take part in the decision; it is for reason to make us feel that we must be happy, whatever it costs. Every age has its own pleasures; those of old age are the most difficult to obtain: *gambling, studying,* if one is still capable of it, the *enjoyment of fine foods, respect,* those are the mainsprings of old age. No doubt these are only consolations. Thank goodness, it is up to us to choose the time of our death, if it is too slow in coming; but as long as we prefer to endure life, we must open ourselves to pleasure by all the doors leading to our soul; we have no other business.

So let us try to be healthy, to have no prejudices, to have passions, to make them serve our happiness, to replace our passions with inclinations, to cherish our illusions, to be virtuous, never to repent, to keep away sad ideas, and never to allow our heart to sustain a spark of inclination for someone whose inclination for us diminishes and who ceases to love us. We must leave love behind one day, if we do indeed age, and that day must be the one when love ceases to make us happy. Lastly, let us think of fostering a taste for study, a taste which makes our happiness depend only on ourselves. Let us preserve ourselves from ambition, and, above all, let us be certain of what we want to be; let us choose for ourselves our path in life, and let us try to strew that path with flowers.

34

Samuel Johnson

Described by the *Oxford Dictionary of National Biography* as "arguably the most distinguished man of letters in English history," Samuel Johnson (1709–1784) was a brilliant essayist, poet, and—famously— the compiler of the celebrated *Dictionary of the English Language*. In the following essay, Johnson maintains that the possibility of happiness is dependent upon religious belief, particularly the belief in a life after death.

Consolation in the Face of Death

Notwithstanding the warnings of Philosophers, and the daily examples of losses and misfortunes which life forces upon our observation, such is the absorption of our thoughts in the business of the present day, such the resignation of our reason to empty hopes of future felicity, or such our unwillingness to foresee what we dread, that every calamity comes suddenly upon us, and not only presses us as a burthen, but crushes as a blow.

There are evils which happen out of the common course of nature, against which it is no reproach not to be provided. A flash of lightning intercepts the traveller in his way. The concussion of an earthquake heaps the ruins of cities upon their inhabitants. But other miseries time brings, though silently yet visibly forward by its even lapse, which yet approach us unseen because we turn our eyes away, and seize us

---

"Consolation in the Face of Death", (London: Penguin, 2009 (1759)), pp. 113–116.

unresisted because we could not arm ourselves against them, but by setting them before us.

That it is vain to shrink from what cannot be avoided, and to hide that from ourselves which must some time be found, is a truth which we all know, but which all neglect, and perhaps none more than the speculative reasoner, whose thoughts are always from home, whose eye wanders over life, whose fancy dances after meteors of happiness kindled by itself, and who examines every thing rather than his own state.

Nothing is more evident than that the decays of age must terminate in death; yet there is no man, says *Tully*, who does not believe that he may yet live another year; and there is none who does not, upon the same principle, hope another year for his parent or his friend; but the fallacy will be in time detected; the last year, the last day must come. It has come and is past. The life which made my own life pleasant is at an end, and the gates of death are shut upon my prospects.

The loss of a friend upon whom the heart was fixed, to whom every wish and endeavour tended, is a state of dreary desolation in which the mind looks abroad impatient of itself, and finds nothing but emptiness and horror. The blameless life, the artless tenderness, the pious simplicity, the modest resignation, the patient sickness, and the quiet death, are remembered only to add value to the loss, to aggravate regret for what cannot be amended, to deepen sorrow for what cannot be recalled.

These are the calamities by which Providence gradually disengages us from the love of life. Other evils fortitude may repel, or hope may mitigate; but irreparable privation leaves nothing to exercise resolution or flatter expectation. The dead cannot return, and nothing is left us here but languishment and grief.

Yet such is the course of nature, that whoever lives long must outlive those whom he loves and honours. Such is the condition of our present existence, that life must one time lose its associations, and every inhabitant of the earth must walk downward to the grave alone and unregarded, without any partner of his joy or grief, without any interested witness of his misfortunes or success.

Misfortune, indeed, he may yet feel, for where is the bottom of the misery of man? But what is success to him that has none to enjoy it. Happiness is not found in self-contemplation; it is perceived only when it is reflected from another.

We know little of the state of departed souls, because such knowledge is not necessary to a good life. Reason deserts us at the brink of the grave, and can give no further intelligence. Revelation is not wholly silent. *There is joy in the Angels of Heaven over one sinner that repenteth*; and surely this joy is not incommunicable to souls disentangled from the body, and made like Angels.

Let Hope therefore dictate, what Revelation does not confute, that the union of souls may still remain; and that we who are struggling with sin, sorrow, and infirmities, may have our part in the attention and kindness of those who have finished their course and are now receiving their reward.

These are the great occasions which force the mind to take refuge in Religion: when we have no help in ourselves, what can remain but that we look up to a higher and a greater Power; and to what hope may we not raise our eyes and hearts, when we consider that the Greatest POWER is the BEST.

Surely there is no man who, thus afflicted, does not seek succour in the *Gospel*, which has brought *Life and Immortality to light*. The Precepts of *Epicurus*, who teaches us to endure what the Laws of the Universe make necessary, may silence but not content us. The dictates of *Zeno*, who commands us to look with indifference on external things, may dispose us to conceal our sorrow, but cannot assuage it. Real alleviation of the loss of friends, and rational tranquillity in the prospect of our own dissolution, can be received only from the promises of him in whose hands are life and death, and from the assurance of another and better state, in which all tears will be wiped from the eyes, and the whole soul shall be filled with joy. Philosophy may infuse stubbornness, but Religion only can give Patience.

===== 🜍 =====

35

Julien Offray de La Mettrie

Julien Offray de La Mettrie (1709–1751) was a French philosopher famous for his relentlessly materialistic account of human nature, elaborated in such works as *Man a Machine* and *Man a Plant*. La Mettrie's work is pregnant with anticipations: his identification of mental processes with brain processes prefigures the theories of materialist theorists of mind in the twentieth century, while his claim that there is no "abrupt transition" between animals and man clearly anticipates aspects of Darwinian theory. The first selection below is drawn from *Man a Machine* and illustrates La Mettrie's mechanistic view of the body and the mind. In the second reading, La Mettrie takes aim at Seneca's theory of the happy life (itself included previously in this volume) and in so doing develops his own (markedly sensuous) conception of what constitutes happiness.

Man a Machine

Descartes and all the Cartesians, among whom have long been counted the Malebrancheans, made the same mistake. They said man consists of two distinct substances, as though they had seen and counted them. . . .

The excellence of reason does not depend on its *immateriality*, a big word empty of meaning, but from its power, extent and clear-sightedness. Thus, a *soul of mud* that could discern at a glance the relations and consequences of an infinity of ideas that are difficult to understand, would obviously be preferable to a foolish and stupid soul made of the more precious elements. To be a philosopher, it is not enough merely to be ashamed like Pliny of the wretchedness of our origin. Our seemingly base beginning is in fact the most precious thing in the world, for which nature seems to have used the most art and ceremony. But just as man would still be the most perfect of all beings even if he came from a source even more vile in appearance, so is his soul lofty whatever its origin, if it is pure, noble, and sublime. And this makes whomever is endowed with it worthy of respect. . . .

Man is a machine so complicated that it is impossible at first to form a clear idea of it, and consequently, to describe it. This is why all the investigations the greatest philosophers have made *a priori*, that is, by wanting to take flight with the wings of the mind, have been in vain. Only *a posteriori*, by unravelling the soul as one pulls out the guts of a body, can one, I do not say discover with clarity what the nature of man is, but rather attain the highest degree of probability on the subject. . . .

[W]ho knows if the reason for man's existence might not lie in this very existence itself? Perhaps he was cast by chance into a tiny corner of the earth, knowing neither how nor why, but only that he must live and die, like those mushrooms that appear from one day to the next, or those flowers that border ditches and cover walls.

Let us not lose our own selves in contemplating the infinite; we are not made to have the least idea of it. It is absolutely impossible for us to go back to the origin of things. It is all the same for our peace of mind whether matter is eternal or created; whether there is a God or none, we will lose no sleep over it. What madness to torment oneself so much over what is impossible to know, and would not make us happier if we knew it. . . .

Now look, all the faculties of the soul depend so much on the proper organization of the brain and the entire body, since these faculties are obviously just this organized brain itself, there is a well-enlightened machine! Because really, why would man's having a share of the natural law make him any less a machine? A few more cog wheels and springs than in the most perfect animals, the brain proportionately nearer the heart so it receives more blood. The same reasons given, what, finally, am I saying? Unknown causes could produce both this delicate conscience so easy to offend, and this remorse, that are no more foreign to matter than thought is, and, in a word, any other faculty supposed here. Is organization therefore sufficient for everything? Yes, once again. Since thought obviously develops with the organs, why would the matter of which they are made not be susceptible to remorse once it has acquired in time the faculty of feeling?

Soul is, therefore, only an empty word to which no idea corresponds. An intelligent person ought to use it only to name the part in us that thinks. Given the least principle of movement, animated bodies have all they need to move, feel, think, repent, and in a word, to act in the physical world and also in the moral, which depends on the physical. . . .

Let us consider the details of these springs of the human machine. Their actions cause all natural, automatic, vital, and animal movements. Does not the body leap back mechanically in terror when one comes upon an unexpected precipice? And do the eyelids not close automatically at the threat of a blow? And as I said before, does not the *pupil* contract automatically in full daylight to protect the retina and enlarge to see in the dark? In the winter, do pores of the skin not close automatically so the cold does not penetrate into the veins? Does the stomach not heave automatically when irritated by poison, a dose of opium, and all emetics? Do the heart, arteries, and muscles not contract automatically when one is asleep, just as when one is awake? Do the lungs not automatically work continually like bellows? Do not the sphincters of the bladder, *rectum*, etc. close automatically? . . .

I will not comment further on all the small subordinate springs everyone knows about. But there is another, more subtle and marvelous, that animates everything. It is the source of all our feelings, pleasures, passions, and thoughts, for the brain has its muscles for thinking as the legs for walking. I mean that impetuous autonomous principle that Hippocrates calls . . . the soul. This principle exists and is seated in the brain at the point of origin of the nerves through which it exercises its rule over all the rest of the body. . . .

To be a machine, to feel, think, know good from evil like blue from yellow, in a word, to be born with intelligence and a sure instinct for morality, and yet to be only an animal, are things no more contradictory than to be an ape or parrot and know how to find sexual pleasure. And since the occasion presents itself for saying so, who would ever have divined *a priori* that shooting off a gob of sperm during copulation would ever make one feel such divine pleasure, and that from it would be born a tiny creature who one day, following certain laws, could enjoy the same delights? Thought is so far from being incompatible with organized matter that it seems to me to be just another of its properties, such as electricity, the motive faculty, impenetrability, extension, etc. . . .

Let us, therefore, conclude boldly that man is a machine, and that the entire universe contains only one single diversely modified substance. . . . Deny it if you can!

Anti-Seneca

Philosophers agree on happiness as they do on everything else. For some it resides in what is dirtiest and most shameless; they can be recognized by their cynical air and they never blush. For others it consists in sensual pleasure, understood in different ways: sometimes it is pleasure given by the most refined sexuality, and sometimes it is the same pleasure, but moderate and reasonable, and subject not to the debauched whims of an inflamed imagination but to the needs of nature alone; for some, it is the sensuality of the mind concerned with the search for the truth, or delighted with its possession, while for others, it is the satisfaction of the mind, the aim and purpose of all our actions, which Epicurus again dubbed sensual pleasure. This word is dangerously ambiguous and is the reason why his disciples have taken from his teaching a very different fruit from that which this great man was entitled to expect. Some have placed the sovereign good in all the perfections of the mind and the body. For Zeno it consisted in honour and virtue. Seneca, the most illustrious of the Stoics, or rather of the Eclectics (for he was Epicurean and Stoic at the same time, and he chose and took what he found best in each sect), added the knowledge of truth, without defining explicitly which truth.

In the midst of so many other superficial opinions, about which I shall say nothing, few philosophers have had enough taste to place happiness in the continuation of those sweet habits which constitute pure friendship or tender love. But how can one be happy, even on the throne, when one does not live with those one loves! And what misery when one is forced to live with those one detests!

To live peacefully, without ambition and without desire; to make use of riches instead of enjoying them; to keep them without anxiety and to lose them without regret; to be master of them instead of their slave; not to be upset or moved by any passion, or rather not to experience any, and to be contented in both pain and pleasure; to possess a strong, healthy soul in a weak, sick body; to experience neither fear nor fright; to rid oneself of all anxiety; to disdain pleasures and sensuality; to agree to experience pleasure and to be rich without seeking those sources of happiness; to despise life itself; and to achieve virtue by a knowledge of the truth—all

---

La Mettrie, Anti-Seneca (in Machine Man and Other Writings (ed. by Ann Thomson) (Cambridge: Cambridge University Press, 1996), pp. 119–120, 120, 121–122, 123, 123–4, 125–126, 127. Copyright © 1996 Cambridge University Press.

these things constitute the Sovereign Good of Seneca and the Stoics in general, and the perfect bliss which follows from it.

But we shall be Anti-Stoics! Those philosophers are sad, strict and unyielding; we shall be cheerful, sweet-natured and indulgent. They are all soul and ignore their bodies; we shall be all body and ignore our souls. They appear impervious to pleasure or pain; we shall glory in feeling both. They aspire to the sublime and rise above all events, considering themselves to be truly men only to the extent that they cease to be men. As for us, we shall not try to control what rules us; we shall not give orders to our sensations. We shall recognise their dominion and our slavery and try to make it pleasant for us, convinced as we are that happiness in life lies there; we shall consider ourselves happier when we are more truly men, or more worthy of being men, and when we experience humanity, nature and all the social virtues. We shall accept no others and no other life but this one. . . .

Our organs are capable of feeling or being modified in a way that pleases us and makes us enjoy life. If the impression created by this feeling is short, it constitutes pleasure; if longer, sensuality and if permanent, happiness. It is always the same feeling; only its duration and intensity differ. I have added the latter word because there is no Sovereign Good as exquisite as the great pleasure of love, in which it perhaps consists. . . .

To have everything one wants—a favourable organisation, beauty, science, wit, grace, talents, honours, wealth, health, pleasure and glory—is true, perfect happiness. . . .

What convinces me of the truth of what I have just raised is the fact that I see so many ignorant people who are happy due to their ignorance and their prejudices. While they experience none of that pleasure which self-esteem derives from the discovery of the most sterile of truths, there is a compensation for everything; they experience none of that suffering and sorrow caused by the most important discoveries. They do not care at all whether it is the earth or the sun that revolves, and whether the earth is flattened or rounded. Instead of worrying about the course of nature, they let it follow chance and they themselves bustle gaily on their way, led by their white stick. They take pleasure in eating, drinking, sleeping and vegetating. . . .

In addition, animals can be cited in support of this system. When they are in good health and their appetites are satisfied, they enjoy the pleasant feelings associated with this satisfaction, and consequently this species is happy in its own fashion. Seneca denies this in vain. His opinion is based on the fact that they have no intellectual idea of happiness, as if metaphysical ideas had an influence on well-being and as if it required reflection. If happiness consists in living and dying in tranquillity, then, alas, how much happier than we are animals. . . .

Surely certain remedies are another proof of that happiness which I call organic, automatic or natural, because the soul is not involved at all and can claim no credit for it, as it is independent of its will. I am referring to that pleasant, calm state caused by opium, in which one would like to remain for eternity; it would be the true paradise of the soul if it were permanent. This happy state is only the result of the gentle regularity of the circulation and a pleasant, half-paralytic relaxation of the solid fibres. What wonders are performed by a single grain of narcotic juice added to the blood and flowing with it in the vessels! What magic makes it transmit more happiness to us than the treatises of all the philosophers! And what would be the fate of someone whose organisation was all his life as it is when under the influence of that divine remedy! How happy he would be! . . .

If being deceived by nature is to our advantage, well, let her always deceive us! Let us use our very reason to mislead ourselves if it makes us happier. He who has found happiness has found everything.

But he who has found happiness has not sought it. We do not seek what we have, and if we do not have it, then we will never have it. Philosophy gives loud praise to the advantages it owes to nature. Seneca was unhappy and he wrote about happiness as one writes for a lost dog. It is true that he was a Stoic, a sort of leper well armed against the pleasures of life. I believe that the first member of that sect must have been a hypochondriac. . . .

In any case, in a century as enlightened as ours, in which nature is so well understood that, on this subject at least, we are completely satisfied, it has finally been demonstrated by a thousand unanswerable proofs that there is only one life and one bliss. The first precondition for happiness is feeling, and death removes all feeling. As the only means by which we can feel no longer exist, we can no more feel after death than we can before life. It is easier for an extinguished candle to give light than for a corpse to feel. False philosophy, like theology, can promise us eternal happiness and, lulling us with splendid fantasies, lead us there at the expense of our life or our pleasures. True philosophy, which is very different and much wiser, only admits temporal bliss; it casts roses and flowers in our path and teaches us to gather them.

36
🐦
Thomas Reid

Thomas Reid (1710–1796) was a Scottish philosopher and a great defender of common sense against the onslaughts of philosophical skepticism. The selections below are drawn from Reid's *Essays on the Intellectual Powers of Man* and consist predominantly of a trenchant critique of Locke's theory of personal identity.

Essays on the Intellectual Powers of Man

Essay III, Chapter IV: "of Identity"

Identity in general, I take to be a relation between a thing which is known to exist at one time, and a thing which is known to have existed at another time. If you ask whether they are one and the same, or two different things, every man of common sense understands the meaning of your question perfectly. Whence we may infer with certainty, that every man of common sense has a clear and distinct notion of identity.

If you ask a definition of identity, I confess I can give none; it is too simple a notion to admit of logical definition: I can say it is a relation, but I cannot find words to express the specific difference between this and other relations, though I am in no danger of confounding it with any

Thomas Reid, *Essays on the Intellectual Powers of Man* (Cambridge, MA: MIT Press, 1969 [1785]), Essay III , "Concerning Memory", Chapter IV, pp. 339–340, 340–342, 344, and Chapter VI.

other. I can say that diversity is a contrary relation, and that similitude and dissimilitude are another couple of contrary relations which every man easily distinguishes in his conception from identity and diversity.

I see evidently that identity supposes an uninterrupted continuance of existence. That which has ceased to exist, cannot be the same with that which afterward begins to exist; for this would be to suppose a being to exist after it ceased to exist, and to have had existence before it was produced, which are manifest contradictions. Continued uninterrupted existence is therefore necessarily implied in identity.

Hence we may infer, that identity cannot, in its proper sense, be applied to our pains, our pleasures, our thoughts, or any operation of our minds. The pain felt this day is not the same individual pain which I felt yesterday, though they may be similar in kind and degree, and have the same cause. The same may be said of every feeling, and of every operation of mind. They are all successive in their nature, like time itself, no two moments of which can be the same moment. . . .

When a man loses his estate, his health, his strength, he is still the same person, and has lost nothing of his personality. If he has a leg or an arm cut off, he is the same person he was before. The amputated member is no part of his person, otherwise it would have a right to a part of his estate, and be liable for a part of his engagements. It would be entitled to a share of his merit and demerit, which is manifestly absurd. A person is something indivisible and is what Leibnitz calls a *monad*.

My personal identity, therefore, implies the continued existence of that indivisible thing which I call *myself*. Whatever this self may be, it is something which thinks, and deliberates, and resolves, and acts, and suffers. I am not thought, I am not action, I am not feeling; I am something that thinks, and acts, and suffers. My thoughts, and actions, and feelings, change every moment; they have no continued, but a successive existence; but that *self* or *I*, to which they belong, is permanent, and has the same relation to all the succeeding thoughts, actions and feelings, which I call mine.

Such are the notions that I have of my personal identity. But perhaps it may be said, this may all be fancy without reality. How do you know; what evidence have you, that there is such a permanent self which has a claim to all the thoughts, actions, and feelings, which you call yours?

To this I answer that the proper evidence I have of all this is remembrance. I remember that twenty years ago I conversed with such a person; I remember several things that passed in that conversation; my memory testifies not only that this was done, but that it was done by me who now remember it. If it was done by me, I must have existed at that time, and continued to exist from that time to the present. If the identical person whom I call myself, had not a part in that conversation, my memory is fallacious; it gives a distinct and positive testimony of what is not true. Every man in his senses believes what he distinctly remembers, and every thing he remembers convinces him that he existed at the time remembered.

Although memory gives the most irresistible evidence of my being the identical person that did such a thing, at such a time, I may have other good evidence of things which befell me, and which I do not remember; I know who bare me, and suckled me, but I do not remember these events.

It may here he observed, though the observation would have been unnecessary, if some great philosophers had not contradicted it, that it is not my remembering any action of mine that makes me to be the person who did it. This remembrance makes me to know assuredly that I did it; but I might have done it, though I did not remember it. That relation to me, which is expressed by saying that I did it, would be the same, though I had not the least remembrance of it. To say that my remembering that I did such a thing, or, as some choose to express it, my being conscious that I did it, makes me to have done it, appears to me as great an absurdity as it would be to say, that my belief that the world was created, made it to be created. . . .

It may likewise be observed that the identity of objects of sense is never perfect. All bodies, as they consist of innumerable parts that may be disjoined from them by a great variety of causes, are subject to continual changes of their substance, increasing, diminishing, changing insensibly. When such alterations are gradual, because language could not afford a different name for every different state of such a changeable being, it retains the same name, and is considered as the same thing. Thus we say of an old regiment, that it did such a thing a century ago, though there now is not a man alive who then belonged to it. We say a tree is the same in the seed bed and in the forest. A ship of war, which has successively changed her anchors, her tackle, her sails, her masts, her planks, and her timbers, while she keeps the same name, is the same.

The identity therefore which we ascribe to bodies, whether natural or artificial, is not perfect identity; it is rather something which, for the conveniency of speech, we call identity. It admits of a great change of the subject, providing the change be gradual, sometimes even of a total change. And the changes which in common language are made consistent with identity, differ from those that are thought to destroy it, not in kind, but in number and degree. It has no fixed nature when applied to bodies; and questions about the identity of a body are very often questions about words. But identity, when applied to persons, has no ambiguity, and admits not of degrees or of more and less: it is the foundation of all rights and obligations, and of all accountableness; and the notion of it is fixed and precise.

Chapter VI: "Of Mr. Locke's Account of Personal Identity"

In a long chapter upon identity and diversity, Mr. Locke has made many ingenious and just observations, and some which, I think, cannot be defended. I shall only take notice of the account he gives of our own personal identity. . . .

Identity, as was observed chap. 4, of this Essay, supposes the continued existence of the being of which it is affirmed, and therefore can be applied only to things which have a continued existence. While any being continues to exist, it is the same being; but two beings which have a different beginning or a different ending of their existence, cannot possibly be the same. To this I think Mr. Locke agrees.

He observes very justly, that to know what is meant by the same *person*, we must consider what the word person stands for; and he defines a person to be an intelligent being, endowed with reason and with consciousness, which last he thinks inseparable from thought. . . .

One would think that the definition of a person should perfectly ascertain the nature of personal identity, or wherein it consists, though it might still be a question how we come to know and be assured of our personal identity.

Mr. Locke tells us, however, "that personal identity, that is, the sameness of a rational being, consists in consciousness alone; and, as far as this consciousness can be extended backward to any past action or thought, so far reaches the identity of that person. So that whatever has the consciousness of present and past actions, is the same person to whom they belong."

This doctrine has some strange consequences, which the author was aware of. Such as, that if the same consciousness can be transferred from one intelligent being to another, which he thinks we cannot show to be impossible, then two or twenty intelligent beings may be the same person. And if the intelligent being may lose the consciousness of the actions done by him, which surely is possible, then he is not the person that did those actions; so that one intelligent being may be two or twenty different persons, if he shall so often lose the consciousness of his former actions.

There is another consequence of this doctrine, which follows no less necessarily, though Mr. Locke probably did not see it. It is, that a man may be, and at the same time not be, the person that did a particular action.

Suppose a brave officer to have been flogged when a boy at school, for robbing an orchard, to have taken a standard from the enemy in his first campaign, and to have been made a general in advanced life. Suppose also, which must be admitted to be possible, that when he took the standard, he was conscious of his having been flogged at school; and that when made a general, he was conscious of his taking the standard, but had absolutely lost the consciousness of his flogging.

These things being supposed, it follows, from Mr. Locke's doctrine, that he who was flogged at school is the same person who took the standard; and that he who took the standard is the same person who was made a general. Whence it follows, if there be any truth in logic, that the general is the same person with him who was flogged at school. But the general's consciousness does not reach so far back as his flogging, therefore, according to Mr. Locke's doctrine, he is not the person who was flogged. Therefore the general is, and at the same time is not, the same person with him who was flogged at school.

Leaving the consequences of this doctrine to those who have leisure to trace them, we may observe, with regard to the doctrine itself;

1st, That Mr. Locke attributes to consciousness the conviction we have of our past actions, as if a man may now be conscious of what he did twenty years ago. It is impossible to understand the meaning of this, unless by consciousness be meant memory, the only faculty by which we have an immediate knowledge of our past actions.

Sometimes, in popular discourse, a man says he is conscious that he did such a thing, meaning that he distinctly remembers that he did it. It is unnecessary, in common discourse, to fix accurately the limits between consciousness and memory. This was formerly shown to be the case with regard to sense and memory: and therefore distinct remembrance is sometimes called sense, sometimes consciousness, without any inconvenience.

But this ought to be avoided in philosophy, otherwise we confound the different powers of the mind, and ascribe to one what really belongs to another. If a man can be conscious of what he did twenty years, or twenty minutes ago, there is no use for memory, nor ought we to allow that there is any such faculty. The faculties of consciousness and memory are chiefly distinguished by this, that the first is an immediate knowledge of the present, the second an immediate knowledge of the past.

When, therefore, Mr. Locke's notion of personal identity is properly expressed, it is, that personal identity consists in distinct remembrance: for, even in the popular sense, to say that I am conscious of a past action, means nothing else than that I distinctly remember that I did it.

2dly, It may be observed, that in this doctrine, not only is consciousness confounded with memory, but, which is still more strange, personal identity is confounded with the evidence which we have of our personal identity.

It is very true, that my remembrance that I did such a thing is the evidence I have that I am the identical person who did it. And this, I am apt to think, Mr. Locke meant: but to say that my remembrance that I did such a thing, or my consciousness, makes me the person who did it, is, in my apprehension, an absurdity too gross to be entertained by any man who attends to the meaning of it: for it is to attribute to memory or consciousness, a strange magical power of producing its object, though that object must have existed before the memory or consciousness which produced it.

Consciousness is the testimony of one faculty; memory is the testimony of another faculty: and to say that the testimony is the cause of the thing testified, this surely is absurd, if any thing be, and could not have been said by Mr. Locke, if he had not confounded the testimony with the thing testified.

When a horse that was stolen is found and claimed by the owner, the only evidence he can have, or that a judge or witnesses can have, that this is the very identical horse which was his property, is similitude.

But would it not be ridiculous from this to infer that the identity of a horse consists in similitude only? The only evidence I have that I am the identical person who did such actions, is, that I remember distinctly I did them; or, as Mr. Locke expresses it, I am conscious I did them. To infer from this, that personal identity consists in consciousness, is an argument, which, if it had any force, would prove the identity of a stolen horse to consist solely in similitude.

3dly, Is it not strange that the sameness or identity of a person should consist in a thing which is continually changing, and is not any two minutes the same?

Our consciousness, our memory, and every operation of the mind, are still flowing like the water of a river, or like time itself. The consciousness I have this moment can no more be the same consciousness I had last moment, than this moment can be the last moment. Identity can only be affirmed of things which have a continued existence. Consciousness, and every kind of thought, is transient and momentary, and has no continued existence; and therefore, if personal identity consisted in consciousness, it would certainly follow, that no man is the same person any two moments of his life; and as the right and justice of reward and punishment is founded on personal identity, no man could be responsible for his actions.

But though I take this to be the unavoidable consequence of Mr. Locke's doctrine concerning personal identity, and though some persons may have liked the doctrine the better on this account, I am far from imputing any thing of this kind to Mr. Locke. He was too good a man not to have rejected with abhorrence a doctrine which he believed to draw this consequence after it.

4thly, There are many expressions used by Mr. Locke in speaking of personal identity, which to me are altogether unintelligible, unless we suppose that he confounded that sameness, or identity, which we ascribe to an individual, with the identity which in common discourse is often ascribed to many individuals of the same species.

When we say that pain and pleasure, consciousness and memory, are the same in all men, this sameness can only mean similarity, or sameness of kind, but that the pain of one man can be the same individual pain with that of another man, is no less impossible, than that one man should be another man; the pain felt by me yesterday, can no more be the pain I feel today, than yesterday can be this day; and the same thing may be said of every passion and of every operation of the mind. The same kind or species of operation may be in different men, or in the same man at different times; but it is impossible that the same individual operation should be in different men, or in the same man at different times.

When Mr. Locke therefore speaks of "the same consciousness being continued through a succession of different substances;" when he speaks of "repeating the idea of a past action, with the same consciousness we had of it at the first," and of "the same consciousness extending to actions past and to come;" these expressions are to me unintelligible, unless he means, not the same individual consciousness, but a consciousness that is similar, or of the same kind.

If our personal identity consists in consciousness, as this consciousness cannot be the same individually any two moments, but only of the same kind, it would follow that we are not for any two moments the same individual persons, but the same kind of persons.

As our consciousness sometimes ceases to exist, as in sound sleep, our personal identity must cease with it. Mr. Locke allows, that the same thing cannot have two beginnings of existence, so that our identity would be irrecoverably gone every time we cease to think, if it was but for a moment.

David Hume

Born in Edinburgh, David Hume (1711–1776) is widely regarded both as the greatest of British philosophers and as the paradigm example of a philosophical skeptic. The astounding array of his interests is reflected in the selections below. In the first reading, we see Hume famously rejecting the idea of a "simple and continu'd" self, and replacing this with his "bundle" conception of the self (a conception that bears comparison with the Buddhist view). The second selection consists of Hume's forensic and devastating analysis of the idea of the immortality of the soul. This is followed by Hume's examination of the possibility of free will and then by his dramatic presentation of the ills of the human condition, taken from the *Dialogues Concerning Natural Religion*. Three shorter readings complete the selections from Hume: a trenchant criticism of the Stoic ideal of happiness as constituted by acceptance of the world's happenings (a view, Hume thinks, more likely to "irritate than appease"); a suggestion that human nature is not to be viewed either as selfish or as benevolent but as a *mixture* of both; and, finally and sadly, a somewhat typical expression of eighteenth century racist attitudes, found in a footnote to his essay "Of National Characters."

A Treatise of Human Nature

Book I, Section VI: "Of Personal Identity"

There are some philosophers, who imagine we are every moment intimately conscious of what we call our SELF; that we feel its existence and

From *A Treatise of Human Nature* (Oxford: Clarendon Press, 1888), pp. 251–253.

its continuance in existence; and are certain, beyond the evidence of a demonstration, both of its perfect identity and simplicity. The strongest sensation, the most violent passion, say they, instead of distracting us from this view, only fix it the more intensely, and make us consider their influence on *self* either by their pain or pleasure. To attempt a farther proof of this were to weaken its evidence; since no proof can be deriv'd from any fact, of which we are so intimately conscious; nor is there any thing, of which we can be certain, if we doubt of this.

Unluckily all these positive assertions are contrary to that very experience, which is pleaded for them, nor have we any idea of *self*, after the manner it is here explain'd. For from what impression cou'd this idea be deriv'd? This question 'tis impossible to answer without a manifest contradiction and absurdity; and yet 'tis a question, which must necessarily be answer'd, if we wou'd have the idea of self pass for clear and intelligible. It must be some one impression, that gives rise to every real idea. But self or person is not any one impression, but that to which our several impressions and ideas are suppos'd to have a reference. If any impression gives rise to the idea of self, that impression must continue invariably the same, thro' the whole course of our lives; since self is suppos'd to exist after that manner. But there is no impression constant and invariable. Pain and pleasure, grief and joy, passions and sensations succeed each other, and never all exist at the same time. It cannot, therefore, be from any of these impressions, or from any other, that the idea of self is deriv'd; and consequently there is no such idea.

But farther, what must become of all our particular perceptions upon this hypothesis? All these are different, and distinguishable, and separable from each other, and may be separately consider'd, and may exist separately, and have no need of any thing to support their existence. After what manner, therefore, do they belong to self; and how are they connected with it? For my part, when I enter most intimately into what I call *myself*, I always stumble on some particular perception or other, of heat or cold, light or shade, love or hatred, pain or pleasure. I never can catch *myself* at any time without a perception, and never can observe any thing but the perception. When my perceptions are remov'd for any time, as by sound sleep; so long am I insensible of *myself*, and may truly be said not to exist. And were all my perceptions remov'd by death, and cou'd I neither think, nor feel, nor see, nor love, nor hate after the dissolution of my body, I shou'd be entirely annihilated, nor do I conceive what is farther requisite to make me a perfect non-entity. If any one upon serious and unprejudic'd reflexion, thinks he has a different notion of *himself*, I must confess I can reason no longer with him. All I can allow him is, that he may be in the right as well as I, and that we are essentially different in this particular. He may, perhaps, perceive something simple and continu'd, which he calls *himself*; tho' I am certain there is no such principle in me.

But setting aside some metaphysicians of this kind, I may venture to affirm of the rest of mankind, that they are nothing but a bundle or collection of different perceptions, which succeed each other with an inconceivable rapidity, and are in a perpetual flux and movement. Our eyes cannot turn in their sockets without varying our perceptions. Our thought is still more variable than our sight; and all our other senses and faculties contribute to this change; nor is there any single power of the soul, which remains unalterably the same, perhaps for one moment. The mind is a kind of theatre, where several perceptions successively make their appearance; pass, re-pass, glide away, and mingle in an infinite variety of postures and situations. There is properly no *simplicity* in it at one time, nor *identity* in different; whatever natural propension we may have to imagine that simplicity and identity. The comparison of the theatre must not mislead us. They are the successive perceptions only, that constitute the mind; nor have we the most distant notion of the place, where these scenes are represented, or of the materials, of which it is compos'd.

"On the Immortality of the Soul"

By the mere light of reason it seems difficult to prove the Immortality of the Soul; the arguments for it are commonly derived either from *metaphysical* topics, or *moral*, or *physical*. But in reality it is the gospel, and the gospel alone, that has brought life and immortality to light.

I. Metaphysical topics suppose that the soul is immaterial, and that it is impossible for thought to belong to a material substance.

But just metaphysics teach us, that the notion of substance is wholly confused and imperfect; and that we have no other idea of any substance, than as an aggregate of particular qualities inhering in an unknown something. Matter, therefore, and spirit, are at bottom equally unknown; and we cannot determine what qualities inhere in the one or in the other.

They likewise teach us, that nothing can be decided *a priori* concerning any cause or effect; and that experience, being the only source of our

---

"On the Immortality of the Soul" in Selected Essays (Oxford: Oxford University Press, 1996), pp. 324–331.

judgments of this nature, we cannot know from any other principle, whether matter, by its structure or arrangement, may not be the cause of thought. Abstract reasonings cannot decide any question of fact or existence.

But admitting a spiritual substance to be dispersed throughout the universe, like the ethereal fire of the Stoics, and to be the only inherent subject of thought, we have reason to conclude from *analogy,* that nature uses it after the manner she does the other substance, matter. She employs it as a kind of paste or clay; modifies it into a variety of forms and existences; dissolves after a time each modification, and from its substance erects a new form. As the same material substance may successively compose the bodies of all animals, the same spiritual substance may compose their minds: their consciousness, or that system of thought which they formed during life, may be continually dissolved by death, and nothing interests them in the new modification. The most positive assertors of the mortality of the soul never denied the immortality of its substance; and that an immaterial substance, as well as a material, may lose its memory or consciousness, appears in part from experience, if the soul be immaterial.

Reasoning from the common course of nature, and without supposing any *new* interposition of the supreme cause, which ought always to be excluded from philosophy, what is incorruptible must also be ingenerable. The soul therefore, if immortal, existed before our birth; and if the former existence noways concerned us, neither will the latter. Animals undoubtedly feel, think, love, hate, will, and even reason, though in a more imperfect manner than men: are their souls also immaterial and immortal?

II. Let us now consider the *moral* arguments, chiefly those derived from the justice of God, which is supposed to be further interested in the future punishment of the vicious and reward of the virtuous.

But these arguments are grounded on the supposition that God has attributes beyond what he has exerted in this universe, with which alone we are acquainted. Whence do we infer the existence of these attributes?

It is very safe for us to affirm, that whatever we know the Deity to have actually done is best; but it is very dangerous to affirm that he must always do what to us seems best. In how many instances would this reasoning fail us with regard to the present world?

But if any purpose of nature be clear, we may affirm, that the whole scope and intention of man's creation, so far as we can judge by natural reason, is limited to the present life. With how weak a concern from the original inherent structure of the mind and passions, does he ever look further? What comparison either for steadiness or for efficacy betwixt so floating an idea and the most doubtful persuasion of any matter of fact that occurs in commonlife.

There arise indeed in some minds some unaccountable terrors with regard to futurity; but these would quickly vanish were they not artificially fostered by precept and education. And those who foster them, what is their motive? Only to gain a livelihood, and to acquire power and riches in this world. Their very zeal and industry, therefore, are an argument against them.

What cruelty, what iniquity, what injustice in nature, to confine all our concern, as well as all our knowledge to the present life, if there be another scene still waiting us of infinitely greater consequence? Ought this barbarous deceit to be ascribed to a beneficent and wise being? . . .

On the theory of the soul's mortality, the inferiority of women's capacity is easily accounted for. Their domestic life requires no higher faculties either of mind or body. This circumstance vanishes and becomes absolutely insignificant on the religious theory: the one sex has an equal task to perform as the other; their powers of reason and resolution ought also to have been equal, and both of them infinitely greater than at present.

As every effect implies a cause, and that another, till we reach the first cause of all, which is the *Deity*; every thing that happens is ordained by him, and nothing can be the object of his punishment or vengeance.

By what rule are punishments and rewards distributed? What is the divine standard of merit and demerit? Shall we suppose that human sentiments have place in the deity? However bold that hypothesis, we have no conception of any other sentiments.

According to human sentiments, sense, courage, good-manners, industry, prudence, genius, etc., are essential parts of personal merits. Shall we therefore erect an elysium for poets and heroes like that of ancient mythology? Why confine all rewards to one species of virtue?

Punishment, without any proper end or purpose, is inconsistent with *our* ideas of goodness and justice; and no end can be served by it after the whole scene is closed.

Punishment, according to our conception, should bear proportion to the offence. Why then eternal punishment for the temporary offences of so frail a creature as man? Can any one approve of *Alexander's* rage, who intended to exterminate a whole nation because they had they seized his favourite horse *Bucephalus*?

Heaven and hell suppose two distinct species of men, the good and the bad; but the greatest part of mankind float betwixt vice and virtue.

Were one to go round the world with an intention of giving a good supper to the righteous and a sound drubbing to the wicked, he would frequently be embarrassed in his choice, and would find the merits and demerits of most men and women scarcely amount to the value of either. . . .

The chief source of moral ideas is the reflection on the interests of human society. Ought these interests, so short, so frivolous, to be guarded by punishments eternal and infinite? The damnation of one man is a infinitely greater evil in the universe than the subversion of a thousand millions of kingdoms.

Nature has rendered human infancy peculiarly frail and mortal, as it were on purpose to refute the notion of a probationary state; the half of mankind die before they are rational creatures.

III. The *physical* arguments from the analogy of nature are strong for the mortality of the soul; and are really the only philosophical arguments which ought to be admitted with regard to this question, or indeed any question of fact.

Where any two objects are so closely connected that all alterations which we have ever seen in the one are attended with proportionable alterations in the other; we ought to conclude, by all rules of analogy, that, when there are still greater alterations produced in the former, and it is totally dissolved, there follows a total dissolution of the latter.

Sleep, a very small effect on the body, is attended with a temporary extinction, at least a great confusion in the soul.

The weakness of the body and that of the mind in infancy are exactly proportioned; their vigour in manhood, their sympathetic disorder in sickness, their common gradual decay in old age. The step further seems unavoidable; their common dissolution in death.

The last symptoms which the mind discovers, are disorder, weakness, insensibility, and stupidity; the forerunners of its annihilation. The further progress of the same causes increasing, the same effects totally extinguish it.

Judging by the usual analogy of nature, no form can continue when transferred to a condition of life very different from the original one in which it was placed. Trees perish in the water, fishes in the air, animals in the earth. Even so small a difference as that of climate is often fatal. What reason then to imagine, that an immense alteration, such as is made on the soul by the dissolution of its body, and all its organs of thought and sensation, can be effected without the dissolution of the whole?

Every thing is in common betwixt soul and body. The organs of the one are all of them the organs of the other; the existence, therefore, of the one must be dependent on the other.

The souls of animals are allowed to be mortal; and these bear so near a resemblance to the souls of men, that the analogy, from one to the other forms a very strong argument. Their bodies are not more resembling, yet no one rejects the argument drawn from comparative anatomy. The *Metempsychosis* is therefore the only system of this kind that philosophy can hearken to.

Nothing in this world is perpetual; every thing, however seemingly firm, is in continual flux and change: The world itself gives symptoms of frailty and dissolution: How contrary to analogy, therefore, to imagine that one single form, seeming the frailest of any, and subject to the greatest disorders, is immortal and indissoluble? What theory is that! How lightly, not to say how rashly, entertained!

How to dispose of the infinite number of posthumous existences ought also to embarrass the religious theory. Every planet in every solar system, we are at liberty to imagine peopled with intelligent mortal beings, at least we can fix on no other supposition. For these then a new universe must every generation be created beyond the bounds of the present universe, or one must have been created at first so prodigiously wide as to admit of the continual influx of beings. Ought such bold suppositions to be received by any philosophy, and that merely on the pretext of a bare possibility?

When it is asked, whether *Agamemnon, Thersites, Hannibal, Nero,* and every stupid clown that ever existed in *Italy, Scythia, Bactria,* or *Guinea,* are now alive; can any man think, that a scrutiny of nature will furnish arguments strong enough to answer so strange a question in the affirmative? The want of argument without revelation sufficiently establishes the negative. . . . Our insensibility before the composition of the body seems to natural reason a proof of a like state after dissolution.

Were our horrors of annihilation an original passion, not the effect of our general love of happiness, it would rather prove the mortality of the soul: for as nature does nothing in vain, she would never give us a horror against an impossible event. She may give us a horror against an unavoidable event, provided our endeavours, as in the present case, may often remove it to some distance. Death is in the end unavoidable; yet the human species could not be preserved had not nature inspired us with an aversion towards it.

All doctrines are to be suspected which are favoured by our passions; and the hopes and fears which gave rise to this doctrine are very obvious.

It is an infinite advantage in every controversy to defend the negative. If the question be out of the common experienced course of nature, this circumstance is almost if not altogether decisive. By what arguments or analogies can we prove any state of existence, which no one ever saw, and which no way resembles any that ever was seen? Who will repose such trust in any pretended philosophy as to admit upon its testimony the reality of so marvellous a scene? Some new species of logic is requisite for that purpose, and some new faculties of the mind, that they may enable us to comprehend that logic.

Nothing could set in a fuller light the infinite obligations which mankind have to Divine revelation, since we find that no other medium could ascertain this great and important truth.

An Enquiry Concerning Human Understanding

Section VIII: "of Liberty and Necessity"

It might reasonably be expected in questions which have been canvassed and disputed with great eagerness, since the first origin of science and philosophy, that the meaning of all the terms, at least, should have been agreed upon among the disputants; and our enquiries, in the course of two thousand years, been able to pass from words to the true and real subject of the controversy. For how easy may it seem to give exact definitions of the terms employed in reasoning, and make these definitions, not the mere sound of words, the object of future scrutiny and examination? But if we consider the matter more narrowly, we shall be apt to draw a quite opposite conclusion. From this circumstance alone, that a controversy has been long kept on foot, and remains still undecided, we may presume that there is some ambiguity in the expression, and that the disputants affix different ideas to the terms employed in the controversy. . . .

This has been the case in the long disputed question concerning liberty and necessity; and to so remarkable a degree that, if I be not much mistaken, we shall find, that all mankind, both learned and ignorant, have always been of the same opinion with regard to this subject, and that a few intelligible definitions would immediately have put an end to the whole controversy. . . .

I hope, therefore, to make it appear that all men have ever agreed in the doctrine both of necessity and of liberty, according to any reasonable

---

Of liberty and necessity: *An Enquiry Concerning Human Understanding* (Oxford: Clarendon Press, 1902), selections from pp. 80, 81, 81–82, 83, 84, 89, 90–95).

sense, which can be put on these terms; and that the whole controversy has hitherto turned merely upon words. We shall begin with examining the doctrine of necessity.

It is universally allowed that matter, in all its operations, is actuated by a necessary force, and that every natural effect is so precisely determined by the energy of its cause that no other effect, in such particular circumstances, could possibly have resulted from it. . . .

It seems evident that, if all the scenes of nature were continually shifted in such a manner that no two events bore any resemblance to each other, but every object was entirely new, without any similitude to whatever had been seen before, we should never, in that case, have attained the least idea of necessity, or of a connexion among these objects. We might say, upon such a supposition, that one object or event has followed another; not that one was produced by the other. The relation of cause and effect must be utterly unknown to mankind. Inference and reasoning concerning the operations of nature would, from that moment, be at an end; and the memory and senses remain the only canals, by which the knowledge of any real existence could possibly have access to the mind. Our idea, therefore, of necessity and causation arises entirely from the uniformity observable in the operations of nature, where similar objects are constantly conjoined together, and the mind is determined by custom to infer the one from the appearance of the other. These two circumstances form the whole of that necessity, which we ascribe to matter. Beyond the constant *conjunction* of similar objects, and the consequent *inference* from one to the other, we have no notion of any necessity or connexion. . . .

It is universally acknowledged that there is a great uniformity among the actions of men, in all nations and ages, and that human nature remains still the same, in its principles and operations. The same motives always produce the same actions: The same events follow from the same causes. Ambition, avarice, self-love, vanity, friendship, generosity, public spirit: these passions, mixed in various degrees, and distributed through society, have been, from the beginning of the world, and still are, the source of all the actions and enterprises, which have ever been observed among mankind. Would you know the sentiments, inclinations, and course of life of the Greeks and Romans? Study well the temper and actions of the French and English: You cannot be much mistaken in transferring to the former *most* of the observations which you have made with regard to the latter. Mankind are so much the same, in all times and places, that history informs us of nothing new or strange in this particular. Its chief use is only to discover the constant and universal principles of human nature, by showing men in all varieties of circumstances and situations, and furnishing us with materials from which we may form our observations and become acquainted with the regular springs of human action and behaviour. These records of wars, intrigues, factions, and revolutions, are so many collections of experiments, by which the politician or moral philosopher fixes the principles of his science, in the same manner as the physician or natural philosopher becomes acquainted with the nature of plants, minerals, and other external objects, by the experiments which he forms concerning them. Nor are the earth, water, and other elements, examined by Aristotle, and Hippocrates, more like to those which at present lie under our observation than the men described by Polybius and Tacitus are to those who now govern the world.

Should a traveller, returning from a far country, bring us an account of men, wholly different from any with whom we were ever acquainted; men, who were entirely divested of avarice, ambition, or revenge; who knew no pleasure but friendship, generosity, and public spirit; we should immediately, from these circumstances, detect the falsehood, and prove him a liar, with the same certainty as if he had stuffed his narration with stories of centaurs and dragons, miracles and prodigies. And if we would explode any forgery in history, we cannot make use of a more convincing argument, than to prove that the actions ascribed to any person are directly contrary to the course of nature, and that no human motives, in such circumstances, could ever induce him to such a conduct. The veracity of Quintus Curtius is as much to be suspected, when he describes the supernatural courage of Alexander, by which he was hurried on singly to attack multitudes, as when he describes his supernatural force and activity, by which he was able to resist them. So readily and universally do we acknowledge a uniformity in human motives and actions as well as in the operations of body. . . .

The mutual dependence of men is so great in all societies that scarce any human action is entirely complete in itself, or is performed without some reference to the actions of others, which are requisite to make it answer fully the intention of the agent. The poorest artificer, who labours alone, expects at least the protection of the magistrate, to ensure him the enjoyment of the fruits of his labour. He also expects that, when he carries his goods to market, and offers them at a reasonable price, he shall find purchasers, and shall be able, by the money he acquires, to engage others to supply him with those commodities which are requisite for his subsistence. In proportion as men extend their dealings, and render their intercourse with others more complicated, they always comprehend, in their schemes of life, a greater variety of voluntary actions, which they expect, from the proper motives, to co-operate with their own. In all these conclusions they take their measures from past experience, in the same manner as in their reasonings concerning external objects; and firmly believe that men, as well as all the elements, are to continue, in their operations, the same that they have ever found them. A manufacturer reckons upon the labour of his servants for the execution of any work as much as upon the tools which he employs, and would be equally surprised were his expectations disappointed. In short, this experimental inference and reasoning concerning the actions of others enters so much into human life that no man, while awake, is ever a moment without employing it. Have we not reason, therefore, to affirm that all mankind have always agreed in the doctrine of necessity according to the foregoing definition and explication of it?

Nor have philosophers ever entertained a different opinion from the people in this particular, for, not to mention that almost every action of their life supposes that opinion, there are even few of the speculative parts of learning to which it is not essential. What would become of *history,* had we not a dependence on the veracity of the historian according to the experience which we have had of mankind? How could *politics* be a science, if laws and forms of government had not a uniform influence upon society? Where would be the foundation of *morals,* if particular characters had no certain or determinate power to produce particular sentiments, and if these sentiments had no constant operation on actions? And with what pretence could we employ our *criticism* upon any poet or polite author, if we could not pronounce the conduct and sentiments of his actors either natural or unnatural to such characters, and in such circumstances? It seems almost impossible, therefore, to engage either in science or action of any kind without acknowledging the doctrine of necessity, and this *inference* from motive to voluntary actions, from characters to conduct.

And indeed, when we consider how aptly *natural* and *moral* evidence link together, and form only one chain of argument, we shall make no scruple to allow that they are of the same nature, and derived from the same principles. A prisoner who has neither money nor interest, discovers the impossibility of his escape, as well when he considers the obstinacy of the gaoler, as the walls and bars with which he is surrounded; and, in all attempts for his freedom, chooses rather to work upon the stone and iron of the one, than upon the inflexible nature of the other. The same prisoner, when conducted to the scaffold, foresees his death as certainly from the constancy and fidelity of his guards, as from the operation of the axe or wheel. His mind runs along a certain train of ideas: The refusal of the soldiers to consent to his escape; the action of the executioner; the separation of the head and body; bleeding, convulsive motions, and death. Here is a connected chain of natural causes and voluntary actions; but the mind feels no difference between them in passing from one link to another: Nor is less certain of the future event than if it were connected with the objects present to the memory or senses, by a train of causes, cemented together by what we are pleased to call a *physical* necessity. The same experienced union has the same effect on the mind, whether the united objects be motives, volition, and actions; or figure and motion. We may change the name of things; but their nature and their operation on the understanding never change.

Were a man, whom I know to be honest and opulent, and with whom I live in intimate friendship, to come into my house, where I am surrounded with my servants, I rest assured that he is not to stab me before he leaves it in order to rob me of my silver standish; and I no more suspect this event than the falling of the house itself, which is new, and solidly built and founded,—*But he may have been seized with a sudden and unknown frenzy.*—So may a sudden earthquake arise, and shake and tumble my house about my ears. I shall therefore change the suppositions. I shall say that I know with certainty that he is not to put his hand into the fire and hold it there till it be consumed: And this event, I think I can foretell with the same assurance, as that, if he throw himself out at the window, and meet with no obstruction, he will not remain a moment suspended in the air. No suspicion of an unknown frenzy can give the least possibility to the former event, which is so contrary to all the known principles of human nature. A man who at noon leaves his purse full of gold on the pavement at Charing-Cross, may as well expect that it will fly away like a feather, as that he will find it untouched an hour after. Above one half of human reasonings contain inferences of a similar nature, attended with more or less degrees of certainty proportioned to our experience of the usual conduct of mankind in such particular situations.

I have frequently considered, what could possibly be the reason why all mankind, though they have ever, without hesitation, acknowledged the doctrine of necessity in their whole practice and reasoning, have yet discovered such a reluctance to acknowledge it in words, and have rather shown a propensity, in all ages, to profess the contrary opinion. The matter, I think, may be accounted for after the following manner. If we examine the operations of body, and the production of effects from their causes, we shall find that all our faculties can never carry us farther in our knowledge of this relation than barely to observe that particular objects are *constantly conjoined* together, and that the mind is carried, by a *customary transition*, from the appearance of one to the belief of the other. But though this conclusion concerning human ignorance be the result of the strictest scrutiny of this subject, men still entertain a strong propensity to believe that they penetrate farther into the powers of nature, and perceive something like a necessary connexion between the cause and the effect. When again they turn their reflections towards the operations of their own minds, and *feel* no such connexion of the motive and the action; they are thence apt to suppose, that there is a difference between the effects which result from material force, and those which arise from thought and intelligence. But being once convinced that we know nothing farther of causation of any kind than merely the *constant conjunction* of objects, and the consequent *inference* of the mind from one to another, and finding that these two circumstances are universally allowed to have place in voluntary actions; we may be more easily led to own the same necessity common to all causes. And though this reasoning may contradict the systems of many philosophers, in ascribing necessity to the determinations of the will, we shall find, upon reflection, that they dissent from it in words only, not in their real sentiment. Necessity, according to the sense in which it is here taken, has never yet been rejected, nor can ever, I think, be rejected by any philosopher. . . .

But to proceed in this reconciling project with regard to the question of liberty and necessity; the most contentious question of metaphysics, the most contentious science; it will not require many words to prove, that all mankind have ever agreed in the doctrine of liberty as well as in that of necessity, and that the whole dispute, in this respect also, has been hitherto merely verbal. For what is meant by liberty, when applied to voluntary actions? We cannot surely mean that actions have so little connexion with motives, inclinations, and circumstances, that one does not follow with a certain degree of uniformity from the other, and that one affords no inference by which we can conclude the existence of the other. For these are plain and acknowledged matters of fact. By liberty, then, we can only mean *a power of acting or not acting; according to the determinations of the will;* that is, if we choose to remain at rest, we may; if we choose to move, we also may. Now this hypothetical liberty is universally allowed to belong to every one who is not a prisoner and in chains. Here, then, is no subject of dispute.

Dialogues Concerning Natural Religion

Part X

It is opinion, I own, replied Demea, that each man feels, in a manner, the truth of religion within his own breast; and from a consciousness of his imbecility and misery, rather than from any reasoning, is led to seek protection from that Being, on whom he and all nature is dependent. So anxious or so tedious are even the best scenes of life, that futurity is still the object of all our hopes and fears. We incessantly look forward, and endeavour, by prayers, adoration, and sacrifice, to appease those unknown powers, whom we find, by experience, so able to afflict and oppress us. Wretched creatures that we are! What resource for us amidst the innumerable ills of life, did not religion suggest some methods of atonement, and appease those terrors, with which we are incessantly agitated and tormented?

I am indeed persuaded, said Philo, that the best and indeed the only method of bringing every one to a due sense of religion is by just representations of the misery and wickedness of men. And for that purpose a talent of eloquence and strong imagery is more requisite than that of reasoning and argument. For is it necessary to prove, what every one feels within himself? It is only necessary to make us feel it, if possible, more intimately and sensibly.

The people, indeed, replied Demea, are sufficiently convinced of this great and melancholy truth. The miseries of life, the unhappiness of man, the general corruptions of our nature, the unsatisfactory enjoyment of pleasures, riches, honours; these phrases have become almost proverbial in all languages. And who can doubt of what all men declare from their own immediate feeling and experience?

From Hume, David *Dialogues Concerning Natural Religion* (Oxford: Oxford University Press, 1998 [1779]), Part X, pp. 95–100.

In this point, said Philo, the learned are perfectly agreed with the vulgar; and in all letters, *sacred* and *profane*, the topic of human misery has been insisted on with the most pathetic eloquence that sorrow and melancholy could inspire. The poets, who speak from sentiment, without a system, and whose testimony has therefore the more authority, abound in images of this nature. . . .

As to authorities, replied Demea, you need not seek them. Look round this library of Cleanthes. I shall venture to affirm, that except authors of particular sciences, such as chemistry or botany, who have no occasion to treat of human life, there scarce is one of those innumerable writers, from whom the sense of human misery has not, in some passage or other, extorted a complaint and confession of it. At least, the chance is entirely on that side; and no author has ever, so far as I can recollect, been so extravagant as to deny it.

There you must excuse me, said Philo: Leibnitz has denied it; and is perhaps the first who ventured upon so bold and paradoxical an opinion; at least the first who made it essential to his philosophical system.

And by being the first, replied Demea, might he not have been sensible of his error? For is this a subject in which philosophers can propose to make discoveries, especially in so late an age? . . .

And why should man, added he, pretend to an exemption from the lot of all other animals? The whole earth, believe me, Philo, is cursed and polluted. A perpetual war is kindled amongst all living creatures. Necessity, hunger, want, stimulate the strong and courageous: Fear, anxiety, terror, agitate the weak and infirm. The first entrance into life gives anguish to the new-born infant and to its wretched parent: Weakness, impotence, distress, attend each stage of that life: And it is at last finished in agony and horror.

Observe too, says Philo, the curious artifices of nature, in order to embitter the life of every living being. The stronger prey upon the weaker, and keep them in perpetual terror and anxiety. The weaker too, in their turn, often prey upon the stronger, and vex and molest them without relaxation. Consider that innumerable race of insects, which either are bred on the body of each animal, or flying about infix their stings in him. These insects have others still less than themselves, which torment them. And thus on each hand, before and behind, above and below, every animal is surrounded with enemies, which incessantly seek his misery and destruction.

Man alone, said Demea, seems to be, in part, an exception to this rule. For by combination in society, he can easily master lions, tigers, and bears, whose greater strength and agility naturally enable them to prey upon him.

On the contrary, it is here chiefly, cried Philo, that the uniform and equal maxims of nature are most apparent. Man, it is true, can, by combination, surmount all his *real* enemies, and become master of the whole animal creation: But does he not immediately raise up to himself *imaginary* enemies, the dæmons of his fancy, who haunt him with superstitious terrors, and blast every enjoyment of life? His pleasure, as he imagines, becomes, in their eyes, a crime: His food and repose give them umbrage and offence: His very sleep and dreams furnish new materials to anxious fear: And even death, his refuge from every other ill, presents only the dread of endless and innumerable woes. Nor does the wolf molest more the timid flock, than superstition does the anxious breast of wretched mortals.

Besides, consider, Demea; this very society, by which we surmount those wild beasts, our natural enemies; what new enemies, does it not raise to us? What woe and misery does it not occasion? Man is the greatest enemy of man. Oppression, injustice, contumely, violence, sedition, war, calumny, treachery, fraud; by these they mutually torment each other: And they would soon dissolve that society which they had formed, were it not for the dread of still greater ills, which must attend their separation.

But though these external insults, said Demea, from animals, from men, from all the elements, which assault us, form a frightful catalogue of woes, they are nothing in comparison of those, which arise within ourselves, from the distempered condition of our mind and body. How many lie under the lingering torment of diseases? Hear the pathetic enumeration of the great poet.

> Intestine stone and ulcer, colic-pangs,
> Daemoniac frenzy, moping melancholy,
> And moon-struck madness, pining atrophy,
> Marasmus and wide-wasting pestilence.
> Dire was the tossing, deep the groans: DESPAIR
> Tended the sick, busiest from couch to couch.
> And over them triumphant DEATH his dart
> Shook, but delay'd to strike, tho' oft invok'd
> With vows, as their chief good and final hope.[1]

The disorders of the mind, continued Demea, though more secret, are not perhaps less dismal and vexatious. Remorse, shame, anguish, rage,

---

[1] MILTON, *Paradise-Lost*, XI.

disappointment, anxiety, fear, dejection, despair, who has ever passed through life without cruel inroads from these tormentors? How many have scarcely ever felt any better sensations? Labour and poverty, so abhorred by every one, are the certain lot of the far greater number. And those few privileged persons who enjoy ease and opulence, never reach contentment or true felicity. All the goods of life united would not make a very happy man: But all the ills united would make a wretch indeed; and any one of them almost (and who can be free from every one), nay often the absence of one good (and who can possess all) is sufficient to render life ineligible.

Were a stranger to drop, on a sudden, into this world, I would show him, as a specimen of its ills, an hospital full of diseases, a prison crowded with malefactors and debtors, a field of battle strewed with carcases, a fleet floundering in the ocean, a nation languishing under tyranny, famine, or pestilence. To turn the gay side of life to him, and give him a notion of its pleasures; whither should I conduct him? to a ball, to an opera, to court? He might justly think, that I was only showing him a diversity of distress and sorrow.

There is no evading such striking instances, said Philo; but by apologies, which still farther aggravate the charge. Why have all men, I ask, in all ages, complained incessantly of the miseries of life? . . . They have no just reason, says one: These complaints proceed only from their discontented, repining, anxious disposition. . . . And can there possibly, I reply, be a more certain foundation of misery, than such a wretched temper? . . . .

Ask yourself [said Demea], ask any of your acquaintance, whether they would live over again the last ten or twenty years of their life. No! but the next twenty, they say, will be better. . . . Thus at last they find (such is the greatness of human misery; it reconciles even contradictions) that they complain, at once, of the shortness of life, and of its vanity and sorrow.

An Enquiry Concerning Human Understanding

Section VIII, Part II

There are many philosophers who, after an exact scrutiny of all the phenomena of nature, conclude, that the WHOLE, considered as one system, is, in every period of its existence, ordered with perfect benevolence; and

From Hume, David, *Enquiry*, pp. 101–103.

that the utmost possible happiness will, in the end, result to all created beings, without any mixture of positive or absolute ill or misery. Every physical ill, say they, makes an essential part of this benevolent system, and could not possibly be removed, even by the Deity himself, considered as a wise agent, without giving entrance to greater ill, or excluding greater good, which will result from it. From this theory, some philosophers, and the ancient *Stoics* among the rest, derived a topic of consolation under all afflictions, while they taught their pupils that those ills under which they laboured were, in reality, goods to the universe; and that to an enlarged view, which could comprehend the whole system of nature, every event became an object of joy and exultation. But though this topic be specious and sublime, it was soon found in practice weak and ineffectual. You would surely more irritate than appease a man lying under the racking pains of the gout by preaching up to him the rectitude of those general laws, which produced the malignant humours in his body, and led them through the proper canals, to the sinews and nerves, where they now excite such acute torments. These enlarged views may, for a moment, please the imagination of a speculative man, who is placed in ease and security; but neither can they dwell with constancy on his mind, even though undisturbed by the emotions of pain or passion; much less can they maintain their ground when attacked by such powerful antagonists. The affections take a narrower and more natural survey of their object; and by an economy, more suitable to the infirmity of human minds, regard alone the beings around us, and are actuated by such events as appear good or ill to the private system.

The case is the same with *moral* as with *physical* ill. It cannot reasonably be supposed, that those remote considerations, which are found of so little efficacy with regard to one, will have a more powerful influence with regard to the other. The mind of man is so formed by nature that, upon the appearance of certain characters, dispositions, and actions, it immediately feels the sentiment of approbation or blame; nor are there any emotions more essential to its frame and constitution. The characters which engage our approbation are chiefly such as contribute to the peace and security of human society; as the characters which excite blame are chiefly such as tend to public detriment and disturbance: Whence it may reasonably be presumed, that the moral sentiments arise, either mediately or immediately, from a reflection of these opposite interests. What though philosophical meditations establish a different opinion or conjecture; that everything is right with regard to the WHOLE, and that the qualities, which disturb society, are, in the main, as beneficial, and are as suitable to the primary intention of nature as those which more directly promote its happiness and welfare? Are such remote and uncertain speculations able to counterbalance the sentiments which arise from the natural and immediate view of the objects? A man who is robbed of a considerable sum; does he find his vexation for the loss anywise diminished by these sublime reflections? Why then should his moral resentment against the crime be supposed incompatible with them? Or why should not the acknowledgment of a real distinction between vice and virtue be reconcileable to all speculative systems of philosophy, as well as that of a real distinction between personal beauty and deformity? Both these distinctions are founded in the natural sentiments of the human mind: And these sentiments are not to be controuled or altered by any philosophical theory or speculation whatsoever.

An Enquiry Concerning the Principles of Morals

Section IX, Part I

It seems a happiness in the present theory, that it enters not into that vulgar dispute concerning the *degrees* of benevolence or self-love, which prevail in human nature; a dispute which is never likely to have any issue, both because men, who have taken part, are not easily convinced, and because the phenomena, which can be produced on either side, are so dispersed, so uncertain, and subject to so many interpretations, that it is scarcely possible accurately to compare them, or draw from them any determinate inference or conclusion. It is sufficient for our present purpose, if it be allowed, what surely, without the greatest absurdity cannot be disputed, that there is some benevolence, however small, infused into our bosom; some spark of friendship for human kind; some particle of the dove kneaded into our frame, along with the elements of the wolf and serpent. Let these generous sentiments be supposed ever so weak; let them be insufficient to move even a hand or finger of our body, they must still direct the determinations of our mind, and where everything else is equal, produce a cool preference of what is useful and serviceable to

From Hume, David *An Enquiry Concerning the Principles of Morals* (Oxford: Clarendon Press, 1902), pp. 270–271.

mankind, above what is pernicious and dangerous. A *moral distinction*, therefore, immediately arises; a general sentiment of blame and approbation; a tendency, however faint, to the objects of the one, and a proportionable aversion to those of the other. Nor will those reasoners, who so earnestly maintain the predominant selfishness of human kind, be any wise scandalized at hearing of the weak sentiments of virtue implanted in our nature. On the contrary, they are found as ready to maintain the one tenet as the other; and their spirit of satire (for such it appears, rather than of corruption) naturally gives rise to both opinions; which have, indeed, a great and almost an indissoluble connexion together.

"Of National Characters" (note)

I am apt to suspect the negroes to be naturally inferior to the whites. There scarcely ever was a civilized nation of that complexion, nor even any individual eminent either in action or speculation. No ingenious manufactures amongst them, no arts, no sciences. On the other hand, the most rude and barbarous of the whites, such as the ancient GERMANS, the present TARTARS, have still something eminent about them, in their valour, form of government, or some other particular. Such a uniform and constant difference could not happen, in so many countries and ages, if nature had not made an original distinction between these breeds of men. Not to mention our colonies, there are NEGROE slaves dispersed all over EUROPE, of whom none ever discovered any symptoms of ingenuity; though low people, without education, will start up amongst us, and distinguish themselves in every profession. In JAMAICA, indeed, they talk of one negroe as a man of parts and learning; but it is likely he is admired for slender accomplishments, like a parrot who speaks a few words plainly.

From Hume, David, Note to "Of National Characters" concerning "natural inferiority of negroes" (in *Selected Essays*, p. 360).

38

Jean-Jacques Rousseau

"Man is born free and everywhere he is in chains." These famous words, the opening line of his book *The Social Contract*, encapsulate a key contention of the thought of Jean-Jacques Rousseau (1712–1778). The state of nature, or original condition of human beings, was for Rousseau one of peace and freedom, before the emergence of the institution of private property set in motion a disastrous chain of events leading to inequality, war and slavery. In this, Rousseau's conceptions of both human nature and the value of society are diametrically opposed to those of Hobbes. The first two sets of selections—from *A Discourse on the Origin of Inequality* and *The State of War*—express these ideas clearly, and explicitly reveal Rousseau's rejection of Hobbesian ideas. Rousseau's strange and conflicted character emerges in his thoughts on women, the subject of the last two selections: in the passages from *Émile*, Rousseau's treatise on education, a condescending attitude toward women is shown, whilst in the less well-known "On Women" Rousseau's view is more subtle: had they not been deprived of their freedom, women's achievements could have outstripped those of men.

A Discourse on the Origin of Inequality

O man, of whatever country you are, and whatever your opinions may be, behold your history, such as I have thought to read it, not in books written by your fellow-creatures, who are liars, but in nature, which never lies. All

From Rousseau, Jean-Jacques, *A Discourse on the Origin of Inequality* (in *The Social Contract and Discourses* (translated by G.D.H. Cole) (London: J.M. Dent, 1913), selections from pp. 51, 52, 59–60, 61, 70–77, 79–80, 81, 84.

that comes from her will be true; nor will you meet with anything false, unless I have involuntarily put in something of my own. The times of which I am going to speak are very remote: how much are you changed from what you once were! It is, so to speak, the life of your species which I am going to write, after the qualities which you have received, which your education and habits may have depraved, but cannot have entirely destroyed. There is, I feel, an age at which the individual man would wish to stop: you are about to inquire about the age at which you would have liked your whole species to stand still. Discontented with your present state, for reasons which threaten your unfortunate descendants with still greater discontent, you will perhaps wish it were in your power to go back; and this feeling should be a panegyric on your first ancestors, a criticism of your contemporaries, and a terror to the unfortunates who will come after you.

. . .

If we strip this being, thus constituted, of all the supernatural gifts he may have received, and all the artificial faculties he can have acquired only by a long process; if we consider him, in a word, just as he must have come from the hands of nature, we behold in him an animal weaker than some, and less agile than others; but, taking him all round, the most advantageously organized of any. I see him satisfying his hunger at the first oak, and slaking his thirst at the first brook: finding his bed at the foot of the tree which afforded him a repast; and, with that, all his wants supplied.

. . .

I see nothing in any animal but an ingenious machine to which nature hath given senses to wind itself up, and to guard itself, to a certain degree, against anything that might tend to disorder or destroy it. I perceive exactly the same things in the human machine, with this difference, that in the operations of the brute, nature is the sole agent, whereas man has some share in his own operations, in his character as a free agent. The one chooses and refuses by instinct, the other from an act of free will: hence the brute cannot deviate from the rule prescribed to it, even when it would be advantageous for it to do so; and, on the contrary, man frequently deviates from such rules to his own prejudice. Thus a pigeon would be starved to death by the side of a dish of the choicest meats, and a cat on a heap of fruit or grain; though it is certain that either might find nourishment in the foods which it thus rejects with disdain, did it think of trying them. Hence it is that dissolute men run into excesses which bring on fevers and death; because the mind depraves the senses, and the will continues to speak when nature is silent.

Every animal has ideas, since it has senses; it even combines those ideas in a certain degree; and it is only in degree that man differs, in this respect, from the brute. Some philosophers have even maintained that there is a greater difference between one man and another than between some men and some beasts. It is not, therefore, so much the understanding that constitutes the difference between the man and the brute, as the human quality of free agency. Nature lays her commands on every animal, and the brute obeys her voice. Man receives the same impulses but at the same time knows himself at liberty to acquiesce or resist; and it is particularly in his consciousness of this liberty that the spirituality of his soul is displayed.

. . .

Whatever moralists may hold, the human understanding is greatly indebted to the passions, which, it is universally allowed, are also much indebted to the understanding. It is by the activity of the passions that our reason is improved; for we desire knowledge only because we wish to enjoy; and it is impossible to conceive any reason why a person who has neither fears nor desires should give himself the trouble of reasoning. The passions, again, originate in our wants, and their progress depends on that of our knowledge; for we cannot desire or fear anything, except from the idea we have of it, or from the simple impulse of nature. Now savage man, being destitute of every species of enlightenment, can have no passions save those of the latter kind: his desires never go beyond his physical wants. The only goods he recognizes in the universe are food, a female, and sleep: the only evils he fears are pain and hunger. I say pain, and not death: for no animal can know what it is to die; the knowledge of death and its terrors being one of the first acquisitions made by man in departing from an animal state.

. . .

I know it is incessantly repeated that man would in such a state have been the most miserable of creatures; and indeed, if it be true, as I think I have proved, that he must have lived many ages, before he could have either desire or an opportunity of emerging from it, this would only be an accusation against nature, and not against the being which she had thus unhappily constituted. But as I understand the word "miserable," it either has no meaning at all, or else signifies only a painful privation of something, or a state of suffering either in body or soul. I should be glad to have explained to me, what kind of misery a free being, whose heart is at ease and whose body is in health, can possibly suffer. I would like to know which is the more likely to become insupportable to those who take part in it: the life of society or the life of nature. We hardly see anyone around us except people who are complaining of their existence; many even deprive themselves of it if they can and all divine and human laws put together can hardly put a stop to this disorder. I would like to know if anyone has heard of a savage who took it into his head, when he was free, to complain of life and to kill himself. Let us be less arrogant, then, when we judge on which side real misery is found. Nothing, on the other hand, could be more miserable than a savage exposed to the dazzling light of our "civilization," tormented by our passions and reasoning about a state different from his own. It appears that providence most wisely determined that the faculties, which he potentially possessed, should develop themselves only as occasion offered to exercise them, in order that they might not be superfluous or perplexing to him, by appearing before their time, nor slow and useless when the need for them arose. In instinct alone, he had all he required for living in the state of nature; and with a developed understanding he has only just enough to support life in society.

It appears, at first view, that men in a state of nature, having no moral relations or determinate obligations one with another, could not be either good or bad, virtuous or vicious; unless we take these terms in a physical sense, and call, in an individual, those qualities vices which may be injurious to his preservation, and those virtues which contribute to it; in which case, he would have to be accounted most virtuous, who put least check on the pure impulses of nature. But without deviating from the ordinary sense of the words, it will be proper to suspend the judgment we might be led to form on such a state, and be on our guard against our prejudices, till we have weighed the matter in the scales of impartiality, and seen whether virtues or vices preponderate among civilized men: and whether their virtues do them more good than their vices do harm; till we have discovered whether the progress of the sciences sufficiently indemnifies them for the mischiefs they do one another, in proportion as they are better informed of the good they ought to do; or whether they would not be, on the whole, in a much happier condition if they had nothing to fear or to hope from any one, than as they are, subjected to universal dependence, and obliged to take everything from those who engage to give them nothing in return.

Above all let us not conclude, with Hobbes, that because man has no idea of goodness, he must be naturally wicked; that he is vicious because he does not know virtue; that he always refuses to do his fellow-creatures services which he does not think they have a right to demand; or that by virtue of the right he justly claims to all he needs, he foolishly imagines himself the sole proprietor of the whole universe. Hobbes had seen clearly the defects of all those modern definitions of natural right: but the consequences which he deduces from his own show that he understands it in an equally false sense. In reasoning on the principles he lays down, he ought to have said that the state of nature, being that in which the care for our own preservation is the least prejudicial to that of others, was consequently the best calculated to promote peace, and the most suitable for mankind. He does say the exact opposite, in consequence of having improperly admitted, as a part of savage man's care for self-preservation, the gratification of a multitude of passions which are the work of society, and have made laws necessary. A bad man, he says, is a robust child. But it remains to be proved whether man in a state of nature is this robust child and, should we grant that he is, what would he infer? Why truly, that if this man, when robust and strong, were dependent on others as he is when feeble, there is no extravagance he would not be guilty of; that he would beat his mother when she was too slow in giving him her breast; that he would strangle one of his younger brothers, if he should be troublesome to him, or bite the leg of another, if he put him to any inconvenience. But that man in the state of nature is both strong and dependent involves two contrary suppositions. Man is weak when he is dependent, and is his own master before he comes to be strong. Hobbes did not reflect that the same cause, which prevents a savage from making use of his reason, as our jurists hold, prevents him also from abusing his faculties, as Hobbes himself allows: so that it may be justly be said that savages are not bad merely because they do not know what it is to be good: for it is neither the development of the understanding nor the restraint of law that hinders them from doing ill; but the peacefulness of their passions, and their ignorance of vice. . . .There is another principle which has escaped Hobbes; which, having been bestowed on mankind, to moderate, on certain occasions, the impetuosity of *amour-propre*, or, before its birth, the desire of self-preservation, tempers the ardour with which he pursues his own welfare, by an innate repugnance at seeing a fellow-creature suffer. I think I need not fear contradiction in holding man to be possessed of the only natural virtue, which could not be denied him by the most violent detractor of human virtue. I am speaking of compassion, which is a disposition suitable to creatures so weak and subject to so many evils as we certainly are: by so much the more universal and useful to mankind, as it comes before any kind of reflection; and at the same time so natural, that the very brutes themselves sometimes give evident proofs of it. Not to mention the tenderness of mothers for their offspring and the perils they encounter to save them from danger, it is well known that horses show a reluctance to trample on living bodies. One animal never passes by the dead body of another of its species without disquiet: some even give their fellows a sort of burial; while the mournful lowings of the cattle when they enter the slaughter-house show the impressions made on them by the horrible spectacle which meets them. We find, with pleasure, the author of *The Fable of the Bees* obliged to own that man is a compassionate and sensible being, and laying aside his cold subtlety of style, in the example he gives, to present us with the pathetic description of a man who, from a place of confinement is compelled to behold a wild beast tear a child from the arms of its mother, grinding its tender limbs with its murderous teeth and tearing its palpitating entrails with its claws. What horrid agitation must not the eye-witness of such a scene experience, although he would not be personally concerned! What anguish would he not suffer at not being able to give any assistance to the mother and the dying infant!

Such is the pure emotion of nature, prior to all kinds of reflection! Such is the force of natural compassion, which the greatest depravity of morals has as yet hardly been able to destroy! for we daily find at our theatres men affected, nay, shedding tears at the sufferings of a wretch who, were he in the tyrant's place, would probably even add to the torments of his enemies; like the bloodthirsty Sulla, who was so sensitive to ills he had not caused, or that Alexander of Pheros who did not dare to go and see any tragedy acted, for fear of being seen weeping with Andromache and Priam, though he could listen without emotion to the citizens who were daily strangled at his command.

> *Mollissima corda*
> *Humano generi dare se natura fatetur*
> *Quae lacrimas dedit.*
>
> Juvenal, *Satires* XV. 131[2]

Mandeville well knew that, in spite of all their morality, men would never have been better than monsters, had not nature bestowed on them a sense of compassion, to aid their reason: but he did not see that from this quality alone flow all those social virtues, of which he denied man the

---

[2] Nature avows she gave the human race the softest hearts, who gave them tears.

possession. But what is generosity, clemency, or humanity but compassion applied to the weak, to the guilty, or to mankind in general? Even benevolence and friendship are, if we judge rightly, only the effects of compassion, constantly set upon a particular object: for how is it different to wish that another person may not suffer pain and uneasiness and to wish him happy? Were it even true that pity is no more than a feeling, which puts us in the place of the sufferer, a feeling obscure yet lively in a savage, developed yet feeble in civilized man; this truth would have no other consequence than to confirm my argument. Compassion must, in fact, be the stronger, the more the animal beholding any kind of distress identifies himself with the animal that suffers. Now, it is plain that such identification must have been much more perfect in a state of nature than it is in a state of reason. It is reason that engenders *amour-propre,* and reflection that confirms it: it is reason which turns man's mind back upon itself, and divides him from everything that could disturb or afflict him. It is philosophy that isolates him, and bids him say, at sight of the misfortunes of others: "Perish if you will, I am secure." Nothing but such general evils as threaten the whole community can disturb the tranquil sleep of the philosopher, or tear him from his bed. A murder may with impunity be committed under his window; he has only to put his hands to his ears and argue a little with himself, to prevent nature, which is shocked within him, from identifying itself with the unfortunate sufferer. Uncivilized man has not this admirable talent; and for want of reason and wisdom, is always foolishly ready to obey the first promptings of humanity. It is the populace that flocks together at riots and street brawls, while the wise man prudently makes off. It is the mob and the market-women, who part the combatants, and stop decent people from cutting one another's throats.

It is then certain that compassion is a natural feeling, which, by moderating the activity of love of self in each individual, contributes to the preservation of the whole species. It is compassion that hurries us without reflection to the relief of those who are in distress: it is this which in a state of nature supplies the place of laws, morals, and virtues, with the advantage that none are tempted to disobey its gentle voice: it is this which will always prevent a sturdy savage from robbing a weak child or a feeble old man of the sustenance they may have with pain and difficulty acquired, if he sees a possibility of providing for himself by other means: it is this which, instead of inculcating that sublime maxim of rational justice, *Do to others as you would have done unto you,* inspires all men with that other maxim of natural goodness, much less perfect indeed, but perhaps more useful; *Do good to yourself with as little evil as possible to others.* In a word, it is rather in this natural feeling than in any subtle argument that we must look for the cause of that repugnance, which every man would experience in doing evil, even independently of the maxims of education. Although it might belong to Socrates and other minds of the like craft to acquire virtue by reason, the human race would long since have ceased to be, had its preservation depended only on the reasonings of the individuals composing it.

With passions so little active, and so good a curb, men, being rather wild than wicked, and more intent to guard themselves against the mischief that might be done them, than to do mischief to others, were by no means subject to very perilous dissensions. They maintained no kind of intercourse with one another, and were consequently strangers to vanity, deference, esteem, and contempt; they had not the least idea of "mine" and "thine" and no true conception of justice; they looked upon every violence to which they were subjected, rather as an injury that might easily be repaired than as a crime that ought to be punished; and they never thought of taking revenge, unless perhaps mechanically and on the spot, as a dog will sometimes bite the stone which is thrown at him. Their quarrels therefore would seldom have very bloody consequences; for the subject of them would be merely the question of subsistence.

. . .

Let us conclude then that man in a state of nature, wandering up and down the forests, without industry, without speech, and without home, an equal stranger to war and to all ties, neither standing in need of his fellow-creatures nor having any desire to hurt them, and perhaps even not distinguishing them one from another; let us conclude that, being self-sufficient and subject to so few passions, he could have no feelings or knowledge but such as befitted his situation; that he felt only his actual necessities, and disregarded everything he did not think himself immediately concerned to notice, and that his understanding made no greater progress than his vanity. If by accident he made any discovery, he was the less able to communicate it to others, as he did not know even his own children. Every art would necessarily perish with its inventor, where there was no kind of education among men, and generations succeeded generations without the least advance; when, all setting out from the same point, centuries must have elapsed in the barbarism of the first ages; when the race was already old, and man remained a child.

. . .

The first man who, having enclosed a piece of ground, bethought himself of saying "This is mine," and found people simple enough to believe him, was the real founder of civil society. From how many crimes, wars, and murders, from how many horrors and misfortunes might not any one have saved mankind, by pulling up the stakes, or filling up the ditch, and crying to his fellows, "Beware of listening to this impostor; you are undone if you once forget that the fruits of the earth belong to us all, and the earth itself to nobody."

The State of War

I open the books on rights and morals, I listen to the scholars and legal experts, and, moved by their "thought-provoking" arguments, I deplore the miseries of nature, I admire the peace and justice established by the civil order, I bless the wisdom of public institutions, and I console myself for being a man by viewing myself as a citizen. Well instructed as to my duties and my happiness, I close the book, I leave the classroom, and I look around me. I see poor wretches groaning under an iron yoke, the human race crushed by a handful of oppressors, a starving mass of people overcome by pain and hunger, whose blood and tears the rich drink in peace, and everywhere the strong armed against the weak with the formidable power of the laws.

All this occurs peacefully and without resistance. It is the tranquility of the companions of Ulysses imprisoned in the Cyclops' cave waiting to be devoured. One can but groan and be quiet. Let us draw an eternal veil over these objects of horror. I lift my eyes and look off in the distance. I see fires and flames, countrysides deserted, and towns sacked. Wild men, where are you dragging these poor wretches? I hear a horrible racket. What an uproar! What cries! I draw near. I see a scene of murders, ten thousand men slaughtered, the dead piled up in heaps, the dying trampled underfoot by horses, everywhere the image of death and agony. This then is the fruit of these peaceful institutions! Pity and indignation rise up from the depths of my heart. Ah, barbarous philosopher! Read us your book on a battlefield! . . .

Who could have imagined without shuddering the mad system of the natural war of each against all? What a strange animal he must be who would believe his good is bound up with the destruction of his entire species! And how can one conceive that this species, so monstrous and so detestable, could last even two generations? Yet this is how far the desire or rather the rage to establish despotism and passive obedience has led one of the finest geniuses who ever lived [Hobbes]. So ferocious a principle was worthy of its purpose.

The state of society that constrains all our natural inclinations cannot, for all that, annihilate them. Despite our prejudices and despite ourselves, they continue to speak to us in the depths of our hearts and often bring us back to the true, which we abandon to pursue chimeras. If this mutual and destructive enmity were an essential part of our constitution, it would therefore still continue to make itself felt and would put us, despite ourselves, at odds with one another, cutting across all social bonds. The frightful hatred of humanity would eat away at man's heart. He would grieve at the birth of his own children; he would rejoice at the death of his brothers; and, on finding someone asleep, his first movement would be to kill him.

The benevolence that causes us to take part in the happiness of our fellowmen, the compassion that identifies us with the one who suffers and distresses us at his pain, would be sentiments unknown and directly contrary to nature. A sensitive and compassionate man would be a monster; and we would naturally be what we have a great deal of difficulty becoming amid the depravation that pursues us.

In vain would the sophist say that this mutual enmity is not innate and immediate but is based on the struggle that inevitably follows from each individual's right to all things. For the sentiment of this alleged right is no more natural to man than the war that he causes to arise from it.

I have already said and I cannot repeat too often that the error of Hobbes and of the philosophers is to confuse natural man with the men they have before their eyes, and to transfer into one system a being that can thrive only in another. Man wants his well-being and everything that can contribute to it; that is indisputable. But naturally this well-being of man is confined to what is physically necessary; for when he has a healthy soul and his body does not suffer, what is there, consistent with his constitution, that is lacking for him to be happy? He who has nothing desires little; he who commands no one has little ambition. But a surplus awakens greed; the more one gets, the more one desires. He who has much wants to have everything; and the mad passion for universal monarchy has never tormented the heart of anyone but a great king. Such is the march of nature; such is the development of the passions. A superficial philosopher observes souls kneaded and fermented a hundred times in the leaven of society and believes he has observed man. But to know him well, one needs to know how to disentangle the natural development of his sentiments, and it is not among the inhabitants of a city that one should look for the first feature of nature imprinted on the human heart.

Thus this analytical method leads to nothing but abysses and mysteries, where the wisest understand the least. Ask why mores are corrupted in proportion as minds are enlightened; unable to find the cause, they will have the nerve to deny the fact. Ask why savages brought among us share neither our passions nor our pleasures and take no interest in all that we desire with great fervor. They will never explain it, or they will explain it only by my principles. They know only what they see, and they have never seen nature. They know perfectly well what a city dweller from London or Paris is; but they will never know what a man is.

But even if it were true that this unlimited and ungovernable greed were as developed in all men as our sophist claims, it would still not produce that state of universal war of each against all, of which Hobbes dares to sketch the odious picture. This unbridled desire to appropriate everything is incompatible with that of destroying all of one's fellowmen; and the victor who, having killed everyone, had the misfortune to remain alone in the world, would enjoy nothing in it for precisely the reason that he would have everything. What are even riches good for, if not to be spent? What use to him is possessing the entire universe if he is its only inhabitant? What? Will his stomach devour all the fruits of the earth? Who will gather for him the crops from all parts of the world? Who will carry word of his empire into the vast wildernesses in which he will never live? What will he do with his treasures, who will consume his provisions, before whose eyes will he display his power? I know. Instead of massacring everyone, he will put them all in irons, at least in order to have slaves. This immediately changes the whole state of the question; and since it is no longer a question of destroying, the state of war is abolished. Let the reader here suspend his judgment. I will not forget to return to this point.

Man is naturally peaceable and timid; at the slightest danger his first movement is to flee; he becomes warlike only by dint of habit and experience. Honor, self-interest, prejudices, vengeance—all the passions that can make him brave perils and death—are alien to him in the state of nature. It is only after having entered into society with another man that he decides to attack someone else, and it is only after having been a citizen that he becomes a soldier. That does not demonstrate strong inclinations to wage war with all his fellowmen. But I am pausing too long over a system as revolting as it is absurd and that has already been refuted a hundred times.

There is then no general war between man and man; and the human species was not formed merely for mutual self-destruction.

Émile

But for her sex, a woman is a man; she has the same organs, the same needs, the same faculties. The machine is the same in its construction; its parts, its working, and its appearance are similar. Regard it as you will the difference is only in degree. . . .

The search for abstract and speculative truths, for principles and axioms in science, for all that tends to wide generalisation, is beyond a woman's grasp; their studies should be thoroughly practical. It is their business to apply the principles discovered by men, it is their place to make the observations which lead men to discover those principles. A woman's thoughts, beyond the range of her immediate duties, should be directed to the study of men, or the acquirement of that agreeable learning whose sole end is the formation of taste; for the works of genius are beyond her reach, and she has neither the accuracy nor the attention for success in the exact sciences; as for the physical sciences, to decide the relations between living creatures and the laws of nature is the task of that sex which is more active and enterprising, which sees more things, that sex which is possessed of greater strength and is more accustomed to the exercise of that strength. Woman, weak as she is and limited in her range of observation, perceives and judges the forces at her disposal to supplement her weakness, and those forces are the passions of man. Her own mechanism is more powerful than ours; she has many levers which may set the human heart in motion. She must find a way to make us desire what she cannot achieve unaided and what she considers necessary or pleasing; therefore she must have a thorough knowledge of man's mind; not an abstract knowledge of the mind of man in general, but the mind of those men who are about her, the mind of those men who have authority over her, either by law or custom. She must learn to divine their feelings from

From Rousseau, Jean-Jacques, *Émile* (translated by Barbara Foxley) (London: J.M. Dent, 1911), pp. 321–322, 349–350.

speech and action, look and gesture. By her own speech and action, look and gesture, she must be able to inspire them with the feelings she desires, without seeming to have any such purpose. The men will have a better philosophy of the human heart, but she will read more accurately in the heart of men. Woman should discover, so to speak, an experimental morality, man should reduce it to a system. Woman has more wit, man more genius; woman observes, man reasons; together they provide the clearest light and the profoundest knowledge which is possible to the unaided human mind; in a word, the surest knowledge of self and of others of which the human race is capable. In this way art may constantly tend to the perfection of the instrument which nature has given us.

On Women

Another subject of admiration for me is the air of confidence with which we make the brilliant enumeration of all the great men that History has celebrated in order to put them into parallel with the small number of Heroines whom it has deigned to remember, and we believe we find our advantage very well in this comparison. Ah, Gentlemen, let the whim of transmitting their annals to posterity come to women, and you will see in what rank you may be placed and whether, perhaps, based on reasons that are more just, they will not award themselves the preeminence that you usurp with so much pride. And, after all, if we entered equitably into the details of all the fine actions to which the times have given birth and if we examine the genuine reasons that might have increased or diminished their number, I do not at all doubt that we would find much more proportion there than we find at first and that the scale might stay just about in equilibrium.

Let us first consider women deprived of their freedom by the tyranny of men, and the latter masters of everything. Crowns, offices, employments, command of armies—everything is in their hands; from the earliest times they have taken hold of them by I know not what natural right that I have never been able to understand very well and that might very well have no other foundation than superior force. Let us also consider the character of the human mind, which wants only what is brilliant, which admires virtue only in the midst of greatness and majesty, which

From Rousseau, Jean-Jacques, "On Women" from *Women, Love, and Family* (ed. by C. Kelly & E. Grace) (Dartmouth, 2009), pp. 63–64.

despises everything greater and more admirable that subject and dependent people can do in their station.

After having speculated about all that, let us enter into the details of the comparison, and, for example, put into parallel Mithridates with Zenobia, Romulus with Dido, Cato of Utica with Lucretia (one of whom gave himself death for the loss of his liberty and the other for that of her honor), the Count de Dunois with Joan of Arc, finally Cornelia, Arria, Artemisia, Fulvia, Elisabeth, the Countess of Thököly, and so many other Heroines of all times with the greatest men; in truth we shall find that the number of the latter outnumber infinitely, but in recompense we shall see in the other sex models as perfect in all sorts of civic and moral virtues. If women had had as great a share as we do in the handling of business, and in the governments of Empires, perhaps they would have pushed Heroism and greatness of courage farther and would have distinguished themselves in greater number. Few of those who have had the good fortune to rule states and command armies remained in mediocrity; they have almost all distinguished themselves by some brilliant point by which they have deserved our admiration for them. It is far from being the case that one could say as much of so many Monarchs who have governed nations: how many of them are there, as Voltaire also said, whose name deserved to be found anywhere but in chronological tables where they are only to serve as an epoch? I repeat it, all proportions maintained, women would have been able to give greater examples of greatness of soul and love of virtue and in greater number than men have ever done if our injustice had not despoiled, along with their freedom, all the occasions to manifest them to the eyes of the world.

I reserve another time for speaking to you about the women who have had a share in the republic of letters and who have adorned it by their works that are ingenious and full of delicacy.

39

Adam Smith

One of the principal figures of the Scottish Enlightenment, Adam Smith (1723–1790) was a highly influential political economist and moral philosopher. He is most famous as the author of *The Wealth of Nations*, commonly regarded as the bible of laissez-faire capitalism. One principal claim of that work is that society benefits from individuals' pursuit of their own self-interest. A brief extract from *The Wealth of Nations* indicates this view. While this may lead one to think of Smith as advancing an egoistic conception of human beings, his account is far more nuanced, as the selections from his *Theory of Moral Sentiments* reveal. Smith there lays great emphasis upon the role of *sympathy* in human motivation, even though this quality may be limited by "the strongest impulses of self-love": these impulses need to be curbed by the voice of conscience. Included here also are Smith's extraordinary ruminations on our sympathy for the dead's wretched fate.

An Inquiry into the Nature and Causes of the Wealth of Nations

This division of labour, from which so many advantages are derived, is not originally the effect of any human wisdom, which foresees and intends that general opulence to which it gives occasion. It is the necessary,

From Smith, Adam, *An Inquiry into the Nature and Causes of the Wealth of Nations* (Oxford: Oxford University Press, 1993 [1776], pp. 21–22.

though very slow and gradual consequence of a certain propensity in human nature which has in view no such extensive utility; the propensity to truck barter, and exchange one thing for another.

Whether this propensity be one of those original principles in human nature, of which no further account can be given; or whether, as seems more probable, it be the necessary consequence of the faculties of reason and speech, it belongs not to our present subject to enquire. It is common to all men, and to be found in no other race of animals, which seem to know neither this nor any other species of contracts. Two greyhounds, in running down the same hare, have sometimes the appearance of acting in some sort of concert. Each turns her towards his companion, or endeavours to intercept her when his companion turns her towards himself. This, however, is not the effect of any contract, but of the accidental concurrence of their passions in the same object at that particular time. Nobody ever saw a dog make a fair and deliberate exchange of one bone for another with another dog. Nobody ever saw one animal by its gestures and natural cries signify to another, this is mine, that yours; I am willing to give this for that. When an animal wants to obtain something either of a man or of another animal, it has no other means of persuasion but to gain the favour of those whose service it requires. A puppy fawns upon its dam, and a spaniel endeavours by a thousand attractions to engage the attention of its master who is at dinner, when it wants to be fed by him. Man sometimes uses the same arts with his brethren, and when he has no other means of engaging them to act according to his inclinations, endeavours by every servile and fawning attention to obtain their good will. He has not time, however, to do this upon every occasion. In civilized society he stands at all times in need of the co-operation and assistance of great multitudes, while his whole life is scarce sufficient to gain the friendship of a few persons. In almost every other race of animals each individual, when it is grown up to maturity, is intirely independent, and in its natural state has occasion for the assistance of no other living creature. But man has almost constant occasion for the help of his brethren, and it is in vain for him to expect it from their benevolence only. He will be more likely to prevail if he can interest their self-love in his favour, and shew them that it is for their own advantage to do for him what he requires of them. Whoever offers to another a bargain of any kind, proposes to do this. Give me that which I want, and you shall have this which you want, is the meaning of every such offer; and it is in this manner that we obtain from one another the far greater part of those good offices which we stand in need of. It is not from the benevolence of the butcher, the brewer, or the baker, that we expect our dinner, but from their regard to their own interest. We address ourselves, not to their humanity but to their self-love, and never talk to them of our own necessities but of their advantages.

The Theory of Moral Sentiments

How selfish soever man may be supposed, there are evidently some principles in his nature, which interest him in the fortune of others, and render their happiness necessary to him, though he derives nothing from it, except the pleasure of seeing it. Of this kind is pity or compassion, the emotion which we feel for the misery of others, when we either see it, or are made to conceive it in a very lively manner. That we often derive sorrow from the sorrow of others, is a matter of fact too obvious to require any instances to prove it; for this sentiment, like all the other original passions of human nature, is by no means confined to the virtuous and humane, though they perhaps may feel it with the most exquisite sensibility. The greatest ruffian, the most hardened violator of the laws of society, is not altogether without it.

As we have no immediate experience of what other men feel, we can form no idea of the manner in which they are affected, but by conceiving what we ourselves should feel in the like situation. Though our brother is upon the rack, as long as we ourselves are at our ease, our senses will never inform us of what he suffers. They never did, and never can, carry us beyond our own person, and it is by the imagination only that we can form any conception of what are his sensations. Neither can that faculty help us to this any other way, than by representing to us what would be our own, if we were in his case. It is the impressions of our own senses only, not those of his, which our imaginations copy. By the imagination we place ourselves in his situation, we conceive ourselves enduring all the same torments, we enter as it were into his body, and become in some measure the same person with him, and thence form some idea of his sensations, and even feel something which, though weaker in degree, is not altogether unlike them. His agonies, when they are thus brought home to ourselves, when we have thus adopted and made them our own, begin at last to affect us, and we then tremble and shudder at the thought

---

From Smith, Adam, *The Theory of Moral Sentiments* (Amherst, NY: Prometheus Books, 2000 [1759]), pp. 3–6, 8–9, 191–194.

of what he feels. For as to be in pain or distress of any kind excites the most excessive sorrow, so to conceive or to imagine that we are in it, excites some degree of the same emotion, in proportion to the vivacity or dullness of the conception.

That this is the source of our fellow-feeling for the misery of others, that it is by changing places in fancy with the sufferer, that we come either to conceive, or to be affected by what he feels, may be demonstrated by many obvious observations, if it should not be thought sufficiently evident of itself. When we see a stroke aimed, and just ready to fall upon the leg or arm of another person, we naturally shrink and draw back our own leg or our own arm; and when it does fall, we feel it in some measure, and are hurt by it as well as the sufferer. The mob, when they are gazing at a dancer on the slack rope, naturally writhe and twist and balance their own bodies as they see him do, and as they feel that they themselves must do if in his situation. Persons of delicate fibres and a weak constitution of body complain, that in looking on the sores and ulcers which are exposed by beggars in the streets, they are apt to feel an itching or uneasy sensation in the corresponding part of their own bodies. The horror which they conceive at the misery of those wretches affects that particular part in themselves more than any other; because that horror arises from conceiving what they themselves would suffer, if they really were the wretches whom they are looking upon, and if that particular part in themselves was actually affected in the same miserable manner. The very force of this conception is sufficient in their feeble frames, to produce that itching or uneasy sensation complained of. Men of the most robust make, observe that in looking upon sore eyes they often feel a very sensible soreness in their own, which proceeds from the same reason; that organ being in the strongest man more delicate than any other part of the body is in the weakest.

Neither is it those circumstances only, which create pain or sorrow, that call forth our fellow-feeling. Whatever is the passion which arises from any object in the person principally concerned, an analogous emotion springs up, at the thought of his situation, in the breast of every attentive spectator. Our joy for the deliverance of those heroes of tragedy or romance who interest us, is as sincere as our grief for their distress, and our fellow-feeling with their misery is not more real than that with their happiness. We enter into their gratitude towards those faithful friends who did not desert them in their difficulties; and we heartily go along with their resentment against those perfidious traitors who injured, abandoned, or deceived them. In every passion of which the mind of man is susceptible, the emotions of the bystander always correspond to what, by bringing the case home to himself, he imagines should he the sentiments of the sufferer.

Pity and compassion are words appropriated to signify our fellow-feeling with the sorrow of others. Sympathy, though its meaning was, perhaps, originally the same, may now, however, without much impropriety, be made use of to denote our fellow-feeling with any passion whatever.

Upon some occasions sympathy may seem to arise merely from the view of a certain emotion in another person. The passions, upon some occasions, may seem to be transfused from one man to another, instantaneously, and antecedent to any knowledge of what excited them in the person principally concerned. Grief and joy, for example, strongly expressed in the look and gestures of any person, at once affect the spectator with some degree of a like painful or agreeable emotion. A smiling face is, to everybody that sees it, a cheerful object; as a sorrowful countenance, on the other hand, is a melancholy one.

. . .

We sympathize even with the dead, and overlooking what is of real importance in their situation, that awful futurity which awaits them, we are chiefly affected by those circumstances which strike our senses, but can have no influence upon their happiness. It is miserable, we think, to be deprived of the light of the sun; to be shut out from life and conversation; to be laid in the cold grave, a prey to corruption and the reptiles of the earth; to be no more thought of in this world, but to be obliterated, in a little time, from the affections, and almost from the memory, of their dearest friends and relations. Surely, we imagine, we can never feel too much for those who have suffered so dreadful a calamity. The tribute of our fellow-feeling seems doubly due to them now, when they are in danger of being forgot by every body; and, by the vain honours which we pay to their memory, we endeavour, for our own misery, artificially to keep alive our melancholy remembrance of their misfortune. That our sympathy can afford them no consolation seems to be an addition to their calamity; and to think that all we can do is unavailing, and that, what alleviates all other distress, the regret, the love, and the lamentations of their friends, can yield no comfort to them, serves only to exasperate our sense of their misery. The happiness of the dead, however, most assuredly is affected by none of these circumstances; nor is it the thought of these things which can ever disturb the profound security of their repose. The idea of that dreary and endless melancholy, which the fancy naturally ascribes to their condition, arises altogether from our joining to the change which has been produced upon them, our own consciousness of that change; from our putting ourselves in their situation, and from our lodging, if I may be allowed to say so, our own living souls in their inanimated bodies, and thence conceiving what would be our emotions in this case. It is from this very illusion of the imagination, that the foresight of our own dissolution is so terrible to us, and that the idea of those circumstances, which undoubtedly can give us no pain when we are dead, makes us miserable while we are alive. And from thence arises one of the most important principles in human nature, the dread of death—the great poison to the happiness, but the great restraint upon the injustice of mankind; which, while it afflicts and mortifies the individual, guards and protects the society.

. . .

As to the eye of the body, objects appear great or small, not so much according to their real dimensions as according to the nearness or distance of their situation; so do they likewise to what may be called the natural eye of the mind and we remedy the defects of both these organs pretty much in the same manner. In my present situation, an immense landscape of lawns and woods, and distant mountains, seems to do no more than cover the little window which I write by, and to be out of all proportion less than the chamber in which I am sitting. I can form a just comparison between those great objects and the little objects around me, in no other way than by transporting myself, at least in fancy, to a different station, from whence I can survey both at nearly equal distances, and thereby form some judgment of their real proportions. Habit and experience have taught me to do this so easily and so readily, that I am scarce sensible that I do it; and a man must be, in some measure, acquainted with the philosophy of vision, before he can be thoroughly convinced how little those distant objects would appear to the eye, if the imagination, from a knowledge of their real magnitudes, did not swell and dilate them.

In the same manner, to the selfish and original passions of human nature, the loss or gain of a very small interest of our own appears to be of vastly more importance, excites a much more passionate joy or sorrow, a much more ardent desire or aversion, than the greatest concern of another with whom we have no particular connection. His interests, as long as they are surveyed from his station, can never be put into the balance with our own, can never restrain us from doing whatever may tend to promote our own, how ruinous soever to him. Before we can make any proper comparison of those opposite interests, we must change our position. We must view them, neither from our own place nor yet from his, neither with our own eyes nor yet with his, but from the place and with the eyes of a third person, who has no particular connection with either, and who judges with impartiality between us. Here, too, habit and experience have taught us to do this so easily and so readily, that we are scarce sensible that we do it; and it requires, in this case, too, some degree of reflection, and even of philosophy, to convince us, how little interest we should take in the greatest concerns of our neighbour, how little we should be affected by whatever relates to him, if the sense of propriety and justice did not correct the otherwise natural inequality of our sentiments.

Let us suppose that the great empire of China, with all its myriads of inhabitants, was suddenly swallowed up by an earthquake, and let us consider how a man of humanity in Europe, who had no sort of connection with that part of the world, would be affected upon receiving intelligence of this dreadful calamity. He would, I imagine, first of all express very strongly his sorrow for the misfortune of that unhappy people, he would make many melancholy reflections upon the precariousness of human life, and the vanity of all the labours of man, which could thus be annihilated in a moment. He would, too, perhaps, if he was a man of speculation, enter into many reasonings concerning the effects which this disaster might produce upon the commerce of Europe, and the trade and business of the world in general. And when all this fine philosophy was over, when all these humane sentiments had been once fairly expressed, he would pursue his business or his pleasure, take his repose or his diversion, with the same ease and tranquility as if no such accident had happened. The most frivolous disaster which could befall himself would occasion a more real disturbance. If he was to lose his little finger to morrow, he would not sleep to-night; but, provided he never saw them, he will snore with the most profound security over the ruin of a hundred millions of his brethren, and the destruction of that immense multitude seems plainly an object less interesting to him than this paltry misfortune of his own. To prevent, therefore, this paltry misfortune to himself, would a man of humanity be willing to sacrifice the lives of a hundred millions of his brethren, provided he had never seen them? Human nature startles with horror at the thought, and the world, in its greatest depravity and corruption, never produced such a villain as could be capable of entertaining it. But what makes this difference? When our passive feelings are almost always so sordid and so selfish, how comes it that our active principles should often be so generous and so noble? When we are always so much more deeply affected by whatever concerns ourselves than by whatever concerns other men; what is it which prompts the generous upon all occasions, and the mean upon many, to sacrifice their own interests to the greater interests of others? It is not the soft power of humanity, it is not that feeble spark of benevolence which Nature has lighted up in the human heart, that is thus capable of counteracting the strongest impulses of self-love. It is a stronger power, a more forcible motive, which exerts itself upon such occasions. It is reason, principle, conscience, the inhabitant of the breast, the man within, the great judge and arbiter of our conduct. It is he who, whenever we are about to act so as to affect the happiness of others, calls to us, with a voice capable of astonishing the most presumptuous of our passions, that we are but one of the multitude, in no respect better than any other in it; and that, when we prefer ourselves so shamefully and so blindly to others, we become the proper objects of resentment, abhorrence, and execration. It is from him only that we learn the real littleness of ourselves, and of whatever relates to ourselves, and the natural misrepresentations of self-love can be corrected only by the eye of this impartial spectator. It is he who shews us the propriety of generosity and the deformity of injustice; the propriety of resigning the greatest interests of our own for the yet greater interests of others; and the deformity of doing the smallest injury to another in order to obtain the greatest benefit to ourselves. It is not the love of our neighbour, it is not the love of mankind, which upon many occasions prompts us to the practice of those divine virtues. It is a stronger love, a more powerful affection, which generally takes place upon such occasions; the love of what is honourable and noble, of the grandeur, and dignity, and superiority of our own characters.

40

Paul-Henri Thiry, Baron d'Holbach

"Man is the work of Nature: he exists in Nature: he is submitted to her laws: he cannot deliver himself from them; nor can he step beyond them even in thought." These words, which are found early on in his *System of Nature*, capture the atheistic and materialistic spirit of the philosophy of Paul-Henri Thiry, Baron d'Holbach (1723–1789). His emphasis on the thoroughly physical nature of human beings, trapped within nature's machinery, shows itself in the selections below, in which d'Holbach exposes what he sees as the illusory character of the belief in both freedom of the will and immortality.

The System of Nature

Those who have pretended that the *soul* is distinguished from the body, is immaterial, draws its ideas from its own peculiar source, acts by its own energies, without the aid of any exterior object, have, by a consequence of their own system, enfranchised it from those physical laws according to which all beings of which we have a knowledge are obliged to act. They have believed that the soul is mistress of its own conduct, is able to regulate its own peculiar operations, has the faculty to determine its will by its own natural energy; in a word, they have pretended that man is a *free agent*.

It has been already sufficiently proved that the soul is nothing more than the body considered relatively to some of its functions more concealed than others: it has been shown that this soul, even when it shall be

From Baron d'Holbach, *The System of Nature* (New York: Lenox Hill, 1970 [trans. by H. D. Robinson, first published 1868]), pp. 88–90, 90–1, 92–93, 95, 116–117, 118–119, 120–121.

supposed immaterial, is continually modified conjointly with the body, is submitted to all its motion, and that without this it would remain inert and dead: that, consequently, it is subjected to the influence of those material and physical causes which give impulse to the body; of which the mode of existence, whether habitual or transitory, depends upon the material elements by which it is surrounded, that form its texture, constitute its temperament, enter into it by means of the aliments, and penetrate it by their subtility. The faculties which are called *intellectual,* and those qualities which are styled *moral,* have been explained in a manner purely physical and natural. In the last place it has been demonstrated that all the ideas, all the systems, all the affections, all the opinions, whether true or false, which man forms to himself, are to be attributed to his physical and material senses. Thus man is a being purely physical; in whatever manner he is considered, he is connected to universal nature, and submitted to the necessary and immutable laws that she imposes on all the beings she contains, according to their peculiar essences or to the respective properties with which, without consulting them, she endows each particular species. Man's life is a line that nature commands him to describe upon the surface of the earth, without his ever being able to swerve from it, even for an instant. He is born without his own consent; his organization does in nowise depend upon himself; his ideas come to him involuntarily; his habits are in the power of those who cause him to contract them; he is unceasingly modified by causes, whether visible or concealed, over which he has no control, which necessarily regulate his mode of existence, give the hue to his way of thinking, and determine his manner of acting. He is good or bad, happy or miserable, wise or foolish, reasonable or irrational, without his will being for any thing in these various states. Nevertheless, in despite of the shackles by which he is bound, it is pretended he is a free agent, or that independent of the causes by which he is moved, he determines his own will, and regulates his own condition.

However slender the foundation of this opinion, of which every thing ought to point out to him the errour, it is current at this day and passes for an incontestable truth with a great number of people otherwise extremely enlightened; it is the basis of religion, which, supposing relations between man and the unknown being she has placed above nature, has been incapable of imagining how man could either merit reward or deserve punishment from this being, if he was not a free agent. Society has been believed interested in this system; because an idea has gone abroad, that if all the actions of man were to be contemplated as necessary, the right of punishing those who injure their associates would no longer exist. At length human vanity accommodated itself to a hypothesis which, unquestionably, appears to distinguish man from all other physical beings, by assigning to him the special privilege of a total independence of all other causes, but of which a very little reflection would have shown him the impossibility.

As a part subordinate to the great whole, man is obliged to experience its influence. To be a free agent, it were needful that each individual was of greater strength than the entire of nature; or that he was out of this nature, who, always in action herself, obliges all the beings she embraces to act, and to concur to her general motion; or, as it has been said elsewhere, to conserve her active existence by the motion that all beings produce in consequence of their particular energies, submitted to fixed, eternal, and immutable laws. In order that man might be a free agent, it were needful that all beings should lose their essences; it would be equally necessary that he himself should no longer enjoy physical sensibility; that he should neither know good nor evil, pleasure nor pain; but if this were the case, from that moment he would no longer be in a state to conserve himself, or render his existence happy; all beings would become indifferent to him; he would no longer have any choice; he would cease to know what he ought to love, what it was right he should fear; he would not have any acquaintance with that which he should seek after, or with that which it is requisite he should avoid. In short, man would be an unnatural being, totally incapable of acting in the manner we behold . . .

The will, as we have elsewhere said, is a modification of the brain, by which it is disposed to action, or prepared to give play to the organs. This will is necessarily determined by the qualities, good or bad, agreeable or painful, of the object or the motive that acts upon his senses, or of which the idea remains with him, and is resuscitated by his memory. In consequence, he acts necessarily, his action is the result of the impulse he receives either from the motive, from the object, or from the idea which has modified his brain, or disposed his will. When he does not act according to this impulse, it is because there comes some new cause, some new motive, some new idea, which modifies his brain in a different manner, gives him a new impulse, determines his will in another way, by which the action of the former impulse is suspended: thus, the sight of an agreeable object, or its idea, determines his will to set him in action to procure it; but if a new object or a new idea more powerfully attracts him, it gives a new direction to his will, annihilates the effect of the former, and prevents the action by which it was to be procured. This is the mode in which reflection, experience, reason, necessarily arrests or suspends the action of man's will: without this he would of necessity have followed the anterior impulse which carried him towards a then desirable object. In all this he always acts according to necessary laws, from which he has no means of emancipating himself.

If when tormented with violent thirst, he figures to himself in idea, or really perceives a fountain, whose limpid streams might cool his feverish want, is he sufficient master of himself to desire or not to desire the object competent to satisfy so lively a want? It will no doubt be conceded, that it is impossible he should not be desirous to satisfy it; but it will be said—if at this moment it is announced to him that the water he so ardently desires is poisoned, he will, notwithstanding his vehement thirst, abstain from drinking it: and it has, therefore, been falsely concluded that he is a free agent. The fact, however, is, that the motive in either case is exactly the same: his own conservation. The same necessity that determined him to drink before he knew the water was deleterious, upon this new discovery equally determines him not to drink; the desire of conserving himself either annihilates or suspends the former impulse; the second motive becomes stronger than the preceding, that is, the fear of death, or the desire of preserving himself necessarily prevails over the painful sensation caused by his eagerness to drink: but, it will he said, if the thirst is very parching, an inconsiderate man without regarding the danger will risk swallowing the water. Nothing is gained by this remark: in this case, the anterior impulse only regains the ascendency; he is persuaded that life may possibly be longer preserved, or that he shall derive a greater good by drinking the poisoned water than by enduring the torment, which, to his mind, threatens instant dissolution: thus the first becomes the strongest and necessarily urges him on to action. Nevertheless, in either case, whether he partakes of the water, or whether he does not, the two actions will be equally necessary; they will be the effect of that motive which finds itself most puissant; which consequently acts in the most coercive manner upon his will. . . .

Choice by no means proves the free agency of man: he only deliberates when he does not yet know which to choose of the many objects that move him, he is then in an embarrassment, which does not terminate until his will is decided by the greater advantage he believes he shall find in the object he chooses, or the action he undertakes. From whence it may be seen, that choice is necessary, because he would not determine for an object, or for an action, if he did not believe that he should find in it some direct advantage. That man should have free agency, it were needful that he should be able to will or choose without motive, or that he could prevent motives coercing his will. Action always being the effect of his will once determined, and as his will cannot be determined but by a motive which is not in his own power, it follows that he is never the master of the determination of his own peculiar will; that consequently he never acts as a free agent. It has been believed that man was a free agent because he had a will with the power of choosing; but attention has not been paid to the fact that even his will is moved by causes independent of himself; is owing to that which is inherent in his own organization, or which belongs to the nature of the beings acting on him. Is he the master of willing not to withdraw his hand from the fire when he fears it will be burnt? Or has he the power to take away from fire the property which makes him fear it? Is he the master of not choosing a dish of meat, which he knows to be agreeable, or analogous to his palate; of not preferring it to that which, he knows to be disagreeable or dangerous? It is always according to his sensations, to his own peculiar experience, or to his suppositions, that he judges of things, either well or ill; but whatever may be his judgment, it depends necessarily on his mode of feeling, whether habitual or accidental, and the qualities he finds in the causes that move him, which exist in despite of himself. . . .

In short, the acts of man are never free; they are always the necessary consequence of his temperament, of the received ideas, and of the notions, either true or false, which he has formed to himself of happiness; of his opinions, strengthened by example, by education, and by daily experience. So many crimes are witnessed on the earth only because every thing conspires to render man vicious and criminal; the religion he has adopted, his government, his education, the examples set before him, irresistibly drive him on to evil: under these circumstances, morality preaches virtue to him in vain. In those societies where vice is esteemed, where crime is crowned, where venality is constantly recompensed, where the most dreadful disorders are punished only in those who are too weak to enjoy the privilege of committing them with impunity, the practice of virtue is considered nothing more than a painful sacrifice of happiness. . . .

Man, then, is not a free agent in any one instant of his life; he is necessarily guided in each step by those advantages, whether real or fictitious, that he attaches to the objects by which his passions are roused: these passions themselves are necessary in a being who unceasingly tends towards his own happiness; their energy is necessary, since that depends on his temperament; his temperament is necessary, because it depends on the physical elements which enter into his composition; the modification of this temperament is necessary, as it is the infallible and inevitable consequence of the impulse he receives from the incessant action of moral and physical beings.

. . .

The reflections presented to the reader in this work, tend to show, what ought to be thought of the human soul, as well as of its operations and faculties: every thing proves, in the most convincing manner, that it acts and moves according to laws similar to those prescribed to the other beings of nature; that it cannot be distinguished from the body; that it is born with it; that it grows up with it; that it is modified in the same progression; in short, every thing ought to make man conclude that it perishes with it. This soul, as well as the body, passes through a state of weakness and infancy; it is in this stage of its existence that it is assailed by a multitude of modifications and of ideas which it receives from exterior objects through the medium of the organs; that it amasses facts; that it collects experience, whether true or false; that it forms to itself a system of conduct, according to which it thinks and acts, and from whence results either its happiness or its misery, its reason or its delirium, its virtues or its vices: arrived with the body at its full powers; having in conjunction with it reached maturity, it does not cease for a single instant to partake in common of its sensations, whether these are agreeable or disagreeable; in consequence it conjointly approves or disapproves its state; like it, it is either sound or diseased, active or languishing, awake or asleep. In old age, man extinguishes entirely, his fibres become rigid, his nerves lose their elasticity, his senses are obtunded, his sight grows dim, his ears lose their quickness, his ideas become unconnected, his memory fails, his imagination cools; what, then, becomes of his soul? Alas! it sinks down with the body; it gets benumbed as this loses its feeling, becomes sluggish as this decays in activity; like it, when enfeebled by years it fulfils its functions with pain; and this substance, which is deemed spiritual or *immaterial*, undergoes the same revolutions, and experiences the same vicissitudes as does the body itself.

In despite of this convincing proof of the materiality of the soul, and of its identity with the body, some thinkers have supposed that although the latter is perishable, the former does not perish; that this portion of man enjoys the especial privilege of *immortality*; that it is exempt from dissolution and free from those changes of form all the beings in nature undergo: in consequence of this, man has persuaded himself that this privileged soul does not die: its immortality above all appears indubitable to those who suppose it spiritual: after having made it a simple being, without extent, devoid of parts, totally different from any thing of which he has a knowledge, he pretended that it was not subjected to the laws of decomposition common to all beings, of which experience shows him the continual operation. . . .

Nothing is more popular than the doctrine of the *immortality of the soul,* nothing is more universally diffused than the expectation of another life. Nature having inspired man with the most ardent love for his existence, the desire of preserving himself for ever was a necessary consequence: this desire was presently converted into certainty; from that desire of existing eternally, which nature has implanted in him, he made an argument to prove that man would never cease to exist. Abbadie says: "Our soul has no useless desires, it desires naturally an eternal life"; and by a very strange logic he concludes, that this desire could not fail to be fulfilled. However this may be, man, thus disposed, listened with avidity to those who announced to him systems so conformable with his wishes. Nevertheless, he ought not to regard as supernatural the desire of existing, which, always was, and always will be, of the essence of man; it ought not to excite surprise if he received with eagerness an hypothesis that flattered his hopes, by promising that his desire would one day be gratified; but let him beware how he concludes, that this desire itself is an indubitable proof of the reality of this future life, with which, for his present happiness, he seems to be far too much occupied. The passion for existence, is in man only a natural consequence of the tendency of a sensible being, whose essence it is to be willing to conserve himself: in the human being, it follows the energy of his soul or keeps pace with the force of his imagination, always ready to realize that which he strongly desires. He desires the life of the body, nevertheless this desire is frustrated; wherefore should not the desire for the life of the soul be frustrated like the other?[3]

The most simple reflection upon the nature of his soul, ought to convince man that the idea of its immortality is only an illusion of the brain. Indeed, what is his soul, save the principle of sensibility? What is it to

---

[3] The partisans of the doctrine of the immortality of the soul, reason thus: "All men desire to live for ever; therefore they will live for ever." Suppose the argument retorted on them: "All men naturally desire to be rich; therefore, all men will one day be rich."

think, to enjoy, to suffer; is it not to feel? What is life, except it be the assemblage of modifications, the congregation of motion, peculiar to an organized being? Thus, as soon as the body ceases to live, its sensibility can no longer exercise itself; therefore it can no longer have ideas, nor in consequence thoughts. Ideas, as we have proved, can only reach man through his senses; now, how will they have it, that once deprived of his senses, he is yet capable of receiving sensations, of having perceptions, of forming ideas? As they have made the soul of man a being separated from the animated body, wherefore have they not made life a being distinguished from the living body? Life in a body is the totality of its motion; feeling and thought make a part of this motion: thus, in the dead man, these motions will cease like all the others.

Indeed, by what reasoning will it be proved, that this soul, which cannot feel, think, will, or act, but by aid of man's organs, can suffer pain, be susceptible of pleasure, or even have a consciousness of its own existence, when the organs which should warn it of their presence, are decomposed or destroyed? Is it not evident that the soul depends on the arrangement of the various parts of the body, and on the order with which these parts conspire to perform their functions or motions? Thus the organic structure once destroyed, can it be doubted the soul will be destroyed also? Is it not seen, that during the whole course of human life, this soul is stimulated, changed, deranged, disturbed, by all the changes man's organs experience? And yet it will be insisted that this soul acts, thinks, subsists, when these same organs have entirely disappeared!

An organized being may be compared to a clock, which, once broken, is no longer suitable to the use for which it was designed. To say, that the soul shall feel, shall think, shall enjoy, shall suffer, after the death of the body, is to pretend, that a clock, shivered into a thousand pieces, will continue to strike the hour, and have the faculty of marking the progress of time. Those who say, that the soul of man is able to subsist notwithstanding the destruction of the body, evidently support the position, that the modification of a body will be enabled to conserve itself, after the subject is destroyed: but this is completely absurd.

. . .

Mortal, led astray by fear! after thy death thine eyes will see no more; thine ears will hear no longer; in the depth of thy grave, thou wilt no more be witness to this scene which thine imagination at present represents to thee under such dismal colours; thou wilt no longer take part in what shall be done in the world; thou wilt no more be occupied with what may befall thine inanimate remains, than thou wast able to be the day previous to that which ranked thee among the beings of thy species. To die, is to cease to think, to feel, to enjoy, to suffer; thy sorrows will not follow thee to the silent tomb. Think of death, not to feed thy fears and to nourish thy melancholy, but to accustom thyself to look upon it with a peaceable eye, and to cheer thee up against those false terrors with which the enemies to thy repose labour to inspire thee!

The fears of death are vain illusions, that must disappear as soon as we learn to contemplate this necessary event under its true point of view. A great man has defined philosophy to be *a meditation on death*; he is not desirous by that to have it understood that man ought to occupy himself sorrowfully with his end, with a view to nourish his fears; on the contrary he wishes to invite him to familiarize himself with an object that nature has rendered necessary to him, and to accustom himself to expect it with a serene countenance. If life is a benefit, if it be necessary to love it, it is no less necessary to quit it, and reason ought to teach him a calm resignation to the decrees of fate: his welfare exacts that he should contract the habit of contemplating without alarm an event that his essence has rendered inevitable: his interest demands that he should not by continual dread imbitter his life, the charms of which he must inevitably destroy, if he can never view its termination but with trepidation. Reason and his interest concur to assure him against those vague terrours with which his imagination inspires him in this respect. If he was to call them to his assistance, they would reconcile him to an object that only startles him because he has no knowledge of it, or because it is only shown to him with those hideous accompaniments with which it is clothed by superstition. Let him, then, endeavour to despoil death of these vain illusions, and he will perceive that it is only the sleep of life; that this sleep will not be disturbed with disagreeable dreams, and that an unpleasant awakening will never follow it. To die, is to sleep; it is to re-enter into that state of insensibility in which he was previous to his birth; before he had senses, before he was conscious of his actual existence. Laws, as necessary as those which gave him birth, will make him return into the bosom of nature from whence he was drawn, in order to reproduce him afterwards under some new form, which it would be useless for him to know: without consulting him, nature places him for a season in the order of organized beings; without his consent, she will oblige him to quit it to occupy some other order.

Let him not complain, then, that nature is callous; she only makes him undergo a law from which she does not exempt any one being she contains.[4] If all are born and perish; if every thing is changed and destroyed; if the birth of a being is never more than the first step towards its end; how is it possible to expect that man, whose machine is so frail, of which the parts are so complicated, the whole of which possesses such extreme mobility, should be exempted from the common law which decrees that even the solid earth he inhabits shall experience change, shall undergo alteration—perhaps be destroyed! Feeble, frail mortal! thou pretendest to exist for ever; wilt thou, then, that for thee alone, eternal nature shall change her undeviating course? Dost thou not behold in those eccentric comets with which thine eyes are sometimes astonished, that the planets themselves are subject to death? Live then in peace, for the season that nature permits thee; and if thy mind be enlightened by reason, thou wilt die without terrour!

---

[4] Seneca: "Man complains of the short duration of life—of the rapidity with which time flies away; yet the greater number of men do not know how to employ either time or life."

==== 🐦 ====

41

Immanuel Kant

One of the greatest of all philosophers, Immanuel Kant (1724–1804) made hugely significant contributions to philosophy, and his three "Critiques"—the *Critique of Pure Reason, Critique of Practical Reason,* and *Critique of Judgment*—are masterful contributions to epistemology, moral philosophy, and aesthetics respectively. The first selection indicates Kant's general reigning in of the pretensions of rational inquiry, and shows how this is applied to the question of the continued persistence of the self after death. In the second, freedom of will—one of the unresolvable metaphysical issues that Kant critiques—is contended to have a practical justification, namely as a presupposition of morality. The extract from *Religion Within the Limits of Reason Alone* concerns the question of the predisposition to good or evil in human nature; while the selection from the *Critique of Practical Reason* contains Kant's justly famous words about the awe-inspiring character of "the starry heavens above me and the moral law within me." The final selections here illustrate Kant's regrettable sexist and racist outlook.

Critique of Pure Reason

Human reason has this peculiar fate that in one species of its knowledge it is burdened by questions which, as prescribed by the very nature of reason itself, it is not able to ignore, but which, as transcending all its powers, it is also not able to answer.

From *Critique of Pure Reason* (trans by Norman Kemp Smith) (London: Macmillan, 1950), pp. 7–9, 377–380.

The perplexity into which it thus falls is not due to any fault of its own. It begins with principles which it has no option save to employ in the course of experience, and which this experience at the same time abundantly justifies it in using. Rising with their aid (since it is determined to this also by its own nature) to ever higher, ever more remote, conditions, it soon becomes aware that in this way—the questions never ceasing—its work must always remain incomplete; and it therefore finds itself compelled to resort to principles which overstep all possible empirical employment and which yet seem so unobjectionable that even ordinary consciousness readily accepts them. But by this procedure human reason precipitates itself into darkness and contradictions; and while it may indeed conjecture that these must be in some way due to concealed errors, it is not in a position to be able to detect them. For since the principles of which it is making use transcend the limits of experience, they are no longer subject to any empirical test. The battle-field of these endless controversies is called metaphysics.

Time was when metaphysics was entitled the Queen of all the sciences; and if the will be taken for the deed, the preeminent importance of her accepted tasks gives her every right to this title of honour. Now, however, the changed fashion of the time brings her only scorn; a matron outcast and forsaken, she mourns like Hecuba: *Modo maxima rerum, tot generis, natisque potens—nunc trahor exul, inops?*[5]

Her government, under the administration of the *dogmatists*, was at first *despotic*. But inasmuch as the legislation still bore traces of the ancient barbarism, her empire gradually through intestine wars gave way to complete anarchy; and the *sceptics*, a species of nomads, despising all settled modes of life, broke up from time to time all civil society. Happily they were few in number, and were unable to prevent its being established ever anew, although on no uniform and self-consistent plan. In more recent times, it has seemed as if an end might be put to all these controversies and the claims of metaphysics receive final judgment, through a certain *physiology* of the human understanding—that of the celebrated Locke. But it has turned out quite otherwise. For however the attempt be made to cast doubt upon the pretensions of the supposed Queen by tracing her lineage to vulgar origins in common experience, this genealogy has, as a matter of fact, been fictitiously invented, and she has still continued to uphold her

---

[5] "Recently at the height of fame and strong in my many sons, I am now penniless and exiled." Ovid, *Metam.* [xiii. 508–10]

claims. Metaphysics has accordingly lapsed back into the ancient time-worn dogmatism, and so again suffers that depreciation from which it was to have been rescued. And now, after all methods, so it is believed, have been tried and found wanting, the prevailing mood is that of weariness and complete *indifferentism*—the mother, in all sciences, of chaos and night, but happily in this case the source, or at least the prelude, of their approaching reform and restoration. For it at least puts an end to that ill-applied industry which has rendered them thus dark, confused, and unserviceable.

But it is idle to feign indifference to such enquiries, the object of which can never be indifferent to our human nature. Indeed these pretended *indifferentists*, however they may try to disguise themselves by substituting a popular tone for the language of the Schools, inevitably fall back, in so far as they think at all, into those very metaphysical assertions which they profess so greatly to despise. None the less this indifference, showing itself in the midst of flourishing sciences, and affecting precisely those sciences, the knowledge of which, if attainable, we should least of all care to dispense with, is a phenomenon that calls for attention and reflection. It is obviously the effect not of levity, but of the matured judgment of the age, which refuses to be any longer put off with illusory knowledge. It is a call to reason to undertake anew the most difficult of all tasks, namely, that of self-knowledge, and to institute a tribunal which will assure to reason its lawful claims, and dismiss all groundless pretensions, not by despotic decrees, but in accordance with its own eternal and unalterable laws. This tribunal is no other than the *critique of pure reason*.

. . .

Rational psychology exists not as *doctrine*, furnishing an addition to our knowledge of the self, but only as *discipline*. It sets impassable limits to speculative reason in this field, and thus keeps us, on the one hand, from throwing ourselves into the arms of a soulless materialism, or, on the other hand, from losing ourselves in a spiritualism which must be quite unfounded so long as we remain in this present life. But though it furnishes no positive doctrine, it reminds us that we should regard this refusal of reason to give satisfying response to our inquisitive probings into what is beyond the limits of this present life as reason's hint to divert our self-knowledge from fruitless and extravagant speculation to fruitful practical employment. Though in such practical employment it is directed always to objects of experience only, it derives its principles from a higher source and determines us to regulate our actions as if our destiny reached infinitely far beyond experience, and therefore far beyond this present life.

From all this it is evident that rational psychology owes its origin simply to misunderstanding. The unity of consciousness, which underlies the categories, is here mistaken for an intuition of the subject as object, and the category of substance is then applied to it. But this unity is only unity in *thought*, by which alone no object is given, and to which, therefore, the category of substance, which always presupposes a given *intuition*, cannot be applied. Consequently this subject cannot be known. The subject of the categories cannot by thinking the categories acquire a concept of itself as an object of the categories. For in order to think them, its pure self-consciousness, which is what was to be explained, must itself be presupposed. Similarly, the subject, in which the representation of time has its original ground, cannot thereby determine its own existence in time. And if this latter is impossible, the former, as a determination of the self (as a thinking being in general) by means of the categories, is equally so.

Thus the expectation of obtaining knowledge which while extending beyond the limits of possible experience is likewise to further the highest interests of humanity, is found, so far as speculative philosophy professes to satisfy it, to be grounded in deception, and to destroy itself in the attempt at fulfilment. Yet the severity of our criticism has rendered reason a not unimportant service in proving the impossibility of dogmatically determining, in regard to an object of experience, anything that lies beyond the limits of experience. For in so doing it has secured reason against all possible assertions of the opposite. That cannot be achieved save in one or other of two ways. Either we have to prove our proposition apodeictically, or, if we do not succeed in this, we have to seek out the sources of this inability, which, if they are traceable to the necessary limits of our reason, must constrain all opponents to submit to this same law of renunciation in respect of all claims to dogmatic assertion.

Yet nothing is thereby lost as regards the right, nay, the necessity, of postulating a future life in accordance with the principles of the practical employment of reason, which is closely bound up with its speculative employment. For the merely speculative proof has never been able to exercise any influence upon the common reason of men. It so stands upon the point of a hair, that even the schools preserve it from falling only so long as they keep it unceasingly spinning round like a top; even in their own eyes it yields no abiding foundation upon which anything could be built. The proofs which are serviceable for the world at large all preserve their entire value undiminished, and indeed, upon the surrender of these dogmatic pretensions, gain in clearness and in natural force. For reason is then located in its own peculiar sphere, namely, the order of ends, which is also at the same time an order of nature; and since it is in itself not only a theoretical but also a practical faculty, and as such is not bound down to natural conditions, it is justified in extending the order of ends, and therewith our own existence, beyond the limits of experience and of life. If we judged according to *analogy with the nature* of living beings in this world, in dealing with which reason must necessarily accept the principle that no organ, no faculty, no impulse, indeed nothing whatsoever is either superfluous or disproportioned to its use, and that therefore nothing is purposeless, but everything exactly conformed to its destiny in life—if we judged by such an analogy we should have to regard man, who alone can contain in himself the final end of all this order, as the only creature that is excepted from it. Man's natural endowments—not merely his talents and the impulses to enjoy them, but above all else the moral law within him—go so far beyond all the utility and advantage which he may derive from them in this present life, that he learns thereby to prize the mere consciousness of a righteous will as being, apart from all advantageous consequences, apart even from the shadowy reward of posthumous fame, supreme over all other values; and so feels an inner call to fit himself, by his conduct in this world, and by the sacrifice of many of its advantages, for citizenship in a better world upon which he lays hold an idea. This powerful and incontrovertible proof is reinforced by our ever-increasing knowledge of purposiveness in all that we see around us, and by contemplation of the immensity of creation, and therefore also by the consciousness of a certain illimitableness in the possible extension of our knowledge, and of a striving commensurate therewith. All this still remains to us; but we must renounce the hope of comprehending, from the merely theoretical knowledge of ourselves, the necessary continuance of our existence.

Groundwork of the Metaphysic of Morals

It is not enough to ascribe freedom to our will, on whatever ground, unless we have sufficient reason for attributing the same freedom to all rational beings, as well. For since morality is a law for us only as *rational beings*, it must be equally valid for all rational beings; and since it must be derived

From *Groundwork of the Metaphysic of Morals* (trans by H.J. Paton) (New York: Harper & Row, 1964), pp. 115–116.

solely from the property of freedom, we have got to prove that freedom too is a property of the will of all rational beings. It is not enough to demonstrate freedom from certain, alleged experiences of human nature (though to do this is in any case absolutely impossible and freedom can be demonstrated only *a priori*): we must prove that it belongs universally to the activity of rational beings endowed with a will. Now I assert that every being who cannot act except *under the Idea of freedom* is by this alone—from a practical point of view—really free; that is to say, for him all the laws inseparably bound up with freedom are valid just as much as if his will could be pronounced free in itself on grounds valid for theoretical philosophy. And I maintain that to every rational being possessed of a will we must also lend the Idea of freedom as the only one under which he can act. For in such a being we conceive a reason which is practical— that is, which exercises causality in regard to its objects. But we cannot possibly conceive of a reason as being consciously directed from outside in regard to its judgements; for in that case the subject would attribute the determination of his power of judgement not to his reason, but to an impulsion. Reason must look upon itself as the author of its own principles independently of alien influences. Therefore as practical reason, or as the will of a rational being, it must be regarded by itself, as free; that is, the will of a rational being can be a will of his own only under the Idea of freedom, and such a will must therefore—from a practical point of view—be attributed to all rational beings.

Religion Within the Limits of Reason Alone

When we say, then, Man is by nature good, or, Man is by nature evil, this means only that there is in him an ultimate ground (inscrutable to us) of the adoption of good maxims or of evil maxims (*i.e.*, those contrary to law), and this he has, being a man; and hence he thereby expresses the character of his species.

We shall say, therefore, of the character (good or evil) distinguishing man from other possible rational beings, that it is *innate* in him. Yet in doing so we shall ever take the position that nature is not to bear the blame (if it is evil) or take the credit (if it is good), but that man himself is its author. But since the ultimate ground of the adoption of our maxims, which must itself

From *Religion Within the Limits of Reason Alone* (New York: Harper & Row, 1960), pp. 17, 21–25. © by Open Court Publishing Company. Reproduced with permission.

lie in free choice, cannot be a fact revealed in experience, it follows that the good or evil in man (as the ultimate subjective ground of the adoption of this or that maxim with reference to the moral law) is termed innate only in *this* sense, that it is posited as the ground antecedent to every use of freedom in experience (in earliest youth as far back as birth) and is thus conceived of as present in man at birth—though birth need not be the cause of it.

. . .

I. Concerning the Original Predisposition to Good in Human Nature

We may conveniently divide this predisposition, with respect to function, into three divisions, to be considered as elements in the fixed character and destiny of man:

1. The predisposition to *animality* in man, taken as a *living* being;
2. The predisposition to *humanity* in man, taken as a living and at the same time a *rational* being;
3. The predisposition to *personality* in man, taken as a rational and at the same time an *accountable* being.

. . .

All of these predispositions are not only good in negative fashion (in that they do not contradict the moral law); they are also predispositions toward good (they enjoin the observance of the law). They are original, for they are bound up with the possibility of human nature. Man can indeed, use the first two contrary to their ends, but he can extirpate none of them. By the predispositions of a being we understand not only its constituent elements which are necessary to it, but also the forms of their combination, by which the being is what it is. They are original if they are involved necessarily in the possibility of such a being, but contingent if it is possible for the being to exist of itself without them. Finally, let it be noted that here we treat only those predispositions, which have immediate reference to the faculty of desire and the exercise of the will.

II. Concerning the Propensity to Evil in Human Nature

By *propensity* I understand the subjective ground of the possibility of an inclination so far as mankind in general is liable to it. A propensity is distinguished from a predisposition by the fact that although it can indeed be innate, it *ought* not to be represented merely thus; for it can also be regarded as having been *acquired* (if it is good), or *brought* by man *upon himself* (if it is evil). Here, however, we are speaking only of the propensity to genuine, that is, moral evil, for since such evil is possible only as a determination of the free will and since the will can be appraised as good or evil only by means of its maxims, this propensity to evil must consist in the subjective ground of the possibility of the deviation of the maxims from the moral law. If, then, this propensity can be considered as belonging universally to mankind (and hence as part of the character of the race), it may be called a *natural* propensity in man to evil. We may add further that the will's capacity or incapacity, arising from this natural propensity, to adopt or not to adopt the moral law into its maxim, may be called *a good or an evil heart*.

In this capacity for evil there can be distinguished three distinct degrees. First, there is the weakness of the human heart in the general observance of adopted maxims, or in other words, the *frailty* of human nature; second, the propensity for mixing unmoral with moral motivating causes (even when it is done with good intent and under maxims of the good), that is, *impurity*; third, the propensity to adopt evil maxims, that is, the *wickedness* of human nature or of the human heart.

First: the frailty of human nature is expressed even in the complaint of an Apostle, "What I would, that I do not!" In other words, I adopt the good (the law) into the maxim of my will, but this good, which objectively, in its ideal conception, is an irresistible incentive, is subjectively, when the maxim is to be followed, the weaker (in comparison with inclination).

Second: the impurity of the human heart consists in this, that although the maxim is indeed good in respect of its object (the intended observance of the law) and perhaps even strong enough for practice, it is yet not purely moral; that is, it has not, as it should have, adopted the law *alone* as its *all-sufficient* incentive: instead, it usually (perhaps, every time) stands in need of other incentives beyond this, in determining the will to do what duty demands; in other words, actions called for by duty are done not purely for duty's sake.

Third: the wickedness or, if you like, the *corruption* of the human heart is the propensity of the will to maxims which neglect the incentives springing from the moral law in favor of others which are not moral. It may also be called the *perversity* of the human heart, for it reverses the ethical order [of priority] among the incentives of a *free* will; and although conduct which is lawfully good (*i.e.*, legal) may be found with it, yet the cast of mind is thereby corrupted at its root (so far as the moral disposition is concerned), and the man is hence designated as evil.

It will be remarked that this propensity to evil is here ascribed (as regards conduct) to men in general, even to the best of them; this must be the case it is to be proved that the propensity to evil in mankind is universal, or, what here comes to the same thing, that it is woven into human nature.

Critique of Practical Reason

Two things fill the mind with ever new and increasing admiration and awe, the oftener and more steadily we reflect on them: the starry heavens above me and the moral law within me. I do not merely conjecture them and seek them as though obscured in darkness or in the transcendent region beyond my horizon: I see them before me, and I associate them directly with the consciousness of my own existence. The former begins at the place I occupy in the external world of sense, and it broadens the connection in which I stand into an unbounded magnitude of worlds beyond worlds and systems of systems and into the limitless times of their periodic motion, their beginning and their continuance. The latter begins at my invisible self, my personality, and exhibits me in a world which has true infinity but which is comprehensible only to the understanding—a world with which I recognize myself as existing in a universal and necessary (and not only, as in the first case, contingent) connection, and thereby also in connection with all those visible worlds. The former view of a countless multitude of worlds annihilates, as it were, my importance as an animal creature, which must give back to the planet (a mere speck in the universe) the matter from which it came, the matter which is for a little time provided with vital force, we know not how. The latter, on the contrary, infinitely raises my worth as that of an intelligence by my personality, in which the moral law reveals a life independent of all animality and even of the whole world of sense—at least so far as it may be inferred from the purposive destination assigned to my existence by this law, a destination which is not restricted to the conditions and limits of this life but reaches into the infinite.

From *Critique of Practical Reason* (New York: Macmillan, 1985), p. 166.

Observations on the Feeling
of the Beautiful and the Sublime

Women have a strong inborn feeling for all that is beautiful, elegant, and decorated. Even in childhood they like to be dressed up, and take pleasure when they are adorned. They are cleanly and very delicate in respect to all that provokes disgust. They love pleasantry and can be entertained by trivialities if only these are merry and laughing. Very early they have a modest manner about themselves, know how to give themselves a fine demeanor and be self-possessed—and this at an age when our well-bred male youth is still unruly, clumsy, and confused. They have many sympathetic sensations, goodheartedness, and compassion, prefer the beautiful to the useful, and gladly turn abundance of circumstance into parsimony, in order to support expenditure on adornment and glitter. They have very delicate feelings in regard to the least offense, and are exceedingly precise to notice the most trifling lack of attention and respect toward them. In short, they contain the chief cause in human nature for the contrast of the beautiful qualities with the noble, and they refine even the masculine sex.

I hope the reader will spare me the reckoning of the manly qualities, so far as they are parallel to the feminine, and be content only to consider both in comparison with each other. The fair sex has just as much understanding as the male, but it is a *beautiful understanding*, whereas ours should be a *deep understanding*, an expression that signifies identity with the sublime.

To the beauty of all actions belongs above all the mark that they display facility, and appear to be accomplished without painful toil. On the other hand, strivings and surmounted difficulties arouse admiration and belong to the sublime. Deep meditation and a long-sustained reflection are noble but difficult, and do not well befit a person in whom unconstrained charms should show nothing else than a beautiful nature. Laborious learning or painful pondering, even if a woman should greatly succeed in it, destroy the merits that are proper to her sex, and because of their rarity they can make of her an object of cold admiration; but at the same time they will weaken the charms with which she exercises her great power over the other sex. A woman who has a head full of Greek, like Mme. Dacier, or carries on fundamental controversies about mechanics, like the Marquise du Châtelet, might as well even have a beard; for perhaps that would express more obviously the mien of profundity for which she strives. The beautiful understanding selects for its objects everything closely related to the finer feeling, and relinquishes to the diligent, fundamental, and deep understanding abstract speculations or branches of knowledge useful but dry. A woman therefore will learn no geometry; of the principle of sufficient reason or the monads she will know only so much as is needed to perceive the salt in a satire which the insipid grubs of our sex have censured. The fair can leave Descartes his vortices to whirl forever without troubling themselves about them, even though the suave Fontenelle wished to afford them company among the planets; and the attraction of their charms loses none of its strength even if they know nothing of what Algarotti has taken the trouble to sketch out for their benefit about the gravitational attraction of matter according to Newton. In history they will not fill their heads with battles, nor in geography with fortresses, for it becomes them just as little to reek of gunpowder as it does the males to reek of musk.

. . .

The Negroes of Africa have by nature no feeling that rises above the trifling. Mr. Hume challenges anyone to cite a single example in which a Negro has shown talents, and asserts that among the hundreds of thousands of blacks who are transported elsewhere from their countries, although many of them have even been set free, still not a single one was ever found who presented anything great in art or science or any other praiseworthy quality, even though among the whites some continually rise aloft from the lowest rabble, and through superior gifts earn respect in the world. So fundamental is the difference between these two races of man, and it appears to be as great in regard to mental capacities as in color. The religion of fetishes so widespread among them is perhaps a sort of idolatry that sinks as deeply into the trifling as appears to be possible to human nature. A bird feather, a cow's horn, a conch shell, or any other common object, as soon as it becomes consecrated by a few words, is an object of veneration and of invocation in swearing oaths. The blacks are very vain but in the Negro's way, and so talkative that they must be driven apart from each other with thrashings.

Among all savages there is no nation that displays so sublime a mental character as those of North America. They have a strong feeling for honor, and as in quest of it they seek wild adventures hundreds of miles abroad, they are still extremely careful to avert the least injury to it when their equally harsh enemy, upon capturing them, seeks by cruel pain to extort cowardly groans from them. The Canadian savage, moreover, is truthful and honest. The friendship he establishes is just as adventurous and enthusiastic as anything of that kind reported from the most ancient and fabled times. He is extremely proud, feels the whole worth of freedom, and even in his education suffers no encounter that would let him feel a low subservience. Lycurgus probably gave statutes to just such savages; and if a lawgiver arose among the Six Nations, one would see a Spartan republic rise in the New World; for the undertaking of the Argonauts is little different from the war-parties of these Indians, and Jason excels Attakullakulla in nothing but the honor of a Greek name. All these savages have little feeling for the beautiful in moral understanding, and the generous forgiveness of an injury, which is at once noble and beautiful, is completely unknown as a virtue among the savages, but rather is disdained as a miserable cowardice. Valor is the greatest merit of the savage and revenge his sweetest bliss. The remaining natives of this part of the world show few traces of a mental character disposed to the finer feelings, and an extraordinary apathy constitutes the mark of this type of race.

If we examine the relation of the sexes in these parts of the world, we find that the European alone has found the secret of decorating with so many flowers the sensual charm of a mighty inclination and of interlacing it with so much morality that he has not only extremely elevated its agreeableness but has also made it very decorous. The inhabitant of the Orient is of a very false taste in this respect. Since he has no concept of the morally beautiful which can be united with this impulse, he loses even the worth of the sensuous enjoyment, and his harem is a constant source of unrest. He thrives on all sorts of amorous grotesqueries, among which the imaginary jewel is only the foremost, which he seeks to safeguard above all else, whose whole worth consists only in smashing it, and of which one in our part of the world generally entertains much malicious doubt—and yet to whose preservation he makes use of very unjust and often loathsome means. Hence there a woman is always in a prison, whether she may be a maid, or have a barbaric, good-for-nothing and always suspicious husband. In the lands of the black, what better can one expect than what is found prevailing, namely the feminine sex in the deepest slavery? A despairing man is always a strict master over anyone weaker, just as with us that man is always a tyrant in the kitchen who outside his own house hardly dares to look anyone in the face. Of course, Father Labat reports that a Negro carpenter, whom he reproached for haughty treatment toward his wives, answered: "You whites are indeed fools, for first you make great concessions to your wives, and afterward you complain when they drive you mad." And it might be that there were something in this which perhaps deserved to be considered; but in short, this fellow was quite black from head to foot, a clear proof that what he said was stupid.

42

Edmund Burke

A vitally important figure in the development of political conserva-
tism, Edmund Burke (1729–1797) was born in Ireland and spent
most of his life actively involved in British political life, sitting as a
member of parliament from 1765 until 1794. In the brief selections
that follow, Burke argues that part of the function of government is to
act as an external restraint upon the unruly impulses and passions of
people. These passages are of interest as a counterpoint to Rousseau's
very different thoughts on the chains that hinder human freedom.

Reflections on the Revolution in France

I flatter myself that I love a manly, moral, regulated liberty as well as any
gentleman of that society, be he who he will; and perhaps I have given as
good proofs of my attachment to that cause, in the whole course of my
public conduct. I think I envy liberty as little as they do, to any other
nation. But I cannot stand forward, and give praise or blame to any thing
which relates to human actions, and human concerns, on a simple view of
the object, as it stands stripped of every relation, in all the nakedness and
solitude of metaphysical abstraction. Circumstances (which with some
gentlemen pass for nothing) give in reality to every political principle
its distinguishing colour, and discriminating effect. The circumstances

From *Reflections on the Revolution in France* (Oxford: Oxford University Press, 1999 [1790]),
pp. 7–9, 60, 246).

are what render every civil and political scheme beneficial or noxious to mankind. Abstractedly speaking, government, as well as liberty, is good; yet could I, in common sense, ten years ago, have felicitated France on her enjoyment of a government (for she then had a government) without enquiry what the nature of that government was, or how it was administered? Can I now congratulate the same nation upon its freedom? Is it because liberty in the abstract may be classed amongst the blessings of mankind, that I am seriously to felicitate a madman, who has escaped from the protecting restraint and wholesome darkness of his cell, on his restoration to the enjoyment of light and liberty? Am I to congratulate an highwayman and murderer, who has broke prison, upon the recovery of his natural rights? . . .

When I see the spirit of liberty in action, I see a strong principle at work; and this, for a while, is all I can possibly know of it. . . . The effect of liberty to individuals is, that they may do what they please: We ought to see what it will please them to do, before we risque congratulations, which may be soon turned into complaints. . . .

Government is not made in virtue of natural rights, which may and do exist in total independence of it; and exist in much greater clearness, and in a much greater degree of abstract perfection: but their abstract perfection is their practical defect. By having a right to every thing they want every thing. Government is a contrivance of human wisdom to provide for human *wants*. Men have a right that these wants should be provided for by this wisdom. Among these wants is to be reckoned the want, out of civil society, of a sufficient restraint upon their passions. Society requires not only that the passions of individuals should be subjected, but that even in the mass and body as well as in the individuals, the inclinations of men should frequently be thwarted, their will controlled, and their passions brought into subjection. This can only be done *by a power out of themselves*; and not, in the exercise of its function, subject to that will and to those passions which it is its office to bridle and subdue. In this sense the restraints on men, as well as their liberties, are to be reckoned among their rights. But as the liberties and the restrictions vary with times and circumstances, and admit of infinite modifications, they cannot be settled upon any abstract rule; and nothing is so foolish as to discuss them upon that principle. . . .

[W]hat is liberty without wisdom, and without virtue? It is the greatest of all possible evils; for it is folly, vice, and madness, without tuition or restraint.

Letter to a Member of the National Assembly

Men are qualified for civil liberty, in exact proportion to their disposition to put moral chains upon their own appetites; in proportion as their love of justice is above their rapacity; in proportion as their soundness and sobriety of understanding is above their vanity and presumption; in proportion as they are more disposed to listen to the counsels of the wise and good, in preference to the flattery of knaves. Society cannot exist unless a controlling power upon will and appetite be placed somewhere, and the less of it there is within, the more there must be without. It is ordained in the eternal constitution of things, that men of intemperate minds cannot be free. Their passions forge their fetters.

From *Reflections on the Revolution in France* (Oxford: Oxford University Press, 1999 [1790]), p. 289.

PART FIVE

Late Modern Writings

43
⚶

William Paley

A great many of the visions of life collected in this anthology emphasize the miseries that human beings have to endure in a heartless world. A notable (and euphoric) counterbalance to such pessimism can be found in the work of the English philosopher and clergyman William Paley (1743–1805). The following passage is taken from Paley's famous book *Natural Theology,* and expresses an extraordinarily upbeat view of the happiness of the world and its inhabitants.

Natural Theology

It is a happy world after all. The air, the earth, the water, teem with delighted existence. In a spring noon, or a summer evening, on whichever side I turn my eyes, myriads of happy beings crowd upon my view. "The insect youth are on the wing." Swarms of new-born *flies* are trying their pinions in the air. Their sportive motions, their wanton mazes, their gratuitous activity, their continual change of place without use or purpose, testify their joy, and the exultation which they feel in their lately discovered faculties. A *bee* amongst the flowers in spring, is one of the cheerfullest objects that can be looked upon. Its life appears to be all enjoyment, so busy and so pleased: yet it is only a specimen of insect life, with which, by reason of the animal being half domesticated, we happen

From William Paley, *Natural Theology* (London: Scott, Webster & Geary, 1838), pp. 278-280, 281-282.

to be better acquainted than we are with that of others. The *whole winged* insect tribe, it is probable, are equally intent upon their proper enjoyments, and under every variety of constitution, gratified, and perhaps equally gratified, by the offices which the author of their nature has assigned to them. But the atmosphere is not the only scene of enjoyment for the insect race. Plants are covered with aphides, greedily sucking their juices, and constantly, as it should seem, in the act of sucking. It cannot be doubted but that this is a state of gratification. What else should fix them so close to the operation, and so long? Other species are *running about* with an alacrity in their motions which carries every mark of pleasure. Large patches of ground are sometimes half covered with these brisk and sprightly natures. If we look to what the *waters* produce, shoals of the fry of fish frequent the margins of rivers, of lakes, and of the sea itself. These are so happy, that they know not what to do with themselves. Their attitudes, their vivacity, their leaps out of the water, their frolics in it (which I have noticed a thousand times with equal attention and amusement), all conduce to show their excess of spirits, and are simply the effects of that excess. Walking by the sea side, in a calm evening, upon a sandy shore, and with an ebbing tide, I have frequently remarked the appearance of a dark cloud, or, rather, very thick mist, hanging over the edge of the water, to the height perhaps of half a yard, stretching along the coast as far as the eye could reach, and always retiring with the water. When this cloud came to be examined, it proved to be nothing else than so much space filled with young *shrimps*, in the act of bounding into the air from the shallow margin of the water, or from the wet sand. If any motion of a mute animal could express delight, it was this: if they had meant to make signs of their happiness, they could not have done it more intelligibly. Suppose then, what I have no doubt of, each individual of this number to be in a state of positive enjoyment, what a sum collectively of gratification and pleasure have we here before our view?

The *young* of all animals appear to me to receive pleasure simply from the exercise of their limbs and bodily faculties, without reference to any end to be attained, or any use to be answered by the exertion. A child, without knowing any thing of the use of language is, in a high degree, delighted with being able to speak. Its incessant repetition of the few articulate sounds, or, perhaps of the single word which it has learnt to pronounce, proves this point clearly. Nor is it least pleased with its first successful endeavours to walk, or rather to run (which precedes walking), although entirely ignorant of the importance of the attainment to its future life and even without applying it to any present purpose. A child is delighted with speaking, without having any thing to say; and with walking, without knowing where to go. And, prior to both these, I am disposed to believe, that the waking hours of infancy are agreeably taken up with the exercise of vision, or, perhaps more properly speaking, with learning to see.

But it is not for youth alone, that the great Parent of creation hath provided. Happiness is found with the purring cat, no less than with the playful kitten; in the arm-chair of dozing age, as well as in either the sprightliness of the dance, or the animation of the chase. To novelty, to acuteness of sensation, to hope, to ardour of pursuit, succeeds, what is, in no inconsiderable degree, an equivalent for them all, "perception of ease." Herein is the exact difference between the young and the old. The young are not happy, but when enjoying pleasure; the old are happy, when free from pain. And this constitution suits with the degrees of animal power which they respectively possess. The vigour of youth was to be stimulated to action by impatience of rest; whilst, to the imbecility of age, quietness and repose become positive gratifications. In one important respect the advantage is with the old. A state of ease is, generally speaking, more attainable than a state of pleasure. A constitution, therefore, which can enjoy ease, is preferable to that which can taste only pleasure. This same perception of ease oftentimes renders old age a condition of great comfort; especially when riding at its anchor, after a busy or tempestuous life. It is well described by Rousseau, to be the interval of repose and enjoyment, between the hurry and the end of life.

. . .

But it will be said, that the instances which we have here brought forward, whether of vivacity or repose, or of apparent enjoyment derived from either, are picked and favourable instances. We answer that they are instances, nevertheless, which comprise large provinces of sensitive existence; that every case which we have described, is the case of millions. At this moment, in every given moment of time, how many myriads of animals are eating their food, gratifying their appetites, ruminating in their holes, accomplishing their wishes, pursuing their pleasures, taking their pastimes? In each individual how many things must go right for it to be at ease; yet how large a proportion out of every species, are so in every assignable instant? Secondly, we contend, in the terms of our original proposition, that throughout the whole of life, as it is diffused in nature, and as far as we are acquainted with it, looking to the average of sensations, the plurality and the preponderancy is in favour of happiness by a vast excess. In our own species, in which perhaps the assertion may be more questionable than any other, the prepollency of good over evil, of health for example, and ease, over pain and distress, is evinced by the very notice which calamities excite. What inquiries does the sickness of our friends produce? What conversation their misfortunes? This shows that the common course of things is in favour of happiness; that happiness is the rule; misery the exception. Were the order reversed, our attention would be called to examples of health and competency, instead of disease and want.

44

Marie Jean Antoine Nicolas de Caritat, Marquis de Condorcet

The Marquis de Condorcet (1743–1794) was a French philosopher and political scientist. The selections that follow are drawn from his principal work, the *Sketch for a Historical Picture of the Progress of the Human Mind*, and illustrate his confidence in the perfectibility and future happiness of human beings. It is to be noted that, well ahead of his time in this regard, Condorcet urged the annihilation of sexual and racial inequality. Condorcet's thoughts on the progress of society and the human mind represent the high-water mark of optimism. A supporter of the French Revolution, Condorcet became one its many victims, dying in prison in 1794.

Sketch for a Historical Picture of the Progress of the Human Mind

Our hopes for the future condition of the human race can be subsumed under three important heads: the abolition of inequality between nations, the progress of equality within each nation, and the true perfection of

---

Condorcet, "Sketch for a Historical Picture of the Progress of the Human Mind", in *Selected Writings* (edited by Keith Michael Baker), Indianapolis: Bobbs-Merrill, 1976, pp. 258–259, 266–267, 274–275, 279–281.

mankind. Will all nations one day attain that state of civilization which the most enlightened, the freest, and the least burdened by prejudices, such as the French and the Anglo-Americans, have attained already? Will the vast gulf that separates these peoples from the slavery of nations under the rule of monarchs, from the barbarism of African tribes, from the ignorance of savages, little by little disappear?

Is there on the face of the earth a nation whose inhabitants have been debarred by nature herself from the enjoyment of freedom and the exercise of reason?

Are those differences which have hitherto been seen in every civilized country in respect of the enlightenment, the resources, and the wealth enjoyed by the different classes into which it is divided, is that inequality between men which was aggravated or perhaps produced by the earliest progress of society, are these part of civilization itself, or are they due to the present imperfections of the social art? Will they necessarily decrease and ultimately make way for a real equality, the final end of the social art, in which even the effects of the natural differences between men will be mitigated and the only kind of inequality to persist will be that which is in the interests of all and which favors the progress of civilization, of education, and of industry, without entailing either poverty, humiliation, or dependence? In other words, will men approach a condition in which everyone will have the knowledge necessary to conduct himself in the ordinary affairs of life, according to the light of his own reason, to preserve his mind free from prejudice, to understand his rights and to exercise them in accordance with his conscience and his creed; in which everyone will become able, through the development of his faculties, to find the means of providing for his needs; and in which at last misery and folly will be the exception, and no longer the habitual lot of a section of society?

Is the human race to better itself, either by discoveries in the sciences and the arts, and so in the means to individual welfare and general prosperity; or by progress in the principles of conduct or practical morality; or by a true perfection of the intellectual, moral, or physical faculties of man, an improvement which may result from a perfection either of the instruments used to heighten the intensity of these faculties and to direct their use or of the natural constitution of man?

In answering these three questions we shall find, in the experience of the past, in the observation of the progress that the sciences and civilization have already made, in the analysis of the progress of the human mind and of the development of its faculties, the strongest reasons for believing that nature has set no limit to the realization of our hopes. . . .

With greater equality of education there will be greater equality in industry and so in wealth; equality in wealth necessarily leads to equality in education: and equality between the nations and equality within a single nation are mutually dependent.

So we might say that a well-directed system of education rectifies natural inequality in ability instead of strengthening it, just as good laws remedy natural inequality in the means of subsistence, and just as in societies where laws have brought about this same equality, liberty, though subject to a regular constitution, will be more widespread, more complete than in the total independence of savage life. Then the social art will have fulfilled its aim, that of assuring and extending to all men enjoyment of the common rights to which they are called by nature.

The real advantages that should result from this progress, of which we can entertain a hope that is almost a certainty, can have no other term than that of the absolute perfection of the human race; since, as the various kinds of equality come to work in its favor by producing ampler sources of supply, more extensive education, more complete liberty, so equality will be more real and will embrace everything which is really of importance for the happiness of human beings. . . .

Among the causes of the progress of the human mind that are of the utmost importance to the general happiness, we must number the complete annihilation of the prejudices that have brought about an inequality of rights between the sexes, an inequality fatal even to the party in whose favor it works. It is vain for us to look for a justification of this principle in any differences of physical organization, intellect, or moral sensibility between men and women. This inequality has its origin solely in an abuse of strength, and all the later sophistical attempts that have been made to excuse it are vain.

We shall show how the abolition of customs authorized, laws dictated by this prejudice, would add to the happiness of family life, would encourage the practice of the domestic virtues on which all other virtues are based, how it would favor the progress of education, and how, above all, it would bring about its wider diffusion; for not only would education be extended to women as well as to men, but it can only really be taken proper advantage of when it has the support and encouragement of the mothers of the family. Would not this belated tribute to equity and good sense put an end to a principle only too fecund of injustice, cruelty, and crime, by removing the dangerous conflict between the strongest and most irrepressible of all natural inclinations and man's duty or the interests of society?. . . .

Once people are enlightened, they will know that they have the right to dispose of their own life and wealth as they choose; they will gradually learn to regard war as the most dreadful of scourges, the most terrible of crimes. The first wars to disappear will be those into which usurpers have forced their subjects in defense of their pretended hereditary rights.

Nations will learn that they cannot conquer other nations without losing their own liberty; that permanent confederations are their only means of preserving their independence; and that they should seek not power but security. Gradually mercantile prejudices will fade away: and a false sense of commercial interest will lose the fearful power it once had of drenching the earth in blood and of ruining nations under pretext of enriching them. When at last the nations come to agree on the principles of politics and morality, when in their own better interests they invite foreigners to share equally in all the benefits men enjoy either through the bounty of nature or by their own industry, then all the causes that produce and perpetuate national animosities and poison national relations will disappear one by one; and nothing will remain to encourage or even to arouse the fury of war.

Organizations more intelligently conceived than those projects of eternal peace which have filled the leisure and consoled the hearts of certain philosophers, will hasten the progress of the brotherhood of nations, and wars between countries will rank with assassinations as freakish atrocities, humiliating and vile in the eyes of nature and staining with indelible opprobrium the country or the age whose annals record them. . . .

Organic perfectibility or deterioration among the various strains in the vegetable and animal kingdom can be regarded as one of the general laws of nature. This law also applies to the human race. No one can doubt that, as preventive medicine improves and food and housing become healthier, as a way of life is established that develops our physical powers by exercise without ruining them by excess, as the two most virulent causes of deterioration, misery and excessive wealth, are eliminated, the average length of human life will be increased and a better health and a stronger physical constitution will he ensured. The improvement of medical practice, which will become more efficacious with the progress of reason and of the social order, will mean the end of infectious and hereditary diseases and illnesses brought on by climate, food, or working conditions. It is reasonable to hope that all other diseases may likewise disappear as their distant causes are discovered. Would it be absurd, then, to suppose that this perfection of the human species might be capable of indefinite progress; that the day will come when death will be due only to extraordinary accidents or to the decay of the vital forces, and that ultimately the average span between birth and decay will have no assignable value? Certainly man will not become immortal, but will not the interval between the first breath that he draws and the time when in the natural course of events, without disease or accident, he expires, increase indefinitely?. . .

Finally may we not extend such hopes to the intellectual and moral faculties? May not our parents, who transmit to us the benefits or disadvantages of their constitution, and from whom we receive our shape and features, as well as our tendencies to certain physical affections, hand on to us also that part of the physical organization which determines the intellect, the power of the brain, the ardor of the soul or the moral sensibility? Is it not probable that education, in perfecting these qualities, will at the same time influence, modify, and perfect the organization itself? Analogy, investigation of the human faculties, and the study of certain facts, all seem to give substance to such conjectures which would further push back the boundaries of our hopes.

These are the questions with which we shall conclude this final stage. How consoling for the philosopher who laments the errors, the crimes, the injustices which still pollute the earth and of which he is often the victim is this view of the human race, emancipated from its shackles, released from the empire of fate and from that of the enemies of its progress, advancing with a firm and sure step along the path of truth, virtue, and happiness! It is the contemplation of this prospect that rewards him for all his efforts to assist the progress of reason and the defense of liberty. He dares to regard these strivings as part of the eternal chain of human destiny; and in this persuasion he is filled with the true delight of virtue and the pleasure of having done some lasting good which fate can never destroy by a sinister stroke of revenge, by calling back the reign of slavery and prejudice. Such contemplation is for him an asylum, in which the memory of his persecutors cannot pursue him; there he lives in thought with man restored to his natural rights and dignity, forgets man tormented and corrupted by greed, fear, or envy; there he lives with his peers in an Elysium created by reason and graced by the purest pleasures known to the love of mankind.

45

Jeremy Bentham

Jeremy Bentham (1748–1832) was an English philosopher and legal theorist, and the principal original architect of the moral theory known as utilitarianism. At the foundation of Bentham's moral theory lay a particular conception of human nature, namely that human beings seek pleasure and avoid pain. In emphasizing this, and its importance for moral action and judgment, Bentham returns us to the ancient principles of Epicureanism. Alongside the famous passage about pleasure and pain being the "sovereign masters" of human life, included here is Bentham's oft-quoted claim about "push-pin" (an unsophisticated children's game) being as good as poetry, a contention that was later to be challenged by John Stuart Mill.

An Introduction to the Principles of Morals and Legislation

Nature has placed mankind under the governance of two sovereign masters, *pain* and *pleasure.* It is for them alone to point out what we ought to do, as well as to determine what we shall do. On the one hand the standard of right and wrong, on the other the chain of causes and effects, are fastened to their throne. They govern us in all we do, in all we say, in all we think: every effort we can make to throw off our subjection,

From *An Introduction to the Principles of Morals and Legislation* (Amherst, NY: Prometheus Books, 1988 [1781]), pp. 1-2, 29-31.

will serve but to demonstrate and confirm it. In words a man may abjure their empire: but in reality he will remain subject to it all the while. The *principle of utility* recognises this subjection, and assumes it for the foundation of that system, the object of which is to rear the fabric of felicity by the hands of reason and of law. Systems which attempt to question it, deal in sounds instead of sense, in caprice instead of reason, in darkness instead of light.

But enough of metaphor and declamation: it is not by such means that moral science is to be improved.

The principle of utility is the foundation of the present work: it will be proper therefore at the outset to give an explicit and determinate account of what is meant by it. By the principle of utility is meant that principle which approves or disapproves of every action whatsoever, according to the tendency which it appears to have to augment or diminish the happiness of the party whose interest is in question: or, what is the same thing in other words, to promote or to oppose that happiness. I say of every action whatsoever; and therefore not only of every action of a private individual, but of every measure of government.

By utility is meant that property in any object, whereby it tends to produce benefit, advantage, pleasure, good, or happiness (all this in the present case comes to the same thing) or (what comes again to the same thing) to prevent the happening of mischief, pain, evil, or unhappiness to the party whose interest is considered: if that party be the community in general, then the happiness of the community: if a particular individual, then the happiness of that individual.

PLEASURES then, and the avoidance of pains, are the *ends* which the legislator has in view: it behoves him therefore to understand their *value*. Pleasures and pains are the *instruments* he has to work with: it behoves him therefore to understand their force, which is again, in other words, their value.

To a person considered *by himself*, the value of a pleasure or pain considered *by itself* will be greater or less, according to the four following circumstances:

1. Its *intensity*.
2. Its *duration*.
3. Its *certainty* or *uncertainty*.
4. Its *propinquity* or *remoteness*.

These are the circumstances which are to be considered in estimating a pleasure or a pain considered each of them by itself. But when the value of any pleasure or pain is considered for the purpose of estimating the tendency of any *act* by which it is produced, there are two other circumstances to be taken into the account; these are,

5. Its *fecundity*, or the chance it has of being followed by sensations of the *same* kind: that is, pleasures, if it be pleasure: pains, if it be a pain.
6. Its *purity*, or the chance it has of *not* being followed by sensations of the *opposite* kind: that is, pains, if it be a pleasure: pleasures, if it be a pain.

These two last, however, are in strictness scarcely to be deemed properties of the pleasure or the pain itself; they are not, therefore, in strictness to be taken into the account of the value of that pleasure or that pain. They are in strictness to be deemed properties only of the act, or other event, by which such pleasure or pain has been produced; and accordingly are only to be taken into the account of the tendency of such act or such event.

To a *number* of persons, with reference to each of whom the value of a pleasure or a pain is considered, it will be greater or less, according to seven circumstances: to wit, the six preceding ones; *viz.*

1. Its *intensity*.
2. Its *duration*.
3. Its *certainty* or *uncertainty*.
4. Its *propinquity* or *remoteness*.
5. Its *fecundity*.
6. Its *purity*.

And one other; to wit:

7. Its *extent*; that is, the number of persons to whom it *extends*; or (in other words) who are affected by it.

The Rationale of Reward

By arts and sciences of curiosity, I mean those which in truth are pleasing, but not in the same degree as the fine arts, and to which at the first glance we might be tempted to refuse this quality. It is not that these arts

From *The Rationale of Reward* in *The Works of Jeremy Bentham*, vol. II (Edinburgh: William Tait, 1843), pp. 253-254.

and sciences of curiosity do not yield as much pleasure to those who cultivate them as the fine arts; but the number of those who study them is more limited. . . .

The utility of all these arts and sciences, . . . the value which they possess, is exactly in proportion to the pleasure they yield. Every other species of pre-eminence which may be attempted to be established among them is altogether fanciful. Prejudice apart, the game of push-pin is of equal value with the arts and sciences of music and poetry. If the game of push-pin furnish more pleasure, it is more valuable than either. Everybody can play at push-pin: poetry and music are relished only by a few. The game of push-pin is always innocent: it were well could the same be always asserted of poetry. Indeed, between poetry and truth there is a natural opposition: false morals, fictitious nature. The poet always stands in need of something false. When he pretends to lay his foundations in truth, the ornaments of his superstructure are fictions; his business consists in stimulating our passions, and exciting our prejudices. Truth, exactitude of every kind, is fatal to poetry. The poet must see everything through coloured media, and strive to make every one else to do the same. It is true, there have been noble spirits, to whom poetry and philosophy have been equally indebted; but these exceptions do not counteract the mischiefs which have resulted from this magic art. If poetry and music deserve to be preferred before a game of push-pin, it must be because they are calculated to gratify those individuals who are most difficult to be pleased.

All the arts and sciences, without exception, inasmuch as they constitute innocent employments, at least of time, possess a species of moral utility, neither the less real or important because it is frequently unobserved. They compete with, and occupy the place of those mischievous and dangerous passions and employments, to which want of occupation and ennui give birth. They are excellent substitutes for drunkenness, slander, and the love of gaming.

46

Pierre-Simon Laplace

Pierre-Simon, Marquis de Laplace (1749–1827) was a French scientist who made significant contributions to the fields of mathematics, physics, and astronomy. As with the contentions of d'Holbach advanced earlier, Laplace's system constitutes a particularly hardline version of determinism.

A Philosophical Essay on Probabilities

All events, even those which on account of their insignificance do not seem to follow the great laws of nature, are a result of it just as necessarily as the revolutions of the sun. In ignorance of the ties which unite such events to the entire system of the universe, they have been made to depend upon final causes or upon hazard, according as they occur and are repeated with regularity, or appear without regard to order; but these imaginary causes have gradually receded with the widening bounds of knowledge and disappear entirely before sound philosophy, which sees in them only the expression of our ignorance of the true causes.

Present events are connected with preceding ones by a tie based upon the evident principle that a thing cannot occur without a cause which produces it. This axiom, known by the name of *the principle of sufficient reason*, extends even to actions which are considered indifferent;

the freest will is unable without a determinative motive to give them birth; if we assume two positions with exactly similar circumstances and find that the will is active in the one and inactive in the other, we say that its choice is an effect without a cause. It is then, says Leibnitz, the blind chance of the Epicureans. The contrary opinion is an illusion of the mind, which, losing sight of the evasive reasons of the choice of the will in indifferent things, believes that choice is determined of itself and without motives.

We ought then to regard the present state of the universe as the effect of its anterior state and as the cause of the one which is to follow. Given for one instant an intelligence which could comprehend all the forces by which nature is animated and the respective situation of the beings who compose it—an intelligence sufficiently vast to submit these data to analysis—it would embrace in the same formula the movements of the greatest bodies of the universe and those of the lightest atom; for it, nothing would be uncertain and the future, as the past, would be present to its eyes. The human mind offers, in the perfection which it has been able to give to astronomy, a feeble idea of this intelligence. Its discoveries in mechanics and geometry, added to that of universal gravity, have enabled it to comprehend in the same analytical expressions the past and future states of the system of the world. Applying the same method to some other objects of its knowledge, it has succeeded in referring to general laws observed phenomena and in foreseeing those which given circumstances ought to produce. All these efforts in the search for truth tend to lead it back continually to the vast intelligence which we have just mentioned, but from which it will always remain infinitely removed. This tendency, peculiar to the human race, is that which renders it superior to animals; and their progress in this respect distinguishes nations and ages and constitutes their true glory.

47

Joseph de Maistre

The extraordinarily violent and reactionary writings of the French philosopher Joseph de Maistre (1753–1821) were intended to counteract and destroy what he saw as principal elements of the eighteenth century worldview: that human beings were at least potentially benevolent, that nature was beneficent, that humans should place their trust in reason and progress, and so on. Against all of this, Maistre stressed the violence inherent in nature and in human beings, the impotence of reason and the primacy of irrationality, and the illusory nature of progress. Maistre's stress on the inescapable violence of the world is uppermost in the following extracts, the selection from his anti-revolutionary *Considerations on France* consisting in part (and very powerfully) of a list of "the long series of massacres that has soiled every page of history."

The St. Petersburg Dialogues

In the immense sphere of living things, the obvious rule is violence, a kind of inevitable frenzy which arms all things *in mutua funera*. Once you leave the world of insensible substances, you find the decree of violent death written on the very frontiers of life. Even in the vegetable kingdom, this law can be perceived: from the huge catalpa to the smallest

From *The St Petersburg Dialogues* (Seventh Dialogue), in *The Works of Joseph de Maistre* (edited by Jack Lively) (New York: Macmillan, 1965), pp. 251–254.

of grasses, how many plants *die* and how many are *killed*! But once you enter the animal kingdom, the law suddenly becomes frighteningly obvious. A power at once hidden and palpable appears constantly occupied in bringing to light the principle of life by violent means. In each great division of the animal world, it has chosen a certain number of animals charged with devouring the others; so there are insects of prey, reptiles of prey, birds of prey, fish of prey, and quadrupeds of prey. There is not an instant of time when some living creature is not devoured by another.

Above all these numerous animal species is placed man, whose destructive hand spares no living thing; he kills to eat, he kills for clothing, he kills for adornment, he kills to attack, he kills to defend himself, he kills for instruction, he kills for amusement, he kills for killing's sake: a proud and terrible king, he needs everything, and nothing can withstand him. He knows how many barrels of oil he can get from the head of a shark or a whale; in his museums, he mounts with his sharp pins elegant butterflies he has caught in flight on the top of Mount Blanc or Chimborazo; he stuffs the crocodile and embalms the hummingbird; on his command, the rattlesnake dies in preserving fluids to keep it intact for a long line of observers. The horse carrying its master to the tiger hunt struts about covered by the skin of this same animal. At one and the same time, man takes from the lamb its entrails for harp strings, from the whale its bones to stiffen the corsets of the young girl, from the wolf its most murderous tooth to polish frivolous manufactures, from the elephant its tusks to make a child's toy; his dining table is covered with corpses. The philosopher can even discern how this permanent carnage is provided for and ordained in the whole scheme of things. But without doubt this law will not stop at man. Yet what being is to destroy him who destroys all else? Man! It is man himself who is charged with butchering man.

But how is he to accomplish this law who is a moral and merciful being, who is born to love, who cries for others as for himself, who finds pleasure in weeping to the extent of creating fictions to make himself weep, to whom finally it has been said that *whoever sheds blood unjustly will redeem it with the last drop of his own*?[1] It is war that accomplishes this decree. Do you not hear the earth itself demanding and crying out for blood? The blood of animals does not satisfy it, nor even that of criminals spilled by the sword of the law. If human justice struck them all, there would be no war; but it can catch up with only a small number of them,

---

[1] Genesis 9:6.

and often it even spares them without suspecting that this cruel humanity contributes to the necessity for war, especially if at the same time another no less stupid and dangerous blindness works to diminish atonement among men. The earth did not cry in vain: war breaks out. Man, seized by a divine fury foreign to both hatred and anger, goes to the battlefield without knowing what he intends or even what he is doing. How can this dreadful enigma be explained? Nothing could be more contrary to his nature, yet nothing is less repugnant to him: he undertakes with enthusiasm what he holds in horror. Have you never noticed that no one ever disobeys on the field of death? They might well slaughter a Nerva or a Henry IV, but they will never say, even to the most abominable tyrant or the most flagrant butcher of human flesh, *We no longer want to follow you.* A revolt on the battlefield, an agreement to unite to repudiate a tyrant is something I cannot remember. Nothing resists, nothing can resist the force that drags man into conflict; an innocent murderer, a passive instrument in a formidable hand, *he plunges unseeing into the abyss he himself has dug; he dies without suspecting that it is he himself who has brought about his death.*[2]

Thus is worked out, from maggots up to man, the universal law of the violent destruction of living beings. The whole earth, continually steeped in blood, is nothing but an immense altar on which every living thing must be sacrificed without end, without restraint, without respite until the consummation of the world, the extinction of evil, the death of death.[3]

Considerations on France

Unhappily, history proves that war is, in a certain sense, the habitual state of mankind, which is to say that human blood must flow without interruption somewhere or other on the globe, and that for every nation, peace is only a respite. . . .

[O]ne must look at the long series of massacres that has soiled every page of history. One sees war raging without interruption, like a continuing fever marked by terrifying paroxysms. I ask the reader to follow the record since the decline of the Roman Republic.

---

[2]   Psalm 9:15.

[3]   1 Corinthians 15:36.

From de Maistre, Joseph, *Considerations on France* (Cambridge: Cambridge University Press, 1994), pp. 24-31.

In one battle Marius exterminated two hundred thousand Cimbri and Teutons. Mithridates slaughtered eighty thousand Romans. Sulla killed ninety thousand men in a battle fought in Boeotia, where he lost ten thousand himself. Soon you see civil wars and proscriptions. Caesar alone killed a million men on the battlefield (before him, Alexander had had this melancholy honour). Augustus closed the temple of Janus momentarily, but he reopened it for centuries by establishing an elective empire. A few good princes gave the state a breathing spell, but war never ceased, and under the rule of the *good* Titus, six hundred thousand men perished in the siege of Jerusalem. The destruction of men brought about by the Roman armies is truly frightening. The late empire is nothing but a series of massacres. To begin with Constantine, what wars and what battles! Licinius loses twenty thousand men at Cibalis, thirty-four thousand at Adrianople, and a hundred thousand at Chrysoupolis. The Nordic peoples begin to move. The Franks, the Goths, the Huns, the Lombards, the Alans, the Vandals, etc. attack the empire and successively tear it to pieces. Attila puts Europe to fire and sword. The Franks kill more than two hundred thousand of his men near Chalons, and the Goths, the following year, cost him more still. In less than a century, Rome was taken and sacked three times; and in a revolt that broke out in Constantinople, forty thousand people were slaughtered. The Goths made themselves masters of Milan and killed three hundred thousand inhabitants. Totila massacred all the inhabitants of Tivoli and ninety thousand men at the sack of Rome.

Mohammed appears; the sword and Koran overrun two-thirds of the world. The Saracens sail from the Euphrates to the Guadalquivir. The immense city of Syracuse is razed to its foundations; they lose thirty thousand men in a single naval combat near Constantinople, and Pelagius kills twenty thousand of them in a land battle. These losses were nothing for the Saracens; but the torrent encountered the genius of the Franks on the plain of Tours, where the son of the first Pepin, in the midst of three hundred thousand cadavers, attached to his name the terrible epithet [Charles *The Hammer*] that distinguishes it still.

Islam is carried to Spain and finds there an indomitable rival. Perhaps never has more glory, more grandeur, and more carnage been seen than in the eight-hundred-year struggle between Christians and Muslims in Spain. Several expeditions, several battles even, cost twenty, thirty, forty, up to eighty thousand lives.

Charlemagne ascends the throne, and there is a half-century of fighting. Every year he decrees death for some portion of Europe. Active everywhere and everywhere the conqueror, he wipes out iron-strong nations as easily as Caesar wiped out the effeminate men of Asia. The Normans begin that long series of ravages and cruelties that still make us shudder. Charlemagne's immense heritage is torn apart; ambition covers it with blood, and the name of the Franks disappears at the battle of Fontenay. All Italy is pillaged by the Saracens while the Normans, Danes, and Hungarians ravage France, Holland, England, Germany, and Greece. The barbarian nations are finally established and tamed. This vein yields no more blood; another is opened immediately with the beginning of the Crusades. All Europe throws itself on Asia; the number of victims can be counted only in myriads. Genghis Khan and his sons subjugate and ravage the world from China to Bohemia. The French, who are involved in crusades against the Muslims, also crusade against the heretics in the cruel Albigensian war. In the battle of Bouvines, thirty thousand men lose their lives. Five years later, eighty thousand Saracens perish at the siege of Damietta. Guelphs and Ghibellines begin the conflict that will stain Italy with blood for so long. The torch of civil war is kindled in Germany. Then the Sicilian Vespers. Under the reigns of Edward and Philip of Valois, France and England hurl themselves at each other more violently than ever and create a new era of carnage. The massacre of Jews. The battle of Poitiers. The battle of Nicopolis. The vanquisher falls under the blows of Tamerlane, who repeats Genghis Khan. The duke of Burgundy has the duke of Orleans assassinated, and the bloody rivalry of these two families begins. The battle of Agincourt. The Hussites put much of Germany to fire and sword. Mohammed II reigns and fights for thirty years. England, forced back within its own frontiers, is torn apart by internal troubles as the houses of York and Lancaster bathe the country in blood. The Burgundian heiress joins her states to the house of Austria, and in this marriage contract it is written that men will slaughter each other for centuries from the Baltic to the Mediterranean. The discovery of the new world means the death sentence for three million Indians. Charles V and Francis I appear on the world stage, and every page of their history is red with human blood. The reign of Suleiman. The battle of Mohacs. The siege of Vienna, the siege of Malta, etc. But it is from the shadow of a cloister that there emerges one of mankind's very greatest scourges. Luther appears; Calvin follows him. The Peasants' Revolt; the Thirty Years' War; the civil war in France; the massacre of the Low Countries; the massacre of Ireland; the massacre of the Cévennes; St. Bartholomew's Day; the murders of Henry II, Henry IV, Mary Stuart, and Charles I; and finally, in our day, from the same source, the French Revolution.

I will not carry this frightful catalogue any further; our own century and the preceding one are too well known. If you go back to the birth of nations, if you come down to our own day, if you examine peoples in all possible conditions from the state of barbarism to the most advanced civilization, you always find war. From this primary cause, and from all the other connected causes, the effusion of human blood has never ceased in the world. Sometimes blood flows less abundantly over some larger area, sometimes it flows more abundantly in a more restricted area, but the flow remains nearly constant.

. . .

Yet there is room to doubt whether this violent destruction is, in general, such a great evil as is believed; at least, it is one of those evils that enters into an order of things where everything is violent and *against nature*, and that produces compensations. First, when the human soul has lost its strength through laziness, incredulity, and the gangrenous vices that follow an excess of civilization, it can be retempered only in blood. Certainly there is no easy explanation of why war produces different effects in different circumstances. But it can be seen clearly enough that mankind may be considered as a tree which an invisible hand is continually pruning and which often profits from the operation. In truth the tree may perish if the trunk is cut or if the tree is *overpruned*; but who knows the limits of the human tree? What we do know is that excessive carnage is often allied with excessive population, as was seen especially in the ancient Greek republics and in Spain under the Arab domination. Platitudes about war mean nothing. One need not be very clever to know that when more men are killed, fewer remain at the moment, just as it is true that the more branches one cuts off, the fewer remain on the tree. But the results of the operation are what must be considered. Moreover, following the same comparison, we may observe that the skilful gardener directs the pruning less towards lush vegetation than towards the fructification of the tree; he wants fruit, not wood or leaves. Now the real *fruits* of human nature—the arts, sciences, great enterprises, lofty conceptions, manly virtues—are due especially to the state of war. We know that nations have never achieved the highest point of the greatness of which they are capable except after long and bloody wars . . . In a word, we can say that blood is the manure of the plant we call *genius*. . . .

There is nothing but violence in the universe; but we are spoiled by a modern philosophy that tells us *all is good*, whereas evil has tainted everything, and in a very real sense, *all is evil*, since nothing is in its place. The keynote of the system of our creation has been lowered, and following the rules of harmony, all the others have been lowered proportionately. *All creation groans,*[4] and tends with pain and effort towards another order of things.

The spectators of great human calamities, especially, are led to these sad meditations. But let us not lose courage: there is no chastisement that does not purify; there is no disorder that eternal love does not turn against the principle of evil. It is gratifying amid the general upheaval to have a presentiment of the plans of Divinity. We will never see the complete picture during our earthly sojourn, and often we will deceive ourselves; but in all possible sciences, except the exact sciences, are we not reduced to conjecture? And if our conjectures are plausible, if there are analogies for them, if they are based on universally accepted ideas, above all if they are consoling and suited to make us better men, what do they lack? If they are not true, they are good; or rather, since they are good, are they not true?

---

[4]   Romans 8:22.

48

Mary Wollstonecraft

Mary Wollstonecraft (1759–1797) was an English philosopher and women's rights advocate. In her *Vindication of the Rights of Woman*, she argues that the perceived inferiority of women to men is nothing natural but merely the result of a deficient education, which encourages women to develop superficial, husband-pleasing characteristics instead of rational and intellectual qualities. Wollstonecraft married the philosopher and anarchist William Godwin in the final year of her life, dying ten days after giving birth to a daughter, Mary Wollstonecraft Shelley, who would later become famous as the author of *Frankenstein*.

A Vindication of the Rights of Woman

After considering the historic page, and viewing the living world with anxious solicitude, the most melancholy emotions of sorrowful indignation have depressed my spirits, and I have sighed when obliged to confess, that either nature has made a great difference between man and man, or that the civilization which has hitherto taken place in the world has been very partial. I have turned over various books written on the subject of education, and patiently observed the conduct of parents and the management of schools; but what has been the result?—a profound conviction that the

A Vindication of the Rights of Woman (Oxford: Oxford University Press, 1999 [1792]), "Introduction" (pp. 71-75).

neglected education of my fellow-creatures is the grand source of the misery I deplore; and that women, in particular, are rendered weak and wretched by a variety of concurring causes, originating from one hasty conclusion. The conduct and manners of women, in fact, evidently prove that their minds are not in a healthy state; for, like the flowers which are planted in too rich a soil, strength and usefulness are sacrificed to beauty; and the flaunting leaves, after having pleased a fastidious eye, fade, disregarded on the stalk, long before the season when they ought to have arrived at maturity.—One cause of this barren blooming I attribute to a false system of education, gathered from the books written on this subject by men who, considering females rather as women than human creatures, have been more anxious to make them alluring mistresses than affectionate wives and rational mothers; and the understanding of the sex has been so bubbled by this specious homage, that the civilized women of the present century, with a few exceptions, are only anxious to inspire love, when they ought to cherish a nobler ambition, and by their abilities and virtues exact respect.

In a treatise, therefore, on female rights and manners, the works which have been particularly written for their improvement must not be overlooked; especially when it is asserted, in direct terms, that the minds of women are enfeebled by false refinement; that the books of instruction, written by men of genius, have had the same tendency as more frivolous productions; and that, in the true style of Mahometanism, they are treated as a kind of subordinate beings, and not as a part of the human species, when improveable reason is allowed to be the dignified distinction which raises men above the brute creation, and puts a natural sceptre in a feeble hand.

Yet, because I am a woman, I would not lead my readers to suppose that I mean violently to agitate the contested question respecting the equality or inferiority of the sex; but as the subject lies in my way, and I cannot pass it over without subjecting the main tendency of my reasoning to misconstruction, I shall stop a moment to deliver, in a few words, my opinion.—In the government of the physical world it is observable that the female in point of strength is, in general, inferior to the male. This is the law of nature; and it does not appear to be suspended or abrogated in favour of woman. A degree of physical superiority cannot, therefore, be denied—and it is a noble prerogative! But not content with this natural pre-eminence, men endeavour to sink us still lower, merely to render us alluring objects for a moment; and women, intoxicated by the adoration which men, under the influence of their senses, pay them, do not seek to obtain a durable interest in their hearts, or to become the friends of the fellow creatures who find amusement in their society.

I am aware of an obvious inference:—from every quarter have I heard exclamations against masculine women; but where are they to be found? If by this appellation men mean to inveigh against their ardour in hunting, shooting, and gaming, I shall most cordially join in the cry; but if it be against the imitation of manly virtues, or, more, properly speaking, the attainment of those talents and virtues, the exercise of which ennobles the human character, and which raise females in the scale of animal being, when they are comprehensively termed mankind;—all those who view them with a philosophic eye must, I should think, wish with me, that they may every day grow more and more masculine.

This discussion naturally divides the subject. I shall first consider women in the grand light of human creatures, who, in common with men, are placed on this earth to unfold their faculties; and afterwards I shall more particularly point out their peculiar designation.

I wish also to steer clear of an error which many respectable writers have fallen into; for the instruction which has hitherto been addressed to women, has rather been applicable to *ladies*, if the little indirect advice, that is scattered through Sandford and Merton, be excepted; but, addressing my sex in a firmer tone, I pay particular attention to those in the middle class, because they appear to be in the most natural state. Perhaps the seeds of false refinement, immorality, and vanity, have ever been shed by the great. Weak, artificial beings, raised above the common wants and affections of their race, in a premature unnatural manner, undermine the very foundation of virtue, and spread corruption through the whole mass of society! As a class of mankind they have the strongest claim to pity; the education of the rich tends to render them vain and helpless, and the unfolding mind is not strengthened by the practice of those duties which dignify the human character.—They only have to amuse themselves, and by the same law which in nature invariably produces certain effects, they soon only afford barren amusement.

But as I purpose taking a separate view of the different ranks of society, and of the moral character of women, in each, this hint is, for the present, sufficient; and I have only alluded to the subject, because it appears to me to be the very essence of an introduction to give a cursory account of the contents of the work it introduces.

My own sex, I hope, will excuse me, if I treat them like rational creatures, instead of flattering their *fascinating* graces, and viewing them as if they were in a state of perpetual childhood, unable to stand alone. I earnestly wish to point out in what true dignity and human happiness consists—I wish to persuade women to endeavour to acquire strength, both of mind and body, and to convince them that the soft phrases, susceptibility of heart, delicacy of sentiment, and refinement of taste, are almost synonymous with epithets of weakness, and that those beings who are only the objects of pity and that kind of love, which has been termed its sister, will soon become objects of contempt.

Dismissing then those pretty feminine phrases, which the men condescendingly use to soften our slavish dependence, and despising that weak elegancy of mind, exquisite sensibility, and sweet docility of manners, supposed to be the sexual characteristics of the weaker vessel, I wish to shew that elegance is inferior to virtue, that the first object of laudable ambition is to obtain a character as a human being, regardless of the distinction of sex; and that secondary views should be brought to this simple touchstone.

This is a rough sketch of my plan; and should I express my conviction with the energetic emotions that I feel whenever I think of the subject, the dictates of experience and reflection will be felt by some of my readers. Animated by this important object, I shall disdain to cull my phrases or polish my style;—I aim at being useful, and sincerity will render me unaffected; for, wishing rather to persuade by the force of my arguments, than dazzle by the elegance of my language, I shall not waste my time in rounding periods, or in fabricating the turgid bombast of artificial feelings, which, coining from the head, never reach the heart.—I shall be employed about things, not words!—and, anxious to render my sex more respectable members of society, I shall try to avoid that flowery diction which has slided from essays into novels, and from novels into familiar letters and conversation.

These pretty superlatives, dropping glibly from the tongue vitiate the taste, and create a kind of sickly delicacy that turns away from simple unadorned truth; and a deluge of false sentiments and overstretched feelings, stifling the natural emotions of the heart, render the domestic pleasures insipid, that ought to sweeten the exercise of those severe duties, which educate a rational and immortal being for a nobler field of action.

The education of women has, of late, been more attended to than formerly; yet they are still reckoned a frivolous sex, and ridiculed or pitied by the writers who endeavour by satire or instruction to improve them. It is acknowledged that they spend many of the first years of their lives in acquiring a smattering of accomplishments; meanwhile strength of body and mind are sacrificed to libertine notions of beauty, to the desire of establishing themselves,—the only way women can rise in the world,— by marriage. And this desire making mere animals of them, when they marry they act as such children may be expected to act:—they dress; they paint, and nickname God's creatures.—Surely these weak beings are only fit for a seraglio! Can they be expected to govern a family with judgment, or take care of the poor babes whom they bring into the world?

If then it can be fairly deduced from the present conduct of the sex, from the prevalent fondness for pleasure which takes place of ambition and those nobler passions that open and enlarge the soul; that the instruction which women have hitherto received has only tended, with the constitution of civil society, to render them insignificant objects of desire—mere propagators of fools!—if it can be proved that in aiming to accomplish them, without cultivating their understandings, they are taken out of their sphere of duties, and made ridiculous and useless when the short-lived bloom of beauty is over,[5] I presume that *rational* men will excuse me for endeavouring to persuade them to become more masculine and respectable.

Indeed the word masculine is only a bugbear: there is little reason to fear that women will acquire too much courage or fortitude; for their apparent inferiority with respect to bodily strength, must render them, in some degree, dependent on men in the various relations of life; but why should it be increased by prejudices that give a sex to virtue, and confound simple truths with sensual reveries?

Women are, in fact, so much degraded by mistaken notions of female excellence, that I do not mean to add a paradox when I assert, that this artificial weakness produces a propensity to tyrannize, and gives birth to cunning, the natural opponent of strength, which leads them to play off those contemptible infantine airs that undermine esteem even whilst they excite desire. Let men become more chaste and modest, and if women do not grow wiser in the same ratio, it will be clear that they have weaker understandings. It seems scarcely necessary to say, that I now speak of the sex in general. Many individuals have more sense than their male relatives; and, as nothing preponderates where there is a constant struggle for an equilibrium, without it has naturally more gravity, some women govern their husbands without degrading themselves, because intellect will always govern.

---

[5] A lively writer, I cannot recollect his name, asks what business women turned of forty have to do in the world?

Thomas Malthus

. . . .

The work of Thomas Robert Malthus (1766–1834) on the nature of population is of considerable importance for discussions of the possibility of human happiness. Whereas certain utopian thinkers saw misery as a contingent feature of human life, vanquishable by an alteration in society and by the improvement of the human intellect, Malthus believed conflict, struggle, and consequently unhappiness to be permanent features of the human condition. This was a result of the fact that human beings reproduce at a rate always exceeding the growth of the food supply. Malthus's work was a key influence on the thought of Darwin, and that most Darwinian of expressions—"struggle for existence"—makes its appearance first of all in Malthus's *Essay on the Principle of Population*. It is worth noting that Karl Marx's response to Malthus's theories differed markedly from Darwin's: Malthus, Marx declared, was "a shameless sycophant of the ruling classes."

. . . .

An Essay on the Principle of Population

The great and unlooked for discoveries that have taken place of late years in natural philosophy, the increasing diffusion of general knowledge from the extension of the art of printing, the ardent and unshackled

Malthus, Thomas, *An Essay on the Principle of Population* (London: Penguin, 1985 [1798]), pp. 67, 69, 70, 71-72, 198-199.

spirit of inquiry that prevails throughout the lettered and even unlettered world, the new and extraordinary lights that have been thrown on political subjects which dazzle and astonish the understanding, and particularly that tremendous phenomenon in the political horizon, the French Revolution, which, like a blazing comet, seems destined either to inspire with fresh life and vigour, or to scorch up and destroy the shrinking inhabitants of the earth, have all concurred to lead many able men into the opinion that we were touching on a period big with the most important changes, changes that would in some measure be decisive of the future fate of mankind.

It has been said that the great question is now at issue, whether man shall henceforth start forwards with accelerated velocity towards illimitable, and hitherto unconceived improvement, or be condemned to a perpetual oscillation between happiness and misery, and after every effort remain still at an immeasurable distance from the wished-for goal. . . .

I have read some of the speculations on the perfectibility of man and of society with great pleasure. I have been warmed and delighted with the enchanting picture which they hold forth. I ardently wish for such happy improvements. But I see great, and, to my understanding, unconquerable difficulties in the way to them. These difficulties it is my present purpose to state, declaring, at the same time, that so far from exulting in them, as a cause of triumph over the friends of innovation, nothing would give me greater pleasure than to see them completely removed . . .

I think I may fairly make two postulata.

First, That food is necessary to the existence of man.

Secondly, That the passion between the sexes is necessary and will remain nearly in its present state. . . .

Assuming then my postulata as granted, I say, that the power of population is indefinitely greater than the power in the earth to produce subsistence for man.

Population, when unchecked, increases in a geometrical ratio. Subsistence increases only in an arithmetical ratio. A slight acquaintance with numbers will shew the immensity of the first power in comparison of the second.

By that law of our nature which makes food necessary to the life of man, the effects of these two unequal powers must be kept equal.

This implies a strong and constantly operating check on population from the difficulty of subsistence. This difficulty must fall somewhere and must necessarily be severely felt by a large portion of mankind.

Through the animal and vegetable kingdoms, nature has scattered the seeds of life abroad with the most profuse and liberal hand. She has been comparatively sparing in the room and the nourishment necessary to rear them. The germs of existence contained in this spot of earth, with ample food, and ample room to expand in, would fill millions of worlds in the course of a few thousand years. Necessity, that imperious all pervading law of nature, restrains them within the prescribed bounds. The race of plants and the race of animals shrink under this great restrictive law. And the race of man cannot, by any efforts of reason, escape from it. Among plants and animals its effects are waste of seed, sickness, and premature death. Among mankind, misery and vice. The former, misery, is an absolutely necessary consequence of it. Vice is a highly probable consequence, and we therefore see it abundantly prevail, but it ought not, perhaps, to be called an absolutely necessary consequence. The ordeal of virtue is to resist all temptation to evil.

This natural inequality of the two powers of population and of production in the earth, and that great law of our nature which must constantly keep their effects equal, form the great difficulty that to me appears insurmountable in the way to the perfectibility of society. All other arguments are of slight and subordinate consideration in comparison of this. I see no way by which man can escape from the weight of this law which pervades all animated nature. No fancied equality, no agrarian regulations in their utmost extent, could remove the pressure of it even for a single century. And it appears, therefore, to be decisive against the possible existence of a society, all the members of which should live in ease, happiness, and comparative leisure; and feel no anxiety about providing the means of subsistence for themselves and families.

Consequently, if the premises are just, the argument is conclusive against the perfectibility of the mass of mankind.

. . .

It is, undoubtedly, a most disheartening reflection that the obstacle in the way to any extraordinary improvement in society is of a nature that we can never hope to overcome. The perpetual tendency in the race of man to increase beyond the means of subsistence is one of the general laws of animated nature which we can have no reason to expect will change. As discouraging as the contemplation of this difficulty must be to those whose exertions are laudably directed to the improvement of the human species, it is evident that no possible good can arise from any endeavours to slur it over or keep it in the background. On the contrary, the most baleful mischiefs may be expected from the unmanly conduct of not daring to face truth because it is unpleasing. Independently of what relates to this great obstacle, sufficient yet remains to be done for mankind to animate us to the most unremitted exertion. But if we proceed without a thorough knowledge and accurate comprehension of the nature, extent, and magnitude of the difficulties we have to encounter, or if we unwisely direct our efforts towards an object in which we cannot hope for success, we shall not only exhaust our strength in fruitless exertions and remain at as great a distance as ever from the summit of our wishes, but we shall be perpetually crushed by the recoil of this rock of Sisyphus.

Arthur Schopenhauer

The profound sense of pessimism that permeates the work of the great German philosopher Arthur Schopenhauer (1788–1860) is fully on display in the readings selected below. Schopenhauer held that all of nature was a blind and insatiable will to live, and that it was this that accounted for the suffering of human life: happiness is not at all a possibility for us. The first selections are drawn from Book Two of Schopenhauer's principal work, *The World as Will and Idea*, and show him arguing that Will is the essence of human beings and, indeed, of all things. His analysis of the egoistic and malicious nature of human beings is next seen, followed by a set of selections on the suffering and meaninglessness of existence. Finally, Schopenhauer's misogyny can be seen in a few pages of his bitter essay "On Women." Few philosophers have addressed the human condition more probingly than Schopenhauer: these selections, accordingly, occupy a vital place in this anthology.

The World as Will and Idea

§ 17. . . . [W]e can never arrive at the real nature of things from without. However much we investigate, we can never reach anything but images and names. We are like a man who goes round a castle seeking in vain

Schopenhauer, Arthur, *The World as Will and Idea* (trans. by R.B.Haldane and J.Kemp) (London: Routledge & Kegan Paul, 1883), Volume 1, pp. 128-130, 133, 140-141, 141-143.

for an entrance, and sometimes sketching the facades. And yet this is the method that has been followed by all philosophers before me.

§ 18. In fact, the meaning for which we seek of that world which is present to us only as our idea, or the transition from the world as mere idea of the knowing subject to whatever it may be besides this, would never be found if the investigator himself were nothing more than the pure knowing subject (a winged cherub without a body). But he is himself rooted in that world; he finds himself in it as an *individual,* that is to say, his knowledge, which is the necessary supporter of the whole world as idea, is yet always given through the medium of a body, whose affections are, as we have shown, the starting-point for the understanding in the perception of that world. His body is, for the pure knowing subject, an idea like every other idea, an object among objects. Its movements and actions are so far known to him in precisely the same way as the changes of all other perceived objects, and would be just as strange and incomprehensible to him if their meaning were not explained for him in an entirely different way. Otherwise he would see his actions follow upon given motives with the constancy of a law of nature, just as the changes of other objects follow upon causes, stimuli, or motives. But he would not understand the influence of the motives any more than the connection between every other effect which he sees and its cause. He would then call the inner nature of these manifestations and actions of his body which he did not understand a force, a quality, or a character, as he pleased, but he would have no further insight into it. But all this is not the case; indeed the answer to the riddle is given to the subject of knowledge who appears as an individual, and the answer is *will.* This and this alone gives him the key to his own existence, reveals to him the significance, shows him the inner mechanism of his being, of his action, of his movements. The body is given in two entirely different ways to the subject of knowledge, who becomes an individual only through his identity with it. It is given as an idea in intelligent perception, as an object among objects and subject to the laws of objects. And it is also given in quite a different way as that which is immediately known to every one, and is signified by the word *will.* Every true act of his will is also at once and without exception a movement of his body. The act of will and the movement of the body are not two different things objectively known, which the bond of causality unites; they do not stand in the relation of cause and effect; they are one and the same, but they are given in entirely different ways,—immediately, and again in perception for the understanding. The action of the body is nothing but the act of the will objectified, *i.e.*, passed into perception.

. . .

We can turn the expression of this truth in different ways and say: My body and my will are one;—or, What as an idea of perception I call my body, I call my will, so far as I am conscious of it in an entirely different way which cannot be compared to any other;—or, My body is the *objectivity* of my will. . . .

. . .

§ 20. . . . Upon this rests the perfect suitableness of the human and animal body to the human and animal will in general, resembling, though far surpassing, the correspondence between an instrument made for a purpose and the will of the maker, and on this account appearing as design, *i.e.*, the teleological explanation of the body. The parts of the body must, therefore, completely correspond to the principal desires through which the will manifests itself; they must be the visible expression of these desires. Teeth, throat, and bowels are objectified hunger; the organs of generation are objectified sexual desire; the grasping hand, the hurrying feet, correspond to the more indirect desires of the will which they express.

. . .

§ 21. Whoever has now gained from all these expositions a knowledge *in abstracto*, and therefore clear and certain, of what every one knows directly *in concreto*, *i.e.*, as feeling, a knowledge that his will is the real inner nature of his phenomenal being,. . . will find that of itself it affords him the key to the knowledge of the inmost being of the whole of nature; for he now transfers it to all those phenomena which are not given to him, like his own phenomenal existence, both in direct and indirect knowledge, but only in the latter, thus merely one-sidedly as *idea* alone. He will recognise this will of which we are speaking not only in those phenomenal existences which exactly resemble his own, in men and animals as their inmost nature, but the course of reflection will lead him to recognise the force which germinates and vegetates in the plant, and indeed the force through which the crystal is formed, that by which the magnet turns to the north pole, the force whose shock he experiences from the contact of two different kinds of metals, the force which appears in the elective affinities of matter as repulsion and attraction, decomposition and combination, and, lastly, even gravitation, which acts so powerfully throughout matter, draws the stone to the earth and the earth to the sun,—all these, I say, he will recognise as different only in their phenomenal existence, but in their inner nature as identical, as that which is directly known to him so intimately and so much better than anything else, and which in its most distinct manifestation is called *will*. It is this application of reflection alone that prevents us from remaining any longer at the phenomenon, and leads us to the *thing in itself.* Phenomenal existence is idea and nothing more. All idea, of whatever kind it may be, all *object,* is *phenomenal* existence, but the *will* alone is a *thing in itself.* As such, it is throughout not idea, but *toto genere* different from it; it is that of which all idea, all object, is the phenomenal appearance, the visibility, the objectification. It is the inmost nature, the kernel, of every particular thing, and also of the whole. It appears in every blind force of nature and also in the preconsidered action of man; and the great difference between these two is merely in the degree of the manifestation, not in the nature of what manifests itself.

On the Basis of Morality

The chief and fundamental incentive in man as in the animal is *egoism,* that is, the craving for existence and well-being. . . . In the animal as in man this egoism is most intimately connected with their innermost core and essence; in fact, it is really identical with essence. As a rule, therefore, all man's actions spring from egoism, and we must always first try to explain a given action with this in mind. In the same way, we generally base on egoism our calculation of all the means whereby we attempt to direct a man toward some goal or other. By its nature, *egoism* is boundless; man has the unqualified desire to preserve his existence, to keep it absolutely free from pain and suffering, which includes all want and privation. He desires to have the greatest possible amount of well-being and every pleasure of which he is capable; in fact, where possible, he attempts to develop within himself fresh capacities for enjoyment. Everything opposing the strivings of his egoism excites his wrath, anger, and hatred, and he will attempt to destroy it as his enemy. If possible, he wants to enjoy everything, to have everything; but as this is impossible, he wants at least to control everything. "Everything for me and nothing for the others" is his motto. Egoism is colossal; it towers above the world; for if every individual were given the choice between his own destruction and that of the rest of the world, I need not say how the decision would go in the vast majority of cases.

Accordingly, everyone makes himself the center of the world, and refers everything to himself. Whatever occurs—for example, the greatest changes in the fate of nations—is first referred to *his* interests; however small and indirect these may be, they are thought of before anything else. There is no greater contrast than that between the profound and exclusive interest everyone takes in his own self and the indifference with which all others as a rule regard it, similar to the indifference with which he regards them. There is even a comic side to seeing innumerable individuals of whom each regards himself alone as *real*, at any rate from a practical point of view, and all others to a certain extent as mere phantoms. This is due ultimately to the fact that everyone is given to himself *directly*, but the rest are given only *indirectly* through their representation in his head; and the directness asserts its right. Thus in consequence of the subjectivity essential to every consciousness, everyone is himself the whole world, for everything objective exists only indirectly, as mere representation of the subject, so that everything is always closely associated with self-consciousness. The only world everyone is actually acquainted with and knows, is carried about by him in his head as his representation, and is thus the center of the world. Accordingly, everyone is all in all to himself; he finds himself to be the holder and possessor of all reality, and nothing can be more important to him than his own self. Now while in his subjective view a man's own self assumes these colossal proportions, in the objective view it shrinks to almost nothing, to a thousand millionth part of the present human race. Now he knows with absolute certainty that this supremely important self, this microcosm whose mere modification or accident appears as the macrocosm—thus the entire world of this self—must disappear in death, which for him is equivalent to the end of the world. These, then, are the elements out of which, on the basis of the will-to-live, egoism grows, and always lies like a broad trench between one man and another. If anyone actually jumps over to help another, it is like a miracle that excites astonishment and wins approval.

On Human Nature

Man is at bottom a savage, horrible beast. We know it, if only in the business of taming and restraining him which we call civilisation. Hence it is that we are terrified if now and then his nature breaks out.

From Schopenhauer, Arthur, *On Human Nature* (London: Swan Sonnenschein, 1897), pp. 18-22.

Wherever and whenever the locks and chains of law and order fall off and give place to anarchy, he shows himself for what he is. But it is unnecessary to wait for anarchy in order to gain enlightenment on this subject. A hundred records, old and new, produce the conviction that in his unrelenting cruelty man is in no way inferior to the tiger and the hyæna. A forcible example is supplied by a publication of the year 1841 entitled *Slavery and the Internal Slave Trade in the United States of North America: being replies to questions transmitted by the British Anti-slavery Society to the American Anti-slavery Society.* This book constitutes one of the heaviest indictments against the human race. No one can put it down without a feeling of horror, and few without tears. For whatever the reader may have ever heard, or imagined, or dreamt, of the unhappy condition of slavery, or indeed of human cruelty in general, it will seem small to him when he reads of the way in which those devils in human form, those bigoted, church-going, strictly Sabbatarian rascals—and in particular the Anglican priests amongst them—treated their innocent black brothers, who by wrong and violence had got into their diabolical clutches.

Other examples are furnished by Tschudi's *Travels in Peru*, in the description which he gives of the treatment of the Peruvian soldiers at the hands of their officers; and by Macleod's *Travels in Eastern Africa*, where the author tells of the cold-blooded and truly devilish cruelty with which the Portuguese in Mozambique treat their slaves. But we need not go for examples to the New World, that obverse side of our planet. In the year 1848 it was brought to light that in England, not in one, but apparently in a hundred cases within a brief period, a husband had poisoned his wife or *vice versâ*, or both had joined in poisoning their children, or in torturing them slowly to death by starving and ill-treating them, with no other object than to get the money for burying them which they had insured in the Burial Clubs against their death. For this purpose a child was often insured in several, even in as many as twenty clubs at once.

Details of this character belong, indeed, to the blackest pages in the criminal records of humanity. But, when all is said, it is the inward and innate character of man, this god *par excellence* of the Pantheists, from which they and everything like them proceed. In every man there dwells, first and foremost, a colossal egoism, which breaks the bounds of right and justice with the greatest freedom, as everyday life shows on a small scale, and as history on every page of it on a large. Does not the recognised need of a balance of power in Europe, with the anxious way in which it is preserved, demonstrate that man is a beast of prey, who no sooner sees a weaker man near him than he falls upon him without fail? and does not the same hold good of the affairs of ordinary life ?

But to the boundless egoism of our nature there is joined more or less in every human breast a fund of hatred, anger, envy, rancour and malice, accumulated like the venom in a serpent's tooth, and waiting only for an opportunity of venting itself, and then, like a demon unchained, of storming and raging. . . .

Gobineau in his work *Les Races Humaines* has called man *l'animal méchant par excellence*. People take this very ill, because they feel that it hits them; but he is quite right, for man is the only animal which causes pain to others without any further purpose than just to cause it. Other animals never do it except to satisfy their hunger, or in the rage of combat. . . . No animal ever torments another for the mere purpose of tormenting, but man does it, and it is this that constitutes that diabolical feature in his character which is so much worse than the merely animal. I have already spoken of the matter in its broad aspect; but it is manifest even in small things, and every reader has a daily opportunity of observing it. For instance, if two little dogs are playing together—and what a genial and charming sight it is—and a child of three or four years joins them, it is almost inevitable for it to begin hitting them with a whip or stick, and thereby show itself, even at that age, *l'animal méchant par excellence*. The love of teasing and playing tricks, which is common enough, may be traced to the same source. For instance, if a man has expressed his annoyance at any interruption or other petty inconvenience, there will he no lack of people who for that very reason will bring it about: *l'animal méchant par excellence!* This is so certain that a man should be careful not to express any annoyance at small evils. On the other hand he should also be careful not to express his pleasure at any trifle, for, if he does so, men will act like the gaoler who, when he found that his prisoner had performed the laborious task of taming a spider, and took a pleasure in watching it, immediately crushed it under his foot: *l'animal méchant par excellence!* This is why all animals are instinctively afraid of the sight, or even of the track of a man, that *animal méchant par excellence!* nor does their instinct play them false; for it is man alone who hunts game for which he has no use and which does him no harm.

It is a fact, then, that in the heart of every man there lies a wild beast which only waits for an opportunity to storm and rage, in its desire to inflict pain on others, or, if they stand in his way, to kill them.

Studies in Pessimism:
"On the Sufferings of the World"

Unless *suffering* is the direct and immediate object of life, our existence must entirely fail of its aim. It is absurd to look upon the enormous amount of pain that abounds everywhere in the world, and originates in needs and necessities inseparable from life itself, as serving no purpose at all and the result of mere chance. Each separate misfortune, as it comes, seems, no doubt, to be something exceptional; but misfortune in general is the rule.

I know of no greater absurdity than that propounded by most systems of philosophy in declaring evil to be negative in its character. Evil is just what is positive; it makes its own existence felt. Leibnitz is particularly concerned to defend this absurdity; and he seeks to strengthen his position by using a palpable and paltry sophism. It is the good which is negative; in other words, happiness and satisfaction always imply some desire fulfilled, some state of pain brought to an end.

This explains the fact that we generally find pleasure to be not nearly so pleasant as we expected, and pain very much more painful.

The pleasure in this world, it has been said, outweighs the pain; or, at any rate, there is an even balance between the two. If the reader wishes to see shortly whether this statement is true, let him compare the respective feelings of two animals, one of which is engaged in eating the other.

The best consolation in misfortune or affliction of any kind will be the thought of other people who are in a still worse plight than yourself; and this is a form of consolation open to every one. But what an awful fate this means for mankind as a whole!

We are like lambs in a field, disporting themselves under the eye of the butcher, who chooses out first one and then another for his prey. So it is that in our good days we are all unconscious of the evil Fate may have presently in store for us—sickness, poverty, mutilation, loss of sight or reason.

No little part of the torment of existence lies in this, that Time is continually pressing upon us, never letting us take breath, but always coming after us like a taskmaster with a whip. If at any moment Time stays his hand, it is only when we are delivered over to the misery of boredom.

From Schopenhauer, Arthur, *Studies in Pessimism* (London: Swan Sonnenschein, 1908), pp. 11-15, 22-25, 28-30, 33-34, 37-39.

But misfortune has its uses; for, as our bodily frame would burst asunder if the pressure of the atmosphere were removed, so, if the lives of men were relieved of all need, hardship and adversity; if everything they took in hand were successful, they would be so swollen with arrogance that, though they might not burst, they would present the spectacle of unbridled folly—nay, they would go mad. And I may say, further, that a certain amount of care or pain or trouble is necessary for every man at all times. A ship without ballast is unstable and will not go straight.

Certain it is that *work, worry, labour* and *trouble,* form the lot of almost all men their whole life long. But if all wishes were fulfilled as soon as they arose, how would men occupy their lives? what would they do with their time? If the world were a paradise of luxury and ease, a land flowing with milk and honey, where every Jack obtained his Jill at once and without any difficulty, men would either die of boredom or hang themselves; or there would be wars, massacres, and murders; so that in the end mankind would inflict more suffering on itself than it has now to accept at the hands of Nature.

In early youth, as we contemplate our coming life, we are like children in a theatre before the curtain is raised, sitting there in high spirits and eagerly waiting for the play to begin. It is a blessing that we do not know what is really going to happen. Could we foresee it, there are times when children might seem like innocent prisoners, condemned not to death, but to life, and as yet all unconscious of what their sentence means. Nevertheless every man desires to reach old age; in other words, a state of life of which it may be said: "It is bad to-day, and it will be worse to-morrow; and so on till the worst of all."

If you try to imagine, as nearly as you can, what an amount of misery, pain and suffering of every kind the sun shines upon in its course, you will admit that it would be much better if on the earth as little as on the moon the sun were able to call forth the phenomena of life; and if, here as there, the surface were still in a crystalline state.

Again, you may look upon life as an unprofitable episode, disturbing the blessed calm of non-existence. And, in any case, even though things have gone with you tolerably well, the longer you live the more clearly you will feel that, on the whole, life is *a disappointment, nay, a cheat.*

If two men who were friends in their youth meet again when they are old, after being separated for a life-time, the chief feeling they will have at the sight of each other will be one of complete disappointment at life as a whole; because their thoughts will be carried back to that earlier time when life seemed so fair as it lay spread out before them in the rosy light of dawn, promised so much—and then performed so little. This feeling will so completely predominate over every other that they will not even consider it necessary to give it words; but on either side it will be silently assumed, and form the ground-work of all they have to talk about.

He who lives to see two or three generations is like a man who sits some time in the conjurer's booth at a fair, and witnesses the performance twice or thrice in succession. The tricks were meant to be seen only once; and when they are no longer a novelty and cease to deceive their effect is gone. . . .

If children were brought into the world by an act of pure reason alone, would the human race continue to exist? Would not a man rather have so much sympathy with the coming generation as to spare it the burden of existence? or at any rate not take it upon himself to impose that burden upon it in cold blood. . . .

Brahma is said to have produced the world by a kind of fall or mistake; and in order to atone for his folly he is bound to remain in it himself until he works out his redemption. As an account of the origin of things, that is admirable! According to the doctrines of *Buddhism*, the world came into being as the result of some inexplicable disturbance in the heavenly calm of Nirvana, that blessed state obtained by expiation, which had endured so long a time—the change taking place by a kind of fatality. This explanation must be understood as having at bottom some moral bearing; although it is illustrated by an exactly parallel theory in the domain of physical science, which places the origin of the sun in a primitive streak of mist, formed one knows not how. Subsequently, by a series of moral errors, the world became gradually worse and worse— true of the physical orders as well—until it assumed the dismal aspect it wears to-day. Excellent! The *Greeks* looked upon the world and the gods as the work of an inscrutable necessity. A passable explanation: we may be content with it until we can get a better. Again, *Ormuzd* and *Ahriman* are rival powers, continually at war. That is not bad. But that a God like Jehovah should have created this world of misery and woe, out of pure caprice, and because he enjoyed doing it, and should then have clapped his hands in praise of his own work, and declared everything to be very good—that will not do at all! In its explanation of the origin of the world, Judaism is inferior to any other form of religious doctrine professed by a civilised nation; and it is quite in keeping with this that it is the only one which presents no trace whatever of any belief in the immortality of the soul.

Even though Leibnitz' contention, that this is the best of all possible worlds, were correct, that would not justify God in having created it. For he is the Creator not of the world only, but of possibility itself; and, therefore, he ought to have so ordered possibility as that it would admit of something better.

There are two things which make it impossible to believe that this world is the successful work of an all-wise, all-good, and, at the same time, all-powerful Being; firstly, the misery which abounds in it everywhere; and secondly, the obvious imperfection of its highest product, man, who is a burlesque of what he should be. These things cannot be reconciled with any such belief. On the contrary, they are just the facts which support what I have been saying; they are our authority for viewing the world as the outcome of our own misdeeds, and therefore, as something that had better not have been. Whilst, under the former hypothesis, they amount to a bitter accusation against the Creator, and supply material for sarcasm; under the latter they form an indictment against our own nature, our own will, and teach us a lesson of humility. They lead us to see that, like the children of a libertine, we come into the world with the burden of sin upon us; and that it is only through having continually to atone for this sin that our existence is so miserable, and that its end is death.

There is nothing more certain than the general truth that it is the grievous *sin of the world* which has produced the grievous *suffering of the world*. I am not referring here to the physical connection between these two things lying in the realm of experience; my meaning is metaphysical. Accordingly, the sole thing that reconciles me to the Old Testament is the story of the Fall. In my eyes, it is the only metaphysical truth in that book, even though it appears in the form of an allegory. There seems to me no better explanation of our existence than that it is the result of some false step, some sin of which we are paying the penalty. . . .

If you accustom yourself to this view of life you will regulate your expectations accordingly, and cease to look upon all its disagreeable incidents, great and small, its sufferings, its worries, its misery, as anything unusual or irregular; nay, you will find that everything is as it should be, in a world where each of us pays the penalty of existence in his own peculiar way. Amongst the evils of a penal colony is the society of those who form it; and if the reader is worthy of better company, he will need no words from me to remind him of what he has to put up with at present. If he has a soul above the common, or if he is a man of genius, he will occasionally feel like some noble prisoner of state, condemned to work in the galleys with common criminals; and he will follow his example and try to isolate himself.

In general however, it should be said that this view of life will enable us to contemplate the so-called imperfections of the great majority of men, their moral and intellectual deficiencies and the resulting base type of countenance, without any surprise, to say nothing of indignation; for we shall never cease to reflect where we are, and that the men about us are beings conceived and born in sin, and living to atone for it. That is what Christianity means in speaking of the sinful nature of man.

Pardon's the word to all![6] Whatever folly men commit, be their shortcomings or their vices what they may, let us exercise forbearance; remembering that when these faults appear in others it is our follies and vices that we behold. They are the shortcomings of humanity, to which we belong; whose faults, one and all, we share; yes, even those very faults at which we now wax so indignant, merely because they have not yet appeared in ourselves. They are faults that do not lie on the surface. But they exist down there in the depths of our nature; and should anything call them forth they will come and show themselves, just as we now see them in others. One man, it is true, may have faults that are absent in his fellow; and it is undeniable that the sum total of bad qualities is in some cases very large; for the difference of individuality between man and man passes all measure.

In fact, the conviction that the world and man is something that had better not have been is of a kind to fill us with indulgence towards one another. Nay, from this point of view, we might well consider the proper form of address to be, not *Monsieur, Sir, mein Herr*, but *my fellow-sufferer, Socî malorum, compagnon de misères!* This may perhaps sound strange, but it is in keeping with the facts; it puts others in a right light; and it reminds us of that which is after all the most necessary thing in life—the tolerance, patience, regard, and love of neighbour, of which everyone stands in need, and which, therefore, every man owes to his fellow.

---

[6] *Cymbeline*, Act V, Sc. 5.

Studies in Pessimism:
"The Vanity of Existence"

A man finds himself, to his great astonishment, suddenly existing, after thousands and thousands of years of non-existence: he lives for a little while; and then, again, comes an equally long period when he must exist no more. . . .

Human life must be some kind of mistake. The truth of this will be sufficiently obvious if we only remember that man is a compound of needs and necessities hard to satisfy; and that even when they are satisfied all he obtains is a state of painlessness, where nothing remains to him but abandonment to boredom. This is direct proof that existence has no real value in itself; for what is boredom but the feeling of the emptiness of life? If life—the craving for which is the very essence of our being—were possessed of any positive intrinsic value, there would be no such thing as boredom at all: mere existence would satisfy us in itself, and we should want for nothing. But as it is, we take no delight in existence except when we are struggling for something; and then distance and difficulties to be overcome make our goal look as though it would satisfy us—an illusion which vanishes when we reach it; or else when we are occupied with some purely intellectual interest—where in reality we have stepped forth from life to look upon it from the outside, much after the manner of spectators at a play. And even sensual pleasure itself means nothing but a struggle and aspiration, ceasing the moment its aim is attained. Whenever we are not occupied in one of these ways, but cast upon existence itself, its vain and worthless nature is brought home to us; and this is what we mean by boredom. The hankering after what is strange and uncommon—an innate and ineradicable tendency of human nature—shows how glad we are at any interruption of that natural course of affairs which is so very tedious.

That this most perfect manifestation of the will to live, the human organism, with the cunning and complex working of its machinery, must fall to dust and yield up itself and all its strivings to extinction— this is the naïve way in which Nature, who is always so true and sincere in what she says, proclaims the whole struggle of this will as in its very essence barren and unprofitable. Were it of any value in itself, anything unconditioned and absolute, it could not thus end in mere nothing.

From Schopenhauer, Arthur, Studies in Pessimism (London: Swan Sonnenschein, 1908), pp. 11-15, 22-25, 28-30, 33-34, 37-39.

If we turn from contemplating the world as a whole, and, in particular, the generations of men as they live their little hour of mock-existence and then are swept away in rapid succession; if we turn from this, and look at life in its small details, as presented, say, in a comedy, how ridiculous it all seems! It is like a drop of water seen through a microscope, a single drop teeming with *infusoria*; or a speck of cheese full of mites invisible to the naked eye. How we laugh as they bustle about so eagerly, and struggle with one another in so tiny a space! And whether here, or in the little span of human life, this terrible activity produces a comic effect.

It is only in the microscope that our life looks so big. It is an indivisible point, drawn out and magnified by the powerful lenses of Time and Space.

Studies in Pessimism: "On Women"

You need only look at the way in which she is formed to see that woman is not meant to undergo great labour, whether of the mind or of the body. She pays the debt of life not by what she does but by what she suffers; by the pains of childbearing and care for the child, and by submission to her husband, to whom she should be a patient and cheering companion. The keenest sorrows and joys are not for her, nor is she called upon to display a great deal of strength. The current of her life should be more gentle, peaceful and trivial than man's, without being essentially happier or unhappier.

Women are directly fitted for acting as the nurses and teachers of our early childhood by the fact that they are themselves childish, frivolous and short-sighted; in a word, they are big children all their life long—a kind of intermediate stage between the child and the full-grown man, who is man in the strict sense of the word. See how a girl will fondle a child for days together, dance with it and sing to it; and then think what a man, with the best will in the world, could do if he were put in her place.

. . .

It is only the man whose intellect is clouded by his sexual impulses that could give the name of *the fair sex* to that undersized, narrow-shouldered, broad-hipped, and short-legged race: for the whole beauty of the sex is bound up with this impulse. Instead of calling them beautiful, there would be more warrant for describing women as the unæsthetic sex. Neither for music, nor for poetry, nor for fine art, have they really

From Schopenhauer, Arthur, *Studies in Pessimism* (op.cit), pp. 105-106, 113-115.

and truly any sense or susceptibility; it is a mere mockery if they make a pretence of it in order to assist their endeavour to please. Hence, as a result of this, they are incapable of taking a *purely objective interest* in anything; and the reason of it seems to me to be as follows. A man tries to acquire *direct* mastery over things, either by understanding them or by forcing them to do his will. But a woman is always and everywhere reduced to obtaining this mastery *indirectly*, namely through a man; and whatever direct mastery she may have is entirely confined to him. And so it lies in woman's nature to look upon everything only as a means for conquering man; and if she takes an interest in anything else it is simulated—a mere roundabout way of gaining her ends by coquetry and feigning what she does not feel. Hence, even Rousseau declared: *Women have, in general, no love of any art; they have no proper knowledge of any; and they have no genius.*[7]

No one who sees at all below the surface can have failed to remark the same thing. You need only observe the kind of attention women bestow upon a concert, an opera, or a play—the childish simplicity, for example, with which they keep on chattering during the finest passages in the greatest masterpieces. If it is true that the Greeks excluded women from their theatres, they were quite right in what they did; at any rate you would have been able to hear what was said upon the stage. In our day, besides, or in lieu of saying, *Let a woman keep silence in the church*, it would be much to the point to say, *Let a woman keep silence in the theatre.* This might, perhaps, be put up in big letters on the curtain.

And you cannot expect anything else of women if you consider that the most distinguished intellects among the whole sex have never managed to produce a single achievement in the fine arts that is really great, genuine, and original; or given to the world any work of permanent value in any sphere. This is most strikingly shown in regard to painting, where mastery of technique is at least as much within their power as within ours—and hence they are diligent in cultivating it; but still, they have not a single great painting to boast of, just because they are deficient in that objectivity of mind which is so directly indispensable in painting. They never get beyond a subjective point of view.

---

[7]   Lettre à d'Alembert. Note xx.

=== 🐦 ===

51

Giacomo Leopardi

....

The poetry of Giacomo Leopardi (1798–1837) expresses deep pessimism about the human condition, never more so than in the poem included below. "To Himself" articulates with great concision a sense of the boredom, bitterness, and emptiness of life.

....

To Himself

Now be for ever still,
Weary my heart. For the last cheat is dead,
I thought eternal. Dead. For us, I know
Not only the dear hope
Of being deluded gone, but the desire.
Rest still for ever. You
Have beaten long enough. And to no purpose
Were all your stirrings; earth not worth your sighs.
Boredom and bitterness
Is life; and the rest, nothing; the world is dirt.
Lie quiet now. Despair

For the last time. Fate granted to our kind
Only to die. And now you may despise
Yourself, nature, the brute
Power which, hidden, ordains the common doom,
And all the immeasurable emptiness of things.

=== ⚓ ===

52

John Stuart Mill

One of the most important of English philosophers, John Stuart Mill (1806–1873) made significant contributions to political and moral philosophy, and was, along with Jeremy Bentham, a key architect of utilitarianism. Three selections are included below. In the first one, from his extraordinary essay on the subject, Mill depicts the sufferings humanity has to endure at the hands of nature. The second selection is excerpted from Mill's celebrated work *Utilitarianism*, and illustrates his conception of the nature and possibility of happiness, depicted as the proper goal of human striving. In the last reading, Mill's progressive political attitudes are clearly on display in his account of the unjustifiable subjection of women.

Three Essays on Religion: "Nature"

In considering this subject it is necessary to divest ourselves of certain preconceptions which may justly he called natural prejudices, being grounded on feelings which, in themselves natural and inevitable, intrude into matters with which they ought to have no concern. One of these feelings is the astonishment, rising into awe, which is inspired (even independently of all religious sentiment) by any of the greater natural phenomena. A hurricane; a mountain precipice; the desert; the ocean, either

From Mill, John Stuart, *Three Essays on Religion* (London: Longman, Green, Longman, Roberts, & Green, 1864), pp. 26–31.

agitated or at rest; the solar system, and the great cosmic forces which hold it together; the boundless firmament, and to an educated mind any single star; excite feelings which make all human enterprises and powers appear so insignificant, that to a mind thus occupied it seems insufferable presumption in so puny a creature as man to look critically on things so far above him, or dare to measure himself against the grandeur of the universe. But a little interrogation of our own consciousness will suffice to convince us, that what makes these phenomena so impressive is simply their vastness. The enormous extension in space and time, or the enormous power they exemplify, constitutes their sublimity; a feeling in all cases, more allied to terror than to any moral emotion. And though the vast scale of these phenomena may well excite wonder, and sets at defiance all idea of rivalry, the feeling it inspires is of a totally different character from admiration of excellence. Those in whom awe produces admiration may be aesthetically developed, but they are morally uncultivated. It is one of the endowments of the imaginative part of our mental nature that conceptions of greatness and power, vividly realized, produce a feeling which though in its higher degrees closely bordering on pain, we prefer to most of what are accounted pleasures. But we are quite equally capable of experiencing this feeling towards maleficent power; and we never experience it so strongly towards most of the powers of the universe, as when we have most present to our consciousness a vivid sense of their capacity of inflicting evil. Because these natural powers have what we cannot imitate, enormous might, and overawe us by that one attribute, it would be a great error to infer that their other attributes are such as we ought to emulate, or that we should be justified in using our small powers after the example which Nature sets us with her vast forces.

For, how stands the fact? That next to the greatness of these cosmic forces, the quality which most forcibly strikes every one who does not avert his eyes from it, is their perfect and absolute recklessness. They go straight to their end, without regarding what or whom they crush on the road. Optimists, in their attempts to prove that "whatever is, is right," are obliged to maintain, not that Nature ever turns one step from her path to avoid trampling us into destruction, but that it would be very unreasonable in us to expect that she should. Pope's "Shall gravitation cease when you go by?" may be a just rebuke to any one who should be so silly as to expect common human morality from nature. But if the question were between two men, instead of between a man and a natural phenomenon, that triumphant apostrophe would be thought a rare piece of impudence.

A man who should persist in hurling stones or firing cannon when another man "goes by," and having killed him should urge a similar plea in exculpation, would very deservedly be found guilty of murder.

In sober truth, nearly all the things which men are hanged or imprisoned for doing to one another, are nature's every day performances. Killing, the most criminal act recognized by human laws, Nature does once to every being that lives; and in a large proportion of cases, after protracted tortures such as only the greatest monsters whom we read of ever purposely inflicted on their living fellow-creatures. If, by an arbitrary reservation, we refuse to account anything murder but what abridges a certain term supposed to be allotted to human life, nature also does this to all but a small percentage of lives, and does it in all the modes, violent or insidious, in which the worst human beings take the lives of one another. Nature impales men, breaks them as if on the wheel, casts them to be devoured by wild beasts, burns them to death, crushes them with stones like the first christian martyr, starves them with hunger, freezes them with cold, poisons them by the quick or slow venom of her exhalations, and has hundreds of other hideous deaths in reserve, such as the ingenious cruelty of a Nabis or a Domitian never surpassed. All this, Nature does with the most supercilious disregard both of mercy and of justice, emptying her shafts upon the best and noblest indifferently with the meanest and worst; upon those who are engaged in the highest and worthiest enterprises, and often as the direct consequence of the noblest acts; and it might almost be imagined as a punishment for them. She mows down those on whose existence hangs the well-being of a whole people, perhaps the prospects of the human race for generations to come, with as little compunction as those whose death is a relief to themselves, or a blessing to those under their noxious influence. Such are Nature's dealings with life. Even when she does not intend to kill, she inflicts the same tortures in apparent wantonness. In the clumsy provision which she has made for that perpetual renewal of animal life, rendered necessary by the prompt termination she puts to it in every individual instance, no human being ever comes into the world but another human being is literally stretched on the rack for hours or days, not unfrequently issuing in death. Next to taking life (equal to it according to a high authority) is taking the means by which we live; and Nature does this too on the largest scale and with the most callous indifference. A single hurricane destroys the hopes of a season; a flight of locusts, or an inundation, desolates a district; a trifling chemical change in an edible root, starves a million of people. The waves of the sea, like banditti seize and appropriate the wealth of the rich and the little all of the poor with the same accompaniments of stripping, wounding, and killing as their human antitypes. Everything in short, which the worst men commit either against life or property is perpetrated on a larger scale by natural agents. Nature has Noyades more fatal than those of Carrier; her explosions of fire damp are as destructive as human artillery; her plague and cholera far surpass the poison cups of the Borgias. Even the love of "order" which is thought to be a following of the ways of Nature, is in fact a contradiction of them. All which people are accustomed to deprecate as "disorder" and its consequences, is precisely a counterpart of Nature's ways. Anarchy and the Reign of Terror are overmatched in injustice, ruin, and death, by a hurricane and a pestilence.

Utilitarianism

The creed which accepts as the foundation of morals, Utility, or the Greatest Happiness Principle, holds that actions are right in proportion as they tend to promote happiness, wrong as they tend to produce the reverse of happiness. By happiness is intended pleasure, and the absence of pain; by unhappiness, pain, and the privation of pleasure. To give a clear view of the moral standard set up by the theory, much more requires to be said; in particular, what things it includes in the ideas of pain and pleasure; and to what extent this is left an open question. But these supplementary explanations do not affect the theory of life on which this theory of morality is grounded—namely, that pleasure, and freedom from pain, are the only things desirable as ends; and that all desirable things (which are as numerous in the utilitarian as in any other scheme) are desirable either for the pleasure inherent in themselves, or as means to the promotion of pleasure and the prevention of pain.

Now, such a theory of life excites in many minds, and among them in some of the most estimable in feeling and purpose, inveterate dislike. To suppose that life has (as they express it) no higher end than pleasure—no better and nobler object of desire and pursuit—they designate as utterly mean and grovelling; as a doctrine worthy only of swine, to whom the followers of Epicurus were, at a very early period, contemptuously likened; and modern holders of the doctrine are occasionally made the subject of equally polite comparisons by its German, French, and English assailants.

From Mill, John Stuart, "Utilitarianism" (in *On Liberty and Other Essays*, Oxford: Oxford University Press, 1991 [1861]), 137-140, 142-145.

When thus attacked, the Epicureans have always answered, that it is not they, but their accusers, who represent human nature in a degrading light; since the accusation supposes human beings to be capable of no pleasures except those of which swine are capable. If this supposition were true, the charge could not be gainsaid, but would then be no longer an imputation; for if the sources of pleasure were precisely the same to human beings and to swine, the rule of life which is good enough for the one would be good enough for the other. The comparison of the Epicurean life to that of beasts is felt as degrading, precisely because a beast's pleasures do not satisfy a human being's conceptions of happiness. Human beings have faculties more elevated than the animal appetites, and when once made conscious of them, do not regard anything as happiness which does not include their gratification. I do not, indeed, consider the Epicureans to have been by any means faultless in drawing out their scheme of consequences from the utilitarian principle. To do this in any sufficient manner, many Stoic as well as Christian elements require to be included. But there is no known Epicurean theory of life which does not assign to the pleasures of the intellect, of the feelings and imagination, and of the moral sentiments, a much higher value as pleasures than to those of mere sensation. It must be admitted, however, that utilitarian writers in general have placed the superiority of mental over bodily pleasures chiefly in the greater permanency, safety, uncostliness, &c., of the former—that is, in their circumstantial advantages rather than in their intrinsic nature. And on all these points utilitarians have fully proved their case; but they might have taken the other, and, as it may be called, higher ground, with entire consistency. It is quite compatible with the principle of utility to recognize the fact, that some *kinds* of pleasure are more desirable and more valuable than others. It would be absurd that while, in estimating all other things, quality is considered as well as quantity, the estimation of pleasures should be supposed to depend on quantity alone.

If I am asked, what I mean by difference of quality in pleasures, or what makes one pleasure more valuable than another, merely as a pleasure, except its being greater in amount, there is but one possible answer. Of two pleasures, if there be one to which all or almost all who have experience of both give a decided preference, irrespective of any feeling of moral obligation to prefer it, that is the more desirable pleasure. If one of the two is, by those who are competently acquainted with both, placed so far above the other that they prefer it, even though knowing it to be attended with a greater amount of discontent, and would not resign it for any quantity of the other pleasure which their nature is capable of, we are justified in ascribing to the preferred enjoyment a superiority in quality, so far outweighing quantity as to render it, in comparison, of small account.

Now it is an unquestionable fact, that those who are equally acquainted with, and equally capable of appreciating and enjoying, both, do give a most marked preference to the manner of existence which employs their higher faculties. Few human creatures would consent to be changed into any of the lower animals, for a promise of the fullest allowance of a beast's pleasures; no intelligent human being would consent to be a fool, no instructed person would be an ignoramus, no person of feeling and conscience would be selfish and base, even though they should be persuaded that the fool, the dunce, or the rascal is better satisfied with his lot than they are with theirs. They would not resign what they possess more than he, for the most complete satisfaction of all the desires which they have in common with him. If they ever fancy they would, it is only in cases of unhappiness so extreme, that to escape from it they would exchange their lot for almost any other, however undesirable in their own eyes. A being of higher faculties requires more to make him happy, is capable probably of more acute suffering, and is certainly accessible to it at more points, than one of an inferior type; but in spite of these liabilities, he can never really wish to sink into what he feels to be a lower grade of existence. We may give what explanation we please of this unwillingness; we may attribute it to pride, a name which is given indiscriminately to some of the most and to some of the least estimable feelings of which mankind are capable: we may refer it to the love of liberty and personal independence, an appeal to which was with the Stoics one of the most effective means for the inculcation of it; to the love of power, or to the love of excitement, both of which do really enter into and contribute to it: but its most appropriate appellation is a sense of dignity, which all human beings possess in one form or other, and in some, though by no means in exact, proportion to their higher faculties, and which is so essential a part of the happiness of those in whom it is strong, that nothing which conflicts with it could be, otherwise than momentarily, an object of desire to them. Whoever supposes that this preference takes place at a sacrifice of happiness—that the superior being, in anything like equal circumstances, is not happier than the inferior—confounds the two very different ideas, of happiness, and content. It is indisputable that the being whose capacities of enjoyment are low, has the greatest chance of having them fully satisfied; and a highly-endowed being will always feel that any happiness which he can look for, as the world is constituted, is imperfect. But he can learn to bear its imperfections, if they are at all bearable; and they will not make him envy the being who is indeed unconscious of the imperfections, but only because he feels not at all the good which those imperfections qualify. It is better to be a human being dissatisfied than a pig satisfied; better to be Socrates dissatisfied than a fool satisfied. And if the fool, or the pig, is of a different opinion, it is because they only know their own side of the question. The other party to the comparison knows both sides.

. . .

According to the Greatest Happiness Principle, as above explained, the ultimate end, with reference to and for the sake of which all other things are desirable (whether we are considering our own good or that of other people), is an existence exempt as far as possible from pain, and as rich as possible in enjoyments, both in point of quantity and quality; the test of quality, and the rule for measuring it against quantity, being the preference felt by those who, in their opportunities of experience, to which must be added their habits of self-consciousness and self-observation, are best furnished with the means of comparison. This, being, according to the utilitarian opinion, the end of human action, is necessarily also the standard of morality; which may accordingly be defined, the rules and precepts for human conduct, by the observance of which an existence such as has been described might be, to the greatest extent possible, secured to all mankind; and not to them only, but, so far as the nature of things admits, to the whole sentient creation.

Against this doctrine, however, arises another class of objectors, who say that happiness, in any form, cannot be the rational purpose of human life and action; because, in the first place, it is unattainable: and they contemptuously ask, What right hast thou to be happy? A question which Mr. Carlyle clenches by the addition, What right, a short time ago, hadst thou even *to be?* Next, they say, that men can do *without* happiness; that all noble human beings have felt this, and could not have become noble but by learning the lesson, of *Entsagen*, or renunciation; which lesson, thoroughly learnt and submitted to, they affirm to be the beginning and necessary condition of all virtue.

The first of these objections would go to the root of the matter were it well founded; for if no happiness is to be had at all by human beings, the attainment of it cannot be the end of morality, or of any rational conduct. Though, even in that case, something might still be said for the utilitarian theory; since utility includes not solely the pursuit of happiness, but the prevention or mitigation of unhappiness; and if the former aim be chimerical, there will be all the greater scope and more imperative need for the latter, so long at least as mankind think fit to live, and do not take refuge in the simultaneous act of suicide recommended under certain conditions by Novalis. When, however, it is thus positively asserted to be impossible that human life should be happy, the assertion, if not something like a verbal quibble, is at least an exaggeration. If by happiness be meant a continuity of highly pleasurable excitement, it is evident enough that this is impossible. A state of exalted pleasure lasts only moments, or in some cases, and with some intermissions, hours or days, and is the occasional brilliant flash of enjoyment, not its permanent and steady flame. Of this the philosophers who have taught that happiness is the end of life were as fully aware as those who taunt them. The happiness which they meant was not a life of rapture; but moments of such, in an existence made up of few and transitory pains, many and various pleasures, with a decided predominance of the active over the passive, and having as the foundation of the whole, not to expect more from life than it is capable of bestowing. A life thus composed, to those who have been fortunate enough to obtain it, has always appeared worthy of the name of happiness. And such an existence is even now the lot of many, during some considerable portion of their lives. The present wretched education, and wretched social arrangements, are the only real hindrance to its being attainable by almost all.

The objectors perhaps may doubt whether human beings, if taught to consider happiness as the end of life, would be satisfied with such a moderate share of it. But great numbers of mankind have been satisfied with much less. The main constituents of a satisfied life appear to be two, either of which by itself is often found sufficient for the purpose: tranquillity, and excitement. With much tranquillity, many find that they can be content with very little pleasure: with much excitement, many can reconcile themselves to a considerable quantity of pain. There is assuredly no inherent impossibility in enabling even the mass of mankind to unite both; since the two are so far from being incompatible that they are in natural alliance, the prolongation of either being a preparation for, and exciting a wish for, the other. It is only those in whom indolence amounts to a vice, that do not desire excitement after an interval of repose; it is only those in whom the need of excitement is a disease, that feel the tranquillity which follows excitement dull and insipid, instead of pleasurable in direct proportion to the excitement which preceded it. When people

who are tolerably fortunate in their outward lot do not find in life sufficient enjoyment to make it valuable to them, the cause generally is caring
for nobody but themselves. To those who have neither public nor private
affections, the excitements of life are much curtailed, and in any case
dwindle in value as the time approaches when all selfish interests must
be terminated by death: while those who leave after them objects of personal affection, and especially those who have also cultivated a fellow
feeling with the collective interests of mankind, retain as lively an interest in life on the eve of death as in the vigour of youth and health.
Next to selfishness, the principal cause which makes life unsatisfactory,
is want of mental cultivation. A cultivated mind—I do not mean that of a
philosopher, but any mind to which the fountains of knowledge have been
opened, and which has been taught, in any tolerable degree, to exercise
its faculties—finds sources of inexhaustible interest in all that surrounds
it; in the objects of nature, the achievements of art, the imaginations of
poetry, the incidents of history, the ways of mankind past and present,
and their prospects in the future. It is possible, indeed, to become indifferent to all this, and that too without having exhausted a thousandth
part of it; but only when one has had from the beginning no moral or
human interest in these things, and has sought in them only the gratification of curiosity.

The Subjection of Women

At present, in the more improved countries, the disabilities of women,
are the only case, save one, in which laws and institutions take persons at
their birth, and ordain that they shall, never in all their lives, be allowed
to compete for certain things. The one exception is that of royalty. Persons still are born to the throne; no one, not of the reigning family, can
ever occupy it, and no one even of that family can, by any means but the
course of hereditary succession, attain it. All other dignities and social
advantages are open to the whole male sex: many indeed are only attainable by wealth, but wealth may be striven for by any one, and is actually
obtained by many men of the very humblest origin. The difficulties, to the
majority, are indeed insuperable without the aid of fortunate accidents;
but no male human being is under any legal ban: neither law nor opinion

From Mill, John Stuart, "The Subjection of Women" (in *On Liberty and Other Essays*, Oxford:
Oxford University Press, 1991 [1869]), pp. 490–492, 493–495.

superadd artificial obstacles to the natural ones. Royalty, as I have said, is excepted: but in this case every one feels it to be an exception—an anomaly in the modern world, in marked opposition to its customs and principles, and to be justified only by extraordinary special expediencies, which though individuals and nations differ in estimating their weight, unquestionably do in fact exist, but in this exceptional case, in which a high social function is, for important reasons, bestowed on birth instead of being put up to competition, all free nations contrive to adhere in substance to the principle from which they nominally derogate; for they circumscribe this high function by conditions avowedly intended to prevent the person to whom it ostensibly belongs from really performing it; while the person by whom it is performed, the responsible minister, does obtain the post by a competition from which no full-grown citizen of the male sex is legally excluded. The disabilities, therefore, to which women are subject from the mere fact of their birth, are the solitary examples of the kind in modern legislation. In no instance except this, which comprehends half the human race, are the higher social functions closed against any one by a fatality of birth which no exertions, and no change of circumstances, can overcome; for even religious disabilities (besides that in England and in Europe they have practically almost ceased to exist) do not close any career to the disqualified person in case of conversion.

The social subordination of women thus stands out an isolated fact in modern social institutions; a solitary breach of what has become their fundamental law; a single relic of an old world of thought and practice exploded in everything else, but retained in the one thing of most universal interest; as if a gigantic dolmen, or a vast temple of Jupiter Olympius, occupied the site of St. Paul's and received daily worship, while the surrounding Christian churches were only resorted to on fasts and festivals. The entire discrepancy between one social fact and all those which accompany it, and the radical opposition between its nature and the progressive movement which is the boast of the modern world, and which has successively swept away everything else of an analogous character, surely affords, to a conscientious observer of human tendencies, serious matter for reflection. It raises a prima facie presumption on the unfavourable side, far outweighing any which custom and usage could in such circumstances create on the favourable; and should at least suffice to make this, like the choice between republicanism and royalty a balanced question. . . .

Neither does it avail anything to say that the *nature* of the two sexes adapts them to their present functions and position, and renders these appropriate to them. Standing on the ground of common sense and the constitution of the human mind, I deny that any one knows, or can know, the nature of the two sexes, as long as they have only been seen in their present relation to one another. If men had ever been found in society without women, or women without men, or if there had been a society of men and women in which the women were not under the control of the men, something might have been positively known about the mental and moral differences which may be inherent in the nature of each. What is now called the nature of women is an eminently artificial thing—the result of forced repression in some directions, unnatural stimulation in others. It may be asserted without scruple, that no other class of dependents have had their character so entirely distorted from its natural proportions by their relation with their masters; for, if conquered and slave races have been, in some respects, more forcibly repressed, whatever in them has not been crushed down by an iron heel, has generally been let alone, and if left with any liberty of development, it has developed *itself* according to its own laws; but in the case of women, a hot-house and stove cultivation has always been carried on of some of the capabilities of their nature, for the benefit and pleasure of their masters. Then, because certain products of the general vital force sprout luxuriantly and reach a great development in this heated atmosphere and under this active nurture and watering, while other shoots from the same root, which are left outside in the wintry air, with ice purposely heaped all round them, have a stunted growth, and some are burnt off with fire and disappear; men, with that inability to recognize their own work which distinguishes the unanalytic mind, indolently believe that the tree grows of itself in the way they have made it grow, and that it would die if one half of it were not kept in a vapour bath and the other half in the snow.

Of all difficulties which impede the progress of thought, and the formation of well-grounded opinions on life and social arrangements, the greatest is now the unspeakable ignorance and inattention of mankind in respect to the influences which form human character. Whatever any portion of the human species now are, or seem to be, such, it is supposed, they have a natural tendency to be: even when the most elementary knowledge of the circumstances in which they have been placed, clearly points out the causes that made them what they are. Because a cottier deeply in arrears to his landlord is not industrious, there are people who think that the Irish are naturally idle. Because constitutions can be overthrown when the authorities appointed to execute them turn their arms against them, there are people who think the French incapable of free government. Because the Greeks cheated the Turks, and the Turks only plundered the Greeks, there are persons who think that the Turks are naturally more sincere: and because women, as is often said, care nothing about politics except their personalities, it is supposed that the general good is naturally less interesting to women than to men. History, which is now so much better understood than formerly, teaches another lesson: if only by showing the extraordinary susceptibility of human nature to external influences, and the extreme variableness of those of its manifestations which are supposed to be most universal and uniform. But in history, as in travelling, men usually see only what they already had in their own minds; and few learn much from history, who do not bring much with them to its study.

Hence, in regard to that most difficult question, what are the natural differences between the two sexes—a subject on which it is impossible in the present state of society to obtain complete and correct knowledge—while almost everybody dogmatizes upon it, almost all neglect and make light of the only means by which any partial insight can be obtained into it. This is an analytic study of the most important department of psychology, the laws of the influence of circumstances on character. For, however great and apparently ineradicable the moral and intellectual differences between men and women might be, the evidence of their being natural differences could only be negative. Those only could be inferred to be natural which could not possibly be artificial—the residuum, after deducting every characteristic of either sex which can admit of being explained from education or external circumstances. The profoundest knowledge of the laws of the formation of character is indispensable to entitle any one to affirm even that there is any difference, much more what the difference is, between the two sexes considered as moral and rational beings; and since no one, as yet, has that knowledge (for there is hardly any subject which, in proportion to its importance, has been so little studied), no one is thus far entitled to any positive opinion on the subject.

53

John Stuart Mill and
Thomas Carlyle

....

In addition to the Mill selections above, below are some extracts from
the published controversy between Mill and Thomas Carlyle on the
"Negro Question," occasioned by the emancipation of slaves throughout the British Empire in 1833, and the subsequent economic and
social upheavals that resulted in the West Indies. Thomas Carlyle
(1795–1881), Victorian essayist, historian and man of letters, offered
a diatribe against the "natural laziness" of the black inhabitants of the
West Indies, regarded by him as inferior human beings. Mill's restrained
yet enraged response attacks both Carlyle's racism and his "gospel of
work," and castigates the incomparably detestable practice of slavery.

....

Thomas Carlyle, "Occasional Discourse on the Negro Question"

The Twenty Millions [the Slavery Abolition Act of 1833 provided twenty
million pounds to be paid to slave owners in compensation for their freed
slaves], a mere trifle despatched with a single dash of the pen, are paid; and
far over the sea, we have a few black persons rendered extremely "free"

Thomas Carlyle, "Occasional Discourse on the Negro Question" (in Thomas Carlyle and
John Stuart Mill, *The Nigger Question and the Negro Question* (Appleton-Century-Crofts,
1971), selections from pp. 4, 9-10, 12, 26-29

indeed. Sitting yonder with their beautiful muzzles up to the ears in pump-kins, imbibing sweet pulps and juices; the grinder and incisor teeth ready for ever new work, and the pumpkins cheap as grass in those rich climates. . . .

And first, with regard to the West Indies, it may be laid down as a principle, . . . That no Black man who will not work according to what ability the gods have given him for working, has the smallest right to eat pumpkin, or to any fraction of land that will grow pumpkin, however plentiful such land may be; but has an indisputable and perpetual *right* to be compelled, by the real proprietors of said land, to do competent work for his living. This is the everlasting duty of all men, black or white, who are born into this world. To do competent work, to labour honestly ac-cording to the ability given them; for that and for no other purpose was each one of us sent into this world. . . .

Do I, then, hate the Negro? No; except when the soul is killed out of him, I decidedly like poor Quashee [Carlyle's name for black men]; and find him a pretty kind of man. With a pennyworth of oil, you can make a handsome glossy thing of Quashee, when the soul is not killed in him! A swift, supple fellow; a merry-hearted, grinning, dancing, singing, af-fectionate kind of creature, with a great deal of melody and amenability in his composition. This certainly is a notable fact: The black African, alone of wild-men, can live among men civilised. While all manner of Caribs and others pine into annihilation in presence of the pale faces, he contrives to continue; does not die of a sullen irreconcilable rage, of rum, of brutish laziness and darkness, and fated incompatibility with his new place; but lives and multiplies, and evidently means to abide among us, if we can find the right regulation for him. . . .

For the rest, I never thought the "rights of Negroes" worth much dis-cussing, nor the rights of men in any form; the grand point, as I once said, is the *mights* of men,—what portion of their "rights" they have a chance of getting sorted out, and realised, in this confused world. . . .

West-India Islands, still full of waste fertility, produce abundant pumpkins: pumpkins, however, you will observe, are not the sole requisite for human well-being. No; for a pig they are the one thing needful: but for a man they are only the first of several things needful. The first is here; but the second and remaining, how are they to be got? . . . Who it may be that has a right to raise pumpkins and other produce on those Islands, perhaps none can, except temporarily, decide. . . . Up to this time it is the Saxon British mainly, they hitherto have cultivated with some manfulness: and when some manfuler class of cultivators, stronger, worthier to have such land, abler to bring fruit from it, shall make their appearance,—they, doubt it not, by fortune of war, and other confused negotiation and vicis-situde, will be declared by Nature and Fact to *be* the worthier, and will become proprietors,—perhaps also only for a time. That is the law, I take it; ultimate, supreme, for all lands in all countries under this sky. . . .

And now observe, my friends, it was not Black Quashee, or those he represents, that made those West-India Islands what they are, or can, by any hypothesis, be considered to have the right of growing pumpkins there. For countless ages, since they first mounted oozy, on the back of earth-quakes, from their dark bed in the Ocean deeps, and reeking saluted the tropical Sun, and ever onwards till the European white man first saw them some three short centuries ago, those Islands had produced mere jungle, savagery, poison-reptiles and swamp-malaria: till the white European first saw them, they were as if not created,—their noble elements of cinnamon, sugar, coffee, pepper black and grey, lying all asleep, waiting the white en-chanter who should say to them, Awake! Till the end of human history and the sounding of the Trump of Doom, they might have lain so, had Quashee and the like of him been the only artists in the game. . . . It was not he, then; it was another than he! Never by art of his could one pumpkin have grown there to solace any human throat; nothing but savagery and reeking putre-faction could have grown there. These plentiful pumpkins, I say therefore, are not his: no, they are another's; they are his only under conditions. . . .

If Quashee will not honestly aid in bringing-out those sugars, cin-namons and nobler products of the West-Indian Islands, for the ben-efit of all mankind, then I say neither will the Powers permit Quashee to continue growing pumpkins there for his own lazy benefit; but will shear him out, by and by, like a lazy gourd overshadowing rich ground; him and all that partake with him,—perhaps in a very terrible manner. For . . . the terrible manner is not yet quite extinct with the Destinies in this Universe; nor will it quite cease, I apprehend, for soft sawder or philanthropic stump-oratory now or henceforth. No; the gods wish be-sides pumpkins, that spices and valuable products be grown in their West Indies:—infinitely more they wish, that manful industrious men occupy their West Indies, not indolent two-legged cattle, however "happy" over their abundant pumpkins! Both these things, we may be assured, the im-mortal gods have decided upon, passed their eternal Act of Parliament for: and both of them, though all terrestrial Parliaments and entities oppose it to the death, shall be done. Quashee, if he will not help in bring-ing out the spices, will get himself made a slave again (which state will be a little less ugly than his present one), and with the beneficent whip, since other methods avail not, will be compelled to work.

John Stuart Mill, "The Negro Question"

Sir,

Your last month's Number contains a speech against the "rights of Negroes," the doctrines and spirit of which ought not to pass without remonstrance. The author issues his opinions, or rather ordinances, under imposing auspices; no less than those of the "immortal gods," "The Powers," "the Destinies," announce through him, not only what *will* be, but what *shall* be done; what they "have decided upon, passed their eternal act of parliament for." This is speaking "as one having authority," but authority from whom? If by the quality of the message we may judge of those who sent it, *not* from any powers to whom just or good men acknowledge allegiance. This so-called "eternal Act of Parliament" is no new law, but the old law of the strongest,—a law against which the great teachers of mankind have in all ages protested:—it is the law of force and cunning; the law that whoever is more powerful than another, is "born lord" of that other, the other being born his "servant," who must be "compelled to work" for him by "beneficent whip," if "other methods avail not." I see nothing divine in this injunction. If "the gods will this, it is the first duty of human beings to resist such gods. Omnipotent these "gods" are not, for powers which demand *human* tyranny and injustice cannot accomplish their purpose unless human beings cooperate. The history of human improvement is the record of a struggle by which inch after inch of ground has been wrung from these maleficent powers, and more and more of human life rescued from the iniquitous dominion of the law of might. Much, very much of this work still remains to do; but the progress made in it is the best and greatest achievement yet performed by mankind, and it was hardly to be expected at this period of the world that we should be enjoined, by way of a great reform in human affairs, to begin *un*doing it.

The age, it appears, is ill with a most pernicious disease, which infects all its proceedings, and of which the conduct of this country in regard to the Negroes is a prominent symptom—the Disease of Philanthropy. "Sunk in deep froth-oceans of Benevolence, Fraternity, Emancipation-principle, Christian Philanthropy, and other most amiable-looking, but most baseless, and, in the end, baleful and all-bewildering jargon," the product of "hearts left destitute of any earnest guidance, and disbelieving that there

From John Stuart Mill, "The Negro Question" (in Thomas Carlyle and John Stuart Mill, *The Nigger Question and the Negro Question* (Appleton-Century-Crofts, 1971)), pp. 38-40, 42-44, 46-47.

ever was any, Christian or heathen," the "human species" is "reduced to believe in rose-pink sentimentalism alone." On this alleged condition of the human species I shall have something to say presently. But I must first set my anti-philanthropic opponent right on a matter of fact. He entirely misunderstands the great national revolt of the conscience of this country against slavery and the slave-trade, if he supposes it to have been an affair of sentiment. It depended no more on humane feelings than any cause which so irresistibly appealed to them must necessarily do. Its first victories were gained while the lash yet ruled uncontested in the barrack-yard and the rod in schools, and while men were still hanged by dozens for stealing to the value of forty shillings. It triumphed because it was the cause of justice; and, in the estimation of the great majority of its supporters, of religion. Its originators and leaders were persons of a stern sense of moral obligation, who, in the spirit of the religion of their time, seldom spoke much of benevolence and philanthropy, but often of duty, crime, and sin. For nearly two centuries had negroes, many thousands annually, been seized by force or treachery and carried off to the West Indies to be worked to death, literally to death; for it was the received maxim, the acknowledged dictate of good economy, to wear them out quickly and import more. In this fact every other possible cruelty, tyranny, and wanton oppression was by implication included. And the motive on the part of the slave-owners was the love of gold; or, to speak more truly, of vulgar and puerile ostentation. I have yet to learn that anything more detestable than this has been done by human beings towards human beings in any part of the earth. . . .

A black man working no more than your contributor affirms that they work, is, he says, "an eye-sorrow," a "blister on the skin of the state," and many other things equally disagreeable; to *work* being the grand duty of man. "To do competent work, to labour honestly according to the ability given them; for that, and for no other purpose, was each one of us sent into this world." Whoever prevents him from his "sacred appointment to labour while he lives on earth" is "his deadliest enemy." If it be "his own indolence" that prevents him, "the first *right* he has" is that all wiser and more industrious persons shall, "by some wise means, compel him to do the work he is fit for." Why not at once say that, by "some wise means," every thing should be made right in the world? While we are about it, wisdom may as well be suggested as the remedy for all evils, as for one only. Your contributor incessantly prays Heaven that all persons, black and white, may be put in possession of this "divine right of being compelled, if permitted will not serve, to do what work they are appointed for." But as this cannot be conveniently managed just yet, he will begin with the blacks, and will make them work *for* certain whites, those whites *not* working at all; that so "the eternal purpose and supreme will" may be fulfilled, and "injustice," which is "for ever accursed," may cease.

This pet theory of your contributor about work, we all know well enough, though some persons might not be prepared for so bold an application of it. Let me say a few words on this "gospel of work"—which, to my mind, as justly deserves the name of a cant as any of those which he has opposed, while the truth it contains is immeasurably farther from being the whole truth than that contained in the words Benevolence, Fraternity, or any other of his catalogue of contemptibilities. To give it a rational meaning, it must first be known what he means by work. Does work mean *every* thing which people *do*? No; or he would not reproach people with doing no work. Does it mean laborious exertion? No; for many a day spent in killing game, includes more muscular fatigue than a day's ploughing. Does it mean *useful* exertion? But your contributor always scoffs at the idea of utility. Does he mean that all persons ought to earn their living? But some earn their living by doing nothing, and some by doing mischief; and the negroes, whom he despises, still do earn by labour the "pumpkins" they consume and the finery they wear.

Work, I imagine, is not a good in itself. There is nothing laudable in work for work's sake. To work voluntarily for a worthy object is laudable; but what constitutes a worthy object? On this matter, the oracle of which your contributor is the prophet has never yet been prevailed on to declare itself. He revolves in an eternal circle round the idea of work, as if turning up the earth, or driving a shuttle or a quill, were ends in themselves, and the ends of human existence. Yet, even in the case of the most sublime service to humanity, it is not because it is work that it is worthy; the worth lies in the service itself, and in the will to render it—the noble feelings of which it is the fruit; and if the nobleness of will is proved by other evidence than work, as for instance by danger or sacrifice, there is the same worthiness. While we talk only of work, and not of its object, we are far from the root of the matter; or if it may be called the root, it is a root without flower or fruit.

In the present case, it seems, a noble object means "spices." "The gods wish, besides pumpkins, that spices and valuable products be grown in their West Indies"—the "noble elements of cinnamon, sugar, coffee, pepper black and grey," "things far nobler than pumpkins." Why so? Is what supports life, inferior in dignity to what merely gratifies the sense of taste? Is it the verdict of the "immortal gods" that pepper is noble, freedom (even freedom from the lash) contemptible? But spices lead "towards commerces, arts, politics, and social developments." Perhaps so; but of what sort? When they must be produced by slaves, the "politics and social developments" they lead to are such as the world, I hope, will not choose to be cursed with much longer.

The worth of work does not surely consist in its leading to other work, and so on to work upon work without end. On the contrary, the multiplication of work, for purposes not worth caring about, is one of the evils of our present condition. When justice and reason shall be the rule of human affairs, one of the first things to which we may expect them to be applied is the question, How many of the so-called luxuries, conveniences, refinements, and ornaments of life, are *worth* the labour which must be undergone as the condition of producing them? The beautifying of existence is as worthy and useful an object as the sustaining of it; but only a vitiated taste can see any such result in those fopperies of so-called civilization, which myriads of hands are now occupied and lives wasted in providing. In opposition to the "gospel of work," I would assert the gospel of leisure, and maintain that human beings *cannot* rise to the finer attributes of their nature compatibly with a life filled with labour. I do not include under the name labour such work, if work it be called, as is done by writers and afforders of "guidance," an occupation which, let alone the vanity of the thing, cannot be called by the same name with the real labour, the exhausting, stiffening, stupefying toil of many kinds of agricultural and manufacturing labourers. To reduce very greatly the quantity of work required to carry on existence, is as needful as to distribute it more equally; and the progress of science, and the increasing ascendancy of justice and good sense, tend to this result. . . .

But the great ethical doctrine of the Discourse, than which a doctrine more damnable, I should think, never was propounded by a professed moral reformer, is, that one kind of human beings are born servants to another kind. "You will have to be servants," he tells the negroes, "to those that are born *wiser* than you, that are born lords of you—servants to the whites, if they are (as what mortal can doubt that they are?) born wiser than you." I do not hold him to the absurd letter of his dictum; it belongs to the mannerism in which he is enthralled like a child in swaddling clothes. By "born wiser," I will suppose him to mean, born more capable of wisdom: a proposition which, he says, no mortal can doubt, but which I will make bold to say, that a full moiety [half] of all thinking persons, who have attended to the subject, either doubt or positively deny. Among the things for which your contributor professes entire disrespect, is the analytical examination of human nature. It is by analytical examination that we have learned whatever we know of the laws of external nature; and if he had not disdained to apply the same mode of investigation to the laws of the formation of character, he would have escaped the vulgar error of imputing every difference which he finds among human beings to an original difference of nature. As well might it be said, that of two trees, sprung from the same stock, one cannot be taller than another but from greater vigour in the original seeding. Is nothing to be attributed to soil, nothing to climate, nothing to difference of exposure—has no storm swept over the one and not the other, no lightning scathed it, no beast browsed on it, no insects preyed on it, no passing stranger stript off its leaves or its bark? If the trees grew near together, may not the one which, by whatever accident, grew up first, have retarded the other's development by its shade? Human beings are subject to an infinitely greater variety of accidents and external influences than trees, and have infinitely more operation in impairing the growth of one another; since those who begin by being strongest, have almost always hitherto used their strength to keep the others weak. What the original differences are among human beings, I know no more than your contributor, and no less; it is one of the questions not yet satisfactorily answered in the natural history of the species. This, however, is well known—that spontaneous improvement, beyond a very low grade,—improvement by internal development, without aid from other individuals or peoples—is one of the rarest phenomena in history; and whenever known to have occurred, was the result of an extraordinary combination of advantages; in addition doubtless to many accidents of which all trace is now lost. No argument against the capacity of negroes for improvement, could be drawn from their not being one of these rare exceptions. It is curious withal, that the earliest known civilization was, we have the strongest reason to believe, a negro civilization. The original Egyptians are inferred, from the evidence of their sculptures, to have been a negro race; it was from negroes, therefore, that the Greeks learnt their first lessons in civilization; and to the records and traditions of these negroes did the Greek philosophers to the very end of their career resort (I do not say with much fruit) as a treasury of mysterious wisdom. But I again renounce all advantage from facts: were the whites born ever so superior in intelligence to the blacks, and competent by nature to instruct and advise them, it would not be the less monstrous to assert that they had therefore a right either to subdue them by force, or circumvent them by superior skill; to throw upon them the toils and hardships of life, reserving for themselves, under the misapplied name of work, its agreeable excitements.

54

Charles Darwin

....

The contribution made by the British naturalist Charles Darwin (1809–1882) to the study of humanity's place in the world can hardly be overstated. The theory of evolution by natural selection, first put forward in *The Origin of Species*, was subsequently applied to human beings in a thoroughgoing manner in *The Descent of Man*: in that later book, humans were shown to have "descended from some pre-existing form" and the differences between humans and nonhuman animals are claimed to be merely differences of degree. After a brief passage from Darwin's early notebooks illustrating his materialist outlook, the first major set of extracts is drawn from *The Origin of Species*, and illustrates the Malthusian vision of permanent struggle that permeates Darwin's conception of existence. The remainder is extracted from the *Descent of Man* and concern the development of humans from an ancient primate ancestor and Darwin's thoughts concerning language, reason and morality, none of which is regarded as a uniquely human possession. A final extract gives a taste of Darwin's views regarding the differences between the sexes.

....

Notebooks 1836–1844 [c. 1838]

Thought (or desires more properly) being hereditary.—it is difficult to imagine it anything but structure of brain hereditary.—analogy points out this.—love of the deity effect of organization. oh you Materialist!...

From *Charles Darwin's Notebooks 1836-1844* (Ithaca, NY: Cornell University Press, 1987), pp. 291, 300.

Why is thought, being a secretion of the brain, more wonderful than gravity a property of matter? It is our arrogance, it is our admiration of ourselves.—

. . .

Man in his arrogance thinks himself a great work, worthy of the interposition of a deity, more humble and I believe true to consider him created from animals.—

On the Origin of Species

Nothing is easier than to admit in words the truth of the universal struggle for life, or more difficult—at least I have found it so—than constantly to bear this conclusion in mind. Yet unless it be thoroughly engrained in the mind, I am convinced that the entire economy of nature, with every fact on distribution, rarity, abundance, extinction, and variation, will be dimly seen or quite misunderstood. We behold the face of nature bright with gladness, we often see superabundance of food; we do not see, or we forget that the birds which are idly singing round us mostly live on insects or seeds, and are thus constantly destroying life; or we forget how largely these songsters, or their eggs, or their nestlings, are destroyed by birds and beasts of prey; we do not always bear in mind, that though food may be superabundant, it is not so at all seasons of each recurring year. . . .

A struggle for existence inevitably follows from the high rate at which all organic beings tend to increase. Every being, which during its natural lifetime produces several eggs or seeds, must suffer destruction during some period of its life, and during some season or occasional year, otherwise, on the principle of geometrical increase, its numbers would quickly become so inordinately great that no country could support the product. Hence, as more individuals are produced than can possibly survive, there must in every case be a struggle for existence, either one individual with another of the same species, or with the individuals of distinct species, or with the physical conditions of life. It is the doctrine of Malthus applied with manifold force to the whole animal and vegetable kingdoms; for in this case there can be no artificial increase of food, and no prudential restraint from marriage. Although some species may be now increasing, more

From *On the Origin of Species* (Oxford: Oxford University Press, 2008 [1859]), pp. 50-52; 63.

or less rapidly, in numbers, all cannot do so, for the world would not hold them.

There is no exception to the rule that every organic being naturally increases at so high a rate, that if not destroyed, the earth would soon be covered by the progeny of a single pair. Even slow-breeding man has doubled in twenty-five years, and at this rate, in a few thousand years, there would literally not be standing room for his progeny. Linnæus has calculated that if an animal plant produced only two seeds—and there is no plant so unproductive as this—and their seedlings next year produced two, and so on, then in twenty years there would be a million plants. The elephant is reckoned the slowest breeder of all known animals, and I have taken some pains to estimate its probable minimum rate of natural increase: it will be under the mark to assume that it breeds when thirty years old, and goes on breeding till ninety years old, bringing forth three pair of young in this interval; if this be so, at the end of the fifth century there would be alive fifteen million elephants, descended from the first pair. . . .

How will the struggle for existence, discussed too briefly in the last chapter, act in regard to variation? Can the principle of selection, which we have seen is so potent in the hands of man, apply in nature? I think we shall see that it can act most effectually. Let it be borne in mind in what an endless number of strange peculiarities our domestic productions, and, in a lesser degree, those under nature, vary; and how strong the hereditary tendency is. Under domestication, it may be truly said that the whole organization becomes in some degree plastic. Let it be borne in mind how infinitely complex and close-fitting are the mutual relations of all organic beings to each other and to their physical conditions of life. Can it, then, be thought improbable, seeing that variations useful in some way to each being in the great complex battle of life, should sometimes occur in the course of thousands of generations? If such do occur, can we doubt (remembering that many more individuals are born than can possibly survive) that individuals having any advantage, however slight, over others, would have the best chance of surviving and of procreating their kind? On the other hand, we may feel sure that any variation in the least degree injurious would be rigidly destroyed. This preservation of favourable variations and the rejection of injurious variations, I call Natural Selection.

The Descent of Man

He who wishes to decide whether man is the modified descendant of some pre-existing form, would probably first enquire whether man varies, however slightly, in bodily structure and in mental faculties; and if so, whether the variations are transmitted to his offspring in accordance with the laws which prevail with the lower animals. Again, are the variations the result, as far as our ignorance permits us to judge, of the same general causes, and are they governed by the same general laws, as in the case of other organisms; for instance, by correlation, the inherited effects of use and disuse, &c.? Is man subject to similar malconformations, the result of arrested development, of reduplication of parts, &c., and does he display in any of his anomalies reversion to some former and ancient type of structure? It might also naturally be enquired whether man, like so many other animals, has given rise to varieties and sub-races, differing but slightly from each other, or to races differing so much that they must be classed as doubtful species? How are such races distributed over the world; and how, when crossed, do they react on each other in the first and succeeding generations? And so with many other points.

The enquirer would next come to the important point, whether man tends to increase at so rapid a rate, as to lead to occasional severe struggles for existence; and consequently to beneficial variations, whether in body or mind, being preserved, and injurious ones eliminated. Do the races or species of men, whichever term may be applied, encroach on and replace one another, so that some finally become extinct? We shall see that all these questions, as indeed is obvious in respect to most of them, must be answered in the affirmative, in the same manner as with the lower animals.

. . .

If it be an advantage to man to stand firmly on his feet and to have his hands and arms free, of which, from his pre-eminent success in the battle of life, there can be no doubt, then I can see no reason why it should not have been advantageous to the progenitors of man to have become more and more erect or bipedal. They would thus have been better able to defend themselves with stones or clubs, to attack their prey, or otherwise to obtain food. The best built individuals would in the long run have succeeded best, and have survived in larger numbers.

From *The Descent of Man* (London: Penguin, 2004 [1871]), pp. 21–22, 71–74, 86, 89–91, 96 & 99, 100–101, 106–108, 120–122 & 123–124, 154–158, 629.

. . .

As the progenitors of man became more and more erect, with their hands and arms more and more modified for prehension and other purposes, with their feet and legs at the same time transformed for firm support and progression, endless other changes of structure would have become necessary. The pelvis would have to be broadened, the spine peculiarly curved, and the head fixed in an altered position, all which changes have been attained by man. . . . Various other structures, which appear connected with man's erect position, might here have been added. It is very difficult to decide how far these correlated modifications are the result of natural selection, and how far of the inherited effects of the increased use of certain parts, or of the action of one part on another. No doubt these means of change often co-operate: thus when certain muscles, and the crests of bone to which they are attached, become enlarged by habitual use, this shews that certain actions are habitually performed and must be serviceable. Hence the individuals which performed them best, would tend to survive in greater numbers.

The free use of the arms and hands, partly the cause and partly the result of man's erect position, appears to have led in an indirect manner to other modifications of structure. The early male forefathers of man were, as previously stated, probably furnished with great canine teeth; but as they gradually acquired the habit of using stones, clubs, or other weapons, for fighting with their enemies or rivals, they would use their jaws and teeth less and less. In this case, the jaws, together with the teeth, would become reduced in size, as we may feel almost sure from innumerable analogous cases.

. . .

As the various mental faculties gradually developed themselves, the brain would almost certainly become larger. No one, I presume doubts that the large proportion which the size of man's brain bears to his body, compared to the same proportion in the gorilla or orang, is closely connected with his higher mental powers.

. . .

My object in this chapter is to show that there is no fundamental difference between man and the higher mammals in their mental faculties.

. . .

To return to our immediate subject: the lower animals, like man, manifestly feel pleasure and pain, happiness and misery. Happiness is never better exhibited than by young animals, such as puppies, kittens, lambs, &c., when playing together, like our own children. Even insects play together, as has been described by that excellent observer, P. Huber who saw ants chasing and pretending to bite each other, like so many puppies.

The fact that the lower animals are excited by the same emotions as ourselves is so well established, that it will not be necessary to weary the reader by many details. Terror acts in the same manner on them as on us, causing the muscles to tremble, the heart to palpitate, the sphincters to be relaxed, and the hair to stand on end. Suspicion, the offspring of fear, is eminently characteristic of most wild animals. It is, I think, impossible to read the account given by Sir E. Tennent, of the behaviour of the female elephants, used as decoys, without admitting that they intentionally practise deceit, and well know what they are about. Courage and timidity are extremely variable qualities in the individuals of the same species, as is plainly seen in our dogs. Some dogs and horses are ill-tempered; and these qualities are certainly inherited. Every one knows how liable animals are to furious rage, and how plainly they show it. Many, and probably true, anecdotes have been published on the long-delayed and artful revenge of various animals. The accurate Rengger, and Brehm state that the American and African monkeys which they kept tame, certainly revenged themselves. Sir Andrew Smith, a zoologist whose scrupulous accuracy was known to many persons, told me the following story of which he was himself an eye-witness; at the Cape of Good Hope an officer had often plagued a certain baboon, and the animal, seeing him approaching one Sunday for parade, poured water into a hole and hastily made some thick mud, which he skilfully dashed over the officer as he passed by, to the amusement of many bystanders. For long afterwards the baboon rejoiced and triumphed whenever he saw his victim.

The love of a dog for his master is notorious; as an old writer quaintly says, "A dog is the only thing on this earth that luvs you more than he luvs himself."

In the agony of death a dog has been known to caress his master, and every one has heard of the dog suffering under vivisection, who licked the hand of the operator; this man, unless the operation was fully justified by an increase of our knowledge, or unless he had a heart of stone, must have felt remorse to the last hour of his life.

As Whewell has well asked, "who that reads the touching instances of maternal affection, related so often of the women of all nations, and of the females of all animals, can doubt that the principle of action is the same in the two cases?" We see maternal affection exhibited in the most trifling details; thus Rengger observed an American monkey (a Cebus) carefully driving away the flies which plagued her infant; and Duvaucel saw a Hylobates washing the faces of her young ones in a stream. So intense is the grief of female monkeys for the loss of their young that it invariably caused the death of certain kinds kept under confinement by Brehm in N. Africa. Orphan monkeys were always adopted and carefully guarded by the other monkeys, both males and females. One female baboon had so capacious a heart that she not only adopted young monkeys of other species, but stole young dogs and cats, which she continually carried about.

. . .

Of all the faculties of the human mind, it will, I presume, be admitted that *Reason* stands at the summit. Only a few persons now dispute that animals possess some power of reasoning. Animals may constantly be seen to pause, deliberate, and resolve.

. . .

The promptings of reason, after very short experience, are well shewn by the following actions of American monkeys, which stand low in their order. Rengger, a most careful observer, states that when he first gave eggs to his monkeys in Paraguay, they smashed them, and thus lost much of their contents; afterwards they gently hit one end against some hard body, and picked off the bits of shell with their fingers. After cutting themselves only *once* with any sharp tool, they would not touch it again, or would handle it with the greatest caution. Lumps of sugar were often given them wrapped up in paper; and Rengger sometimes put a live wasp in the paper, so that in hastily unfolding it they got stung; after this had *once* happened, they always first held the packet to their ears to detect any movement within.

. . .

It has, I think, now been shewn that man and the higher animals, especially the Primates, have some few instincts in common. All have the same senses, intuitions, and sensations—similar passions, affections, and emotions, even the more complex ones, such as jealousy, suspicion, emulation, gratitude, and magnanimity; they practise deceit and are revengeful; they are sometimes susceptible to ridicule, and even have a sense of humour; they feel wonder and curiosity; they possess the same faculties of imitation, attention, deliberation, choice, memory, imagination, the association of ideas, and reason, though in very different degrees. The individuals of the same species graduate in intellect from absolute imbecility to high excellence. They are also liable to insanity, though far less often than in the case of man. Nevertheless, many authors have insisted that man is divided by an insuperable barrier from all the lower animals in his mental faculties. I formerly made a collection of above a score of such aphorisms, but they are almost worthless, as their wide difference and number prove the difficulty, if not the impossibility, of the attempt. It has been asserted that man alone is capable of progressive improvement; that he alone makes use of tools or fire, domesticates other animals, or possesses property; that no animal has the power of abstraction, or of forming general concepts, is self-conscious and comprehends itself; that no animal employs language; that man alone has a sense of beauty, is liable to caprice, has the feeling of gratitude, mystery, &c.; believes in God, or is endowed with a conscience. I will hazard a few remarks on the more important and interesting of these points.

Archbishop Sumner formerly maintained that man alone is capable of progressive improvement. That he is capable of incomparably greater and more rapid improvement than is any other animal, admits of no dispute; and this is mainly due to his power of speaking and handing down his acquired knowledge. With animals, looking first to the individual, every one who has had any experience in setting traps, knows that young animals can be caught much more easily than old ones; and they can be much more easily approached by an enemy. Even with respect to old animals, it is impossible to catch many in the same place and in the same kind of trap, or to destroy them by the same kind of poison; yet it is improbable that all should have partaken of the poison, and impossible that all should have been caught in a trap. They must learn caution by seeing their brethren caught or poisoned. In North America, where the fur-bearing animals have long been pursued, they exhibit, according to the unanimous testimony of all observers, an almost incredible amount of sagacity, caution and cunning; but trapping has been there so long carried on, that inheritance may possibly have come into play. I have received several accounts that when telegraphs are first set up in any district, many birds kill themselves by flying against the wires, but that in the course of a very few years they learn to avoid this danger, by seeing, as it would appear, their comrades killed.

. . .

Language—This faculty has justly been considered as one of the chief distinctions between man and the lower animals. But man, as a highly competent judge, Archbishop Whately remarks, "is not the only animal that can make use of language to express what is passing in his mind, and can understand, more or less, what is so expressed by another." In

Paraguay the *Cebus azarae* when excited utters at least six distinct sounds, which excite in other monkeys similar emotions. The movements of the features and gestures of monkeys are understood by us, and they partly understand ours, as Rengger and others declare. It is a more remarkable fact that the dog, since being domesticated, has learnt to bark in at least four or five distinct tones. Although barking is a new art, no doubt the wild parent-species of the dog expressed their feelings by cries of various kinds. With the domesticated dog we have the bark of eagerness, as in the chase; that of anger, as well as growling; the yelp or howl of despair, as when shut up; the baying at night; the bark of joy, as when starting on a walk with his master; and the very distinct one of demand or supplication, as when wishing for a door or window to be opened. According to Houzeau, who paid particular attention to the subject, the domestic fowl utters at least a dozen significant sounds.

The habitual use of articulate language is, however, peculiar to man; but he uses, in common with the lower animals, inarticulate cries to express his meaning, aided by gestures and the movements of the muscles of the face. This especially holds good with the more simple and vivid feelings, which are but little connected with our higher intelligence. Our cries of pain, fear, surprise, anger, together with their appropriate actions, and the murmur of a mother to her beloved child, are more expressive than any words. That which distinguishes man from the lower animals is not the understanding of articulate sounds, for, as every one knows, dogs understand many words and sentences. In this respect they are at the same stage of development as infants, between the ages of ten and twelve months, who understand many words and short sentences, but cannot yet utter a single word. It is not the mere articulation which is our distinguishing character, for parrots and other birds possess this power. Nor is it the mere capacity of connecting definite sounds with definite ideas; for it is certain that some parrots, which have been taught to speak, connect unerringly words with things, and persons with events. The lower animals differ from man solely in his almost infinitely larger power of associating together the most diversified sounds and ideas; and this obviously depends on the high development of his mental powers.

. . .

I fully subscribe to the judgment of those writers who maintain that of all the differences between man and the lower animals, the moral sense or conscience is by far the most important. This sense, as Mackintosh remarks, "has a rightful supremacy over every other principle of human action," it is summed up in that short but imperious word *ought*, so full of high significance. It is the most noble of all the attributes of man, leading him without a moment's hesitation to risk his life for that of a fellow-creature; or after due deliberation, impelled simply by the deep feeling of right or duty, to sacrifice it in some great cause. Immanuel Kant exclaims, "Duty! Wondrous thought, that workest neither by fond insinuation, flattery, nor by any threat, but merely by holding up thy naked law in the soul, and so extorting for thyself always reverence, if not always obedience; before whom all appetites are dumb, however secretly they rebel; whence thy original?"[8]

This great question has been discussed by many writers of consummate ability; and my sole excuse for touching on it is the impossibility of here passing it over; and because, as far as I know, no one has approached it exclusively from the side of natural history. The investigation possesses, also, some independent interest, as an attempt to see how far the study of the lower animals throws light on one of the highest psychical faculties of man.

The following proposition seems to me in a high degree probable—namely, that any animal whatever, endowed with well-marked social instincts, the parental and filial affections being here included, would inevitably acquire a moral sense or conscience, as soon as its intellectual powers had become as well, or nearly as well developed, as in man. For, *firstly*, the social instincts lead an animal to take pleasure in the society of its fellows, to feel a certain amount of sympathy with them and to perform various services for them. The services may be of a definite and evidently instinctive nature; or there may be only a wish and readiness, as with most of the higher social animals, to aid their fellows in certain general ways. But these feelings and services are by no means extended to all the individuals of the same species, only to those of the same association. *Secondly*, as soon as the mental faculties had become highly developed, images of all past actions and motives would be incessantly passing through the brain of each individual; and that feeling of dissatisfaction, or even misery, which invariably results, as we shall hereafter see, from any unsatisfied instinct, would arise, as often as it was perceived that the enduring and always present social instinct had yielded to some other instinct, at the time stronger, but neither enduring in its nature, nor leaving behind it a very vivid impression. It is clear that many instinctive desires, such as that of hunger, are in their nature of short duration; and after

---

[8]   "Metaphysics of Ethics," translated by J. W. Semple, Edinburgh p. 136.

being satisfied, are not readily or vividly recalled. *Thirdly*, after the power of language had been acquired, and the wishes of the community could be expressed, the common opinion how each member ought to act for the public good, would naturally become in a paramount degree the guide to action. But it should be borne in mind that however great weight we may attribute to public opinion, our regard for the approbation and disapprobation of our fellows depends on sympathy, which, as we shall see, forms an essential part of the social instinct, and is indeed its foundation-stone. *Lastly*, habit in the individual would ultimately play a very important part in guiding the conduct of each member; for the social instinct, together with sympathy, is, like any other instinct, greatly strengthened by habit, and so consequently would be obedience to the wishes and judgment of the community.

. . .

Sociability—Animals of many kinds are social; we find even distinct species living together; for example, some American monkeys; and united flocks of rooks, jackdaws, and starlings. Man shews the same feeling in his strong love for the dog, which the dog returns with interest. Every one must have noticed how miserable horses, dogs, sheep, &c., are when separated from their companions, and what strong mutual affection the two former kinds, at least, shew on their reunion. It is curious to speculate on the feelings of a dog, who will rest peacefully for hours in a room with his master or any of the family, without the least notice being taken of him; but if left for a short time by himself, barks or howls dismally. We will confine our attention to the higher social animals; and pass over insects, although, some of these are social, and aid one another in many important ways. The most common mutual service in the higher animals is to warn one another of danger by means of the united senses of all. Every sportsman knows, as Dr. Jaeger remarks, how difficult it is to approach animals in a herd or troop. Wild horses and cattle do not, I believe, make any danger-signal; but the attitude of any one of them who first discovers an enemy, warns the others. Rabbits stamp loudly on the ground with their hind-feet, as a signal: sheep and chamois do the same with their forefeet, uttering likewise a whistle. Many birds, and some mammals, post sentinels, which in the case of seals are said generally to be the females. The leader of a troop of monkeys acts as the sentinel, and utters cries expressive both of danger and of safety. Social animals perform many services for each other: horses nibble, and cows lick each other, on any spot which itches; monkeys search each other for external parasites;

and Brehm states that after a troop of the *Cercopithecus griseo-viridis* has rushed through a thorny brake, each monkey stretches itself on a branch, and another monkey sitting by, "conscientiously" examines its fur, and extracts every thorn or burr.

Animals also render more important services to one another: thus wolves and some other beasts of prey hunt in packs, and aid one another in attacking their victims. Pelicans fish in concert. The Hamadryas baboons turn over stones to find insects, &c.; and when they come to a large one, as many as can stand round, turn it over together and share the booty.

. . .

Turning now to the social and moral faculties. In order that primeval men, or the ape-like pregenitors of man, should become social, they must have acquired the same instinctive feelings, which impel other animals to live in a body; and they no doubt exhibited the same general disposition. They would have felt uneasy when separated from their comrades, for whom they would have felt some degree of love; they would have warned each other of danger, and have given mutual aid in attack or defence. All this implies some degree of sympathy, fidelity, and courage. Such social qualities, the paramount importance of which to the lower animals is disputed by no one, were no doubt acquired by the progenitors of man in a similar manner, namely, through natural selection, aided by inherited habit. When two tribes of primeval man, living in the same country, came into competition, if (other circumstances being equal) the one tribe included a great number of courageous, sympathetic and faithful members, who were always ready to warn each other of danger, to aid and defend each other, this tribe would succeed better and conquer the other. Let it be borne in mind how all-important in the never-ceasing wars of savages, fidelity and courage must be. The advantage which disciplined soldiers have over undisciplined hordes follows chiefly from the confidence which each man feels in his comrades. Obedience, as Mr. Bagehot has well shewn, is of the highest value, for any form of government is better than none. Selfish and contentious people will not cohere, and without coherence nothing can be effected. A tribe rich in the above qualities would spread and be victorious over other tribes: but in the course of time it would, judging from all past history, be in its turn overcome by some other tribe still more highly endowed. Thus the social and moral qualities would tend slowly to advance and be diffused throughout the world.

But, it may be asked, how within the limits of the same tribe did a large number of members first become endowed with these social and moral qualities, and how was the standard of excellence raised? It is extremely doubtful whether the offspring of the more sympathetic and benevolent parents, or of those who were the most faithful to their comrades, would be reared in greater numbers than the children of selfish and treacherous parents belonging to the same tribe. He who was ready to sacrifice his life, as many a savage has been, rather than betray his comrades, would often leave no offspring to inherit his noble nature. The bravest men, who were always willing to come to the front in war, and who freely risked their lives for others, would on an average perish in larger numbers than other men. Therefore it hardly seems probable, that the number of men gifted with such virtues, or that the standard of their excellence, could be increased through natural selection, that is, by the survival of the fittest; for we are not here speaking of one tribe being victorious over another.

Although the circumstances, leading to an increase in the number of those thus endowed within the same tribe, are too complex to be clearly followed out, we can trace some of the probable steps. In the first place, as the reasoning powers and foresight of the members became improved, each man would soon learn that if he aided his fellow-men, he would commonly receive aid in return. From this low motive he might acquire the habit of aiding his fellows; and the habit of performing benevolent actions certainly strengthens the feeling of sympathy which gives the first impulse to benevolent actions. Habits, moreover, followed during many generations probably tend to be inherited.

But another and much more powerful stimulus to the development of the social virtues, is afforded by the praise and the blame of our fellow-men. To the instinct of sympathy, as we have already seen, it is primarily due, that we habitually bestow both praise and blame on others, whilst we love the former and dread the latter when applied to ourselves; and this instinct no doubt was originally acquired, like all the other social instincts, through natural selection. At how early a period the progenitors of man in the course of their development, became capable of feeling and being impelled by, the praise or blame of their fellow-creatures, we cannot of course say. But it appears that even dogs appreciate encouragement, praise, and blame. The rudest savages feel the sentiment of glory, as they clearly show by preserving the trophies of their prowess, by their habit of excessive boasting, and even by the extreme care which they take of their personal appearance and decorations; for unless they regarded the opinion of their comrades, such habits would be senseless.

They certainly feel shame at the breach of some of their lesser rules, and apparently remorse, as shewn by the case of the Australian who grew thin and could not rest from having delayed to murder some other woman, so as to propitiate his dead wife's spirit. Though I have not met with any other recorded case, it is scarcely credible that a savage, who will sacrifice his life rather than betray his tribe, or one who will deliver himself up as a prisoner rather than break his parole, would not feel remorse in his inmost soul, if he had failed in a duty, which he held sacred.

We may therefore conclude that primeval man, at a very remote period, was influenced by the praise and blame of his fellows. It is obvious, that the members of the same tribe would approve of conduct which appeared to them to be for the general good, and would reprobate that which appeared evil. To do good unto others—to do unto others as ye would they should do unto you—is the foundation-stone of morality. It is, therefore, hardly possible to exaggerate the importance during rude times of the love of praise and the dread of blame. A man who was not impelled by any deep, instinctive feeling, to sacrifice his life for the good of others, yet was roused to such actions by a sense of glory, would by his example excite the same wish for glory in other men, and would strengthen by exercise the noble feeling of admiration. He might thus do far more good to his tribe than by begetting offspring with a tendency to inherit his own high character.

With increased experience and reason, man perceives the more remote consequences of his actions, and the self-regarding virtues, such as temperance, chastity, &c., which during early times are, as we have before seen, utterly disregarded, come to be highly esteemed or even held sacred. . . . Ultimately our moral sense or conscience becomes a highly complex sentiment—originating in the social instincts, largely guided by the approbation of our fellow-men, ruled by reason, self-interest, and in later times by deep religious feelings, and confirmed by instruction and habit.

It must not be forgotten that although a high standard of morality gives but a slight or no advantage to each individual man and his children over the other men of the same tribe, yet that an increase in the number of well-endowed men and an advancement in the standard of morality will certainly give an immense advantage to one tribe over another. A tribe including many members who, from possessing in a high degree the spirit of patriotism, fidelity, obedience, courage, and sympathy, were always ready to aid one another, and to sacrifice themselves for the common good, would be victorious over most other tribes; and this would be natural selection. At all times throughout the world tribes have supplanted other tribes; and as morality is one important element in their success, the standard of morality and the number of well-endowed men will thus everywhere tend to rise and increase.

   . . .

Difference in the Mental Powers of the two Sexes—With respect to differences of this nature between man and woman, it is probable that sexual selection has played a highly important part. I am aware that some writers doubt whether there is any such inherent difference; but this is at least probable from the analogy of the lower animals which present other secondary sexual characters. No one disputes that the bull differs in disposition from the cow, the wild-boar from the sow, the stallion from the mare, and, as is well known to the keepers of menageries, the males of the larger apes from the females. Woman seems to differ from man in mental disposition, chiefly in her greater tenderness and less selfishness; and this holds good even with savages. . . . Woman, owing to her maternal instincts, displays these qualities towards her infants in an eminent degree; therefore it is likely that she would often extend them towards her fellow-creatures. Man is the rival of other men; he delights in competition, and this leads to ambition which passes too easily into selfishness. These latter qualities seem to be his natural and unfortunate birthright. It is generally admitted that with woman the powers of intuition, of rapid perception, and perhaps of imitation, are more strongly marked than in man; but some, at least, of these faculties are characteristic of the lower races, and therefore of a past and lower state of civilisation.

The chief distinction in the intellectual powers of the two sexes is shewn by man's attaining to a higher eminence, in whatever he takes up, than can woman—whether requiring deep thought, reason, or imagination, or merely the use of the senses and hands. If two lists were made of the most eminent men and women in poetry, painting, sculpture, music (inclusive both of composition and performance), history, science, and philosophy, with half-a-dozen names under each subject, the two lists would not bear comparison. We may also infer, from the law of the deviation from averages, so well illustrated by Mr. Galton, in his work on "Hereditary Genius," that if men are capable of a decided preeminence over women in many subjects, the average of mental power in man must be above that of woman.

55

=== 𝕭 ===

Frederick Douglass

....

Born into slavery in Maryland, Frederick Douglass (1818–1895) escaped in 1838 and became an active and prominent member of the abolitionist movement. His many writings and speeches on slavery include the classic work of autobiography *My Bondage and My Freedom*. What follows is an extract from a lecture on the nature of slavery, delivered in Rochester, New York, in 1850. In it, Douglass describes how the humanity of a person "possessing a soul, eternal and indestructible; capable of endless happiness, or immeasurable woe" is "smitten and blasted" by the dreadful institution of slavery.

....

The Nature of Slavery

More than twenty years of my life were consumed in a state of slavery. My childhood was environed by the baneful peculiarities of the slave system. I grew up to manhood in the presence of this hydra-headed monster—not as a master—not as an idle spectator—not as the guest of the slaveholder—but as as A SLAVE, eating the bread and drinking the cup of slavery with the most degraded of my brother-bondmen, and sharing with them all the painful conditions of their wretched lot. In consideration of these facts, I feel that I have a right to speak, and to speak *strongly*. Yet, my friends, I feel bound to speak truly.

"The Nature of Slavery" (London: Penguin, 2003 [1855]), pp. 326-332.

Goading as have been the cruelties to which I have been subjected—bitter as have been the trials through which I have passed—exasperating as have been, and still are, the indignities offered to my manhood—I find in them no excuse for the slightest departure from truth in dealing with any branch of this subject.

First of all, I will state, as well as I can, the legal and social relation of master and slave. A master is one—to speak in the vocabulary of the southern states—who claims and exercises a right of property in the person of a fellow-man. This he does with the force of the law and the sanction of southern religion. The law gives the master absolute power over the slave. He may work him, flog him, hire him out, sell him, and, in certain contingencies, *kill* him, with perfect impunity. The slave is a human being, divested of all rights—reduced to the level of a brute—a mere "chattel" in the eye of the law—placed beyond the circle of human brotherhood—cut off from his kind—his name, which the "recording angel" may have enrolled in heaven, among the blest, is impiously inserted in a *master's ledger*, with horses, sheep, and swine. In law, the slave has no wife, no children, no country, and no home. He can own nothing, possess nothing, acquire nothing, but what must belong to another. To eat the fruit of his own toil, to clothe his person with the work of his own hands, is considered stealing. He toils that another may reap the fruit; he is industrious that another may live in idleness; he eats unbolted meal that another may eat the bread of fine flour; he labors in chains at home, under a burning sun and biting lash, that another may ride in ease and splendor abroad; he lives in ignorance that another may be educated; he is abused that another may be exalted; he rests his toil-worn limbs on the cold, damp ground that another may repose on the softest pillow; he is clad in coarse and tattered raiment that another may he arrayed in purple and fine linen; he is sheltered only by the wretched hovel that a master may dwell in a magnificent mansion; and to this condition he is bound down as by an arm of iron.

From this monstrous relation there springs an unceasing stream of most revolting cruelties. The very accompaniments of the slave system stamp it as the offspring of hell itself. To ensure good behavior, the slaveholder relies on the whip; to induce proper humility, he relies on the whip; to rebuke what he is pleased to term insolence, he relies on the whip; to supply the place of wages as an incentive to toil, he relies on the whip; to bind down the spirit of the slave, to imbrute and destroy his manhood, he relics on the whip, the chain, the gag, the thumb-screw, the pillory,

the bowie-knife, the pistol, and the blood-hound. These are the necessary and unvarying accompaniments of the system. Wherever slavery is
found, these horrid instruments are also found. Whether on the coast of
Africa, among the savage tribes, or in South Carolina, among the refined
and civilized, slavery is the same, and its accompaniments one and the
same. It makes no difference whether the slaveholder worships the God
of the christians, or is a follower of Mahomet, he is the minister of the
same cruelty, and the author of the same misery. *Slavery* is always *slavery*;
always the same foul, haggard, and damning scourge, whether found in
the eastern or in the western hemisphere.

There is a still deeper shade to be given to this picture. The physical
cruelties are indeed sufficiently harassing and revolting; but they are as
a few grains of sand on the sea shore, or a few drops of water in the great
ocean, compared with the stupendous wrongs which it inflicts upon the
mental, moral, and religious nature of its hapless victims. It is only when
we contemplate the slave as a moral and intellectual being, that we can
adequately comprehend the unparalleled enormity of slavery, and the intense criminality of the slaveholder. I have said that the slave was a man.
"What a piece of work is man! How noble in reason! How infinite in faculties! In form and moving how express and admirable! In action how
like an angel! In apprehension how like a God! the beauty of the world!
the paragon of animals!"

The slave is a man, "the image of God," but "a little lower than the
angels"; possessing a soul, eternal and indestructible; capable of endless
happiness, or immeasurable woe; a creature of hopes and fears, of affections and passions, of joys and sorrows, and he is endowed with those
mysterious powers by which man soars above the things of time and sense,
and grasps, with undying tenacity, the elevating and sublimely glorious
idea of a God. It is *such* a being that is smitten and blasted. The first work
of slavery is to mar and deface those characteristics of its victims which
distinguish *men* from *things*, and *persons* from *property*. Its first aim is
to destroy all sense of high moral and religious responsibility. It reduces
man to a mere machine. It cuts him off from his Maker, it hides from him
the laws of God, and leaves him to grope his way from time to eternity
in the dark, under the arbitrary and despotic control of a frail, depraved,
and sinful fellow-man. As the serpent-charmer of India is compelled to
extract the deadly teeth of his venomous prey before he is able to handle
him with impunity, so the slaveholder must strike down the conscience of
the slave before he can obtain the entire mastery over his victim.

It is, then, the first business of the enslaver of men to blunt, deaden, and destroy the central principle of human responsibility. Conscience is, to the individual soul, and to society, what the law of gravitation is to the universe. It holds society together; it is the basis of all trust and confidence; it is the pillar of all moral rectitude. Without it, suspicion would take the place of trust; vice would be more than a match for virtue; men would prey upon each other, like the wild beasts of the desert; and earth would become a *hell*.

Nor is slavery more adverse to the conscience than it is to the mind. This is shown by the fact, that in every state of the American Union, where slavery exists, except the state of Kentucky, there are laws absolutely prohibitory of education among the slaves. The crime of teaching a slave to read is punishable with severe fines and imprisonment, and, in some instances, with *death itself.*

Nor are the laws respecting this matter a dead letter. Cases may occur in which they are disregarded, and a few instances may be found where slaves may have learned to read; but such are isolated cases, and only prove the rule. The great mass of slaveholders look upon education among the slaves as utterly subversive of the slave system. I well remember when my mistress first announced to my master that she had discovered that I could read. His face colored at once with surprise and chagrin. He said that "I was ruined, and my value as a slave destroyed; that a slave should know nothing but to obey his master; that to give a negro an inch would lead him to take an ell; that having learned how to read, I would soon want to know how to write; and that by-and-by I would be running away." I think my audience will bear witness to the correctness of this philosophy, and to the literal fulfillment of this prophecy.

It is perfectly well understood at the south, that to educate a slave is to make him discontented with slavery, and to invest him with a power which shall open to him the treasures of freedom; and since the object of the slaveholder is to maintain complete authority over his slave, his constant vigilance is exercised to prevent everything which militates against, or endangers, the stability of his authority. Education being among the menacing influences, and, perhaps, the most dangerous, is, therefore, the most cautiously guarded against.

It is true that we do not often hear of the enforcement of the law, punishing as a crime the teaching of slaves to read, but this is not because of a want of disposition to enforce it. The true reason or explanation of the matter is this: there is the greatest unanimity of opinion among the white population in the south in favor of the policy of keeping the slave in ignorance. There is, perhaps, another reason why the law against education is so seldom violated. The slave is too poor to be able to offer a temptation sufficiently strong to induce a white man to violate it; and it is not to be supposed that in a community where the moral and religious sentiment is in favor of slavery, many martyrs will he found sacrificing their liberty and lives by violating those prohibitory enactments.

As a general rule, then, darkness reigns over the abodes of the enslaved, and "how great is that darkness!"

We are sometimes told of the contentment of the slaves, and are entertained with vivid pictures of their happiness. We are told that they often dance and sing; that their masters frequently give them wherewith to make merry; in fine, that they have little of which to complain. I admit that the slave does sometimes sing, dance, and appear to be merry. But what does this prove? It only proves to my mind, that though slavery is armed with a thousand stings, it is not able entirely to kill the elastic spirit of the bondman. That spirit will rise and walk abroad, despite of whips and chains, and extract from the cup of nature occasional drops of joy and gladness. No thanks to the slaveholder, nor to slavery, that the vivacious captive may sometimes dance in his chains; his very mirth in such circumstances stands before God as an accusing angel against his enslaver.

It is often said, by the opponents of the anti-slavery cause, that the condition of the people of Ireland is more deplorable than that of the American slaves. Far be it from me to underrate the sufferings of the Irish people. They have been long oppressed; and the same heart that prompts me to plead the cause of the American bondman, makes it impossible for me not to sympathize with the oppressed of all lands. Yet I must say that there is no analogy between the two cases. The Irishman is poor, but he is not a slave. He may be in rags, but he is not a slave. He is still the master of his own body, and can say with the poet, "The hand of Douglass is his own." "The world is all before him, where to choose"; and poor as may be my opinion of the British parliament, I cannot believe that it will ever sink to such a depth of infamy as to pass a law for the recapture of fugitive Irishmen! The shame and scandal of kidnapping will long remain wholly monopolized by the American congress. The Irishman has not only the liberty to emigrate from his country, but he has liberty at home. He can write, and speak, and cooperate for the attainment of his rights and the redress of his wrongs.

The multitude can assemble upon all the green hills and fertile plains of the Emerald Isle; they can pour out their grievances, and proclaim their wants without molestation; and the press, that "swift-winged messenger," can bear the tidings of their doings to the extreme bounds of the civilized world. They have their "Conciliation Hall," on the banks of the Liffey, their reform clubs, and their newspapers; they pass resolutions, send forth addresses, and enjoy the right of petition. But how is it with the American slave? Where may he assemble? Where is his Conciliation Hall? Where are his newspapers? Where is his right of petition? Where is his freedom of speech? his liberty of the press? and his right of locomotion? He is said to be happy; happy men can speak. But ask the slave what is his condition—what his state of mind—what he thinks of enslavement? and you had as well address your inquiries to the *silent dead*. There comes no *voice* from the enslaved. We are left to gather his feelings by imagining what ours would be, were our souls in his soul's stead.

If there were no other fact descriptive of slavery, than that the slave is dumb, this alone would be sufficient to mark the slave system as a grand aggregation of human horrors.

Most who are present, will have observed that leading men in this country have been putting forth their skill to secure quiet to the nation. A system of measures to promote this object was adopted a few months ago in congress. The result of those measures is known. Instead of quiet, they have produced alarm; instead of peace, they have brought us war; and so it must ever be.

While this nation is guilty of the enslavement of three millions of innocent men and women, it is as idle to think of having a sound and lasting peace, as it is to think there is no God to take cognizance of the affairs of men. There can be no peace to the wicked while slavery continues in the land. It will be condemned; and while it is condemned there will be agitation. Nature must cease to be nature; man must become monsters; humanity must be transformed; christianity must be exterminated; all ideas of justice and the laws of eternal goodness must be utterly blotted out from the human soul,—ere a system so foul and infernal can escape condemnation, or this guilty republic can have a sound, enduring peace.

56
Karl Marx

The writings of Karl Marx (1818–1883), German philosopher, economist, and revolutionary socialist, contain a wealth of insights on the nature of the human condition. The selections included here constitute a small sampling of these insights. The first, drawn from *The Communist Manifesto* (a work co-authored with Friedrich Engels), illustrates Marx's view of the essentially conflict-ridden nature of human life, the conflicts in question always being between oppressors and oppressed. The second discusses the impoverished and alienated nature of the laboring classes under capitalism. Finally, a selection is included which reveals a central contention of Marx's (historical materialist) outlook, namely that human nature is shaped by economics. The malleability of human nature is a central claim of Marxist theory. "All history," he wrote in *The Poverty of Philosophy*, "is nothing but a continuous transformation of human nature."

The Communist Manifesto

The history of all hitherto existing society is the history of class struggles.

Freeman and slave, patrician and plebeian, lord and serf, guildmaster and journeyman, in a word, oppressor and oppressed, stood in constant opposition to one another, carried on an uninterrupted, now

From Karl Marx, *The Communist Manifesto*, from *Selected Writings* (edited by Lawrence H. Simon) (Indianapolis: Hackett Publishing Company, 1994), pp. 158–159, 168–169.

hidden, now open fight, a fight that each time ended, either in a revolutionary reconstitution of society at large, or in the common ruin of the contending classes.

In the earlier epochs of history, we find almost everywhere a complicated arrangement of society into various orders, a manifold gradation of social rank. In ancient Rome we have patricians, knights, plebeians, slaves; in the Middle Ages, feudal lords, vassals, guild-masters, journeymen, apprentices, serfs; in almost all of these classes, again, subordinate gradations.

The modern bourgeois society that has sprouted from the ruins of feudal society has not done away with class antagonisms. It has but established new classes, new conditions of oppression, new forms of struggle in place of the old ones.

Our epoch, the epoch of the bourgeoisie, possesses, however, this distinctive feature: it has simplified the class antagonisms. Society as a whole is more and more splitting up into two great hostile camps, into two great classes directly facing each other: Bourgeoisie and Proletariat.

. . .

Hitherto, every form of society has been based, as we have already seen, on the antagonism of oppressing and oppressed classes. But in order to oppress a class, certain conditions must be assured to it under which it can, at least, continue its slavish existence. The serf, in the period of serfdom, raised himself to membership in the commune, just as the petty bourgeois, under the yoke of feudal absolutism, managed to develop into a bourgeois. The modern labourer, on the contrary, instead of rising with the progress of industry, sinks deeper and deeper below the conditions of existence of his own class. He becomes a pauper, and pauperism develops more rapidly that population and wealth. And here it becomes evident, that the bourgeoisie is unfit any longer to be the ruling class in society, and to impose its conditions of existence upon society as an over-riding law. It is unfit to rule because it is incompetent to assure an existence to its slave within his slavery, because it cannot help letting him sink into such a state, that it has to feed him, instead of being fed by him. Society can no longer live under this bourgeoisie, in other words, its existence is no longer compatible with society.

The essential condition for the existence, and for the sway of the bourgeois class, is the formation and augmentation of capital; the condition for capital is wage-labour. Wage-labour rests exclusively on competition between labourers. The advance of industry, whose involuntary promoter is the bourgeoisie, replaces the isolation of the labourers, due to competition, by their revolutionary combination, due to association. The development of Modern Industry, therefore, cuts from under its feet the very foundation on which the bourgeoisie produced and appropriates products. What the bourgeoisie, therefore, produces, above all, is its own grave-diggers. Its fall and the victory of the proletariat are equally inevitable.

Economic and Philosophic Manuscripts

Alienated Labor

We have proceeded from the presuppositions of political economy. We have accepted its language and its laws. We presupposed private property, the separation of labor, capital and land, hence of wages, profit of capital and rent, likewise the division of labor, competition, the concept of exchange value, etc. From political economy itself, in its own words, we have shown that the worker sinks to the level of a commodity, the most miserable commodity; that the misery of the worker is inversely proportional to the power and volume of his production; that the necessary result of competition is the accumulation of capital in a few hands and thus the revival of monopoly in a more frightful form; and finally that the distinction between capitalist and landowner, between agricultural laborer and industrial worker, disappears and the whole society must divide into the two classes of *proprietors* and propertyless *workers*.

Political economy proceeds from the fact of private property. It does not explain private property. It grasps the actual, *material* process of private property in abstract and general formulae which it then takes as *laws*. It does not *comprehend* these laws, that is, does not prove them as proceeding from the nature of private property. Political economy does not disclose the reason for the division between capital and labor, between capital and land. When, for example, the relation of wages to profits is determined, the ultimate basis is taken to be the interest of the capitalists; that is, political economy assumes what it should develop. Similarly competition is referred to at every point and explained from external circumstances. Political economy teaches us nothing about the extent to which these external, apparently accidental circumstances are simply the expression of a necessary development. We have seen how political

---

From Karl Marx, *Economic and Philosophic Manuscripts*, from *Selected Writings*, pp. 58-65.

economy regards exchange itself as an accidental fact. The only wheels which political economy puts in motion are *greed* and the *war among the greedy, competition.*

Just because political economy does not grasp the interconnections within the movement, the doctrine of competition could stand opposed to the doctrine of monopoly, the doctrine of freedom of craft to that of the guild, the doctrine of the division of landed property to that of the great estate. Competition, freedom of craft, and division of landed property were developed and conceived only as accidental, deliberate, forced consequences of monopoly, the guild, and feudal property, rather than necessary, inevitable, natural consequences.

We now have to grasp the essential connection among private property, greed, division of labor, capital and landownership, and the connection of exchange with competition, of value with the devaluation of men, of monopoly with competition, etc., and of this whole alienation with the *money-system.*

Let us not put ourselves in a fictitious primordial state like a political economist trying to clarify things. Such a primordial state clarifies nothing. It merely pushes the issue into a gray, misty distance. It acknowledges as a fact or event what it should deduce, namely the necessary relation between two things, for example, between division of labor and exchange. In such a manner theology explains the origin of evil by the fall of man. That is, it asserts as a fact in the form of history what it should explain.

We proceed from a *present* fact of political economy.

The worker becomes poorer the more wealth he produces, the more his production increases in power and extent. The worker becomes a cheaper commodity the more commodities he produces. The *increase in value* of the world of things is directly proportional to the *decrease in value* of the human world. Labor not only produces commodities. It also produces itself and the worker as a *commodity*, and indeed in the same proportion as it produces commodities in general.

This fact simply indicates that the object which labor produces, its product, stands opposed to it as an *alien thing*, as a *power independent* of the producer. The product of labor is labor embodied and made objective in a thing. It is the *objectification* of labor. The realization of labor is its objectification. In the viewpoint of political economy this realization of labor appears as the *diminution of* the worker, the objectification as the *loss of and subservience to the object*, and the appropriation as *alienation*, as externalization.

So much does the realization of labor appear as diminution that the worker is diminished to the point of starvation. So much does objectification appear as loss of the object that the worker is robbed of the most essential objects not only of life but also of work. Indeed, work itself becomes a thing of which he can take possession only with the greatest effort and with the most unpredictable interruptions. So much does the appropriation of the object appear as alienation that the more objects the worker produces, the fewer he can own and the more he falls under the domination of his product, of capital.

All these consequences follow from the fact that the worker is related to the *product of his labor* as to an *alien* object. For it is clear according to this premise: The more the worker exerts himself, the more powerful becomes the alien objective world which he fashions against himself, the poorer he and his inner world become, the less there is that belongs to him. It is the same in religion. The more man attributes to God, the less he retains in himself. The worker puts his life into the object; then it no longer belongs to him but to the object. The greater this activity the poorer is the worker. What the product of his work is, he is not. The greater this product is, the smaller he is himself. The *externalization* of the worker in his product means not only that his work becomes an object, an *external* existence, but also that it exists *outside him* independently, alien, an autonomous power, opposed to him. The life he has given to the object confronts him as hostile and alien.

A Contribution to the Critique of Political Economy

... In the social production of their existence, men inevitably enter into definite relations, which are independent of their will, namely relations of production appropriate to a given stage in the development of their material forces of production. The totality of these relations of production constitutes the economic structure of society, the real foundation, on which arises a legal and political superstructure and to which correspond definite forms of social consciousness. The mode of production of material life conditions the general process of social, political, and intellectual life. It is not the consciousness of men that determines their

From Karl Marx, *A Contribution to the Critique of Political Economy*, from *Selected Writings*, pp. 210–212.

existence, but their social existence that determines their consciousness. At a certain stage of development, the material productive forces of society come into conflict with the existing relations of production or—this merely expresses the same thing in legal terms—with the property relations within the framework of which they have operated hitherto. From forms of development of the productive forces these relations turn into their fetters. Then begins an era of social revolution. The changes in the economic foundation lead sooner or later to the transformation of the whole immense superstructure. In studying such transformations it is always necessary to distinguish between the material transformation of the economic conditions of production, which can be determined with the precision of natural science, and the legal, political, religious, artistic, or philosophic—in short, ideological forms in which men become conscious of this conflict and fight it out. Just as one does not judge an individual by what he thinks about himself, so one cannot judge such a period of transformation by its consciousness, but, on the contrary, this consciousness must be explained from the contradictions of material life, from the conflict existing between the social forces of production and the relations of production. No social formation is ever destroyed before all the productive forces for which it is sufficient have been developed, and new superior relations of production never replace older ones before the material conditions for their existence have matured within the framework of the old society. Mankind thus inevitably sets itself only such tasks as it is able to solve, since closer examination will always show that the problem itself arises only when the material conditions for its solution are already present or at least in the course of formation. In broad outline, the Asiatic, ancient, feudal, and modern bourgeois modes of production may be designated as epochs marking progress in the economic development of society. The bourgeois relations of production are the last antagonistic form of the social process of production—antagonistic not in the sense of individual antagonism but of an antagonism that emanates from the individuals' social conditions of existence—but the productive forces developing within bourgeois society create also the material conditions for a solution of this antagonism. The prehistory of human society accordingly closes with this social formation.

57

Friedrich Nietzsche

The following brief extracts from the writings of the German philosopher Friedrich Nietzsche (1844–1900) illustrate his distinctive contributions to themes explored throughout this anthology: his attack on dualism in the powerful "Despisers of the Body," from *Thus Spake Zarathustra*; his musings on "bad conscience" and how wild instincts are in the case of human beings turned inwards and transformed into a kind of sickness; his exposure of the idea of free will as being merely an "error"; and—from *The Gay Science*—his conception of eternal recurrence, regarded as a world-affirming alternative to the belief in the immortality of the soul, and his memorable recommendation for a happy life: *live dangerously.*

Thus Spake Zarathustra

"The Despisers of the Body"

To the despisers of the body will I speak my word. I wish them neither to learn afresh, nor teach anew, but only to bid farewell to their own bodies,—and thus be dumb.

"Body am I, and soul"—so saith the child. And why should one not speak like children?

"The Despisers of the Body", from *Thus Spake Zarathustra* (in The Philosophy of Nietzsche (New York: Modern Library, 1937), pp. 32-34.

But the awakened one, the knowing one, saith: "Body am I entirely, and nothing more; and soul is only the name of something in the body."

The body is a big sagacity, a plurality with one sense, a war and a peace, a flock and a shepherd.

An instrument of thy body is also thy little sagacity, my brother, which thou callest "spirit"—a little instrument and plaything of thy big sagacity.

"Ego," sayest thou, and art proud of that word. But the greater thing—in which thou art unwilling to believe—is thy body with its big sagacity; it saith not "ego," but doeth it.

What the sense feeleth, what the spirit discerneth, hath never its end in itself. But sense and spirit would fain persuade thee that they are the end of all things: so vain are they.

Instruments and playthings are sense and spirit: behind them there is still the Self. The Self seeketh with the eyes of the senses, it hearkeneth also with the ears of the spirit.

Ever hearkeneth the Self, and seeketh; it compareth, mastereth, conquereth, and destroyeth. It ruleth, and is also the ego's ruler.

Behind thy thoughts and feelings, my brother, there is a mighty lord, an unknown sage—it is called Self; it dwelleth in thy body, it is thy body.

There is more sagacity in thy body than in thy best wisdom. And who then knoweth why thy body requireth just thy best wisdom?

Thy Self laugheth at thine ego, and its proud prancings. "What are these prancings and flights of thought unto me?" it saith to itself. "A by-way to my purpose. I am the leading-string of the ego, and the prompter of its notions."

The Self saith unto the ego: "Feel pain!" And thereupon it suffereth, and thinketh how it may put an end thereto—and for that very purpose it *is meant* to think.

The Self saith unto the ego: "Feel pleasure!" Thereupon it rejoiceth, and thinketh how it may ofttimes rejoice—and for that very purpose it *is meant* to think.

To the despisers of the body will I speak a word. That they despise is caused by their esteem. What is it that created esteeming and despising and worth and will?

The creating Self created for itself esteeming and despising, it created for itself joy and woe. The creating body created for itself spirit, as a hand to its will.

Even in your folly and despising ye each serve your Self, ye despisers of the body. I tell you, your very Self wanteth to die, and turneth away from life.

No longer can your Self do that which it desireth most:—create beyond itself. That is what it desireth most; that is all its fervour.

But it is now too late to do so;—so your Self wisheth to succumb, ye despisers of the body.

To succumb—so wisheth your Self, and therefore have ye become despisers of the body. For ye can no longer create beyond yourselves.

And therefore are ye now angry with life and with the earth. And unconscious envy is in the sidelong look of your contempt.

I go not your way, ye despisers of the body! Ye are no bridges for me to the Superman!—

"Old and Young Women"

. . . Everything in woman is a riddle, and everything in woman hath one solution—it is called pregnancy.

Man is for woman a means: the purpose is always the child. But what is woman for man?

Two different things wanteth the true man: danger and diversion. Therefore wanteth he woman, as the most dangerous plaything.

Man shall be trained for war, and woman for the recreation of the warrior: all else is folly. . . .

Then answered me the old woman: "Many fine things hath Zarathustra said . . . And now accept a little truth by way of thanks!". . .

"Give me, woman, thy little truth!" said I. And thus spake the old woman:

"Thou goest to women? Do not forget thy whip!"—

The Genealogy of Morals

At this juncture I cannot avoid trying to give a tentative and provisional expression to my own hypothesis concerning the origin of the bad conscience: it is difficult to make it fully appreciated, and it requires continuous meditation, attention, and digestion. I regard the bad conscience as the

From Nietzsche, Friedrich, "Old and Young Women", in *Thus Spake Zarathustra* (in The Philosophy of Nietzsche (New York: Modern Library, 1937), pp. 68-69, 70.
From Nietzsche, Friedrich, *The Genealogy of Morals* (in The Philosophy of Nietzsche), pp. 701-703.

serious illness which man was bound to contract under the stress of the most radical change which he has ever experienced—that change, when he found himself finally imprisoned within the pale of society and of peace.

Just like the plight of the water-animals, when they were compelled either to become land-animals or to perish, so was the plight of these half-animals, perfectly adapted as they were to the savage life of war, prowling, and adventure—suddenly all their instincts were rendered worthless and "switched off." Henceforward they had to walk on their feet—"carry themselves," whereas heretofore they had been carried by the water: a terrible heaviness oppressed them. They found themselves clumsy in obeying the simplest directions, confronted with this new and unknown world they had no longer their old guides—the regulative instincts that had led them unconsciously to safety—they were reduced, were those unhappy creatures, to thinking, inferring, calculating, putting together causes and results, reduced to that poorest and most erratic organ of theirs, their "consciousness." I do not believe there was ever in the world such a feeling of misery, such a leaden discomfort—further, those old instincts had not immediately ceased their demands! Only it was difficult and rarely possible to gratify them: speaking broadly, they were compelled to satisfy themselves, by new and, as it were, hole-and-corner methods. All instincts which do not find a vent without, *turn inwards*—this is what I mean by the growing "internalisation" of man: consequently we have the first growth in man, of what subsequently was called his soul. The whole inner world, originally as thin as if it had been stretched between two layers of skin, burst apart and expanded proportionately, and obtained depth, breadth, and height, when man's external outlet became *obstructed*. These terrible bulwarks, with which the social organisation protected itself against the old instincts of freedom (punishments belong pre-eminently to these bulwarks), brought it about that all those instincts of wild, free, prowling man became turned backwards *against man himself*. Enmity, cruelty, the delight in persecution, in surprises, change, destruction—the turning all these instincts against their own possessors: this is the origin of the "bad conscience." It was man, who, lacking external enemies and obstacles, and imprisoned as he was in the oppressive narrowness and monotony of custom, in his own impatience lacerated, persecuted, gnawed, frightened, and ill-treated himself; it was this animal in the hands of the tamer, which beat itself against the bars of its cage; it was this being who, pining and yearning for that desert home of which it had been deprived, was compelled to create out of its own self, an adventure, a torture-chamber, a hazardous and perilous desert—it was this fool, this homesick and desperate prisoner—who invented the "bad conscience." But thereby he introduced that most grave and sinister illness, from which mankind has not yet recovered, the suffering of man from the disease called man, as the result of a violent breaking from his animal past, the result, as it were, of a spasmodic plunge into a new environment and new conditions of existence, the result of a declaration of war against the old instincts, which up to that time had been the staple of his power, his, joy, his formidableness. Let us immediately add that this fact of an animal ego turning against itself, taking part against itself, produced in the world so novel, profound, unheard-of, problematic, inconsistent, and *pregnant* a phenomenon, that the aspect of the world was radically altered thereby. In sooth, only divine spectators could have appreciated the drama that then began, and whose end baffles conjecture as yet—a drama too subtle, too wonderful, too paradoxical to warrant its undergoing a nonsensical and unheeded performance on some random grotesque planet! Henceforth man is to be counted as one of the most unexpected and sensational lucky shots in the game of the "big baby" of Heracleitus, whether he be called Zeus or Chance—he awakens on his behalf the interest, excitement, hope, almost the confidence, of his being the harbinger and forerunner of something, of man being no end, but only a stage, an interlude, a bridge, a great promise.

Twilight of the Idols

The error of free will.—We no longer have any sympathy today with the concept of "free will": we know only too well what it is—the most infamous of all the arts of the theologian for making mankind "accountable" in his sense of the word, that is to say for *making mankind dependent on him.* . . . I give here only the psychology of making men accountable.—Everywhere accountability is sought, it is usually the instinct for *punishing and judging* which seeks it. One has deprived becoming of its innocence if being in this or that state is traced back to will, to intentions, to accountable acts: the doctrine of will has been invented essentially for the purpose of punishment, that is of *finding guilty*. The whole of the old-style psychology, the psychology of will, has as its precondition the desire of its authors, the priests at the head of the ancient communities, to create for themselves a *right* to ordain punishments—or their desire to create for God a right to do so. . . . Men were thought of as "free" so that they could become *guilty*: consequently, every action *had* to be thought of as willed, the origin of every action as lying in the consciousness (—whereby the most *fundamental* falsification *in psychologicis* was made into the very principle of psychology). . . . Today, when we have started to move in the *reverse* direction, when we immoralists especially are trying with all our might to remove the concept of guilt and the concept of punishment from the world and to purge psychology, history, nature, the social institutions and sanctions of them, there is in our eyes no more radical opposition than that of the theologians, who continue to infect the innocence of becoming with "punishment" and "guilt" by the means of the concept of the "moral world-order." Christianity is a hangman's metaphysics.

The Gay Science

283 *Preparatory human beings.*—I welcome all signs that a more virile, warlike age is about to begin, which will restore honor to courage above all. For this age shall prepare the way for one yet higher, and it shall gather the strength that this higher age will require some day—the age that will carry heroism into the search for knowledge and that will *wage wars* for the sake of ideas and their consequences. To this end we now need many preparatory courageous human beings who cannot very well leap out of nothing, any more than out of the sand and slime of present-day civilization and metropolitanism—human beings who know how to be silent, lonely, resolute, and content and constant in invisible activities; human beings who are bent on seeking in all things for what in them must be *overcome*; human beings distinguished as

much by cheerfulness, patience, unpretentiousness, and contempt for all great vanities as by magnanimity in victory and forbearance regarding the small vanities of the vanquished; human beings whose judgment concerning all victors and the share of chance in every victory and fame is sharp and free; human beings with their own festivals, their own working days, and their own periods of mourning, accustomed to command with assurance but instantly ready to obey when that is called for—equally proud, equally serving their own cause in both cases; more endangered human beings, more fruitful human beings, happier beings! For believe me: the secret for harvesting from existence the greatest fruitfulnesss and the greatest enjoyment is—to *live dangerously!* Build your cities on the slopes of Vesuvius! Send your ships into uncharted seas! Live at war with your peers and yourselves! Be robbers and conquerors as long as you cannot be rulers and possessors, you seekers of knowledge! Soon the age will be past when you could be content to live hidden in forests like shy deer. At long last the search for knowledge will reach out for its due; it will want to *rule* and *possess*, and you with it!

. . .

341 *The greatest weight*—What, if some day or night a demon were to steal after you into your loneliest loneliness and say to you: "This life as you now live it and have lived it, you will have to live once more and innumerable times more; and there will be nothing new in it, but every pain and every joy and every thought and sigh and everything unutterably small or great in your life will have to return to you, all in the same succession and sequence—even this spider and this moonlight between the trees, and even this moment and I myself. The eternal hourglass of existence is turned upside down again and again, and you with it, speck of dust!"

Would you not throw yourself down and gnash your teeth and curse the demon who spoke thus? Or have you once experienced a tremendous moment when you would have answered him: "You are a god and never have I heard anything more divine." If this thought gained possession of you, it would change you as you are or perhaps crush you. The question in each and every thing, "Do you desire this once more and innumerable times more?" would lie upon your actions as the greatest weight. Or how well disposed would you have to become to yourself and to life to *crave nothing more fervently* than this ultimate eternal confirmation and seal?

PART SIX

Twentieth Century and Contemporary Voices

58

===== 🐝 =====

Sigmund Freud

One of the towering cultural figures of the twentieth century, Sigmund Freud (1856–1939) was the creator of psychoanalysis, which is both a theory of the workings of the mind and a therapeutic technique for the treatment of mental illnesses. Freud lived in Vienna for most of his long life, but Hitler's invasion of Austria in 1938 forced him into asylum in London, where he died the following year. Five selections from Freud's voluminous writings are included below. The first is a succinct summary of his mature theory of the mind, famously anatomized as consisting of ego, id, and superego. The second reading is taken from *Civilization and Its Discontents*, and illustrates Freud's deeply pessimistic view of the human condition (the possibility of happiness, he tells us, has not been included in the plan of creation). Also from *Civilization and Its Discontents*, the third reading shows Freud immersing himself in the debate between Hobbes and Rousseau, speculating as to how it might be that civilization has contributed to human misery while simultaneously affirming that most Hobbesian of positions: the ineradicable aggression of the human person. Freud's criticisms of Marxist optimism are here also noteworthy. In "On Transience" Freud strikes a more upbeat note, suggesting that the brevity of life adds to our enjoyment of it. The final selection offers a glimpse into Freud's notorious view of the psychology of women, condemned to a sense of inferiority as a consequence of "penis envy."

The Psychical Apparatus

Psycho-analysis makes a basic assumption, the discussion of which is reserved to philosophical thought but the justification for which lies in its results. We know two kinds of things about what we call our psyche (or mental life): firstly, its bodily organ and scene of action, the brain (or nervous system) and, on the other hand, our acts of consciousness, which are immediate data and cannot be further explained by any sort of description. . . .

We have arrived at our knowledge of this psychical apparatus by studying the individual development of human beings. To the oldest of these psychical provinces or agencies we give the name of *id*. It contains everything that is inherited, that is present at birth, that is laid down in the constitution—above all, therefore, the instincts, which originate from the somatic organization and which find a first psychical expression here [in the id] in forms unknown to us.

Under the influence of the real external world around us, one portion of the id has undergone a special development. From what was originally a cortical layer, equipped with the organs for receiving stimuli and with arrangements for acting as a protective shield against stimuli, a special organization has arisen which henceforward acts as an intermediary between the id and the external world. To this region of our mind we have given the name of *ego*.

Here are the principal characteristics of the ego. In consequence of the pre-established connection between sense perception and muscular action, the ego has voluntary movement at its command. It has the task of self-preservation. As regards *external* events, it performs that task by becoming aware of stimuli, by storing up experiences about them (in the memory), by avoiding excessively strong stimuli (through flight), by dealing with moderate stimuli (through adaptation) and finally by learning to bring about expedient changes in the external world to its own advantage (through activity). As regards *internal* events, in relation to the id, it performs that task by gaining control over the demands of the instincts, by deciding whether they are to be allowed satisfaction, by postponing that satisfaction to times and circumstances favourable in the external world or by suppressing their excitations entirely. It is guided in its activity by

From Freud, Sigmund, *An Outline of Psycho-Analysis* (Standard Edition Vol. XXIII), Part I, Chapter I, "The Psychical Apparatus" (pp. 144–147).

consideration of the tensions produced by stimuli, whether these tensions are present in it or introduced into it. The raising of these tensions is in general felt as *unpleasure* and their lowering as *pleasure*. It is probable, however, that what is felt as pleasure or unpleasure is not the *absolute* height of this tension but something in the rhythm of the changes in them. The ego strives after pleasure and seeks to avoid unpleasure. An increase in unpleasure that is expected and foreseen is met by a *signal of anxiety*; the occasion of such an increase, whether it threatens from without or within, is known as a *danger*. From time to time the ego gives up its connection with the external world and withdraws into the state of sleep, in which it makes far-reaching changes in its organization. It is to be inferred from the state of sleep that this organization consists in a particular distribution of mental energy.

The long period of childhood, during which the growing human being lives in dependence on his parents, leaves behind it as a precipitate the formation in his ego of a special agency in which this parental influence is prolonged. It has received the name of *super-ego*. In so far as this super-ego is differentiated from the ego or is opposed to it, it constitutes a third power which the ego must take into account.

An action by the ego is as it should be if it satisfies simultaneously the demands of the id, of the super-ego and of reality—that is to say, if it is able to reconcile their demands with one another. The details of the relation between the ego and the super-ego become completely intelligible when they are traced back to the child's attitude to its parents. This parental influence of course includes in its operation not only the personalities of the actual parents but also the family, racial and national traditions handed on through them, as well as the demands of the immediate social *milieu* which they represent. In the same way, the super-ego, in the course of an individual's development, receives contributions from later successors and substitutes of his parents, such as teachers and models in public life of admired social ideals. It will be observed that, for all their fundamental difference, the id and the super-ego have one thing in common: they both represent the influences of the past—the id the influence of heredity, the super-ego the influence, essentially, of what is taken over from other people—whereas the ego is principally determined by the individual's own experience, that is by accidental and contemporary events.

This general schematic picture of a psychical apparatus may be supposed to apply as well to the higher animals which resemble man mentally. A super-ego must be presumed to be present wherever, as is the case with man, there is a long period of dependence in childhood. A distinction between ego and id is an unavoidable assumption. Animal psychology has not yet taken in hand the interesting problem which is here presented.

Civilization and Its Discontents

Life, as we find it, is too hard for us; it brings us too many pains, disappointments and impossible tasks. In order to bear it we cannot dispense with palliative measures. "We cannot do without auxiliary constructions," as Theodor Fontane tells us. There are perhaps three such measures: powerful deflections, which cause us to make light of our misery; substitutive satisfactions, which diminish it; and intoxicating substances, which make us insensitive to it. Something of the kind is indispensable. Voltaire has deflections in mind when he ends *Candide* with the advice to cultivate one's garden; and scientific activity is a deflection of this kind, too. The substitutive satisfactions, as offered by art, are illusions in contrast with reality, but they are none the less psychically effective, thanks to the role which phantasy has assumed in mental life. The intoxicating substances influence our body and alter its chemistry. It is no simple matter to see where religion has its place in this series. We must look further afield.

The question of the purpose of human life has been raised countless times; it has never yet received a satisfactory answer and perhaps does not admit of one. Some of those who have asked it have added that if it should turn out that life has *no* purpose, it would lose all value for them. But this threat alters nothing. It looks, on the contrary, as though one had a right to dismiss the question, for it seems to derive from the human presumptuousness, many other manifestations of which are already familiar to us. Nobody talks about the purpose of the life of animals, unless, perhaps, it may be supposed to lie in being of service to man. But this view is not tenable either, for there are many animals of which man can make nothing, except to describe, classify and study them; and innumerable species of animals have escaped even this use, since they existed and became extinct before man set eyes on them. Once again, only religion can answer the question of the purpose of life. One can hardly be wrong in concluding that the idea of life having a purpose stands and falls with the religious system.

We will therefore turn to the less ambitious question of what men themselves show by their behaviour to be the purpose and intention of their lives. What do they demand of life and wish to achieve in it? The answer to this can hardly be in doubt. They strive after happiness; they want to become happy and to remain so. This endeavour has two sides, a positive and a negative aim. It aims, on the one hand, at an absence of pain and unpleasure, and, on the other, at the experiencing of strong feelings of pleasure. In its narrower sense the word "happiness" only relates to the last. In conformity with this dichotomy in his aims, man's activity develops in two directions, according as it seeks to realize—in the main, or even exclusively—the one or the other of these aims.

As we see, what decides the purpose of life is simply the programme of the pleasure principle. This principle dominates the operation of the mental apparatus from the start. There can be no doubt about its efficacy, and yet its programme is at loggerheads with the whole world, with the macrocosm as much as with the microcosm. There is no possibility at all of its being carried through; all the regulations of the universe run counter to it. One feels inclined to say that the intention that man should be "happy" is not included in the plan of "Creation." What we call happiness in the strictest sense comes from the (preferably sudden) satisfaction of needs which have been dammed up to a high degree, and it is from its nature only possible as an episodic phenomenon. When any situation that is desired by the pleasure principle is prolonged, it only produces a feeling of mild contentment. We are so made that we can derive intense enjoyment only from a contrast and very little from a state of things. Thus our possibilities of happiness are already restricted by our constitution. Unhappiness is much less difficult to experience. We are threatened with suffering from three directions: from our own body, which is doomed to decay and dissolution and which cannot even do without pain and anxiety as warning signals; from the external world, which may rage against us with overwhelming and merciless forces of destruction; and finally from our relations to other men. The suffering which comes from this last source is perhaps more painful to us than any other. We tend to regard it as a kind of gratuitous addition, although it cannot be any less fatefully inevitable than the suffering which comes from elsewhere.

It is no wonder if, under the pressure of these possibilities of suffering, men are accustomed to moderate their claims to happiness—just as the pleasure principle itself, indeed, under the influence of the external world, changed into the more modest reality principle—, if a man thinks himself happy merely to have escaped unhappiness or to have survived his suffering, and if in general the task of avoiding suffering pushes that of obtaining pleasure into the background. Reflection shows that the accomplishment of this task can be attempted along very different paths; and all these paths have been recommended by the various schools of worldly wisdom and put into practice by men. An unrestricted satisfaction of every need presents itself as the most enticing method of conducting one's life, but it means putting enjoyment before caution, and soon brings its own punishment. The other methods, in which avoidance of unpleasure is the main purpose, are differentiated according to the source of unpleasure to which their attention is chiefly turned. Some of these methods are extreme and some moderate; some are one-sided and some attack the problem simultaneously at several points. Against the suffering which may come upon one from human relationships the readiest safeguard is voluntary isolation, keeping oneself aloof from other people. The happiness which can be achieved along this path is, as we see, the happiness of quietness. Against the dreaded external world one can only defend oneself by some kind of turning away from it, if one intends to solve the task by oneself. There is, indeed, another and better path: that of becoming a member of the human community, and, with the help of a technique guided by science, going over to the attack against nature and subjecting her to the human will. Then one is working with all for the good of all. But the most interesting methods of averting suffering are those which seek to influence our own organism. In the last analysis, all suffering is nothing else than sensation; it only exists in so far as we feel it, and we only feel it in consequence of certain ways in which our organism is regulated.

The crudest, but also the most effective among these methods of influence is the chemical one—intoxication. I do not think that anyone completely understands its mechanism, but it is a fact that there are foreign substances which, when present in the blood or tissues, directly cause us pleasurable sensations; and they also so alter the conditions governing our sensibility that we become incapable of receiving unpleasurable impulses. The two effects not only occur simultaneously, but seem to be intimately bound up with each other. But there must be substances in the chemistry of our own bodies which have similar effects, for we know at least one pathological state, mania, in which a condition similar to intoxication arises without the administration of any intoxicating drug. Besides this, our normal mental life exhibits oscillations between a comparatively easy liberation of pleasure and a comparatively difficult one, parallel with which there goes a diminished or an increased receptivity to unpleasure. It is greatly to be regretted that this toxic side of mental processes has so far escaped scientific examination. The service rendered by intoxicating media in the struggle for happiness and in keeping misery at a distance is so highly prized as a benefit that individuals and peoples alike have given them an established place in the economics of their libido. We owe to such media not merely the immediate yield of pleasure, but also a greatly desired degree of independence from the external world. For one knows that, with the help of this "drowner of cares" one can at any time withdraw from the pressure of reality and find refuge in a world of one's own with better conditions of sensibility. As is well known, it is precisely this property of intoxicants which also determines their danger and their injuriousness. They are responsible, in certain circumstances, for the useless waste of a large quota of energy which might have been employed for the improvement of the human lot.

The complicated structure of our mental apparatus admits, however, of a whole number of other influences. Just as a satisfaction of instinct spells happiness for us, so severe suffering is caused us if the external world lets us starve, if it refuses to sate our needs. One may therefore hope to be freed from a part of one's sufferings by influencing the instinctual impulses. This type of defence against suffering is no longer brought to bear on the sensory apparatus; it seeks to master the internal sources of our needs. The extreme form of this is brought about by killing off the instincts, as is prescribed by the worldly wisdom of the East and practised by Yoga. If it succeeds, then the subject has, it is true, given up all other activities as well—he has sacrificed his life; and, by another path, he has once more only achieved the happiness of quietness. We follow the same path when our aims are less extreme and we merely attempt to *control* our instinctual life. In that case, the controlling elements are the higher psychical agencies, which have subjected themselves to the reality principle. Here the aim of satisfaction is not by any means relinquished; but a certain amount of protection against suffering is secured, in that non-satisfaction is not so painfully felt in the case of instincts kept in dependence as in the case of uninhibited ones. As against this, there is an undeniable diminution in the potentialities of enjoyment. The feeling of happiness derived from the satisfaction of a wild instinctual impulse untamed by the ego is incomparably more intense than that derived from sating an instinct that has been tamed. The irresistibility of perverse instincts, and perhaps the attraction in general of forbidden things, finds an economic explanation here.

Another technique for fending off suffering is the employment of the displacements of libido which our mental apparatus permits of and through which its function gains so much in flexibility. The task here is that of shifting the instinctual aims in such a way that they cannot come up against frustration from the external world. In this, sublimation of the instincts lends its assistance. One gains the most if one can sufficiently heighten the yield of pleasure from the sources of psychical and intellectual work. When that is so, fate can do little against one. A satisfaction of this kind, such as an artist's joy in creating, in giving his phantasies body, or a scientist's in solving problems or discovering truths, has a special quality which we shall certainly one day be able to characterize in metapsychological terms. At present we can only say figuratively that such satisfactions seem "finer and higher." But their intensity is mild as compared with that derived from the sating of crude and primary instinctual impulses; it does not convulse our physical being. And the weak point of this method is that it is not applicable generally: it is accessible to only a few people. It presupposes the possession of special dispositions and gifts which are far from being common to any practical degree. And even to the few who do possess them, this method cannot give complete protection from suffering. It creates no impenetrable armour against the arrows of fortune, and it habitually fails when the source of suffering is a person's own body.

While this procedure already clearly shows an intention of making oneself independent of the external world by seeking satisfaction in internal, psychical processes, the next procedure brings out those features yet more strongly. In it, the connection with reality is still further loosened; satisfaction is obtained from illusions, which are recognized as such without the discrepancy between them and reality being allowed to interfere with enjoyment. The region from which these illusions arise is the life of the imagination; at the time when the development of the sense of reality took place, this region was expressly exempted from the demands of reality-testing and was set apart for the purpose of fulfilling wishes which were difficult to carry out. At the head of these satisfactions through phantasy stands the enjoyment of works of art—an enjoyment which, by the agency of the artist, is made accessible even to those who are not themselves creative. People who are receptive to the influence of art cannot set too high a value on it as a source of pleasure and consolation in life. Nevertheless the mild narcosis induced in us by art can do no more than bring about a transient withdrawal from the pressure of vital needs, and it is not strong enough to make us forget real misery.

Another procedure operates more energetically and more thoroughly. It regards reality as the sole enemy and as the source of all suffering, with which it is impossible to live, so that one must break off all relations with it if one is to be in any way happy. The hermit turns his back on the world and will have no truck with it. But one can do more than that; one can try to re-create the world, to build up in its stead another world in which its most unbearable features are eliminated and replaced by others that are in conformity with one's own wishes. But whoever, in desperate defiance, sets out upon this path to happiness will as a rule attain nothing. Reality is too strong for him. He becomes a madman, who for the most part finds no one to help him in carrying through his delusion. It is asserted, however, that each one of us behaves in some one respect like a paranoic, corrects some aspect of the world which is unbearable to him by the construction of a wish and introduces this delusion into reality. A special importance attaches to the case in which this attempt to procure a certainty of happiness and a protection against suffering through a delusional remoulding of reality is made by a considerable number of people in common. The religions of mankind must be classed among the mass-delusions of this kind. No one, needless to say, who shares a delusion ever recognizes it as such.

I do not think that I have made a complete enumeration of the methods by which men strive to gain happiness and keep suffering away and I know, too, that the material might have been differently arranged. One procedure I have not yet mentioned—not because I have forgotten it but because it will concern us later in another connection. And how could one possibly forget, of all others, this technique in the art of living? It is conspicuous for a most remarkable combination of characteristic features. It, too, aims of course at making the subject independent of Fate (as it is best to call it), and to that end it locates satisfaction in internal mental processes, making use, in so doing, of the displaceability of the libido of which we have already spoken. But it does not turn away from the external world; on the contrary, it clings to the objects belonging to that world and obtains happiness from an emotional relationship to them. Nor is it content to aim at an avoidance of unpleasure—a goal, as we might call it, of weary resignation; it passes this by without heed and holds fast to the original, passionate striving for a positive fulfilment of happiness. And perhaps it does in fact come nearer to this goal than any other method. I am, of course, speaking of the way of life which makes love the centre of everything, which looks for all satisfaction in loving and being loved. A psychical attitude of this sort comes naturally enough to all of us; one of the forms in which love manifests itself—sexual love—has given us our most intense experience of an overwhelming sensation of pleasure and has thus furnished us with a pattern for our search for happiness. What is more natural than that we should persist in looking for happiness along the path on which we first encountered it? The weak side of this technique of living is easy to see; otherwise no human being would have thought of abandoning this path to happiness for any other. It is that we are never so defenceless against suffering as when we love, never so helplessly unhappy as when we have lost our loved object or its love. But this does not dispose of the technique of living based on the value of love as a means to happiness. There is much more to be said about it.

We may go on from here to consider the interesting case in which happiness in life is predominantly sought in the enjoyment of beauty, wherever beauty presents itself to our senses and our judgement—the beauty of human forms and gestures, of natural objects and landscapes and of artistic and even scientific creations. This aesthetic attitude to the goal of life offers little protection against the threat of suffering, but it can compensate for a great deal. The enjoyment of beauty has a peculiar, mildly intoxicating quality of feeling. Beauty has no obvious use; nor is there any clear cultural necessity for it. Yet civilization could not do without it. The science of aesthetics investigates the conditions under which things are felt as beautiful, but it has been unable to give any explanation of the nature and origin of beauty, and, as usually happens, lack of success is concealed beneath a flood of resounding and empty words. Psychoanalysis, unfortunately, has scarcely anything to say about beauty either. All that seems certain is its derivation from the field of sexual feeling. The love of beauty seems a perfect example of an impulse inhibited in its aim. "Beauty" and "attraction" are originally attributes of the sexual object. It is worth remarking that the genitals themselves, the sight of which is always exciting, are nevertheless hardly ever judged to be beautiful; the quality of beauty seems, instead, to attach to certain secondary sexual characters.

In spite of the incompleteness [of my enumeration], I will venture on a few remarks as a conclusion to our enquiry. The programme of becoming happy, which the pleasure principle imposes on us, cannot be fulfilled; yet we must not—indeed, we cannot—give up our efforts to bring it nearer to fulfilment by some means or other. Very different paths may be taken in that direction, and we may give priority, either to the positive aspect of the aim, that of gaining pleasure, or to its negative one, that of avoiding unpleasure. By none of these paths can we attain all that we desire. Happiness, in the reduced sense in which we recognize it as possible, is a problem of the economics of the individual's libido. There is no golden rule which applies to everyone: every man must find out for himself in what particular fashion he can be saved. All kinds of different factors will operate to direct his choice. It is a question of how much real satisfaction he can expect to get from the external world, how far he is led to make himself independent of it, and, finally, how much strength he feels he has for altering the world to suit his wishes. In this, his psychical constitution will play a decisive part, irrespectively of the external circumstances. The man who is predominantly erotic will give first preference to his emotional relationships to other people; the narcissistic man, who inclines to be self-sufficient, will seek his main satisfactions in his internal mental processes; the man of action will never give up the external world on which he can try out his strength. As regards the second of these types, the nature of his talents and the amount of instinctual sublimation open to him will decide where he shall locate his interests. Any choice that is pushed to an extreme will be penalized by exposing the individual to the dangers which arise if a technique of living that has been chosen as an exclusive one should prove inadequate. Just as a cautious businessman avoids tying up all his capital in one concern, so, perhaps, worldly wisdom will advise us not to look for the whole of our satisfaction from a single aspiration. Its success is never certain, for that depends on the convergence of many factors, perhaps on none more than on the capacity of the psychical constitution to adapt its function to the environment and then to exploit that environment for a yield of pleasure. A person who is born with a specially unfavourable instinctual constitution, and who has not properly undergone the transformation and rearrangement of his libidinal components which is indispensable for later achievements, will find it hard to obtain happiness from his external situation, especially if he is faced with tasks of some difficulty. As a last technique of living, which will at least bring him substitutive satisfactions, he is offered that of a flight into neurotic illness—a flight which he usually accomplishes when he is still young. The man who sees his pursuit of happiness come to nothing in later years can still find consolation in the yield of pleasure of chronic intoxication; or he can embark on the desperate attempt at rebellion seen in a psychosis.

Religion restricts this play of choice and adaptation, since it imposes equally on everyone its own path to the acquisition of happiness and protection from suffering. Its technique consists in depressing the value of life and distorting the picture of the real world in a delusional manner—which presupposes an intimidation of the intelligence. At this price, by forcibly fixing them in a state of psychical infantilism and by drawing them into a mass-delusion, religion succeeds in sparing many people an individual neurosis. But hardly anything more. There are, as we have said, many paths which *may* lead to such happiness as is attainable by men, but there is none which does so for certain. Even religion cannot keep its promise. If the believer finally sees himself obliged to speak of God's "inscrutable decrees," he is admitting that all that is left to him as a last possible consolation and source of pleasure in his suffering is an unconditional submission. And if he is prepared for that, he could probably have spared himself the *détour* he has made.

. . .

Our enquiry concerning happiness has not so far taught us much that is not already common knowledge. And even if we proceed from it to the problem of why it is so hard for men to be happy, there seems no greater prospect of learning anything new. We have given the answer already by pointing to the three sources from which our suffering comes: the superior power of nature, the feebleness of our own bodies and the inadequacy of the regulations which adjust the mutual relationships of human beings in the family, the state and society. In regard to the first two sources, our judgement cannot hesitate long. It forces us to acknowledge those sources of suffering and to submit to the inevitable. We shall never completely master nature; and our bodily organism, itself a part of that nature, will always remain a transient structure with a limited capacity for adaptation and achievement. This recognition does not have a paralysing effect. On the contrary, it points the direction for our activity. If we cannot remove all suffering, we can remove some, and we can mitigate some: the experience of many thousands of years has convinced us of that. As regards the third source, the social source of suffering, our attitude is a different one. We do not admit it at all; we cannot see why the regulations made by ourselves should not, on the contrary, be a protection and a benefit for every one of us. And yet, when we consider how unsuccessful we have been in precisely this field of prevention of suffering, a suspicion dawns on us that here, too, a piece of unconquerable nature may lie behind—this time a piece of our own psychical constitution.

When we start considering this possibility, we come upon a contention which is so astonishing that we must dwell upon it. This contention holds that what we call our civilization is largely responsible for our misery, and that we should be much happier if we gave it up and returned to primitive conditions. I call this contention astonishing because, in whatever way we may define the concept of civilization, it is a certain fact that all the things with which we seek to protect ourselves against the threats that emanate from the sources of suffering are part of that very civilization.

How has it happened that so many people have come to take up this strange attitude of hostility to civilization? I believe that the basis of it was a deep and long-standing dissatisfaction with the then existing state of civilization and that on that basis a condemnation of it was built up, occasioned by specific historical events. I think I know what the last and the last but one of those occasions were. I am not learned enough to trace the chain of them far back enough in the history of the human species; but a factor of this kind hostile to civilization must already have been at work in the victory of Christendom over the heathen religions. For it was very closely related to the low estimation put upon earthly life by the Christian doctrine. The last but one of these occasions was when the progress of voyages of discovery led to contact with primitive peoples and races. In consequence of insufficient observation and a mistaken view of their manners and customs, they appeared to Europeans to be leading a simple, happy life with few wants, a life such as was unattainable by their visitors with their superior civilization. Later experience has corrected some of those judgements. In many cases the observers had wrongly attributed to the absence of complicated cultural demands what was in fact due to the bounty of nature and the ease with which the major human needs were satisfied. The last occasion is especially familiar to us. It arose when people came to know about the mechanism of the neuroses, which threaten to undermine the modicum of happiness enjoyed by civilized men. It was discovered that a person becomes neurotic because he cannot tolerate the amount of frustration which society imposes on him in the service of its cultural ideals, and it was inferred from this that the abolition or reduction of those demands would result in a return to possibilities of happiness.

. . .

The tendency on the part of civilization to restrict sexual life is no less clear than its other tendency to expand the cultural unit. Its first, totemic, phase already brings with it the prohibition against an incestuous choice of object, and this is perhaps the most drastic mutilation which man's erotic life has in all time experienced. Taboos, laws and customs impose further restrictions, which affect both men and women. Not all civilizations go equally far in this; and the economic structure of the society also influences the amount of sexual freedom that remains. Here, as we already know, civilization is obeying the laws of economic necessity, since a large amount of the psychical energy which it uses for its own purposes has to be withdrawn from sexuality. In this respect civilization behaves towards sexuality as a people or a stratum of its population does which has subjected another one to its exploitation. Fear of a revolt by the suppressed elements drives it to stricter precautionary measures. A high-water mark in such a development has been reached in our Western European civilization. A cultural community is perfectly justified, psychologically, in starting by proscribing manifestations of the sexual life of children, for there would be no prospect of curbing the sexual lusts of adults if the ground had not been prepared for it in childhood. But such a community cannot in any way be justified in going to the length of actually *disavowing* such easily demonstrable, and, indeed, striking phenomena. As regards the sexually mature individual, the choice of an object is restricted to the opposite sex, and most extra-genital satisfactions are forbidden as perversions. The requirement, demonstrated in these prohibitions, that there shall be a single kind of sexual life for everyone, disregards the dissimilarities, whether innate or acquired, in the sexual constitution of human beings; it cuts off a fair number of them from sexual enjoyment, and so becomes the source of serious injustice. The result of such restrictive measures might be that in people who are normal—who are not prevented by their constitution—the whole of their sexual interests would flow without loss into the channels that are left open. But heterosexual genital love, which has remained exempt from outlawry, is itself restricted by further limitations, in the shape of insistence upon legitimacy and monogamy. Present-day civilization makes it plain that it will only permit sexual relationships on the basis of a solitary, indissoluble bond between one man and one woman, and that it does not like sexuality as a source of pleasure in its own right and is only prepared to tolerate it because there is so far no substitute for it as a means of propagating the human race.

. . .

[M]en are not gentle creatures who want to be loved, and who at the most can defend themselves if they are attacked; they are, on the contrary, creatures among whose instinctual endowments is to be reckoned a powerful share of aggressiveness. As a result, their neighbour is for them not only a potential helper or sexual object, but also someone who tempts them to satisfy their aggressiveness on him, to exploit his capacity for work without compensation, to use him sexually without his consent, to seize his possessions, to humiliate him, to cause him pain, to torture and to kill him. *Homo homini lupus.*[1] Who, in the face of all his experience of life and of history, will have the courage to dispute this assertion? As a rule this cruel aggressiveness waits for some provocation or puts itself at the service of some other purpose, whose goal might also have been reached by milder measures. In circumstances that are favourable to it, when the mental counter-forces which ordinarily inhibit it are out of action, it also manifests itself spontaneously and reveals man as a savage beast, to whom consideration towards his own kind is something alien. Anyone who calls to mind the atrocities committed during the racial migrations or the invasions of the Huns, or by the people known as Mongols under Jenghiz Khan and Tamerlane, or at the capture of Jerusalem by the pious Crusaders, or even, indeed, the horrors of the recent World War— anyone who calls these things to mind will have to bow humbly before the truth of this view.

The existence of this inclination to aggression, which we can detect in ourselves and justly assume to be present in others, is the factor which disturbs our relations with our neighbour and which forces civilization into such a high expenditure [of energy]. In consequence of this primary mutual hostility of human beings, civilized society is perpetually threatened with disintegration. The interest of work in common would not hold it together; instinctual passions are stronger than reasonable interests. Civilization has to use its utmost efforts in order to set limits to man's aggressive instincts and to hold the manifestations of them in check by psychical reaction-formations. Hence, therefore, the use of methods intended to incite people into identifications and aim-inhibited

---

[1] "Man is a wolf to man." Derived from Plautus, Asinaria II, iv, 88.

relationships of love, hence the restriction upon sexual life, and hence too the ideal's commandment to love one's neighbour as oneself—a commandment which is really justified by the fact that nothing else runs so strongly counter to the original nature of man. In spite of every effort, these endeavours of civilization have not so far achieved very much. It hopes to prevent the crudest excesses of brutal violence by itself assuming the right to use violence against criminals, but the law is not able to lay hold of the more cautious and refined manifestations of human aggressiveness. The time comes when each one of us has to give up as illusions the expectations which, in his youth, he pinned upon his fellow-men, and when he may learn how much difficulty and pain has been added to his life by their ill-will. At the same time, it would be unfair to reproach civilization with trying to eliminate strife and competition from human activity. These things are undoubtedly indispensable. But opposition is not necessarily enmity; it is merely misused and made an *occasion* for enmity.

The communists believe that they have found the path to deliverance from our evils. According to them, man is wholly good and is well-disposed to his neighbour; but the institution of private property has corrupted his nature. The ownership of private wealth gives the individual power, and with it the temptation to ill-treat his neighbour; while the man who is excluded from possession is bound to rebel in hostility against his oppressor. If private property were abolished, all wealth held in common, and everyone allowed to share in the enjoyment of it, ill-will and hostility would disappear among men. Since everyone's needs would be satisfied, no one would have any reason to regard another as his enemy; all would willingly undertake the work that was necessary. I have no concern with any economic criticisms of the communist system; I cannot enquire into whether the abolition of private property is expedient or advantageous.[2] But I am able to recognize that the psychological premises on which the system is based are an untenable illusion. In abolishing private property we deprive the human love of aggression of one of its instruments, certainly a strong one, though certainly not the strongest; but we have in no

---

[2] Anyone who has tasted the miseries of poverty in his own youth and has experienced the indifference and arrogance of the well-to-do, should be safe from the suspicion of having no understanding or good will towards endeavours to fight against the inequality of wealth among men and all that it leads to. To be sure, if an attempt is made to base this fight upon an abstract demand, in the name of justice, for equality for all men, there is a very obvious objection to be made—that nature, by endowing individuals with extremely unequal physical attributes and mental capacities, has introduced injustices against which there is no remedy.

way altered the differences in power and influence which are misused by aggressiveness, nor have we altered anything in its nature. Aggressiveness was not created by property. It reigned almost without limit in primitive times, when property was still very scanty, and it already shows itself in the nursery almost before property has given up its primal, anal form; it forms the basis of every relation of affection and love among people (with the single exception, perhaps, of the mother's relation to her male child). If we do away with personal rights over material wealth, there still remains prerogative in the field of sexual relationships, which is bound to become the source of the strongest dislike and the most violent hostility among men who in other respects are on an equal footing. If we were to remove this factor, too, by allowing complete freedom of sexual life and thus abolishing the family, the germ-cell of civilization, we cannot, it is true, easily foresee what new paths the development of civilization could take; but one thing we can expect, and that is that this indestructible feature of human nature will follow it there.

On Transience

Not long ago I went on a summer walk through a smiling countryside in the company of a taciturn friend and of a young but already famous poet. The poet admired the beauty of the scene around us but felt no joy in it. He was disturbed by the thought that all this beauty was fated to extinction, that it would vanish when winter came, like all human beauty and all the beauty and splendour that men have created or may create. All that he would otherwise have loved and admired seemed to him to be shorn of its worth by the transience which was its doom.

The proneness to decay of all that is beautiful and perfect can, as we know, give rise to two different impulses in the mind. The one leads to the aching despondency felt by the young poet, while the other leads to rebellion against the fact asserted. No! it is impossible that all this loveliness of Nature and Art, of the world of our sensations and of the world outside, will really fade away into nothing. It would be too senseless and too presumptuous to believe it. Somehow or other this loveliness must be able to persist and to escape all the powers of destruction.

But this demand for immortality is a product of our wishes too unmistakable to lay claim to reality: what is painful may none the less be true.

From Freud, Sigmund, "On Transience" (SE Vol.XIV), pp. 305–307.

I could not see my way to dispute the transience of all things, nor could I insist upon an exception in favour of what is beautiful and perfect. But I did dispute the pessimistic poet's view that the transience of what is beautiful involves any loss in its worth.

On the contrary, an increase! Transience value is scarcity value in time. Limitation in the possibility of an enjoyment raises the value of the enjoyment. It was incomprehensible, I declared, that the thought of the transience of beauty should interfere with our joy in it. As regards the beauty of Nature, each time it is destroyed by winter it comes again next year, so that in relation to the length of our lives it can in fact be regarded as eternal. The beauty of the human form and face vanish for ever in the course of our own lives, but their evanescence only lends them a fresh charm. A flower that blossoms only for a single night does not seem to us on that account less lovely. Nor can I understand any better why the beauty and perfection of a work of art or of an intellectual achievement should lose its worth because of its temporal limitation. A time may indeed come when the pictures and statues which we admire to-day will crumble to dust, or a race of men may follow us who no longer understand the works of our poets and thinkers, or a geological epoch may even arrive when all animate life upon the earth ceases; but since the value of all this beauty and perfection is determined only by its significance for our own emotional lives, it has no need to survive us and is therefore independent of absolute duration.

These considerations appeared to me incontestable; but I noticed that I had made no impression either upon the poet or upon my friend. My failure led me to infer that some powerful emotional factor was at work which was disturbing their judgement, and I believed later that I had discovered what it was. What spoilt their enjoyment of beauty must have been a revolt in their minds against mourning. The idea that all this beauty was transient was giving these two sensitive minds a foretaste of mourning over its decease; and, since the mind instinctively recoils from anything that is painful, they felt their enjoyment of beauty interfered with by thoughts of its transience.

Mourning over the loss of something that we have loved or admired seems so natural to the layman that he regards it as self-evident. But to psychologists mourning is a great riddle, one of those phenomena which cannot themselves be explained but to which other obscurities can be traced back. We possess, as it seems, a certain amount of capacity for love—what we call libido—which in the earliest stages of development is directed towards our own ego. Later, though still at a very early time, this libido is diverted from the ego on to objects, which are thus in a sense taken into our ego. If the objects are destroyed or if they are lost to us, our capacity for love (our libido) is once more liberated; and it can then either take other objects instead or can temporarily return to the ego. But why it is that this detachment of libido from its objects should be such a painful process is a mystery to us and we have not hitherto been able to frame any hypothesis to account for it. We only see that libido clings to its objects and will not renounce those that are lost even when a substitute lies ready to hand. Such then is mourning.

My conversation with the poet took place in the summer before the war. A year later the war broke out and robbed the world of its beauties. It destroyed not only the beauty of the countrysides through which it passed and the works of art which it met with on its path but it also shattered our pride in the achievements of our civilization, our admiration for many philosophers and artists and our hopes of a final triumph over the differences between nations and races. It tarnished the lofty impartiality of our science, it revealed our instincts in all their nakedness and let loose the evil spirits within us which we thought had been tamed for ever by centuries of continuous education by the noblest minds. It made our country small again and made the rest of the world far remote. It robbed us of very much that we had loved, and showed us how ephemeral were many things that we had regarded as changeless.

We cannot be surprised that our libido, thus bereft of so many of its objects, has clung with all the greater intensity to what is left to us, that our love of our country, our affection for those nearest us and our pride in what is common to us have suddenly grown stronger. But have those other possessions, which we have now lost, really ceased to have any worth for us because they have proved so perishable and so unresistant? To many of us this seems to be so, but once more wrongly, in my view. I believe that those who think thus, and seem ready to make a permanent renunciation because what was precious has proved not to be lasting, are simply in a state of mourning for what is lost. Mourning, as we know, however painful it may be, comes to a spontaneous end. When it has renounced everything that has been lost, then it has consumed itself and our libido is once more free (in so far as we are still young and active) to replace the lost objects by fresh ones equally or still more precious. It is to be hoped that the same will be true of the losses caused by this war. When once the mourning is over, it will be found that our high opinion of the riches of civilization has lost nothing from our discovery of their fragility. We shall build up again all that war has destroyed, and perhaps on firmer ground and more lastingly than before.

Some Psychical Consequences of the Anatomical Distinction Between the Sexes

In examining the earliest mental shapes assumed by the sexual life of children we have been in the habit of taking as the subject of our investigations the male child, the little boy. With little girls, so we have supposed, things must be similar, though in some way or other they must nevertheless be different. The point in development at which this difference lay could not be clearly determined.

In boys the situation of the Oedipus complex is the first stage that can be recognized with certainty. It is easy to understand, because at that stage a child retains the same object which he previously cathected with his libido—not as yet a genital one—during the preceding period while he was being suckled and nursed. The fact, too, that in this situation he regards his father as a disturbing rival and would like to get rid of him and take his place is a straightforward consequence of the actual state of affairs. I have shown elsewhere how the Oedipus attitude in little boys belongs to the phallic phase, and how its destruction is brought about by the fear of castration—that is, by narcissistic interest in their genitals. The matter is made more difficult to grasp by the complicating circumstance that even in boys the Oedipus complex has a double orientation, active and passive, in accordance with their bisexual constitution; a boy also wants to take his *mother's* place as the love-object of his *father*—a fact which we describe as the feminine attitude.

. . .

In little girls the Oedipus complex raises one problem more than in boys. In both cases the mother is the original object; and there is no cause for surprise that boys retain that object in the Oedipus complex. But how does it happen that girls abandon it and instead take their father as an object? In pursuing this question I have been able to reach some conclusions which may throw light precisely on the prehistory of the Oedipus relation in girls.

Freud, S. (1927). Some psychological consequences of anatomical distinction between the sexes. International Journal of Psycho-Analysis, 8, 133–142.

Every analyst has come across certain women who cling with especial intensity and tenacity to the bond with their father and to the wish in which it culminates of having a child by him. We have good reason to suppose that the same wishful phantasy was also the motive force of their infantile masturbation, and it is easy to form an impression that at this point we have been brought up against an elementary and unanalysable fact of infantile sexual life. But a thorough analysis of these very cases brings something different to light—namely, that here the Oedipus complex has a long prehistory and is in some respects a secondary formation.

The old paediatrician Lindner [1879] once remarked that a child discovers the genital zones (the penis or the clitoris) as a source of pleasure while indulging in sensual sucking (thumbsucking). I shall leave it an open question whether it is really true that the child takes the newly found source of pleasure in exchange for the recent loss of the mother's nipple—a possibility to which later phantasies (fellatio) seem to point. Be that as it may, the genital zone is discovered at some time or other, and there seems no justification for attributing any psychical content to the first activities in connection with it. But the first step in the phallic phase which begins in this way is not the linking-up of the masturbation with the object-cathexes of the Oedipus complex, but a momentous discovery which little girls are destined to make. They notice the penis of a brother or playmate, strikingly visible and of large proportions, at once recognize it as the superior counterpart of their own small and inconspicuous organ, and from that time forward fall a victim to envy for the penis.

There is an interesting contrast between the behaviour of the two sexes. In the analogous situation, when a little boy first catches sight of a girl's genital region, he begins by showing irresolution and lack of interest; he sees nothing or disavows what he has seen, he softens it down or looks about for expedients for bringing it into line with his expectations. It is not until later, when some threat of castration has obtained a hold upon him, that the observation becomes important to him: if he then recollects or repeats it, it arouses a terrible storm of emotion in him and forces him to believe in the reality of the threat which he has hitherto laughed at. This combination of circumstances leads to two reactions, which may become fixed and will in that case, whether separately or together or in conjunction with other factors, permanently determine the boy's relations to women: horror of the mutilated creature or triumphant contempt for her. These developments, however, belong to the future, though not to a very remote one.

A little girl behaves differently. She makes her judgement and her decision in a flash. She has seen it and knows that she is without it and wants to have it.

Here what has been named the masculinity complex of women branches off. It may put great difficulties in the way of their regular development towards femininity, if it cannot be got over soon enough. The hope of some day obtaining a penis in spite of everything and so of becoming like a man may persist to an incredibly late age and may become a motive for strange and otherwise unaccountable actions. Or again, a process may set in which I should like to call a "disavowal," a process which in the mental life of children seems neither uncommon nor very dangerous but which in an adult would mean the beginning of a psychosis. Thus a girl may refuse to accept the fact of being castrated, may harden herself in the conviction that she *does* possess a penis, and may subsequently be compelled to behave as though she were a man.

The psychical consequences of envy for the penis, in so far as it does not become absorbed in the reaction-formation of the masculinity complex, are various and far-reaching. After a woman has become aware of the wound to her narcissism, she develops, like a scar, a sense of inferiority. When she has passed beyond her first attempt at explaining her lack of a penis as being a punishment personal to herself and has realized that that sexual character is a universal one, she begins to share the contempt felt by men for a sex which is the lesser in so important a respect, and, at least in holding that opinion, insists on being like a man.

59

W. E. B. Du Bois

W. E. B. Du Bois (1868–1963) was an American sociologist and civil rights activist. Leader of the Niagara Movement, a group pressing for equal rights for African-Americans, Du Bois was born in Massachusetts, but ended his days as a citizen of Ghana. In the following extract from *The Souls of Black Folk*, Du Bois introduces the concept of "double consciousness," which denotes the internal conflict felt by members of a subordinated group when they struggle to reconcile the two cultures (here: African and American) composing their identity.

The Souls of Black Folk

Between me and the other world there is ever an unasked question: unasked by some through feelings of delicacy; by others through the difficulty of rightly framing it. All, nevertheless, flutter round it. They approach me in a half-hesitant sort of way, eye me curiously or compassionately, and then, instead of saying directly, How does it feel to be a problem? they say, I know an excellent colored man in my town; or, I fought at Mechanicsville; or, Do not these Southern outrages make your blood boil? At these I smile, or am interested, or reduce the boiling to a

---

From Du Bois, W. E. B., *The Souls of Black Folk* (New York: Dover, 1994 [1903]), pp. 1–3.

simmer, as the occasion may require. To the real question, How does it feel to be a problem? I answer seldom a word.

And yet being a problem is a strange experience,—peculiar even, for one who has never been anything else, save perhaps in babyhood and in Europe. It is in the early days of rollicking boyhood that the revelation first bursts upon one, all in a day, as it were. I remember well when the shadow swept across me. I was a little thing, away up in the hills of New England, where the dark Housatonic winds between Hoosac and Taghkanic to the sea. In a wee wooden schoolhouse, something put it into the boys' and girls' heads to buy gorgeous visiting-cards—ten cents a package—and exchange. The exchange was merry, till one girl, a tall newcomer, refused my card,—refused it peremptorily, with a glance. Then it dawned upon me with a certain suddenness that I was different from the others; or like, mayhap, in heart and life and longing, but shut out from their world by a vast veil. I had thereafter no desire to tear down that veil, to creep through; I held all beyond it in common contempt, and lived above it in a region of blue sky and great wandering shadows. That sky was bluest when I could beat my mates at examination time, or beat them at a foot-race, or even beat their stringy heads. Alas, with the years all this fine contempt began to fade; for the worlds I longed for, and all their dazzling opportunities, were theirs, not mine. But they should not keep these prizes, I said; some, all, I would wrest from them. Just how I would do it I could never decide: by reading law, by healing the sick, by telling the wonderful tales that swam in my head,—some way. With other black boys the strife was not so fiercely sunny: their youth shrunk into tasteless sycophancy, or into silent hatred of the pale world about them and mocking distrust of everything white; or wasted itself in a bitter cry, Why did God make me an outcast and a stranger in mine own house? The shades of the prison-house closed round about us all: walls strait and stubborn to the whitest, but relentlessly narrow, tall, and unscalable to sons of night who must plod darkly on in resignation, or beat unavailing palms against the stone, or steadily, half hopelessly, watch the streak of blue above.

After the Egyptian and Indian, the Greek and Roman, the Teuton and Mongolian, the Negro is a sort of seventh son, born with a veil, and gifted with second-sight in this American world,—a world which yields him no true self-consciousness, but only lets him see himself through the revelation of the other world. It is a peculiar sensation, this double-consciousness, this sense of always looking at one's self through the eyes of others, of measuring one's soul by the tape of a world that looks on in amused contempt and pity. One ever feels his two-ness,—an American, a Negro; two souls, two thoughts, two unreconciled strivings; two warring ideals in one dark body, whose dogged strength alone keeps it from being torn asunder.

The history of the American Negro is the history of this strife,—this longing to attain self-conscious manhood, to merge his double self into a better and truer self. In this merging he wishes neither of the older selves to be lost. He would not Africanize America, for America has too much to teach the world and Africa. He would not bleach his Negro soul in a flood of white Americanism, for he knows that Negro blood has a message for the world. He simply wishes to make it possible for a man to be both a Negro and an American, without being cursed and spit upon by his fellows, without having the doors of Opportunity closed roughly in his face.

60

Ludwig Wittgenstein

Regarded by many as the greatest philosopher of the twentieth century, Ludwig Wittgenstein (1889–1951) is mainly known for his contributions to the philosophy of language. In this extract, Wittgenstein explores the question of the meaning of life and happiness.

Notebooks 1914–1916

11.6.16

What do I know about God and the purpose of life?
I know that this world exists.
That I am placed in it like my eye in its visual field.
That something about it is problematic, which we call its meaning.
That this meaning does not lie in it but outside it.
That life is the world.
That my will penetrates the world.
That my will is good or evil.
Therefore that good and evil are somehow connected with the meaning of the world.

Notebooks, 1914–1916 by ANSCOMBE, G.E. ; WITTGENSTEIN, LUDWIG Reproduced with permission of UNIV OF CHICAGO PRESS in the format Republish in a book via Copyright Clearance Center.

The meaning of life, i.e., the meaning of the world, we can call God.
And connect with this the comparison of God to a father.
To pray is to think about the meaning of life.
I cannot bend the happenings of the world to my will: I am completely powerless.
I can only make myself independent of the world—and so in a certain sense master it—by renouncing any influence on happenings.

5.7.16

The world is independent of my will.
Even if everything that we want were to happen, this would still only be, so to speak, a grace of fate, for what would guarantee it is not any logical connexion between will and world, and we could not in turn will the supposed physical connexion.
If good or evil willing affects the world it can only affect the boundaries of the world, not the facts, what cannot be portrayed by language but can only be shewn in language.
In short, it must make the world a wholly different one.
The world must, so to speak, wax or wane as a whole. As if by accession or loss of meaning.
As in death, too, the world does not change but stops existing.

6.7.16.

And in this sense Dostoievsky is right when he says that the man who is happy is fulfilling the purpose of existence.
Or again we could say that the man is fulfilling the purpose of existence who no longer needs to have any purpose except to live. That is to say, who is content.
The solution of the problem of life is to be seen in the disappearance of this problem.
But is it possible for one so to live that life stops being problematic? That one is *living* in eternity and not in time?

7.7.16.

Isn't this the reason why men to whom the meaning of life had become clear after long doubting could not say what this meaning consisted in?. . .

8.7.16.

To believe in a God means to understand the question about the meaning of life.

To believe in a God means to see that the facts of the world are not the end of the matter.

To believe in God means to see that life has a meaning.

The world is *given* me, i.e., my will enters into the world completely from outside as into something that is already there.

(As for what my will is, I don't know yet.)

That is why we have the feeling of being dependent on an alien will.

However this may be, at any rate we *are* in a certain sense dependent, and what we are dependent on we can call God.

In this sense God would simply be fate, or, what is the same thing: The world—which is independent of our will.

I can make myself independent of fate.

There are two godheads: the world and my independent I.

I am either happy or unhappy, that is all. It can be said: good or evil do not exist.

A man who is happy must have no fear. Not even in face of death.

Only a man who lives not in time but in the present is happy.

For life in the present there is no death.

Death is not an event in life. It is not a fact of the world.

If by eternity is understood not infinite temporal duration but non-temporality, then it can be said that a man lives eternally if he lives in the present.

In order to live happily I must be in agreement with the world. And that is what "being happy" *means*.

I am then, so to speak, in agreement with that alien will on which I appear dependent. That is to say: "I am doing the will of God."

Fear in face of death is the best sign of a false, i.e., a bad, life.

When my conscience upsets my equilibrium, then I am not in agreement with Something. But what is this? Is it *the world*?

Certainly it is correct to say: Conscience is the voice of God.

For example: it makes me unhappy to think that I have offended such and such a man. Is that my conscience?

Can one say: "Act according to your conscience whatever it may be"?

Live happily!

Martin Heidegger

....

Martin Heidegger (1889–1976) was one of the most important philosophers of the twentieth century and a central figure in the existentialist tradition. His best-known book, *Being and Time*, constitutes a sustained investigation into "the question of being," and in so doing Heidegger reflects probingly (though in extraordinarily difficult and tortured prose) on the human condition (the condition of being-in-the-world). In this extract, Heidegger introduces the idea of "being-towards-death" as definitive of *Dasein* (literally "being there," his term for the distinctive form of existence peculiar to human beings), and discusses the ways in which people attempt to evade thinking about its inevitability.

....

Being and Time

50. Preliminary Sketch of the Existential-Ontological Structure of Death

From our considerations of totality, end, and that which is still outstanding, there has emerged the necessity of Interpreting the phenomenon of death as Being-towards-the-end, and of doing so in terms of Dasein's

---

basic state. Only so can it be made plain to what extent Being-a-whole, as constituted by Being towards-the-end, is possible in Dasein itself in conformity with the structure of its Being. We have seen that care is the basic state of Dasein. The ontological signification of the expression "care" has been expressed in the "definition": "ahead-of-itself-Being-already-in (the world) as Being-alongside entities which we encounter (within-the-world)." In this are expressed the fundamental characteristics of Dasein's Being: existence, in the "ahead-of-itself"; facticity, in the "Being-already-in"; falling, in the "Being-alongside." If indeed death belongs in a distinctive sense to the Being of Dasein, then death (or Being-towards-the-end) must be defined in terms of these characteristics.

We must, in the first instance, make plain in a preliminary sketch how Dasein's existence, facticity, and falling reveal themselves in the phenomenon of death.

The Interpretation in which the "not-yet"—and with it even the uttermost "not-yet," the end of Dasein—was taken in the sense of something still outstanding, has been rejected as inappropriate in that it included the ontological perversion of making Dasein something present-at-hand. Being-at-an-end implies existentially Being-towards-the-end. The uttermost "not-yet" has the character of something *towards which* Dasein *comports itself.* The end is impending for Dasein. Death is not something not yet present-at-hand, nor is it that which is ultimately still outstanding but which has been reduced to a minimum. *Death is something that stands before us—something impending.*

However, there is much that can impend for Dasein as Being-in-the-world. The character of impendence is not distinctive of death. On the contrary, this Interpretation could even lead us to suppose that death must be understood in the sense of some impending event encountered environmentally. For instance, a storm, the remodelling of the house, or the arrival of a friend, may be impending; and these are entities which are respectively present-at-hand, ready-to-hand, and there-with-us. The death which impends does not have this kind of Being.

But there may also be impending for Dasein a journey, for instance, or a disputation with Others, or the forgoing of something of a kind which Dasein itself can be—its own possibilities of Being, which are based on its Being with Others.

Death is a possibility-of-Being which Dasein itself has to take over in every case. With death, Dasein stands before itself in its ownmost potentiality-for-Being. This is a possibility in which the issue is nothing less than Dasein's Being-in-the-world. Its death is the possibility of no-longer being-able-to-be-there. If Dasein stands before itself as this possibility, it has been *fully* assigned to its ownmost potentiality-for-Being. When it stands before itself in this way, all its relations to any other Dasein have been undone. This ownmost non-relational possibility is at the same time the uttermost one.

As potentiality-for-Being, Dasein cannot outstrip the possibility of death. Death is the possibility of the absolute impossibility of Dasein. Thus death reveals itself as that *possibility which is one's ownmost, which is non-relational, and which is not to be outstripped*. As such, death is something *distinctively* impending. Its existential possibility is based on the fact that Dasein is essentially disclosed to itself, and disclosed, indeed, as ahead-of-itself. This item in the structure of care has its most primordial concretion in Being-towards-death. As a phenomenon. Being-towards-the-end becomes plainer as Being towards that distinctive possibility of Dasein which we have characterized.

This ownmost possibility, however, non-relational and not to be outstripped, is not one which Dasein procures for itself subsequently and occasionally in the course of its Being. On the contrary, if Dasein exists, it has already been *thrown* into this possibility. Dasein does not, proximally and for the most part, have any explicit or even any theoretical knowledge of the fact that it has been delivered over to its death, and that death thus belongs to Being-in-the-world. Thrownness into death reveals itself to Dasein in a more primordial and impressive manner in that state-of-mind which we have called "anxiety." Anxiety in the face of death is anxiety "in the face of" that potentiality-for-Being which is one's ownmost, nonrelational, and not to be outstripped. That in the face of which one has anxiety is Being-in-the-world itself. That about which one has this anxiety is simply Dasein's potentiality-for-Being. Anxiety in the face of death must not be confused with fear in the face of one's demise. This anxiety is not an accidental or random mood of "weakness" in some individual; but, as a basic state-of-mind of Dasein, it amounts to the disclosedness of the fact that Dasein exists as thrown Being *towards* its end. Thus the existential conception of "dying" is made clear as thrown Being towards its ownmost potentiality-for-Being, which is non-relational and not to be outstripped. Precision is gained by distinguishing this from pure disappearance, and also from merely perishing, and finally from the "Experiencing" of a demise.

Being-towards-the-end does not first arise through some attitude which occasionally emerges, nor does it arise as such an attitude; it belongs essentially to Dasein's thrownness, which reveals itself in a state-of-mind (mood) in one way or another. The factical "knowledge" or "ignorance" which prevails in any Dasein as to its ownmost Being-towards-the-end, is only the expression of the existentiell possibility that there are different ways of maintaining oneself in this Being. Factically, there are many who, proximally and for the most part, do not know about death; but this must not be passed off as a ground for proving that Being-towards-death does not belong to Dasein "universally." It only proves that proximally and for the most part Dasein covers up its ownmost Being-towards-death, fleeing *in the face* of it. Factically, Dasein is dying as long as it exists, but proximally and for the most part, it does so by way of *falling*. For factical existing is not only generally and without further differentiation a thrown potentiality-for-Being-in-the-world, but it has always likewise been absorbed in the "world" of its concern. In this falling Being-alongside, fleeing from uncanniness announces itself; and this means now, a fleeing in the face of one's ownmost Being-towards-death. Existence, facticity, and falling characterize Being-towards-the-end, and are therefore constitutive for the existential conception of death. *As regards its ontological possibility, dying is grounded in care.*

But if Being-towards-death belongs primordially and essentially to Dasein's Being, then it must also be exhibitable in everydayness, even if proximally in a way which is inauthentic. And if Being-towards-the-end should afford the existential possibility of an existentiell Being-a-whole for Dasein, then this would give phenomenal confirmation for the thesis that "care" is the ontological term for the totality of Dasein's structural whole. If, however, we are to provide a full phenomenal justification for this principle, a *preliminary sketch* of the connection between Being-towards-death and care is not sufficient. We must be able to see this connection above all in that *concretion* which lies closest to Dasein—its everydayness.

51. Being-towards-death and the Everydayness of Dasein

In setting forth average everyday Being-towards-death, we must take our orientation from those structures of everydayness at which we have earlier arrived. In Being-towards-death, Dasein comports itself *towards itself* as a distinctive potentiality-for-Being. But the Self of everydayness is the "they." The "they" is constituted by the way things have been publicly interpreted, which expresses itself in idle talk. Idle talk must accordingly make manifest the way in which everyday Dasein interprets for itself its Being-towards-death. The foundation of any interpretation is an act of understanding, which is always accompanied by a state-of-mind, or, in other words, which has a mood. So we must ask how Being-towards-death is disclosed by the kind of understanding which, with its state-of-mind, lurks in the idle talk of the "they." How does the "they" comport itself understandingly towards that ownmost possibility of Dasein, which is non-relational and is not to be outstripped? What state-of-mind discloses to the "they" that it has been delivered over to death, and in what way?

In the publicness with which we are with one another in our everyday manner, death is "known" as a mishap which is constantly occurring—as a "case of death." Someone or other "dies," be he neighbour or stranger. People who are no acquaintances of ours are "dying" daily and hourly. "Death" is encountered as a well-known event occurring within-the-world. As such it remains in the inconspicuousness characteristic of what is encountered in an everyday fashion. The "they" has already stowed away an interpretation for this event. It talks of it in a "fugitive" manner, either expressly or else in a way which is mostly inhibited, as if to say, "One of these days one will die too, in the end; but right now it has nothing to do with us."

The analysis of the phrase "one dies" reveals unambiguously the kind of Being which belongs to everyday Being-towards-death. In such a way of talking, death is understood as an indefinite something which, above all, must duly arrive from somewhere or other, but which is proximally *not yet present-at-hand* for oneself and is therefore no threat. The expression "one dies" spreads abroad the opinion that what gets reached, as it were, by death, is the "they." In Dasein's public way of interpreting, it is said that "one dies," because everyone else and oneself can talk himself into saying that "in no case is it I myself," for this "one" is the *"nobody."* "Dying" is levelled off to an occurrence which reaches Dasein, to be sure, but belongs to nobody in particular. If idle talk is always ambiguous, so is this manner of talking about death. Dying, which is essentially mine in such a way that no one can be my representative, is perverted into an event of public occurrence which the "they" encounters. In the way of talking which we have characterized, death is spoken of as a "case" which is constantly occurring. Death gets passed off as always something "actual"; its character as a possibility gets concealed, and so are the other two items that belong to it—the fact that it is non-relational and that it is not to be outstripped. By such ambiguity, Dasein puts itself in the position of losing itself in the "they" as regards a distinctive potentiality-for-Being which belongs to Dasein's ownmost Self. The "they" gives its approval, and aggravates the *temptation* to cover up from oneself one's ownmost Being-towards-death. This evasive concealment in the face of death dominates everydayness so stubbornly that, in Being with one another, the "neighbours" often still keep talking the "dying person" into the belief that he will escape death and soon return to the tranquillized everydayness of the world of his concern. Such "solicitude" is meant to "console" him. It insists upon bringing him back into Dasein, while in addition it helps him to keep his ownmost non-relational possibility-of-Being completely concealed. In this manner the "they" provides a *constant tranquillization about death*. At bottom, however, this is a tranquillization not only for him who is "dying" but just as much for those who "console" him. And even in the case of a demise, the public is still not to have its own tranquillity upset by such an event, or be disturbed in the carefreeness with which it concerns itself. Indeed the dying of Others is seen often enough as a social inconvenience, if not even a downright tactlessness, against which the public is to be guarded.

But along with this tranquillization, which forces Dasein away from its death, the "they" at the same time puts itself in the right and makes itself respectable by tacitly regulating the way in which *one* has to comport oneself towards death. It is already a matter of public acceptance that "thinking about death" is a cowardly fear, a sign of insecurity on the part of Dasein, and a sombre way of fleeing from the world. *The "they" does not permit us the courage for anxiety in the face of death.* The dominance of the manner in which things have been publicly interpreted by the "they," has already decided what state-of-mind is to determine our attitude towards death. In anxiety in the face of death, Dasein is brought face to face with itself as delivered over to that possibility which is not to be outstripped. The "they" concerns itself with transforming this anxiety into fear in the face of an oncoming event. In addition, the anxiety which has been made ambiguous as fear, is passed off as a weakness with which no self-assured Dasein may have any acquaintance. What is "fitting" according to the unuttered decree of the "they," is indifferent tranquillity as to the "fact" that one dies. The cultivation of such a "superior" indifference *alienates* Dasein from its ownmost nonrelational potentiality-for-Being.

But temptation, tranquillization, and alienation are distinguishing marks of the kind of Being called "*falling*." As falling, everyday

Being-towards-death is a constant *fleeing in the face of death*. Being-*towards*-the-end has the mode of *evasion in the face of it*—giving new explanations for it, understanding it inauthentically, and concealing it. Factically one's own Dasein is always dying already; that is to say, it is in a Being-towards-its-end. And it hides this Fact from itself by recoining "death" as just a "case of death" in Others—an everyday occurrence which, if need be, gives us the assurance still more plainly that "oneself" is still "living." But in thus foiling and fleeing *in the face of* death, Dasein's everydayness attests that the very "they" itself already has the definite character of *Being-towards-death*, even when it is not explicitly engaged in "thinking about death." *Even in average everydayness, this ownmost potentiality-for-Being, which is non-relational and not to be outstripped, is constantly an issue for Dasein. This is the case when its concern is merely in the mode of an untroubled indifference* **towards** *the uttermost possibility of existence.*

In setting forth everyday Being-towards-death, however, we are at the same time enjoined to try to secure a full existential conception of Being-towards-the-end, by a more penetrating Interpretation in which falling Being-towards-death is taken as an evasion *in the face of death*. *That in the face of which one flees* has been made visible in a way which is phenomenally adequate. Against this it must be possible to project phenomenologically the way in which evasive Dasein itself understands its death.

62

H. H. Price

H. H. Price (1899–1984) was a Welsh philosopher with interests in parapsychology. He was Wykeham Professor of Logic at the University of Oxford and also president of the Society for Psychical Research. In what follows, Price makes a valiant attempt to describe what life after death (conceived here as disembodied existence) might be like.

Two Conceptions of the Next World

On the face of it, there are two different ways of conceiving of the Next World, and they correspond to two different conceptions of survival itself.

First there is what I shall call the *embodied* conception of survival, and secondly there is the *disembodied* conception of it. According to the first, personality (or finite personality at any rate) cannot possibly exist without some kind of embodiment. At death a person loses his physical body. So, after death, he must have a body of some other kind, composed of some "higher" kind of matter which is not perceptible by means of our present physical sense-organs. Those who accept this conception of survival usually maintain that each of us does in fact have such a "higher" body even in this present life, as well as a physical body, and that even in

From Price, H.H., "Two Conceptions of the Next World", in *Essays in the Philosophy of Religion* (Oxford: Clarendon Press, 1972), pp. 100–101, 104–113.

this life the two bodies may occasionally be separated, in the "out of the body" experiences which are sometimes reported.

According to the second or "disembodied" conception of survival, what survives death is just the mind or spirit, and this is regarded as a wholly immaterial entity. Its essential attributes are consciousness, memory, volition, and the capacity for having emotions. It would, of course, be admitted that in this present life there is constant interaction between the immaterial soul and the material organism. But at death this interaction ceases; indeed, on this view death just *is* the termination of soul-body interaction, and afterwards the soul is supposed to exist and to have experiences in a completely disembodied state.

. . .

Disembodied Survival

Let us now turn to the other conception of survival, what I called the "disembodied" conception of it. If we take this view of survival, it is not easy to see at first sight how there could be a Next *World* at all. What kind of experiences could a wholly immaterial soul be supposed to have? As it has no sense-organs of any sort, surely it will have to spend the whole of its time in pure thought, contemplating the *a priori* truths of logic and mathematics which are independent of the data of the senses? Such a conception of the after-life may seem to many people exceedingly dreary and unsatisfying, however satisfactory it might be to logicians and mathematicians like Descartes. Of course, we might have to put up with it whether it satisfied us or not. If we do exist in a completely disembodied state after death, and if it is really true that a completely disembodied soul or spirit can have no experiences at all except purely intellectual ones, we must just make the best of it, however unsatisfying such an after-life may seem to us.

But I do not think that the disembodied conception of survival really does have these rather unwelcome implications. It is true that a completely disembodied soul would have no sense-organs and therefore no sense-experiences. But it would still have *memory*. Indeed, it must, if there is personal survival at all. Without this, a surviving personality could not retain its personal identity; the surviving entity could not be the same person as the late Mr. Robinson who formerly lived in Church Street, Kensington, and worked in the Westminster Bank. Unless we "take our memories with us" when we leave the physical body, there can be no *personal* survival at all. For the same reason, we must "take" our characters with us too—the emotional and conative dispositions which we have acquired during our embodied life on earth. Otherwise we shall not continue to be the same persons after death as we were before. Let us suppose that in our disembodied state we also retain the power of imagination, even though we lose the capacity for having sense-experiences.

A World of Mental Images

On these assumptions, it is not too difficult to form some idea of what the Next World might be like according to the "disembodied" conception of survival. The obvious suggestion is that it would be a kind of *dream-world*: or to put it the other way round, the dreams we have in this present life would be a kind of foretaste of the experiences we might expect to have after death. In dreams we are cut off from sensory stimuli. The sense-organs cease to operate. But this does not at all prevent us from having experiences, sometimes very vivid and exciting ones. The perceptible objects we are aware of when awake are replaced by mental images, and these mental images are the product of our own memories and desires. If we retain our memories and desires after death (and there can be no personal survival unless we do) these memories and desires may continue to manifest themselves by means of mental images, as they do in this present life when we are dreaming. Life after death on this view would be a kind of dream from which we never wake up.

In this present life we wake up eventually from our dreams. After a time the sense-organs begin to operate again. The dream-images fade away, and we are forced to attend again to our physical environment. Our nose is applied to the grindstone once more, whether we like it or not. But suppose we could no longer wake up. Suppose that someone's sense-organs ceased to operate altogether because his body had died. Then he would just go on dreaming. He would have passed from this world to the Other World or the Next World. This "passage" from the one world to the other would not of course be a change of place. It would be a change of consciousness, somewhat like the one which occurs now when we fall asleep and begin to dream, except that this time the change would be irreversible. Henceforth the disembodied mind or soul would live wholly in a world constructed out of its own memories and desires.

Here it is important to remember that many of our dream-images are spatial entities. If our dream is of the visual type (as most people's dreams probably are) our dream-images have shape, size, and position; at any rate they have position in relation to one another. If you dream of a mountain landscape, for instance, there may be an image of a spiky-topped mountain on the left, and an image of a round-topped mountain on the right, with a torrent flowing down between them. But though these dream-images have spatial properties, they are not located in *physical* space. From the point of view of the physicist or geographer these images are nowhere, because no position can be assigned to any of them in a map of the physical universe. They are spatial entities, but the space in which they are is not physical space. They are in a space of their own.

Next, we may notice that such an image-world would appear perfectly real to the disembodied soul itself, as dream-objects usually do now when we are actually dreaming. We only call them "unreal" by contrast with the world we are aware of when we wake up again. But if we no longer had any waking perception to contrast them with, we should no longer regard them as "unreal."

We are sometimes told in mediumistic communications that many discarnate personalities are at first unable to realize that they are dead. This, I think, is perfectly credible on the view of the Next World which we are now discussing. The memories and desires of these newly deceased persons would supply them with images of the same old familiar scenes, and it might not be at all easy for them to discover that what they are now aware of is no longer the physical world, but a world of vivid and coherent mental images. Among these images there might be one which closely resembled the physical body which the discarnate person had when he was alive. He might have a "dream body," so to speak, as well as a dream-environment.

In time, however, he might gradually discover that the *causal laws* which apply to the world he is now experiencing are rather different from those he was familiar with in earthly life. He might notice, for instance, that if he desires to be in a certain place, he instantaneously finds himself in it, without passing through any intermediate place on the way; or that when he thinks of something, it immediately presents itself before him in a visible form. He would then be driven to the conclusion that he is no longer in the physical world after all. For though the objects he is aware of might closely resemble physical objects in having shapes, sizes, colours, etc. (as dream-objects often do now), it would gradually become clear to him that the causal laws which apply to them are not the laws of physics, but are much more like the laws of psychology.

Conceivably a *very* dogmatic materialist might never succeed in realizing that he was dead and in the Other World. He might prefer to believe that he had been transported to another planet. It might even be (as I think is asserted in some mediumistic communications) that a very firm disbelief in survival would prevent the surviving personality from having any post-mortem experiences at all. Then he would never know that he had survived, because he preferred not to know. But I should suppose that this result would be unlikely if his disbelief in survival was of a purely theoretical kind, without any strong desire or emotion to reinforce it.

A Subjective Other World?

It may seem at first sight that such an image-world as I have described would be something purely subjective, and that each discarnate personality would be confined as it were to his own private dream, without any means of contact with other discarnate personalities. Perhaps the Next World of a *very* self-centred person really is like that: a pretty terrifying prospect if you come to think of it. . . . .

But though on the theory we are discussing there would certainly have to be *many* Next Worlds (not the same one for all) it does not really follow that each of them would be wholly private. Telepathy must be taken into account. Even in this present life telepathic dreams are not infrequent, and there are also occasional telepathic hallucinations. In this present life, it is likely that many telepathically received impressions fail to reach consciousness at all, owing to the pressure of biological needs which force us to pay attention to our physical environment. In a disembodied state, this inhibiting influence would be removed. So there might be a common image-world which is the joint product of many telepathically interacting personalities.

Nevertheless, there would still be *many* Next Worlds, and not just one. The material world in which we live now has what one might call "unrestricted publicity." In principle, any macroscopic object in it can be observed by anyone, provided that he moves his body to the appropriate place and has the normal equipment of sense-organs. But in the universe as a whole, perhaps this unrestricted publicity is something rather exceptional.

Another—and connected—characteristic of the material world, is that in it people with very different moral characters are intermingled, so to speak, and saints and sinners can rub shoulders with one another.

Perhaps this is rather exceptional too. For in the next life, if there is one, it is to be expected that only *like-minded* personalities will share a common world—personalities whose memories and desires are sufficiently similar to allow of continuous telepathic interaction. If so, each group of like-minded personalities would have a different next world, public to all the members of that particular group but private to the group as a whole. Each "goes to his own place" and "birds of a feather flock together." Something of this kind is asserted in many religious traditions. You will remember the "great gulf fixed" between the Next World of Lazarus and the Next World of Dives in the Gospel parable. The "great gulf," I suggest, was a consequence of the *un*like-mindedness between Dives and those like-minded with him, on the one hand, and Lazarus and those like-minded with him, on the other. Between these two groups of persons, there could be no telepathic interaction.

The Two Theories Compared

Let us now compare these two theories of the Next World. According to the first, which corresponds with the "embodied" conception of survival, the Next World is a quasi-physical world, though not located in physical space. According to the second, which corresponds with the "disembodied" conception of survival, it is a world of mental images produced by the memories and desires of the surviving personalities. I hope I have succeeded in showing that both these theories are more or less intelligible and coherent, and that both of them deserve serious consideration.

I expect that most of you prefer the first theory, the quasi-physical theory which goes with the embodied conception of survival. A dream-like Next World composed of nothing but mental images may seem to you somehow "thin" and unsatisfying. We may emphasize, as I did, that a world of mental images need not be purely private. A number of like-minded personalities, who interact telepathically with each other, could have a common image-world. Again, we may insist, as I also did, that an image-world could be just as orderly and coherent as this present material world in which we now live, though its causal laws would be different from the laws of physics. But even so, I suspect you will still find this theory somehow unsatisfying, however agreeable it may seem to a professional philosopher.

Of course, even though it is unsatisfying, it may be all that we are going to get. Assuming we survive, we may have to put up with a dream-like existence after death, even though many of us would prefer something different. But I think that behind this feeling of dissatisfaction there is an important point of principle which needs to be brought into the open and stated explicitly. It is a point about the concept of personality itself. It might be argued that a person has to have a body in order to be a person: or at any rate that a *finite* person has to have a body. (We are not concerned here with the infinite personality of God.)

Embodiment and Social Relations

Why does a person need a body? (It is a philosopher's business to consider silly questions like this, which sensible adults do not ask, though tiresome children might.) As I have said already, the Pythagoreans, and some of the Platonists, thought that the body is a kind of prison and that it is better to be completely disembodied. For surely, one would rather be out of prison than in it. Were they mistaken? In this present life a person *must* have a body, in order to perceive and act upon his physical environment. But though he does need a body while he is in this world, why should he need one in the next?

The answer which is at the back of people's minds (though seldom explicitly stated) is that a person needs a body in order to be a *social* being. It might be argued that no one can be a person unless he has social relations with other persons. According to Christian theism, the most important of all social relationships is the relation of loving, and no one can be a person unless he is at least capable of being related in this way to other persons.

Let us consider this "social dimension" of personality. There are two different reasons why a social being needs a body. To understand what they are, we have to think of the body not as an anatomist or physiologist thinks of it, but rather as a painter or a dramatist thinks of it. First, it is a means by which inner states of mind *express* themselves in some overt and perceptible manner. To put it rather extravagantly: in order to be a person you must have a *face* which other persons can look at, and recognize and respond to. You do not absolutely need to be able to talk; but if you cannot talk, you do need to be able to make expressive gestures. It comes to this: without some means of expressing oneself one cannot enter into social relations at all. And one function of the body is to provide a person with means of expressing himself.

But it has another function as well. In order to enter into social relations of a permanent kind (friendship, for example) a person has to be recognizable—recognizable, for instance, as the *same* "Dear old So-and-so" whom you met years ago. Unless persons remained recognizable over considerable periods of time, no such relations as love or friendship would be possible, though very evanescent social relations—of what you might call the "sherry party" sort—could no doubt exist. And how can a person be recognizable unless he has a body, by means of which he can be identified as the same person whom one met previously?

It follows from this that if a newly dead person is to be recognized by his friends who are in the Next World already, his post-mortem body must resemble has former physical body fairly closely, at least so far as its outward appearance goes. To speak extravagantly again, he must have more or less the same face as he had in his earthly life.

Similarly, if he in his turn is to recognize his friends in the Next World, their post-mortem bodies must not be too different in outward appearance from those they had when he previously knew them in earthly life, though there might be minor differences (comparable to those between the body one has at the age of twenty and the body one has at the age of sixty). Internally, the post-mortem body might be quite different from the physical body, but outwardly it must *look like* the physical body, as of course the occultists and the spiritualists say it does.

The body then is not the prison of the soul, or at any rate that is not all it is. It is the means by which the soul expresses itself and makes itself recognizable to others.

An Image Body

I think these considerations do suggest that *personal* existence, in anything like the form in which we know it now, requires that one should be in some way embodied. But it does not follow from this that the image-theory of the Next World must be mistaken. Here let me remind you again that the body we are discussing now is the body as the artist conceives of it—the painter or the dramatist—and not the body as the anatomist or physiologist conceives of it. The conception of disembodied survival might still be correct, if one thinks of embodiment in the way that anatomists and physiologists do. In order to be a person (or at any rate to be a finite person) one needs to have some sort of body; and it must be not too unlike one's physical body in outward appearance, if one is to be recognizable by others as being the same person after death as one was before. But it need not have anything at all like the complicated internal mechanism which the physical body has. It need not have any internal mechanism, so long as it serves the essential function of expressing one's mental states, and enabling one to be recognized by others. One must have a face, but one need not have a skull, or a cerebral cortex.

Now it seems to me that an *image-body* could perform these functions perfectly well. In order to perform them, it does have to be a spatial entity. But as we have seen already, mental images do have spatial properties, though they are not located in physical space. It is also true that one's body has to be a public entity—public, that is, to all those other persons with whom one has social relations. But as we have also seen, a world of mental images could have some degree of publicity, if we suppose that it is the joint product of the memories and desires of a number of telepathically interacting personalities. It is true that in such an image-world one could not have social relations with *all* the other personalities that there are, but only with those who are sufficiently like-minded with oneself. If one were a very nasty person indeed (exceedingly self-centred or very cruel) one might have to share one's Next World with only a very few others. But I think that if there is life after death at all, we have to suppose that there are many Next Worlds and not just a single one which is common to all of us, regardless of the different memories, emotions, and desires which each of us brings with him when he gets there.

======= ⚘ =======

63

Gilbert Ryle

Gilbert Ryle (1900–1976) was a significant figure in the British tradition of "ordinary language philosophy." His most celebrated work, *The Concept of Mind* (from which the following selections are drawn), is a sustained attack on Cartesian dualism. In what follows, Ryle isolates what he sees as the root mistake of dualism.

Descartes' Myth

The Official Doctrine

There is a doctrine about the nature and place of minds which is so prevalent among theorists and even among laymen that it deserves to be described as the official theory. Most philosophers, psychologists and religious teachers subscribe, with minor reservations, to its main articles and, although they admit certain theoretical difficulties in it, they tend to assume that these can be overcome without serious modifications being made to the architecture of the theory. It will be argued here that the central principles of the doctrine are unsound and conflict with the whole body of what we know about minds when we are not speculating about them.

The official doctrine, which hails chiefly from Descartes, is something like this. With the doubtful exceptions of idiots and infants in arms every human being has both a body and a mind. Some would prefer to say that every human being is both a body and a mind. His body and his mind are ordinarily harnessed together, but after the death of the body his mind may continue to exist and function.

Human bodies are in space and are subject to the mechanical laws which govern all other bodies in space. Bodily processes and states can be inspected by external observers. So a man's bodily life is as much a public affair as are the lives of animals and reptiles and even as the careers of trees, crystals and planets.

But minds are not in space, nor are their operations subject to mechanical laws. The workings of one mind are not witnessable by other observers; its career is private. Only I can take direct cognisance of the states and processes of my own mind. A person therefore lives through two collateral histories, one consisting of what happens in and to his body, the other consisting of what happens in and to his mind. The first is public, the second private. The events in the first history are events in the physical world, those in the second are events in the mental world.

It has been disputed whether a person does or can directly monitor all or only some of the episodes of his own private history; but, according to the official doctrine, of at least some of these episodes he has direct and unchallengeable cognisance. In consciousness, self-consciousness and introspection he is directly and authentically apprised of the present states and operations of his mind. He may have great or small uncertainties about concurrent and adjacent episodes in the physical world, but he can have none about at least part of what is momentarily occupying his mind.

It is customary to express this bifurcation of his two lives and of his two worlds by saying that the things and events which belong to the physical world, including his own body, are external, while the workings of his own mind are internal. This antithesis of outer and inner is of course meant to be construed as a metaphor, since minds, not being in space, could not be described as being spatially inside anything else, or as having things going on spatially inside themselves. But relapses from this good intention are common and theorists are found speculating how stimuli, the physical sources of which are yards or miles outside a person's skin, can generate mental responses inside his skull, or how decisions framed inside his cranium can set going movements of his extremities.

Even when "inner" and "outer" are construed as metaphors, the problem how a person's mind and body influence one another is notoriously charged with theoretical difficulties. What the mind wills, the legs, arms and the tongue execute; what affects the ear and the eye has something to do with what the mind perceives; grimaces and smiles betray the mind's moods and bodily castigations lead, it is hoped, to moral improvement. But the actual transactions between the episodes of the private history and those of the public history remain mysterious, since by definition they can belong to neither series. They could not be reported among the happenings described in a person's autobiography of his inner life, but nor could they be reported among those described in some one else's biography of that person's overt career. They can be inspected neither by introspection nor by laboratory experiment. They are theoretical shuttlecocks which are forever being bandied from the physiologist back to the psychologist and from the psychologist back to the physiologist.

Underlying this partly metaphorical representation of the bifurcation of a person's two lives there is a seemingly more profound and philosophical assumption. It is assumed that there are two different kinds of existence or status. What exists or happens may have the status of physical existence, or it may have the status of mental existence. Somewhat as the faces of coins are either heads or tails, or somewhat as living creatures are either male or female, so, it is supposed, some existing is physical existing, other existing is mental existing. It is a necessary feature of what has physical existence that it is in space and time; it is a necessary feature of what has mental existence that it is in time but not in space. What has physical existence is composed of matter, or else is a function of matter; what has mental existence consists of consciousness, or else is a function of consciousness.

There is thus a polar opposition between mind and matter, an opposition which is often brought out as follows. Material objects are situated in a common field, known as "space," and what happens to one body in one part of space is mechanically connected with what happens to other bodies in other parts of space. But mental happenings occur in insulated fields, known as "minds," and there is, apart maybe from telepathy, no direct causal connection between what happens in one mind and what happens in another. Only through the medium of the public physical world can the mind of one person make a difference to the mind of another. The mind is its own place and in his inner life each of us lives the life of a ghostly Robinson Crusoe. People can see, hear and jolt one another's bodies, but they are irremediably blind and deaf to the workings of one another's minds and inoperative upon them.

What sort of knowledge can be secured of the workings of a mind? On the one side, according to the official theory, a person has direct knowledge of the best imaginable kind of the workings of his own mind. Mental states and processes are (or are normally) conscious states and processes, and the consciousness which irradiates them can engender no illusions and leaves the door open for no doubts. A person's present thinkings, feelings and willings, his perceivings, rememberings and imaginings are intrinsically "phosphorescent"; their existence and their nature are inevitably betrayed to their owner. The inner life is a stream of consciousness of such a sort that it would be absurd to suggest that the mind whose life is that stream might be unaware of what is passing down it. . . .

Besides being currently supplied with these alleged immediate data of consciousness, a person is also generally supposed to be able to exercise from time to time a special kind of perception, namely inner perception, or introspection. He can take a (non-optical) "look" at what is passing in his mind. Not only can he view and scrutinize a flower through his sense of sight and listen to and discriminate the notes of a bell through his sense of hearing; he can also reflectively or introspectively watch, without any bodily organ of sense, the current episodes of his inner life. This self-observation is also commonly supposed to be immune from illusion, confusion or doubt. A mind's reports of its own affairs have a certainty superior to the best that is possessed by its reports of matters in the physical world. Sense-perceptions can, but consciousness and introspection cannot, be mistaken or confused.

On the other side, one person has no direct access of any sort to the events of the inner life of another. He cannot do better than make problematic inferences from the observed behaviour of the other person's body to the states of mind which, by analogy from his own conduct, he supposes to be signalized by that behaviour. Direct access to the workings of a mind is the privilege of that mind itself; in default of such privileged access, the workings of one mind are inevitably occult to everyone else. For the supposed arguments from bodily movements similar to their own to mental workings similar to their own would lack any possibility of observational corroboration. Not unnaturally, therefore, an adherent of the official theory finds it difficult to resist this consequence of his premises, that he has no good reason to believe that there do exist minds other than his own. Even if he prefers to believe that to other human bodies there are harnessed minds not unlike his own, he cannot claim to be able to discover their individual characteristics, or the particular things that they undergo and do. Absolute solitude is on this showing the ineluctable destiny of the soul. Only our bodies can meet.

As a necessary corollary of this general scheme there is implicitly prescribed a special way of construing our ordinary concepts of mental powers and operations. The verbs, nouns and adjectives, with which in ordinary life we describe the wits, characters and higher-grade performances of the people with whom we have do, are required to be construed as signifying special episodes in their secret histories, or else as signifying tendencies for such episodes to occur. When someone is described as knowing, believing or guessing something, as hoping, dreading, intending or shirking something, as designing this or being amused at that, these verbs are supposed to denote the occurrence of specific modifications in his (to us) occult stream of consciousness. Only his own privileged access to this stream in direct awareness and introspection could provide authentic testimony that these mental-conduct verbs were correctly or incorrectly applied. The onlooker, be he teacher, critic, biographer or friend, can never assure himself that his comments have any vestige of truth. Yet it was just because we do in fact all know how to make such comments, make them with general correctness and correct them when they turn out to be confused or mistaken, that philosophers found it necessary to construct their theories of the nature and place of minds. Finding mental-conduct concepts being regularly and effectively used, they properly sought to fix their logical geography. But the logical geography officially recommended would entail that there could be no regular or effective use of these mental-conduct concepts in our descriptions of, and prescriptions for, other people's minds.

The Absurdity of the Official Doctrine

Such in outline is the official theory. I shall often speak of it, with deliberate abusiveness, as "the dogma of the Ghost in the Machine." I hope to prove that it is entirely false, and false not in detail but in principle. It is not merely an assemblage of particular mistakes. It is one big mistake and a mistake of a special kind. It is, namely, a category-mistake. It represents the facts of mental life as if they belonged to one logical type or category (or range of types or categories), when they actually belong to another. The dogma is therefore a philosopher's myth. . . .

I must first indicate what is meant by the phrase "Category-mistake." This I do in a series of illustrations.

A foreigner visiting Oxford or Cambridge for the first time is shown a number of colleges, libraries, playing fields, museums, scientific departments and administrative offices. He then asks "But where is the University? I have seen where the members of the Colleges live, where the Registrar works, where the scientists experiment and the rest. But I have not yet seen the University in which reside and work the members of your University." It has then to be explained to him that the University is not another collateral institution, some ulterior counterpart to the colleges, laboratories and offices which he has seen. The University is just the way in which all that he has already seen is organized. When they are seen and when their co-ordination is understood, the University has been seen. His mistake lay in his innocent assumption that it was correct to speak of Christ Church, the Bodleian Library, the Ashmolean Museum *and* the University, to speak, that is, as if "the University" stood for an extra member of the class of which these other units are members. He was mistakenly allocating the University to the same category as that to which the other institutions belong. . . .

One more illustration. A foreigner watching his first game of cricket learns what are the functions of the bowlers, the batsmen, the fielders, the umpires and the scorers. He then says "But there is no one left on the field to contribute the famous element of team-spirit. I see who does the bowling, the batting and the wicketkeeping; but I do not see whose role it is to exercise *esprit de corps.*" Once more, it would have to be explained that he was looking for the wrong type of thing. Team-spirit is not another cricketing-operation supplementary to all of the other special tasks. It is, roughly, the keenness with which each of the special tasks is performed, and performing a task keenly is not performing two tasks. Certainly exhibiting team-spirit is not the same thing as bowling or catching, but nor is it a third thing such that we can say that the bowler first bowls *and* then exhibits team-spirit or that a fielder is at a given moment *either* catching *or* displaying *esprit de corps.*

These illustrations of category-mistakes have a common feature which must be noticed. The mistakes were made by people who did not know how to wield the concepts *University* . . . and *team-spirit*. Their puzzles arose from inability to use certain items in the English vocabulary.

The theoretically interesting category-mistakes are those made by people who are perfectly competent to apply concepts, at least in the situations with which they are familiar, but are still liable in their abstract thinking to allocate those concepts to logical types to which they do not belong. An instance of a mistake of this sort would be the following story. A student of politics has learned the main differences between the British, the French and the American Constitutions, and has learned also the difference and connections between the Cabinet, Parliament, the various Ministries, the Judicature and the Church of England. But he still becomes embarrassed when asked questions about the connections between the Church of England, the Home Office and the British Constitution. For while the Church and the Home Office are institutions, the British Constitution is not another institution in the same sense of that noun. So inter-institutional relations which can be asserted or denied to hold between the Church and the Home Office cannot be asserted or denied to hold between either of them and the British Constitution. "The British Constitution" is not a term of the same logical type as "the Home Office" and, "the Church of England." In a partially similar way, John Doe may be a relative, a friend, an enemy or a stranger to Richard Roe; but he cannot be any of these things to the Average Taxpayer. He knows how to talk sense in certain sorts of discussions about the Average Taxpayer, but he is baffled to say why he could not come across him in the street as he can come across Richard Roe.

It is pertinent to our main subject to notice that, so long as the student of politics continues to think of the British Constitution as a counterpart to the other institutions, he will tend to describe it as a mysteriously occult institution; and so long as John Doe continues to think of the Average Taxpayer as a fellow-citizen, he will tend to think of him as an elusive insubstantial man, a ghost who is everywhere yet nowhere.

My destructive purpose is to show that a family of radical category-mistakes is the source of the double-life theory. The representation of a person as a ghost mysteriously ensconced in a machine derives from this argument. Because, as is true, a person's thinking, feeling and purposive doing cannot be described solely in the idioms of physics, chemistry and physiology, therefore they must be described in counterpart idioms. As the human body is a complex organized unit, so the human mind must be another complex organised unit, though one made of a different sort of stuff and with a different sort of structure. Or, again, as the human body, like any other parcel of matter, is a field of causes and effects, so the mind must be another field of causes and effects, though not (Heaven be praised) mechanical causes and effects.

The Origin of the Category-Mistake

One of the chief intellectual origins of what I have yet to prove to be the Cartesian category-mistake seems to be this. When Galileo showed that his methods of scientific discovery were competent to provide a mechanical theory which should cover every occupant of space, Descartes found in himself two conflicting motives. As a man of scientific genius he could not but endorse the claims of mechanics, yet as a religious and moral man he could not accept, as Hobbes accepted, the discouraging rider to those claims, namely that human nature differs only in degree of complexity from clockwork. The mental could not be just a variety of the mechanical.

He and subsequent philosophers naturally but erroneously availed themselves of the following escape-route. Since mental-conduct words are not to be construed as signifying the occurrence of mechanical processes, they must be construed as signifying the occurrence of non-mechanical processes; since mechanical laws explain movements in space as the effects of other movements in space, other laws must explain some of the non-spatial workings of minds as the effects of other non-spatial workings of minds. The difference between the human behaviours which we describe as intelligent and those which we describe as unintelligent must be a difference in their causation; so, while some movements of human tongues and limbs are the effects of mechanical causes, others must be the effects of non-mechanical causes, i.e., some issue from movements of particles of matter, others from workings of the mind.

The differences between the physical and the mental were thus represented as differences inside the common framework of the categories of "thing," "stuff," "attribute," "state," "process," "change," "cause" and "effect." Minds are things, but different sorts of things from bodies; mental processes are causes and effects, but different sorts of causes and effects from bodily movements. And so on. Somewhat as the foreigner expected the University to be an extra edifice, rather like a college but also considerably different, so the repudiators of mechanism represented minds as extra centres of causal processes, rather like machines but also considerably different from them. Their theory was a para-mechanical hypothesis.

. . .

When two terms belong to the same category, it is proper to construct conjunctive propositions embodying them. Thus a purchaser may say that he bought a left-hand glove and a right-hand glove, but not that he bought a left-hand glove, a right-hand glove and a pair of gloves. "She came home in a flood of tears and a sedan-chair" is a well-known joke based on the absurdity of conjoining terms of different types. It would have been equally ridiculous to construct the disjunction "She came home either in a flood of tears or else in a sedan-chair." Now the dogma of the Ghost in the Machine does just this. It maintains that there exist both bodies and minds; that there occur physical processes and mental processes; that there are mechanical causes of corporeal movements and mental causes of corporeal movements. I shall argue that these and other analogous conjunctions are absurd; but, it must be noticed, the argument will not show that either of the illegitimately conjoined propositions is absurd in itself. I am not, for example, denying that there occur mental processes. Doing long division is a mental process and so is making a joke. But I am saying that the phrase "there occur mental processes" does not mean the same sort of thing as "there occur physical processes," and, therefore, that it makes no sense to conjoin or disjoin the two.

If my argument is successful, there will follow some interesting consequences. First, the hallowed contrast between Mind and Matter will be dissipated, but dissipated not by either of the equally hallowed absorptions of Mind by Matter or of Matter by Mind, but in quite a different way. For the seeming contrast of the two will be shown to be as illegitimate as would be the contrast of "she came home in a flood of tears" and "she came home in a sedan-chair." The belief that there is a polar opposition between Mind and Matter is the belief that they are terms of the same logical type.

It will also follow that both Idealism and Materialism are answers to an improper question. The "reduction" of the material world to mental states and processes, as well as the "reduction" of mental states and processes to physical states and processes, presuppose the legitimacy of the disjunction "Either there exist minds or there exist bodies (but not both)." It would be like saying, "Either she bought a left-hand and a right-hand glove or she bought a pair of gloves (but not both)."

It is perfectly proper to say, in one logical tone of voice, that there exist minds, and to say, in another logical tone of voice, that there exist bodies. But these expressions do not indicate two different species of existence, for "existence" is not a generic word like "coloured" or "sexed." They indicate two different senses of "exist," somewhat as "rising" has different senses in "the tide is rising," "hopes are rising," and "the average age of death is rising." A man would be thought to be making a poor joke who said that three things are now rising, namely the tide, hopes and the average age of death. It would be just as good or bad a joke to say that there exist prime numbers and Wednesdays and public opinions and navies; or that there exist both minds and bodies.

64

Jean-Paul Sartre

Jean-Paul Sartre (1905–1980) was a French existentialist philosopher and novelist. The first selection is drawn from his philosophical novel *Nausea,* and dramatically reveals Sartre's view of the gratuitous and meaningless nature of human life; in the second, taken from his widely read book *Existentialism and Humanism,* Sartre explores the concept of freedom and its significance in human life: we are, as he famously wrote, "condemned to be free."

Nausea

I was in the municipal park just now. The root of the chestnut tree plunged into the ground just underneath my bench. I no longer remembered that it was a root. Words had disappeared, and with them the meaning of things, the methods of using them, the feeble landmarks which men have traced on their surface. I was sitting, slightly bent, my head bowed, alone in front of that black, knotty mass, which was utterly crude and frightened me. And then I had this revelation.

It took my breath away. Never, until these last few days, had I suspected what it meant to "exist." I was like the others, like those who walk along the sea-shore in their spring clothes. I used to say like them: "The sea *is* green; that white speck up there *is* a seagull," but I didn't feel that it

From Sartre, Jean-Paul, *Nausea* (trans. by Robert Baldick) (Harmondsworth: Penguin, 1965), pp. 182–185.

existed, that the seagull was an "existing seagull"; usually existence hides itself. It is there, around us, in us, it is *us*, you can't say a couple of words without speaking of it, but finally you can't touch it. When I believed I was thinking about it, I suppose that I was thinking nothing, my head was empty, or there was just one word in my head, the word "to be." Or else I was thinking . . . how can I put it? I was thinking *appurtenances*, I was saying to myself that the sea belonged to the class of green objects, or that green formed part of the sea's qualities. Even when I looked at things, I was miles from thinking that they existed: they looked like stage scenery to me. I picked them up in my hands, they served me as tools, I foresaw their resistance. But all that happened on the surface. If anybody had asked me what existence was, I should have replied in good faith, that it was nothing, just an empty form which added itself to external things, without changing anything in their nature. And then, all of a sudden, there it was, as clear as day: existence had suddenly unveiled itself. It had lost its harmless appearance as an abstract category: it was the very stuff of things, that root was steeped in existence. Or rather the root, the park gates, the bench, the sparse grass on the lawn, all that had vanished; the diversity of things, their individuality, was only an appearance, a veneer. This veneer had melted, leaving soft, monstrous masses, in disorder— naked, with a frightening, obscene nakedness.

I took care not to make the slightest movement, but I didn't need to move in order to see, behind the trees, the blue columns and the lamp- post of the bandstand, and the Velleda in the middle of a clump of laurel bushes. All those objects . . . how can I explain? They embarrassed me; I would have liked them to exist less strongly, in a drier, more abstract way, with more reserve. The chestnut tree pressed itself against my eyes. Green rust covered it half way up; the bark, black and blistered, looked like boiled leather. The soft sound of the water in the Masqueret Fountain flowed into my ears and made a nest there, filling them with sighs; my nostrils overflowed with a green, putrid smell. All things, gently, tenderly, were letting themselves drift into existence like those weary women who abandon themselves to laughter and say: "It does you good to laugh," in tearful voices; they were parading themselves in front of one another, they were abjectly admitting to one another the fact of their existence. I realized that there was no half-way house between nonexistence and this rapturous abundance. If you existed, you had to *exist to that extent*, to the point of mildew, blisters, obscenity. In another world, circles and melodies kept their pure and rigid lines. But existence is a curve. Trees, midnight-blue pillars, the happy bubbling of a fountain, living smells, wisps of heat haze floating in the cold air, a red-haired man digesting on a bench: all these somnolences, all these digestions taken together had a vaguely comic side. Comic. . . . No: it didn't go as far as that, nothing that exists can be comic; it was like a vague, almost imperceptible analogy with certain vaudeville situations. We were a heap of existents inconvenienced, embarrassed by ourselves, we hadn't the slightest reason for being there, any of us, each existent, embarrassed, vaguely ill at ease, felt superfluous in relation to the others. *Superfluous*: that was the only connexion I could establish between those trees, those gates, those pebbles. It was in vain that I tried to count the chestnut trees, to *situate* them in relation to the Velleda, to compare their height with the height of the plane trees: each of them escaped from the relationship in which I tried to enclose it, isolated itself, overflowed. I was aware of the arbitrary nature of these relationships, which I insisted on maintaining in order to delay the collapse of the human world of measures, of quantities, of bearings; they no longer had any grip on things. *Superfluous*, the chestnut tree, over there, opposite me, a little to the left. *Superfluous*, the Velleda. . . .

And *I*—weak, languid, obscene, digesting, tossing about dismal thoughts—*I too was superfluous*. Fortunately, I didn't feel this, above all I didn't understand it, but I was uneasy because I was afraid of feeling it (even now I'm afraid of that—I'm afraid that it might take me by the back of my head and lift me up like a ground-swell). I dreamed vaguely of killing myself, to destroy at least one of these superfluous existences. But my death itself would have been superfluous. Superfluous, my corpse, my blood on these pebbles, between these plants, in the depths of this charming park. And the decomposed flesh would have been superfluous in the earth which would have received it, and my bones, finally, cleaned, stripped, neat and clean as teeth, would also have been superfluous; I was superfluous for all time.

Existentialism and Humanism

And when we speak of "abandonment"—a favourite word of Heidegger— we only mean to say that God does not exist, and that it is necessary to draw the consequences of his absence right to the end. The existentialist

From Sartre, Jean-Paul, *Existentialism and Humanism* (trans. by Philip Mairet) (London: Methuen, 1948), pp. 32–35.

is strongly opposed to a certain type of secular moralism which seeks to suppress God at the least possible expense. Towards 1880, when the French professors endeavoured to formulate a secular morality, they said something like this:—God is a useless and costly hypothesis, so we will do without it. However, if we are to have morality, a society and a law-abiding world, it is essential that certain values should be taken seriously; they must have an *à priori* existence ascribed to them. It must be considered obligatory *à priori* to be honest, not to lie, not to beat one's wife, to bring up children and so forth; so we are going to do a little work on this subject, which will enable us to show that these values exist all the same, inscribed in an intelligible heaven although, of course, there is no God. In other words—and this is, I believe, the purport of all that we in France call radicalism—nothing will be changed if God does not exist; we shall re-discover the same norms of honesty, progress and humanity, and we shall have disposed of God as an out-of-date hypothesis which will die away quietly of itself. The existentialist, on the contrary, finds it extremely embarrassing that God does not exist, for there disappears with Him all possibility of finding values in an intelligible heaven. There can no longer be any good *à priori*, since there is no infinite and perfect consciousness to think it. It is nowhere written that "the good" exists, that one must he honest or must not lie, since we are now upon the plane where there are only men. Dostoievsky once wrote "If God did not exist, everything would be permitted"; and that, for existentialism, is the starting point. Everything is indeed permitted if God does not exist, and man is in consequence forlorn, for he cannot find anything to depend upon either within or outside himself. He discovers forthwith, that he is without excuse. For if indeed existence precedes essence, one will never be able to explain one's action by reference to a given and specific human nature; in other words, there is no determinism—man is free, man *is* freedom. Nor, on the other hand, if God does not exist, are we provided with any values or commands that could legitimise our behaviour. Thus we have neither behind us, nor before us in a luminous realm of values, any means of justification or excuse. We are left alone, without excuse. That is what I mean when I say that man is condemned to be free. Condemned, because he did not create himself, yet is nevertheless at liberty, and from the moment that he is thrown into this world he is responsible for everything he does. The existentialist does not believe in the power of passion. He will never regard a grand passion as a destructive torrent upon which a man is swept into certain actions as by fate, and which, therefore, is an excuse for them. He thinks that man is responsible for his passion. Neither will an existentialist think that a man can find help through some sign being vouchsafed upon earth for his orientation: for he thinks that the man himself interprets the sign as he chooses. He thinks that every man, without any support or help whatever, is condemned at every instant to invent man. As Ponge has written in a very fine article, "Man is the future of man." That is exactly true. Only, if one took this to mean that the future is laid up in Heaven, that God knows what it is, it would be false, for then it would no longer even be a future. If, however, it means that, whatever man may now appear to be, there is a future to be fashioned, a virgin future that awaits him—then it is a true saying. But in the present one is forsaken.

≈ 𝔰 ≈

Hannah Arendt

Hannah Arendt (1906–1975) was a German-Jewish philosopher and political theorist. Forced to leave Germany in 1933, she finally settled in the United States where she lived the remainder of her life. Her many books include *The Human Condition*, *The Origins of Totalitarianism*, and *Eichmann in Jerusalem*, from which the following extracts are drawn. Arendt's report on the trial of the Nazi war criminal Adolf Eichmann is famous for, among other things, introducing the idea of "the banality of evil": according to Arendt, Eichmann was neither an ideologue nor a fanatic, but an exceedingly average person motivated by a desire for promotion and with a marked inability to think for himself. Arendt's account of this type of personality is clearly of value in discussions concerning one of the themes of this anthology: the natural goodness or badness of human beings.

Eichmann in Jerusalem

Despite all the efforts of the prosecution, everybody could see that this man was not a "monster," but it was difficult indeed not to suspect that he was a clown. And since this suspicion would have been fatal to the whole enterprise, and was also rather hard to sustain in view of the sufferings he and his like had caused to millions of people, his worst clowneries were hardly noticed and almost never reported. What could you do with a man who first declared, with great emphasis, that the one thing he had learned in an ill-spent life was that one should never take an oath ("Today no man, no judge could ever persuade me to make a sworn statement, to declare something under oath as a witness. I refuse it, I refuse it for moral reasons. Since my experience tells me that if one is loyal to his oath, one day he has to take the consequences, I have made up my mind once and for all that no judge in the world or any other authority will ever be capable of making me swear an oath, to give sworn testimony. I won't do it voluntarily and no one will be able to force me"), and then, after being told explicitly that if he wished to testify in his own defense he might "do so under oath or without an oath," declared without further ado that he would prefer to testify under oath? Or who, repeatedly and with a great show of feeling, assured the court, as he had assured the police examiner, that the worst thing he could do would be to try to escape his true responsibilities, to fight for his neck, to plead for mercy—and then, upon instruction of his counsel, submitted a handwritten document, containing his plea for mercy?

As far as Eichmann was concerned, these were questions of changing moods, and as long as he was capable of finding, either in his memory or on the spur of the moment, an elating stock phrase to go with them, he was quite content, without ever becoming aware of anything like "inconsistencies." As we shall see, this horrible gift for consoling himself with clichés did not leave him in the hour of his death.

. . .

Adolf Eichmann went to the gallows with great dignity. He had asked for a bottle of red wine and had drunk half of it. He refused the help of the Protestant minister, the Reverend William Hull, who offered to read the Bible with him: he had only two more hours to live, and therefore no "time to waste." He walked the fifty yards from his cell to the execution chamber calm and erect, with his hands bound behind him. When the guards tied his ankles and knees, he asked them to loosen the bonds so that he could stand straight. "I don't need that," he said when the black hood was offered him. He was in complete command of himself, nay, he was more: he was completely himself. Nothing could have demonstrated this more convincingly than the grotesque silliness of his last words. He began by stating emphatically that he was a *Gottgläubiger,* to express in common Nazi fashion that he was no Christian and did not believe in life after death. He then proceeded: "After a short while, gentlemen, *we shall all meet again.* Such is the fate of all men. Long live Germany, long live Argentina, long live Austria. *I shall not forget them.*" In the face of death, he had found the cliché used in funeral oratory. Under the gallows, his memory played him the last trick; he was "elated" and he forgot that this was his own funeral.

It was as though in those last minutes he was summing up the lesson that this long course in human wickedness had taught us—the lesson of the fearsome, word-and-thought-defying *banality of evil.*

. . .

Foremost among the larger issues at stake in the Eichmann trial was the assumption current in all modern legal systems that intent to do wrong is necessary for the commission of a crime. On nothing, perhaps, has civilized jurisprudence prided itself more than on this taking into account of the subjective factor. Where this intent is absent, where, for whatever reasons, even reasons of moral insanity, the ability to distinguish between right and wrong is impaired, we feel no crime has been committed. We refuse, and consider as barbaric, the propositions "that a great crime offends nature, so that the very earth cries out for vengeance; that evil violates a natural harmony which only retribution can restore; that a wronged collectivity owes a duty to the moral order to punish the criminal" (Yosal Rogat). And yet I think it is undeniable that it was precisely on the ground of these long-forgotten propositions that Eichmann was brought to justice to begin with, and that they were, in fact, the supreme justification for the death penalty. Because he had been implicated and had played a central role in an enterprise whose open purpose was to eliminate forever certain "races" from the surface of the earth, he had to be eliminated. And if it is true that "justice must not only be done but must be seen to be done," then the justice of what was done in Jerusalem would have emerged to be seen by all if the judges had dared to address their defendant in something like the following terms:

> You admitted that the crime committed against the Jewish people during the war was the greatest crime in recorded history, and you admitted your role in it. But you said you had never acted from base motives, that you had never had any inclination to kill anybody, that you had never hated Jews, and still that you could not have acted otherwise and that you did not feel guilty. We find this difficult, though not altogether impossible, to believe; there is some, though not very much, evidence against you in this matter of motivation and conscience that could be proved beyond reasonable doubt. You also said

that your role in the Final Solution was an accident and that almost anybody could have taken your place, so that potentially almost all Germans are equally guilty. What you meant to say was that where all, or almost all, are guilty, nobody is. This is an indeed quite common conclusion, but one we are not willing to grant you. And if you don't understand our objection, we would recommend to your attention the story of Sodom and Gomorrah, two neighboring cities in the Bible, which were destroyed by fire from Heaven because all the people in them had become equally guilty. This, incidentally, has nothing to do with the newfangled notion of "collective guilt," according to which people supposedly are guilty of, or feel guilty about, things done in their name but not by them—things in which they did not participate and from which they did not profit. In other words, guilt and innocence before the law are of an objective nature, and even if eighty million Germans had done as you did, this would not have been an excuse for you.

Luckily, we don't have to go that far. You yourself claimed not the actuality but only the potentiality of equal guilt on the part of all who lived in a state whose main political purpose had become the commission of unheard-of crimes. And no matter through what accidents of exterior or interior circumstances you were pushed onto the road of becoming a criminal, there is an abyss between the actuality of what you did and the potentiality of what others might have done. We are concerned here only with what you did, and not with the possible noncriminal nature of your inner life and of your motives or with the criminal potentialities of those around you. You told your story in terms of a hard-luck story, and, knowing the circumstances, we are, up to a point, willing to grant you that under more favorable circumstances it is highly unlikely that you would ever have come before us or before any other criminal court. Let us assume, for the sake of argument, that it was nothing more than misfortune that made you a willing instrument in the organization of mass murder; there still remains the fact that you have carried out, and therefore actively supported, a policy of mass murder. For politics is not like the nursery; in politics obedience and support are the same. And just as you supported and carried out a policy of not wanting to share the earth with the Jewish people and the people of a number of other nations—as though you and your superiors had any right to determine who should and who should not inhabit the world—we find that no one, that is, no member of the human race, can be expected to want to share the earth with you. This is the reason, and the only reason, you must hang.

. . .

There is of course no doubt that the defendant and the nature of his acts as well as the trial itself raise problems of a general nature which go far beyond the matters considered in Jerusalem. . . . I would not have been surprised if people had found my treatment inadequate, and I would have welcomed a discussion of the general significance of the entire body of facts, which could have been all the more meaningful the more directly it referred to the concrete events. I also can well imagine that an authentic controversy might have arisen over the subtitle of the book; for when I speak of the banality of evil, I do so only on the strictly factual level, pointing to a phenomenon which stared one in the face at the trial. Eichmann was not Iago and not Macbeth, and nothing would have been farther from his mind than to determine with Richard III "to prove a villain." Except for an extraordinary diligence in looking out for his personal advancement, he had no motives at all. And this diligence in itself was in no way criminal; he certainly would never have murdered his superior in order to inherit his post. He *merely*, to put the matter colloquially, *never realized what he was doing.* It was precisely this lack of imagination which enabled him to sit for months on end facing a German Jew who was conducting the police interrogation, pouring out his heart to the man and explaining again and again how it was that he reached only the rank of lieutenant colonel in the S.S. and that it had not been his fault that he was not promoted. In principle he knew quite well what it was all about, and in his final statement to the court he spoke of the "revaluation of values prescribed by the [Nazi] government." He was not stupid. It was sheer thoughtlessness—something by no means identical with stupidity—that predisposed him to become one of the greatest criminals of that period. And if this is "banal" and even funny, if with the best will in the world one cannot extract any diabolical or demonic profundity from Eichmann, that is still far from calling it commonplace. It surely cannot be so common that a man facing death, and, moreover, standing beneath the gallows, should be able to think of nothing but what he has heard at funerals all his life, and that these "lofty words" should completely becloud the reality of his own death. That such remoteness from reality and such thoughtlessness can wreak more havoc than all the evil instincts taken together which, perhaps, are inherent in man—that was, in fact, the lesson one could learn in Jerusalem. But it was a lesson, neither an explanation of the phenomenon nor a theory about it.

66

=== ॐ ===

Simone de Beauvoir

· ·

In this selection from the introduction to her *The Second Sex*, Simone de Beauvoir (1908–1986) develops and applies the existentialist emphasis on subjectivity and freedom to the question of the place in society and thought of women—and, by extension, any group that has been defined by a set of stereotyped characteristics. She deals with the way in which women have been objectified and treated as mysterious Other.

· ·

The Second Sex

But first we must ask: what is a woman? "*Tota mulier in utero,*" says one, "woman is a womb." But in speaking of certain women, connoisseurs declare that they are not women, although they are equipped with a uterus like the rest. All agree in recognizing the fact that females exist in the human species; today as always they make up about one half of humanity. And yet we are told that femininity is in danger; we are exhorted to be women, remain women, become women. It would appear, then, that every female human being is not necessarily a woman; to be so considered she must share in that mysterious and threatened reality known as femininity. Is this attribute something secreted by the ovaries? Or is it a Platonic essence, a product of the philosophic imagination? Is a rustling petticoat enough to bring it down to earth? Although some women try zealously to incarnate this essence, it is hardly patentable. It is frequently described in vague and dazzling terms that seem to have been borrowed from the vocabulary of the seers, and indeed in the times of St. Thomas it was considered an essence as certainly defined as the somniferous virtue of the poppy.

But conceptualism has lost ground. The biological and social sciences no longer admit the existence of unchangeably fixed entities that determine given characteristics, such as those ascribed to woman, the Jew, or the Negro. Science regards any characteristic as a reaction dependent in part upon a *situation*. If today femininity no longer exists, then it never existed.

But does the word *woman*, then, have no specific content? This is stoutly affirmed by those who hold to the philosophy of the enlightenment, of rationalism, of nominalism; women, to them, are merely the human beings arbitrarily designated by the word *woman*. Many American women particularly are prepared to think that there is no longer any place for woman as such; if a backward individual still takes herself for a woman, her friends advise her to be psychoanalysed and thus get rid of this obsession. In regard to a work, *Modern Woman: The Lost Sex*, which in other respects has its irritating features, Dorothy Parker has written: "I cannot be just to books which treat of woman as woman. . . . My idea is that all of us, men as well as women, should be regarded as human beings." But nominalism is a rather inadequate doctrine, and the anti-feminists have had no trouble in showing that women simply *are not* men. Surely woman is, like man, a human being; but such a declaration is abstract. The fact is that every concrete human being is always a singular, separate individual. To decline to accept such notions as the eternal feminine, the black soul, the Jewish character, is not to deny that Jews, Negroes, women exist today—this denial does not represent a liberation for those concerned, but rather a flight from reality. Some years ago a well-known woman writer refused to permit her portrait to appear in a series of photographs especially devoted to women writers; she wished to be counted among the men. But in order to gain this privilege she made use of her husband's influence! Women who assert that they are men lay claim none the less to masculine consideration and respect. I recall also a young Trotskyite standing on a platform at a boisterous meeting and getting ready to use her fists, in spite of her evident fragility. She was denying her feminine weakness; but it was for love of a militant male whose equal she wished to be. The attitude of defiance of many American women proves that they are haunted by a sense of their femininity. In truth, to go for a walk with one's eyes open is enough to demonstrate that humanity is divided into two classes of individuals whose clothes, faces, bodies, smiles, gaits, interests, and occupations are manifestly different. Perhaps these differences are superficial, perhaps they are destined to disappear. What is certain is that they do most obviously exist.

If her functioning as a female is not enough to define woman, if we decline also to explain her through "the eternal feminine," and if nevertheless we admit, provisionally, that women do exist, then we must face the question: what is a woman?

To state the question is, to me, to suggest, at once, a preliminary answer. The fact that I ask it is in itself significant. A man would never set out to write a book on the peculiar situation of the human male. But if I wish to define myself, I must first of all say: "I am a woman"; on this truth must be *based* all further discussion. A man never begins by presenting himself as an individual of a certain sex; it goes without saying that he is a man. The terms *masculine* and *feminine* are used symmetrically only as a matter of form, as on legal papers. In actuality the relation of the two sexes is not quite like that of two electrical poles, for man represents both the positive and the neutral, as is indicated by the common use of *man* to designate human beings in general; whereas woman represents only the negative, defined by limiting criteria, without reciprocity. In the midst of an abstract discussion it is vexing to hear a man say: "You think thus and so because you are a woman"; but I know that my only defence is to reply: "I think thus and so because it is true," thereby removing my subjective self from the argument. It would be out of the question to reply: "And you think the contrary because you are a man," for it is understood that the fact of being a man is no peculiarity. A man is in the right in being a man; it is the woman who is in the wrong. It amounts to this: just as for the ancients there was an absolute vertical with reference to which the oblique was defined, so there is an absolute human type, the masculine. Woman has ovaries, a uterus; these peculiarities imprison her in her subjectivity, circumscribe her within the limits of her own nature. It is often said that she thinks with her glands. Man superbly ignores the fact that his anatomy also includes glands, such as the testicles, and that they secrete hormones. He thinks of his body as a direct and normal connection with the world, which he believes he apprehends objectively, whereas he regards the body of woman as a hindrance, a prison, weighed down by everything peculiar to it. "The female is a female by virtue of a certain *lack* of qualities," said Aristotle; "we should regard the female nature as afflicted with a natural defectiveness." And St. Thomas for his part pronounced woman to be an "imperfect man," an "incidental" being. This is symbolized in Genesis where Eve is depicted as made from what Bossuet called "a supernumerary bone" of Adam.

Thus humanity is male and man defines woman not in herself but as relative to him; she is not regarded as an autonomous being. Michelet writes: "Woman, the relative being . . ." And Benda is most positive in his *Rapport d'Uriel*: "The body of man makes sense in itself quite apart from that of woman, whereas the latter seems wanting in significance by itself. . . . Man can think of himself without woman. She cannot think of herself without man." And she is simply what man decrees; thus she is called "the sex," by which is meant that she appears essentially to the male as a sexual being. For him she is sex—absolute sex, no less. She is defined and differentiated with reference to man and not he with reference to her; she is the incidental, the inessential as opposed to the essential. He is the Subject, he is the Absolute—she is the Other.

. . .

Now, what peculiarly signalizes the situation of woman is that she—a free and autonomous being like all human creatures—nevertheless finds herself living in a world where men compel her to assume the status of the Other. They propose to stabilize her as object and to doom her to immanence since her transcendence is to be overshadowed and for ever transcended by another ego (*conscience*) which is essential and sovereign. The drama of woman lies in this conflict between the fundamental aspirations of every subject (ego)—who always regards the self as the essential— and the compulsions of a situation in which she is the inessential. How can a human being in woman's situation attain fulfilment? What roads are open to her? Which are blocked? How can independence be recovered in a state of dependency? What circumstances limit woman's liberty and how can they be overcome? These are the fundamental questions on which I would fain throw some light. This means that I am interested in the fortunes of the individual as defined not in terms of happiness but in terms of liberty.

67

Albert Camus

Albert Camus (1913–1960) was a French philosopher and novelist. One of his most important books is *The Myth of Sisyphus*, from which the following selections are drawn. By means of an investigation into suicide—the "one truly serious philosophical problem," as he calls it—Camus develops his philosophy of the absurd. The absurd, he contends, is generated by the contradiction between human needs (for reason and happiness) and "the unreasonable silence of the world."

The Myth of Sisyphus

Suicide has never been dealt with except as a social phenomenon. On the contrary, we are concerned here, at the outset, with the relationship between individual thought and suicide. An act like this is prepared within the silence of the heart, as is a great work of art. The man himself is ignorant of it. One evening he pulls the trigger or jumps. Of an apartment-building manager who had killed himself I was told that he had lost his daughter five years before, that he had changed greatly since and that that experience had "undermined" him. A more exact word cannot be imagined. Beginning to think is beginning to be undermined. Society has but little connection with such beginnings. The worm is in man's heart. That

Approximately one thousand nine hundred and forty-four words from THE MYTH OF SISYPHUS by Albert Camus, translated by Justin O'Brien. (Penguin Classics, 1955). Copyright © Justin O'Brien. The moral right of the translator has been asserted.

is where it must be sought. One must follow and understand this fatal game that leads from lucidity in the face of experience to flight from light.

There are many causes for a suicide and generally the most obvious ones were not the most powerful. Rarely is suicide committed (yet the hypothesis is not excluded) through reflection. What sets off the crisis is almost always unverifiable. Newspapers often speak of "personal sorrows" or of "incurable illness." These explanations are plausible. But one would have to know whether a friend of the desperate man had not that very day addressed him indifferently. He is the guilty one. For that is enough to precipitate all the rancours and all the boredom still in suspension.

But if it is hard to fix the precise instant the subtle step when the mind opted for death, it is easier to deduce from the act itself the consequences it implies. In a sense, and as in melodrama, killing yourself amounts to confessing. It is confessing that life is too much for you or that you do not understand it. Let's not go too far in such analogies, however, but rather return to everyday words. It is merely confessing that that "is not worth the trouble." Living, naturally, is never easy. You continue making the gestures commanded by existence for many reasons, the first of which is habit. Dying voluntarily implies that you have recognized, even instinctively, the ridiculous character of that habit, the absence of any profound reason for living, the insane character of that daily agitation and the uselessness of suffering.

What then is that incalculable feeling that deprives the mind of the sleep necessary to life? A world that can be explained even with bad reasons is a familiar world. But, on the other hand, in a universe suddenly divested of illusions and lights, man feels an alien, a stranger. His exile is without remedy since he is deprived of the memory of a lost home or the hope of a promised land. This divorce between man and his life, the actor and his setting, is properly the feeling of absurdity. . . .

At any street corner the feeling of absurdity can strike any man in the face. . . .

It happens that the stage-sets collapse. Rising, tram, four hours in the office or factory, meal, tram, four hours of work, meal, sleep and Monday, Tuesday, Wednesday, Thursday, Friday and Saturday, according to the same rhythm—this path is easily followed most of the time. But one day the "why" arises and everything begins in that weariness tinged with amazement. "Begins"—this is important. Weariness comes at the end of the acts of a mechanical life, but at the same time it inaugurates the impulse of consciousness. It awakens consciousness and provokes what follows.

What follows is the gradual return into the chain or it is the definitive awakening. At the end of the awakening comes, in time, the consequence: suicide or recovery. In itself weariness has something sickening about it. Here, I must conclude that it is good. For everything begins with consciousness and nothing is worth anything except through it. There is nothing original about these remarks. But they are obvious; that is enough for a while, during a sketchy reconnaissance in the origins of the absurd. Mere "anxiety," as Heidegger says, is at the source of everything.

Likewise and during every day of an unillustrious life, time carries us. But a moment always comes when we have to carry it. We live on the future: "tomorrow," "later on," "when you have made your way," "you will understand when you are old enough." Such irrelevancies are wonderful, for after all, it's a matter of dying. Yet a time comes when a man notices or says that he is thirty. Thus he asserts his youth. But simultaneously he situates himself in relation to time. He takes his place in it. He admits that he stands at a certain point on a curve that he acknowledges having to travel to its end. He belongs to time and, by the horror that seizes him, he recognizes his worst enemy. Tomorrow, he was longing for tomorrow, whereas everything in him ought to reject it. The revolt of the flesh is the absurd.

. . .

Of whom and of what indeed can I say: "I know that!" This heart within me I can feel, and I judge that it exists. This world I can touch, and I likewise judge that it exists. There ends all my knowledge, and the rest is construction. For if I try to seize this self of which I feel sure, if I try to define and to summarize it, it is nothing but water slipping through my fingers. I can sketch one by one all the aspects it is able to assume, all those likewise that have been attributed to it, this upbringing, this origin, this ardour or these silences, this nobility or this vileness. But aspects cannot be added up. This very heart which is mine will for ever remain indefinable to me. Between the certainty I have of my existence and the content I try to give to that assurance, the gap will never be filled. For ever I shall be a stranger to myself. In psychology as in logic, there are truths but no truth. Socrates' "Know thyself" has as much value as the "be virtuous" of our confessionals. They reveal a nostalgia at the same time as an ignorance. They are sterile exercises on great subjects. They are legitimate only precisely in so far as they are approximate.

And here are trees and I know their gnarled surface, water and I feel its taste. These scents of grass and stars at night, certain evenings when the heart relaxes—how shall I negate this world whose power and strength I feel? Yet all the knowledge on earth will give me nothing to assure me that this world is mine. You describe it to me and you teach me to classify it. You enumerate its laws and in my thirst for knowledge I admit that they are true. You take apart its mechanism and my hope increases. At the final stage you teach me that this wondrous and multi-coloured universe can be reduced to the atom and that the atom itself can be reduced to the electron. All this is good and I wait for you to con-tinue. But you tell me of an invisible planetary system in which electrons gravitate around a nucleus. You explain this world to me with an image. I realize then that you have been reduced to poetry: I shall never know. Have I the time to become indignant? You have already changed theories. So that science that was to teach me everything ends up in a hypothesis, that lucidity founders in metaphor, that uncertainty is resolved in a work of art. What need had I of so many efforts? The soft lines of these hills and the hand of evening on this troubled heart teach me much more. I have returned to my beginning. I realize that if through science I can seize phenomena and enumerate them, I cannot for all that apprehend the world. Were I to trace its entire relief with my finger, I should not know any more. And you give me the choice between a description that is sure but that teaches me nothing and hypotheses that claim to teach me but that are not sure. A stranger to myself and to the world, armed solely with a thought that negates itself as soon as it asserts, what is this condition in which I can have peace only by refusing to know and to live, in which the appetite for conquest bumps into walls that defy its assaults? To will is to stir up paradoxes. Everything is ordered in such a way as to bring into being that poisoned peace produced by thoughtlessness, lack of heart or fatal renunciations.

Hence the intelligence, too, tells me in its way that this world is absurd. Its contrary, blind reason, may well claim that all is clear. I was waiting for proof and longing for it to be right. But, despite so many pre-tentious centuries and over the heads of so many eloquent and persuasive men, I know that is false. On this plane, at least, there is no happiness if I cannot know. That universal reason, practical or ethical, that deter-minism, those categories that explain everything are enough to make a decent man laugh. They have nothing to do with the mind. They negate its profound truth which is to be enchained. In this unintelligible and limited universe, man's fate henceforth assumes its meaning. A horde of irrationals has sprung up and surrounds him until his ultimate end. In his recovered and now studied lucidity, the feeling of the absurd becomes clear and definite. I said that the world is absurd but I was too hasty. This world in itself is not reasonable, that is all that can be said. But what is absurd is the confrontation of the irrational and the wild longing for clarity whose call echoes in the human heart. The absurd depends as much on man as on the world. For the moment it is all that links them together. It binds them one to the other as only hatred can weld two creatures together. This is all I can discern clearly in this measureless universe where my adventure takes place. Let us pause here. If I hold to be true that absurdity that determines my relationship with life, if I become thoroughly imbued with that sentiment that seizes me in face of the world's scenes, with that lucidity imposed on me by the pursuit of a science, I must sacrifice everything to these certainties and I must see them squarely to be able to maintain them. Above all, I must adapt my behaviour to them and pursue them in all their consequences. I am speaking here of decency. But I want to know beforehand if thought can live in those deserts.

. . .

The experiences called to mind here were born in the desert that we must not leave behind. At least it is essential to know how far they went. At this point of his effort man stands face to face with the irrational. He feels within him his longing for happiness and for reason. The absurd is born of this confrontation between the human need and the unreasonable silence of the world. This must not be forgotten. This must be clung to because the whole consequence of a life can depend on it. The irrational, the human nostalgia, and the absurd that is born of their encounter—these are the three characters in the drama that must necessarily end with all the logic of which an existence is capable.

68

P. F. Strawson

Sir Peter Strawson (1919–2006) was Waynflete Professor of
Metaphysical Philosophy at the University of Oxford. In this selection from his book *Individuals,* Strawson argues that a disembodied
existence would be something very unattractive indeed, an attenuated existence little different from complete annihilation.

Persons

Earlier, when I was discussing the concept of a pure individual consciousness, I said that though it could not exist as a primary concept to be used
in the explanation of the concept of a person. . ., yet it might have a logically secondary existence. Thus, within our actual conceptual scheme,
each of us can quite intelligibly conceive of his or her individual survival of bodily death. The effort of imagination is not even great. One has
simply to think of oneself as having thoughts and memories as at present, visual and auditory experiences largely as at present, even, perhaps—
though this involves certain complications—some quasi-tactual and
organic sensations as at present, whilst (*a*) having no perceptions of a
body related to one's experience as one's own body is, and (*b*) having no
power of initiating changes in the physical condition of the world, such

as one at present does with one's hands, shoulders, feet and vocal cords. Condition (*a*) must be expanded by adding that no one else exhibits reactions indicating that he perceives a body at the point which one's body would be occupying if one were seeing and hearing in an embodied state from the point from which one is seeing and hearing in a disembodied state. One could, of course, imagine condition (*a*) being fulfilled, in both its parts, without condition (*b*) being fulfilled. This would be a rather vulgar fancy, in the class of the table-tapping spirits with familiar voices. But suppose we take disembodiment strictly in the sense that we imagine both (*a*) and (*b*) fulfilled. Then two consequences follow, one of which is commonly noted, the other of which is perhaps insufficiently attended to. The first is that the strictly disembodied individual is strictly solitary, and it must remain for him indeed an utterly empty, though not meaningless, speculation, as to whether there are other members of his class. The other, and less commonly noticed point, is that in order to retain his idea of himself as an individual, he must always think of himself as *disembodied*, as a *former* person. That is to say, he must contrive still to have the idea of himself as a member of a class or type of entities with whom, however, he is now debarred from entering into any of those transactions the past fact of which was the condition of his having any idea of himself at all. Since then he has, as it were, no personal life of his own to lead, he must live much in the memories of the personal life he did lead; or he might, when this living in the past loses its appeal, achieve some kind of attenuated vicarious personal existence by taking a certain kind of interest in the human affairs of which he is a mute and invisible witness—much like that kind of spectator at a play who says to himself: "That's what I should have done (or said)" or "If I were he, I should. . . ." In proportion as the memories fade, and this vicarious living palls, to that degree his concept of himself as an individual becomes attenuated. At the limit of attenuation there is, *from the point of view of his survival as an individual*, no difference between the continuance of experience and its cessation. Disembodied survival, on such terms as these, may well seem unattractive. No doubt it is for this reason that the orthodox have wisely insisted on the resurrection of the body.

69

John Hick

John Hick (1922–2012) was one of the most respected philosophers of religion of the twentieth century, and made significant contributions to debates concerning religious pluralism and the theological problem of evil. In the following reading from his book *Philosophy of Religion*, Hick seeks to provide an intelligible account of the possibility of an afterlife, conceived of as a resurrection of the body. The aim of the thought experiments undertaken by Hick is to counter a standard objection to the concept of resurrection, namely that there are no grounds for concluding that a resurrected person would be the same as the person who had died, since a break in bodily continuity violates criteria of identity.

Human Destiny: Immortality and Resurrection

What does "the resurrection of the dead" mean? Saint Paul's discussion provides the basic Christian answer to this question.[3] His conception of the general resurrection (distinguished from the unique resurrection of Jesus) has nothing to do with the resuscitation of corpses in a cemetery. It concerns God's re-creation or reconstitution of the human psychophysical individual, not as the organism that has died but as a *soma pneumatikon*,

---

[3] I Corinthians 15.

Hick, John, PHILOSOPHY OF RELIGION, 3rd Ed., © 1983. Reprinted by permission of Pearson Education, Inc. New York, New York.

a "spiritual body," inhabiting a spiritual world as the physical body inhabits our present material world.

A major problem confronting any such doctrine is that of providing criteria of personal identity to link the earthly life and the resurrection life. Paul does not specifically consider this question, but one may perhaps develop his thought along lines such as the following.

Suppose, first, that someone—John Smith—living in the United States were suddenly and inexplicably to disappear before the eyes of his friends, and that at the same moment an exact replica of him were inexplicably to appear in India. The person who appears in India is exactly similar in both physical and mental characteristics to the person who disappeared in America. There is continuity of memory, complete similarity of bodily features including fingerprints, hair and eye coloration, and stomach contents, and also of beliefs, habits, emotions, and mental dispositions. Further, the "John Smith" replica thinks of himself as being the John Smith who disappeared in the United States. After all possible tests have been made and have proved positive, the factors leading his friends to accept "John Smith" as John Smith would surely prevail and would cause them to overlook even his mysterious transference from one continent to another, rather than treat "John Smith," with all of John Smith's memories and other characteristics, as someone other than John Smith.

Suppose, second, that our John Smith, instead of inexplicably disappearing, dies, but that at the moment of his death a "John Smith" replica, again complete with memories and all other characteristics, appears in India. Even with the corpse on our hands, we would, I think, still have to accept this "John Smith" as the John Smith who had died. We would just have to say that he had been miraculously re-created in another place.

Now suppose, third, that on John Smith's death the "John Smith" replica appears, not in India, but as a resurrection replica in a different world altogether, a resurrection world inhabited only by resurrected persons. This world occupies its own space distinct from that with which we are now familiar. That is to say, an object in the resurrection world is not situated at any distance or in any direction from the objects in our present world, although each object in either world is spatially related to every other object in the same world.

This supposition provides a model by which one may begin to conceive of the divine re-creation of the embodied human personality. In this model, the element of the strange and mysterious has been reduced to a minimum by one's following the view of some of the early Church

Fathers that the resurrection body has the same shape as the physical body,[4] and ignoring Paul's own hint that it may be as unlike the physical body as a full grain of wheat differs from the wheat seed.[5]

What is the basis for this Judaic-Christian belief in the divine re-creation or reconstitution of the human personality after death? There is, of course, an argument from authority, in that life after death is taught throughout the New Testament (although very rarely in the Old Testament). More basically, though, belief in the resurrection arises as a corollary of faith in the sovereign purpose of God, which is not restricted by death and which holds us in being beyond our natural mortality. In a similar vein it is argued that if it be the divine plan to create finite persons to exist in fellowship with God, then it contradicts both that intention and God's love for the human creatures if God allows men and women to pass out of existence when the divine purpose for them still remains largely unfulfilled.

It is this promised fulfillment of God's purpose for the individual, in which the full possibilities of human nature will be realized, that consti-tutes the "heaven" symbolized in the New Testament as a joyous banquet in which all and sundry rejoice together.

---

[4]   For example, Irenaeus, *Against Heresies*, Book II, Chap. 34, para. 1.

[5]   I Corinthians 15:37.

70

Bernard Williams

Sir Bernard Williams (1929–2002) was described by *The Times* newspaper as the "most brilliant and most important British moral philosopher of his time." The following selections from Williams pertain to discussions about the possibility and desirability of a life after death. The first is a short extract from a paper called "Personal Identity and Individuation," wherein Williams argues for the necessity of bodily continuity in the determination of personal identity. This conclusion poses an enormous challenge to those conceptions of immortality involving a dramatic break in spatio-temporal continuity (resurrection and reincarnation), and is the kind of objection that John Hick (in the selection above) was attempting to meet. In the extracts from "The Makropulos Case," Williams contends that, far from being a desirable state of affairs, personal immortality would inevitably be tedious.

Personal Identity and Individuation

Suppose someone undergoes a sudden and violent change of character. Formerly quiet, deferential, church-going and home-loving, he wakes up one morning and has become, and continues to be, loud-mouthed, blasphemous and bullying. Here we might ask the question

(a) Is he the same person as he used to be?

There seem to be two troubles with the formulation of this question, at least as an *identity* question. The first is a doubt about the reference of the second "he": if asked the question "as *who* used to be?," we may well want to say "this person," which answers the original question (a) for us. This is not a serious difficulty, and we can easily avoid it by rephrasing the question in some such way as

(b) Is this person the same as the person who went to sleep here last night?

We do not, however, *have* to rephrase the question in any such way; we can understand (a) perfectly well, and avoid paradox, because our use of personal pronouns and people's names is malleable. It is a reflection of our concept of "a person" that some references to *him* cannot be understood as references to *his body* or to parts of it, and that others can; and that these two sorts of reference can readily occur in one statement ("He was embarrassed and went red.") In the case of (a), the continuity of reference for "he" can be supplied by the admitted continuity of reference of "his body," and the more fundamental identity question can be discussed in these terms without any serious puzzlement.

The second difficulty with (a) is that it is too readily translated into

(c) Is he the same sort of person as he used to be? or possibly

(d) Has he the same personality as he used to have? But (c) and (d) are not identity questions in the required sense. For on any interpretation, "sort of person," and on one interpretation, "personality," are quality-terms, and we are merely asking whether the same subject now has different qualities, which is too easy to answer.

. . .

Suppose the man who underwent the radical change of character—let us call him Charles—claimed, when he woke up, to remember witnessing certain events and doing certain actions which earlier he did not claim to remember; and that under questioning he could not remember witnessing other events and doing other actions which earlier he did remember. Would this give us grounds for saying that he now was or had, in some particular sense, a different personality?

. . .

Let us now go back to the case of Charles. We may suppose that our enquiry has turned out in the most favourable possible way, and that all the events he claims to have witnessed and all the actions he claims to have done point unanimously to the life-history of some one person in the past—for instance, Guy Fawkes. Not only do all Charles' memory-claims that can be checked fit the pattern of Fawkes' life as known to historians, but others that cannot be checked are plausible, provide explanations of unexplained facts, and so on. Are we to say that Charles is now Guy Fawkes, that Guy Fawkes has come to life again in Charles' body, or some such thing?

Certainly the temptation to say something on this pattern is very strong. It is difficult to insist that we *couldn't* say that Charles (or sometime Charles) had become Guy Fawkes; this is certainly what the newspapers would say if they heard of it. But newspapers are prone to exaggeration, and this might be an exaggeration. For why shouldn't we say that Charles had, except for his body, become just like Guy Fawkes used to be; or perhaps that Charles clairvoyantly—i.e., mysteriously—knows all about Guy Fawkes and his *ambiance*? In answer to this, it will be argued that this is just what memory was introduced to rule out; granted that we need similar personal characteristics, skills, and so on as necessary conditions of the identification, the final—and, granted these others, sufficient—condition is provided by memories of seeing just *this*, and doing just *that*, and it is these that pick out a particular man. But perhaps this point is fundamentally a logical trick. Granted that in a certain context the expressions "the man who did A," "the man who saw E," do effectively individuate, it is logically impossible that two different persons should (correctly) remember being the man who did A or saw E; but it is not logically impossible that two different persons should *claim* to remember being this man, and this is the most we can get.

This last argument is meant to show only that we are not forced to accept the description of Charles' condition as his being identical with Guy Fawkes. I shall now put forward an argument to strengthen this contention and to suggest that we should not be justified in accepting this description. If it is logically possible that Charles should undergo the changes described, then it is logically possible that some other man should simultaneously undergo the same changes; e.g. that both Charles and his brother Robert should be found in this condition. What should we say in that case? They cannot both be Guy Fawkes; if they were, Guy Fawkes would be in two places at once, which is absurd. Moreover, if they were both identical with Guy Fawkes, they would be identical with each other, which is also absurd. Hence we could not say that they were both identical with Guy Fawkes. We might instead say that one of them was identical with Guy Fawkes, and that the other was just like him; but this would be an utterly vacuous manoeuvre, since there would be *ex hypothesi* no principle determining which description was to apply to which. So it would be best, if anything, to say that both had mysteriously become like Guy Fawkes, clairvoyantly knew about him, or something like this. If this would be the best description of each of the two, why would it not be the best description of Charles if Charles alone were changed?

. . .

We can then say that Charles has the same character, and the same supposed past, as Fawkes; which is just the same as to say that they are in these respects exactly similar. This is not to say that they are identical at all. The only case in which identity and exact similarity could be distinguished, as we have just seen, is that of the body—"same body" and "exactly similar body" really do mark a difference. Thus I should claim that the omission of the body takes away all content from the idea of personal *identity*.

I should like to make one last point about this example. This turns on the fact, mentioned before, that in order to describe Charles' change of identity, we must be able to identify some one person who might plausibly be supposed to have seen and done all the things that Charles now claims to remember having seen and done; otherwise there would be nothing to pin down Charles' memory claims as other than random feats of clairvoyance. We succeeded in doing this, just by discovering that Charles' memory claims fitted Fawkes' life. This could be done only by knowing what Fawkes did, and what Fawkes did could be known only by reference to witnesses of Fawkes' activities, and these witnesses must have seen Fawkes' *body*. In order for their accounts to be connected into the history of one person, it is necessary to rely on the continuity of this body.

The Makropulos Case: Reflections on the Tedium of Immortality

My title is that, as it is usually translated into English, of a play by Karel Čapek which was made into an opera by Janaček and which tells of a woman called Elina Makropulos, *alias* Emilia Marty, *alias* Ellian Macgregor, alias a number of other things with the initials "EM," on whom her father, the Court physician to a sixteenth-century Emperor, tried out an elixir of life. At the time of the action she is aged 342. Her unending life has come to a state of boredom, indifference and coldness. Everything is joyless: "in the end it is the same," she says, "singing and silence." She refuses to take the elixir again; she dies; and the formula is deliberately destroyed by a young woman among the protests of some older men.

EM's state suggests at least this, that death is not necessarily an evil, and not just in the sense in which almost everybody would agree to that, where death provides an end to great suffering, but in the more intimate sense that it can be a good thing not to live too long. It suggests more than that, for it suggests that it was not a peculiarity of EM's that an endless life was meaningless. That is something I shall follow out later. First, though, we should put together the suggestion of EM's case, that death is not necessarily an evil, with the claim of some philosophies and religions that death is necessarily not an evil. Notoriously, there have been found two contrary bases on which that claim can be mounted: death is said by some not to be an evil because it is not the end, and by others, because it is. . . .

No-one need deny that since, for instance, we grow old and our powers decline, much may happen to increase the reasons for thinking death a good thing. But these are contingencies. We might not age; perhaps, one day, it will be possible for some of us not to age. If that were so, would it not follow then that, more life being *per se* better than less life, we should have reason so far as that went (but not necessarily in terms of other inhabitants) to live for ever? EM indeed bears strong, if fictional, witness against the desirability of that; but perhaps she still laboured under some contingent limitations, social or psychological, which might once more be eliminated to bring it about that really other things were equal. Against this, I am going to suggest that the supposed contingencies are not really contingencies; that an endless life would be a meaningless one; and that we could have no reason for living eternally a human life. There is no desirable or significant property which life would have more of, or have more unqualifiedly, if we lasted for ever. . . .

If one pictures living for ever as living as an embodied person in the world rather as it is, it will be a question, and not so trivial as may seem, of what age one eternally is. EM was 342; because for 300 years she had been 42. This choice (if it was a choice) I am personally, and at present, well disposed to salute—if one had to spend eternity at any age, that seems an admirable age to spend it at. Nor would it necessarily be a less good age for a woman: that at least was not EM's problem, that she was too old at the age she continued to be at. Her problem lay in having been at it for too long. Her trouble was, it seems, boredom: a boredom connected with the fact that everything that could happen and make sense to one particular human being of 42 had already happened to her. Or, rather, all the sorts of things that could make sense to one woman of a certain character; for EM has a certain character, and indeed, except for her accumulating memories of earlier times, and no doubt some changes of style to suit the passing centuries, seems always to have been much the same sort of person.

. . .

The more one reflects to any realistic degree on the conditions of EM's unending life, the less it seems a mere contingency that it froze up as it did. That it is not a contingency, is suggested also by the fact that the reflections can sustain themselves independently of any question of the particular character that EM had; it is enough, almost, that she has a human character at all. Perhaps not quite. One sort of character for which the difficulties of unending life would have less significance than they proved to have for EM might be one who at the beginning was more like what she is at the end: cold, withdrawn, already frozen. For him, the prospect of unending cold is presumably less bleak in that he is used to it. But with him, the question can shift to a different place, as to why he wants the unending life at all; for, the more he is at the beginning like EM is at the end, the less place there is for categorical desire to keep him going, and to resist the desire for death. In EM's case, her boredom and distance from life both kill desire and consist in the death of it; one who is already enough like that to sustain life in those conditions may well be one who had nothing to make him want to do so. But even if he has, and we conceive of a person who is stonily resolved to sustain for ever an already stony existence, his possibility will be of no comfort to those, one hopes a larger party, who want to live longer because they want to live more.

. . .

[W]e have moved a little away from the very direct response which EM's case seemed to provide to the hope that one would never die. But perhaps we have moved not nearly far enough. Nothing of this, and nothing much like this, was in the minds of many who have hoped for immortality; for it was not in this world that they hoped to live for ever. As one might say, their hope was not so much that they would never die as that they would live after their death, and while that in its turn can be represented as the hope that one would not really die, or, again, that it was not really oneself that would die, the change of formulation could point to an after-life sufficiently unlike this life, perhaps, to earth the current of doubt that flows from EM's frozen boredom.

But in fact this hope has been and could only be modelled on some image of a more familiar untiring or unresting or unflagging activity or satisfaction; and what is essentially EM's problem, one way or another, remains.

In general we can ask, what it is about the imaged activities of an eternal life which would stave off the principal hazard to which EM succumbed, boredom. The Don Juan in Hell joke, that heaven's prospects are tedious and the devil has the best tunes, though a tired fancy in itself, at least serves to show up a real and (I suspect) a profound difficulty, of providing any model of an unending, supposedly satisfying, state or activity which would not rightly prove boring to anyone who remained conscious of himself and who had acquired a character, interests, tastes and impatiences in the course of living, already, a finite life. The point is not that for such a man boredom would be a tiresome consequence of the supposed states or activities, and that they would be objectionable just on the utilitarian or hedonistic ground that they had this disagreeable feature. If that were all there was to it, we could imagine the feature away, along no doubt with other disagreeable features of human life in its present imperfection. The point is rather that boredom, as sometimes in more ordinary circumstances, would be not just a tiresome effect, but a reaction almost perceptual in character to the poverty of one's relation to the environment. Nothing less will do for eternity than something that makes boredom *unthinkable*. What could that be? Something that could be guaranteed to be at every moment utterly absorbing? But if a man has and retains a character, there is no reason to suppose that there is anything that could be that. If, lacking a conception of the guaranteedly absorbing activity, one tries merely to think away the reaction of boredom, one is no longer supposing an improvement in the circumstances, but merely an impoverishment in his consciousness of them. Just as being bored can be a sign of not noticing, understanding or appreciating enough, so equally not being bored can be a sign of not noticing, or not reflecting, enough. One might make the immortal man content at every moment, by just stripping off from him consciousness which would have brought discontent by reminding him of other times, other interests, other possibilities. Perhaps, indeed, that is what we have already done, in a more tempting way, by picturing him just now as at every moment totally absorbed—but that is something we shall come back to.

Of course there is in actual life such a thing as justified but necessary boredom. Thus—to take a not entirely typical example—someone who was, or who thought himself, devoted to the radical cause might eventually admit to himself that he found a lot of its rhetoric excruciatingly boring. He might think that he ought not to feel that, that the reaction was wrong, and merely represented an unworthiness of his, an unregenerate remnant of intellectual superiority. However, he might rather feel that it would not necessarily be a better world in which no-one was bored by such rhetoric and that boredom was, indeed, a perfectly worthy reaction to this rhetoric after all this time; but for all that, the rhetoric might be necessary. A man at arms can get cramp from standing too long at his post, but sentry-duty can after all be necessary. But the threat of monotony in eternal activities could not be dealt with in that way, by regarding immortal boredom as an unavoidable ache derived from standing ceaselessly at one's post. (This is one reason why I said that boredom in eternity would have to be *unthinkable*.) For the question would be unavoidable, in what campaign one was supposed to be serving, what one's ceaseless sentry-watch was for.

Some philosophers have pictured an eternal existence as occupied in something like intense intellectual enquiry. Why that might seem to solve the problem, at least for them, is obvious. The activity is engrossing, self-justifying, affords, as it may appear, endless new perspectives, and by being engrossing enables one to lose oneself. It is that last feature that supposedly makes boredom unthinkable, by providing something that is, in that earlier phrase, at every moment totally absorbing. But if one is totally and perpetually absorbed in such an activity, and loses oneself in it, then as those words suggest, we come back to the problem of satisfying the conditions that it should be me who lives for ever, and that the eternal life should be in prospect of some interest. Let us leave aside the question of people whose characteristic and most personal interests are remote from such pursuits, and for whom, correspondingly, an immortality promised in terms of intellectual activity is going to make heavy demands on some theory of a "real self" which will have to emerge at death. More interesting is the content and value of the promise for a person who *is*, in this life, disposed to those activities. For looking at such a person as he now is, it seems quite unreasonable to suppose that those activities would have the fulfilling or liberating character that they do have for him, if they were in fact all he could do or conceive of doing. If they are genuinely fulfilling, and do not operate (as they can) merely as a compulsive diversion, then the ground and shape of the satisfactions that the intellectual enquiry offers him, will relate to *him*, and not just to the enquiry. The *Platonic introjection*, seeing the satisfactions of studying what is timeless and impersonal as being themselves timeless and impersonal, may be a deep illusion, but it is certainly an illusion.

. . .

. . . I also know, if what has gone before is right, that an eternal life would be unliveable. In part, as EM's case originally suggested, that is because categorical desire will go away from it: in those versions, such as hers, in which I am recognisably myself, I would eventually have had altogether too much of myself. There are good reasons, surely, for dying before that happens. But equally, at times earlier than that moment, there is reason for not dying. Necessarily, it tends to be either too early or too late. EM reminds us that it can be too late, and many, as against Lucretius, need no reminding that it can be too early. If that is any sort of dilemma, it can, as things still are and if one is exceptionally lucky, be resolved, not by doing anything, but just by dying shortly before the horrors of not doing so become evident. Technical progress may, in more than one direction, make that piece of luck rarer. But as things are, it is possible to be, in contrast to EM, *felix opportunitate mortis*—as it can be appropriately mistranslated, lucky in having the chance to die.

71

Robert Nozick

Robert Nozick (1938–2002) was an American philosopher, and author of *Anarchy, State, and Utopia*, a now-classic statement of libertarian political philosophy. In the following selection, Nozick uses the thought-experiment of an "experience machine" to show that there is more to life than the pursuit of pleasure. If successful, this thought-experiment presents a considerable challenge to hedonistic (e.g., Benthamite) views regarding what really matters in human life.

The Experience Machine

There are also substantial puzzles when we ask what matters other than how *people's* experiences feel "from the inside." Suppose there were an experience machine that would give you any experience you desired. Superduper neuropsychologists could stimulate your brain so that you would think and feel you were writing a great novel, or making a friend, or reading an interesting book. All the time you would be floating in a tank, with electrodes attached to your brain. Should you plug into this machine for life, preprogramming your life's experiences? If you are worried about missing out on desirable experiences, we can suppose that business enterprises have researched thoroughly the lives of many others.

You can pick and choose from their large library or smorgasbord of such experiences, selecting your life's experiences for, say, the next two years. After two years have passed, you will have ten minutes or ten hours out of the tank, to select the experiences of your *next* two years. Of course, while in the tank you won't know that you're there; you'll think it's all actually happening. Others can also plug in to have the experiences they want, so there's no need to stay unplugged to serve them. (Ignore problems such as who will service the machines if everyone plugs in.) Would you plug in? *What else can matter to us, other than how our lives feel from the inside?* Nor should you refrain because of the few moments of distress between the moment you've decided and the moment you're plugged. What's a few moments of distress compared to a lifetime of bliss (if that's what you choose), and why feel any distress at all if your decision *is* the best one?

What does matter to us in addition to our experiences? First, we want to *do* certain things, and not just have the experience of doing them. In the case of certain experiences, it is only because first we want to do the actions that we want the experiences of doing them or thinking we've done them. (But *why* do we want to do the activities rather than merely to experience them?) A second reason for not plugging in is that we want to *be* a certain way, to be a certain sort of person. Someone floating in a tank is an indeterminate blob. There is no answer to the question of what a person is like who has long been in the tank. Is he courageous, kind, intelligent, witty, loving? It's not merely that it's difficult to tell; there's no way he is. Plugging into the machine is a kind of suicide. It will seem to some, trapped by a picture, that nothing about what we are like can matter except as it gets reflected in our experiences. But should it be surprising that what *we are* is important to us? Why should we be concerned only with how our time is filled, but not with what we are?

Thirdly, plugging into an experience machine limits us to a man-made reality, to a world no deeper or more important than that which people can construct. There is no *actual* contact with any deeper reality, though the experience of it can be simulated. Many persons desire to leave themselves open to such contact and to a plumbing of deeper significance. This clarifies the intensity of the conflict over psychoactive drugs, which some view as mere local experience machines, and others view as avenues to a deeper reality; what some view as equivalent to surrender to the experience machine, others view as following one of the reasons *not* to surrender!

We learn that something matters to us in addition to experience by imagining an experience machine and then realizing that we would not use it. We can continue to imagine a sequence of machines each designed to fill lacks suggested for the earlier machines. For example, since the experience machine doesn't meet our desire to *be* a certain way, imagine a transformation machine which transforms us into whatever sort of person we'd like to be (compatible with our staying us). Surely one would not use the transformation machine to become as one would wish, and thereupon plug into the experience machine! So something matters in addition to one's experiences *and* what one is like. Nor is the reason merely that one's experiences are unconnected with what one is like. For the experience machine might be limited to provide only experiences possible to the sort of person plugged in. Is it that we want to make a difference in the world? Consider then the result machine, which produces in the world any result you would produce and injects your vector input into any joint activity. We shall not pursue here the fascinating details of these or other machines. What is most disturbing about them is their living of our lives for us. Is it misguided to search for *particular* additional functions beyond the competence of machines to do for us? Perhaps what we desire is to live (an active verb) ourselves, in contact with reality. (And this, machines cannot do *for* us.) Without elaborating on the implications of this, which I believe connect surprisingly with issues about free will and causal accounts of knowledge, we need merely note the intricacy of the question of what matters *for people* other than their experiences. Until one finds a satisfactory answer, and determines that this answer does not *also* apply to animals, one cannot reasonably claim that only the felt experiences of animals limit what we may do to them.

72

Genevieve Lloyd

Born in 1941, Genevieve Lloyd was the first woman to be appointed a professor of philosophy in Australia, taking up that position at the University of New South Wales in 1987. In her book *The Man of Reason*—from which the following selections are taken—Lloyd discusses the identification of reason with maleness. In the extracts below, she first discusses the case of Descartes and then addresses the historically conditioned nature of philosophical activity.

The Man of Reason

Descartes saw his method as opening the way to a new egalitarianism in knowledge. In a letter written shortly after the publication of the *Discourse on Method*, he commented that his thoughts on method seemed to him appropriate to put in a book where he wished that "even women" might understand something. From our perspective, this tone might sound patronizing, but the remark is to be understood against the background of associations between earlier Renaissance versions of method and pedagogical procedures. By and large, it was only boys who were given systematic formal education outside the home. The exclusion of women from method was a direct consequence of their exclusion from the schools in which it was pursued. Descartes's egalitarian intentions come out also in his insistence on writing the *Discourse on Method* in the vernacular, rather than in Latin, the learned language of the schools. The work, he stressed, should appeal to those who avail themselves only of their natural reason in its purity. The point was political as well as practical. The use of Latin was in many ways the distinguishing mark of the learned. Women, being educated mostly at home rather than in the schools, had no direct access to the learned, Latin-speaking world. The teaching of Latin to boys thus marked the boundaries between the private world of the family, in which the vernacular was used, and the external world of learning, to which males had access. The accessibility of the new method even to women was thus a powerful symbol of the transformation which it marked in the relationship between method and autonomous, individual reasoning.

In place of the subtleties of scholastic disputation, which can only, he thought, obscure the mind's natural clarity, Descartes offered a few supposedly simple procedures, the rationale of which was to remove all obstacles to the natural operations of the mind. The general rubric of the method was to break down the more complex operations of the mind into their simplest forms and then recombine them in an orderly series. The complex and obscure is reduced to simple, self-evident "intuitions," which the mind scrutinizes with "steadfast, mental gaze," then combines in orderly chains of deductions. Anyone who follows this method can feel assured that "no avenue to the truth is closed to him from which everyone else is not also excluded, and that his ignorance is due neither to a deficiency in his capacity nor to his method of procedure."

Descartes's method, with its new emphasis on the privacy of the mind's natural operations, promised to make knowledge accessible to all, even to women. Such was his intent. The lasting influence of his method, however, was something quite different, though no less a product of his radical separation of mind and body. In the context of associations already existing between gender and Reason, his version of the mind-body relationship produced stark polarizations of previously existing contrasts. This came about not through any intellectual move made within his system, but as a by-product of his transformation of the relations between Reason and its opposites. Descartes strongly repudiated his medieval predecessors' idea of a divided soul, which had Reason—identified with the authentic character of a human being—struggling with lesser parts of the soul. For him, the soul was not to be divided into higher (intellectual) and lower (sensitive) parts; it was an indivisible unity, identified with pure intellect. . . .

Arduous as the grasp of the metaphysical basis of Descartes's method may be, the method itself was supposed to be accessible to all. And within the terms of the system there is, in all this, no differentiation between male and female minds. Both must be seen as equally intellectual substances, endowed with good sense or Reason. The difference in intellectual achievement between men and women, no less that that between different men, must arise not from some being more rational than others, but "solely from the fact that our thoughts pass through diverse channels and the same objects are not considered by all." But removing method from the restraints of public pedagogy did not, in practice, make knowledge any more accessible to women. Descartes's method may be essentially private and accessible to all. But for him, no less than Bacon, the new science was, none the less, a collective endeavour. It is by "joining together the lives and labours of many," he says in the concluding section of the *Discourse on Method*, that science will progress. It is through a corporate exercise, however non-corporeal may be its ultimate metaphysical foundation, that the new science will advance, rendering humanity the promised goal of becoming "masters and possessors of nature." Descartes thought his account of the mind opened the way to a newly egalitarian pursuit of knowledge. But the channels through which those basically equal resources of Reason had to flow remained more convoluted, even for noble women, than for men. Elizabeth poignantly expressed the situation in one of her letters to Descartes:

> the life I am constrained to lead does not allow me enough free time to acquire a habit of meditation in accordance with your rules. Sometimes the interests of my household, which I must not neglect, sometimes conversations and civilities I cannot eschew, so thoroughly deject this weak mind with annoyances or boredom that it remains, for a long time afterward, useless for anything else.

The realities of the lives of women, despite their supposed equality in Reason, precluded them, too, from any significant involvement in the collective endeavours of science, the developing forms of which quickly outstripped the private procedures of Descartes's method.

It is not just impinging social realities, however, which militate against sexual equality in this new version of Reason's relations with science. There are aspects of Descartes's thought which—however unintentionally—provided a basis for a sexual division of mental labour whose influence is still very much with us. Descartes's emphasis on the equality of Reason had less influence than his formative contribution to the ideal of a distinctive kind of Reason—a highly abstract mode of thought, separable, in principle, from the emotional complexities and practical demands of ordinary life. This was not the only kind of thought which Descartes recognized as rational. In the Sixth Meditation he acknowledged that the inferior senses, once they have been set aside from the search for truth—where they can only mislead and distort—are reliable guides to our well-being. To trust them is not irrational. He does not maintain that we are rational only when exercising arduous pure thought, engaged in intellectual contemplation and assembling chains of deduction. Indeed, he thinks it is not rational to spend an excessive amount of time in such purely intellectual activity. None the less, through his philosophy, Reason took on special associations with the realm of pure thought, which provides the foundations of science, and with the deductive ratiocination which was of the essence of his method. And the sharpness of his separation of the ultimate requirements of truth-seeking from the practical affairs of everyday life reinforced already existing distinctions between male and female roles, opening the way to the idea of distinctive male and female consciousness.

We owe to Descartes an influential and pervasive theory of mind, which provides support for a powerful version of the sexual division of mental labour. Women have been assigned responsibility for that realm of the sensuous which the Cartesian Man of Reason must transcend, if he is to have true knowledge of things. He must move on to the exercise of disciplined imagination, in most of scientific activity; and to the rigours of pure intellect, if he would grasp the ultimate foundations of science. Woman's task is to preserve the sphere of the intermingling of mind and body, to which the Man of Reason will repair for solace, warmth and relaxation. If he is to exercise the most exalted form of Reason, he must leave soft emotions and sensuousness behind; woman will keep them intact for him. The way was thus opened for women to be associated with not just a lesser presence of Reason, but a different kind of intellectual character, construed as complementary to "male" Reason. This crucial development springs from the accentuation of women's exclusion from Reason, now conceived—in its highest form—as an attainment.

. . .

What exactly does the "maleness" of Reason amount to? It is clear that what we have in the history of philosophical thought is no mere succession of surface misogynist attitudes, which can now be shed, while leaving intact the deeper structures of our ideals of Reason. There is more at stake than the fact that past philosophers believed there to be flaws in female character. Many of them did indeed believe that women are less rational than men; and they have formulated their ideals of rationality with male paradigms in mind. But the maleness of Reason goes deeper than this. Our ideas and ideals of maleness and femaleness have been formed within structures of dominance—of superiority and inferiority, "norms" and "difference," "positive" and "negative," the "essential" and the "complementary." And the male-female distinction itself has operated not as a straightforwardly descriptive principle of classification, but as an expression of values. We have seen that the equation of maleness with superiority goes back at least as far as the Pythagoreans. What is valued—whether it be odd as against even numbers, "aggressive" as against "nurturing" skills and capacities, or Reason as against emotion—has been readily identified with maleness. Within the context of this association of maleness with preferred traits, it is not just incidental to the feminine that female traits have been construed as inferior—or, more subtly, as "complementary"—to male norms of human excellence. Rationality has been conceived as transcendence of the feminine; and the "feminine" itself has been partly constituted by its occurrence within this structure.

. . .

Philosophers have defined their activity in terms of the pursuit of Reason, free of the conditioning effects of historical circumstance and social structures. But despite its professed transcendence of such contingencies, Philosophy has been deeply affected by, as well as deeply affecting, the social organization of sexual difference. The full dimensions of the maleness of Philosophy's past are only now becoming visible. Despite its aspirations to timeless truth, the History of Philosophy reflects the characteristic preoccupations and self-perceptions of the kinds of people who have at any time had access to the activity. Philosophers have at different periods been churchmen, men of letters, university professors. But there is one thing they have had in common throughout the history of the activity: they have been predominantly male; and the absence of women from the philosophical tradition has meant that the conceptualization of Reason has been done exclusively by men. It is not surprising that the results should reflect their sense of Philosophy as a male activity. There have of course been female philosophers throughout the western tradition. But, like Philo's or Augustine's women of Reason, they have been philosophers despite, rather than because of, their femaleness; there has been no input of femaleness into the formation of ideals of Reason.

. . .

Philosophers can take seriously feminist dissatisfaction with the maleness of Reason without repudiating either Reason or Philosophy. Such criticisms of ideals of Reason can in fact be seen as continuous with a very old strand in the western philosophical tradition; it has been centrally concerned with bringing to reflective awareness the deeper structures of inherited ideals of Reason. Philosophy has defined ideals of Reason through exclusions of the feminine. But it also contains within it the resources for critical reflection on those ideals and on its own aspirations. Fortunately, Philosophy is not necessarily what it has in the past proudly claimed to be—a timeless rational representation of the real, free of the conditioning effects of history.

73

David Lewis

David Lewis (1941–2001) was one of the brightest in a constellation of inventive and important Australian philosophers of the later twentieth century. In this piece, he sets forth a type of materialism that is able to account for mental states in beings with very different structures or who behave differently from the norm. This functionalism (to be distinguished from the simple functionalism he identifies with behaviorism) became the dominant theory in philosophy of mind. It is also the main target of Paul Churchland's eliminativism in the next selection.

Mad Pain and Martian Pain

There might be a strange man who sometimes feels pain, just as we do, but whose pain differs greatly from ours in its causes and effects. Our pain is typically caused by cuts, burns, pressure, and the like; his is caused by moderate exercise on an empty stomach. Our pain is generally distracting; his turns his mind to mathematics, facilitating concentration on that but distracting him from anything else. Intense pain has no tendency whatever to cause him to groan or writhe, but does cause him to cross his legs and snap his fingers. He is not in the least motivated to prevent pain or to get rid of it. In short, he feels pain but his pain does not at all occupy the typical causal role of pain. He would doubtless seem to us to be some sort of madman, and that is what I shall call him, though of course the sort of madness I have imagined may bear little resemblance to the real thing.

I said there might be such a madman.

I don't know how to prove that something is possible, but my opinion that this is a possible case seems pretty firm. If I want a credible theory of mind, I need a theory that does not deny the possibility of mad pain. I needn't mind conceding that perhaps the madman is not in pain in *quite* the same sense that the rest of us are, but there had better be some straightforward sense in which he and we are both in pain.

Also, there might be a Martian who sometimes feels pain, just as we do, but whose pain differs greatly from ours in its physical realization. His hydraulic mind contains nothing like our neurons. Rather, there are varying amounts of fluid in many inflatable cavities, and the inflation of any one of these cavities opens some valves and closes others. His mental plumbing pervades most of his body—in fact, all but the heat exchanger inside his head. When you pinch his skin you cause no firing of C-fibers— he has none—but, rather, you cause the inflation of many smallish cavities in his feet. When these cavities are inflated, he is in pain. And the effects of his pain are fitting: his thought and activity are disrupted, he groans and writhes, he is strongly motivated to stop you from pinching him and to see to it that you never do again. In short, he feels pain but lacks the bodily states that either are pain or else accompany it in us.

There might be such a Martian; this opinion too seems pretty firm. A credible theory of mind had better not deny the possibility of Martian pain. I needn't mind conceding that perhaps the Martian is not in pain in *quite* the same sense that we Earthlings are, but there had better be some straightforward sense in which he and we are both in pain.

A credible theory of mind needs to make a place both for mad pain and for Martian pain. Prima facie, it seems hard for a materialist theory to pass this twofold test. As philosophers, we would like to characterize pain a priori. (We might settle for less, but let's start by asking for all we want.) As materialists, we want to characterize pain as a physical phenomenon. We can speak of the place of pain in the causal network from stimuli to inner states to behavior. And we can speak of the physical processes that go on when there is pain and that take their place in that causal network. We seem to have no other resources but these. But the lesson of mad pain is that pain is associated only contingently with its causal role, while the lesson of Martian pain is that pain is connected only contingently with its physical realization. How can we characterize pain a priori in terms of causal role and physical realization, and yet respect both kinds of contingency?

A simple identity [between mental and brain states] theory straightforwardly solves the problem of mad pain. It goes just as straightforwardly wrong about Martian pain. A simple behaviorism or functionalism goes the other way: right about the Martian, wrong about the madman. The theories that fail our twofold test so decisively are altogether too simple. (Perhaps they are too simple ever to have had adherents.) It seems that a theory that can pass our test will have to be a mixed theory. It will have to be able to tell us that the madman and the Martian are both in pain, but for different reasons: the madman because he is in the right physical state, the Martian because he is in a state rightly situated in the causal network.

. . .

Our view is that the concept of pain, or indeed of any other experience or mental state, is the concept of a state that occupies a certain causal role, a state with certain typical causes and effects. It is the concept of a state apt for being caused by certain stimuli and apt for causing certain behavior. Or, better, of a state apt for being caused in certain ways by stimuli plus other mental states and apt for combining with certain other mental states to jointly cause certain behavior. It is the concept of a member of a system of states that together more or less realize the pattern of causal generalizations set forth in commonsense psychology. (That system may be characterized as a whole and its members characterized afterward by reference to their place in it.)

If the concept of pain is the concept of a state that occupies a certain causal role, then whatever state does occupy that role is pain. If the state of having neurons hooked up in a certain way and firing in a certain pattern is the state properly apt for causing and being caused, as we materialists think, then that neural state is pain. But the concept of pain is not the concept of that neural state. . . . The concept of pain, unlike the concept of that neural state which in fact is pain, would have applied to some different state if the relevant causal relations had been different. Pain might have not been pain. The occupant of the role might have not occupied it. Some other state might have occupied it instead. Something that is not pain might have been pain.

. . .

We may say that some state *occupies a causal role for a population*. We may say this whether the population is situated entirely at our actual world, or partly at our actual world and partly at other worlds, or entirely at other worlds. If the concept of pain is the concept of a state that occupies that role, then we may say that a state *is pain for a population*. Then we may say that a certain pattern of firing of neurons is pain for the population of actual Earthlings and some but not all of our otherworldly counterparts, whereas the inflation of certain cavities in the feet is pain for the population of actual Martians and some of their otherworldly counterparts. Human pain is the state that occupies the role of pain for humans. Martian pain is the state that occupies the same role for Martians. . . .

The thing to say about Martian pain is that the Martian is in pain because he is in a state that occupies the causal role of pain for Martians, whereas we are in pain because we are in a state that occupies the role of pain for us.

Now, what of the madman? He is in pain, but he is not in a state that occupies the causal role of pain for him. He is in a state that occupies that role for most of us, but he is an exception. The causal role of a pattern of firing of neurons depends on one's circuit diagram, and he is hooked up wrong.

His state does not occupy the role of pain for a population comprising himself and his fellow madmen. But it does occupy that role for a more salient population—mankind at large. He is a man, albeit an exceptional one, and a member of that larger population.

We have allowed for exceptions. I spoke of the definitive syndrome of *typical* causes and effects. Armstrong spoke of a state *apt for* having certain causes and effects; that does not mean that it has them invariably. Again, I spoke of a system of states that *comes near to* realizing common-sense psychology. A state may therefore occupy a role for mankind even if it does not at all occupy that role for some mad minority of mankind.

The thing to say about mad pain is that the madman is in pain because he is in the state that occupies the causal role of pain for the population comprising all mankind. He is an exceptional member of that population. The state that occupies the role for the population does not occupy it for him.

. . .

If the causal facts are right, then also we characterize pain as a physical phenomenon. By allowing for exceptional members of a population, we associate pain only contingently with its causal role. Therefore we do not deny the possibility of mad pain, provided there is not too much of it. By allowing for variation from one population to another (actual or merely possible) we associate pain only contingently with its physical realization. Therefore we do not deny the possibility of Martian pain. If different ways of filling in the relativity to population may be said to yield different senses of the word "pain," then we plead ambiguity. The madman is in pain in one sense, or relative to one population. The Martian is in pain in another sense, or relative to another population. (So is the mad Martian.)

Paul Churchland

Paul Churchland (1942–) is professor emeritus of philosophy at the University of California–San Diego. He is perhaps the leading exponent of the position in philosophy of mind known as "eliminative materialism": the position that the everyday concepts of beliefs, hopes, feelings (and so on) are part of an outmoded "folk psychology" that is destined to be replaced (or eliminated) by a more accurate neuroscientific account of the nature of human mental experience. What follows is a statement and defense of that dramatic contention.

In Defense of Eliminative Materialism

Eliminative Materialism

The identity theory was called into doubt not because the prospects for a materialist account of our mental capacities were thought to be poor, but because it seemed unlikely that the arrival of an adequate materialist theory would bring with it the nice one-to-one match-ups, between the concepts of folk psychology and the concepts of theoretical neuroscience, that intertheoretic reduction requires. The reason for that doubt was the great variety of quite different physical systems that could instantiate the required functional organization. *Eliminative materialism* also doubts

Churchland, Paul M., Matter and Consciousness, 2073 word excerpt from pages 43–49, © 1984 Massachusetts Institute of Technology, by permission of The MIT Press.

that the correct neuroscientific account of human capacities will produce a neat reduction of our common-sense framework, but here the doubts arise from a quite different source.

As the eliminative materialists see it, the one-to-one match-ups will not be found, and our common-sense psychological framework will not enjoy an intertheoretic reduction, *because our common-sense psychological framework is a false and radically misleading conception of the causes of human behavior and the nature of cognitive activity.* On this view, folk psychology is not just an incomplete representation of our inner natures; it is an outright misrepresentation of our internal states and activities. Consequently, we cannot expect a truly adequate neuroscientific account of our inner lives to provide theoretical categories that match up nicely with the categories of our common-sense framework. Accordingly, we must expect that the older framework will simply be eliminated, rather than be reduced, by a matured neuroscience.

Historical Parallels

As the identity theorist can point to historical cases of successful intertheoretic reduction, so the eliminative materialist can point to historical cases of the outright elimination of the ontology of an older theory in favor of the ontology of a new and superior theory. . . .

It used to be thought that when a piece of wood burns, or a piece of metal rusts, a spiritlike substance called "phlogiston" was being released: briskly, in the former case, slowly in the latter. Once gone, that "noble" substance left only a base pile of ash or rust. It later came to be appreciated that both processes involve, not the loss of something, but the *gaining* of a substance taken from the atmosphere: oxygen. Phlogiston emerged, not as an incomplete description of what was going on, but as a radical misdescription. Phlogiston was therefore not suitable for reduction to or identification with some notion from within the new oxygen chemistry, and it was simply eliminated from science.

. . .[O]ur history also includes the elimination of certain widely accepted "observables." Before Copernicus' views became available, almost any human who ventured out at night could look up at *the starry sphere of the heavens,* and if he stayed for more than a few minutes he could also see that it *turned,* around an axis through Polaris. . . . In the end, however, we learned to reinterpret our visual experience of the night sky within a very different conceptual framework, and the turning sphere evaporated.

Witches provide another example. Psychosis is a fairly common affliction among humans, and in earlier centuries its victims were standardly seen as cases of demonic possession, as instances of Satan's spirit itself, glaring malevolently out at us from behind the victims' eyes. That witches exist was not a matter of any controversy. One would occasionally see them, in any city or hamlet, engaged in incoherent, paranoid, or even murderous behavior. But observable or not, we eventually decided that witches simply do not exist. We concluded that the concept of a witch is an element in a conceptual framework that misrepresents so badly the phenomena to which it was standardly applied that literal application of the notion should be permanently withdrawn. Modern theories of mental dysfunction led to the elimination of witches from our serious ontology.

The concepts of folk psychology—belief, desire, fear, sensation, pain, joy, and so on—await a similar fate, according to the view at issue. And when neuroscience has matured to the point where the poverty of our current conceptions is apparent to everyone, and the superiority of the new framework is established, we shall then be able to set about reconceiving our internal states and activities, within a truly adequate conceptual framework at last. Our explanations of one another's behavior will appeal to such things as our neuropharmacological states, the neural activity in specialized anatomical areas, and whatever other states are deemed relevant by the new theory. Our private introspection will also be transformed, and may be profoundly enhanced by reason of the more accurate and penetrating framework it will have to work with—just as the astronomer's perception of the night sky is much enhanced by the detailed knowledge of modern astronomical theory that he or she possesses.

The magnitude of the conceptual revolution here suggested should not be minimized: it would be enormous. And the benefits to humanity might be equally great. If each of us possessed an accurate neuroscientific understanding of (what we now conceive dimly as) the varieties and causes of mental illness, the factors involved in learning, the neural basis of emotions, intelligence, and socialization, then the sum total of human misery might be much reduced. The simple increase in mutual understanding that the new framework made possible could contribute substantially toward a more peaceful and humane society. Of course, there would be dangers as well: increased knowledge means increased power, and power can always be misused.

Arguments for Eliminative Materialism

The arguments for eliminative materialism are diffuse and less than decisive, but they are stronger than is widely supposed. . . .

First, the eliminative materialist will point to the widespread explanatory, predictive, and manipulative failures of folk psychology. So much of what is central and familiar to us remains a complete mystery from within folk psychology. We do not know what *sleep* is, or why we have to have it, despite spending a full third of our lives in that condition. (The answer, "For rest," is mistaken. Even if people are allowed to rest continuously, their need for sleep is undiminished. Apparently, sleep serves some deeper functions, but we do not yet know what they are.) We do not understand how *learning* transforms each of us from a gaping infant to a cunning adult or how differences in *intelligence* are grounded. We have not the slightest idea how *memory* works, or how we manage to retrieve relevant bits of information instantly from the awesome mass we have stored. We do not know what *mental illness* is, nor how to cure it.

In sum, the most central things about us remain almost entirely mysterious from within folk psychology. And the defects noted cannot be blamed on inadequate time allowed for their correction, for folk psychology has enjoyed no significant changes or advances in well over 2,000 years, despite its manifest failures. Truly successful theories may be expected to reduce, but significantly unsuccessful theories merit no such expectation.

This argument from explanatory poverty has a further aspect. So long as one sticks to normal brains, the poverty of folk psychology is perhaps not strikingly evident. But as soon as one examines the many perplexing behavioral and cognitive deficits suffered by people with *damaged* brains, one's descriptive and explanatory resources start to claw the air. . . .

The second argument tries to draw an inductive lesson from our conceptual history. Our early folk theories of motion were profoundly confused, and were eventually displaced entirely by more sophisticated theories. Our early folk theories of the structure and activity of the heavens were wildly off the mark, and survive only as historical lessons in how wrong we can be. Our folk theories of the nature of fire, and the nature of life, were similarly cockeyed. And one could go on, since the vast majority of our past folk conceptions have been similarly exploded. All except folk psychology, which survives to this day and has only recently begun to feel pressure. But the phenomenon of conscious intelligence is surely a more complex and difficult phenomenon than any of those just listed. So far as accurate understanding is concerned, it would be a *miracle* if we had got *that* one right the very first time, when we fell down so badly on all the others. Folk psychology has survived for so very long, presumably, not because it is basically correct in its representations, but because the phenomena addressed are so surpassingly difficult that any useful handle on them, no matter how feeble, is unlikely to be displaced in a hurry.

A third argument attempts to find an a priori advantage for eliminative materialism over the identity theory and functionalism. It attempts to counter the common intuition that eliminative materialism is distantly possible; perhaps, but is much less probable than either the identity theory or functionalism. The focus again is on whether the concepts of folk psychology will find vindicating match-ups in a matured neuroscience. The eliminativist bets no; the other two bet yes. . . .

Arguments Against Eliminative Materialism

The initial plausibility of this rather radical view is low for almost everyone, since it denies deeply entrenched assumptions. That is at best a question-begging complaint, of course, since those assumptions are precisely what is at issue. But the following line of thought does attempt to mount a real argument.

Eliminative materialism is false, runs the argument, because one's introspection reveals directly the existence of pains, beliefs, desires, fears, and so forth. Their existence is as obvious as anything could be.

The eliminative materialist will reply that this argument makes the same mistake that an ancient or medieval person would be making if he insisted that he could just see with his own eyes that the heavens form a turning sphere, or that witches exist. The fact is, all observation occurs within some system of concepts, and our observation judgments are only as good as the conceptual framework in which they are expressed. In all three cases—the starry sphere, witches, and the familiar mental states—precisely what is challenged is the integrity of the background conceptual frameworks in which the observation judgments are expressed. To insist on the validity of one's experiences, *traditionally interpreted*, is therefore to beg the very question at issue. For in all three cases, the question is whether we should reconceive the nature of some familiar observational domain.

A second criticism attempts to find an incoherence in the eliminative materialist's position. The bald statement of eliminative materialism is that the familiar mental states do not really exist. But that statement is meaningful, runs the argument, only if it is the expression of a certain *belief*, and an *intention* to communicate, and a *knowledge* of the language, and so forth. But if the statement is true, then no such mental states exist, and the statement is therefore a meaningless string of marks or noises, and cannot be true. Evidently, the assumption that eliminative materialism is true entails that it cannot be true.

The hole in this argument is the premise concerning the conditions necessary for a statement to be meaningful. It begs the question. If eliminative materialism is true, then meaningfulness must have some different source. To insist on the "old" source is to insist on the validity of the very framework at issue. . . .

A final criticism draws a much weaker conclusion, but makes a rather stronger case. Eliminative materialism, it has been said, is making mountains out of molehills. It exaggerates the defects in folk psychology, and underplays its real successes. Perhaps the arrival of a matured neuroscience will require the elimination of the occasional folk-psychological concept, continues the criticism, and a minor adjustment in certain folk-psychological principles may have to be endured. But the large-scale elimination forecast by the eliminative materialist is just an alarmist worry or a romantic enthusiasm.

Perhaps this complaint is correct. And perhaps it is merely complacent. Whichever, it does bring out the important point that we do not confront two simple and mutually exclusive possibilities here: pure reduction versus pure elimination. Rather, these are the end points of a smooth spectrum of possible outcomes, between which there are mixed cases of partial elimination and partial reduction. Only empirical research . . . can tell us where on that spectrum our own case will fall. Perhaps we should speak here, more liberally, of "revisionary materialism," instead of concentrating on the more radical possibility of an across-the-board elimination. Perhaps we should. But it has been my aim . . . to make it at least intelligible to you that our collective conceptual destiny lies substantially toward the revolutionary end of the spectrum.

75

=== 🐢 ===

Patricia Smith Churchland

Patricia Smith Churchland (1943–) is UC President's Professor of
Philosophy Emerita at the University of California–San Diego. She
specializes in neurophilosophy, a field that operates at the intersec-
tion of philosophy and neuroscience. In the following selection from
her book *Brain-Wise*, Churchland builds on the materialist identification of mental states with brain states to argue that there can be no
life after death, rejecting the apparent evidence drawn from parapsy-
chological phenomena such as near-death experiences and the recollection of previous lives.

Brain-Wise

Is There Life after Death?

As discussed in earlier chapters, the preponderance of evidence supports
the hypothesis that mental states are brain states and mental processes
are brain processes. On this hypothesis, what thing exists to survive the
death of the brain? What kind of substance would it be, and how could it
have the emotions, knowledge, preferences, and memories that the brain
had when it was alive? How can it be related to those activities in the

Churchland, Patricia, *Brain-Wise: Studies in Neurophilosophy*, 1638 word excerpt from pages
393–396, © 2002 Massachusetts Institute of Technology, by permission of The MIT Press.

brain that make me me? Reasonable answers need to be forthcoming if the hypothesis that there is life after death is to win credibility.

So far as I can determine, there are no answers that cohere enough to make some sense of the life-after-death hypothesis. The preponderance of the evidence indicates that when the brain degenerates, mental functions are compromised, and when the brain dies, mental functions cease. The suggestion that the whole body is resurrected after death does address the problem, but so far the evidence for resurrection is not persuasive. Old graves contain old bones, and decaying flesh is devoured by scavengers.

Is there any positive evidence that *something*, we know not what, does in fact live on after the death of the brain? There are, certainly, many reports that purport to provide confirming evidence. Because I cannot consider them all here, I shall restrict myself to the following pertinent observations. So many of the claims that rest on the intervention of a psychic medium have been shown to be fraudulent that a general suspicion of these claims is as prudent as the general suspicion one has toward get-rich-quick investments. Many claims to a previous life are either openly concocted, confabulated, or a matter of unwitting selectivity of evidence. By "selectivity of evidence" I mean that one pays attention to events that, with suitable interpretation, could be construed as confirming one antecedently favored hypothesis, while ignoring or explaining away in ad hoc fashion events that could be disconfirming.

For a made-up illustration of selectivity of evidence concerning an afterlife and a previous life, consider this story. A child draws a picture of a scene with a farmhouse, apple trees in the yard, a dog sleeping under the tree, and so forth. It reminds his mother of Great Grandfather Smith's house. Indeed, little Billy has some of Great Grandfather Smith's physical traits, including his curly red hair and his hot temper. The mother asks the child about his picture, and the source of his ideas. "Do you remember ever seeing a place like this?" she queries. If she *prompts* him, the child will begin to agree, as psychologists have repeatedly shown, that he remembers this place, remembers the dog, and so forth. Later he may quite innocently embellish all these "memories" with details from parental conversation, family albums, and so forth. Billy may even discover, perhaps without conscious knowledge, that he is encouraged to *confabulate* his earlier life, where his confabulations get conceptualized as the *recovery of hidden memories*.

Great Grandfather Smith, in Billy's "recovered memories," killed a grizzly with a mere bowie knife, built a snow house in a blizzard, and talked to quail and coyote. Nobody else remembers these events, but that is not troubling, since Grandfather was somewhat reserved. His mother, we may imagine, does not work hard to test the hypothesis that Billy is the reincarnation of Great Grandfather Smith. When she does ask a question about Great Grandfather Smith's life that Billy *cannot* answer, this is soothingly explained away by saying that Billy has forgotten that particular of his previous life. She ignores countervailing evidence, she tends to notice or remember only confirming evidence. This is not because she is openly mendacious. Quite the contrary. She is inadvertently fooling *herself*. She *wants* to believe. This fable illustrates selectivity in considering evidence, and it is something to which we all are prone. Consequently, we have to work hard to be as tough-minded with respect to hypotheses we *hope* are true as we are with respect to those we *fear* are true.

Whether all accounts of reincarnation share the weaknesses illustrated in the fable is not known, but because so many that have been studied do, and because one does not want to be gullible, we need to exercise careful scrutiny, case by individual case. Why do we not all enthusiastically believe Shirley McLaine's claims of her earlier, colorful lives? Partly, I think, because her accounts seem to suffer from the selectivity-of-evidence problem just outlined, partly because her claims are conveniently untestable, but also because they have the indelible stamp of fantasy. Her "earlier lives" are enviably glamorous; they are not the lives of a poor peasant grubbing about with running sores and bent back. Typically, reports of previous lives are replete with storybook appeal: handsome heroes, beautiful queens, and romantic deeds. Surely, there were many more hungry, stooped peasants than there were pining, gothic princesses, yet these tend not to be the "previous lives" channeling reveals. Or is it perhaps that only glamorous persons are reincarnated and the humble ones stay dead?

Recently, evocative descriptions provided by patients who very nearly died have become a source of interest to our question. Visual experiences involving tunnels with shimmering lights at the far end, feelings of great peacefulness, feelings that one is being led on a journey, and sometimes the experience of seeming to see one's body below on a gurney are typical of experiences called "near-death experiences." These experiences are alleged to be evidence that the patients have experienced the otherworld of the afterlife. As always, we must weigh the evidence for and against, and reflect on whether there might be more down-to-earth explanations.

Several obstacles suggest that caution is in order. First, these experiences seem to be somewhat unusual (about 35 percent) among those patients who are very close to death but who revive. *Selectivity of evidence* makes them seem to confirm an afterlife, despite the existence of other cases where the resuscitated patient reports no such experiences.

Second, the conditions are not those of a controlled experiment, and one wants to know whether any of these patients are *encouraged* to "remember" events that, in their current stressful circumstances, they attribute to experiences "while dead."

Third, the reports are reports from patients whose brains are under great stress; they are anoxic (oxygen deprived) and awash in norepinephrine, precisely *because* they are close to death. Brains under stress may produce many abnormal activities, including involuntary movements, strange speech, unusual eye movements, and unusual experiences. Severe anoxia, for example in drowning, is known to result in feelings of peacefulness, once the panic phase has passed. Some people have used self-strangulation as a means of inducing anoxic ecstasy. Anoxia resulting from breathing nitrous oxide (so-called laughing gas) can produce ecstatic feelings and feelings of having glimpsed profound truths. William James says he experienced "metaphysical illuminations" while intoxicated on nitrous oxide, though what he wrote on these occasions was, by his admission, sheer gibberish. Nitrous oxide stimulates neurons that release endorphins (the brain's endogenous opiates), which is why it can be used as an anesthetic. Endogenous endorphin release, along with some suggestibility perhaps, is the probable cause of ecstatic effects. In this respect, therefore, the problem is similar to the problem with the reports from the cases of temporal-lobe epileptics who experience "religious feelings" during a seizure.

Fourth, . . . out-of-body experiences, as well as other disorienting and depersonalizing experiences, can be produced artificially, for example with the anesthetic ketamine or with LSD. It is not unlikely that the neuronal explanations for the ketamine experiences and the near-death experiences are very similar. Moreover, as Francis Crick has pointed out in conversation, the out-of-body claims could be tested a little more directly by asking whether the patient saw an object that could be seen only if he was where he said he was, such as floating out the hospital window. So far as I can tell, this sort of test has not been systematically undertaken.

Although the skepticism and caution with respect to claims about past and future lives are justified, we should keep an open mind about the possibility that a genuinely testable case will emerge. If a prima facie case does emerge, it will indeed be of the greatest importance to examine it carefully and systematically, to avoid inadvertent contamination of memory, to do everything possible to rule out fraud, to check the claims against what is known about the facts, to consider other possible explanations, and so forth. The record of examined cases makes one less than optimistic that such a case will survive scrutiny, but one must not rule out the possibility that it will.

But is the prospect of extinction not unsettling? Is it not disappointing and frightening? It may be all these things, but it need not be. One can live a richly purposeful life of love and work—of family, community, wilderness, music, and so forth—cognizant that it makes sense to make the best of *this* life. Arguably, it is less painful to accept that miseries are just a part of life than that they are punishment or trials or that one's prayers are being ignored. Arguably, it is comforting to assume that matters of justice and desert need to be addressed in the here and now, not deferred to an afterlife. Finding peaceful solutions, redressing wrongs, seeking reconciliation and compromise, expressing love, maximizing the significance of each day that one is alive—these things may make more sense than pinning too much hope on an iffy hereafter. When all is said and done, the truth is still the truth, however grim it turns out to be. If there is no life after death—if that *is* the truth—then wishing it were otherwise will not make it otherwise.

76

John Gray

John Gray (1948–) is a philosopher and political theorist, and was until his retirement Professor of European Thought at the London School of Economics. His book *Straw Dogs*—from which the following selection is taken—constitutes an attack on both humanism and the idea of progress. Gray depicts humanity as a rapacious species, something akin to a virulent infestation destructive to the world around us.

Disseminated Primatemaia

James Lovelock has written:

> Humans on the Earth behave in some ways like a pathogenic organism, or like the cells of a tumour or neoplasm. We have grown in numbers and disturbance to Gaia, to the point where our presence is perceptibly disturbing. . . . the human species is now so numerous as to constitute a serious planetary malady. Gaia is suffering from *Disseminated Primatemaia*, a plague of people.

Around 65 million years ago the dinosaurs and three quarters of all other species suddenly perished. The cause is disputed, but many scientists believe the mass extinction was the result of a meteorite colliding with the Earth. Today species are disappearing at a rate that is set to surpass

John Gray, *Straw Dogs* (New York: Farrar, Strauss and Giroux, 2002), pp. 6–12.

that last great extinction. The cause is not any cosmic catastrophe. As Lovelock says, it is a plague of people.

"Darwin's dice have rolled badly for Earth," [E. O.] Wilson points out. The lucky throw that brought the human species to its present power has meant ruin for countless other life forms. When humans arrived in the New World around twelve thousand years ago, the continent abounded in mammoths, mastodons, camels, giant ground sloths and dozens of similar species. Most of these indigenous species were hunted to extinction. North America lost over 70 per cent and South America 80 per cent of its large mammals, according to [Jared] Diamond.

The destruction of the natural world is not the result of global capitalism, industrialisation, "Western civilisation" or any flaw in human institutions. It is a consequence of the evolutionary success of an exceptionally rapacious primate. Throughout all of history and prehistory, human advance has coincided with ecological devastation.

It is true that a few traditional peoples lived in balance with the Earth for long periods. The Inuit and the Bushmen stumbled into ways of life in which their footprint was slight. We cannot tread the Earth so lightly. *Homo rapiens* has become too numerous.

The study of population is not a very exact science. No one forecast the population collapse that is occurring in post-communist European Russia, or the scale of the fall in fertility that is under way in much of the world. The margin of error in calculations of fertility and life expectancy is large. Even so, a further large increase is inevitable. As [Reg] Morrison observes, "Even if we assume a declining birth rate due to social factors and a rising death rate due to starvation, disease and genocide, the present global population of over 6 billion will grow by at least 1.2 billion by the year 2050."

A human population of approaching 8 billion can be maintained only by desolating the Earth. If wild habitat is given over to human cultivation and habitation, if rainforests can be turned into green deserts, if genetic engineering enables ever-higher yields to be extorted from the thinning soils—then humans will have created for themselves a new geological era, the Eremozoic, the Era of Solitude, in which little remains on the Earth but themselves and the prosthetic environment that keeps them alive.

It is a hideous vision, but it is only a nightmare. Either the Earth's self-regulating mechanisms will make the planet less habitable for humans or the side effects of their own activities will cut short the current growth in their numbers.

Lovelock suggests four possible outcomes of *disseminated primate-maia*: "destruction of the invading disease organisms; chronic infection; destruction of the host; or symbiosis—a lasting relationship of mutual benefit to the host and invader."

Of the four outcomes, the last is the least likely. Humanity will never initiate a symbiosis with the Earth. Even so, it will not destroy its planetary host, Lovelock's third possible outcome. The biosphere is older and stronger than they will ever be. As [Lynn] Margulis writes, "No human culture, despite its inventiveness, can kill life on this planet, were it even to try."

Nor can humans chronically infect their host. True, human activity is already altering the planetary balance. The production of greenhouse gases has changed global ecosystems irreversibly. With worldwide industrialisation, such changes can only accelerate. In a worst-case scenario that some scientists are taking seriously, climate change could wipe out populous coastal countries such as Bangladesh and trigger agricultural failure in other parts of the world, spelling disaster for billions of people, before the end of the present century.

The scale of the change afoot cannot be known with certainty. In a chaotic system even the near future cannot be predicted accurately. Yet it seems likely that the conditions of life are shifting for much of humankind, with large segments of it facing much less hospitable climates. As Lovelock has suggested, climate change may be a mechanism through which the planet eases its human burden.

As a side effect of climate change, new patterns of disease could trim the human population. Our bodies are bacterial communities, linked indissolubly with a largely bacterial biosphere. Epidemiology and microbiology are better guides to our future than any of our hopes or plans.

War could have a major impact. Writing at the turn of the nineteenth century, Thomas Malthus named war as being one of the ways—along with recurrent famines—in which population and resources were kept in balance. Malthus's argument was satirised in the twentieth century by Leonard C. Lewin:

> Man, like all other animals, is subject to the continuing process of adapting to the limitations of his environment. But the principal mechanism he has utilised for this purpose is unique among living creatures. To forestall the inevitable historical cycles of inadequate food supply, post-Neolithic man destroys surplus members of his own species by organised warfare.

The irony is misplaced. War has rarely resulted in any long-term reduction of human numbers. Yet today its impact could be considerable. It is not only that weapons of mass destruction—notably biological and (soon) genetic weapons—are more fearsome than before. More, their impact on the life-support systems of human society is likely to be greater. A globalised world is a delicate construction. A vastly greater population than hitherto is dependent on far-flung supply networks, and any war on the scale of the larger conflicts of the twentieth century could have the effect of culling the population in the way Malthus described.

In 1600 the human population was about half a billion. In the 1990s it increased by the same amount. People who are now over forty have lived through a doubling of the world's human population. It is natural for them to think that these numbers will be maintained. Natural, but—unless humans really are different from all other animals—mistaken.

The human population growth that has taken place over the past few hundred years resembles nothing so much as the spikes that occur in the numbers of rabbits, house mice and plague rats. Like them, it can only be short-lived. Already fertility is falling throughout much of the world. As Morrison observes, humans are like other animals in responding to stress. They react to scarcity and overcrowding by tuning down the reproductive urge:

> Many other animals seem to have a hormone-regulated response to environmental stress that switches their metabolism into a more economical mode whenever resources become scarce. Inevitably, the energy-hungry processes of reproduction are the first to be targeted. . . . The telltale hormonal signature of this process . . . has been identified in captive lowland gorillas, and in women.

In responding to environmental stress by ceasing to breed, humans are no different from other mammals.

The current spike in human numbers may come to an end for any number of reasons—climate change, new patterns of disease, the side effects of war, a downward spiral in the birth rate, or a mix of these and other, unknown factors. Whatever brings about its end, it is an aberration:

> [if] the human plague is really as normal as it looks, then the collapse curve should mirror the population growth curve. This means that the bulk of the collapse will not take much more than one hundred

years, and by the year 2150 the biosphere should be safely back to its preplague population of Homo sapiens—somewhere between 0.5 and 1 billion.

Humans are like any other plague animal. They cannot destroy the Earth, but they can easily wreck the environment that sustains them. The most likely of Lovelock's four outcomes is a version of the first, in which *disseminated primatemaia* is cured by a large-scale decline in human numbers.

Patricia Hill Collins

....

Black feminism emerged from the perception that traditional feminism was tainted by racism and that the civil rights movement did not sufficiently address sexism, and it stresses the "intersectional" nature of oppressive structures. The philosophical and epistemological elements of black feminism are explored in the work of Patricia Hill Collins (1948–), Distinguished University Professor of Sociology at the University of Maryland, College Park. In the following extracts from her *Black Feminist Thought: Knowledge, Consciousness and the Politics of Empowerment*, Collins discusses two distinct epistemologies: "one representing elite White male interests and the other expressing Black feminist concerns." Her probing and critical reflections on the partiality of apparently universal contentions are of considerable significance in assessing a great many of the extracts included in this anthology.

....

Black Feminist Thought

Tracing the origin and diffusion of Black feminist thought or any comparable body of specialized knowledge reveals its affinity to the power of the group that created it. . . .

Black feminist thought's core themes of work, family, sexual politics, motherhood, and political activism rely on paradigms that emphasize

---

the importance of intersecting oppressions in shaping the U.S. matrix of domination. But expressing these themes and paradigms has not been easy because Black women have had to struggle against White male interpretations of the world.

In this context, Black feminist thought can best be viewed as subjugated knowledge. Traditionally, the suppression of Black women's ideas within White-male-controlled social institutions led African-American women to use music, literature, daily conversations, and everyday behavior as important locations for constructing a Black feminist consciousness. . . .

Epistemology constitutes an overarching theory of knowledge. It investigates the standards used to assess knowledge or why we believe what we believe to be true. Far from being the apolitical study of truth, epistemology points to the ways in which power relations shape who is believed and why. For example, various descendants of Sally Hemmings, a Black woman owned by Thomas Jefferson, claimed repeatedly that Jefferson fathered her children. These accounts forwarded by Jefferson's African-American descendants were ignored in favor of accounts advanced by his White progeny. Hemmings's descendants were routinely disbelieved until their knowledge claims were validated by DNA testing. . . .

In producing the specialized knowledge of U.S. Black feminist thought, Black women intellectuals often encounter two distinct epistemologies: one representing elite White male interests and the other expressing Black feminist concerns. Whereas many variations of these epistemologies exist, it is possible to distill some of their distinguishing features that transcend differences among the paradigms within them. Epistemological choices about whom to trust, what to believe, and why something is true are not benign academic issues. Instead, these concerns tap the fundamental question of which versions of truth will prevail. . . .

Two political criteria influence knowledge validation processes. First, knowledge claims are evaluated by a group of experts whose members bring with them a host of sedimented experiences that reflect their group location in intersecting oppressions. No scholar can avoid cultural ideas and his or her placement in intersecting oppressions of race, gender, class, sexuality, and nation. In the United States, this means that a scholar making a knowledge claim typically must convince a scholarly community controlled by elite White avowedly heterosexual men holding U.S. citizenship that a given claim is justified. Second, each community of experts must maintain its credibility as defined by the larger population in which it is situated and from which it draws its basic, taken-for-granted knowledge. This means that scholarly communities that challenge basic beliefs held in U.S. culture at large will be deemed less credible than those that support popular ideas. For example, if scholarly communities stray too far from widely held beliefs about Black womanhood, they run the risk of being discredited.

When elite White men or any other overly homogeneous group dominates knowledge validation processes, both of these political criteria can work to suppress Black feminist thought. Given that the general U.S. culture shaping the taken-for-granted knowledge of the community of experts is permeated by widespread notions of Black female inferiority, new knowledge claims that seem to violate this fundamental assumption are likely to be viewed as anomalies. Moreover, specialized thought challenging notions of Black female inferiority is unlikely to be generated from within White-male-controlled academic settings because both the kinds of questions asked and the answers to them would necessarily reflect a basic lack of familiarity with Black women's realities. Even those who think they are familiar can reproduce stereotypes. Believing that they are already knowledgeable, many scholars staunchly defend controlling images of U.S. Black women as mammies, matriarchs, and jezebels, and allow these commonsense beliefs to permeate their scholarship. . . .

Criteria for methodological adequacy associated with positivism illustrate the standards that Black women scholars, especially those in the social sciences, would have to satisfy in legitimating Black feminist thought. . . . Positivist approaches aim to create scientific descriptions of reality by producing objective generalizations. Because researchers have widely differing values, experiences, and emotions, genuine science is thought to be unattainable unless all human characteristics except rationality are eliminated from the research process. By following strict methodological rules, scientists aim to distance themselves from the values, vested interests, and emotions generated by their class, race, sex, or unique situation. By decontextualizing themselves, they allegedly become detached observers and manipulators of nature.

Several requirements typify positivist methodological approaches. First, research methods generally require a distancing of the researcher from her or his "object" of study by defining the researcher as a "subject" with full human subjectivity and by objectifying the "object" of study. A second requirement is the absence of emotions from the research process. Third, ethics and values are deemed inappropriate in the research process, either as the reason for scientific inquiry or as part of the research process itself. Finally, adversarial debates, whether written or oral, become the preferred method of ascertaining truth: The arguments that can withstand the greatest assault and survive intact become the strongest truths.

Such criteria ask African-American women to objectify ourselves, devalue our emotional life, displace our motivations for furthering knowledge about Black women, and confront in an adversarial relationship those with more social, economic, and professional power. . . .

An ethic of personal accountability also characterizes Black feminist epistemology. Not only must individuals develop their knowledge claims through dialogue and present them in a style proving their concern for their ideas, but people are expected to be accountable for their knowledge claims. Zilpha Elaw's description of slavery reflects this notion that every idea has an owner and that the owner's identity matters: "Oh, the abominations of slavery! . . . Every case of slavery, however lenient its inflictions and mitigated its atrocities, indicates an oppressor, the oppressed, and oppression." For Elaw abstract definitions of slavery mesh with the personal identities of slavery's perpetrators and its victims. African-Americans consider it essential for individuals to have definite positions on issues and assume full responsibility for arguing their validity.

Assessments of an individual's knowledge claims simultaneously evaluate an individual's character, values, and ethics. Within this logic, many African-Americans reject prevailing beliefs that probing into an individual's personal viewpoint is outside the boundaries of discussion. Rather, all views expressed and actions taken are thought to derive from a central set of core beliefs that cannot be other than personal. . . . Knowledge claims made by individuals respected for their moral and ethical connections to their ideas will carry more weight than those offered by less respected figures.

An example drawn from an undergraduate class session where the students were all Black women illustrates the uniqueness of this portion of the knowledge validation process. During one class discussion I asked the students to evaluate a prominent Black male scholar's analysis of Black feminism. Instead of removing the scholar from his context in order to dissect the rationality of his thesis, my students demanded facts about the author's personal biography. They were especially interested in specific details of his life, such as his relationships with Black women, his marital status, and his social class background. By requesting data on dimensions of his personal life routinely excluded in positivist approaches to knowledge validation, they invoked lived experience as a criterion of meaning. They used this information to assess whether he really cared about his topic and drew on this ethic of caring in advancing their knowledge claims about his work. Furthermore, they refused to evaluate the rationality of his written ideas without some indication of his personal credibility as an ethical human being. The entire exchange could only have occurred as a dialogue among members of a group that had established a solid enough community to employ an alternative epistemology in assessing knowledge claims. . . .

Rather than emphasizing how a Black women's standpoint and its accompanying epistemology differ from those of White women, Black men, and other collectivities, Black women's experiences serve as one specific social location for examining points of connection among multiple epistemologies. Viewing Black feminist epistemology in this way challenges additive analyses of oppression claiming that Black women have a more accurate view of oppression than do other groups. Such approaches suggest that oppression can be quantified and compared and that adding layers of oppression produces a potentially clearer standpoint. One implication of some uses of standpoint theory is that the more subordinated the group, the purer the vision available to them. This is an outcome of the origins of standpoint approaches in Marxist social theory, itself reflecting the binary thinking of its Western origins. Ironically, by quantifying and ranking human oppressions, standpoint theorists invoke criteria for methodological adequacy that resemble those of positivism. Although it is tempting to claim that Black women are more oppressed than everyone else and therefore have the best standpoint from which to understand the mechanisms, processes, and effects of oppression, this is not the case.

Instead, those ideas that are validated as true by African-American women, African-American men, Latina lesbians, Asian-American women, Puerto Rican men, and other groups with distinctive standpoints, with each group using the epistemological approaches growing from its unique standpoint, become the most "objective" truths. Each group speaks from its own standpoint and shares its own partial, situated knowledge. But because each group perceives its own truth as partial, its knowledge is unfinished. Each group becomes better able to consider other groups' standpoints without relinquishing the uniqueness of its own standpoint or suppressing other groups' partial perspectives. "What is always needed in the appreciation of art, or life," maintains Alice Walker, "is the larger perspective.

Connections made, or at least attempted, where none existed before, the straining to encompass in one's glance at the varied world the common thread, the unifying theme through immense diversity." Partiality, and not universality, is the condition of being heard; individuals and groups forwarding knowledge claims without owning their position are deemed less credible than those who do.

Alternative knowledge claims in and of themselves are rarely threatening to conventional knowledge. Such claims are routinely ignored, discredited, or simply absorbed and marginalized in existing paradigms. Much more threatening is the challenge that alternative epistemologies offer to the basic process used by the powerful to legitimate knowledge claims that in turn justify their right to rule. If the epistemology used to validate knowledge comes into question, then all prior knowledge claims validated under the dominant model become suspect. Alternative epistemologies challenge all certified knowledge and open up the question of whether what has been taken to be true can stand the test of alternative ways of validating truth. The existence of a self-defined Black women's standpoint using Black feminist epistemology calls into question the content of what currently passes as truth and simultaneously challenges the process of arriving at that truth.

===== 𝔰 =====

Grace Jantzen

....

Grace Jantzen (1948–2006) was a Canadian philosopher who until her untimely death was professor of religion, culture, and gender at Manchester University, UK. In the following piece, Jantzen explores the motives that lie at the root of the belief in immortality and finds them all deficient, arguing that the religious life does not require belief in a life after death.

....

Do We Need Immortality?

The doctrine of life after death is often taken to be an essential ingredient in Christian theology. Baron Friedrich Von Hügel, when he said that "Religion, in its fullest development, essentially requires, not only this our little span of earthly years, but a life beyond," was only echoing the words of St. Paul: "If in this life only we have hope in Christ, we are of all men most miserable.". . . In this article I propose to look behind the arguments for and against the possibility of life after death, to investigate the various motives for wanting it, ranging from the frivolously irreligious to the profound. I shall argue that the belief in immortality is not so central to Christian thought and practice as is often believed, and indeed that a rich Christian faith does not require a doctrine of life after death in order to be profound and meaningful.

Grace Jantzen. "Do We Need Immortality?", Modern Theology 1:1, 1984, pp. 25–31.

I. Self-Regarding Motives

To begin with the obvious, our desire for immortality is not a desire for just any sort of continued existence: the less musical among us might prefer extinction to an eternity of playing harps and singing hymns, and given a choice, we would all prefer extinction to hell. H. H. Price has offered a picture of a life after death which is entirely the product of our desires—but which might turn out to be a highly undesirable state. In his description, the post-mortem world is a world in which our wishes would immediately fulfil themselves, a world whose laws "would be more like the laws of Freudian psychology than the laws of physics." As Price points out, this might be much less pleasant than we might have thought, because our desires, when we include all those we have repressed, are not in mutual harmony. They incorporate, for instance, desires for punishment and suffering for the wrongs we have done.... Price's point is that if all our repressed desires suddenly came true, this would be horrifying, and we would have to set about the difficult process of altering our characters so that when we get what we want, we want what we get.

The popular desire for immortality is very little like this. Life after death is often pictured, rather, as the fulfilment of longings for pleasure: it will be a paradise where there will be no more suffering and pain, where we will be happily reunited with those we love in perpetual feasting and gladness. It must be admitted that some religious pictures of heaven reinforce this frankly hedonistic conception. In the Koran we find that heaven is a beautiful garden filled with fruits and flowers. "There the Muslims drink the wine they have been denied on earth, wine that has no after-effects. It is brought to them by handsome youths, and dark-eyed houris wait on their every pleasure." Similar descriptions of a hedonistic paradise of feasting and delight can be found in Christian writings, except that the dark-eyed houris are conspicuously absent, probably because of Christianity's long-standing suspicion of the sorts of delights the presence of these creatures would signal.

One of the appeals of such a description of paradise is that in this eternal delight there is no more separation from those we love; we are all eternally reunited. This, however, might prove a mixed blessing. Apart from the fact that with some of those we love, the relationship improves if there are periods of space between our togetherness, there is also the consideration that heaven would not be a private party—everyone is invited. Now, what might it be like to find oneself at the heavenly feast seated next to a Neanderthal man? Surely conversation would lag, and it is doubtful whether the silences could be filled by enjoyment of the same food. Christianity has sometimes avoided this social embarrassment by consigning the vast majority of mankind to hell, but that is not a possibility with which many of us could acquiesce and still enjoy the feast.

The point behind these frivolous comments is that it is not quite so easy to give a picture of unending delight as might be thought; it is against scenarios of this sort that Bernard Williams' comments on the tedium of immortality have some point. A paradise of sensuous delights would become boring; it would in the long run be pointless and utterly unfulfilling. We can perhaps imagine ways of making a very long feast meaningful; we do, after all, cope with lengthy terrestrial social occasions by choosing interesting conversational partners, and making the dinner occasions not merely for food and drink but also for stimulating discussion and for giving and receiving friendship the value of which extends beyond the termination of the dinner. But if the feasting literally never came to an end, if there were no progress possible from the sensuous enjoyment of paradise to anything more meaningful, then we might well wish, like Elina Makropulos, to terminate the whole business and destroy the elixir of youth. It is important to notice, however, that on this view survival is tedious simply because there is no progress, no point to the continued existence except the satisfaction of hedonistic desires. But this picture is much too simple-minded; Christians (and Muslims too, of course) have long recognized this, and have taken the hedonistic descriptions of the Scriptures as symbolic of something more meaningful than eternal self-indulgence, as we shall see.

Death is sometimes seen as evil because it means the curtailment of projects; immortality would be required to give significance to life because it would allow those projects to be meaningfully continued. Of course, most of our projects would not require all eternity to complete. But even in this life, one enterprise leads to another, and provided endless progress were possible, we might pursue an endless series of challenging and absorbing tasks, each one developing into another, without any risk of boredom. This might also give more point to some of our earthly projects: the painstaking acquisition of languages and techniques would be worthwhile beyond the few years we have to employ them here. This way of thinking about survival is probably more attractive to an intellectual whose current projects could easily be extended into the future, than, say, to a labourer who considers the prospect of endless projects as enough to make him feel tired already. Still, given the opportunity, perhaps he too would develop interests which he would genuinely like to pursue.

The notion that life after death would provide an opportunity for the fulfilment of projects is not, of course, presented as an argument for the likelihood of survival but as an argument for its desirability. But does it succeed? There is considerable pull toward saying that it does, especially for those who have far more interests than they can possibly develop even assuming an average life-span. An after-life would be one in which we could all pursue what we are really interested in without worrying about earning daily bread or having the notion that the project itself is fulfilling—so that a fulfilled person is one who completes fulfilling projects—but then we have gone round in a circle. Personal fulfilment involves something like actualizing our potential, completing projects which "do ourselves justice." But this then is problematical again: what is meant by "our potential"? If it means the whole variety of things that many of us would enjoy doing and could do well with suitable training, then this life is much too short for fulfilment, and immortality appears attractive.

But while this shows that immortality may be desirable (for some people in some forms) it is possible to give an alternative account of fulfilment which does not require survival. . . . [I]f we take seriously the fact that our existence will terminate, this will affect our choice about life: if we will not live forever, then we must do while we can those things which are really important to do. On this view, a fulfilled person would be a person who picked such projects for his life that were genuinely worthwhile and suitable for his abilities and aptitudes, and was able to bring them to completion: Einstein, who lived to an old age and had accomplished significant projects would be described as fulfilled, but a person who never had any projects at all, and lived in continuous aimless frustration, "In the evening saying 'Would it were morning' and in the morning saying 'Would it were evening'" would not be so describable. Neither would be the person who had projects but died before he could accomplish them. We do distinguish fulfilled and unfulfilled people in these ways, without reference to immortality. This does not of course mean that immortality is not desirable, especially for those who through no fault of their own are not able to complete their projects in their life-times. But it does mean that we do not have to postulate an after-life to make sense of the very concept of fulfilled and meaningful human life.

Also, if death is a limit, this gives a significance and urgency to our choices which they would not otherwise have. If we could go on pursuing an endless series of projects, it might not matter very much which ones we chose first: we could always do others later. Nor would it matter how vigourously we pursued them—for there would always be more time—nor how challenging they were or how well they developed us and brought out the best in us—for there would always be other opportunities. But if fulfilment is something which must be reached in this life if it is to be reached at all, we will be far less cavalier about the choices we make affecting our own fulfilment, and also, very importantly, in our relationships with others for whose fulfilment we are partly responsible. A great many of our projects, and arguably the most significant of them, have to do not merely with ourselves but with others: our fulfilment is not simply a matter of, say, satisfying our individual intellectual curiosities, but is bound up with the fulfilment of family, friends, students. If we really have only this life, then enjoyment and fulfilment cannot be postponed to another, either for ourselves or for those we care about.

II. Moral Motives

It is sometimes argued that immortality is required on moral grounds. Such an argument can take the Kantian form: immortality is necessary as a postulate of practical reason. Since the *summum bonum* involves happiness as well as virtue, and since in this life we often find a disparity between the two, it is necessary to postulate a life after death where the imbalance will be redressed. Otherwise the universe is ultimately unjust, out of joint.

I do not wish to linger long over this, but simply make three points, none of them original. First, maybe we should just admit that the universe is out of joint; it hardly seems obvious, even (or especially) from the point of view of Christian theology, that it is not. Second, even if it is, that does not rob morality—even on a Kantian system—of its point. An act of intrinsic worth is still worthwhile even if it will never receive any happiness in reward; furthermore, morality retains its meaning even if we are all going to perish. (It is not pointless for the dying to show kindness to one another.) Those who say that if there is no life after death then nothing—including morality—in this life is meaningful, are implicitly admitting that there is nothing in this life which is worthwhile for its own sake, independent of eternal consequences; that everything, even love, is only a means to an end, and an end which this life cannot give. Kant himself could not have accepted such a view. Third, the Kantian view of reward has a peculiarity. What sort of happiness is it which is to be the reward of virtue? Suppose we think of it as some variant of the hedonistic paradise described earlier: then for reasons already given, the more moral one was—the more one valued that which was intrinsically good—the less happiness one would find in such ultimately pointless eternal self-indulgence. On the other hand, if Kant was speaking of the satisfactions of fulfilment rather than of hedonistic utopia, then for the one who truly pursues virtue, becoming virtuous will itself be the fulfilment; virtue will be its own reward.

A more interesting argument for the requirement of immortality arises, not from the idea that virtue needs to be rewarded, but from the fact that none of us is sufficiently virtuous. If part of the point of life is moral development, and none of us develops fully in this life, would it not be desirable for this process to continue beyond the grave? There is considerable connection between this argument and the previous ones; except that here there is no request for happiness as a compensation for virtue, but rather for fulfilment of the very virtue that one has sought, albeit with only moderate success. There are at least two aspects of this, which I shall consider separately.

The first is encapsulated by Dostoyevsky in *The Brothers Karamazov*. "Surely I haven't suffered simply that I, my crimes and my sufferings, may manure the soil of the future harmony for somebody else. I want to see with my own eyes the hind lie down with the lion and the victim rise up and embrace his murderer. I want to be there when everyone suddenly understands what it has all been for." This is not a desire for happiness in any hedonistic sense, but a desire to see the point, the fruition of all one's efforts. It is a natural enough human desire, of course; yet I do not think that it can be used as an argument that morality requires immortality, for the assumption here surely is that all the toil and suffering does have a point, whether we are there to understand it in the end or not. Even if we are not present at the final denouement, this does not make working toward it less worthwhile, for once again, the value of doing that cannot depend on what we individually get out of it. Although Dostoyevsky here touches, as he so often does, a very deep nerve of desire, he surely cannot be interpreted to mean that if that desire remains forever unfulfilled, there was no meaning to the suffering in the first place.

The second aspect of the longing for immortality is the longing for perfection in virtue. This is part of what prompted the more positive conceptions of purgatory, where that was seen not as a place of retributive punishment until one had suffered proportionately to the sins one had committed on earth, but rather as a place of moral purification and advance. . . . This, clearly, is not an unworthy motive for desiring life after death (though in more cynical moments one might wonder how universally it is shared—how many people desire immortality because they truly want to become better). Yet it too has some problems.

In the first place, it is not obvious that simple extension of life would result in moral improvement: more time can be opportunity for deterioration as well as for advance; the person who says, "I would be better, if only I had a little longer" is justifiably suspect. Still, although time does not automatically produce growth, it may be true that it is necessary for growth. But once again it is worth thinking about the concept of death as a limit. If immortality is denied, and if moral growth is valued; there is an urgency to moral improvement, both for oneself and for others, which might easily be ignored if it were thought that there was endless time available. And as we have already seen, it will not do to say that such moral improvement, with its struggle and frequent failure, would be worthless if all ends at death, for this would hold true only if moral improvement were a means to an end, rather than intrinsically valuable.

III. Religious Motives

Those who say that immortality will be the scene of moral progress do not, of course, usually have in mind nothing but temporal extension to bring this about: as Fichte once said, "By the mere getting oneself buried, one cannot arrive at blessedness." Rather, they believe that in the life after death there will be some strong inducements to improvement. In Price's non-theistic purgatory the unpleasantness of getting what we want may lead us to revise our desires and characters, while according to some theistic conceptions of purgatory, the punishments for our sins will purge us—sometimes in Clockwork Orange fashion—of our innate sinfulness. The most interesting theory of inducement to moral perfection, and one that forms a bridge to specifically religious arguments for the need for immortality, is the idea that the lure of divine love, more obvious in the next life than in this one, will progressively wean us from our self-centeredness and purify us so that at last our response will be perfect love reciprocated. John Hick, in his discussion of universal salvation, argues that given the assumption that man has been created by God and is "basically oriented towards him, there is no final opposition between

God's saving will and our human nature acting in freedom." Thus God, extending his love ever again towards us, will not take "no" for an answer but will ultimately woo successfully, not by overriding our freedom, but by winning us over so that eventually we freely choose him and his perfection. Hick says, "if there is continued life after death, and if God is ceaselessly at work for the salvation of his children, it follows that he will continue to be at work until the work is done; and I have been arguing that it is logically possible for him eventually to fulfil his saving purpose without at any point overriding our human freedom."

But even granting Hick's basic assumptions of humanity's created bias toward God, God in loving pursuit of men and women, and endless time for "the unhurried chase," there are still problems with his conclusion. It is not clear that genuine freedom could be preserved while still guaranteeing the ultimate result: surely if there is freedom there is always the possibility of refusal. . . .

It is important to see the implications of human freedom for a Christian doctrine of redemption. One aspect of choice not sufficiently considered is its finality. Of course decisions can sometimes be reversed: we can often change our minds. And when we do so, when there is genuine repentance and conversion, Christianity teaches that God "makes all things new," brings creativity out of chaos, Easter out of Calvary. But the fact that we can sometimes freely change our minds is not the same as saying that in the end it makes no difference what our intermediate choices are because ultimately we will all (freely) be brought to the same goal. If it is true that whether I choose p or not-p, in the end I will get p, the idea of choice has been robbed of all significance—and that is so even if I can be persuaded that in the end it will really be p that I do want. So if I perpetually choose selfishness and distrust and dishonesty, and my character is formed by these choices, it seems perverse to say that eventually these choices will be reversed and I will attain the same moral perfection as I would have if I had all along chosen integrity and compassion. Part of what it means to be free is that our choices have consequences; it is playing much too lightly with the responsibility of freedom to suggest that these consequences, at least in their effects upon ourselves, are always reversible, even if only in the endless life to come. For that matter, if everyone is perfected, then even the consequences of our choices upon others will finally be overridden: all, in the end, will be as though no one had ever chosen evil at all. Morally revolting as is the thought of God committing people to eternal flames, one of the reasons why traditional theology has so long retained a doctrine of hell is surely to guard this aspect of freedom: there is no such thing as automatic salvation.

In spite of the strong reinforcement which the belief in immortality receives from Scripture and Christian tradition, a surprising amount can also be found which calls into question the idea that immortality is a religious requirement. In the first place, it is sometimes held that, of all the evils and suffering in this world, death is the worst. On a traditional theistic view, evil must eventually be overcome, and all the wrongs made good; and this requires that death, "the last enemy," may not be proud. Death, too, shall die, when all who have ever lived will live again. This assumes, of course, that death is an evil; and if what I have said about death as a limit is correct, then that cannot be retained without some qualifications. Still, although death is not the worst evil, and not an unqualified evil, this does not amount to saying that it is not an evil at all; consequently in a world where evil was eradicated, death, too, would have no place.

But can this be used as an argument for a religious requirement of life after death? I am not sure that it can. If the perfect world dawns, death will perhaps not be found in it; but does this mean that death in this very imperfect world is followed by immortality? One might argue that only if it is, is God just: the sufferings of this present world can only be justified by the compensation of eternal life. But this, in the first place, is shocking theodicy: it is like saying that I may beat my dog at will provided that I later give him a dish of his favourite liver chowder. What happens after death—no matter how welcome—does not make present evil good. But if life after death cannot be thought of as a compensation for otherwise unjustified present evils, surely death itself—permanent extinction—must be an evil from which a Christian may hope to escape? Well, on what grounds? We do not escape other evils and sufferings which a perfect world would not contain: why should we expect to escape this one? A Christian surely must recognize that there are many aspects of the problem of evil which he cannot explain; maybe he should just accept that death is another one. But would not death make the problem of evil not just more mysterious than it already is, but actually in principle unsolvable? Wouldn't we have to conclude that God is unjust? I don't know. If we can retain a belief in divine justice amid present evil and suffering, horrific as it is, I am not sure that relinquishing the prospect of life after death would necessarily alter the case. Of course it might tip the balance psychologically, making us "of all men, most miserable," but that is another matter. If the present evils can be relegated to the mysterious purposes of God, it seems presumptuous to assume that these purposes could not include our extinction.

A very persuasive argument for the requirement for immortality for Christian theology gathers up strands from several of these lines of thought, but places special emphasis on the personal love of God. If, as Christians maintain, God loves and values each of us individually, then we can trust him not to allow us to perish forever. We are worth more to him than that. Thus Helen Oppenheimer, in her discussion of problems of life after death, recognizes the great philosophical complexities regarding personal identity, resurrection, and the rest, but finally says that if we believe in God at all, we must also believe that if we keep on looking we will find the solution to these problems, because it is as unthinkable that a loving God would permit a relationship with one he loves to be severed by extinction of that loved one as it is to think that we would willingly allow our dearest friends to perish if it were in our power to provide them with a full and rich life.

This approach has the merit, first, of not pretending that the puzzles of identity and/or resurrection are easily solvable, second, of treating death seriously, and third, of placing the doctrine of immortality within the context of a doctrine of personal relationship with God. Death is not seen as a mild nuisance which can be quickly left behind never to be repeated; immortality is not automatic, and could not be expected at all were it not for the intervention of an omnipotent God. It is only because Christianity stakes itself on the unfailing love of God, following the man who dared to call God "Father" rather than "Judge," that life after death can even be considered.

But even though this seems to me a sounder starting place, given basic assumptions of Christian theology, than the belief that human beings are endowed with naturally immortal souls, I still have problems with it. It is comforting to be told that the love of God will not allow the termination of a relationship with him; it is also much more religiously satisfying to see this relationship as of central importance, and all the descriptions of the delights of paradise as mere symbolic gropings after the enjoyment of this divine fellowship. Nevertheless, Christian theology does hold that there are other things which are precious to God and which, in spite of that, perish forever. Christian theologians increasingly recognize that it is not the case that the whole earth, every primrose, every songbird, all the galaxies of all the heavens, exist for the benefit of humanity alone. Yet if it is true that God brought about the existence of all these things and takes delight in them; then it is also true that some of the things he delights in perish forever: a popular book of natural history estimates that 99 per cent of all species of animals which have lived on earth are now extinct.

We cannot have it both ways. "Are not three sparrows sold for a farthing?" Jesus asked. "Yet not one of them falls to the ground without your heavenly Father's knowledge." These words of Jesus have often (and rightly) been taken as his teaching of the tender concern of the Father for all his creatures; what has not been noticed so often is that Jesus never denies that sparrows do fall. If the analogy which Jesus is drawing to God's care for persons (who, he says, "are of more value than many sparrows") is taken to its logical conclusion, the implication, surely, is not that we will not die but that our death will not go unnoticed. If a Christian admits that God allows some things which he values to perish, it will need further argument to show why this should not also be true of human beings: the primroses, presumably, are not loved less simply because they are temporary.

But perhaps they are temporary because they are loved less? Because they are not of such enduring worth to God (as human beings are) they are allowed to perish? This still leaves me uneasy. It is one thing to believe that we are individually valued by God, and valued perhaps in a way that other things are not; it is quite another to say that this value must result in our immortality. How can we be so sure? The analogy with persons we love whom we would not willingly allow to perish assumes that our relationship with God is in this respect just like our relationship with them. But even if we accept this analogy as the best we have for our relationship with God, we must still admit that there must be considerable disanalogies as well: how do we know that the case of endless preservation is not one of them? We may believe that God looks upon us with love and compassion, but that does not seem to me to be any guarantee that he wills our everlasting existence—that is a further (very large) step. We are taught, to be sure, that God wishes to bring us to eternal life; but it is a glaring confusion to equate eternal life with endless survival. As the notion of eternal life is used in the Johannine writings, for instance, it is spoken of as a present possession, a quality of life, not a limitless quantity; nor is it something that happens after death but in this present lifetime.

Furthermore, if there were no life after death, this in itself would not mean that religion would be pointless. Just as that which is morally valuable is valuable for its own sake and not for the reward it can bring, so also trust in God, if it is worthwhile at all, is worthwhile even if it cannot

.go on forever. A relationship with another human being does not become pointless just because at some time it will end with the death of one of the partners; why should it be thought that a relationship with God would be pointless if one day it too should end? Shneur Zalman, the Jewish founder of the Chabad, once exclaimed, "Master of the Universe! I desire neither Paradise nor Thy bliss in the world to come. I desire Thee and Thee alone." And the hymn of Fénelon has become the common property of Christendom:

> My God I love Thee: not because I hope for heaven thereby,
> Nor yet because who love Thee not are lost eternally . . .
> Not for the sake of winning heaven, nor of escaping hell;
> Not from the hope of gaining aught, not seeking a reward;
> But as thyself hast loved me, O ever loving Lord . . .
> Solely because thou art my God and my most loving King.[6]

It is true, of course, that these words (and many more examples could be given) were written by men who did believe in immortality; the point, however, is that according to them, the value of the relationship with God, the vision of God, cannot be measured by measuring its temporal duration.

But perhaps it will still be objected that if God will one day allow me to perish, this shows that all the teaching about his love for me is a vast fraud—if he really loved me, he would preserve my life. I can only reply that for reasons already given, this does not seem obvious to me. I cannot forget the primroses. They perish. Must we conclude that they are not precious to God?

I am not arguing that there is no life beyond the grave or that it is irrational to hope for it or for Christians to commit their future to God in trust. But if what I have said is correct, then it would be presumptuous to be confident that life after death is a matter of course, guaranteed, whatever the problems, by the requirements of morality and religion. We should not neglect the significant change of verb in the Nicene Creed: from affirmations "I believe in God," "I believe in Jesus Christ," and so on, we come to the rather more tentative "And I look for the resurrection of the dead and the life of the world to come." Christian faith and Christian commitment bases itself not first and foremost on a hope of survival of death, but on the intrinsic value of a relationship with God, without any reservations about what the future holds—here or hereafter.

---

6   Quoted from *Hymns Ancient and Modern*, 106.

Charles W. Mills

....

Born in Jamaica in 1951, Charles Mills is a social and political philosopher, currently John Evans Professor of Moral and Intellectual
Philosophy at Northwestern University, Illinois. In the following
selection from his collection of essays, *Blackness Visible*, Mills explores black underrepresentation in the discipline of philosophy,
tracing this to a racially exclusivist trait of philosophy as traditionally
undertaken.

....

Non-Cartesian *Sums:* Philosophy and the African-American Experience

Some years ago, I taught, for the first time, an introductory course in
African-American philosophy. . . . The course forced me to think more
systematically about the issue of philosophy and race than I had ever done
before. Though my general area of specialization is ethics and social and
political philosophy, and I am African-American (at least in the extended
sense that the Caribbean is part of the Americas), my main research interests and publication focus had not been in this particular area. So I
had to do more preparatory work than usual to come up with a course

structure, since at that time, because of the relatively undeveloped state of African-American philosophy, I found nothing appropriate in my search for a suitable introductory text, with articles that would cover a broad range of philosophical topics from an African-American perspective and that would be accessible to undergraduates with little or no background in the subject. Often the structure of a textbook provides an organizing narrative and an expository framework for a course. Here, by contrast, I had to think the course out and locate and assign readings from a variety of sources. And in order to put them all together, of course, I had to work out what African-American philosophy really was, how it was related to mainstream (Western? European/Euro-American? Dead White Guys'?) philosophy—where it challenged and contradicted it, where it supplemented it, and where it was in a theoretical space of its own.

The natural starting point of my reflections was blacks and philosophy itself. There are as yet so few recognized black philosophers that the term still has something of an oxymoronic ring to it, causing double takes and occasional quickly suppressed reactions of surprise when one is introduced. As a result, I would imagine that most black philosophers think about philosophy and race to some extent, even if they don't actually write or publish in the area. What exactly is it about philosophy that so many black people find alienating, which would explain the fact, a subject of ongoing discussion in the *APA Proceedings and Addresses*, that blacks continue to be far more underrepresented here than in most other humanities and that black graduate students generally steer away from philosophy?

I reject explanations that attribute this pattern entirely to present-day (as against past) racist exclusion. Rather, I suggest that a major contributory cause is the self-sustaining dynamic of the "whiteness" of philosophy, not the uncontroversial whiteness of skin of most of its practitioners but what could be called, more contestably, the *conceptual* or *theoretical* whiteness of the discipline. This alone would be sufficient to discourage black graduate students contemplating a career in the academy, so that, through mechanisms familiar to those who study the reproduction of dynamic systems, certain defining traits are perpetuated unchallenged or only weakly challenged, and the socialization and credentialing of newcomers proceeds in a way that maintains the "persistently monochromatic" character of the profession.

This notion is hard to tease out; it is a pretheoretical intuition, and as with all intuitions, it can be hard to convey to those who do not, in this case because of their color, spontaneously feel it in the first place. But I will make the attempt, using gender as a comparison, because of the interesting similarities and interesting differences, and because the line of argument here is far better known, even by those who do not accept it.

In an enlightening paper in *Teaching Philosophy*, Thomas Wartenberg described the experience, from the perspective of a white male instructor, of trying to see his assigned texts from the viewpoint of his female students and gradually developing a revelatory sense of the "schizophrenic relationship" they would be bound to have to works characterized by "a systematic denigration of the nature of women." There is no mystery, then, about why women are likely to feel at least some initial discomfort with classic philosophy. But the response of blacks poses more of a challenge, because for the most part blacks are simply not mentioned in classic philosophy texts. Whole anthologies could be and have been filled by the misogynistic statements of various famous philosophers, and entire books could be and have been written on the inconsistencies between the ostensibly general moral and political prescriptions of famous philosophers and their proclaimed views on the status of women. But in Western philosophy there is no rationale for black subordination in particular (as against arguments for slavery in general) that can compare in detail and in theoretical centrality to the rationale for female subordination. A collection of explicitly racist statements about blacks from the major works of the central figures in the Anglo-American canon would not be a particularly thick document. It is more that issues of race do not even arise than that blacks are continually being put down.

What, then, is the source for blacks of a likely feeling of alienness, strangeness, of not being entirely at home in this conceptual world? The answer has to be sought at another level, in a taxonomy of different kinds of silences and invisibility. The position of women in society had to be theoretically confronted by Western thinkers (after all, they were right *there* as mothers, sisters, wives) in a way that the position of enslaved blacks did not. The embarrassing moral and political problems posed by the fate of slaves could more readily be ignored, dealt with by not saying anything about them. As David Brion Davis observes in his book on slavery in Western culture: "[N]o protest against the traditional theory [of slavery] emerged from the great seventeenth-century authorities on law, or from such philosophers and men-of-letters as Descartes, Malebranche, Spinoza, Pascal, Bayle, or Fontenelle. . . . The inherent contradiction of human slavery had always generated dualisms in thought, but by the sixteenth and seventeenth centuries Europeans had arrived at the greatest dualism of all—the momentous division between an increasing devotion to liberty in Europe and an expanding mercantile system based on Negro [slave] labor in America. For a time most jurists and philosophers met this discrepancy simply by ignoring it."

So the result is a silence—a silence not of tacit inclusion but rather of exclusion: the black experience is not subsumed under these philosophical abstractions, despite their putative generality. An enlightening metaphor might be the notion of a parallel universe that partially overlaps with the familiar (to whites) one but then, because of crucial variations in the initial parameters, goes radically askew. For the inhabitants of this universe, the standard geometries are of limited cartographic use, conceptual apparatuses predicated on assumptions that do not hold true. It is not a question of minor deviations, which, with a bit of bending and twisting here and there, can be accommodated within the framework. Rather, so to speak, some of the Euclidean axioms have to be rejected; a reconceptualization is necessary because the structuring logic is different. The peculiar features of the African-American experience—racial slavery, which linked biological phenotype to social subordination, and which is chronologically located in the modern epoch, ironically coincident with the emergence of liberalism's proclamation of universal human equality—are not part of the experience represented in the abstractions of European or Euro-American philosophers. And those who have grown up in such a universe, asked to pretend that they are living in the other, will be cynically knowing, exchanging glances that signify "There the white folks go again." They know that what is in the books is largely mythical as a *general* statement of principles, that it was never intended to be applicable to them in the first place, but that within the structure of power relations, as part of the routine, one has to pretend that it does.

Thus there is a feeling, not to put too fine a point on it, that when you get right down to it, a lot of philosophy is just white guys jerking off. Either philosophy is not about real issues in the first place but about pseudo-problems; or when it is about real problems, the emphases are in the wrong places; or crucial facts are omitted, making the whole discussion pointless; or the abstractness is really a sham for what we all know but are not allowed to say out loud. The impatience or indifference that I have sometimes detected in black students seems to derive in part from their sense that there is something strange in spending a whole course describing the logic of different moral ideals, for example, without ever mentioning that *all of them* were systematically violated for blacks. So it is not merely that the ideal was not always attained but that, more fundamentally, *this was never actually the ideal in the first place.* A lot of moral philosophy will then seem to be based on pretense, the claim that these were the principles that people strove to uphold, when in fact the real principles were the racially exclusivist ones.

The example of Locke here is paradigmatic of the kind of guilty silence I am talking about: the pillar of constitutionalist liberal democracy; the defender of the natural equality of all men; and the opponent of patriarchalism, of enslavement resulting from a war of aggression, of *all* hereditary slavery, who nevertheless had no difficulty reconciling his principles with investments in the Atlantic slave trade and a part in writing the Carolina slave constitution. Women are, of course, also unequal in the Lockean polity, but their subordination is at least addressed, explained (inconsistently) on the basis of natural disadvantage. But nothing at all is formally said in the *Second Treatise of Government* about justifying *black* subordination: blacks are just outside the scope of these principles. Similarly, in the two most widely used contemporary political texts, John Rawls's *A Theory of Justice* and Robert Nozick's *Anarchy, State, and Utopia,* it will certainly be noticed by blacks, if not commented on, that U.S. slavery and its aftermath barely appear. The only slavery Rawls mentions is that of antiquity, while Nozick's thoughts on the possible need for rectificatory reparations occupy a few sentences and an endnote reference. So the focus on "ideal theory" (Rawls) here will seem in part ideological, a steering away from disquieting questions and unresolved issues. It is a generalism, an abstractness, which is covertly particularistic and concrete, in that it is really based on a white experience for which these realities were not central, not that important.

And it is because of this *interconnection* between "white" principles and black philosophy that it is not really accurate, at least for African-Americans, to characterize the issue purely in terms of promoting "multiculturalism" and "cultural diversity." This description would be fair enough in the case of geographically and historically discrete communities, with different cultures and worldviews, coming into contact through voluntary immigration. But in the case of the African-American experience, what is involved is a subject population simultaneously linked to and excluded from the dominant group—the "sixty percent solution" of the Constitution, the 1857 *Dred Scott* v. *Sanford* decision that blacks in America had no rights that whites were bound to respect—whose culture and worldview are, as a consequence, deeply motivated by the necessity of doing a critique *of* the dominant view. A lot of black thought has simply revolved around the insistent demand that whites *live up to their own (ostensibly universalist) principles,* so that African-Americans such as David Walker could challenge American slavery and white supremacy in the name of the Declaration of Independence, and the Saint-Domingue (Haitian) revolutionaries who triumphed over French colonial slavery could be described as "black Jacobins" acting in the name of the "Rights of Man." Thus African retentions in the "New World" and the elements of a syncretic new culture growing out of slavery were necessarily intellectually shaped in their development by the experience of resistance to white oppression in a way that African thought developing on the home continent in the precolonial period was not. *African*-Americans, as such writers as James Baldwin and Ralph Ellison have always pointed out, are also African-*Americans*, with the result that a relationship simultaneously of influence by and opposition to white theory and practice imprints their cognition from the start. What is involved, then, is not so much a purely externalist collision of different cultures as a (partially) internalist critique of the dominant culture by those who accept many of the culture's principles but are excluded by them. In large measure, this critique has involved telling white people things that they do not know and do not want to know, the main one being that this alternative (nonideal) universe *is* the actual one and that the local reality in which whites are at home is only a nonrepresentative part of the larger whole.

Back to the course and the problem of finding an organizing principle for it. Obviously, African-American philosophy comprises not just the philosophical writings of black people, because then any article—on the Gettier problem, on counterfactuals, on bivalence, on the French Enlightenment—would count, and of course there are such articles. The unifying theme had to be something like the struggles of people of African descent in the Americas against the different manifestations of white racism. . . . The political, economic, social, and legal dimensions of this struggle were clear enough and well documented. But how exactly was the philosophical aspect of this struggle to be characterized?

I decided that "personhood," or the lack of it, could provide an ingress to this universe, and that I would work with the concept of a "subperson" as my central organizing notion. This strategy arguably captures the defining feature of the African-American experience under conditions of white supremacy (both slavery and its aftermath): that white racism so structured the world as to have negative ramifications for every sphere of black life—juridical standing, moral status, personal/racial identity, epistemic reliability, existential plight, political inclusion, social metaphysics, sexual relations, aesthetic worth.

What is a (racial) "subperson"? (The term, of course, is a translation of the useful German *Untermensch*.) What are its specific differentiae? A subperson is not an inanimate object, like a stone, which has (except perhaps for some green theorists) zero moral status. Nor is it simply a nonhuman animal, which (again, before recent movements to defend "animal rights") would have been regarded, depending on one's Kantian or Benthamite sympathies, as outside the moral community altogether, or at best as a member with a significantly lower utility-consuming co-efficient. Rather, the peculiar status of a subperson is that it is an entity which, because of phenotype, seems (from, of course, the perspective of the categorizer) human in some respects but not in others. It is a human (or, if this word already seems normatively loaded, a humanoid) who, though adult, is not fully a person. And the tensions and internal contra-dictions in this concept capture the tensions and internal contradictions of the black experience in a white-supremacist society. To be an African-American was to be, in Aristotle's conceptualization, a living tool, prop-erty with a soul, whose moral status was tugged in different directions by the dehumanizing requirements of slavery on the one hand and the (grudging and sporadic) white recognition of the objective properties blacks possessed on the other, generating an insidious array of cognitive and moral splits in both black and white consciousness. . . . This, then, is a more illuminating starting point than the assumption that in general all humans have been recognized as persons (the "default mode" so to speak). In other words, one would be taking the historical reality of a partitioned social ontology as the starting point rather than the ideal ab-straction of universal equality, qualified with an embarrassed marginal asterisk or an endnote to say that there were some exceptions.

If this is your foundation, then the nature of your perspective on the world and the philosophy that grows organically out of it are bound to be radically different. Even after emancipation, you are categorized on the basis of your color as an inferior being, since modern racial slavery (unlike the slavery of antiquity) ties phenotype to subordination. So you are seen as having less mental capacity, with rights on a sliding scale from zero to a ceiling well below that of your white co-humans, a creature deemed to have no real history, who has made no global contribution to civilization, and who in general can be encroached upon with impunity. Once you have faced this social ontology without evasion and circumlocution, then the kind of problems with which you must grapple, the existential plight, the array of concepts found useful, the set of paradigmatic dilemmas, the range of concerns, is going to be significantly different from that of the mainstream white philosopher. And this means that many of the crucial episodes and foundational texts (The Great Moments in Western Philosophy) that make up the canon and the iconography of the Western tradition will have little or no resonance.

As an illustration, let me contrast two kinds of paradigmatic philosophical situations and two kinds of selves or *sums*, the Cartesian self with which we are all familiar and an Ellisonian one that will be unfamiliar to many readers. I think that these selves epitomize the different kind of problematic involved.

The enunciation of the Cartesian *sum* can be construed as a crucial episode in European modernity. Here we have vividly portrayed the plight of the individual knower torn free from the sustaining verities of the dissolving feudal world, which had provided authority and certainty, and entering tentatively into the cognitive universe of an (as yet unrecognized) revolutionizing individualist capitalism, where all that is solid melts into air. So the crucial question is posed: "What can I know?" And out of this question, of course, comes modern epistemology, with the standard moves we all know, the challenges of skepticism, the danger of degeneration into solipsism, the idea of being enclosed in our own possibly unreliable perceptions, the question whether we can be certain other minds exist, the scenario of brains in a vat, and so forth. The Cartesian plight, represented as an allegedly universal predicament, and the foundationalist solution of knowledge of one's own existence thus become emblematic, a kind of pivotal scene for a whole way of doing philosophy and one that involves a whole program of assumptions about the world and (taken-for-granted) normative claims about what is philosophically important.

Contrast this *sum* with a different kind, that of Ralph Ellison's classic novel of the black experience, *Invisible Man*. What are the problems that this individual faces? Is the problem global doubt? Not at all; such a doubt would never be possible, because the whole point of subordinate black experience, or the general experience of oppressed groups, is that the subordinated are in no position to doubt the existence of the world and other people, especially that of their oppressors. It could be said that only those most solidly attached to the world have the luxury of doubting its reality, whereas those whose attachment is more precarious, whose existence is dependent on the goodwill or ill temper of others, are those compelled to recognize that it exists. The first is a function of power, the second of subjection. If your daily existence is largely defined by oppression, by *forced* intercourse with the world, it is not going to occur to you that doubt about your oppressor's existence could in any way be a serious or pressing philosophical problem; this idea will simply seem frivolous, a perk of social privilege.

The dilemmas of Ellison's black narrator, the philosophical predicament, are therefore quite different. His problem is his "invisibility," the fact that whites do not see him, take no notice of him, not because of physiological deficiency but because of the psychological "construction of their *inner* eyes" which conceptually erases his existence. He is not a full person in their eyes, and so he either is not taken into account at all in their moral calculations or is accorded only diminished standing. If they did not have power over him, this white moral derangement would not matter, but they do. So his problem is to convince them that he exists, not as a physical object, a lower life form, a thing to be instrumentally treated, but as a person in the same sense that they are, and not as a means to their ends. Moreover, because of the intellectual domination these beings have over his world, he may also be frequently assailed by self-doubts, doubts about whether he *is* a real person who deserves their respect or perhaps an inferior being who deserves the treatment he has received. The *sum* here, then—the *sum* of those seen as subpersons—will be quite different. From the beginning it will be relational, not monadic; dialogic, not monologic: one is a subperson precisely because *others*—persons—have categorized one as such and have the power to enforce their categorization. African-American philosophy is thus inherently, definitionally *oppositional*, the philosophy produced by property that does not remain silent but insists on speaking and contesting its status. So it will be a *sum* that is metaphysical not in the Cartesian sense but in the sense of challenging a *social* ontology; not the consequent of a proof but the beginning of an affirmation of one's self-worth, one's reality as a person, and one's militant insistence that others recognize it also. In the words of Ellison's nameless narrator: "[Y]ou often doubt if you really exist. . . . You ache with the need to convince yourself that you do exist in the real world, that you're a part of all the sound and anguish, and you strike out with your fists, you curse and you swear to make them recognize you. And, alas, it's seldom successful."

The universalizing pretensions of Western philosophy, which by its very abstractness and distance from vulgar reality seemed to be all-inclusive of human experience, are thereby shown to be illusory. White (male) philosophy's confrontation of Man and Universe, or even Person and Universe, is really predicated on taking personhood for granted and thus excludes the differential experience of those who have ceaselessly had to fight to have their personhood recognized in the first place. Without even recognizing that it is doing so, Western philosophy abstracts *away* from what has been the central feature of the lives of Africans transported against their will to the Americas: the denial of black humanity and the reactive, defiant assertion of it. Secure in the uncontested *sum* of the leisurely Cartesian derivation, whites find it hard to understand the metaphysical rage and urgency permeating the *non*-Cartesian *sums* of those invisible native sons and daughters who, since nobody knows their name, have to be the men who cry "I am!" and the women who demand "And ain't I a woman?" From the beginning, therefore, the problems faced by those categorized as persons and those categorized as subpersons will be radically different. One can no longer speak with quite such assurance of *the* problems of philosophy; rather, these are problems for *particular* groups of human beings, and for others there will be different kinds of problems that are far more urgent. A relativizing of the discipline's traditional hierarchies of importance and centrality thus becomes necessary.